THE ROUGH GUIDE TO

PANAMA

WITHDRAWN

This third edition updated by
Sara Humphreys

with additional contributions by
Raffa Calvo

**ROUGH
GUIDES**

Contents

Introduction to

Panama

Never has a country been so defined by its location. From the summit of Volcán Barú – Panama's highest peak – it's possible to watch the sun rise over both the Atlantic and Pacific oceans, light slowly spreading across the water to reveal two glittering archipelagos. For centuries this slender isthmus has provided an invaluable shortcut between the two seas; you can witness it yourself, tramping the old mule trails of the Spanish conquistadors or gliding past forested islands along the world's most famous canal. Panama is a "biological corridor", too, linking the vast land masses of the Americas, and harbours tremendous biodiversity within its cloud-forested highlands, glorious palm-fringed islands, vast mangrove tracts and towering rainforests. The country also boasts Central America's most ebullient capital city, and if you're after riotous partying, be it at a small village festival or throughout the hedonistic marathon of Carnaval, you're in the right place.

Panama's compact size means the vast majority of its sights are **easily accessible**. From the comfort of your hotel in the capital, you can head out in the morning to hike through spectacular, primate-packed rainforest, or explore crumbling colonial forts, and the same evening be swinging your hips to salsa or dining by candlelight in a downtown hot spot. The ancient and modern, artificial and natural are irresistibly juxtaposed: vast container ships transiting the Canal slice through primeval rainforests teeming with fluorescent frogs and elusive wild cats, just thirty minutes by dugout from where Emberá villagers practise subsistence agriculture. Visiting the country's fringes and interior, you can explore uninhabited islands and untracked jungle, basing yourself in small towns, friendly villages and remote ecolodges.

Despite these attractions, Panama has often been overlooked as a tourist destination, overshadowed by its neighbour Costa Rica, and sometimes mistakenly viewed as a US annexe – thanks to the US occupation of the former Canal Zone and the dollarized economy. Add to that Panama's not entirely undeserved reputation for money-laundering and the current trend of attracting North American retirees, and it's perhaps not surprising that tourists have been slow to appreciate the country's multifaceted identity and outstanding natural beauty. Yet the US is only one of many **cultural influences** – which derive from Spain and other parts of Europe, West Africa, the West Indies, China, India and the Middle East – fused with the fascinating heritage of the eight **indigenous peoples** that survived the Spanish Conquest. Many of these indigenous communities welcome tourists, sharing their traditional skills, customs and modern-day challenges.

Panama's complexities and contradictions confront you at every turn, which can intrigue and frustrate in equal measure. The Panamanian government is actively promoting international **tourism**, yet there's often very little information on offer. The colourful traditional attire of Panama's indigenous populations is used unashamedly in promotional images, but the people themselves are frequently ignored by their government. Many inhabit the tropical rainforests of Panama's national parks and reserves, which remain tantalizingly underdeveloped and desperately underfunded; covering more than a third of Panama's land and marine territory, these ostensibly protected areas are threatened by government-sanctioned hydroelectric and mining projects, as well as by land-hungry cattle-farmers.

It's hard to visit Panama and not be both amazed and perturbed by the pace of change in this small, young nation, as skyscrapers gobble up Panama City's skyline and new roads and farms push deeper into the forests. Outside the big attractions, though, it's easy enough to get off the beaten track. Seek out and spend time in the country's **less-visited corners** – far-flung islands, isolated mountain hamlets, remote indigenous communities and untamed national parks – and you'll be afforded greater insights into this compelling, beautiful and often surprising country.

PANAMA

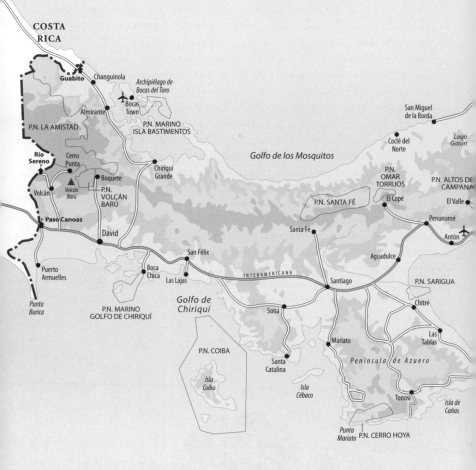

CARIBBEAN SEA

COSTA
RICA

Guabito
Changuinola
Archipiélago de
Bocas del Toro
Almirante
Bocas
Town
P.N. MARINO
ISLA BASTIMENTOS

San Miguel
de la Borda

Coclé del
Norte

Lago
Gatún

Golfo de los Mosquitos

P.N. LA AMISTAD

Río
Sereno
Cerro
Punta
Chiriquí
Grande

P.N.
OMAR
TORRIJOS

P.N. ALTOS DE
CAMPANA

Boquete
P.N. SANTA FÉ
El Copé
El Valle

Volcán
Volcán
Barú
P.N.
VOLCÁN
BARÚ

Penonomé

Paso Canoas
David
Santa Fé
Aguadulce
Antón

San Félix
P.N. SARIGUA

Puerto
Armuelles
Boca
Chica
INTERAMERICANA
Santiago
Chitré

Las Lajas
Soná

Punta
Burica
P.N. MARINO
GOLFO DE CHIRIQUÍ
Golfo de
Chiriquí
Mariato
Las
Tablas

P.N. COIBA
Santa
Catalina
Península de Azuero

Isla
Coiba
Isla
Cébaco
Tonosí
Isla de
Cañas

Punta
Mariato
P.N. CERRO HOYA

N

0   50
kilometres

FACT FILE

- Though Panama has one of the highest **GDP** growth rates in Latin America – around 5.8 percent in 2016 – it also has the second highest level of income **inequality**.

- Panama hosts 987 species of **bird**, including the odd-looking three-wattled bellbird, resident in the Chiriquí Highlands, whose extraordinary "bonk" call can be heard almost 1km away.

- Panama City's new 14km **metro** line cost an estimated $1.88 billion, with a further $2.2 billion earmarked for a second line due for completion in 2019.

- The original **Panama Canal** took more than 60 million pounds of dynamite to blast through the isthmus; the ships laden with the explosives each contained twenty thousand boxes that all had to be unloaded by hand.

- The **Guna**, Panama's most high-profile indigenous people, have one of the highest rates of albinism in the world with one in 150 being born a "moon child".

Where to go

The vast majority of visitors fly in to cosmopolitan **Panama City**, where brash skyscrapers stare across the bay at the rocky peninsula of **Casco Viejo**, the city's rapidly transforming colonial centre, whose elegantly restored mansions, churches and leafy plazas demand at least a day's leisurely exploration. If you're planning a short visit, it's easy to base yourself in the city and make daily forays to the monumental **Panama Canal** and the Spanish **colonial forts** of San Lorenzo and Portobelo. Should the frenetic energy and interminable traffic din of the city's clogged arteries get too much, an exhilarating excursion to the **Archipiélago de las Perlas**, or a relaxing outing birdwatching in the **Parque Nacional Soberanía** or kayaking down the **Río Chagres** are all possible without forgoing the epicurean delights of the capital's sophisticated bars and restaurants in the evening.

After Panama City, the country's most popular tourist area is the Caribbean archipelago of **Bocas del Toro**, close to the Costa Rican border. Its deserted stretches of sand, powerful surf and colourful coral reefs are matched by an often-forgotten mainland that offers spectacular wilderness hiking as well as wildlife viewing in the Humedales de San San Pond Sak. Bocas's bohemian vibe and Afro-Caribbean culture contrasts with the vast archipelago of **Guna Yala**, which extends for hundreds of kilometres along Panama's eastern Caribbean coast, and is home to Panama's most politically independent and culturally distinct indigenous people, the Guna. Here you can live out your desert-island fantasies swinging in a hammock and sleeping in simple cane *cabañas* on picture-postcard cays of white sand and coconut palms. With more time, you can experience the aquatic wonderlands off the Pacific coast, with world-class scuba diving, snorkelling and sport fishing in the mangrove-rich protected marine parks of the **Golfo de Chiriquí**, and **Coiba**, the penal colony turned wildlife reserve. The latter is generally reached from the laidback surfing hot spot of **Santa Catalina**.

From there it's a short hop east to the rolling pastureland and quaint villages of the **Azuero Peninsula**, a region that revels in its colonial heritage. Once neglected by visitors, its joyous festivals, including the country's most ardent **Carnaval**, overflow with enthusiastic accordion and violin playing, colourful costumes, masks, rodeos and lashings of seco – Panama's potent national tipple – and provide ample opportunities to interact with the outgoing populace.

ARTS AND CRAFTS IN PANAMA

It may not have the sprawling markets of Mexico or Guatemala, but Panama's arts and crafts are thriving, and reflect the country's multi-ethnic make-up. From appliqué textiles to coiled basketry, woodcarving to mask-making, here's our pick of the top five crafts:

Basketry and woodcarving Head for the Darién to pick up some exquisite Emberá basketry in villages such as Mogué and La Chunga, or smooth cocobolo and tagua carvings of animals in Wounaan communities such as Puerto Lara. **See p.284, p.287 & p.278.**

Beaded necklaces Though once fashioned out of dyed pebbles, shells and bone worn by Ngäbe and Buglé warriors, these modern-day colourful *nguñunkua* (*chaquira* in Spanish) still make beautiful adornments. You'll find them sold in stalls along the Interamericana near Tolé. **See p.204.**

Devil masks Although made for festivals around the country, the most famous mask-makers hail from La Villa de los Santos and Chitré, their workshops stuffed full of terrifying salivating dragon or gargoyle-like monsters in kaleidoscopic colours. **See p.159.**

Molas Guna women's distinctive multicoloured, embroidered *molas* are transformed into everything from cushion covers to Christmas stockings using traditional geometric designs or modern-day icons such as Batman. They're widely available everywhere in Guna Yala, and you'll find them on the street corners of Panama City. **See p.85, p.134 & p.259.**

Straw hats Panama's hats may not be Panama hats – those are made in Ecuador – but some finely woven specimens are available: consider buying a *sombrero pintao* in La Pintada, or an *ocueño* in Ocú. **See p.143 & p.161.**

The dorsal mountain range dividing Panama's two coasts rises dramatically from the Pacific coastal plains that constitute the country's agricultural heartlands, with the most impressive peaks in the spectacular **national parks** of Chiriquí's **Western Highlands**, surrounding the alpine towns of **Boquete** and the less touristed **Cerro Punta**, which lie either side of brooding **Volcán Barú**. Here it's hard to resist the allure of verdant cloud forests filled with orchids, quetzals and hummingbirds, precision rows of shade-grown coffee plantations and fast-flowing rivers, perfect for whitewater rafting, and a range of adventure activities. Further east, the **Cordillera Central** hosts more parks and rainforested peaks laced with waterfalls above the small communities of **El Copé**, **Santa Fé** and **El Valle**, all of which offer rewarding hiking, birdwatching and horseriding.

Few visitors venture east of Panama City to the **Darién** jungle, which has gained almost mythical status, as much for FARC guerrillas and drug-traffickers as for its spectacular scenery and wildlife. Requiring patience, money and more than a smattering of Spanish, the rewards are ample: sinuous river journeys by dugout, great canopies of cathedral-like rainforests sheltering some of Panama's most spectacular fauna, and remote Emberá and Wounaan communities, keen to share their skills and culture with visitors.

ABOVE NGÄBE *CHAQUIRA* **OPPOSITE FROM TOP** HARPY EAGLE; FESTIVAL DE LA MEJORANA; GUNA YALA FROM THE AIR

Author picks

To research this guide, the authors spent countless hours hunched over in dugout canoes, tramping though steamy rainforests and fending off sandflies as they journeyed from the cocktail bars of Bocas to Emberá and Wounaan villages deep in the Darién. Here are some of their personal picks.

Thrilling boat trip The Humedales de San San Pond Sak (p.240) are at their best at sunrise as the mist clears; glide through the wetlands spotting herons and hawks, sloths and snakes, and the extraordinary-looking manatee.

Wow-factor birdwatching After a dawn hike through the Darién rainforest, and a lengthy stakeout of a nest, the sight of a majestic adult harpy eagle swooping down to feed its chick is truly special (p.285).

Exhilarating flight Peering out of your eight-seater twin-prop over Guna Yala (p.252) will leave you gasping at the countless tiny specks of white sand dotted with coconut palms that dazzle in translucent turquoise shallows.

Panoramic views The vistas from the summit of Cerro Ancón (p.68) take your breath away: on one side the city with its shimmering skyscrapers dwarfing the colonial architecture of Casco Viejo, on the other a procession of vast ships passing through the Panama Canal.

Challenging hike It's hard to beat the four-day trek across the cordillera from Boquete to Bocas (p.187), hiking through cloud forest, traversing rivers and sleeping in Ngäbe villages, with the reward of a soak in the Caribbean at the end.

Fabulous fiesta While the extreme hedonism of Carnaval grabs the headlines, tiny Guararé's Festival de la Mejorana (p.165) is a more mellow but equally joyous affair, including heavy doses of *pindín* – upbeat folk music featuring accordion-playing – and competitions in traditional skills.

Lipsmacking ice cream The sweltering heat of Panama City is best alleviated by a cone from *Granclement* (p.80): choose from mouthwatering sorbets and unusually flavoured *helados* from Earl Grey tea to vanilla and walnut.

> Our author recommendations don't end here. We've flagged up our favourite places – a perfectly sited hotel, an atmospheric café, a special restaurant – throughout the Guide, highlighted with the ★ symbol.

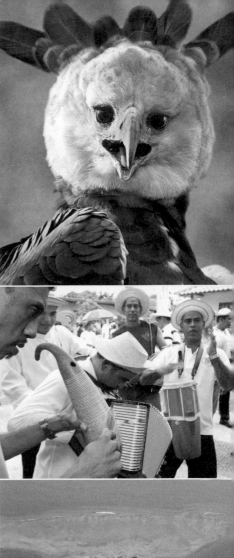

When to go

Squeezed between seven and nine degrees north of the equator, Panama is located firmly within the **tropics**, with a climate to match: relentlessly hot and humid in the lowlands, cooling off fractionally to give balmy nights, whereas in the highlands, temperatures vary significantly with altitude, and can be chilly at night.

Most travellers visit during the shorter **dry season** (*verano*, "summer"), which runs from mid-December to the end of April, and with good reason. Azure skies predominate, at least on the drier Pacific plains, sheltered by Panama's mountainous spine. The firmer going underfoot makes it easier to travel on unpaved roads and explore the rainforests, and the reduced rainwater run-off ensures clearer waters to swim in. The dry season also includes the lively holiday periods of Christmas, New Year, Carnaval and Holy Week, when flights and hotels in popular tourist spots are at a premium.

You'll avoid the crowds and the price hikes in the **rainy season** (*invierno*, "winter"), which stretches roughly from May to mid-December. Although the mountainous and rainforested regions in Panama are best avoided during the wettest months, since peaks are constantly swathed in cloud and tracks are boggy, if you stick to the lowland areas on the Pacific coast, the downpours, while frequent and intense, rarely last more than a few hours, leaving plenty of sunny, dry periods to enjoy. In particular, the otherwise parched Azuero Peninsula offers much more picturesque scenery during its understated rainy season.

By contrast, the **Caribbean coast** receives almost twice as much rain as the Pacific, with virtually no recognizable dry season. Regional variations impact here too: the trade winds (strongest Dec–Feb) make the water choppy and outer islands inaccessible in Bocas del Toro and Guna Yala, while Bocas enjoys two relatively dry spells around March and October.

AVERAGE DAILY TEMPERATURES AND RAINFALL

	Jan	Feb	Mar	Apr	May	Jun	Jul	Aug	Sep	Oct	Nov	Dec
PANAMA CITY												
Max/min (°C)	30/22	31/22	32/23	32/23	31/24	30/23	30/23	31/23	30/23	30/23	30/23	30/23
Max/min (°F)	86/71	87/71	89/73	89/73	87/75	86/73	86/73	87/73	86/73	86/73	86/73	86/73
Rainfall (mm)	33	18	13	74	201	203	178	198	198	262	254	137
BOQUETE												
Max/min (°C)	25/13	27/13	28/14	29/14	28/15	27/14	27/14	27/14	27/14	28/14	27/14	27/13
Max/min (°F)	77/55	80/56	82/58	84/59	82/59	80/58	81/58	81/58	80/57	83/57	81/56	82/56
Rainfall (mm)	2.5	38	81	231	472	432	467	660	546	925	376	121
BOCAS DEL TORO												
Max/min (°C)	31/20	31/20	31/21	31/21	32/22	32/22	32/22	32/22	32/22	32/22	32/22	31/21
Max/min (°F)	88/68	88/68	88/70	88/70	90/72	90/72	90/72	90/72	90/72	90/72	90/72	88/70
Rainfall (mm)	204	235	188	323	273	287	387	346	254	219	390	485

OPPOSITE FROM TOP SURFER, SANTA CATALINA; LOTTERY STALL, CHITRÉ

17

things not to miss

It's not possible to see everything Panama has to offer in one trip – and we don't suggest you try. What follows, in no particular order, is a selective taste of the country's highlights: remote islands, great coffee, colonial architecture and unique wildlife. All highlights are colour-coded by chapter and have a page reference to take you straight into the Guide, where you can find out more.

1

1 ARCHIPIÉLAGO DE LAS PERLAS
Page 120
A myriad of idyllic tropical islands ringed with white-sand beaches and azure waters.

2 STAY IN AN EMBERÁ VILLAGE
Pages 104 & 283
Challenge the cultural stereotypes by experiencing village life with the Emberá or Wounaan in the forests of the Darién and Chagres national parks.

3 BIRDWATCHING
Page 37
Get close to the country's 987 bird species – including dazzling hummingbirds, the resplendent quetzal and, pictured here, the blue-crowned motmot.

4 COLONIAL ARCHITECTURE
Pages 110, 148 & 57
From ruined Caribbean fortresses to Baroque Pacific churches, Panama possesses some fine Conquest-era buildings, including Panama City's Catedral Metropolitana with its gleaming spires.

5 CASCO VIEJO
Page 56

Hip bars and chic restaurants rub shoulders with colonial churches and leafy plazas in Panama City's historic centre.

6 SANTA FÉ DE VERAGUAS
Page 207

A fresh climate, picturesque waterfalls and an abundance of glorious orchids make this village an appealing retreat.

7 PANAMA CANAL
Page 95

Experience the twentieth century's greatest engineering feat with a transit through the locks.

8 ISLAND LIFE IN GUNA YALA
Page 246

Sleep in a cane-and-thatch *cabaña* amid swaying coconut palms, and dip into the warm Caribbean waters.

9 SANTA CATALINA
Page 210

Surfing hot spot with glorious sunsets and a wealth of outdoor adventures.

10 THE CHIRIQUÍ HIGHLANDS
Page 184

Get up close to spectacular scenery – including fast-flowing rivers and dazzling waterfalls.

11 SNORKELLING AND DIVING
Pages 227, 254 & 211

The coral reefs of the Caribbean offer superb snorkelling; for world-class diving, head to Isla Coiba.

12 COFFEE IN BOQUETE
Page 187

Learn to detect floral, caramel, citrus and spice aromas in some of the world's finest gourmet coffee estates.

13 CHILLING IN BOCAS
Page 222

Laidback bars, party hostels, mellow lodges and Caribbean cuisine make Bocas a fine spot to let your hair down for a few days.

14 DARIÉN BOAT TRIPS
Page 276

Glide upriver into one of the world's last remaining wilderness areas, viewing vast buttress roots, tangled vines and the soaring forest canopy.

15 GUNA CULTURE
Page 264

Learn about the rich cultural traditions of the island-dwelling Guna.

16 FESTIVALS
Page 37

Panama's diverse heritage has resulted in a fascinating array of festivals, from the wild Carnaval party in Las Tablas to the vibrant, rebellious celebration of Afro-Colonial culture in the Caribbean's annual *congos*.

17 HIKING
Page 38

The combination of magnificent views, picturesque waterfalls and lush forest makes hiking in central and western Panama a constant delight.

12

13

14

Itineraries

These itineraries cover the length and breadth of the isthmus, from idyllic Caribbean beaches to steaming rainforests. Limited roads and facilities in the Canal area and eastern Panama mean that in many cases the capital will necessarily serve as a hub, either as a base for day-trips or as a transit point during longer excursions.

THE GRAND TOUR

A grand tour of Panama is manageable in two weeks, mostly using the capital as a base but with a few nights in appealing provincial towns and tropical beach hideaways. For a richer experience, take it at a more leisurely pace.

❶ **Panama City** Get to know the vibrant capital, exploring its sights and nightlife and hopping out on a wealth of day-trips. **See p.52**

❷ **The Canal** Watch giant container ships squeeze through the locks, or experience a partial transit by boat. **See p.95**

❸ **Parque Nacional Soberanía** A short bus ride beyond the Miraflores Locks, this accessible park offers excellent rainforest hiking and birdwatching. **See p.98**

❹ **San Lorenzo** The forts at Portobelo may boast more cannons, but San Lorenzo's atmospheric location, towering above the Río Chagres, is unbeatable. **See p.110**

❺ **Guna Yala** Accessible as a day-trip from the capital, but better as a three-day escape: stay in cane-and-thatch *cabañas* on tranquil tropical beaches. **See p.246**

❻ **El Valle** Flower-filled crater town, surrounded by scenic hills, two hours west of Panama City by bus. An ideal place to unwind for a couple of days. **See p.134**

❼ **Boquete** Two bus changes away, in the Chiriquí Highlands, this scenic centre of gourmet coffee production and adventure activities merits at least three days. **See p.184**

❽ **Bocas del Toro** A trip across the cordillera takes you to bohemian Bocas – enjoy diving, surfing and snorkelling by day, and drinking, dining and partying by night. Great day-trips, too. **See p.218**

SAND, SEA AND SURF

You could spend sixteen to eighteen days enjoying the best beaches, surf spots, islands and marine reserves of Panama's Caribbean and Pacific coastlines.

❶ **Playa Bluff** A flight or overnight bus trip from the capital takes you to Bocas Town; Playa Bluff is its finest beach. Relax in a Caribbean eco-retreat overlooking a 5km expanse of deserted sand and pounding surf, and in season watch turtles lay their eggs. **See p.225**

❷ **Golfo de Chiriquí** A lengthy bus journey across the cordillera brings you to Boca Chica village; book into a boutique lodging and kayak around the coastal mangroves and secluded coves of the nearby Pacific islands. **See p.202**

❸ **Santa Catalina** Panama's top surfing spot has a world-class break, a good beach for novices and a mellow après-surf scene. **See p.210**

ABOVE GUNA YALA

❹ Isla Coiba A short boat trip away, Coiba is a diver's paradise, with great snorkelling too. See p.213

❺ Playa Reina, Mariato This little-known beach hotel on the western Azuero offers plenty of water-based fun, plus stunning sunsets. See p.176

❻ Archipiélago de las Perlas Accessible by boat or plane from Panama City, Isla Contadora, with its splendid beaches, makes a good base for sailing out to the archipelago's deserted cays and islands. See p.120

❼ Western Guna Yala Laze away your days in idyllic cays, palm-topped islands and translucent warm waters – the quintessential Caribbean paradise. See p.254

CULTURES AND CRAFTS

By swapping modern hotel comforts for basic rural lodgings, you'll gain great insights into Panama's cultural and colonial heritage. Count on two or three nights per stop, adding a five-day Emberá stay in the Darién if you're feeling adventurous.

❶ Naso communities The provincial town of Changuinola, a flight or bus ride away from Panama City, is the launch pad for trips up the Río Teribe to visit Seiyik, seat of the Naso monarch, and to float downriver on a bamboo raft. See p.242

❷ Silico Creek Stay in traditional *cabañas* in this Ngäbe village, learning about organic perma-culture and tasting artisanal chocolate.. See p.238

❸ Santa Fé de Veraguas A long bus journey takes you to this delightful mountain village, where a tour of the coffee cooperative gives a fascinating taste of the community's history. See p.207

❹ An Azuero festival Head southeast to laidback Las Tablas, and aim to time your trip to coincide with one of the peninsula's many riotous festivals: heady mixes of the religious and profane, colonial and indigenous, traditional and modern. See p.155 & p.165

❺ Azueran crafts On your way back to Panama City, drop in to see the devil mask-makers of Chitré and the women's hat-making cooperative in nearby Ocú. See p.159 & p.161

❻ Casco Viejo, Panama City Steeped in colonial history, the capital's old city centre is also awash with shops and stalls selling crafts – jewellery, clothing, baskets, masks, hats, carvings – made in far-flung communities around the country. See p.56

❼ Guna Yala After a bumpy plane or jeep ride to the *comarca* from the capital, experience first-hand how the women make their colourful *molas* and *winis*. See p.254

❽ Emberá homestay A full day's travel each way (by bus and dugout) from Panama City brings you to the welcoming Darién community of La Chunga. Gain insights into the culture, from basketry to medicinal plants, and sleep in an open-sided *bujía* (wooden house on stilts). See p.287

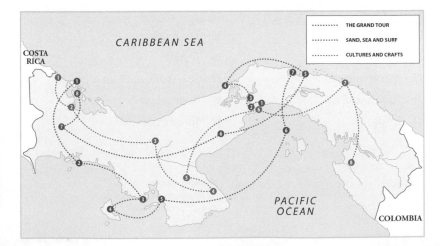

CARNAVAL DANCER, PANAMA CITY

Basics

Getting there

The vast majority of visitors to Panama arrive by air, landing at Tocumen International Airport in Panama City. Seats are generally more expensive and more heavily subscribed during the dry season (late Dec to April), especially the peak holiday periods of Christmas, Easter and Carnaval (usually in Feb) when many Panamanians living in the US return home. Thus, high season broadly counts as December through to the end of April, low season May to November. Though flights are easily booked online it is still sometimes cheaper to make arrangements via a travel agent – bearing in mind the crucial distinction between Panama City in Central America (airport code PTY) and the Panama City in Florida (airport code PFN).

Panama's reliable no-frills **national carrier**, Copa Airlines (W copaair.com), often offers the best rates and has an efficient online booking service. It flies to and from several US cities and numerous destinations in Latin America and the Caribbean, with three connecting flights a day from Tocumen to the airport at David, capital of Chiriquí province, in the far west of the country. The new **Panamá Pacífico International Airport**, formerly the US Howard Air Force base in the Canal Zone, 9km southwest of Balboa, accommodates a couple of Latin American low-cost airlines and charter flights.

Visitors travelling down from **Central America** may choose to make the longer but cheaper bus journey through Costa Rica, generally along the Pan-American Highway via the Pacific border crossing at Paso Canoas, though there are a couple of other border posts at Río Sereno in the Western Highlands and at Guabito on the Caribbean (or Atlantic) coast in Bocas del Toro.

Alternatives to flying from **South America** are a great deal more complicated, involving a number of boat and bus journeys on the Caribbean side, and are only for the adventurous. Cruise ship visitors will dock at the cruise ship terminals in either Colón, at the Caribbean end of the Panama Canal, or on the Calzada de Amador in Panama City, on the Pacific side. Sailing boats carrying backpackers from Cartagena usually unload passengers in Puerto Lindo or Portobelo, along the coast in Colón province. Other yacht arrivals will probably call in at the Balboa Yacht Club on the Calzada de Amador or at the Shelter Bay Marina west of Colón.

Visas and red tape

Tourists from **most European countries**, plus the US, Canada, Australia, New Zealand and South Africa, do not need a visa. They can get their passport stamped for ninety days on arrival provided they can produce a passport valid for at least six months after departure, an onward (or return) bus or plane ticket and proof of funds (usually $500 or a credit card).

That said, check for the latest **regulations** at a Panamanian consulate in advance and don't forget that if you are transiting via the US, you will need a transit visa, or a visa waiver (ESTA) application in advance of travel (see W usimmigrationsupport .org), as well as a machine-readable passport. The Panamanian immigration authorities' website is also worth checking (W migracion.gob.pa).

If you are arriving from one of the WHO-listed yellow fever countries you may be asked to produce your vaccination certificate (see p.33).

The only way to **extend your stay** is to pop over to Costa Rica for a couple of days before returning, brandishing a return bus ticket.

Flights from the US and Canada

There are numerous **direct flights**: Delta (W delta .com), United (W united.com) and American Airlines (W aa.com) alongside Copa (W copaair.com) and Avianca (W avianca.com) fly daily to Panama City from various US cities, including Miami – the main portal, offering several daily connections – plus New York, Washington, Los Angeles and Orlando.

A BETTER KIND OF TRAVEL

At Rough Guides we are passionately committed to travel. We believe it helps us understand the world we live in and the people we share it with – and of course tourism is vital to many developing economies. But the scale of modern tourism has also damaged some places irreparably, and climate change is accelerated by most forms of transport, especially flying. All Rough Guides' flights are carbon-offset, and every year we donate money to a variety of environmental charities.

Including the relevant taxes, return **fares** from Miami, for example, range from US$700 (low season) to US$900 (high season), from New York or Washington US$750–1100 and from Los Angeles US$750–1000.

There are no direct flights from **Canada**; connections have to be made in the US or Mexico, making it at least a nine-hour journey, with typical prices of Can$800–1100. Slightly cheaper, direct charter flights can sometimes be bought in high season through Transat (W transat.com) from Calgary, Montréal and Toronto or through Sunwing (W flysunwing.ca) from Montréal and Toronto to **Río Hato** airport at Playa Blanca.

Flights from the UK and Ireland

Although there are currently no direct flights from the **UK** or **Ireland**, Lufthansa (W lufthansa.com) operates five flights a week from Frankfurt, and generally offers the cheapest deal from London and Ireland (£600–800 return). It's slightly more expensive to travel with KLM (W klm.com), which offers daily flights to Panama City from Amsterdam, and Air France (W airfrance.com), which makes the trip five times a week from Paris. Iberia (W iberia.com) has frequent, but even more expensive departures from several Spanish cities. The cheapest route from the UK or Ireland is sometimes via the US with a US carrier (see p.24), though the lengthier flying time and the extra hassle of clearing US immigration generally makes this less appealing than flying via Europe.

Flights from Australia, New Zealand and South Africa

It is a long, expensive haul to Panama from Australia, New Zealand and South Africa, with no direct flights. Most routes from **Australia** (Aus$3500–4000) and New Zealand (NZ$4000–4400) travel via the US, generally passing through Los Angeles, though flights via Santiago or Buenos Aires are also possible with journey time (26hr-plus) staying much the same. From **South Africa** (30hr-plus), you can travel via London, South America or the US (ZAR$19,000–22,000).

Flights from Central and South America

Various countries in **Latin America** have direct connections with Panama City, generally either through Avianca or, more usually, Copa, which connects with more than forty destinations across Latin America and the Caribbean. In Costa Rica,

award-winning Nature Air (W natureair.com) operates daily flights from San José to Bocas del Toro (US$360 return, including carbon offsetting), while Panama's domestic carrier Air Panama (W airpanama.com) makes six trips a week (except Sun) from San José to Panama City (from US$226 return). Copa's low-cost airline, Wingo (W wingo.com) offers cheap connections with several Colombian destinations (Medellín from $160 return, for example) as well as San José in Costa Rica ($228 return) – note that flights land at the new **Panamá Pacífico** airport (see p.73). Low-cost airline Viva Colombia (W vivacolombia.co) also uses the new airport and other South American budget airlines are said to be considering flights here.

Buses from Central America

It is possible to travel overland along the **Pan-American Highway** from Tapachula in Mexico to Panama City (with drop-offs at David and Santiago), with **Ticabus** (W ticabus.com; US$144 one way). Buses are comfortable and air-conditioned, offering the obligatory diet of Hollywood movies; they pick up (and drop off) passengers at the major Central American cities on the way, though you will have to spend a couple of nights in hotels, which increases the cost. **Transportes Galgos** (W transgalgosintergt.com) will also get you to Guatemala City from Tapachula (US$30 one way), from where you can transfer to Ticabus. **Agencia Tracopa** (W tracopacr.com) operates a twice-daily service from San José to David (US$21 one way).

Boats from Colombia

The only break in the 50,000km or so Pan-American Highway is an 87km stretch of swamp and mountainous jungle between Carepa on the Colombian border and Yaviza in Panama, in what is known as the **Darién Gap** (see p.43 & p.279). Up until the early 1990s, thrashing your way through here **overland** was a famous challenge for adventurers. However, crossing the Darién Gap has been forbidden for several years – the presence of drug-traffickers, Colombian paramilitaries and smugglers make it extremely dangerous, with the threat of death or kidnapping adding to the usual jungle hazards.

A (somewhat) safer alternative for those wanting to save money on air fares is to travel by **boat** along the Caribbean coast, though if you are out of luck with the weather, timings and bookings, the overall saving is likely to be negligible. Still, an adventure of sorts is guaranteed. This route requires a reasonable command of Spanish or a travelling companion who

SAILING BETWEEN COLOMBIA AND PANAMA – THE CLASSIC BACKPACKER ROUTE

A popular passage between Colombia and Panama involves a four- to five-day **sailing trip** between **Cartagena** or **Sapzurro** (close to the Colombia–Panama border) – taking in some of the more remote tropical islands of Guna Yala – and Cartí (see p.251), from where it's another US$40 to reach Panama City; Portobelo (see p.112); or Puerto Lindo (see p.117). Typically backpacker rates are US$500–550 per person from Cartagena (US$450–500 from Sapzurro), including food and non-alcoholic drinks, though some deals require you to help around the ship, be it crewing or cooking. In addition to being cheaper, the Sapzurro route has the advantage of avoiding the roughest seas by hugging the coast, thereby affording more time to explore Guna Yala. Be prepared to hang around at your departure point for a few days, since preparations can take some time. **Horror stories** abound of drunken captains and poorly maintained boats, so do your homework; hostel recommendations of particular captains can be helpful, but should be viewed critically since hostels usually receive commission for supplying passengers. You're best getting the lowdown from other people who have made the trip. Bear in mind, too, that this trip is **seasonal** – sailing between November and February can be dangerous with rough seas, so much so that some captains do not make the crossing during that period.

can speak the language. A **multiday sailing trip** from Cartagena or Sapzurro in Colombia to Colón province is another possibility (see box above).

To make the coastal journey from Colombia, it is first necessary to get to **Turbo**, a small city in the Antioquia department on the Pan-American Highway (accessible by regular buses from Medellín, which are safe during the day), or the nicer **Necoclí**, which lies nearer Cartagena. Both have a regular morning launch (8–9am) to **Capurganá** (2hr 30min from Turbo, US$21; 1hr 30min from Necoclí, US$23), a burgeoning low-key Caribbean resort unreachable by road. Note that in high season (Dec–April) there is usually more than one departure a day from Turbo. From Capurganá it is possible to sail to **Puerto Obaldía** (1hr; around US$10, depending on numbers), a small military outpost across the border in Panama, at the eastern end of Guna Yala. Since there is no regular crossing to Puerto Obaldía, departure times and charges from Capurganá depend on numbers, though the place is pleasant enough to hang out in for a few days while you're waiting for fellow travellers to roll up. Note also that both sea crossings can be exceedingly rough (especially between Nov and Feb) and are not for the faint-hearted; the boats are small and the waves loom large, though life jackets are provided. A large plastic bag to cover your luggage is a must, as well as waterproof protection for yourself.

Moving on from Puerto Obaldía, you can fly to Albrook Airport, the domestic airport in Panama City (1hr; US$105), with Air Panama (daily except Sat), though timings can vary. Alternatively, if you're feeling adventurous and are prepared to hang around in Puerto Obaldía, you can get a ride on one of the speedboats bound for Cartí, at the western end of Guna Yala. Note that this will be as expensive as flying (see p.268) and can be horrifically uncomfortable if the waves are high.

Red tape

Before leaving Colombia, get an exit stamp from **immigration** at Capurganá (daily 9am–5pm) and an entry stamp for Panama on arrival in Puerto Obaldía (daily 8am–4pm). Military police will meet the boat and escort you to the relevant authorities. Your belongings will be thoroughly searched for drugs and you are likely to be required to show proof of onward travel, possibly a yellow fever vaccination certificate (see p.33), and sufficient funds (a credit card will do) to cover your stay. A serious grilling and further searches may await you at customs and immigration at Albrook Airport in Panama City.

Agents and operators

Only a handful of operators offer Panama-only tours; most combine a visit with Costa Rica or other countries in Central America. While packages are convenient, it's cheapest to book your flight to Panama using a regular travel agent and then arrange your itinerary with a Panama City-based tour operator (see p.76).

Audley Travel UK ☎ 01993 838 675, ⓦ audleytravel.com. Several packages to Panama (eleven to nineteen days), including birdwatching and a highlights tour taking in Panama City, the Canal, Bocas and Guna Yala.

Journey Latin America UK ☎ 020 3811 6508, ⓦ journey latinamerica.co.uk. Long-established UK-based tour operator offering tailor-made itineraries and tours; includes trips combining Panama with Costa Rica and other countries, as well as a Panama highlights package.

North South Travel UK ☎ 01245 608291, ✆ northsouthtravel
.co.uk. Friendly, competitive travel agency, offering discounted fares
worldwide. Profits are used to support projects in the developing world,
especially the promotion of sustainable tourism.

STA Travel UK ☎ 0333 321 0099, US ☎ 1 800 781 4040, Australia
☎ 134 782, New Zealand ☎ 0800 474 400, South Africa ☎ 0861
781 781; ✆ statravel.co.uk. Worldwide specialists in independent
travel; also student IDs, travel insurance, car rental and more. Good
discounts for students and under-26s.

Travel CUTS Canada ☎ 1800 667 2887, US ☎ 1 800 592 2887;
✆ travelcuts.com. Canadian youth and student travel firm offering
discount flights and several trips combining Panama with Costa Rica and
other Central American countries.

Tucan Travel UK ☎ 020 8896 1600 or ☎ 0800 804 8435, US
☎ 1 855 444 9110; ✆ tucantravel.com. Award-winning small travel
operator offering Panama in combination with Costa Rica and other
Central American destinations on some of their adventure overland tours.

USIT Ireland ☎ 01 602 1906, ✆ usit.ie. Ireland's main student and
youth travel specialists.

Wild Planet Adventures US ☎ 1 800 9904376, ✆ wildplanet
adventures.com. Multi-award-winning company offering excellent
wildlife-focused adventure holidays (eight or thirteen days) to Panama, led
by naturalist guides. Also scuba diving in Coiba and tailor-made tours.

Getting around

**Panama has a fairly comprehensive and
very efficient bus network, used by the
majority of the population, which will
get you around most of the mainland,
though the level of comfort varies
enormously. Along the western section
of the Interamericana – the Panamanian
section of the Pan-American Highway –
luxury vehicles with reclinable seats, air
conditioning, nonstop videos and
on-board toilets speed along for several
hours for a handful of dollars, while at
the other end of the scale chivas –
converted pickup trucks packed like the
proverbial sardine can – grind their way
up twisting mountain roads to remote
villages for not a lot less.**

There are many good paved **roads** in central and
western Panama, even to small villages up in the
mountains, and dirt roads are also generally well
graded, though in the rainy season (roughly May to
mid-Dec) they can soon become a quagmire. East
of Panama City are few roads of any description.

For the longer trips from Panama City – over the
Cordillera Central to Bocas, deep into the Darién or to
the more distant islands of Guna Yala – an **internal
flight** on **Air Panama**, Panama's domestic airline, will

FINDING YOUR WAY

Panama is not without its frustrations:
streets often have several names, rarely
marked on a signpost; **telephone
numbers** change frequently, especially
for mobile phones and even for
government offices; and **websites** are
often not updated, or domain names left
to lapse – all of which makes contacting
people difficult. Moreover, the **pace of
change** in Panama at the moment is
phenomenal: new places to stay are
mushrooming; bars, discos and
restaurants, especially in Panama City
and tourist areas, regularly open, close,
move or change name, often lasting the
summer partying and tourist season, but
failing to make it through winter. This
Guide will help you navigate this dynamic
country, but it's always worth checking
details on the ground.

save a lot of time. Indeed with only one road –
sometimes impassable in the rainy season – into
Guna Yala, climbing aboard a plane is sometimes the
only way into the archipelago. And to hop from
island to island in Guna Yala or ease upriver to visit
Emberá villages in the Darién, the main mode of
transport is a motorized **dugout** (*cayuco* or *piragua*).

By bus

The vast brick building fronted by battalions of
buses just down the road from Albrook Airport on
the edge of Panama City is the Gran Terminal de
Transportes de Panamá – or **Albrook bus terminal**
– the hub of the **national bus system**. Most of the
capital's local transport and all international and
regional buses leave from here (see p.73).

The main centres, such as Santiago, Chitré and
David, also have large efficient **bus terminals** on
the outskirts of town complete with toilets, left-
luggage facilities and restaurants. From these,
regional connections and local buses – usually a
mixture of battered Toyota minivans with extra
fold-down aisle seating and the more comfortable
Coasters – head out into the countryside in centrif-
ugal fashion. In the smaller settlements, minibuses
or *chivas* hang out in the plaza or main street
waiting for an adequate number of passengers.
Generally, the more **rural** the location, the more
laissez-faire the bus timetable and the more likely it
is that passengers will be picked up anywhere
along the route.

Along most regional **bus routes** from Panama City, transport runs from 5.30/6am until 9/10pm, whereas the first buses heading into the capital from the provinces may leave from 1 to 4am to ensure passengers arrive for the start of the commercial day. Local transport in the provinces usually peters out around 6.30 or 7pm. Unless stated otherwise, all the bus services we list throughout this Guide are **daily** – but note that departures are often less frequent at weekends and in very rural areas, the last bus may not leave at all. The **timetables** for many routes can be consulted online at ⓦ thebusschedule.com/pa, which is kept reasonably up to date.

The **Interamericana** is punctuated with official and unofficial (generally at a major intersection) bus stops where you can flag down transport. Bear in mind that on Friday and Sunday afternoons, and at either end of a holiday period, when buses are jam-packed, you might be left stranded for hours.

Ticket prices range from $5–6 for a two-hour ride in moderate comfort to $15 for a relaxing seven-hour recline from Panama City all the way to David. There are set prices for every route, often posted on the bus window, and tourists are rarely overcharged – if in doubt about a fare ask a local on the bus. **Luggage** generally goes for free, either on the roof or in the luggage compartment, although surfboards sometimes incur extra charges. Security is not usually an issue.

Booking ahead for busy holiday periods and international journeys is a must, though it is only possible for international and some long-haul domestic routes. You'll need to go in person to the travel company ticket office, usually in the bus terminal, in Panama City, David or Changuinola, to buy the ticket in cash.

By plane

Flying within Panama is a convenient and safe experience, though you might have your heart in your mouth landing in the more flimsy twin-props at some of the more remote airstrips of Guna Yala and the Darién. All internal flights depart from or arrive at Marcos A. Gelabert Airport (☎238 2700), more commonly known as **Albrook Airport** (after the former US Air Force base it occupies), which lies 3km northwest of Panama City centre.

Air Panama (ⓦ airpanama.com), the country's one **domestic airline**, operates out of Albrook, and serves around twenty destinations: the major urban areas, several locations along the largely inaccessible Comarca de Guna Yala and currently two destinations in the Darién, which are impossible to reach by road. Propeller planes seating forty to fifty passengers generally ply the urban routes, while smaller puddle-hoppers operate in the Darién and Guna Yala to suit the shorter runways – sometimes only as long as the island they're on.

Prices remain constant irrespective of the season, with the maximum one-way domestic fare currently around $105 (including taxes) and many much cheaper. Luggage allowances are 12kg plus 2.3kg carry-on, but full-size surfboards incur an extra charge of $20.

Compared with the long-distance buses, plane **timetables** are fairly sketchily adhered to, especially in Guna Yala and the Darién. Flights to David, Bocas and Guna Yala are booked up quickly in advance of a holiday weekend.

By car

Away from the traffic hell that is Panama City, **driving** in Panama is generally fairly straightforward, with very good, well-signposted roads connecting the main urban centres, though it can be a different story in some of the more remote or mountainous areas.

The **Interamericana** (also called the Carretera Panamericana in Panama), Panama's main thoroughfare – part of the Pan-American Highway that travels almost 48,000km from Alaska to Chile – runs 486km from the Costa Rican border at Paso Canoas in the west, skirting several major cities, crossing the canal and bludgeoning its way through the capital before continuing another 282km and grinding to an abrupt halt in Yaviza in the eastern Darién.

Traffic for the Azuero Peninsula peels off onto the **Carretera Nacional** at Divisa, 34km east of Santiago, and branches off north across the Cordillera Central at Chiriquí for the sinuous journey across the continental divide down to the islands of Bocas del Toro on western Panama's only transisthmian route. Though an excellent paved road, it is sometimes blocked by landslides during the wettest months of the rainy season (roughly May to mid-Dec).

The only other routes across the isthmus lie east of the canal. The frequently log-jammed **Transístmica** links the capital with the country's second city of Colón; the faster **Autopista Panamá–Colón**, a toll road aimed at improving commercial traffic, runs parallel. An hour east of Panama City, beyond Chepo, a roller coaster of a road heads north from the Interamericana at El Llano, heading 40km over the mountains to Cartí, providing the only road link with Guna Yala. It's accessible most of the year, but although it's paved, only 4WD vehicles are granted access. Further east, the final stretch of the Interamericana as far as **Yaviza** is completely paved, but every year after heavy rain a section or two gets damaged, resulting in a quagmire. Expect an increasing number of police **checkpoints** along this stretch of road, as well as along the western section of the Interamericana, as you near the Costa Rican border.

Despite Panama's decent road network, **driving at night** is best avoided because there's little illumination outside the urban centres, and drink driving, one of the main causes of accidents nationally, is common. Though there is a legal limit of 86mg, it is rarely adhered to or enforced.

If you are involved in a car **accident**, Panamanian law requires that you should not move the vehicles but should wait near them until the traffic police (*Transito*) arrive; a statement from them is required in order to file any insurance claim. Unless otherwise indicated the **speed limits** are 40km/h in urban areas, 60km/h on secondary roads and 100km/h on primary roads but these limits are neither widely advertised nor followed. Two of the most **dangerous** roads are the Interamericana, along which copious buses and heavy trucks thunder, and the route across the Cordillera Central to Bocas del Toro, when bad weather can make the hairpin bends even more scary.

Hitching is possible, though with all the obvious attendant risks, on the main thoroughfares, but it is unlikely anyone will stop. In the rural areas, where there is no or at best infrequent bus service, it is quite usual to thumb a lift on the back of a private pickup, though you should offer to pay at least the equivalent of a bus fare.

Car rental

Renting a car makes it easier to explore some out-of-the-way spots – though if you're staying in Panama City and the Canal area it's much more convenient to use buses and taxis. You'll find all the usual international **car rental firms** represented. The larger firms have their head offices at Tocumen International Airport, with many running a downtown office and sometimes branches at Albrook and David airports too. Some operators have offices in other major cities and tourist towns. Rental **costs** vary greatly, so shop around and note that rates fluctuate according to season and demand. You may get a better deal if you book online in advance.

Virtually all rental vehicles have air conditioning. A manual economy car is the cheapest option (from approximately $25/day, or $140/week, including taxes and basic insurance cover). For a 4WD, which is probably only necessary if you want to get off the beaten track and into the national parks, bank on

paying almost double that. **Fuel** costs $3.50–4 a gallon (about $1/litre) and petrol stations (often 24hr) are liberally sprinkled along the main roads.

The **minimum age** for most car rental companies is 25 but 23 will suffice for some firms provided a credit card is produced as security. A driving licence – international or from your country of origin – as well as a passport will need to be shown.

By taxi

Taxis, generally in the form of a 4WD twin cab, are also a practical way of reaching rural locations that are poorly served by public transport. Official cabs are yellow, with their licence number printed on the door, though in the countryside you may come across unofficial drivers whose service is generally just as reliable.

Taxis are widely available in most **urban centres** and can save you from melting in the heat. Panama City cabs ostensibly charge fixed rates according to zones (which are rarely adhered to) or generally agreed prices for particular routes (see p.75). Most central trips within the capital during the day should not exceed $4; in other urban centres it should not exceed a couple of dollars. Across the country, a small surcharge is added for more than two passengers and prices are higher at night. While most taxi drivers are very honest, in Panama City and tourist areas like Boquete some might try to take advantage – make local enquiries about the going rates and agree on a price before getting in. The establishment of an **Uber** system in Panama City has helped to curb some drivers overcharging.

Taxi drivers can also be hired as **tourist guides**, though most will only speak Spanish – ask at your accommodation for a recommended driver. There is no set charge, but around $15 an hour is the going rate in the capital for a driver who speaks English, $10–12 an hour for a driver who can only speak Spanish. Petrol costs also need to be factored in if you want to cover a substantial distance. A full day-trip round the Canal area (both Pacific and Atlantic sides), for example, might cost around $140 but you'll need to shop around.

By boat

Panama boasts more than 1500 islands so it's almost inevitable you'll require water transport at some stage, be it smooth sightseeing in a Canal transit or a bumpy water-taxi ride in Bocas. Fairly robust **ferries** equipped with life jackets and radio transmitters leave Panama City for Isla Taboga and the Archipiélago de las Perlas, according to regular timetables. In the remoter regions of eastern Guna Yala, meanwhile, you could be seated on a plank in a leaking motorized **dugout** bailing out with a yoghurt carton, having spent a couple of hours asking round for a ride. Frequent **water-taxis** serve Bocas from Almirante for fixed fares ($6), whereas any trip to the Pacific island of Coiba may mean getting a group of interested people together and negotiating a deal with a fisherman.

Travelling by motorized dugout or occasionally, if you're lucky, in a slightly more comfy **skiff** (*panga*), is the norm among the communities of Guna Yala and the Darién. If a boat is already heading the way you want to travel, as a **colectivo**, you can travel *como pasajero*, and the fare will be cheaper. Otherwise, private boat rental, or **viaje especial** (which needs to cover fuel and the boat operator's time), can be expensive; awareness of the going price for diesel will help when it comes to haggling, as will knowledge of the amount of fuel necessary to cover the distance given the size of the engine. Note that the seaworthiness of vessels varies enormously; many are overloaded and lack life jackets even when heading for long trips on potentially hazardous waters. Every few months a boat somewhere sinks or capsizes and people **drown**. Make sure you check out your transport thoroughly before committing to a journey.

By bike

Away from the Interamericana and Panama City, **cycling** is pleasant – with wonderful views and quiet roads – and growing in popularity both as recreation and a means of transport (though you won't find cycle lanes or cycle routes). Mountain bike **rental** is on the increase in tourist areas such as El Valle, Boquete, Bocas and Santa Fé, though the quality of the machine on offer varies ($3–5/hr, $10–15/day). In Panama City you'll find rental places on the Calzada de Amador, which actually possesses a cycle path, as does the recently inaugurated Cinta Costera. Exodus (Ⓦexodus.co.uk) and Explore (Ⓦexplore.co.uk) offer **cycling holidays** in Panama.

Accommodation

From secluded mountain ecolodges to thatched cane cabañas on deserted islands, from backpackers' party hostels to smart boutique hotels, Panama offers a wide range of accommodation. Panama City has the greatest variety, though prices are generally a lot higher than elsewhere. In touristy areas such as Bocas and Boquete prices are creeping up and more lodgings now exist at the higher end of the market, with an increasing number of comfortable lodges (often foreign-owned) and B&Bs – but there is still little outside Panama City that could truly be described as luxury. In Guna Yala you could just as likely be sleeping in a hammock, while in the Darién you might be snoozing on a thin mattress on an open-sided raised traditional Emberá dwelling.

Types of hotel

Posadas and **lodges** usually offer a fair degree of comfort in pleasant natural surroundings, whereas places prefaced with **hospedaje**, **pensión** or **residencial** are generally much simpler small family-owned lodgings. The word **cabaña** may conjure up an image of a simple thatched hut in an idyllic natural setting, but can just as easily mean a dark, windowless cement cell in an unremarkable location. **Hostal** may signify a place with dorms for backpackers but is also a synonym for a family-run hotel. The term **hotel**, too, can cover a mixed bag from a plush international five-star high-rise to a dilapidated shack, and also includes the famous by-the-hour push-button motel, often referred to as **un push**, which rents out rooms short-term for sexual liaisons. In no way unique to Panama, they are scattered all over the country, most visibly along the Interamericana, with such enticing names as *Sueño Lindo* (Sweet Dreams) or *Las Mil y Una Noches* (Thousand and One Nights). As for the much-abused prefix "eco", it may simply denote pleasant natural surroundings, and is no guarantee of sustainable environmental practices or social responsibility.

ACCOMMODATION PRICES

For each accommodation option listed in this Guide we give the cheapest rate for a **double room** (one double bed) for one night in high season (outside public holidays), including tourist tax, with a private bathroom where available; we state in the reviews if only shared bathrooms are available. Dorm beds and camping are quoted per person, unless otherwise stated, as are prices for **homestays**.

Facilities

Neither name nor price is much of an indication of what you'll get for your money, though a private **bathroom** is often squeezed into even fairly rudimentary and minuscule lodgings. In the lowlands, even the cheapest establishments usually have **air conditioning**, though not necessarily **hot water**; in the highlands air conditioning and fans are unnecessary and usually absent though hot water is almost always available. **Wi-fi** is widely available, and almost always free. Guna Yala and the Darién are the two exceptions: in the former there is virtually no wi-fi, and in the latter coverage is limited and unreliable. As in most other Latin American countries, toilet paper should not be put down the **toilet**, but into the adjacent wastebasket, because it can clog the system in all but the most modern top-end hotels. If in doubt, enquire at reception.

Breakfast is not always provided, and where it is available, it may not be included in the rates. In our reviews we presume breakfast is not included unless otherwise stated.

Hostels

Panama's **hostel** scene is expanding as the country attracts increasing numbers of backpackers. Most hostels have common areas, shared kitchens, free wi-fi or internet access and bags of useful information about the surrounding area. Currently there are about two dozen in the country – mainly in Panama City, Bocas, Boquete, David and Santa Catalina. Advance **booking**, where allowed, is advisable in high season. A dorm bunk varies in price from around $11 to $17, occasionally including coffee or a light breakfast, and increasingly including air conditioning in lowland areas. Some establishments also offer private rooms at around $25–35. Some of the **national parks** and protected areas offer dorm accommodation (usually $15/person/night) and a shared kitchen.

Camping

There is virtually no organized **camping** in Panama, though a few lodgings allow tents if asked and some places provide tents to rent in summer (Dec–April). In rural communities you can almost always find someone willing to let you to camp on their land for a small fee. Alternatively, there are long swathes of empty beaches to pitch a tent on, although you should always seek local advice, since they are not universally safe; beach campers in touristy areas such as Santa Clara and Isla Bastimentos have periodically been subject to thefts and muggings. The **national parks** seem more set up for camping, with set fees (usually $6/person a night), but the sites rarely offer facilities beyond those shared with the park wardens at the park entrance: a toilet, cold-water shower and rudimentary kitchen with limited utensils.

Homestays

Homestays, a good budget accommodation option, often help the local economy more directly while providing an opportunity to engage in cross-cultural interaction. They may also be the only option during major fiestas in a town that is short of formal lodgings. In indigenous communities, such as in Guna Yala and the Darién, a homestay is frequently the norm when overnighting in a village; you will need to arrange this with the chief or tourist coordinator on arrival (see pp.252–253 & p.283).

Pricing and taxes

Most mid-range and high-end accommodation operates a dual **pricing system**: high-season rates (mid-Dec to April) generally coincide with the dry season, whereas the rest of the year counts as low season, when it's possible to find significant discounts, especially for online bookings. On top of high-season rates, some establishments in Panama City and the major holiday destinations hike their prices even higher for Carnaval, Easter (Semana Santa), Christmas and New Year. Some lodgings in places that are primarily weekend retreats, such as Isla Grande and El Valle, charge more from Friday to Sunday, occasionally demanding a two- or three-night minimum stay over the weekend.

Places with more than nine rooms are subject to a ten-percent **tourist tax** (though even smaller lodgings sometimes charge), which is not always included in the advertised rate. Note too that in mid-range hotels a double room often means a room with two double beds and you might have to specify one double bed (*una cama doble*, or *una cama matrimonial*) if you want to keep costs down. Room costs are usually based on two people sharing, but many rooms have an extra single bed, which a third person can have for an extra $10–15. Children under 12 are often allowed to stay for free.

Food and drink

Panamanian cuisine is infused with numerous culinary influences, notably Afro-Antillean, indigenous, Spanish, Chinese and American. Cosmopolitan Panama City offers the greatest variations in terms of gastronomy and price, from a $3–4 plate of noodles and chicken in the public market to ornate fusion cuisine served on damask tablecloths. You can take your pick from a host of world cuisines, including American – and thankfully not just McDonald's and KFC.

In the capital, **Panamanian food** rarely features on the menus of the mid- to high-end restaurants, outside a few tourist-oriented venues, but in markets, hole-in-the-wall restaurants and out in the interior, it's much easier to find local specialities – often heavy on starch and frequently fried.

Outside the capital and the major tourist destinations of Boquete and Bocas, there is less variety and dining is often more informal and a lot cheaper; travellers on a tight budget can easily find simple well-cooked food in *fondas* (basic restaurants), which offer *comida corriente* – also known as the *menú del día* – (meal of the day) for very little. **Vegetarians** will be challenged since, as elsewhere in Central America, even the veggie staple of beans and rice can be cooked in pork fat. Your best bet is to head for a Chinese restaurant, which exist in most towns, or one of the proliferating pizzerias, or to stock up with the fresh fruit and vegetables that abound in local markets.

Predominantly self-service **cafeterías** – the Panamanian equivalent of American diners – keep going from around 6 or 7am until 11pm or midnight in the urban centres. Out in the countryside, local restaurants and **fondas** may also open for all three meals but shut shortly after nightfall, depending on demand.

Breakfast

Panama's filling **desayuno típico** (traditional breakfast) is aimed at sustaining workers for a hard day in the fields. Deep-fried favourites include tortillas (thick cornmeal cakes), *carimañolas* (mashed boiled yuca – cassava or manioc – stuffed with ground beef) and *hojaldres* (discs of sweetened leavened dough, which at best are delightfully crispy and tasty but at worst are chewy

---

TRADITIONAL DISHES

PANAMANIAN MAINS

Non-vegetarians should not leave Panama without sampling the **national dish**, *sancocho*. Variations are served in many parts of Latin America and even within Panama the meal is prepared in numerous ways; essentially it's a hearty chicken-based soup with large chunks of yuca and other filling root vegetables, or maybe even plantain and sweetcorn, flavoured with cilantro – a herb similar to coriander but more pungent – exemplifying the Caribbean culinary influence. Other Panamanian variations of ubiquitous **Latin dishes** include the unappetizing-sounding *ropa vieja* ("old clothes" – spicy shredded beef over rice), *ceviche* (white fish, shrimp or octopus marinated in lime juice with chopped onion and garlic plus hot pepper and fresh coriander) and *mondongo* (a slow-cooked tripe- and chorizo-based stew with root vegetables, laced with garlic and coriander or cilantro).

COASTAL CUISINE

Seafood is a Panamanian staple in both the Pacific and Caribbean lowlands. In the latter, the Afro-Antillean influence is dominant – typical dishes include rice cooked in coconut milk and seafood prepared with spices and judicious amounts of lime. *Corvina* (sea bass) is the most widely eaten fish, but you can also find snapper, grouper, dorado, shrimp, langoustines, crab and lobster, though you should refuse the last four if offered them during the closed season (Dec 1–April 15 in the Pearl Islands, March 1–June 30 along the Caribbean coast) unless you know they have come from a freezer. Locally farmed trout is a speciality of the Chiriquí Highlands.

GREENS AND SPICES

While starch and carbohydrates abound in most traditional foods, **greenery** is scarce. Don't be surprised if your salad accompaniment is merely a lettuce leaf supporting a slice of tomato and a couple of onion rings. Green vegetables are even conspicuous by their absence in many restaurants outside the capital, though they can often be found in local markets. Spices are generally used sparingly, but there's usually some *salsa picante* on the table to help add a kick.

and dripping in grease). Costa Rica's national dish, *gallo pinto* (literally "speckled rooster"), is also popular, a moist rice, beans and onions mix often accompanied with a dollop of *natilla* – a local sour cream that is also lavished on strawberries in the Chiriquí Highlands – and fried or scrambled eggs.

For something lighter, head for a **panadería** (bakery) for a pastry and a shot of coffee, or pick up fresh fruit at the local market. In the more expensive hotels in Panama City and in European- or North American-owned establishments outside the capital, you can also expect combinations of cereals, fruit, yoghurt and toast.

Lunch and dinner

Lunch in formal dining establishments is usually served from noon until 3pm, dinner from 6 or 7pm until around 10pm, with the midday meal usually offering better value for money.

While it's possible to grab a light **lunch** – a flaky *empanada* (pasty) with a beef-, pork-, chicken or cheese-based filling or an *emparedado* (sandwich) – in urban areas, for most Panamanians lunch is the main meal of the day. In the *fondas* and cheaper restaurants ordering an *almuerzo* or *menú del día* (lunch of the day) will get you a filling plate of chicken with rice, plus beans or lentils, or maybe fish and plantain down on the coast, for $3–4. Some places throw in a soup starter and dessert to give you a three-course set meal at very little extra cost. Posher restaurants in the city will sometimes offer a *menú ejecutivo* – a fancier and pricier set menu – but still good value – to their business clientele.

Set-meal **cenas** (dinner of the day) are available in the early evening in some places. Otherwise, **evening eating** is generally more low-key.

Mid-range and high-end restaurants often add the seven-percent sales tax (ITBMS) on top of the bill, and some even add an obligatory ten-percent **service charge** – recently outlawed, in theory – which is not always included on the menu price list. Where meal prices are quoted in the Guide we have factored in these extra charges.

Street food and snacks

Street food, though not widespread, can range from chunks of fresh pineapple or watermelon to plantain crisps (*platanitos*) deep-fried on the spot. Small **roadside grills** often serve *carne en palito* (meat on a little stick) – fairly tiny kebabs comprising slivers of (occasionally spicy) marinated beef, which take the edge off your appetite. During the day, you'll also see men pushing carts laden with fluorescent liquids and blocks of ice around the main squares, peddling **raspados** – paper cones filled with shavings of ice, drizzled over with a sickly flavoured liquid, made still sweeter by a slurp of condensed milk and much loved by kids.

Alcoholic drinks

Beer is the most popular alcoholic drink; Panama's four main labels – Soberana, Panamá, Balboa and Atlas – are all fairly inoffensive lagers, with Balboa, the current favourite, slightly more full-bodied. Balboa Ice and Panamá Lite are low-alcohol additions to the range. Though none of these will set the pulses of beer aficionados racing, when ice-cold they do hit the spot. You'll pay a dollar to swig out of a bottle in a local *cantina*, and up to $6 to have your beer served in a frosted glass on a serviette in a plush nightclub. Imported beers such as Heineken and Budweiser, and even Guinness, are available in Panama City and tourist towns but are more expensive. Over the last couple of years, craft beers have made an appearance in the major tourist/expat areas; bank on paying $5–6 a bottle.

The national tipple, the transparent, throat-singeing **seco** (a rough sugar-cane spirit), is significantly more potent (35 percent) and more commonly consumed by men in the interior, particularly during fiestas – as is rum. **Chicha fuerte**, a potent fermented maize brew, is made in bulk for special celebrations, particularly among indigenous and *campesino* communities. Another lethal home-brew favoured by *campesinos* is **vino de palma**, made from fermented palm sap, whereas *guarapo* is sugar-cane juice distilled to knockout strength. **Wine** – usually Chilean or Californian – is becoming increasingly available at reasonable prices in Panama City and in tourist areas such as Bocas and Boquete.

Non-alcoholic drinks

Fruit-based drinks feature prominently; in most parts of the country you can enjoy them with ice, safe in the knowledge that the water is drinkable (see opposite). Mango, pineapple, soursop, passion fruit, tamarind and a host of other fruits can be savoured in a range of forms: as a *jugo natural* (pure fruit juice), a *licuado* (a fresh fruit, water and sugar shake), a *batido* (a milk shake) or a *chicha* (a sweet maize-based fruit concoction, not to be confused with its alcoholic cousin *chicha fuerte*). The similar-sounding **chicheme**, a tasty Panamanian speciality of ground maize, milk, vanilla and cinnamon, most revered in La Chorrera, should be sampled, as should **pipa** – fresh coconut water sipped through a straw straight from the shell.

Outside the country, Panama's reputation as the world leader in producing gourmet **coffee** is a secret known only to connoisseurs; you can sample the most prized beans in Boquete and Panama City, though elsewhere you're more likely to be sipping the more mundane but perfectly satisfying Café Duran, which will be strong and is sometimes offered with condensed milk. While black **tea** is widely available in cities and tourist areas, tea lovers will usually have to content themselves with herbal varieties elsewhere – chamomile (*manzanilla*) or cinnamon (*canela*) are the most common.

Iced **tap water** is generally served on arrival in restaurants, except where water quality is poor – Bocas, the Darién and Guna Yala – in which case you'll need to order mineral water.

Health

In the years when the transisthmus railroad and Canal were under construction, Panama was synonymous with disease, in particular yellow fever, malaria and cholera. Thankfully, times have changed, and most of Panama poses little threat to your health: yellow fever has been eradicated; malaria only persists in a few isolated areas; tap water is safe to drink in most of the country; and sophisticated medical care is widely available in the main population centres. Your most likely medical ailment will be travellers' diarrhoea from a change of diet and climate, or sunburn from overdoing it on the beach.

That said, you should ensure that your basic **inoculations** are up to date and consult a travel medical centre professional to help you decide what other precautions to take. If you intend only to explore the Canal area and chill on the beach, you'll probably need little more than sun block and insect repellent, but if you're bent on venturing into the Darién jungle, all kinds of insect- and water-borne hazards need to be considered. **Medical insurance** is essential (see p.35 & p.43).

Inoculations

Most inoculations that involve multiple jabs need six to eight weeks to complete. There are no compulsory vaccinations to visit Panama but in addition to ensuring that your **routine injections** are current (tetanus, diphtheria and polio, and MMR), hepatitis A and typhoid are generally recommended, though you can also have a combined hepatitis A and B jab, advisable for long-term travellers. **Yellow fever** is nearly always flagged up as a hazard on health websites in relation to Panama, although the last documented case was in 1974. Nevertheless, there is still deemed to be a very slight risk of the disease in the Darién and remoter parts of Guna Yala. Moreover, since November 2008 the Panamanian government has required travellers entering the country from countries where yellow fever is listed as endemic, such as Colombia and Brazil, to carry proof of vaccination at least ten days prior to entry – ironic given that Panama is also on the list – though this requirement is rarely enforced.

Rabies is another potential hazard, more from vampire bats in cattle-ranching areas than from feral dogs, and one that should only really be considered by travellers expecting to spend time in the remoter rural areas.

General precautions

A major plus is that **tap water** in most of Panama is safe to drink, which means the usual travel worries about avoiding ice in drinks and salads washed in ordinary water can be dispensed with. The exceptions are in Guna Yala, much of the Darién and the remoter parts of Bocas. On the main tourist islands of Guna Yala and Bocas bottled water, though expensive, is widely available, but it is less easily obtained in the Darién. That said, since disposing of non-organic waste such as plastic bottles is a particularly acute environmental issue in these areas, try to bring a water filter or use water purification tablets as much as possible. These are rarely available in Panama City (see p.38) so bring them with you. While vile-tasting chlorine or iodine tablets are still effective and widely available, most companies now produce tablets to neutralize the unpleasant aftertaste. Seek advice on the relative merits of chlorine versus iodine; the latter, for example, though considered more effective against giardia parasites, is generally not recommended for pregnant women. Campers with their own stove can of course boil water to sterilize it.

Since food safety is related to water safety and to food storage, exercise common sense when eating **salads** or **unpeeled fruit** in the few areas in Panama where the water is not potable. **Street food**, though frequently very tasty, is another potential minefield, particularly at fiestas when mounds of chicken and rice stand around in the hot sun for hours. Make sure the food is well cooked in front of you and, if the stall has been dishing up food all day, that any raw meat or fish has been stored in a cooler box with ice before cooking – and avoid anything swimming in mayonnaise.

Intestinal problems

Travellers' **diarrhoea** (TD) lasting a few days is the most common ailment encountered, as likely to be due to the change in diet and climate as to contaminated food or water-carrying bacteria, viruses or parasites. If you're afflicted by the runs, the best cure is to rest and rehydrate, drinking plenty of clean water with rehydration salts. Sachets of Dioralyte or Electolade are worth keeping in your first-aid kit, though equivalents are easily found in pharmacies in the major urban centres. Diarrhoea remedies such as Imodium and Lomotil should only be used in emergencies, such as when embarking on a long-distance plane journey or a jungle trek, since stopping the flow is not actually healthy. If symptoms persist, especially if there is blood in the stool or vomiting occurs, consult a doctor, who will probably prescribe a course of antibiotics.

Sunburn and dehydration

Skin cancer is on the increase, largely because of overexposure to UV radiation – indeed it is the most prevalent form of cancer in the US. In the fierce tropical sun of Panama, a high-factor sun cream (SPF 15 or higher with both UVA and UVB protection), a sun hat and sunglasses are an absolute must. Up to forty percent of the sun's rays can be reflected back up from water or sand, even if you're sitting in the shade; nor is an overcast day free from damaging UV light. When travelling in a dugout – a likely scenario if exploring the Darién or Guna Yala – you could be faced with hours without any protection. Serious sunburn, sunstroke and heatstroke are therefore all very real health hazards and far more likely than catching a tropical disease. Keeping up your fluid intake to avoid **dehydration** is essential.

Malaria

There is low risk of **malaria** in more remote areas of the Caribbean lowlands in Bocas and Veraguas, and a slightly higher risk east of the Canal, in the Darién and in more isolated areas of Guna Yala. Transmitted by a parasite in the saliva of an infected anopheles mosquito (active from dusk to dawn), its symptoms – fever, chills, headaches and muscle pains – are easily confused with flu.

It is most effectively combated through **prevention** – wearing long loose sleeves and trousers for protection, dousing yourself in repellent and sleeping under a mosquito net or in screened rooms. Most effective chemical insect **repellents** contain DEET, with the 25–35 percent varieties considered adequate for most needs. However, a few recent studies have started to raise questions about DEET's possible neurological side-effects as well as damage to the environment. Whatever the medical opinions on the subject, you have to wonder about a solution that will melt your pen if it gets too close. Recently, more organic, non-chemical products, based on oils such as eucalyptus, citronella, cedar or verbena, are appearing on the market. They are generally more expensive but give less fierce protection, which wears off much more quickly. They can be effective enough when used with other preventive measures, although if you are in a malarial area you might want to stick to DEET. Mosquito **coils** are widely available across Panama, even in small villages; if you're seeking a natural alternative, candles can help deter the insects. In neither case should they be used in enclosed indoor environments. It's a good idea to carry a travel mosquito **net** if you're intending to travel widely in the Darién or spend time in the national parks.

A range of **anti-malarial tablets** are on the market, all of which should be bought prior to arriving in Panama and started in advance of visiting the malarial area, though a public medical centre (*centro de salud*) in a malarial area should stock a supply for post-exposure treatment. West of the Canal, chloroquine is the drug of choice, generally taken once a week a fortnight in advance of entering a malarial area and for four weeks afterwards. East of the Canal, where mosquitoes are chloroquine-resistant, mefloquine (also known as Larium) is often prescribed, though it can have particularly severe side effects. Malarone is a less controversial alternative but is currently the most expensive anti-malarial drug on the market. It is taken daily only two days before entering an infected area, to be continued for a week after leaving. Whatever you choose, it is important to finish the course of anti-malarials because of the time lag between bite and infection. If you become ill with flu-like symptoms after returning home, consult a doctor and inform them you've been to a malarial risk area.

Other bites and stings

Taking steps to avoid being bitten by **insects** is of paramount importance (see opposite). In addition to malaria, mosquitoes can transmit **dengue fever**, which induces flu-like symptoms similar to malaria but with more extreme aches and has been on the increase in Central America and the Caribbean in recent years. **Sandflies** (*chitras*) are a more likely pest for travellers, proliferating during the rainy season (roughly May to mid-Dec), and not only at the beach; they're almost invisible, so you will become aware of them only when they bite. Sandfly bites itch more and for longer than mosquito bites – calamine lotion or antihistamine cream will usually reduce the aggravation. In forested rural areas in various parts of Panama bites from an infected sandfly can cause cutaneous leishmaniasis, whose symptoms can remain dormant for up to six months before sores and swellings break out on the skin. Though there is no vaccine, the disease is treatable through a series of jabs.

An overfamiliarity with Indiana Jones films can lead to the misconception that the greatest danger in the rainforest is a **snake bite**. While Panama has its share of venomous snakes – bushmaster, fer-de-lance and coral for starters – you are unlikely to see one, let alone get bitten. Nevertheless, donning long trousers and closed shoes, or (even better) boots, reduces the risk, as does avoiding walking in the forest at night. Should a snake manage to get its fangs into you, immobilize the affected area, apply a light-pressure bandage (not tourniquet) above and below the bite and seek immediate medical attention. Even a local medical centre should have some antivenin.

There's a whole host of **other beasts** on land that may bite or sting, but only when threatened – scorpions (more commonly seen at night) and some spiders, for example – while in the sea jellyfish, sting rays and fire coral can all be painful. If you are prone to allergic reactions to bites and stings, make sure you carry some antihistamine tablets, which can reduce swelling and itchiness, as well as antihistamine cream or calamine lotion to cool and ease the pain.

Accessing medical care

Both state and private **medical care** is very good in Panama, particularly in Panama City; many doctors work in the public-sector hospitals in the morning and run private clinics in the afternoon. The main problem the public sector faces is a lack of resources, particularly in the more rural villages, so most Panamanians who can afford private health care, as well as almost all expats, will head for a **private clinic**, where service is likely to be more immediate. The average cost of a consultation with a private doctor starts at $50, provided no X-rays or laboratory tests need doing, whereas a doctor at the local government-run clinic will see you for $5.

While **travel insurance** may cover costs, it will only do so after you file a claim on your return; you still need to be able to access sufficient funds to cover the bills at the time. Many doctors in the main cities have trained in the US at some stage and so speak good English. The US Embassy has a list of **bilingual doctors** in Panama City on its website (Ⓦ panama.usembassy.gov/medical2010.html).

Medical resources for travellers

There are a number of useful **online resources**, though their information may not be sufficiently nuanced for your needs. The websites listed here generally note travel medical centres, where you can get jabs, and give general advice on the most common ailments and diseases that you might encounter. Travel medical centre professionals generally have access to more detailed and specific health information; you are strongly advised to consult them as well as carrying out your own research.

US AND CANADA

Canadian Society for International Health ☎ 613 241 5785, Ⓦ csih.org. Extensive list of travel health centres.

Centers for Disease Control and Prevention (CDC) ☎ 1 800 232 4636, ☎ 1 888 232 6348 (24hr health helpline), Ⓦ cdc.gov /travel. Official US government travel health site that's laden with info

Public Health Agency of Canada Ⓦ phac-aspc.gc.ca. Distributes free pamphlets on travel health and provides a comprehensive list of travel clinics in the country.

Travellers' Medical and Vaccination Centre Ⓦ tmvc.com. List of travel health centres in Canada and vaccination costs plus brief travel health tips.

UK AND IRELAND

Fitfortravel Ⓦ fitfortravel.nhs.uk. Excellent NHS (Scotland) public access site with country-specific advice, the latest health bulletins and information on immunizations.

Hospital for Tropical Diseases Travel Clinic ☎ 020 7388 9600 (Travel Clinic), ☎ 020 7950 7799 (24hr Travellers Healthline Advisory Service – see website for additional country-specific information), Ⓦ www.thehtd.org/TravelClinic.aspx. Mainly aimed at travellers suffering from allergies or with complex medical conditions.

MASTA (Medical Advisory Service for Travellers Abroad) ☎ 0870 606 2782, Ⓦ masta-travel-health.com. List of affiliated travel clinics where you can get vaccinations and detailed country-specific health briefs.

National Travel Health Network and Centre ⓦ nathnac.org. Excellent website for health professionals and the travelling public providing factsheets on travel health risks and a free database of country-specific health info.

STA Travel UK ⓦ statravel.co.uk/travel-clinic.htm. List of STA travel clinics in England and vaccination prices; full-time students with student card can get a ten-percent discount.

Tropical Medical Bureau ☎ 1850 487 674, international ☎ 00 353 1 2715 210, ⓦ tmb.ie. List of travel clinics in Ireland and country-specific info from US consular service.

AUSTRALASIA AND SOUTH AFRICA

Travellers' Medical and Vaccination Centre ⓦ traveldoctor .com.au. User-friendly site listing travel clinics in Australia, New Zealand and South Africa plus accessible factsheets on travel health and postings of health alerts worldwide.

The media

Aside from one government TV channel and one radio station, the media in Panama is privately owned. The five national daily Spanish-language newspapers – and three Chinese-language papers, catering to the country's sixty-thousand-strong Chinese-Panamanian community – are widely available from street vendors in urban areas, and in supermarkets countrywide. It's hard to escape TV in Panama – screens adorn most eating and drinking establishments, even upmarket restaurants, and are standard in most hotel rooms.

Newspapers

The most respected **paper** is *La Prensa* (ⓦ prensa .com), which also produces informative supplements with in-depth writing and interesting features on tourism, history and culture. *La Estrella de Panamá* (ⓦ laestrella.com.pa) and *Panamá América* (ⓦ pa-digital.com.pa) also count as "quality press", with *El Siglo* (ⓦ elsiglo.com) and *La Crítica* (ⓦ critica.com.pa) the popular tabloid options.

Given the large US expat population, there is no shortage of **English-language news**. Aside from the imported *Miami Herald International Edition* and *USA Today*, there is the online *The Panama News* (ⓦ thepanamanews.com), which has the mantra "writing for thinking people not cattle". It pulls no punches and frequently contains features that border on the libellous but, picking through them

with healthy scepticism, you will gain some valuable insights into the dirty side of politics and business.

Liberally sprinkled round hotel lobbies and restaurants around the country, the **free bilingual weekly** *The Visitor/El Visitante* (ⓦ thevisitorpanama .com) offers a bland summary of Panamanian news, features and a decent listings section of events in the main tourist zones of Panama City, Bocas and Boquete. The latter two expat enclaves also produce **free English-language monthlies**: *The Bocas Breeze* (ⓦ thebocasbreeze.com) and *The Bajareque* (ⓦ elbajareque.net). Primarily run by and for expats, they occasionally contain some useful listings.

TV and radio

On evenings in a bar or *cafetería* you're likely to catch an unremittingly awful soap opera (*telenovela*) on one of Panama's six terrestrial **television** channels. Many middle-class Panamanians have access to cable TV with channels in Spanish and English.

Check out ⓦ coolpanama.com for a list of **radio stations**, frequencies and their musical preferences.

Festivals

Panama is awash with festivals and public holidays. Alongside the numerous commemorations of historical events, there are copious Catholic celebrations – including each town's patron-saint bash, agricultural fairs and cultural extravaganzas that reflect the country's ethnic diversity. Whatever the differences in the details, they all demand the ability to survive several days and nights of music, dancing and processions, fuelled on mountains of street food and gallons of booze. Head and shoulders above the rest stands Carnaval – generally referred to in the plural as Los Carnavales – a five-day marathon of hedonism at its most outlandish in the tiny Azuero town of Las Tablas (see box, p.167). Major festivals are listed opposite and in the relevant sections of the Guide. Public holidays are listed in our "Opening hours and public holidays" section (see p.47).

A festival calendar

JANUARY

Feria de las Flores y del Café Mid-Jan. Ten-day celebration in Boquete to mark the coffee harvest with carpets of flowers, food and craft stalls. Daytime family entertainment is followed by night-time discos.

FEBRUARY

Revolución Dule Feb 25. Celebrates the Guna Revolution of 1925, their Independence Day, with colourful reenactments of battles against the Panamanian authorities held across the *comarca*.

Carnaval Five days ending at dawn on Ash Wednesday. Wild partying and processions – celebrated countrywide, but especially in Las Tablas and Panama City, with an aquatic parade on the Saturday in Penonomé.

MARCH

Semana Santa or Holy Week March–April. Celebrated everywhere, but most colourfully on the Azuero Peninsula.

Festival de los Diablos y Congos Usually the second or third weekend of March. Vibrant biennial weekend event (next held in 2019 and 2021) in Portobelo, showcasing Afro-Colonial culture and resistance to the Spanish conquest in a mass of devilish costumes and dances.

APRIL

Feria de las Orquídeas Five days in early April. Boquete festival featuring copious orchids, craft stalls and cultural events.

Feria Internacional de Azuero Ten days in April. Major agricultural fair in La Villa de Los Santos with stalls, presentations and competitions reflecting the area's colonial and cattle-farming traditions.

MAY AND JUNE

Festival de Corpus Christi Late May/early June. Celebrated across the country but most spectacularly in La Villa de Los Santos, with processions and dramatic devil dances.

JULY

Fiestas Patronales de la Virgen del Carmen July 16. On Isla Taboga the Holy Virgin gets to circumnavigate the island in a procession of decorated boats.

Fiestas Patronales de la Santa Librada July 20–22. A mix of religious and folkloric parades in Las Tablas, incorporating the Festival de la Pollera, which showcases Panama's gorgeous national dress.

AUGUST

Festival del Manito Ocueño Thurs–Sun, dates vary. In Ocú, on the Azuero Peninsula, this lively folk festival features a mock duel and peasant wedding.

SEPTEMBER

Festival de la Mejorana Late Sept. Panama's premier folk festival, in Guararé, on the Azuero Peninsula, involving five days of music, dancing and parades.

OCTOBER

Feria de Isla Tigre Mid-Oct. Multiday festivity of Guna culture, celebrated in Isla Tigre (Digir Dubu), Guna Yala.

Festival del Cristo Negro Oct 21. The most revered pilgrimage in the country, attracting thousands bedecked in purple robes to Portobelo.

NOVEMBER

Primer Grito de la Independencia Nov 10. The "First Cry of Independence", celebrated in La Villa de los Santos as part of "El Mes de la Patria". Patriotic flag-waving parades and marching bands, attended by the president.

Sports and outdoor activities

Both inside and outside the parks, Panama offers a host of outdoor activities, from swinging through the canopy on a zip line to tracking tapir prints in the mud of the Darién or lolling on a deserted beach. Some of these pursuits can be experienced as efficient packages from Panama City; others will need to be arranged more informally on the spot and a few require no organization whatsoever. Already renowned as a world-class birdwatching and sport fishing destination, Panama is also developing a reputation for outstanding diving, whitewater rafting and wilderness hiking.

Several excellent **tour operators**, providing knowledgeable bilingual or multilingual naturalist guides work out of Panama City and offer tours around the country (see p.76), though for the more distant locations, such as Boquete or Coiba, you are better off looking for operators closer to the destination; they are listed in the relevant chapters of the Guide.

Birdwatching

Panama offers first-class **birdwatching**. Boasting more than 990 species of bird, including 55 varieties of hummingbird and spectacular show birds such as the emerald-and-ruby resplendent quetzal (easy to see in the Chiriquí Highlands), the country also contains the world's largest concentration of harpy eagles (most likely to be spotted in the Darién or in Amistad). Though Panama acts as a magnet for serious twitchers laden with tripods, checklists and hefty avian tomes (see p.313), it might persuade even those who have viewed birdwatching as a dull pastime, involving hours of trying to identify one indistinguishable brown bird from another, to think again. It's hard not to be impressed by the dazzling flashes of parrots and macaws in flight or the ludicrous painted bills of toucans swooping across the treetops.

Since many of these glamorous birds spend much of their time tantalizingly high up in the canopy, it is worth splashing out on at least a small pair of binoculars, which will significantly enhance your birdwatching experience. So too will engaging a **guide**. Alongside the big-name tour operators in the capital (see p.76) there are small-scale specialists, such as Birding Panama (Ⓦbirdingpanama.com) and Birding in Panama (Ⓦbirdinginpanama.com), as well as numerous local residents scattered across the country, whose contact details are given in the relevant chapters of the Guide. Daily rates for a professional bilingual naturalist guide contracted in the capital can range from $150–170 per person, partly depending on how far you travel, but if you want something less expensive or just want someone to be able to point out some of the more obvious species, engaging a local from one of the villages for a few hours can cost as little as $15. A good way to start off is to attend one of the regular birdwatching-for-beginners walks (donations welcome) in the Parque Natural Metropolitano in Panama City; organized by the Panama Audubon Society (Ⓣ232 5977, Ⓦfacebook.com/audubonpanama), they are open to all.

Hiking

Panama also affords a myriad **hiking** opportunities. Vast wilderness areas such as La Amistad and the Darién are ideal for adventurous multiday hikes across the isthmus, often involving bivouacking, staying in indigenous villages, fording rivers and wading through metres of mud. Aside from the Panama City operators, guides can be engaged locally in places such as Santa Fé, Boquete and Cerro Punta, at far less cost, though you'll need some Spanish. If you fancy a more modest outing, parks in the canal basin offer a range of trails from a gentle circular route to a reasonably strenuous rainforest tramp following in the footsteps of the conquistadors. Note you'll need warm clothes for the chilly nights in the peaks of western Panama.

Basic hiking and camping gear can often be bought at any of the Novey or Do It Center shops in the main cities, but the best selection (albeit still fairly limited) is found at the outlets of **Outdoor Adventure** in Albrook Mall (Ⓣ303 6120), Multiplaza (Ⓣ302 4828) and Multicentro (Ⓣ302 0157) in Panama City, and also in Chitré and Santiago. Matawi is a new, expensive specialist shop for climbing and hiking gear in the Sky Business Centre, Av Balboa (Ⓦmatawigear.com), in the capital. Do It Center in Albrook Mall sometimes stocks water filters and water purification tablets, but you are better off bringing them with you.

Rafting and kayaking

The fast-flowing rivers that tumble down from the highlands of western and central Panama, carving their way through dramatic scenery, have put Panama on the map for **whitewater rafting** and **kayaking**. The top destination is the Río Chiriquí Viejo, which runs parallel with the Costa Rican border. Though the descent is shorter and slightly less wild since its damming for a hydroelectric project, it's still an impressive run, with Category II to IV rapids. The rivers are at their wildest during the heavy rains (roughly May to mid-Dec), but you'll manage to find enough water flowing somewhere to raft and kayak year-round. Boquete operators (see p.187) are best placed to organize Chiriquí destinations, while companies in the capital head for rivers in the Chagres basin or in neighbouring Coclé province.

Sea-kayaking is growing in popularity, offering a great way to explore rocky coastlines and mangroves, and to access remote beaches among the islands of Guna Yala, or round Coiba and Boca Chica in Chiriquí.

Diving and snorkelling

Diving in the **Pacific** can be truly spectacular, particularly in the Golfo de Chiriquí and the Archipiélago de las Perlas. Pick the right time of year (see p.308) and you're likely to spot manta rays, moray eels, sharks, schools of dolphins and migrating humpback and sperm whales – some scuba operators offer whale-watching tours. Large pelagic fish such as marlin, sailfish, amberjack, dorado and tuna also abound, which reel in sport fishing enthusiasts too. The jewel in this marine crown is Isla Coiba; located on the edge of the second-largest reef on the Pacific side of the Americas, it offers world-class diving.

Among the coral reefs of Bocas and Portobelo on the **Caribbean** side, diving can also be enjoyable, if not as spectacular as at some other Caribbean destinations. Visibility can vary enormously, especially after heavy rain. However, the rainbow-coloured soft corals of Cayo Crawl off Isla Bastimentos make for breathtaking **snorkelling** and there are plenty of other fun spots to explore.

Reputable local **dive shops** operate out of Bocas, Portobelo, Santa Catalina, Isla Contadora and Pedasí, on the Azuero Peninsula, while Scuba Panama (☎ 261 3841, Ⓦ scubapanama.com), the country's oldest outfit, organizes expeditions from Panama City.

Surfing

With two long coastlines, Panama offers hundreds of waves of all kinds to suit novices and expert **surfers**. Away from the renowned hot spots you can have the beach almost to yourself, though the surfing infrastructure (hostels, bars, restaurants and regular public transport) may also be lacking.

Local surfers confined to Panama City tend to dash to the nearby Pacific beaches of **Coclé** for a weekend escape, such as El Palmar and Playa Malibu. For top-drawer surfing on the **Pacific coast** (generally best April–Nov), head for the internationally renowned breaks round **Santa Catalina**. In April waves here can reach 4m or more, with the high season continuing until August (though a good ride on 2m breakers is guaranteed year-round). **Playa Venao**, on the south coast of the Azuero Peninsula, arguably offers the country's best-known beach break, and also attracts international competitions; the more remote **Cambutal**, which has beach and point breaks, and can catch big waves, lies further west. On the eastern side of the peninsula, the small town of **Pedasí** is within reach of several surfing spots; **Playa Morrillo**, on the western flank, is up-and-coming.

On the **Caribbean coast** (best Dec–March), **Bocas del Toro** is the standout, offering varied breaks for beginners and experts – including the monster reef bottom wave of Silverbacks – plus welcoming bars and a decent après-surf scene. Less-well-known surfing spots lie **east of Portobelo**, such as Isla Grande or Nombre de Dios and Palenque.

Ⓦ surfeapanama.com and the Panamanian surfing association's Facebook page, Ⓦ facebook.com /surfAPS, offer **information** (in Spanish); check also Magic Seaweed (Ⓦ magicseaweed.com) for the swell history and forecasts for the best-known spots.

Sport fishing

According to one reading of the indigenous language Cueva, Panama means "abundance of fish", and the country offers some phenomenal **fishing**. The Bahía de Piñas on the Pacific coast of the Darién, location of the exclusive *Tropic Star Lodge* (Ⓦ tropicstarlodge.com), is widely considered to be the world's top saltwater fishing destination,

with the Golfo de Chiriquí, and Coiba in particular, a close second and the Islas Perlas not far behind.

Foreign-owned **fishing lodges** are mush rooming along the Pacific coast, most of which offer multiday package deals that cover accommodation, meals and fishing excursions costing up to several thousand dollars. Recommended outfits include Panama Big Game Fishing (Ⓦ panama -sportfishing.com), Coiba Adventure Sportfishing (Ⓦ coibaadventure.com) and Pesca Panama (Ⓦ pescapanama.com).

Other activities

The Boquete Tree Trek (see p.187) can justifiably be considered the **canopy adventure** to top them all, boasting a dozen zip lines – more modest versions exist in El Valle (see p.137), near Portobelo (see box, p.116) and on Isla Bastimentos (see p.235). Similar adrenaline surges are guaranteed when **kitesurfing** at Punta Chame on the Pacific coast (see p.132).

Pass by any small fishing village and you can usually find a **boatman** willing to take you for a chug round the mangroves, drop you off for a laze on a deserted beach or even throw a line for a spot of fishing. Similarly relaxing is a plod along an empty beach or through the rainforest on **horseback**, which offers the chance to soak up the scenery without frightening the wildlife – though don't necessarily expect a safety helmet, or a saddle that fails to remind you what you've been doing for the next week.

Mountain-bikers in search of company might consider contacting Boa Panama (Ⓦ facebook.com /groups/boapanama) for English- and Spanish-speaking contacts; this association of recreational off-road cycling enthusiasts organizes weekend outings.

Spectator sports

With a highly ranked national team, and a number of successful major-league baseball stars to its credit, **baseball** is Panama's national sport. An inexpensive and captivating evening's entertainment awaits if you attend one of the fiercely contested national-league matches that take place in the dry season (late Dec to April) – check Ⓦ fedebeis.com for fixtures – particularly in the more intimate stadiums in the interior. Under the floodlights, a raucous spirit prevails, with people partying in the stands and screaming to the accompaniment of brass bands and drums, with plenty of tasty street-food on hand.

Close behind comes **boxing**, which has produced more Panamanian world champions than any other sport. Of these, two stand out: "Panama Al Brown", a bantamweight from Colón, who became the first Latin American world champion in 1929, and Roberto Durán, who won numerous world titles at various weights during the 1970s and 80s.

Less illustrious, though still given passionate support when the occasion demands, the national **football** team won its first international trophy in 2009, triumphing in the Central American championships. Generally, though, the team can do with all the help it can muster so if you fancy going to cheer them on, check out Ⓦ panamafutbol.com, although the professional league matches played out in the low-key stadiums in the interior, at Santiago or David, may provide greater entertainment.

Panama also excels in **horse racing**, which you can see in Panama City (see p.84).

National parks

Almost a quarter of Panama's land lies within the boundaries of its fourteen national parks – add in reserves, refuges and other protected areas, and the figure is more than a third. Under siege on all sides from urban development, pollution and deforestation (see p.309), these

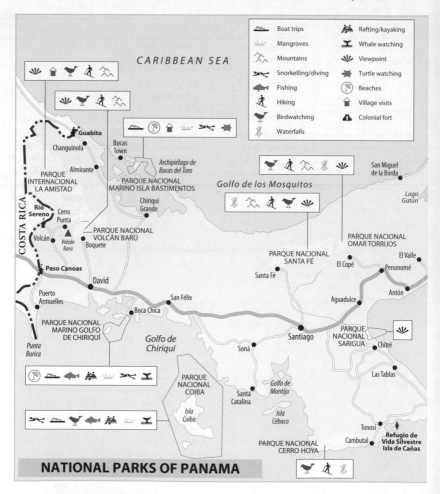

NATIONAL PARKS OF PANAMA

nevertheless constitute one of Panama's major attractions: you can trek through pristine rainforest, explore Spanish colonial forts, haul yourself up volcanic peaks or swim with sharks and manta rays. Some, such as the legendary Darién, Central America's largest wilderness, and Cerro Hoya, at the tip of the Azuero Peninsula, are particularly inaccessible and involve a lot of planning, persever-ance and often money to reach; others, such as Camino de Cruces and Soberanía, are a stone's throw from Panama City, making an easy day-trip and providing a great opportunity to see some of Panama's dazzling birdlife.

Panama's ecosystems are astonishingly diverse – little surprise given that the country stands at the crossroads of two oceans and two continents, a vital link in the biological corridor between North and South America. Since the country is so slender, many of the parks offer a hugely varied **topography**. Several straddle the continental divide, ranging from lofty moss-covered cloud forest pierced by rugged peaks to humid lowland rainforest; others protect dense swathes of mangrove, harbouring caimans, crocodiles and crustaceans while protecting vital mud flats for thousands of migratory birds. The three **marine parks** offer coral reefs, turquoise waters and islands encircled with sugar-sand beaches and coated in tropical forest that supports everything from

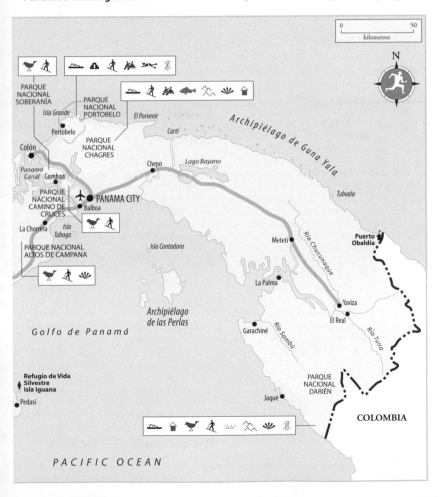

PAYING NATIONAL PARK FEES

In theory, **park fees** (including the daily entry and accommodation costs) have to be paid in advance, in a branch of the Banco Nacional, into MiAmbiente's current account. The deposit slip needs to be made out to MiAmbiente/Fondo de Vida Silvestre; account no: 1-00000-46528. This effectively means that you have to decide before you visit a park how many days you intend to stay there. Be sure to hold on to the receipt to show the MIA office as proof of payment.

However, the reality on the ground is more varied. For Darién and Coiba, pre-payment is essential (see p.280 & p.212) but for most other parks you can usually pay cash at the regional MIA office or in the park itself. We've covered the details where necessary in this Guide, but if in doubt, ask the relevant park desk officer in the Áreas Protegidas section of MIA's head office in Panama City (☎ 500 0855, ⓦ miambiente.gob.pa).

---

fluorescent poison dart frogs to primordial iguanas. Ruined colonial fortresses, a crumbling Devil's Island penitentiary and a rare tract of dry tropical forest also lie within national park boundaries.

Visiting the parks

Panama's national parks are managed by the **Ministry of the Environment** (Ministerio de Ambiente) – upgraded in 2015 from being a mere department (Autoridad del Ambiente de Panamá, or ANAM). Although the ANAM acronym is still widely used, the ministry has been formally branded as **MiAmbiente**, or **MIA** (ⓦ miambiente .gob.pa). Dealing with tourists is in theory the job of Panama's national tourist agency, the ATP (see p.48), but MIA staff in the regional and local offices, as well as the *guardaparques* (park wardens) are often very helpful and likely to be of more direct use, though they will only speak Spanish.

MIA offices are generally open from Monday to Friday from 8am to 4pm. If you need a permit, to book accommodation or to hire a guide, it's best to drop by the regional or larger town offices to sort matters out in advance. If this is not possible, you can usually organize something on the spot – though not for the Darién or Coiba – see box above. Indeed, in theory, there should be a full-time resident warden at each park entrance although in practice, it is not always the case, in which case any facilities will be locked. If you decide to organize your visit by telephoning one of the MIA offices, ask to talk to someone *in* Áreas Protegidas, and note that most MIA employees only speak Spanish.

With tourism very much a fledgling business in Panama, it may be some time before there is an integrated approach and anything like standardized **facilities** across the national parks. In most places, you will need to ask the park warden, and possibly hire them as a guide (for around $20–25/day) since maps and trail signs are conspicuously absent.

Since 2016, **park fees** have been standardized at $5 per day for foreigners, except in Coiba (see p.215). Officially you'll pay $6 per person to camp – though again, there are anomalies; Soberanía charges $6 per tent, for example (see p.100) – or $15 for a bed for the night. Be aware that many park bunkhouses (*refugios*) are in a poor state of repair, and may lack basic utensils. The method for **paying park fees** is somewhat convoluted (see box above).

Travel essentials

Costs

Costs are higher than in countries such as Guatemala and Nicaragua, and have risen to Costa Rican levels in some areas. Staying in dorms, eating in inexpensive local restaurants and using public transport you can easily survive on $40–50 a day, less if camping, with anything from $50–90 on top for a day's guided excursion – snorkelling, surfing, fishing, horseriding or kayaking, for instance.

Staying in more comfortable accommodation and eating in more touristy restaurants can mean a daily food and lodgings budget of $100 with excursions and maybe car rental (minimum $25/day) on top, though a lot depends on whether you stay in Panama City and the Canal area, where prices are significantly higher, or make for the interior.

High-end accommodation – only really available in Panama City and at a handful of resorts across the rest of the country – will set you back more than $250 a night, with a three-course meal (without drinks) in one of the city's top restaurants averaging $50. **Tipping** should not add too much to any costs (see p.46).

Crime and personal safety

The presence of FARC guerrillas and cocaine smugglers in the Darién jungle has helped promote the popular misconception that Panama is a dangerous country to visit. In fact, even though crime seems to be on the increase, especially in urban areas, Panama is still much safer than most other Central American states, with only a few areas to avoid or in which to take special care.

The eastern strip of the **Darién** and **Guna Yala** that borders Colombia tops the danger list as a no-go area; it contains the fabled Darién Gap, which has long held a fascination for travellers seeking adventure by hacking through jungle to the border. While this was difficult but feasible, it is now very dangerous and prohibited; since the 1990s several travellers attempting the overland route have been kidnapped or killed. There are still ways of visiting the Darién safely both in an organized group and as an independent traveller, and for crossing to Colombia on the Caribbean side by boat (see box, p.25), all of which can provide excitement without putting your life in acute danger.

The second major trouble spot is **Colón**, where extreme caution needs to be exercised even during the day (see box, p.107). **Panama City** also has several areas to avoid, generally poor neighbourhoods with inadequate housing and high unemployment. **Violent crime** is on the increase, but ninety percent of this is estimated to be drug-related, often among rival gangs; petty crime too is on the rise in some areas, especially where there are significant economic disparities between the general population and those who are making decent money from tourism, such as in Bocas. That said, by far the vast majority of visitors enjoy their time in Panama without incident, with the main issues being theft of money and/or passport and the odd traffic accident. The usual common-sense guidelines apply.

The police

If you are a **victim of crime**, report to the Policía de Turismo (Tourist Police) in Panama City (see p.86) or the main police station in other towns. Even though your possessions are unlikely to be recovered, a police report (*denuncia*) will be required to make an insurance claim. At the police station, you will probably need to present your ID, which by law you should always carry with you, though it is acceptable to carry a photocopy of your passport details provided it also includes a copy of the entry date stamp on the same page.

Culture and etiquette

No society is homogenous but Panama is particularly diverse, and customs vary widely. Overall,

though, people are very courteous – driving in Panama City aside – and quite formal. **Greetings** are customary before any exchange, such as asking for information, and the "usted" form of address is preferred to the "tu" form, which is reserved for close friends – although this is beginning to change among younger people or those who have spent significant periods of time out of the country. This formality is also reflected in **clothing**, particularly by the urban middle classes, who like to dress up to go out. Dress is also important on the beach; no nude sunbathing is permitted in Panama, except on one beach on Isla Contadora (see p.122), and beachwear should stay on the beach – cover your body in town.

Suitably modest attire (covered shoulders) is appreciated in churches. When visiting **indigenous communities**, cultural sensitivity is particularly important as regards dress, alcohol and photography (see box, p.255).

Drugs

Drugs are widely available in Panama, **marijuana** and **cocaine** in particular, and you're quite likely to be offered something at some stage. However, possession of either is illegal and makes those caught liable for a prison sentence. While the police might – and only might – turn a blind eye to a joint being smoked discreetly on a deserted beach, being caught with weed trying to cross a border can have serious consequences. Possession of cocaine is punished very heavily, in part because Panama is a known transit point for drugs heading from Colombia to the US.

Electricity

The **voltage** in Panama is 110 volts and sockets take flat two- and occasionally three-pronged plugs. **Power cuts** and subsequent surges occur fairly frequently so if travelling with a laptop you may want to bring a surge protector. In many remote parts of the country, such as some islands of Guna Yala and in much of the Darién, in national parks or in isolated villages, there is limited or no electricity at night, so a torch is essential.

Insurance

It would be unwise to head for Panama without **insurance** that covers theft, loss, illness, injury and flight cancellation. Before you take out a new policy, make sure that you aren't already covered: some all-risks home insurance policies may cover your

ROUGH GUIDES TRAVEL INSURANCE

Rough Guides has teamed up with WorldNomads.com to offer great **travel insurance** deals. Policies are available to residents of over 150 countries, with cover for a wide range of **adventure sports**, 24hr emergency assistance, high levels of medical and evacuation cover and a stream of **travel safety information**. Roughguides.com users can take advantage of their policies online 24/7, from anywhere in the world – even if you're already travelling. And since plans often change when you're on the road, you can extend your policy and even claim online. Roughguides.com users who buy travel insurance with WorldNomads.com can also leave a positive footprint and donate to a community development project. For more information, go to ⓦ**roughguides.com/travel-insurance**.

possessions while abroad, and many private medical schemes also apply when overseas. In Canada, provincial health plans usually provide some cover for medical treatment when out of the country. Some student insurance packages also include vacation travel. When shopping around for a policy, bear in mind that what are termed **dangerous sports**, which usually include the likes of scuba diving and white-water rafting, sometimes require an additional premium to be paid. Should you have to seek medical attention, keep all receipts, and if you lose something valuable, get a police report (*denuncia*). Whatever the situation you will still need to access sufficient funds to cover such emergencies (hence the usefulness of a credit card) while on your trip, and apply for reimbursement on your return home.

Internet

Where internet connectivity is available, almost all hostels and most hotels offer free **wi-fi**. There are also numerous government wi-fi hot spots, though you have to register and the speed is very slow. However, internet access – along with mobile phone coverage – is very limited in the **Darién** and **Guna Yala**. In the former, wi-fi is restricted to a few places in the major settlements of Metetí, La Palma, Yaviza and Garachiné; in the latter it is only available in Puerto Obaldía, unless you manage to catch a signal outside a government office on one of the larger village-islands. We indicate in the Guide where wi-fi is available in these regions, though even then you should bear in mind that the service is often unreliable, especially in the rainy season (roughly May to mid-Dec).

In general, the exponential spread of smart-phones has led to a decline in the number of internet cafés across the country, though in most towns the local **library**, at the very least, usually has a couple of PCs. Rates are generally $1 an hour – note that the "@" sign is usually achieved by pressing ALT, "6" and "4" keys simultaneously.

Language

Spanish is the official language of Panama and the first language of more than two million of the population, though a recorded thirteen other first languages are spoken across the country. The latter are mainly indigenous but include Panamanian **Creole English**, preferred by around 100,000 Afro-Antillean Panamanians, primarily resident in Bocas, Colón and Panama City, and **Cantonese** or **Hakka**, spoken by around sixty thousand Chinese-Panamanians. While many urban middle-class Panamanians speak **English**, some of whom are bilingual, the "everybody-speaks-English" myth is easily dispelled. Official estimates reckon around fourteen percent of the population can communicate in English but in small towns and rural areas you'll find many speak virtually no English and in a number of the remote indige-nous communities some villagers, especially women, do not even speak Spanish. Your travel experience in the country will be greatly enhanced by learning at least the basics of Spanish before you arrive. The Language section in the Contexts chapter of this Guide is a useful starting point (see p.314).

Learning Spanish in Panama

A good way of getting to grips with Spanish is to attend a **language school**. This also gives you an entrance into Panamanian life, especially if you take up the cultural immersion or homestay options and become involved in the volunteering projects on offer. Most schools run an extracurricular programme, which almost inevitably includes salsa classes and excursions, while some courses specialize in language learning combined with activities such as scuba diving or surfing.

Group, small-group (two to four people) and one-to-one tuition is usually available; group classes, the cheapest option, generally comprise four hours of lessons per day at rates of around

$230–320 per week, not including board and lodging. Make sure the institution is registered, that staff are qualified and that the teaching methodology is not just "chalk and talk" before committing any money. Ⓦ goabroad.com/language-study -abroad contains a list of recommended schools.

LANGUAGE SCHOOLS

Habla Ya Panama Plaza Los Establos, Boquete 20–22 ☎ 720 1294; Av "G" Norte, Bocas Town ☎ 757 7352; 1st St, Le Bleu Building 2A, Panama City ☎ 730 8344, Ⓦ hablayapanama.com.
Spanish by the River Entrada a Palmira, Alto Boquete ☎ 720 3456, Ⓦ spanishatlocations.com.
Spanish by the Sea Calle 4a, behind *Hotel Bahía*, Bocas del Toro, Isla Colón ☎ 757 9518.
Spanish Panama Edif Americana 1A, Vía Argentina, Panama City ☎ 213 3121, Ⓦ spanishpanama.com.

Laundry

Most mid-range and top-end hotels offer a **laundry** service, while aparthotels (see p.77) and some hostels have their own washing machines for guest use. Otherwise you could find a *lavamático* (not as easy to locate in Panama City as in the provinces), an old-fashioned launderette where you bundle your clothes into a machine, and then a dryer, for no more than $5 per load, including detergent and conditioner. The more ubiquitous *lavanderías*, which more closely resemble dry cleaners, usually cost slightly more, especially if you want clothes ironed.

LGBT travellers

Homosexuality was finally decriminalized in Panama in 2008, which illustrates not only the country's prevailing social conservatism but also the fact that things are changing. The Asociación de Hombres y Mujeres Nuevos de Panamá (AHMN) – at the time of writing only the Chiriquí chapter was online (Ⓦ facebook.com/AHMNPCH) – is active in campaigning for LGBT rights and low-key Gay Pride marches have been held since 2005. The LGBT scene is discreet; the clutch of nightclubs is not widely advertised (see Ⓦ ellgeebe.com). However, on the Panama pages of LGBT travel websites (for example Ⓦ purpleroofs.com/centralamerica /panama.html, Ⓦ gayjourney.com/hotels/panama .htm and Ⓦ globalgayz.com) the number of openly "gay-friendly" accommodation listings, though small, is gradually increasing. In general, hotels in Panama City and North American- and European-run establishments are likely to be more tolerant.

Mail

It is reliable, but if speed is of the essence the standard Panamanian **postal service** is probably not for you; a postcard from Panama can take five to ten days to reach North America (25¢ stamp) and a couple of weeks or longer to meander to Europe (35¢ stamp), Australasia or South Africa (60¢ stamp). While post offices (*correos*) are relatively elusive in Panama City (see p.86), they are more visible in the provinces; they are marked on the maps in this Guide. Opening hours, though generally Monday to Friday 8am to 5pm and Saturday 8am to noon, do vary. For a speedier delivery, you can send your letter or parcel express from the post office, though this service is not available for Europe. Alternatively, use one of the more expensive private mailing or courier services widely available, such as Fedex (Ⓦ fedex.com/pa) or Mail Boxes Etc. (Ⓦ mbe.com).

Post offices also offer an *entrega general* (**poste restante**) service, keeping letters for up to a month. Passport ID needs to be shown when claiming post and you can't collect on behalf of another person. The sender should address items as follows: receiver's name, Entrega General, name of town, name of province, Republica de Panamá. If you are receiving post in Panama City then the postal zone also needs to be specified – enquire at the branch in question.

Maps

Country and city **maps** of Panama are increasing in number and quality though there's still some way to go. There are also some rudimentary trail maps for the parks in the former Canal Zone, usually available from the park offices. International Travel Maps (1:300,000; available online at Ⓦ itmb.com and Ⓦ amazon.com; $12) – updated in 2014 – and National Geographic (Ⓦ nationalgeographic.com) both produce good maps of Panama, though the latter updated only the text, not the map itself, in 2016. In Panama itself, large-scale maps are available in Panama City at the Instituto Geográfico Nacional Tommy Guardia (Mon–Fri 8am–4pm; ☎ 507 9686) on Avenida Simón Bolívar, opposite the entrance to the university; that said, some are several years out of date and would really only be of use if you were planning some wilderness hiking.

Money

Panama adopted **US dollars** (referred to as *dólares* or *balboas*) as its currency in 1904, shortly after separation from Colombia. Apart from a seven-day print flurry in 1941, producing what is known as the "seven-day-dollar" (now a collector's item), the country has always used US paper currency, though it mints its own coinage: 1, 5, 10, 25 and 50 centavo pieces, and a dollar coin, which are used alongside US coins. Both $100 and $50 notes are often difficult to spend, so try to have $10 or $20 as the largest denominations you carry. **Travellers' cheques** are virtually obsolete.

Most **banks** are open from 8am to 3.30pm Monday to Friday, and from 9am to noon on Saturday, though busier branches in the capital have extended hours; almost all branches have ATMs, as do many large supermarkets.

It is difficult to **change foreign currency** in Panama – convert any cash into US dollars as soon as you can. There are two Travelex currency exchange counters in Tocumen International Airport, and several branches of Red Plus (Ⓦ gruporedplus.com) in the city, which are open every day: Multicentro houses the main office, but there are also branches in Albrook Mall, Multiplaza and Metro Mall. Foreign banks will generally change their own currencies. Current **exchange rates** can be checked at Ⓦ xe.com.

Money transfers can easily be carried out through Western Union (Ⓦ westernunion.com), which has more than one hundred offices sprinkled around the isthmus, with a concentration in Panama City.

Cards and ATMs

With more than a thousand **ATMs** across the country, the most convenient way to access your money is by drawing out cash on a credit card (you'll need your PIN). **Debit cards** such as Maestro and Cirrus are valid in many ATMs though they sometimes do not actually work in practice. Most home banks charge a fee for credit and debit card withdrawal – check before departure – and almost all ATMs in Panama levy $5.25 per transaction (except Scotiabank). You can avoid paying the ATM fee by withdrawing cash against your credit/debit card over the counter at a bank. Make sure to inform your bank at home that you are travelling to Panama before you leave so that they don't block your credit or debit card when you try to use it, although note that your card may still be blocked when undertaking swipe rather than chip-and-pin transactions.

Visa and MasterCard are the most widely accepted **credit cards** across the country, both at ATMs (recognizable by the red *Sistema Clave* sign outside) and to pay for services such as plane tickets, tourist hotels, restaurants, goods in shops

and car rental. Banistmo, which took over HSBC in Panama, is the best bank to seek out if you wish to withdraw cash against your credit card.

Most establishments in **Bocas del Toro**, **Guna Yala** and the **Darién** only accept **cash**; denominations of $20 and below are preferred because of problems with counterfeit $50 and $100 notes. Note that there is only one ATM in the whole of Guna Yala (in Narganá), one in the archipelago of Bocas del Toro (in Bocas Town, Isla Colón), and just two in the Darién (in Metetí and La Palma).

Note also that heading into a major holiday weekend, ATMs at holiday destinations may run out of money, especially if there is only one machine in town.

Bargaining and tipping

Bargaining for goods is not the norm in Panama. If you're buying several items from a single stall in a craft market you can usually negotiate a slight discount (*descuento*), but it's rarely the lengthy social ritual it can be in some countries. Bear in mind too that while $40 for an intricate *mola* or $70 for a Panama hat may seem like a lot, they are likely to have taken several weeks to make.

Tipping is not universally expected and should be reserved for good service. While ten percent is customary in mid-range (or more expensive) restaurants, it should not be automatic. In local *fondas* you might round up a $2.80 lunch to $3. Porters in hotels are usually tipped $0.50–1 per bag; the going rate at Tocumen International Airport is $1 per bag. In hotels you might consider leaving a tip of $1–2 per day for the person who has cleaned your room, but it's not *de rigueur*. It's not usual to tip taxi drivers or guides on organized tours. If, however, you hire the services of a park warden (*guardaparque*) to take you on a guided hike, you should ask what the going rate is; if there isn't one, $15–20 should be adequate for a full-day outing.

Overtipping is not helpful; it sets a precedent which other travellers may not be able to live up to, and can upset the micro-economy, particularly in small villages.

Opening hours and public holidays

Opening hours vary but generally businesses are open Monday to Saturday from 8/9am to 5/6pm. Government office hours are Monday to Friday 8am to 4pm. Shops usually open their doors Monday to Saturday from 9am to 6pm, though places selling souvenirs and crafts to tourists may

PUBLIC HOLIDAYS

Jan 1 Año Nuevo. New Year's Day.
Jan 9 Día de los Mártires. Martyrs' Day, in remembrance of those killed by US troops in the 1964 flag riots.
Feb Carnaval. Five days up to and including Ash Wednesday.
March/April Viernes Santo. Good Friday.
May 1 Día del Trabajo. Labour Day.
Nov 3 Separación de Panamá de Colombia. Anniversary of the 1903 separation from Colombia and primary Independence Day.
Nov 4 Día de la Bandera. Flag Day.
Nov 5 Día de Colón. Celebrating Colón's separation from Colombia.
Nov 10 Primer Grito de la Independencia. "First Cry for Independence", marking the unilateral declaration of independence from Spain in La Villa de Los Santos.
Nov 28 4 Independencia de Panamá de España. Celebrating independence from Spain in 1821.
Dec 8 Día de la Madre. Mother's Day.
Dec 25 Día de Navidad. Christmas Day.

---

open on Sundays too, and Chinese-Panamanian supermarkets often open early (6.30–7am) until late (10pm–midnight); some of the larger outlets of the major supermarket chains, e.g. Super 99, Extra and El Rey, are open 24 hours.

Churches rarely have official opening hours; most are open from around 8am until early evening, with the odd one closing for lunch.

Most government offices, businesses and shops close during the several national **public holidays**. When the public holidays fall on or near a weekend the government often grants a *puente* (bridge), at the last minute, usually for a Monday or a Friday, making a long weekend and prompting a mass exodus from the city to the beach or the countryside, with a scramble for plane tickets and accommodation – check **⦿** qppstudio.net/publicholidays.htm. Note that services shut down in Panama City on August 15 to celebrate the foundation of Panamá La Vieja, while other towns and cities have their own multiday festivities during which most places close.

Over some public holidays, as well as during national elections, *ley seca* (literally **dry law**) is enacted, which means that alcohol can't be bought or consumed during that period, and nightclubs and other places of entertainment remain closed, although black market booze is fairly easy to get hold of and in remote areas, the law is less rigorously observed.

Phones

Apart from very remote villages, where the lone phone box – assuming it works – may be the community's only means of communication with the outside world, **phone boxes** are becoming less common. Easy to use, with instructions in English as well as Spanish, some phones accept both coins (5¢, 10¢ and 25¢) and cards; others only accept prepaid phonecards (generally $3, $5 and $10) which you can buy at shops, Cable & Wireless offices and local pharmacies. Note that some cards can only be used for either international or local calls but not both. Seven-digit phone numbers denote **landlines** – the first three digits comprise the area code – whereas eight-digit numbers are for **mobile phones**.

Making a call

To make a call **to Panama** you need to dial the international prefix (generally 00), followed by 507 – the country code for Panama – followed by the number. Local calls to landlines anywhere in Panama cost a pittance and are usually free from a hotel room. International calls are also relatively cheap provided you do not use a hotel phone. Some internet cafés (and Cable & Wireless offices) also have phone booths and offer decent rates for international calls as well as a degree of comfort, quiet and privacy. Off-peak time for international calls is between 6pm and 6am, and at weekends.

Mobile phones

Mobile phones have mushroomed in Panama, which now has as many different numbers – almost 3.5 million – as it does people. Mobiles have transformed the lives of some indigenous communities that live far from the main population centres, and can be very useful for travellers too, especially in the more remote areas when wanting to confirm transport or a reservation from a dugout in the Darién. Crucially, though, **coverage** varies among the four service providers – Mas Móvil (from Cable & Wireless), Digicel, Movistar and Clarocom – in particular regions, especially in the Darién and Guna Yala, where your need is likely to be greatest. Ask locally which provider is best before you buy a SIM

USEFUL PHONE NUMBERS

Ambulance Red Cross **⦿**455;
Seguro Social **⦿** 107 – both are free
Directory enquiries ⦿ 102
International operator ⦿ 106
Police ⦿ 104 (including traffic police)

CALLING HOME FROM PANAMA

To **make an international call from Panama**, dial the international access code (in Panama it's 00), then the destination's country code, before the rest of the number. Note that the initial zero is omitted from the area code when dialling the UK, Ireland, Australia and New Zealand from abroad.

Australia 0061 + area code minus initial zero

Ireland 00353 + area code minus initial zero

New Zealand 0064 + area code minus initial zero

South Africa 0027 + area code

UK 0044 + area code minus initial zero

US and Canada 001 + area code

---

card. If you have an unlocked mobile phone on an 850 GSM (the setting for much of the Americas), you can easily buy a SIM card on arrival for a few dollars, from numerous corner shops in Panama City, or from Albrook bus terminal. Only expensive phone packages (around $40) are available at Tocumen International Airport. Once the initial credit has expired, you can buy prepaid airtime cards from shops around the country. Alternatively, you might consider renting a mobile or satellite phone; the executive business hotels can usually procure one for you. Incoming calls are all free in Panama.

Photography

The dazzling sunlight of any tropical country, especially in the dry season (late Dec to April), can make it difficult to take decent **photographs**. The best times for the light are just after dawn and late afternoon to dusk, but since the sun rises and sets quickly it doesn't give you much time. If you need to purchase any photographic equipment, such as camera batteries or memory cards, Panafoto in Panama City (Ⓦpanafoto.com) is really your only bet.

People are fascinating subjects, but be sensitive. If you want to photograph one or more human beings, rather than a market scene with people in it, you should ask their permission. In indigenous villages in particular, ask the village chief or the head of the tourist committee what the protocol is – some villages do not permit photography at all. Tour groups to a village may be encouraged to snap away but you should still ask for permission from the

individuals concerned. In Guna Yala, in particular, each island has its own regulations (see p.255).

Senior travellers

Given that Panama is one of the world's top **retirement** destinations, especially for North Americans, Panamanians are well used to meeting older foreign travellers. Though senior Panamanian and resident foreign retirees are eligible for incredible **discounts** on everything from flights to cinema tickets, visitors generally are not.

Time

Panama is four hours behind **Greenwich Mean Time** throughout the year, the same as **Eastern Standard Time** in the US, though note time changes for daylight-saving hours. Panama is one hour ahead of Costa Rica. If in doubt, consult Ⓦtimeanddate.com.

Toilets

Public toilets are thin on the ground in Panama. You will generally find them in airports and bus terminals, which require payment of a few cents to an attendant, who in return will hand you an inadequate few sheets of paper – always travel with an emergency toilet roll. Other options are fast-food joints, cafeterias and petrol stations. Most places outside top-end or very modern hotels with their own septic system require you to throw used toilet paper into an adjacent basket – alas sometimes missing altogether from the most rudimentary establishments. In Guna Yala and parts of Bocas, a toilet cistern is no guarantee of a water treatment system; everything may still flush straight out to sea.

Tourist information

The official **tourist agency**, the Autoridad de Turismo Panamá (ATP; Ⓦatp.gob.pa), has a slowly improving website (in English too) at Ⓦvisit panama.com, though the swanky air-conditioned tourist offices in the major towns and resort areas are still not geared up to assisting passing tourists. You may be lucky enough to get a map and, if you have a specific question, the employee will probably do their best to help you, but do not expect lists of local accommodation or tourist attractions, nor assume the person will speak English. **Reception staff** at a good hostel or hotel are a far better bet for reliable information.

The Visitor/El Visitante (Ⓦthevisitorpanama.com), a free, weekly tourist promotion **magazine** in English and Spanish, available in hotels and touristy restaurants throughout the country – as well as online – lists attractions and upcoming events; there are a number of other sources, too (see p.84). Panama's **national parks** and other protected areas, which encompass many of the country's natural wonders, are administered by the Ministry for the Environment, or MiAmbiente (see box, p.42).

Travellers with disabilities

Organized tourism is in its infancy in Panama and awareness of the needs and rights of **people with disabilities** is a fairly recent phenomenon – they were only granted equal rights by law in 1999. As a result, Panama isn't really geared up to accommodate travellers with disabilities. That said, Tocumen International Airport and many mid-range and luxury hotels in Panama City have "wheelchair access", though none addresses the spectrum of special needs. The three resorts mentioned in our "Travelling with children" section (see below) also advertise "disabled access" (as in "wheelchair access") and most cruise ships that take in Panama tend to be suitably equipped. Eco-Adventure International (Ⓦeaiadventure.com), and DisabledHolidays.com (Ⓦdisabledholidays.com) both organize customized **tours** to Panama for travellers with disabilities.

Travelling with children

Latin cultures are very family-oriented and Panama is no exception. While there is no pre-packaged entertainment for **children** such as theme parks, there's plenty to enjoy, including boat trips, snorkelling, horseriding, exploring the Canal and walking in the rainforest. Many **hotels** have extra beds or pull-outs in rooms for children and under-12s are often free, with older kids admitted at discount rates. The large resort hotels – the *Decameron* at Farallón on the Pacific coast (Ⓦdecameron.com), the *Hotel Meliá* on Lago Gatún (Ⓦmelia.com) and the *Gamboa Rainforest Resort* (see p.101) – have special activities laid on and child-minding services. Small B&Bs and ecolodges sometimes do not permit children or have a minimum age of 12 or 14.

Habla Ya Language Centre (Ⓦhablayapanama.com) in Boquete offers family and children's **Spanish courses**, while various tour operators in the UK and North America (check out Ⓦwildland.com in the US, Ⓦfamiliesworldwide.co.uk in the UK, and Ⓦaudleytravel.com for both the US and UK) include **family-oriented itineraries**. Travelling to Guna Yala and to the Darién, which can be challenging enough for adults, is very hard work with kids in tow. Sticking to Panama City and the Canal area, the Pacific beach resorts, El Valle, Bocas and Boquete is much easier and more enjoyable all round, especially if you're on a modest budget.

Volunteering

It's possible to arrange **voluntary work**, which can be carried out on a tourist visa, in advance. Try one of the various reputable international agencies, such as Volunteer Abroad (Ⓦgoabroad.com/volunteer-abroad), or directly through the websites of Panamanian organizations; alternatively you may be able to show up on the spot. Key areas include conservation or social development projects, usually in poor, marginalized communities. Before you plunge into volunteering, do your homework to ensure that the programme is bona fide and sustainable and that you are sufficiently skilled and experienced for the job. If training is provided, ensure that there is adequate time devoted to it – often a problem if organizations are hard-stretched.

Volunteering in projects, particularly with marginalized or vulnerable groups, is fraught with ethical dilemmas, which usually have no easy or "right" solution and can have unexpected negative side effects. While a couple of weeks on a turtle monitoring project may be fine, social development projects need long-term commitment since a constant rotation of volunteers can be unsettling for individuals and communities, especially for vulnerable groups such as young children. Moreover, as unemployment escalates in Panama, you should ask yourself whether you are taking away a job that a Panamanian could be paid to do.

That said, there are several well-established **programmes** in Panama. In Bocas del Toro, turtle conservation projects abound (see box, p.236), and the Smithsonian Tropical Research Institute takes on volunteers too (Ⓦstri.si.edu/english/visit_us/volunteers/index.php).

Panama City

1

Panama City

Proudly positioned in the crook of land overlooking the Pacific, the soaring skyline of Panama City surveys the ocean before it, much as Vasco Nuñez de Balboa did when he chanced upon the body of water after a bloody journey south across the isthmus almost five hundred years ago. From its inception, the city has been situated on one of the world's great crossroads, and it has thrived on trade, attracting migrants from all over the world to a cosmopolitan melting pot bubbling with energy and ambition. Panama has long been considered a bridge between two continents and nowhere is this divided identity more apparent than in the capital, where glitzy skyscrapers, laser-lit nightclubs and chic restaurants more reminiscent of Miami than Latin America are juxtaposed with colonial churches, clamouring street vendors and chaotic traffic. Though it is the undisputed political, economic and social centre of Panama and home to 1.5 million – more than a third of the country's population – the city has very little in common with the rest of the country, which is often vaguely referred to as "el interior".

On the southwest end of the bay stands the old city centre of **Casco Viejo**, a jumble of immaculately restored colonial buildings, crumbling ruins and run-down housing on a rocky promontory, while a few kilometres to the northeast rise the shimmering skyscrapers of **El Cangrejo** and **Marbella**, the modern banking and commercial district, and the penthouse apartments of **Punta Paitilla** and **Punta Pacífica**. Further east, amid sprawling suburbs whose tentacles extend 30km along the coast, stand the ruins of **Panamá Viejo**, the first European city to be founded on the Pacific coast of the Americas, while west of the city centre the former US Canal Zone town of **Balboa**, with its clipped lawns and restrained utilitarian architecture, retains a distinctly North American character despite having been turned over to full Panamanian control in 1999. In the background, the Panamanian flag proudly flies on the summit of **Cerro Ancón**, a surprising oasis of greenery on what was once a major US military base.

For the vast majority of visitors to Panama, the capital provides their first point of contact. Many spend their entire stay here, since it makes a good base from which to explore many of the country's attractions while enjoying the material comforts of sophisticated city living – the Canal, a handful of national parks and the Caribbean coast as far as Portobelo can all be visited on **day-trips**. Other visitors, keen to leave behind the frenzied construction and thronging streets and escape into Panama's outstanding wilderness areas, still linger a couple of days to savour the colonial architecture of Casco Viejo and the vitality of the modern city, including its many bars and restaurants.

While it is easy to tire of Panama City's irrepressible energy, oppressive heat and relentless traffic, it's as simple to escape to nearby places of real tranquillity: the

PARQUE SANTA ANA

Highlights

① Casco Viejo Perched on a rocky promontory, the evocative colonial centre has ancient churches, leafy plazas and grand buildings. **See p.56**

② Amador Causeway Take a perfect afternoon promenade, soaking up the views while marvelling at the architecture of Frank Gehry's biodiversity museum, followed by a sundowner on Isla Flamenco. **See p.67**

③ Cerro Ancón Vantage point offering an unparalleled panorama of towering skyscrapers and the imposing Canal. **See p.68**

④ Parque Natural Metropolitano A patch of tropical rainforest within the city limits – perfect for birdwatching. **See p.70**

⑤ Panamá Viejo Crumbling remains of the original Panama City, set in mud flats and mangroves on the edge of the metropolis. **See p.70**

⑥ Nightlife From rooftop cocktails in skyscraper bars to cheap beer in low-key indie joints, from salsa, techno or reggaeton in alfresco discos to fancy dining in the colonial centre, Panama City has a nightlife scene for everyone. **See p.82**

⑦ Isla Taboga The perfect day-trip from the bustle of the city, offering a lovely boat trip across the mouth of the Canal, a laidback fishing village and pleasant scenic walks. **See p.87**

HIGHLIGHTS ARE MARKED ON THE MAP ON P.54

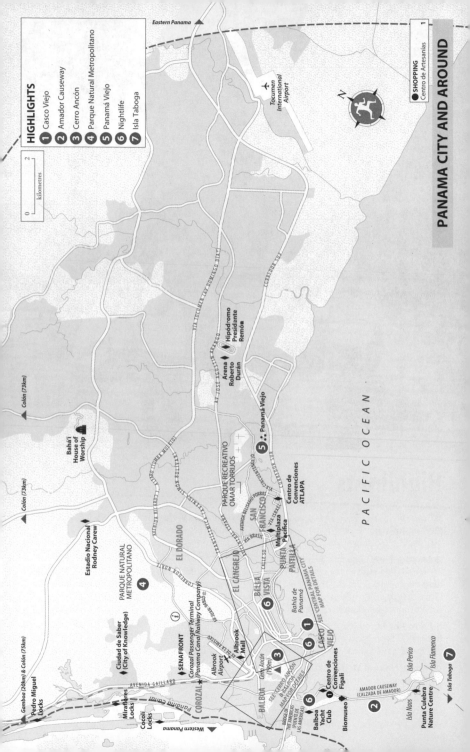

PANAMA CITY AND AROUND

HIGHLIGHTS

1. Casco Viejo
2. Amador Causeway
3. Cerro Ancón
4. Parque Natural Metropolitano
5. Panamá Viejo
6. Nightlife
7. Isla Taboga

SHOPPING

Centro de Artesanías

0   1   2
kilometres

Eastern Panama

Tocumen International Airport

Bahá'í House of Worship

Colón (73km)
Colón (73km)

Hipódromo Presidente Remón

Arena Roberto Durán

PARQUE RECREATIVO OMAR TORRIJOS

Centro de Convenciones ATLAPA

5 Panamá Viejo

PACIFIC OCEAN

Estadio Nacional Rodney Carew

PARQUE NATURAL METROPOLITANO

Ciudad de Saber (City of Knowledge)

4 PARQUE NATURAL METROPOLITANO

EL DORADO

EL CANGREJO

SAN FRANCISCO

Multiplaza Pacífica

BELLA VISTA

PUNTA PAITILLA

6

Bahía de Panamá

1

SENAFRONT

Corozal Passenger Terminal (Panama Canal Railway Company)

Albrook Mall

Albrook Airport

Cerro Ancón (199m)

3

SEE "CENTRAL PANAMA CITY MAP FOR DETAILS

CASCO VIEJO

6

Gamboa (20km) & Colón (75km)
Western Panama

Pedro Miguel Locks

Miraflores Locks

Cocolí Locks

AVENIDA GAILLARD

Panama Canal

COROZAL

BALBOA

SEE "CERRO ANCÓN MAP" FOR DETAILS

BRIDGE OF THE AMERICAS (PUENTE DE LAS AMÉRICAS)

Balboa Yacht Club

Biomuseo

Centro de Convenciones Figali

6

AMADOR CAUSEWAY (CALZADA DE AMADOR)

2

Isla Naos

Isla Perico

Punta Culebra Nature Centre

Isla Flamenco

Isla Taboga

7

Amador Causeway, a breezy breakwater offering fabulous views of the Canal and the city skyline; **Isla Taboga**, the sleepy "Island of Flowers" an hour's boat ride off the coast; or the **Parque Natural Metropolitano**, the only natural tropical rainforest within the limits of a Latin American capital.

Brief history

Modern-day Panama City, named **Panamá Nuevo**, was established by the Spanish in 1673, two years after the original settlement, **Panama Viejo**, had been sacked by the Welsh buccaneer Henry Morgan (see p.293). The new city developed in the area known today as **Casco Viejo**, on a rocky peninsula jutting out into the bay, 8km southwest of the old capital, and a more defendable and salubrious site than its swampy predecessor.

The Gold Rush and the railroad

Once the Spanish had rerouted their treasure fleet around Cape Horn in 1746, Panama City's commercial importance as a trade route slowly began to decline, only substantially picking up again in the mid-nineteenth century due to the isthmus's popularity as a transit point in the **California Gold Rush** and the completion of the **Panama Railroad** in 1855. The railroad, and subsequently the French and US canal construction efforts, brought immense prosperity and a wealth of new cultural influences that transformed the city and its inhabitants, who by 1920 totalled almost sixty thousand.

The Canal

Whereas the **Canal**, completed in 1914, confirmed Panama City's importance as a global trading centre, the outbreak of World War I, the waterway's official inauguration, opened the floodgates to large-scale **US military occupation** of the Panama Canal Zone, the 8km strip of land either side of the waterway under US jurisdiction. During World War II, defence installations proliferated and the predominantly US population topped one hundred thousand. Though other migrants continued to pour in, the lives of the city's population were regulated by the US military in the adjacent Canal Zone, who controlled everything from refuse collection and water supply to construction permits, and whose affluence and spending power inevitably shaped commercial development. No surprise then that Panama City found itself at the forefront of increasing nationalist sentiment that periodically erupted into violence, most notably in the flag riots of 1964 (see p.299). Only after the handover of the Canal had been assured, in the canal treaty of 1977, could the capital, and the country, start to plan its own path.

Modern times

The introduction of banking secrecy laws in the 1970s led to the rapid expansion of the financial services sector, including an influx of **narco-dollars**. Despite the tightening of banking regulations, El Cangrejo remains a hive of intrigue. Some of the luxury high-rise apartments there and in Punta Paitilla, and further east in Punta Pacífica and Costa del Este, stand empty, the astronomical rents paid by their fictitious occupants providing a useful means of laundering money.

The handover of the last US bases to Panamanian control at the end of 1999 released huge amounts of real estate, enabling the city to expand further along the coast, though its spread inland is still checked by the backdrop of hills that form the protected Panama Canal Basin. This has resulted in ever increasing **traffic congestion**; in response, millions of dollars have been recently spent on a **metro** line – Central America's first – and the Cinta Costera, a four-lane highway around the Bahía de Panama, which includes a controversial ring road around Casco Viejo. A second metro line is planned and further funds have been earmarked for another **bridge** over the Canal, which should also help extend the metro westwards.

1

Casco Viejo and around

Most of Panama City's historical monuments and tourist attractions are concentrated in the colonial city centre of **San Felipe** – more commonly called **Casco Viejo** (sometimes Casco Antiguo) – which is the best place to start your explorations. For centuries the heart of Panama City's social and political life, and still home to the presidential palace, Casco Viejo, after decades of neglect, was declared a UNESCO World Heritage Site in 1997 and is gradually being restored to its former glory. The subsequent gentrification is not without its problems: while upmarket restaurants and cafés sit alongside chic offices and apartments in renovated colonial buildings, poor families are gradually being squeezed out and prices are rocketing. That said, Casco Viejo is an exceedingly pleasant place to visit – and the visible presence of the tourist police means it is safe to explore, during the day at least. **Caution** should still be exercised when walking around at night, however; stick to the well-lit streets, and avoid straying into the adjacent neighbourhoods of El Chorrillo and Santa Ana.

The best way to see Casco Viejo is to **walk** – you can get there by taxi or by taking any bus, or the metro, to Plaza Cinco de Mayo.

Avenida Central

From Plaza Cinco de Mayo you can walk up **Avenida Central**, past Parque Santa Ana and the famous *Café Coca Cola* (see p.79), as it narrows into a cobbled street, passing through the now invisible city walls into the historic centre. The rows of lottery ticket sellers – who number more than ten thousand across the country – doing a brisk trade

■ ACCOMMODATION		● EATING				■ DRINKING & NIGHTLIFE		● SHOPPING	
American Trade Hotel	6	Café Coca-Cola	2	The Fish Market	5	Danilo's Jazz Club	5	Casa Latina Panamá	2
The Central Hotel	4	Caffè Per Due	4	Fonda León	9	Mojitos (sin Mojitos)	6	Galería de Arte Indígena	3
Las Clementinas	2	Calicanto	7	Granclement	6	Piña Cala Vera	1	Reprosa	1
Los Cuatro Tulipanes	5	Casa Sucre		Mähaló	11	Relic	2	La Ronda	4
Hospedaje Casco Viejo	1	Coffee House	1	René Café	3	Tántalo	3		
Luna's Castle	1	Donde José	4	Super Gourmet	8	Teatro Amador	4		
Magnolia Inn	3								

on the left-hand pavement provide an obvious clue to the function of the striking blue-and-white-striped Art Deco building – one of two homes of the national lottery (the other lies on Avenida Perú). A little further along on the left is the gleaming white-and-cream Neoclassical **Casa de la Municipalidad**, seat of the city government.

Iglesia de la Merced

C 10 at Av Central • Daily 6am–7pm • Free

Next door to the Casa de la Municipalidad stands the crumbling Baroque facade of the city's oldest church, **Iglesia de la Merced**, which in 1680 was reconstructed on its present site using the original stones from Panamá Viejo. The facade is the best-preserved section of the church, which gives way inside to some poorly conceived twentieth-century restoration work, though the gilded wooden altar retains some appeal.

Plaza de la Catedral

Midway down Avenida Central the street opens out into the old quarter's most impressive square, **Plaza de la Catedral** – also known as Plaza Mayor and Plaza de la Independencia, since the proclamations of independence from Spain and separation from Colombia were both made here (the newly restored *Central Hotel*, on the east side of the plaza, played a starring role in both events). Numerous busts of the nation's founding fathers are scattered beneath the shady trees surrounding the striking central gazebo, with the Republic's first president, Manuel Amador Guerrero, taking pride of place.

A **craft market** is held in the plaza on the last weekend of the month, and the first non-bank-holiday Sunday of the month sees a **flea market** (10am–5pm). In addition, free evening **concerts** are frequently held on balmy summer nights.

Catedral Metropolitana

Plaza de la Catedral • Closed for renovations; due to reopen 2019 • Free

Flanked by white towers sparkling with inlaid mother-of-pearl, the hybrid Neoclassical and Baroque olive-and-cream sandstone facade of the **Catedral Metropolitana** dominates the plaza. It was built between 1688 and 1796 using stone brought from the ruins of Panamá Viejo (see box, p.71). Three of its bells were also recovered from its ruined predecessor, and reputedly owe their distinctive tone to a gold ring thrown by Queen Isabella I of Spain into the molten metal from which they were cast. The interior is tatty in places, though the large altarpiece carved from seven types of Italian marble is suitably imposing. To its right lies a trapdoor marking the entrance to tunnels – not open to visitors – designed as escape routes, connecting the cathedral to the churches of La Merced and San José.

Museo de Historia de Panamá

Palacio Municipal, Plaza de la Catedral • Mon–Fri 8am–4pm • $1 • ☎ 228 6231

Southeast of the cathedral is the splendid Neoclassical **Palacio Municipal**, built in 1910 on the site of the former city hall. On the ground floor, the **Museo de Historia de Panamá** offers a cursory introduction to Panamanian history, focusing on symbols of independence such as the national flag, the national anthem and the coat of arms, alongside an eclectic mixture of maps and artefacts (explanations in Spanish). Despite some recent interactive additions, it will probably only appeal to history buffs. The languorous nude reclining in the entrance hall represents Panama bathing in the waters of the two oceans.

Museo del Canal Interoceánico

Plaza de la Catedral • Tues–Sun 9am–5pm • $10; audioguides in English or Spanish $3; prebooked guided tours in English $15/person (including entry); three people minimum • ☎ 211 1649, ⊛ museodelcanal.com

Housed in a three-storey French colonial building, complete with mansard roof and shutters, the excellent **Museo del Canal Interoceánico** offers a comprehensive account

1

of both the French and US endeavours to build a canal across the isthmus, and of the protracted handover of the Canal to Panama's control (see p.295, p.297 & p.299). Take a sweater – the air conditioning is fierce.

The highly polished marble entrance hall bears witness to the museum's former life as the city's grandest hotel. The bulk of the exhibition lies on the **second floor**, expounding the history of the transisthmian route, from the first Spanish attempt to find a passage to Asia to the contemporary management of the Canal. Although the museum is rather text-heavy (in Spanish – the most conspicuous sign in English asks visitors to refrain from sitting on an original Panama Railroad waiting-room bench), there are plenty of photographs, video montages and maps offering striking comparisons between the different working conditions of the French and US canal eras which bring to life the huge scale of the achievements.

The **third floor** displays cover the apartheid living conditions of gold and silver roll employees (see p.297), more information and artefacts from the US Canal drama and a barrage of press reports on the deteriorating Panamanian–US relations that eventually led to the handover of the Canal.

The museum has a small **shop** selling modern and original Canal memorabilia.

Palacio Presidencial

Av Eloy Alfaro, between C 6 and C 5 • To arrange a free guided tour (Tues, Thurs & Fri mornings; 1hr), a letter in Spanish suggesting possible dates needs to be emailed or hand-delivered to the Oficina de Guías several days in advance (Mon–Fri 8am–4pm; ☎ 527 9740, ask for Sra Griselda Bernal, ✉ gbernal@presidencia.gob.pa), at the back of the yellow building on the waterfront by C 4 – bring your passport

Built in 1673 as an opulent private mansion for a corrupt colonial judge, the present-day **Palacio Presidencial** went on to serve as a customs house, teacher training college and even a prison. In 1922 it was rebuilt as the presidential residence in grandiose neo-Moorish style under the orders of President Belisario Porras. It is commonly known as the "Palacio de las Garzas" after the white egrets given to Porras by his poet friend Ricardo Miró; white egrets have lived freely around the patio fountain ever since, alongside a pair of elegant blue cranes donated by the South African government. The streets around the palace are closed to traffic and pedestrians but visitors are allowed access via Calle 5 to view the exterior of the building during the day.

It is also possible to take a free **guided tour**, which is well worth the hassle (see above) even though it only covers a few rooms. After admiring the marble floor and mother-of-pearl-encrusted columns of the Moorish vestibule, you are taken up to the first floor and the long **Salón Amarillo** (Yellow Hall), used for official ceremonies. From the presidential throne to the gilt mirrors and heavy drapes, the room is replete with shades of gold, amber and mustard, while striking murals by Roberto Lewis offer a selective romp through Panama's history. In the adjoining **Comedor del Palacio** (Dining Room), where state banquets are held, Lewis's distinctive murals are even more prominent, depicting idyllic country scenes. Secreted away at the far end of the dining room is the **Salón del Cabinete** (Cabinet Room), which contains portraits of all Panama's presidents.

Plaza Bolívar and around

A block back from the waterfront on Avenida B, elegant **Plaza Bolívar**, dotted with manicured trees, provides the perfect spot for a glass of wine or a meal at its pavement café-restaurants. At lunchtime the peace is periodically interrupted by the cries of primary-school children spilling out of class seeking out snow-cones (*raspados*) from the waiting vendors.

Simón Bolívar monument

Rebuilt after a fire in 1756, the plaza was dedicated in 1883 to **Simón Bolívar**, whose central **statue**, crowned by a condor, dominates the space. The monument was erected in 1926 to commemorate one hundred years since the Amphyctionic Congress – the first **Panamerican gathering**, organized by Bolívar, aimed at unifying the newly independent Latin American countries in their relations with Spain. Although "El Libertador" (The Liberator) failed to attend the congress, and his dreams of unity ultimately foundered, it was considered a historic event.

Palacio Bolívar and Salón Bolívar

Northeastern corner of Plaza Bolívar • Mon–Fri 8am–4pm • Free

The **Palacio Bolívar**, whose impressive peach-and-white facade extends along the eastern edge of the square, is well worth a peek. Having served as part of a convent, military barracks and a school, the building now houses the Ministry of Foreign Affairs, among other government offices. It has been beautifully restored, its courtyard – the **Plaza de los Libertadores** – boasting a magnificent translucent roof allowing in lots of natural light. From a raised platform at the far side a bronze bust of the visionary Liberator looks on. To the right as you enter is the **Salón Bolívar**, formerly the chapter house of a Franciscan monastery where the Amphyctionic Congress took place, and now a small museum. It contains a replica of the Liberator's gold ceremonial sword, encrusted with more than a thousand diamonds, and the congress's original documents.

Iglesia y Convento de San Francisco de Asís

Southeastern corner of Plaza Bolívar • Daily 7am–7pm • Free

On the southeastern corner of the plaza, next to the Palacio Bolívar (see above), the recently renovated **Iglesia y Convento de San Francisco de Asís** has finally reopened after years of neglect. Established by the Franciscans in the seventeenth century, it was later taken over by the Jesuits, who were responsible for its present design, adding the imposing bell tower in 1918 – which is still closed due to a lack of funding. Get a welcome blast of cool air conditioning as you check out the restrained interior, which features delightful modern stained-glass windows laden with Franciscan symbolism, and, framing the main altar, a beautifully restored mural composed of Venetian mosaic.

Iglesia San Felipe de Neri

Plaza Bolívar at Av "B" and C 4 • Daily 7am–7pm • Free

Built in 1688, **Iglesia San Felipe de Neri** was one of Casco Viejo's earliest churches; it served as a shrine to the cathedral and then, much later, as a children's home and orphanage.

Teatro Nacional

Eastern end of Av "B" • Closed for renovations • ☎ 262 3525

The handsome **Teatro Nacional** was one of the first grand national buildings to be commissioned by the newly independent Panamanian state. Built on the site of a former convent and designed by Italian architect Genaro Ruggieri, the magnificent Italianate Neoclassical edifice, with a splendid Baroque interior, opened its doors to the public in 1908. Despite initial success, the global depression of the 1930s brought a slump in the venue's fortunes, and it became a cinema for a while before falling into neglect. After substantial restoration work, the theatre reopened in 1974 with a performance by Margot Fonteyn, the British ballerina and long-term Panama resident, whose bronze bust adorns the foyer, alongside that of Roberto Lewis, whose allegorical frescoes depicting the birth of the nation can be seen on the vaulted ceiling. It is hoped that the current renovations will be completed by early 2019, when occasional theatrical productions (see p.85) should resume.

The ramparts

Two hundred metres southeast of the Teatro Nacional, steps lead up to **Paseo Esteban Huertas**, a delightful, breezy, bougainvillea-covered promenade that runs some 400m along the top of what were the ramparts. The walkway along the defensive seawall is a favourite haunt of smooching couples – earning it the nickname Paseo de los Inamorados – and Guna traders displaying their handicrafts to passing tourists. At the far end, before descending the steps into the Plaza de Francia, you get fine views across the bay. Peek over the wall and you can glimpse the windows of the dungeons where prisoners were allegedly left at low tide to drown when the high tide flooded the cells.

Plaza de Francia

Plaza de Francia, at the southeastern tip of Casco Viejo, is an irregularly shaped space bounded by the seawall and the renovated arches of **Las Bóvedas** (vaults), Spanish dungeons that also functioned as storehouses, prison cells and barracks for the fort that occupied the plaza until the early twentieth century. They now contain a chic restaurant of the same name. Formerly the Plaza de Armas, the city's main square, the space is dominated by a substantial monument dedicated to the thousands of workers who died during the disastrous French attempt to build the Canal (see p.295). The central **obelisk** is topped by a proud Gallic cockerel and ringed by busts of the key figures involved, including Ferdinand de Lesseps, the French diplomat who first conceived of the canal yet whose ignorance and vanity were central to the project's ultimate failure (see p.295). Behind, vast marble tablets chronologically outline the bare bones of the dream to build a transisthmian waterway.

The Neoclassical **French Embassy** overlooks the square from the north, fronted by a huge statue of former Panamanian president Pablo Arosemena. The large gleaming-white building to the east is home to the **Instituto Nacional de Cultura** (INAC), the body responsible for maintaining the country's museums. It was spruced up for the James Bond film *Quantum of Solace*, in which it featured as a Bolivian hotel. Adjacent is the intimate Teatro Anita Villalaz (see p.85).

Iglesia y Convento de Santo Domingo

Av "A" at C 3 • Closed for restoration

Restoration work is ongoing at the ruined **Iglesia y Convento de Santo Domingo**. Completed in 1678, it is most famous for the **Arco Chato** (flat arch) over its main entrance – which remains open to the public. Just 10.6m high, but spanning some 15m with no keystone or external support, it was reputedly cited as evidence of Panama's seismic stability when the US Senate was debating where to build an interoceanic canal. Ironically, the arch inexplicably collapsed just after the centenary celebrations for Panama's independence in 2003, but has subsequently been restored.

Museo de Arte Religioso Colonial

Av "A" at C 3 • Mon–Fri 9.30am–3.30pm • Free • ☎ 501 4127

The single room of the **Museo de Arte Religioso Colonial** has a small collection of religious paintings, silverwork and sculpture dating back to the colonial era. Realistically, the detailed information panels will only be of interest to colonial-history buffs who can read Spanish.

Iglesia de San José

Av "A" at C 8 • Mon–Fri 9am–noon & 2–5pm, Sat 9am–noon

The **Iglesia de San José**, built in 1673 but subsequently remodelled, is exceptional only for being home to the legendary Baroque **Altar de Oro** (Golden Altar), which illuminates the otherwise gloomy interior. A carved mahogany extravaganza gilded with 22-carat gold leaf, it was one of the few treasures to survive Henry Morgan's ransacking of Panamá Viejo in 1671 thanks, apparently, to having been painted or covered in mud to disguise its true value. Legend has it that when Morgan demanded to see the gold, the priest explained its absence by pleading poverty, even persuading the buccaneer to make a donation to the church.

Plaza Herrera

At the western limit of Casco Viejo is **Plaza Herrera**, a pleasant square lined with elegant nineteenth-century houses, named in honour of General Tomás Herrera, the military leader of Panama's first short-lived independence attempt in 1840 (see p.295). His equestrian monument stands in the centre of the plaza. Just off Plaza Herrera to the west lies **Bastión Mano de Tigre** (Tiger Hand Bastion), a crumbling and indistinct pile of masonry that is the last remaining section of the city's original defensive walls on the landward side. To the north a gleaming white facade announces the restored *American Trade Hotel* (see p.77), which dates back to 1917.

In contrast, tucked away at the western end of the square is a striking wooden residential building, named **La Boyacá** after a nineteenth-century gunboat and with a frontage carved like the prow of a ship. Beyond, the road soon dissolves into the poor barrio and no-go area of **El Chorrillo**, which was devastated during the US invasion, leaving hundreds dead and thousands homeless. The neighbourhood has since been rebuilt, but the coloured concrete tenements that replaced the old wooden slum housing are already run-down. Despite a substantial increase in police presence, and investment in leisure facilities, it's still a **dangerous** place, day or night.

Parque Santa Ana

Parque Santa Ana, the social hub of the impoverished neighbourhood of Santa Ana, marks the transition between the old colonial centre of Casco Viejo and the more commercial modern city. As the centre of activity outside the city walls in the early nineteenth century, it hosted colourful markets and bullfights; now it offers some respite from the swirling traffic, and is often populated by many of the locality's older residents, discussing the latest news. The pedestrianized section of Avenida Central starts on the park's northeastern side, where a row of shoe-shine booths provides another social focus.

Central Panama City

In contrast to the relative calm of the city's historical centre and ancient remains, the **modern** streets of **central Panama City** reverberate with traffic noise and pavements are packed with people squeezing in and out of the patchwork of shops, banks, hotels and restaurants or threading their way through street vendors, hawkers and other pedestrians. Wedge-shaped central Panama City stretches 3km around the Bahía de Panamá, from **Avenida Central** and **Plaza Cinco de Mayo** – home to the central government buildings – to **Punta Paitilla**, encompassing the older residential and commercial districts of **Calidonia** and **La Exposición**, fanning out to include **Bella Vista** and the newer, plusher financial districts of **Marbella** and **El Cangrejo**.

Avenida Central

The pedestrianized stretch of **Avenida Central**, from Parque Santa Ana north as far as Plaza Cinco de Mayo, is one of the city's oldest and most colourful shopping districts. Air conditioning and loud music blast out from the huge, predominantly Hindu-owned superstores that sell cheap clothing, electronics and household goods, while hawkers flog pirate DVDs and cheap sunglasses, and vendors quench the thirst of shoppers with fruit

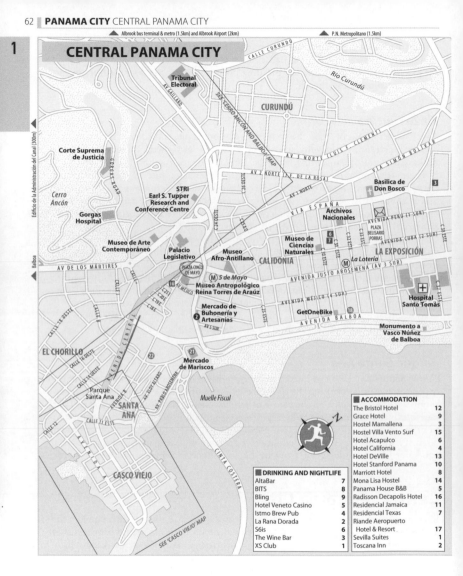

CENTRAL PANAMA CITY

Albrook bus terminal & metro (1.5km) and Albrook Airport (2km)　　P.N. Metropolitano (1.5km)

CALLE CURUNDÚ
Río Curundú
CURUNDÚ

Tribunal Electoral
AV. GAILLARD
CERRO ANCÓN AND BALBOA RD.

AV. 3 NORTE (LUIS F. CLEMENT)
VÍA SIMÓN BOLÍVAR

Corte Suprema de Justicia
AV. 2 NORTE (F. DE LA ROSA)
AV. 1 NORTE

Basilica de Don Bosco

Cerro Ancón
STRI Earl S. Tupper Research and Conference Centre

VÍA ESPAÑA
Archivos Nacionales
AVENIDA PERÚ (E SUR)
PLAZA BELISARIO PORRAS
AVENIDA CUBA (2 SUR)

Gorgas Hospital
Palacio Legislativo
Museo Afro-Antillano
CALIDONIA
Museo de Ciencias Naturales

Museo de Arte Contemporáneo
PLAZA CINCO DE MAYO
La Lotería
LA EXPOSICIÓN

AV. DE LOS MÁRTIRES
5 de Mayo
AVENIDA JUSTO AROSEMENA (AV 3 SUR)

Balboa

Museo Antropológico Reina Torres de Araúz
AV. MÉJICO
AVENIDA MÉJICO (4 SUR)

Hospital Santo Tomás

Mercado de Buhonería y Artesanías
AV. S SUR
GetOneBike
AVENIDA BALBOA

EL CHORRILLO
Monumento a Vasco Núñez de Balboa

Parque Santa Ana
SANTA ANA
Mercado de Mariscos

AVENIDA CENTRAL
Muelle Fiscal

CASCO VIEJO
CINTA COSTERA
SEE 'CASCO VIEJO' MAP

■ ACCOMMODATION	
The Bristol Hotel	12
Grace Hotel	9
Hostel Mamallena	3
Hostel Villa Vento Surf	15
Hotel Acapulco	6
Hotel California	4
Hotel DeVille	13
Hotel Stanford Panama	10
Marriott Hotel	8
Mona Lisa Hostel	14
Panama House B&B	5
Radisson Decapolis Hotel	16
Residencial Jamaica	11
Residencial Texas	7
Riande Aeropuerto Hotel & Resort	17
Sevilla Suites	1
Toscana Inn	2

■ DRINKING AND NIGHTLIFE	
AltaBar	7
BITS	8
Bling	9
Hotel Veneto Casino	5
Istmo Brew Pub	4
La Rana Dorada	2
S6is	6
The Wine Bar	3
XS Club	1

or sugar cane juice. Nowhere is the city's cultural diversity more evident, a kaleidoscope of Hindus in saris, Guna women in traditional costume, bearded Muslims in robes and skullcaps, *interioranos* in sombreros, Chinese, Afro-Antillanos and Latinos. In the evening, in the pedestrianized area round Cinco de Mayo, extra food stalls pop up selling kebabs and sausages and as the night wears on, prostitutes tout for custom. Exercise **caution** when walking around the streets either side of Avenida Central and north of Parque Santa Ana, and avoid wandering around the side streets at night.

Plaza Cinco de Mayo and around

The pedestrian zone of Avenida Central spills out into the busiest square in the city centre, **Plaza Cinco de Mayo**, where the traffic mayhem takes over again. To the east the square is

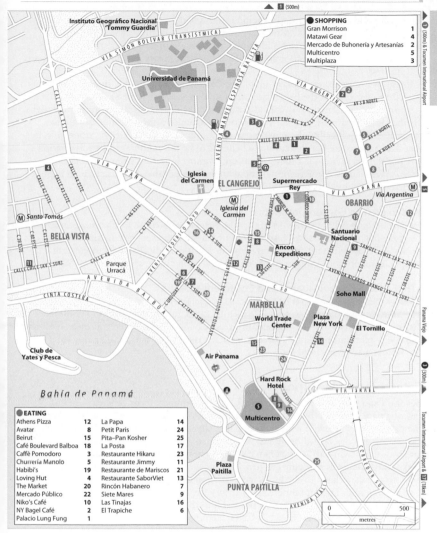

bordered by the neglected Neoclassical building that was originally the proud Panama Railroad Pacific terminal; the national **anthropological museum** here is due to reopen soon.

On the northwestern side of the plaza is the rather uninspiring **Palacio Legislativo** (Legislative Palace), which stands in the raised **Parque José Antonio Remón Cantera**, named after a former president who was mysteriously gunned down at the hippodrome in 1955. Peer behind the towering black monolith at its centre and you are greeted by an enormous, rather unflattering head of the murdered president, protruding from the granite.

Museo Antropológico Reina Torres de Araúz

Plaza Cinco de Mayo • ☎ 501 4151 • Ⓜ Cinco de Mayo

The **Museo Antropológico Reina Torres de Araúz (MARTA)**, named after Panama's foremost anthropologist, is home to Panama's finest anthropological collection.

1

Languishing in the old railroad's Pacific terminus, the exhibits have been hidden from the public since 2010, ostensibly due to the lack of funds to carry out the necessary renovations on the building; however, the museum is due to open again in 2019. Despite a major theft of almost three hundred pieces in 2003, the collection is still impressive.

The most eye-catching displays are of **pre-Columbian gold**, mainly **huacas** – precious objects recovered from the burial sites of prominent *caciques* (chiefs). These include weapons, tools and intricately carved jewellery, often in fantastical zoomorphic designs. The beautifully painted, primarily ceremonial, **ceramics** comprise three distinctive regional designs. Possibly the most intriguing exhibits, however, are the **stone** objects that date back to the **Barriles culture** – believed to be the country's oldest civilization (see p.291). These include ornate ceremonial *metates* (grinding stones) and curious large carved figures, some seemingly depicting chiefs or other prominent men being carried on the shoulders of slaves.

Museo de Arte Contemporáneo

Between Av de los Mártires and C San Blas • Tues–Sat 10am–5pm, Sun 10am–4pm • $5 • ☎ 262 8012, ⓦ macpanama.org • Ⓜ Cinco de Mayo

The privately owned **Museo de Arte Contemporáneo** houses a permanent collection of works by Panamanian artists in a range of media. It periodically hosts interesting temporary exhibitions; photos of the entire collection can be seen on the website.

STRI Earl S. Tupper Research and Conference Centre

Av Roosevelt • Mon–Fri 9am–5pm • Free • ☎ 212 8000, ⓦ stri.si.edu • Ⓜ Cinco de Mayo

The Smithsonian Tropical Research Institute's **Earl S. Tupper Research and Conference Centre**, set in leafy grounds, hosts an impressive bookshop (see p.86), a research library and a very pleasant, modestly priced cafeteria. Visits to Isla Barro Colorado (see p.102) can be arranged at the bookshop.

Calidonia and La Exposición

Beyond Plaza Cinco de Mayo, Avenida Central continues north. The city's main thoroughfare remains a busy shopping street as it runs through **CALIDONIA** – where the pavements are packed with stalls flogging cheap goods – and **LA EXPOSICIÓN**. Consisting of a dense grid of streets, where the sound of construction work is never far away, these twin barrios are crammed with cheap hotels, with a sprinkling of small parks and a couple of museums to provide welcome relief. This older section of the modern city dates back to the boom construction eras of the Panama Railroad and Canal in the mid- and late nineteenth century (see p.294 & p.295), when a large number of West Indian immigrants poured into the city. The area's population expanded yet further when non-US-Canal labourers and their families – again, primarily West Indian – were gradually forced out of the newly created Canal Zone (see p.297) in the early twentieth century.

Museo Afro-Antillano

Av Justo Arosemena (also known as Av 3 Sur) at C 24 • Tues–Sun 9.30am–3.45pm • $1 • ☎ 501 4130, ⓦ samaap.org • Ⓜ Cinco de Mayo

Housed in an unmarked wooden former church, the **Museo Afro-Antillano** is dedicated to the history and culture of Panama's large West Indian population. The Church of the Christian Mission, as it was then, constituted the social centre of the barrio of El Marañón, once a thriving Afro-Antillean community dating back to the construction of the railroad (see p.294). As property prices escalated in the 1970s and developers moved in, residents were forced out to the suburbs. The community has maintained a precarious toehold in the centre of the city through this small but worthwhile museum, which highlights the pivotal role that Afro-Antilleans played in the construction of the railroad and the Canal. The photographs, tools and period furniture, with captioning in English, provide a sharp reminder of the harsh working and living conditions of black, "silver roll" Canal workers, which contrasted acutely with the privileges of white American "gold roll" employees, in the days of the Canal Zone. The museum also helps organize the annual **Afro-Antillean Fair** that takes place during Carnaval at the Centro de Convenciones ATLAPA (see p.85).

Plaza Belisario Porras
Av Perú, between C 33 and C 34 • Ⓜ La Lotería

Plaza Belisario Porras honours the country's three-time president and founding father. Amid the neatly trimmed flowerbeds rises a vast monument in which Porras cuts a dashing figure, overlooked by splendidly restored government buildings and the balustraded Spanish Embassy.

Basílica de Don Bosco
Daily 6am–6pm • Free • Ⓜ La Lotería

With your back to the Belisario Porras monument, looking up Calle Ecuador to Avenida Central, you can spy the rose window of the neo-Romanesque **Basílica de Don Bosco**, built in the 1950s. As well as being pleasantly airy with some lovely stained glass, the place is a glittering blue mass of modern mosaics, crafted in Italy and brought to Panama for the centennial celebrations.

Bella Vista, El Cangrejo and Marbella

The neighbouring areas of Bella Vista, Marbella and El Cangrejo form the financial and commercial core of Panama City – what is often nebulously referred to as the Área Bancaria. **BELLA VISTA**, either side of Calle 50, once a leafy barrio brimming with 1930s colonial mansions, has all but been taken over by modern high-rise buildings. To the north on Vía España stands the incongruous twentieth-century neo-Gothic wedding cake of the **Iglesia del Carmen**. Particularly impressive when illuminated at night, the stained-glass windows along the aisles depict tropical flowers, while those higher up in the nave relate tales from the Old and New Testaments. The neo-Byzantine mosaic altarpiece also grabs your attention.

The church marks the beginning of **EL CANGREJO**, home to many of Panama City's classier hotels and restaurants, as well as upmarket stores and shopping centres. This, and the adjacent areas of Bella Vista and **MARBELLA**, are among the city's nightlife zones.

Avenida Balboa and the Cinta Costera

The sweeping arc of **Avenida Balboa**, which connects the city's historic heartland, Casco Viejo, to its symbols of industrial progress, Punta Paitilla, now forms part of the **Cinta Costera**. The aim of this multimillion-dollar land reclamation project was to ease traffic congestion by constructing a parallel dual carriageway alongside a promenade complete with trees, benches and leisure facilities. Although the project has delivered more concrete than the green spaces that were originally promised, it has marginally improved the traffic flow, and its jogging path and cycleway are well used by residents (see box, p.66). The Cinta Costera is also the focus of Panama City's Carnavales, which, outside the Azuero, are the country's most extravagant.

Mercado de Mariscos
Southern end of the Cinta Costera • Mon–Sat 6am–6pm; closed first Mon of the month for fumigation • Ⓜ Cinco de Mayo

The distinctive blue-roofed **Mercado de Mariscos** is a fabulous place to wander around. All shapes and sizes of seafood are on sale, some waving their antennae at you from tanks. You can observe the comings and goings from a table upstairs at the *Restaurante*

1

GETTING ACTIVE ON THE CINTA COSTERA

Sunday mornings on the Cinta Costera offer a spread of recreational activities, most of them free. **Cycling** is the main event; during **Ciclovía Panamá** (6am–noon) the regular cycleway is extended northeast all the way to the museum at Panamá Viejo, from where you can pedal southwest as far as the Estadio Maracaná, the other side of Casco Viejo – 15km one way. Around three hundred free bikes are available for this weekly event, on a first-come-first-served basis; you'll find them opposite the *Hilton Hotel* at Calle Alquilino de la Guardia, in the middle of the Cinta Costera (you'll need to show your passport). Otherwise, you can rent a bike (see p.75), or, if you're staying at *Luna's Castle*, use one of the bikes they loan for free to guests (see p.77). You're likely to need to navigate your way through joggers, skateboarders and assorted others while on your bike.

Alongside the Sunday cycling, there's plenty of **jogging**, plus free **exercise classes** at 7 and 8am: choose from yoga, boxercise and Zumba. Turn up suitably attired at the Fuente Anayansi, and treat yourself to a *raspado* when you've finished. Classes are also held on weekdays, in the early mornings and evenings, for a few dollars.

de Mariscos (see p.80), or head around the back and catch the buzz of the *cevicherías* and fish stalls overlooking the busy public dock (*muelle fiscal*).

Monumento a Vasco Núñez de Balboa and around

The Cinta Costera's main sight, midway along, is the magnificent **Monumento a Vasco Núñez de Balboa**. Erected in 1913, it shows the sixteenth-century explorer atop a globe, sword in one hand and flag in the other; once looking out in perpetual triumph on the southern ocean he "discovered", he now seems a tad lost in the traffic. Set back across Avenida Balboa is the grand Neoclassical facade of **Hospital Santo Tomás**, the largest public medical facility in the country.

Parque Urracá

A further 800m along the embankment from the Balboa monument, the pleasant **Parque Urracá** is named after the indigenous chief who famously defeated the Spaniards and later escaped from captivity (see box, p.292). Hemmed in by high-rises, this welcome green space comes alive in the late afternoons at weekends as locals congregate to play football and socialize.

Punta Paitilla, Punta Pacífica and San Francisco

Jutting out into the sea at the northeastern end of the bay, the artificial peninsula of **PUNTA PAITILLA**, packed with more than fifty shimmering skyscrapers, constitutes one of Panama City's most emblematic views. Built around 1970, the forty-storey high-rises and their luxury apartments, many of which lie empty due to absent or fictitious owners, became one of the city's most exclusive residential areas. It's also a major Jewish neighbourhood, with a synagogue and kosher food stores and restaurants in the vicinity.

Around the headland, the newer skyscrapers of **PUNTA PACÍFICA** house yet more opulent ocean-view residences, with the sail-shaped Trump Tower easily the most distinctive. Both exclusive enclaves form part of the broader district of **SAN FRANCISCO**, which is also gradually falling prey to Panama's skyscraper addiction. The area's two main landmarks are the **Centro de Convenciones ATLAPA**, the city's main convention centre (see p.85), and Parque Recreativo Omar Torrijos, generally shortened to **Parque Omar**, the city's second largest green space after the Parque Metropolitano. Hundreds of residents take their morning exercise here, or laze about at weekends, and there's a lovely outdoor swimming pool (see box, p.76).

Former Canal Zone

1

Established in 1903 to protect the Canal, the **former Canal Zone** ran the length of the waterway, extending approximately 8km either side of it but excluding Panama City and Colón. Under US military control until 1977, it was jointly administered by the US and Panamanian authorities until the eventual handover in 1999 (see p.299). Though gradually being swallowed up by Panama City's urban sprawl, **Balboa** – which was effectively the administrative capital of the "Zone" – still retains some of its pleasant leafy landscaping and original architecture, most notably the palatial **Canal Administration Building** and exclusive residential enclave of Quarry Heights. Above, **Cerro Ancón** affords splendid views of the city and Canal, including south to the **Amador Causeway**, which marks the Pacific entrance to the Canal, and north to the forested **Parque Natural Metropolitano**.

Amador Causeway

Away from the deafening traffic, pollution and stultifying heat of downtown Panama City, the refreshing breezes of the **Amador Causeway** (Calzada de Amador) – the Canal's Pacific breakwater – make it an attractive weekend recreational area for middle-class Panamanians as well as a draw for tourists. Over the last decade the causeway's popularity has waxed and waned; currently, it is on the up again, following a multimillion-dollar facelift that has seen a new dual carriageway, a regular bus service – including the hop-on-hop-off tourist bus (see p.75) – a cycleway, park benches and four viewpoints. As a result, the bars and restaurants are beginning to fill once more; you can wine and dine while enjoying close-ups of transiting ships or more distant views of the Paitilla skyline. Nearer the mouth of the causeway stands the **Centro de Convenciones Figali** – currently closed for renovations – with the city's best **craft market** squeezed in alongside (see p.86). More practically, the causeway is the departure point for **ferries** to Taboga and the Archipiélago de las Perlas as well as for Canal tours (see p.89, p.123 & box, p.95). Consisting of three interconnecting islands – islas **Naos**, **Perico** and **Flamenco** – the 3km causeway first came into existence in 1913, to help prevent crosscurrents silting up the entry to the Canal. Its strategic location, protruding out into the bay, resulted in Isla Flamenco becoming the site for a US military base. Flamenco also hosts the command centre for the Autoridad del Canal de Panamá (ACP), which controls all traffic transiting the Canal.

The best way to explore the area is on foot or by **bike**; you can rent cycles at several places (see p.75).

Biomuseo

Amador Causeway • Tues–Fri 10am–4pm, Sat & Sun 1am–5pm • $18 • ☏ 830 6700, ⊕ biomuseopanama.com • Metrobuses run down the causeway from outside Albrook bus terminal

The unmissable, crumpled technicolour rooftop at the entrance to the causeway proper heralds the **Biomuseo** – designed by famed architect **Frank Gehry** – which, after almost fifteen years of political wrangling, finally opened in 2014. By far the city's best museum, it has a hefty price tag to match the hype.

Aimed at highlighting Panama's rich **biodiversity** due to its unique position as a land bridge between the two Americas, the Biomuseo also devotes space to Panama's **human history**. Although the permanent exhibition comprises just eight rooms, plus a couple of outdoor exhibits, its state-of-the-art interactive screens and large-scale audiovisual presentations are undeniably impressive. The **Panamarama** room is particularly striking, its ten-screen, surround-sound romp through Panama's ecosystems, accompanied by drumming and jungle noises, an assault on the senses. Other rooms focus on the geological formation of the isthmus, the ways in which the marine life in the two oceans evolved, and the interconnectedness of various ecosystems. Outside, the

1

biodiversity park, still in its infancy, intends to continue the theme; endemic and native plants are to be selected either on aesthetic grounds or because of what they tell us about Panama's biodiversity.

Inevitably, there is both a **gift shop** and **café** on site.

Isla Naos

Isla Naos is the location of a marine research centre for the Smithsonian Tropical Research Institute (STRI), which maintains a small reserve on the adjoining peninsula, Punta Culebra. The **Punta Culebra Nature Centre** (March–Dec Tues–Fri 1–5pm, Sat & Sun 10am–6pm; Jan–Feb Tues–Sun 10am–6pm; $5; ⓦstri.si.edu) is probably only worth popping into if you are travelling with young children. Set in a rare patch of tropical dry forest, the reserve offers a small visitor's centre, a couple of pools containing marine life and a short trail through the forest, where you should keep an eye out for green iguanas and two-toed sloths. Next to the reserve entrance is the departure point for the ferry to Taboga (see p.89).

Isla Perico and Isla Flamenco

At the end of the causeway, the neglected strip mall of **Isla Perico** tends to be ignored in favour of **Isla Flamenco**, which features a cruise terminal and a flash marina sheltering sleek yachts and motorboats, surrounded by priccy bars and restaurants – a real tourist trap for unwary cruise-ship visitors, though its wonderful views make the island a choice spot for a sundowner.

Cerro Ancón

Visible from most of the surrounding area, the huge Panamanian flag fluttering in the breeze on the summit of **Cerro Ancón** (199m) is one of the city's most distinctive landmarks. The hill itself affords sweeping **vistas** of both the city and the Canal; what's more, it is topped with a protected area of secondary **forest** harbouring white-tailed deer, agoutis, sloths, toucans, Geoffroy's tamarin and white-faced capuchin monkeys, and is well worth climbing (see box below).

By the mirador overlooking the city, and below the flagpole, sits the serene bronze figure of poet **Amelia Denis de Icaza**, who is remembered for *Al Cerro Ancón*; written in 1900, it served as a nationalist rallying cry.

Steps down the eastern side of hill, by the main gate, lead to the theme-park-style **Mi Pueblito** (Tues–Sun 9am–9pm; free), a set of four rather tacky replica villages recreating traditional architectural styles and flogging overpriced crafts. The main incentive is the

---

WALKING UP CERRO ANCÓN

One of the highlights of Panama City is undoubtedly a **walk up Cerro Ancón** in the early morning or late afternoon, when you're likely to encounter keel-billed toucans croaking from the treetops and a host of other wildlife.

To get there on foot, cross Avenida de los Mártires, behind the Palacio Legislativo on Plaza Cinco de Mayo, and cut through to the road that winds through the old Gorgas Hospital and Supreme Court. Skirting round the northern side of the hill, the road divides: to the right, it drops down to the Canal Administration Building, while ahead it climbs to **Quarry Heights**, the former US military command centre. These days it is an exclusive leafy residential area (renamed Altos de Ancón) and is worth a short detour for its unique Zonian wooden architecture. From the Quarry Heights security gate, it's a twenty- to thirty-minute hike to the **summit**; take the first left, then immediate right. A few hundred metres later you'll come to a locked gate, which, at the time of writing had been closed to vehicles for several months for fear of subsidence in the road. Pedestrians and cyclists can slip through the side gate, whereas taxis will have to deposit their passengers ($5 one way; $10–12 including wait time).

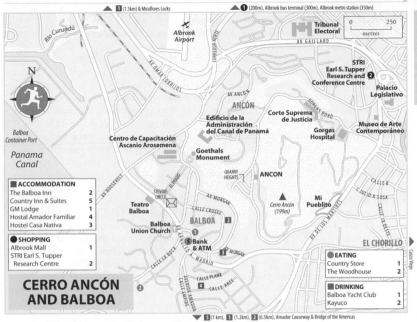

CERRO ANCÓN AND BALBOA

café-restaurant on the pseudo-Spanish colonial square, whose fresh fruit juices aid recovery from any physical exertion on the hill.

Edificio de la Administración del Canal de Panamá

Western slope of Cerro Ancón • No hours; tell the security guard that you want to see the "*murales*" – you may have to present ID

The stately **Edificio de la Administración del Canal de Panamá** (Canal Administration Building), which dominates the hill's western slope, houses four arresting **murals** that celebrate in graphic detail the Herculean achievement of building the Canal. Decorating an elegant domed marble rotunda, just inside the main entrance, they were painted by New York artist William Van Ingen, known for his work in the Library of Congress in Washington DC. A series of evocative lithographs adorn the outer walls of the rotunda.

Balboa

West of Cerro Ancón lies the district of **BALBOA**, whose centre, **El Prado**, is a palm-lined grassy rectangle measured to match the length and width of an original lock chamber. El Prado extends from the Goethals Monument at the foot of the administration building steps to Stevens Circle at the far end, by the main road. When George Goethals took over as chief engineer of the Canal in 1907, he surveyed all that his predecessor, John Stevens, had achieved and prophetically wrote to his son, "Mr Stevens has done an amount of work for which he will never get any credit, or if he gets any, will not get enough". Nowhere is this more evident than in the monuments to their labours: while **Stevens Circle** consists of a small and rather neglected memorial down the far end of the Prado, the cream marble **Goethals Monument** monolith stands tall at the foot of the Canal Authority's seat of power, with water cascading over three stepped marble platforms – symbolizing the three sets of locks – into a pool below.

1

Centro de Capacitación Ascanio Arosemena

Edif. 704 • Mon–Fri 7.15am–4.15pm • Free • ☎ 272 1111 • To reach the displays, enter the former school gates, taking the first right turn through a building, across a courtyard and into a second building

Diagonally across from the Goethals Monument stands the former Balboa High School, site of the dramatic "flag riots" of 1964 (see p.299); the 21 Panamanians who died in the skirmish are honoured in a memorial near the back of the building. Today, the old school houses the **Centro de Capacitación Ascanio Arosemena**, which, in addition to providing technical training to Canal employees, contains a small but evocative Canal exhibition with bilingual labelling. If your Spanish is not up to the Canal museum in Casco Viejo (see p.57) this display will give you a good enough flavour, its **memorabilia** ranging from porcelain from the *Tivoli Hotel* – the grandest hotel of the Canal Zone era – to Goethals' hat rack, along with an excellent collection of **photographs** of the Canal construction.

Teatro Balboa and beyond

A stroll down the Prado takes you to Avenida Arnulfo Arias Madrid, across which stands the faded Art Deco **Teatro Balboa** (see p.85), worth peeking inside for its splendid mosaic floors. Turning left along the main road, you hit the main intersection with Calle la Boca, where you cannot fail to notice the vainglorious bronze **monument** to former president Arnulfo Arias Madrid (see p.298), standing on the end of what looks like a giant seesaw with citizens imploring his help crawling towards him.

Parque Natural Metropolitano

The main entrance and park office are 200m along Av Juan Pablo II beyond the junction with Av Ascanio Villalaz • Daily 6am–5pm; office Mon–Fri 8am–5pm, Sat 8am–1pm • $4; 2hr guided tours $50/group of up to five people, in English or Spanish; 24hr notice needed • ☎ 232 5552, ⊛ parquemetropolitano.org

Though it's not quite far enough from the city centre to escape the hum of traffic, the **Parque Natural Metropolitano** nevertheless offers genuine tranquillity. A hilly patch of semi-deciduous tropical forest, the park offers excellent **birdwatching** and glimpses of the city and Canal area from three lookouts and five short but well-marked **trails**. Arriving early in the morning enhances your chances of seeing sloths entwined around branches, agoutis or koatis snuffling in the undergrowth and colourful and abundant birdlife, including golden-collared mannakins, slaty-tailed trogons and red-lored Amazon parrots. On the first Sunday of the month, Panama's Audubon Society leads **guided birdwatching** walks, open to all ($7; see ⊛ facebook.com/audubonpanama).

Park trails

The most interesting meander is the 1.7km **Camino del Mono Tití**, named after the Geoffroy's tamarin monkeys that can occasionally be sighted when making the moderate climb to the viewpoint. From the main park entrance, you'll need to walk 1km along the **Sendero El Roble**, so called because of the pink-flowering oak trees along the path. To make a circular route, walk the Mono Tití trail one way, returning via the steeper but shorter **Sendero La Cienaguita** ("little marsh" – only visible in the rainy season). You can pick up a free **map** at the main entrance, but it's hard to get lost since the park is only about two square kilometres and the trails are well signed.

Panamá Viejo

Vía Cincentenario • Museum Tues–Sun 8.30am–4.30pm; Plaza Mayor & bell tower Tues–Sun 8.30am–4.30pm • Museum & bell tower $12; tickets sold at the museum and at the entrance to the Plaza Mayor • ☎ 226 8915, ⊛ panamaviejo.org • Metrobuses from the front of Albrook bus terminal run along the Cinta Costera and stop outside the museum (every 30min; 30min); to catch the return bus, wait on the corner of the road heading back into the city, close to the pedestrian crossing near the bell tower

You'll need some imagination to reconstruct the neglected ruins of sixteenth-century Panamá La Vieja, or **PANAMÁ VIEJO**, as it's more often called, which was once the premier colonial city on the isthmus (see box below). Yet while there's no comparison with the magnificent Maya sites elsewhere in Central America, the view from the **bell tower** alone makes a half-day visit worthwhile.

Museo del Sitio de Panamá la Vieja

The **Museo del Sitio de Panamá la Vieja**, with some summaries in English, should be your first port of call. The top floor displays items discovered during excavations, which are described in greater detail on the ground floor. There are some exquisitely preserved **pre-Columbian artefacts** – though labels are often frustratingly absent – together with pottery, coins and utensils from colonial times, and a useful interactive **scale model** of the city in 1671.

The convents

Outside the museum, you can backtrack 100m to peer over at the **Puente del Matadero** ("Bridge of the Slaughterhouse"), named after the neighbouring abattoir, which marked the western limit of the old city. Returning east along the shoreline, continue along the gravel path a few hundred metres past extensive mud flats being probed by hundreds of migrating waders. Passing the scarcely visible or recognizable Iglesia y Convento de la Merced – which survived Morgan's assault and was relocated to Casco Viejo – and the Iglesia y Convento de San Francisco, cross the road and turn east down Calle de la Empedrada. To the left stands the well-preserved **Iglesia del Convento de la Concepción**, the city's only convent for women, built in 1597. Look over the nearby wall and you'll find the impressive remains of the convent's seventeenth-century reservoir. The tour continues past the skeletal remnants of the Jesuit Iglesia y Convento de la Compañia de Jesús before reaching the Cincuentenario.

Plaza Mayor

The vast open space of the **Plaza Mayor** is overlooked by the imposing cathedral **bell tower**, one of Panama's most distinctive landmarks. The view from the top allows you to appreciate the city's former grandeur. The plaza was the social hub of the city, hosting events from political rallies to bullfights, and surrounded by the most prestigious

---

PANAMÁ VIEJO'S TREASURE TRAIL

Nuestra Señora de la Asunción de Panamá, to give Panamá Viejo its full name, was established in 1519 by the infamous Pedro Arias de Ávila. Despite the surprisingly swampy location, Panama City prospered as the Pacific terminal of the Spanish Crown's **treasure trail**, sending silks and spices from the East and plundered silver and gold from Peru to Europe via the isthmus. By the early seventeenth century, it boasted an impressive cathedral, seven convents, numerous churches, a hospital, two hundred warehouses and around five thousand houses. Being on the crucial trade route necessitated the construction of a huge customs house, a treasury and a mint; these were built in the most heavily fortified area of the Casas Reales (Royal Houses), the symbol of the Spanish Crown's might, originally separated from the rest of the city by a moat and wooden palisade.

Following the Welsh pirate Henry Morgan's sacking of the city in 1671 (see p.293), the place was razed to the ground. Little more than a pile of rubble now remains of these once impressive buildings – some of the original stones were quarried for construction of the new city, after which the site was largely neglected – but the **Iglesia del Convento de la Concepción** and the cathedral **bell tower** have been restored.

1

buildings, including to the east the Cabildo (City Hall) and the cathedral – **La Catedral de la Nuestra Señora de la Asunción**. The stone edifice that replaced the original wooden structure was completed between 1619 and 1629. The magnificently restored belfry now has a modern staircase, which is worth climbing for the views. Sporadic free guided tours are conducted in English and Spanish but depend on numbers, available staff and the weather. Enquire at the entry kiosk near the tower, or at the museum.

Leaving the cathedral by the vestibule, you can just make out the remains of the **Casa Alarcón**; formerly the domicile of the bishop, this nobleman's home dating back to the 1640s is the largest known and best-preserved private house on the site. Beyond lies the crumbling Dominican Iglesia y Convento de Santo Domingo.

The northern remains

A few hundred metres north along the Cincuentenario, little remains of the **Iglesia de San José**, which survived the fire of 1671 and contained the splendid golden altar that now sits in the church of the same name in Casco Viejo (see p.60). At the old northern city limit, a couple of hundred metres beyond, Panamá Viejo's famous **Puente del Rey** (King's Bridge) still spans the Río Gallinero, where it marked the gateway to the Camino Real, the conquistadors' mule trail across the isthmus. If you explore that far, exercise **caution**, since the surrounding Río Abajo neighbourhood is an impoverished barrio and tourist muggings are not unknown.

Bahá'í House of Worship

Apartado 143, Zona 15 · Daily 9am–6pm; Sun service 10am (30min) · Free · ☎ 231 1191 · Ⓜ San Isidro, at the end of the line; follow the signs to the main exit, where a courtesy shuttle can take you up to the temple (9am–5pm; Mon 4 buses, Tues–Sat 7 buses, Sun 14 buses) – keep alert as you exit San Isidro metro, as muggings have been reported

In the foothills of the Cordillera Central, the **Bahá'í House of Worship** – the hilltop dome that resembles an alien spaceship – offers splendid vistas across the eastern suburbs to the Pacific. It's the focus of attention for an estimated sixty thousand Bahá'í followers in Panama and following the opening of a nearby metro station in 2015, it's attracting increasing numbers of tourists.

The Bahá'í faith, which developed in nineteenth-century Persia, is one of the world's youngest religions, and emphasizes equality and respect among religions and people. Panama was singled out for Latin America's first Bahá'í house of worship on account of a Bahá'í prophecy made in the early twentieth century that recognized the country's strategic location as a bridge between the Americas, and anticipated that the Canal would enhance its importance as a mean of accessing countries in other parts of the world.

Interested visitors can attend the Sunday service or simply wander through the delightful flower-filled gardens.

ARRIVAL AND DEPARTURE   PANAMA CITY

Panama City is the country's transport hub for both international and national traffic, with two international airports, one domestic airport, a port, a cruise ship terminal and a gigantic bus terminal. When it comes to moving on, most people use the country's efficient and extensive **bus system**, though internal **flights** are plentiful, reasonably priced and simple to arrange – and particularly useful for reaching the islands of Guna Yala and Bocas del Toro. **Car rental** is also easy, though fairly pricey (see p.28), but worth it if you're heading off the beaten track.

BY PLANE

TOCUMEN INTERNATIONAL AIRPORT

Most visitors enter Panama through Tocumen International Airport (Aeropuerto Internacional de Tocumen; ☎ 238 2703), about 24km northeast of Panama City.

Facilities The airport has a couple of (often unstaffed) tourist information desks, a bank, ATMs, a left luggage office and nine car-rental desks.

Phone and internet A Cable & Wireless office upstairs provides internet and international phone facilities.

Expensive mobile-phone packages are also for sale in the arrivals hall but you can get a better deal in town (see p.47).

Taxis Most passengers take a private or *colectivo* taxi into the city. The official taxi service provider has a desk in the exit hall displaying the official rates, which you should consult if in doubt. At the time of writing, private taxis for one or two passengers cost $30 for central Panama City; $35 for Albrook and Cerro Ancón; and $38 for the Amador Causeway. *Colectivos* cost $15/person for three or more passengers – exit by the main terminal door, and cross the road to the *colectivo* taxi stand.

Buses You can only travel to the city centre by bus if you have been to Panama before and have a Metrobus card (see p.75), since the cards are currently not sold at the airport. If you have a card, leave the arrivals hall, turn right, walk past *Restaurante Selles* and head across the car park for the bus stop across the main road, outside the terminal. You can catch Metrobuses (see p.74) to Albrook bus terminal (6am–midnight; every 20–40min; 45min–1hr, longer in rush hour); make sure you take the "Corredor" services, which take the faster toll road. If you arrive after dark, take a taxi; hanging round the bus stop at night can be risky.

Getting to the airport Metrobuses displaying "Tocumen Corredor" leave from the front of Albrook bus terminal (6am–midnight; every 20–40min; 45min–1hr, longer in rush hour), picking up passengers at the new Cinco de Mayo–Marañon metro station and at stops along the Cinta Costera. Passengers alight at a bus stop 200m from the terminal entrance.

PANAMÁ PACÍFICO INTERNATIONAL AIRPORT

Charter flights and a couple of low-cost Colombian airlines – Viva Colombia (🔘 vivacolombia.co) and Wingo (🔘 wingo .com) – use the new Panamá Pacífico International Airport, formerly the US Howard Air Force base, in the Canal Zone, 9km southwest of Balboa. Other Latin American airlines are likely to start using this airport in the near future.

Taxis Taxis to central Panama City cost $22.

ALBROOK AIRPORT

Domestic flights from the one domestic carrier, Air Panama (🔘 316 9000, 🔘 airpanama.com), touch down at low-key Albrook Airport (officially Aeropuerto International Marcos A. Gelabert; 🔘 238 2700), 3km northwest of the city centre. Air Panama serves around twenty destinations, including two in Colombia and San José in Costa Rica. While in theory Air Panama accepts online credit-card bookings, the website rarely works. Nor is credit-card payment over the phone accepted, though you can make a phone reservation using a credit card for flights from Guna Yala (see p.252). You need to buy a ticket in person at the airport (daily 5am–6pm) or at their office on Av Balboa (Mon–Fri 8am–6pm, Sat 8am–1pm).

Facilities Several car rental firms have offices here; there's also an ATM and a tourist desk.

Taxis Taxis to most places in the city should not top $3–4, although the more luxurious cabs waiting outside the terminal will charge you double the fare of a taxi flagged down on the road, which is easy to do during the day.

BY BUS

All regional buses arrive at the upper level of Albrook bus terminal (officially Gran Terminal de Transportes de Panamá, more commonly referred to as "El Terminal"), the national bus terminal. It lies 3km northwest of the city centre, near Albrook Airport.

Getting into town Local buses, including the new Metrobuses (see p.74), leave from ground level at the front of the terminal. Taxis also stop here and can take you to your lodgings; this should cost no more than $3–4 for one or two passengers for a central area such as Casco Viejo or El Cangrejo, but they may try to charge more if you arrive late at night or don't seem to know what you're doing. The terminal is also at the end of the new metro line (see p.75), which can get you to Plaza Cinco de Mayo – from where you can walk to Casco Viejo – or El Cangrejo.

Getting to the bus terminal To get to the bus terminal from the city centre, take a bus bound for Albrook on Vía España, along the Cinta Costera/Av Balboa, or at the side of the Palacio Legislativo off Plaza Cinco de Mayo. Alternatively, take the metro (see p.75) from El Cangrejo or Plaza Cinco de Mayo.

Onward travel by bus Several major destinations are served by more than one company, some of which offer express and (cheaper) stopping buses – ticket prices charged by all companies will be the same. To catch a bus out of town, first buy your ticket from the appropriate ticket office inside the terminal before passing through a turnstile to a numbered departure bay at the back. To do this you'll need a RapiPass, a rechargeable swipe card (*tarjeta magnética*) used on Metrobuses, the metro and the bus terminal turnstiles (10¢). You can buy the RapiPass for $2 (plus the credit you want to put on it) at a kiosk in the bus terminal.

Travelling to Costa Rica Ticabus (🔘 314 6385, 🔘 ticabus.com), with an office at the terminal, runs overnight and daytime buses (daily 11am & 11.55pm; 15–16hr; $55 & $40, respectively) to San José, Costa Rica. Advance booking is advisable. Alternatively, take a Panachif (🔘 314 6885, 🔘 transporte10pa.es.tl) bus to Paso Canoas (see box, p.213) at the border (daily; 9 regular buses & 3 express at 10pm, 11pm & midnight; $17 regular, $21 express), via David, and transfer to Costa Rican transport there.

1

MAJOR DOMESTIC BUS ROUTES

DESTINATION	FREQUENCY	DURATION
Antón	5.20am–8pm; every 20min	2hr
Bayano (via Chepo)	4am–4.40pm; every 40min	2hr
Chame	5.30am–9pm; every 20min	1hr 10min
Changuinola	6pm & 6.30pm (7pm during busy periods)	10hr (via Almirante, for Bocas)
Chitré	6am–7pm; every 30min	3hr 30min
Colón	express bus: 4.40am–10pm; approximately every 30min	1hr 15min
	regular bus: 4am–midnight; every 20–30min	1hr 45min
David	4.30am–8.30pm; two companies each run buses every 1hr–1hr30min; both have express services at 10pm, 11pm & midnight	express 6–7hr
El Copé	6am–6.30pm; every 30min	3hr
El Valle (de Antón)	7am–7pm; every 25–30min	2hr
Gamboa	5am (6am Sat & Sun)–11.15pm; 16 buses	50min
Las Tablas	6am–7pm; hourly	4hr
Metetí	4.15am–4.30pm; 9 buses	5–6hr
Penonomé	4.50am–10.45pm; every 20min	2hr
San Carlos	6am–8.30pm; every 20min	1hr 20min
Santiago	3.15am–9.15pm; hourly (note that all buses for David also stop in Santiago)	3hr 30min
Soná (for Santa Catalina)	6.45am–5.30pm; every 2hr	5hr
Yaviza	Midnight express bus; buses for Metetí will continue to Yaviza if there is demand; otherwise change in Metetí to a local bus.	6–7hr

GETTING AROUND

Panama City's vast urban sprawl continues to expand at an alarming rate, and navigating your way around can at first seem daunting. However, places of interest to tourists are concentrated in a few areas easily accessible by **bus** or **taxi**, or, in the case of Casco Viejo, **on foot**. Avoid travelling at **rush hour** (Mon–Fri 7.30–9am & 4.30–6.30pm), when traffic grinds to a halt in horn-honking mayhem. The new **metro** so far only has one line but it provides a quick way of travelling between El Cangrejo, Plaza Cinco de Mayo (with walking access to Casco Viejo) and Albrook bus terminal. At the time of writing, a second line was under construction, which should also connect with Tocumen International Airport.

BY BUS

Types of bus There are two types of public bus. Best known, but being phased out, are the slow, dilapidated chicken buses, known in Panama as *diablos rojos*, or red devils, on account of the devil-may-care attitude of many of the drivers. Though they operate on fixed routes – destinations are painted on the windscreen – some drivers will pick up and drop off at other places as the whim takes them, and there are no fixed timetables. The newer, a/c Metrobuses also operate on fixed routes without timetables, and use designated, less frequent stops.

1

Fares and passes Travelling by bus is the cheapest way to get about, costing a mere 25–35¢ for any trip within the metropolitan boundary (except the buses that use Corredores – express toll roads – which cost $1.25). On the *diablos rojos* you pay 25¢ cash on exit. Metrobus journeys cost 35¢; for these you need a prepaid Metro or RapiPass swipe card (*tarjeta magnética*; $2, plus the credit you want to load onto it). Metro cards are available at supermarkets (such as El Rey on Vía España and El Machetazo on Av Central), Albrook bus terminal, metro stations and a kiosk on Plaza Cinco de Mayo; the RapiPass can only be bought in Albrook bus terminal (see p.73).

Routes The city's main arteries and bus routes run vaguely southwest to northeast along Av Balboa and the Cinta Costera, Av Central (which becomes Av España) and Av Justo Arosemena (Av 3 Sur). All buses circulate every few minutes on the busiest routes, from 5.30/6am until 11pm/ midnight; less frequently on Sun.

Getting to Casco Viejo Buses don't run into Panama City's historical centre, Casco Viejo; you'll need to catch a bus that passes Plaza Cinco de Mayo, then walk up the pedestrianized section of Av Central. Alternatively, take a bus that goes to the Cinta Costera; get off at the first stop and walk back along the bay, past the Mercado de Mariscos.

Hop-on-hop-off sightseeing bus The red city sight-seeing double-decker bus (ⓦcitytourspanama.com; one-day pass $33, two-day pass $35) is a disappointment in terms of giving an informative overview of the city's main attractions, thanks to a limited route and often unintelligible commentary. However, it can be a cost-efficient way for solo travellers wanting to visit the Miraflores Locks, Casco Viejo, the Biodiversity Museum and Amador Causeway in a short space of time.

BY METRO

Route Panama City's new metro system – Central America's first – currently has just one line, with twelve stations, though a second line is planned. It runs from the Albrook bus terminal via Plaza Cinco de Mayo and northwards towards El Cangrejo and beyond, as far as the districts of Los Andes and San Isidro.

Fares At the time of writing metro fares had yet to be determined. To pay you will need a rechargeable metro or RapiPass swipe card (*tarjeta magnética*; $2); they're sold at the stations, Albrook bus terminal, supermarkets and a kiosk on Plaza Cinco de Mayo.

BY TAXI

Taxis are plentiful – around 28,000 in the city at the last count – and relatively cheap.

Fares Taxis are supposed to follow an overcomplicated zonal pricing schedule (see ⓦtransito.gob.pa) set by the transport authorities, but in practice the price is often down to supply and demand, your negotiating skills in Spanish and whether they want to take you. For most destinations in the city you shouldn't pay more than $3–4 during normal working hours, the exception being to Panamá Viejo or the Amador Causeway, where prices may be inflated (usually to a minimum of $5) because the driver is concerned about finding a passenger for the return trip – that said, the arrival of Uber in the capital has curbed to some extent the tendency to overcharge tourists. If you're unsure, ask around for the current rates beforehand and agree a price before getting in. Note that the more comfortable a/c tourist taxis hovering outside the mid- to high-end hotels, recognizable by the SET licence plates, charge much higher rates.

Tours Taxi drivers often serve as chauffeurs and unofficial city tour guides; you may be charged anything between $12–15/hr.

BY BIKE

You would need to have a death wish to cycle in most of Panama City. The exceptions are along the Cinta Costera and the Amador Causeway, where the cycleways and the general lack of traffic and fumes make for a pleasant ride. There is even a popular Ciclovía (cycling festival) every Sun morning (see box, p.66).

Bike rental and repairs GetOneBike, C 30 Este just off Av Balboa (Mon–Sat 10am–7pm; ☎395 2224, ⓦgetonebike .com) rents a range of high-quality cycles from $10/day for a single-speed bike to $40/weekend or $70/week for a multi-geared mountain bike; helmet and lock are included. It also offers bike repairs and bike tours of the city. Bicicletas Moses, by *Las Pencas* on the Amador Causeway (Mon–Fri noon– 8pm, Sat & Sun 8am–8pm; ☎211 3671), rents bikes by the hour ($3.50/hr), plus tandems and pedal buggies for two or four ($12–18/hr). Rates vary according to demand, so check in advance. You will need to present ID at both places.

BY CAR

Although rental cars are available at both airports and along Vía España near El Cangrejo, the city's cheap and plentiful buses and taxis mean there is no need to rent a car until you're ready to leave. Besides, the free-for-all attitude of many drivers makes driving a stressful experience.

INFORMATION

Tourist information The main office of the Autoridad de Turismo Panamá (ATP) is behind the ATLAPA Convention Centre on Vía Israel in San Francisco, but it is not set up to deal with tourists. The hostels and some of the more upmarket hotels and tour operators are much better sources of information.

Maps Free city maps of variable quality abound, generally marked with whichever hotels, restaurants and tourist services have bought ad space.

1

ACTIVITIES AND TOURS

Several excellent **tour operators** in Panama City offer bilingual guiding in English and Spanish on day- and multiday excursions. Specialist tour operators for Guna Yala and Darién have been listed in the relevant chapters (see p.253 & p.276).

Ancon Expeditions ☎269 9415, ⓦanconexpeditions .com. Very professional, expensive outfit, offering top-notch bilingual naturalist guiding services for single- and multiday adventures: birdwatching across Panama, trekking in the Darién (see box, p.276) or exploring the cloud forests of Chiriquí ($2825 for a fully inclusive four-day tour for two people). The unique experiences offered in the private reserve of Punta Patiño in the Darién and the birding expertise are likely to be worth the expense, but the inflated rates for a Panama Canal transit or Emberá village tour are harder to justify.

Aventuras Panamá 32 C 63 Oeste ☎260 0044, ⓦaventuraspanama.com. Adventure tours, chiefly kayaking and whitewater rafting along a variety of rivers within a couple of hours of Panama City in Panamá and Coclé provinces. $165 for a day's kayaking down the Chagres to Fuerte San Lorenzo.

Barefoot Panama ☎6780 3010, ⓦbarefootpanama .com. Well-regarded US-run organization specializing in customized adventure and ecotours to cater for all tastes, with one-day and multiday itineraries. Try their one-day Caribbean adventure, which includes zip lining, snorkelling and visiting the forts of Portobelo ($150).

Ecocircuitos Albrook Plaza, second floor, no. 31 ☎314 0068, ⓦecocircuitos.com. Actively involved in promoting sustainable tourism and supporting community-based projects, this outfit offers a wide range of day- and multiday excursions including kayaking, jungle trekking

– $985 for a four-day hike along the Camino Real (minimum four people) – and yoga retreats.

Emberá Tours ☎250 1165 or ☎6519 7121, ⓦemberatourspanama.com. Run by Garceth Cunampio, an English-speaking Emberá guide who organizes day or overnight excursions to Emberá Puru on the Chagres ($150/$200), wildlife-viewing trips round Lago Gatún and longer expeditions to the Darién, on request.

Panamá Orgánica ☎6079 6825, ⓔpanamaorganica @gmail.com. Small outfit specializing in bespoke budget tours to hard-to-access areas such as the Darién and Guna Yala, working with local communities and independent operators. They can also help arrange transport to Colombia and day-trips from Panama City. Two weeks' notice; minimum two people.

Sendero Panamá ☎6429 8163, ⓦsenderopanama .com. Run by certified bilingual naturalist guides, at the upper end of the market, this company offers a range of acclaimed day-trips and multiday adventures.

Whale Watching Panama ☎6758 7600, ⓦwhale watchingpanama.com. Day-trips from Panama City in small boats around Taboga (from $175) and the Islas Perlas (from $200) – both need a minimum of six people – to spot humpback whales in the migration season (July–Oct). Sightings are almost guaranteed in the Pearl Islands, and you have a 75/80 percent chance of spotting a humpback on the Taboga trip.

RECREATIONAL ACTIVITIES

Many visitors to Panama are expressly here for the wealth of **outdoor activities**, all of which can be enjoyed on a day-trip from the capital, either independently or on a tour (see above). There are also options within the city itself, some of them free. Head for the **Cinta Costera** (see box, p.66) or the following:

CIUDAD DE SABER (CITY OF KNOWLEDGE)

The **Ciudad de Saber (City of Knowledge)**, opposite the Miraflores Locks and accessible by bus (see p.97), contains some fabulous sports facilities run by the Kiwanis (Mon–Fri 8am–9pm, Sat & Sun 8am–6pm; ☎317 0208, ⓦciudaddeportivakiwanis.org). Set in a green recreational park, they provide a great escape from the city congestion and high-rises, and are open to all – though they can be busy at weekends. The large open-air **swimming pool** is a big draw (Tues–Sun 8am–4.45pm; $4) for which you'll need to wear a cap. There's also a **gym** and **tennis courts**, and plenty of picnic space.

PARQUE OMAR

Leafy **Parque Recreativo Omar Torrijos**, on Av Porras, San Francisco, has tennis courts, a jogging route, an outdoor pool (Tues–Fri 11am–9pm, Sat 6am–9pm, Sun 6am–6pm; $2) and lots of space to picnic. Though closer to the city centre than the Ciudad de Saber, and cheaper, the facilities are not quite as pristine and access is trickier: you'll need to present a current medical certificate, and two passport photos, which will get you a pass, valid for a couple of years ($3). Less hassle are the free **exercise classes**, from yoga to Zumba, given in the park by qualified instructors (6–8am & 4–7pm). Just roll up and join in.

ACCOMMODATION

There are **accommodation** options to suit all tastes and all budgets in Panama City, but beds can be in short supply at busy times such as Carnaval or Christmas, when it is essential to **book in advance**. Some mid-range hotels offer special business rates (open to all) and most mid-range and high-end hotels offer substantial **discounts** for online bookings. Note that hotels located on a major bus route, such as Vía España or Av Perú, can get **noisy** from around 5.30–6.00am, when the traffic starts up and the horn honking begins, until late at night, so ask for a room at the back on one of the higher floors. As for **facilities**, hot water is standard in hotels (though not necessarily in hostels) and most have a/c, cable TV and wi-fi (free in budget and mid-range accommodation, often charged for in the expensive hotels). Families or anyone staying a week or more might consider an **aparthotel** – these have kitchen/lounge/dining facilities and offer hotel services such as cleaning, laundry and breakfast. Long-term rentals and corporate rates are often negotiable.

CASCO VIEJO

Many budget travellers opt for the backpacker hostels in Casco Viejo, the old colonial centre, where there are also some very comfortable choices. The restoration of many of the historic buildings and absence of buses make it a pleasant retreat from the congestion and the pollution of the rest of the city. Lively bars and restaurants have also made it a popular nightlife destination, though most places are relatively pricey.

★ **American Trade Hotel** Plaza Herrera ☎ 211 2000, ⓦ acehotel.com/panama; map p.56. Overlooking an elegant plaza, a gleaming white facade proudly announces Casco Viejo's first fully restored grand hotel. White and wood predominate in light airy rooms, many of which have their own balustraded balcony. Every detail has been considered, from plush bathrobes to fully stocked minibars, with modern comforts carefully blended into the historical structure. Substantial discounts for advance booking online. **$195**

The Central Hotel Plaza de la Catedral ☎ 309 0300, ⓦ centralhotelpanama.com; map p.56. Despite oozing history, Panama's recently renovated Canal-era hotel somehow lacks character – lost perhaps when ensuring the (small) rooms have all the comforts and amenities of a modern five-star hotel. The views from the rooftop pool and bar, though, are amazing. **$319**

Las Clementinas C 11 and Av "B" ☎ 228 7613, ⓦ lasclementinas.com; map p.56. Half a dozen beautifully decorated suites (sleeping two to four), with hand-painted tiles, wooden floors and a combination of antiques and stylish modern furnishings. All have lofty ceilings, fully equipped kitchens and access to a fabulous rooftop terrace. Service is top-notch. **$198**

★ **Los Cuatro Tulipanes** Casa las Monjas, Av Central, between C 3 and C 4 ☎ 211 0877, ⓦ loscuatrotulipanes .com; map p.56. Bohemian chic, with a range of sumptuous apartments in beautifully restored colonial houses, plus traditional hotel services if required. Weekly rates ($1260) and substantial discounts in low season. Three-night minimum stay preferred. **$210**

Hospedaje Casco Viejo C 8 and Av "A" ☎ 211 2127, ⓦ hospedajecascoviejo.com; map p.56. Clean, relaxed and surprisingly spacious hostel with fan-ventilated dorms and private rooms (shared bathroom for $5 less) in a quiet street by the Iglesia de San José. The cold-water showers have seen better days, but you can't complain for the price. Small shared kitchen, interior patio and a cosy rooftop terrace. Basic breakfast included. Dorms **$13**, doubles **$35**

★ **Luna's Castle** C 9 Este, between Av "B" and Av Alfaro ☎ 262 1540, ⓦ lunascastlehostel.com; map p.56. Boasting bags of character and a laidback vibe, this backpacker party venue is set in a rambling property with a balcony overlooking a square. It offers large dorms (fan or a/c) – with curtained bunks for privacy – and a handful of doubles, with a big shared kitchen, solar hot water, laundry, lounge areas, book exchange, free bike use, ping pong, free pancake breakfast and on-site bars. Just don't expect much sleep. Dorms **$16**, doubles **$37**

Magnolia Inn C 8 and Boquete, behind the cathedral ☎ 202 0872, ⓦ magnoliapanama.com; map p.56. Lovingly restored, this colonial mansion is part boutique hotel, part luxury hostel. Superior dorms have a/c and private reading lights, plus use of a beautifully furnished, comfortable dining and lounge area; the cheaper "ballroom dorm" – somewhat reminiscent of a hospital wing, despite the piano and three-piece suite – has fans. The variously priced hotel rooms offer affordable luxury. Dorms **$15**, doubles **$88**

CALIDONIA AND LA EXPOSICIÓN

Calidonia and La Exposición offer a wide selection of unexceptional but affordable modern hotels and *pensiones*. The streets off the main arteries are not very safe at night, however, and some of the hotels offer rooms by the hour – though usually on a separate floor. Also, places to eat are few and far between, though generally quite cheap.

Hostel Mamallena Primera C Perejil, off Vía España ☎ 6676 6163, ⓦ mamallena.com; map pp.62–63. Popular backpacker place where you can chill in a hammock on the communal balcony or in the courtyard garden, or lounge in front of the TV. Dorms have a/c and quality mattresses while private rooms (also a/c) share bathrooms. The friendly, helpful staff have bags of info and deals on trips, and there are plenty of extras – PCs with Skype; complimentary tea, coffee and all-day pancake breakfasts; cheap airport transfers; washing machine – and

1

renovations on the way. Only the location could be improved. Dorms $13, doubles $33

Hotel Acapulco C 30, between Av Cuba and Av Perú ☎225 3832, ⌨hotelacapulcopanama.com; map pp.62–63. A travellers' favourite for its solid value and friendly service. Some of the well-maintained, functional rooms (a/c, hot water, cable TV) have small balconies; other pluses include late check-out and an on-site restaurant. $39

Hotel Stanford Panama Plaza Cinco de Mayo ☎262 4930, ⌨hotelstanfordpa.com; map pp.62–63. A fantastic location overlooking the busy plaza, and recently refurbished en-suite rooms, each with fridge, safe and desk, at affordable rates. Go for a room with a bay view but away from the bar, casino and rooftop terrace, which often throbs to the beat of weekend parties. $48

Residencial Jamaica Av Cuba at C 38 Este ☎225 9870; map pp.62–63. Hidden behind a nicely trimmed hedge, *Jamaica* offers an excellent deal for the price – and is often full. Rooms are bright and clean, with a/c and cable TV. $26

Residencial Texas C 31, between Av Perú and Cuba, beside the national lottery ☎225 1467, ✉hoteltexas @mixmail.com; map pp.62–63. Friendly, secure place offering good-value rooms with spotless tiled bathrooms, decent hot showers and good mattresses, though the furniture is tired. $32

BELLA VISTA, EL CANGREJO & MARBELLA

Bella Vista, Marbella and El Cangrejo, which form the hub of the modern city's nightlife and commercial activity, have the densest concentration of accommodation. Although hotel prices are generally high, the number of hostels in this area is steadily increasing too, and you're within striking distance of many restaurants, bars, clubs, shops and casinos. If you keep to the well-lit streets, it's fairly safe to stroll around here at night.

The Bristol Hotel Av Aquilino de la Guardia at C 50 ☎264 0000, ⌨thebristol.com; map pp.62–63. From the moment you glide across its gleaming marble foyer, this good-value boutique hotel exudes exclusivity. Rooms are elegant and sumptuously furnished, with vast marble bathrooms and 24hr butler service. Spa services and an award-winning restaurant, too. $164

Hostel Villa Vento Surf C 47 at C Margarita A. de Vallarino ☎397 6001, ⌨villaventosurfhostels.com; map pp.62–63. Modern hostel in the heart of the banking district but within reach of restaurants and nightlife. There's one en-suite fan-ventilated room and small a/c dorms with comfortable bunks. Guests have a kitchen and a lounge, where surf videos are *de rigueur* and which opens out onto the pool and BBQ patio – the hostel's main draw. Dorms $15, double $35

Hotel California Vía España at C 43 Este ☎263 7736, ⌨hotelcaliforniapanama.net; map pp.62–63. Not the most convenient location, but this is a very popular hotel,

offering good-value rooms (single, double and triple), pleasant service and a rooftop jacuzzi. $44

★**Hotel DeVille** C Beatríz M. Cabal at C 50 ☎206 3100, ⌨hoteldevillepanamacity.com; map pp.62–63. In the heart of the financial district, this boutique hotel provides the best value for quality accommodation with personalized service. Elegant, spacious suites possess dark wooden French-style furniture and opulent marble bathrooms. Breakfast included. $78

Marriott Hotel C 52 at Ricardo Arias ☎210 9100, ⌨marriothotels.com; map pp.62–63. A *Marriott* that truly merits its five-star rating, with excellent rooms and service plus full business amenities, pool and casino – located in the middle of the financial district. $145

Mona Lisa Hostel C 54 Este, Casa 3a ☎6985 7578, ⌨casamonalisapty.com; map pp.62–63. More Dalí than Da Vinci, this eclectically designed hostel – vibrant murals, marble floors, fancy cornices, astroturf lawn – is super-friendly, secure and conveniently located, with a view of El Tornillo skyscraper from the terrace. It has a decent kitchen, a couple of TV lounges, BBQ facilities, ping pong and table football, and – occasionally – karaoke. A/c dorms, doubles and family rooms all share bathrooms. Pancake breakfast included. Dorms $13, doubles $44

Radisson Decapolis Hotel Av Balboa, Multicentro ☎215 5000, ⌨radisson.com/panamacitypan; map pp.62–63. Brash or stylish (depending on your viewpoint), this thirty-floor glass-and-steel edifice, with touches of modern art, leads into the Multicentro Mall and Majestic Casino. The big, tasteful guestrooms have all the frills – go for an upper-floor room with an ocean view. There's an on-site restaurant (excellent breakfast buffet included in rates), sushi bar and pool. Big discounts for advance booking. $151

Sevilla Suites C Eusebio A. Morales, opposite Rincón Suizo ☎213 0016, ⌨sevillasuites.com; map pp.62–63. Smart aparthotel aimed at the business market, in a convenient location. The nicely furnished suites have kitchenettes and living/dining areas. Enjoy breakfast (included in the rates) on the patio after a few lengths in the rooftop pool or a session in the mini-gym. $79

★**Toscana Inn** C "D" at C Eusebio A. Morales ☎265 001, ⌨toscanainnhotel.com; map pp.62–63. Top mid-range hotel in an excellent location, with warmly decorated en-suite rooms with all modern amenities and efficient, friendly service. Good buffet breakfast included in the rates. $80

FORMER CANAL ZONE

There are an increasing number of lodgings scattered round the former Canal Zone, an area that includes the Amador Causeway, Balboa and Cerro Ancón, stretching to Albrook, Clayton and Miraflores Locks. These often offer greater tranquillity than the city-centre hotels and, in some cases,

1

superb views, though they are some distance from the main watering holes, which means you will need to spend more on taxis.

The Balboa Inn Las Cruces 2311a, Balboa ☎314 1520, ⓦ balboainnpanama.com; map p.69. In the quiet residential area of Balboa, yet close to bus and taxi routes, this established B&B offers simple, nicely furnished rooms with excellent beds and plenty of light. The delightful garden breakfast terrace allows you to birdwatch while you enjoy your full American breakfast. $81

Country Inn & Suites Amador Causeway ☎211 4500, ⓦ panamacanalcountry.com; map p.69. A standard motel in a stunning location, right by the Canal entrance. Pay the extra $15 to watch the ships from your balcony – otherwise you may get a view of the car park. The large, bright rooms are equipped with all conveniences. There's an on-site *TGI Friday's* and a couple of pools. Breakfast included. $73

GM Lodge C Las Bromelias 143b ☎6656 0766, Ereservas@GMLodgepa.com; map p.69. Convenient for early flights from Albrook Airport and fine if you've got your own transport, this otherwise out-of-the-way B&B is in a tranquil residential suburb. It offers a high level of comfort for the price: sparkling white-walled bedrooms enlivened by vibrant artwork, spotless modern bathrooms, large beds and a pleasant outdoor pool and patio area. $66

★**Hostal Amador Familiar** Av Amador, by the playground, Ancón ☎314 1251, ⓦ hostalamador familiar.com; map p.69. Maroon three-storey Canal Zone building with a laidback atmosphere, attracting a good mix of Panamanians and overseas visitors. Some of the basic, compact en-suite rooms (with fan or a/c) need a bit of TLC – but there's a washing machine, cheap airport transfers and a pleasant outdoor open-sided kitchen-cum-social-area

where you prepare your complimentary DIY breakfast. Dorms $15, doubles $33

Hostel Casa Nativa Av Morgan 2465, Balboa ☎6091 3746, ⓦ casanativapanama.com; map p.69. Fauvist murals announce your arrival at this mellow backpackers' retreat in a Canal-era house at the foot of Cerro Ancón. Brightly painted dorms with wooden floors, a/c and private bathrooms share two well-equipped kitchens and a semi-open social area, with hammocks, overlooking the garden. Dorms $14, double $30

OTHER AREAS

Grace Hotel Twist Tower, C 54 Este and C Samuel Lewis, Obarrio ☎280 6400, ⓦ gracehotels.com/panama; map pp.62–63. Occupying the ground floor and various upper floors of a quirkily designed skyscraper, this luxurious place exudes urban chic. The airy rooms have floor-to-ceiling windows, understated colours – with the odd flash of royal blue – and glitzy bathrooms; amenities include a gym, spa, outdoor rooftop plunge pool and jacuzzi, and a fine-dining restaurant. Good online rates. $154

Panama House B&B C Primera 32, El Carmen ☎263 4366, ⓦ panamahousebb.com; map pp.62–63. A hostel-type B&B that attracts a wide age range with its restful patio and garden, shared kitchen, helpful travel advice and free breakfast and laundry. It's popular, so usually full; book well ahead. Dorms are better value than the doubles. Dorms $17, doubles $50

Riande Aeropuerto Hotel & Resort Av Tocumen, Tocumen ☎291 9012, ⓦ hotelesriande.com/aeropuerto; map pp.62–63. It's not a base for your stay, but this motel-like joint does the job if you've an early flight (or a late arrival) at Tocumen; it's a couple of minutes away and offers free airport transfer. $99

EATING

Panama City's **cosmopolitan** nature is reflected in its restaurants: anything from US fast food to Greek, Italian, Chinese, Peruvian, Japanese and French cuisine can be found, along with traditional Panamanian dishes and excellent seafood. **Bookings** are advisable at weekends, if there's live music or a show, and during holiday periods. Outside the five-star hotels, **Casco Viejo** is the place for fine dining, with very few budget choices, whereas Bella Vista, Marbella and El Cangrejo have a greater range of restaurants both high-end and more moderately priced. New places are opening in Obarrio and San Francisco, with a handful of restaurants sprinkled along the **Amador Causeway**. Cheap hot and cold **takeaway** meals are available from the Rey supermarket (daily 24hr) on Vía España, while the **food courts** in the numerous shopping malls (see p.85) are popular at weekends.

CASCO VIEJO

In the evenings the city's smart set jam the streets of Casco Viejo with their 4WDs, heading for the neighbourhood's many chic restaurants in converted colonial houses. There are also a few open-air dining locations, where you can soak up the historic surroundings, and a couple of hole-in-the-wall joints serving meals for less than $4.

Café Coca-Cola Plaza Santa Ana, C 12 at Av Central ☎228 7687; map p.56. The self-proclaimed "oldest café in

Panama" and something of an institution among the city's older residents, who gather to drink good coffee, read the paper and discuss the news. Affordable, filling Panamanian staples – fish with *patacones* or chicken with rice (mains $6–7) – plus generously portioned breakfasts cooked to order. Daily 7am–11pm.

Caffè Per Due Av "A" at C 3 ☎228 0547; map p.56. Italian-owned and -operated, this little gem serves scrumptious oven-crisped pizzas ($9–12) and salads

1

($6–8) and is a popular spot for afternoon coffee and cake. Tues–Sun 9am–10pm.

★**Calicanto** C José de Obaldía ☎390 3385, ⓦfacebook.com/calicantopty; map p.56. The corner-café appearance of this small, unassuming Italian restaurant belies the quality of its cuisine – and its espresso. The usual pastas and pizzas are joined by *arancini*, home-made bread and fresh salads. But the *pièce de résistance* is their signature dish – a plateful of stuffed pyramidal pizza parcels spread over a sumptuous salad topped with a huge blob of home-made *burrata* ($27). It's enough for two, but leave room for the tiramisu. Mains from $11. Mon & Wed–Sun noon–9pm.

Casa Sucre Coffee House Av "B" and C 8 ☎393 6130, ⓦcasasucrecoffeehouse.com; map p.56. Laidback, arty café decked out with eclectic antiques and a similarly eclectic spread of coffee-table books. They serve gourmet coffees, deli sandwiches, all-day breakfasts and the signature dish, a filling soup served in a bread bowl ($9). Free wi-fi. Mon–Thurs 7.30am–8pm, Fri & Sat 7.30am–10pm, Sun 8am–7pm.

Donde José Av Central and C 11 ☎262 1682, ⓦdondejose.com; map p.56. The hottest table in town is a unique dining experience choreographed by Cordon Bleu-trained owner-chef José Olmedo Carles. He personally takes the sixteen diners through a multicourse gourmet tasting menu ($70), often using lesser-known Panamanian ingredients, such as the jobo fruit, toro or peach-palm, in innovative ways. An open kitchen backed by an angled mirror allows you to watch the chefs at work. Book well in advance and be on time. Tues–Sat, sittings 7pm & 9.30pm.

The Fish Market Av Central at C 10 ☎6721 6445, ⓦfacebook.com/Fish.Market.Panama; map p.56. Bohemian venue offering a changing menu of high-quality gourmet seafood served in plastic bowls out of a trailer truck for around $10–13. Enjoy your meal in an open-air courtyard, accompanied by occasional live music at weekends. Tues–Sat 6–11.30pm.

Fonda León Av "A" at C 5; map p.56. Squeezed between high-end establishments, this cafeteria-style restaurant has been feeding the average Panamanian for more than thirty years. True it's heavy on fried food and carbohydrates, but you can sometimes find fresh veg, and $4 will get you a full plate of rice, beans, potato salad and chicken stew. Daily 7am–7pm.

★**Granclement** Av Central at C 4 ☎223 6277, ⓦgranclement.com; map p.56. A fabulous indulgence after tramping the streets of Casco Viejo, this French-style artisanal ice-cream parlour offers unusual flavours – basil, lavender, Earl Grey – as well as chocolate every which way and an array of mouthwatering sorbets, though at a price ($2.50 for a large scoop). Mon–Thurs 11.30am–8pm, Fri & Sat 11.30am–9.30pm, Sun noon–8pm.

★**Mähalō** Av "A" at C 5 ☎399 3432, ⓦmahalopanama .com; map p.56. This delightful, trendy courtyard café is the perfect spot to linger over Sun brunch, chat over a glass of wine and eat healthily; quinoa, beetroot and avocado feature strongly in burgers, exotic salads, dips, soups and sandwiches ($8–12). Board games, pilates, yoga, and live music on Thurs & Sat evenings. Daily 8.30am–10.30pm.

★**René Café** Plaza Catedral at C 7 ☎262 3487, ⓦfacebook.com/renecafepty; map p.56. An intimate place, with Provençal-style ambience and an open-plan kitchen turning out international and Panamanian fusion cuisine. There's an excellent-value three-course lunchtime set menu ($11); in the evening $27 gets you six starters/ tapas, a substantial main course and dessert. Drinks are moderately priced (small bottle of wine only $5; beer $3). Mon–Sat 10am–3pm & 6–10pm.

Super Gourmet Av "A" at C 6 ☎212 3487, ⓦsuper gourmetcascoviejo.com; map p.56. Upmarket café serving delicious deli sandwiches and excellent light lunches ($7–10). Set yourself up for the day with a full breakfast (from around $7). Free wi-fi. Mon–Sat 8am–5pm, Sun 10am–4pm.

CALIDONIA AND LA EXPOSICIÓN

Reflecting their working-class populations, most dining options in these neighbourhoods are inexpensive and particularly busy at lunchtimes, serving up traditional Panamanian dishes.

Café Boulevard Balboa Av Balboa at C 31 Este ☎225 0914; map pp.62–63. An a/c oasis of civilization in the dust, noise and endless construction work outside, lively with a smart lunchtime business crowd. Specializing in toasted sandwiches ($6–9), the menu also includes more filling Panamanian dishes and a good-value three-course *menú del día* for around $8. Mon–Sat 6.30am–1am.

Mercado Público Av "B" and Av Balboa; map pp.62–63. A dozen *fondas* serving heaps of tasty hot food – noodles or rice with fried vegetables and strips of meat or chicken – for less than $4, with communal seating. Mon–Sat 4am–3pm.

★**Restaurante de Mariscos** Av Balboa, above the Mercado de Mariscos; map pp.62–63. The catch couldn't be any fresher, landing straight from the boat onto your plate. Crab, conch, octopus, lobster, langoustines, shrimp, snapper, dorado – it's all there, and can be accompanied with coconut rice, fried yuca or *patacones*; just don't expect too many vegetables (mains from $9). Cheaper food is available downstairs, around the back, at the row of *cevicherías*. Daily 11am–6pm.

BELLA VISTA, EL CANGREJO & MARBELLA

From the converted colonial mansions of Bella Vista to the neon lights of El Cangrejo, this area offers by far the greatest variety of dining and drinking venues, mainly at the mid to high end of the price scale.

★**Avatar** Av Argentina at Vía España ☎393 9066; map pp.62–63. Eschew the tacky neon-and-chrome nightclub decor inside and seat yourself on the patio to savour the city's best Indian food. This is veggie heaven, with subtle flavours and textures infusing all the dishes. A main with all the trimmings – roti, dahl, basmati rice – washed down with a mango lassi, comes to $20–25. Daily 11.30am–10.30pm.

Beirut C 49a Este at Av Justo Arosemena, opposite the Marriott ☎214 3815; map pp.62–63. A grotto-like ceiling, faux vines, murals and mosaics provide the setting for appetizers (from $7) and better-value, large combo platters, with mains from around $14. Hookah rental and belly-dancing at weekends. Daily noon–11pm.

★**Caffè Pomodoro** Vía Veneto, Plaza Downtown Cangrego, El Cangrejo ☎387 4455, ⍓pomodoropanam.com; map pp.62–63. Extremely popular Italian place, with a pleasant outdoor terrace, offering simple pastas and small pizzas ($7–12) plus more sophisticated Italian dishes such as clams in white wine ($18). Mon–Sat 8am–11pm, Sun–9am–10pm.

Churrería Manolo Vía Argentina 12 ☎264 3965, ⍓churrerianmanolo.com; map pp.62–63. Café specializing in sweet cigar-shaped *churro* pastries for a little over a dollar; they also serve coffee, sandwiches and more substantial mains ($9–12). Daily 7am–1am.

Habibi's C Uruguay at C 48 ☎264 3647, ⍓habibis panama.com; map pp.62–63. This buzzing corner terrace is a well-established gathering spot for groups heading off to party. Prices are high: the weekday lunchtime *menú ejecutivo* costs $11. Stick to the tasty Middle Eastern dishes; meze platters start at $14 for one person, going up to $48 for six. Belly-dancing Fri & Sat. Mon–Sat noon–late, Sun 3pm–late.

Loving Hut C Manuel Espinosa Batista, Edif. Cali ☎240 5621, ⍓lovinghut.com/pa; map pp.62–63. Part of a global veggie and vegan chain, this no-nonsense *cafetería* dishes up delicious, inexpensive food. You can "pick and mix" a healthy plateful for less than $5. Mon–Sat 10.30am–8.30pm.

The Market C 48 and C Uruguay ☎264 9401, ⍓marketpanama.com; map pp.62–63. This trendy venue, its walls bedecked with wine bottles, is the place to come for a juicy Aberdeen Angus steak (from $21) or a deli burger (around $13). Save space for a key lime pie or cheesecake. Weekend brunch too. Mon–Fri 7am–11pm, Sat 11.30am–11pm, Sun 11.30am–9pm.

Niko's Café C 51 Este at Vía España ☎223 0111, ⍓nikoscafe.com; map pp.62–63. The unpromising frontage masks a city institution. This no-frills *cafetería* is the original in a chain that now numbers nine outlets (there are others in Albrook bus terminal and El Dorado Mall and on C 50). Good-value hot dishes – seafood, meat and generic pasta options plus sides – for around $5–6, to take out or eat in. Daily 24hr.

★**NY Bagel Café** Cabeza de Einstein, C Arturo Motta at Vía Argentina ☎390 6051, ⍓newyorkbagelcafe.com; map pp.62–63. A popular hangout for travellers, expats and local business folk, serving a wide variety of their namesake plus breakfast specials, fruit smoothies, good coffee (free refills) and more. Most items $6–10. Free wi-fi. Mon–Fri 7am–8pm, Sat 8am–8pm, Sun 8am–3pm.

La Papa C 51 Este at Av Federico Boyd ☎265 5800, ⍓lapapa.net; map pp.62–63. There's a vast and varied menu – with diverse prices to match – at this popular Colombian restaurant. Expect large portions of well-prepared dishes (mains from $13): substantial salads, wraps, kebabs, steaks and paellas, plus Colombian specialities such as *arepas* and *ajaico* (a hearty chicken and potato soup served with capers, cream and avocado). Daily 11.30am–3.30pm & 6.30–10.30pm.

Petit Paris C 53 Este opposite Felipe Motta ☎391 8778, ⍓petitparispanama.com; map pp.62–63. A genuine French-run patisserie-boulangerie-bistro serving beautifully prepared food at Parisian prices. Forget the delicious bread and quiches and indulge in the exquisitely crafted cakes and chocolates ($5–7), to be enjoyed with great coffee or a hot chocolate. Free wi-fi and live music Wed evenings. Daily 7am–10pm.

★**La Posta** C 49 at C Uruguay ☎269 1076, ⍓lapostapanama.com; map pp.62–63. The 1950s Havana ambience of this beautifully restored mansion, set in lush tropical gardens, makes it a favourite among Panama City's elite. The tiled floors, wooden ceiling fans and Cuban music enhance your appreciation of the gourmet cuisine – start off with pork and yuca *carimañolas*, perhaps, followed by tuna with quinoa and feta cheese – and prices are not as exorbitant as they might be (mains from around $22, bottles of wine under $28). Mon–Fri noon–2.30pm & 6.45–10.30pm, Sat 6.45–10.30pm.

Restaurante Hikaru C Anastacio Ruíz ☎203 5087, ⍓hikaru-restaurant; map pp.62–63. The place to come for Japanese food: beautifully presented fresh sashimi, sushi and hot mains (from around $13) in a minimalist space. At weekday lunchtimes choose from one of three menus – each includes miso soup, salad and a main ($9–11). Mon–Fri noon–3pm & 6–11pm, Sat & Sun 6–11pm.

Restaurante Jimmy C Manuel M. Icaza at Vía España ☎223 1523, ⍓parilladajimmy.com; map pp.62–63. Popular 24hr restaurant-cafeteria in the heart of El Cangrejo, with a wide choice of Panamanian and Greek food, plenty of light bites and fresh, strong coffee. Mains from around $9. A second, larger, open-air version serving succulent barbecued dishes sits opposite the ATLAPA Convention Centre on C Cincuentenario (daily 11.30am–11.30pm). Daily 24hr.

Rincón Habanero Vía Argentina, opposite El Trapiche ☎213 2560, ⍓facebook.com/restaurante rinconhabanero; map pp.62–63. Sample a slice of Cuba

1

in this dark, wood-panelled restaurant, from the rum (have a mojito) to the cigars and even on the plasma screen. The handful of cosy tables are always packed with people tucking into Cuban classics ($12–14) featuring copious black beans, accompanied by hot salsa tunes. Mon–Sat 11am–11pm.

Siete Mares C Guatemala at Vía Argentina ☎ 264 0144; map pp.62–63. This place generally delivers on its reputation for the best seafood in Panama City. Mains (from around $17) include corvina with crab in Pernod, and jumbo shrimps in passion-fruit sauce, and the ambience, from the glass waterfall at the entrance to the piano-bar accompaniment (Mon–Sat from 8pm), is sophisticated. Daily 11.30am–11pm.

Las Tinajas C 51 at Av Federico Boyd ☎ 263 7890, ⓦ tinajaspanama.com; map pp.62–63. This delightful colonial Bella Vista mansion is a favourite with tour groups, who flock here to experience authentic Panamanian food and a traditional dance show involving swishing *polleras* and devil dances (see box, p.163). Grab a table early to ensure a decent view of the tiny stage. Shows Tues–Sat 9pm; $10, provided you spend at least $15 on food and drink. Try the *surtido de mariscos*, a platter of seafood appetizers. Mon–Sat 11.30am–11pm.

El Trapiche Vía Argentina between C Guatemala and Av 2B Norte ☎ 269 4353, ⓦ eltrapicherestaurante .com; map pp.62–63. Frequently billed as the place for tourists to try traditional food, such as *mondongo* (tripe and chorizo stew) and *tamal de olla* (local *tamale* without the leaf wrapping), though it attracts Panamanians too. Prices are moderate (mains $8–13) and there's a lively atmosphere on the terrace, but the quality is variable. Daily 7am–11pm.

OBARRIO

Athens Pizza C 57 Este at Vía España ☎ 223 1464, ⓦ athenspizzapanama.com; map pp.62–63. Eat tasty filling meals from around $8, surrounded by images of Greece. Greek dishes, including salads, abound, and the pizza provides great comfort food. Mon & Wed–Sun 11am–11pm.

Restaurante SaborViet C 54 Este ☎ 388 9960, ⓦ facebook.com/sabor.vietnamita; map pp.62–63. Classic Vietnamese dishes such as *bun cha* (grilled pork and

rice noodles) and *pho bo* (broth with rice noodles and beef) accompanied by pleasingly fresh vegetables. A treat for the palate and the wallet (mains from less than $10). Daily 11.30am–10pm.

BALBOA, ANCON AND THE AMADOR CAUSEWAY

The Amador Causeway provides a cool, breezy setting with fabulous views across the bay. The downside is that a taxi there and back (there are few and infrequent buses) will add another $10–15 to your bill.

★**Country Store** C John F. Wallace 2361, Balboa ☎ 203 5824, ⓦ countrystorepanama.webs.com; map p.69. In an unlikely location hidden behind a bank, this is a great, mellow place for fresh, mainly organic dishes, featuring sautéed vegetables and delicate aromatic sauces (mains from $12). Sit indoors or out on the plant-filled patio. The live band on Sat nights, playing blues, jazz or rock, is a real plus. Tues–Thurs 11.30am–9.30pm, Fri & Sat 11.30am–10.30pm, Sun 10.30am–5pm.

The Woodhouse C La Boca, La Boca ☎ 314 1242; map p.69. Surprisingly tasty food and efficient, friendly service in this unassuming open-sided sports bar/grill. Try the *camarones al ajillo* with yuca chips. Mains $9–15. Daily noon–11pm.

OTHER AREAS

Palacio Lung Fung Transístmica and C 62 Oeste, Los Ángeles ☎ 260 4011, ⓦ facebook.com/lungfung panama; map pp.62–63. It's some way from the action, but every taxi driver knows this vast Chinese-style palace, whose thousand-seater upstairs ballroom with its glittering chandeliers is packed at weekends with Panamanians enjoying the *dim sum* breakfast (until 11.30am). The food is average but the social experience makes it well worthwhile. Daily 7am–11pm.

Pita-Pan Kosher Bal Harbour, Punta Paitilla ☎ 264 2786; map pp.62–63. An illuminated 3D mural of Jerusalem welcomes you to this casual, slightly chaotic *cafetería*, popular with Jewish families. They serve appetizing, moderately priced dishes, with lots of veggie options – hummus, *baba ghanoush* and falafel – alongside the ubiquitous pasta and pizza and even kosher sushi. Mon–Thurs 7.30am–8pm, Fri 7.30am–5pm, Sun 9am–9pm.

DRINKING AND NIGHTLIFE

Panama City arguably has the best **clubbing** in Central America, although many places feel like imitations of Miami nightspots. In addition, there are plenty of **bars**, plus live music **venues** putting on rock concerts. **Casco Viejo** is the nightlife hub, attracting both the smart set and more bohemian revellers; in addition to the permanent places, the odd derelict building or courtyard provide temporary venues during the high season (mid-Dec to April), offering music and a spot to hang out, chat and drink cheap beer – nose around and follow the music. In addition to the listings below, you could try the **Zona de la Rumba**, on the Amador Causeway, before Centro de Convenciones Figali; this constantly revolving strip mall of discos, bars and restaurants to suit every mood is the kind of place you'll love or loathe (Tues–Sat 9pm–late).

ESSENTIALS

Clubs and bars Clubs are called *discotecas* – ask for a club and you'll end up at a strip joint. Bars and *discotecas* open, close and reinvent themselves at an alarming rate: the current hot spots are in and around Casco Viejo, with a sprinkling around C Uruguay in Bella Vista, spreading out towards El Cangrejo and Marbella, where you'll hear everything from techno to reggae and reggaeton to salsa. In the smarter bars and clubs you'll need to dress up – no shorts or sandals.

Costs Local beers cost around $4–6, with imports, spirits and cocktails at $8–10. If you're in a group, buying a bottle of spirits between you (which can sometimes get the entry charge waived) or a *cubetazo* (bucket of beer) will help keep costs down. *Discoteca* entry, generally $10–20, may include an open bar up until a certain time and the usual "Ladies' Night" enticements.

Casinos Several large casinos are conveniently located near or in the high-end hotels. The larger ones, such as the Majestic (in Multicentro by the *Radisson Decapolis Hotel*) and the *Hotel Veneto* Casino, often have live music at weekends.

What's on To find out what's on, pick up a copy of *La Prensa* (w prensa.com) or the free weekly *The Visitor/El Visitante* (w thevisitorpanama.com); w thepanamadigest.com and w quehaypahoypanama.com also have events listings, and w panamarock.com has gig listings.

CASCO VIEJO

BARS

Mojitos (sin Mojitos) Plaza Herrera w mojitossin mojitos.com; map p.56. This small, intimate cellar-like bar, draped with foliage, and buzzing with expats, locals and travellers, is a must for a night out in Casco Viejo, offering affordable drinks (though no mojitos!), tasty home-made meat- and veggie burgers, and the occasional live act. Tues–Sat 6pm–late.

Relic Luna's Castle, C 9 Este between Av "B" and Av Alfaro ☎ 262 1540, w relicbar.com; map p.56. Funky plant-filled basement courtyard and dungeon-like bar with subdued lighting and wooden tables, and a playlist of indie, hip-hop and rock. It attracts travellers from the adjoining hostel, but the (relatively) inexpensive drinks and casual vibe reel in many Panamanians too. At weekends it's so crammed you can hardly get in the door and the lack of a/c can take its toll. Tues–Sat from 8pm.

Tántalo Tántalo Hotel, Av "B" between C 8 and C 9 ☎ 262 4030, w tantalo.com/roofbar; map p.56. The original Casco Viejo rooftop bar has stellar views – get here early to bag your high stool. Watch the city skyline light up while sipping one of their signature cocktails – try the Bacardi grape mojito ($7). There's something happening most nights, with body painting and live artists on "Artes

Martes" (Tues) and Latin dancing on Wed. Food served until 9pm. $10 cover at weekends. Daily 5pm–late.

CLUB

Teatro Amador Av Central between C 11 and C 13 ☎ 212 1565, w teatroamador.com; map p.56. This converted theatre, with VIP balcony, cage-dancers and a large dancefloor, is currently the hottest dance place in the city, presided over by a DJ and attracting international Latin acts. Cover charge $10–15. Thurs–Sat 10pm–late.

LIVE MUSIC

Danilo's Jazz Club American Trade Hotel, Plaza Herrera ☎ 211 2000, w es.acehotel.com/panama/jazz–club; map p.56. Backed by Grammy-award-winning Panamanian jazz great Danilo Pérez (to whose foundation some of the proceeds go), this fifty-seater club is a major venue for the annual international jazz festival in January, also organized by Pérez (w panamajazzfestival.com), and regularly hosts international guest artists. Bar menu available. Cover charge. Wed–Sat 7pm–1am, Sun 3–10pm.

Piña Cala Vera C 11 at C Eloy Alfaro ☎ 6245 1377, w facebook.com/pinacalavera; map p.56. Funky, bohemian cultural space owned by Panamanian musician Cienfue, aimed at encouraging and promoting new musicians – rock artists in particular. The distinctive decor features umbrellas hanging from the ceiling and a host of recycled materials. Cheap beer and occasional cover charge. Tues–Sat 7pm–late, Sun 4pm–late.

BELLA VISTA, EL CANGREJO & MARBELLA

BARS

BITS Hard Rock Hotel, Av Balboa by Multicentro ☎ 380 1111, w hrhpanamamegapolis.com/unforgettable -nightlife.htm; map pp.62–63. The *Bar in the Sky* is just that: Latin America's highest rooftop bar, on the 62nd floor, with indoor and outdoor seating offering 360-degree views of the glittering city lights from behind a glass surround. Mon–Sat 8pm–late.

Istmo Brew Pub C Eusebio A. Morales at Vía Veneto; map pp.62–63. If you're craving something other than the standard *cerveza*, try this half open-air, half dungeon-like bar – they offer tasty beer on tap brewed on site (from $5) in beautiful copper kegs, plus bottled imports from all over. The pool table, darts, football matches on TV and occasional live bands also bring in the punters. Daily 4.30pm–late.

★ **La Rana Dorada** Vía Argentina at Einstein's Head ☎ 269 2989, w laranadorada.com; map pp.62–63. Brasserie-bar popular with young expat and middle-class Panamanians, serving beer, cocktails and food. The home-brewed beer and the trendy location attract crowds that spill out onto the street. Its sibling bar in Casco Viejo (Av Eloy Alfaro at C 11; ☎ 212 2680) is equally popular. Daily noon–late.

1

SPECTATOR SPORTS

Catching a **baseball** game at the Estadio Nacional Rod Carew (about 8km northeast of the city centre on Vía Ricardo J. Alfaro, off the Corredor Norte) is a real treat and worth the taxi fare. **Horse racing** has a rich tradition in Panama; you can see races at the Hipódromo Presidente Remón (races Thurs 5.30pm, Sat & Sun 2pm; ☎ 217 6060, ✆ hipodromo.com), 10km east of the centre on the way to Tocumen International Airport. Panama's resurgence as a global **boxing** powerhouse has encouraged an increased number of bouts in the capital, above all in the slick new Arena Roberto Durán, named after Panama's former megastar. Check the press for details.

S6is C Uruguay between C 48 and C 49 ☎ 264 5237, ✆ facebook.com/BarS6isPanama; map pp.62–63. A mainstay of the party scene, popular with various age groups, this small cocktail lounge with DJ can get packed at weekends. It's pronounced "seis". Thurs–Sat 8pm–late.

The Wine Bar Vía Veneto, Plaza Downtown Cangrejo, El Cangrejo ☎ 387 4455, ✆ elwinebar.com; map pp.62–63. A long-standing favourite that provides a convivial setting amid faux vines, bottles galore and murals of rustic scenes. Choose from more than two hundred bottles, or just enjoy a glass while chilling out to mellow live music (Mon–Fri after 9pm, Sat & Sun after 7.30pm). Wood-fired pizzas and other comfort food available. Daily 5pm–midnight.

CLUBS

AltaBar C 47 at C Uruguay ☎ 390 2582, ✆ altabar panama.com; map pp.62–63. This club, a current hot spot just off C Uruguay, also has an upstairs terrace bar-restaurant with sports screens and bar. The dancefloor (Wed–Sat), bar and stage are downstairs behind ornate black-and-gold doors, surrounded by fluorescent white seating. Big-name DJs tend to hold sway, but there are occasional live acts. Thurs is usually ladies' night, with themed nights, karaoke and other events at other times. Entry $10–15. Tues–Fri 6pm–late, Sat 8pm–late.

Bling Hard Rock Hotel, Av Balboa, by Multicentro ☎ 380 1111, ✆ hrhpanamamegapolis.com/unforgettable-nightlife.htm; map pp.62–63. A Vegas-style laser-light disco with VIP tables, hot DJs and dancers. The usual features apply: two-for-one drinks, ladies' nights (women usually have free entry before 11pm) and cover charges

(from $10) for DJs or live music. Thurs–Sat 9pm–late.

CASINO

Hotel Veneto Casino Vía Veneto at C Eusebio A. Morales ☎ 340 8686, ✆ venetopanama.com; map pp.62–63. Dull by day, but a festive atmosphere by night, especially at weekends, drawing a mixed crowd of casual and smart dressers who come to socialize, eat, listen to live music and watch sports on the myriad screens as much as to gamble. Daily 24hr.

OTHER AREAS

BARS

Balboa Yacht Club Amador Causeway ☎ 314 0168, ✆ balboayachtclub.com.pa; map p.69. With a pleasant, family-friendly waterside location this is the perfect spot for a sundowner, watching the ships exit the Canal and the yachts bobbing at their moorings. The beer's cheap and the pub grub is decent enough: wings, scampi, tacos and the like ($10–17). Live music Fri & Sat. Daily 11am–late.

Kayuco Isla Flamenco, Amador Causeway ☎ 314 1998; map p.69. With outdoor tables overlooking the marina, this is by far the liveliest place in the area to enjoy sundowners accompanied by sizzling grilled seafood (snacks $5; mixed grill for two around $12). Daily noon–late.

CLUB

XS Club (formerly Icon Club) Av Juan Pablo II at Tumba Muerto, La Locería ☎ 6230 0378, ✆ bit.ly/2qizxC; map pp.62–63. The city's biggest gay club, featuring laser lights, foam parties, dancing boys and drag acts. Cover charge for events (up to $20). Thurs–Sun 9pm–3am.

ENTERTAINMENT

While there's no shortage of places to go drinking, dancing or clubbing in Panama City, other more high-brow entertainment is harder to come by: **classical concerts** (see ✆ conciertospanama.org) and **theatrical presentations** (see ✆ bit.ly/2qryLDn) are sporadic and **opera** is extremely rare (✆ operapanama.com). Check *La Prensa* (✆ prensa.com), *The Visitor/El Visitante* (✆ thevisitorpanama.com), ✆ thepanamadigest.com and ✆ quehaypahoypanama.com for events listings. **Cinema**, on the other hand, is becoming increasingly popular, with multiplexes including 3-D, IMAX and VIP screens proliferating in the city's malls. Screenings predominantly consist of the latest Hollywood offerings, generally in English with subtitles (*subtitulada*), though sometimes dubbed (*doblada*); check out ✆ cinespanama.com. There are also several **bowling alleys**, including one in Albrook Mall.

Ateneo Ciudad de Saber, Edif. 182, Clayton, Ancón ☎ 306 3700, ✆ ciudaddelsaber.org/es/servicios/ateneo.

Seven-hundred-seat auditorium with a small stage and cinema screen for theatrical, musical and movie presentations.

Centro de Convenciones ATLAPA Vía Israel, San Francisco ☎ 521 7000, ⓦ atlapa.gob.pa. The centre has two auditoriums: Teatro Anayansi, seating almost three thousand, hosts pop, jazz, classical, ballet, circus acts and even ice-skating, with plays and beauty pageants in the smaller Teatro La Huaca.

Teatro Anita Villalaz Plaza de Francia, Casco Viejo ☎ 501 4020. Once part of the Supreme Court, this intimate 250-seater hosts a range of cultural activities, from poetry readings to reggae nights.

Teatro Balboa Av Arnulfo Arias Madrid, Balboa ☎ 228 0327. Spacious Art Deco theatre, staging all kinds of events, including concerts by the resident National Symphony Orchestra (ⓦ facebook.com/OSNPANAMA).

Teatro En Círculo Av 6C Norte, El Carmen ☎ 261 5375, ⓣ teatroencirculo.org. One of the premier venues for plays (in Spanish), staged a few times a year.

Teatro Nacional Av "B" between C 3 and C 4, Casco Viejo ☎ 262 3525. Occasional classical concerts, ballets and operas staged in the sumptuous Rococo interior of the capital's premier artistic venue. Closed for renovations at the time of writing (see p.59).

Theatre Guild of Ancón Foot of Cerro Ancón, by the police station ⓦ anconguild.com. Community theatre established to entertain Zonians and still putting on English-speaking productions.

SHOPPING

Despite the hype about duty-free **shopping** in Panama City, there's actually very little around and though the streets are bulging with malls and shops, you're unlikely to be overly impressed by either the selection or the prices – indigenous **crafts** and other **souvenirs** aside. **Av Central**, leading from Plaza Cinco de Mayo to Santa Ana, is the place to browse if you're after cheap clothes or electronics, while **Vía España** in El Cangrejo contains an eclectic mix of bargain stores, would-be chic boutiques and tourist-oriented shops; the Gran Morrison department store here is useful (see p.86), and there's an El Rey supermarket (24hr).

MALLS

Albrook Mall By Albrook bus terminal ⓦ albrookmall .com; map p.69. The largest mall in Latin America: a two-storey kilometre of retail therapy with discount stores, a handful of more upmarket boutiques and a vast food court. Also banks, ATMs, an Apple Store, a cinema and Super 99 – the nearest supermarket for anyone staying in Balboa or Cerro Ancón. Mon–Thurs 10am–8pm, Fri & Sat 10am–9pm, Sun 10.30am–7pm.

Multicentro Av Balboa, Paitilla ⓦ multicentropanama .com; map pp.62–63. Convenient shopping centre for Marbella, with a cinema and a good kosher supermarket in the basement (ⓦ facebook.com/deliKpanama.com). Mon–Thurs 10am–8pm, Fri & Sat 10am–9pm, Sun 11am–7pm.

Multiplaza Vía Israel, Punta Pacífica; map pp.62–63. More than 350 shops, with many upmarket boutiques, such as Paul Smith, Carolina Herrera, Gucci and Tiffany, plus a cinema.

ARTS AND CRAFTS

If a *mola* is on the shopping list, you'll probably get the best prices from the Guna craftspeople who spread out their wares on the pavements around Casco Viejo and Vía Veneto; they can often organize you a trip to Guna Yala too. You'll also find high-quality *molas*, along with good basketry and woodcarvings, in shops dotted round Casco Viejo, though the prices are higher than elsewhere in the city; Vía Veneto is another good area to look. Craft markets are also a good option; the stalls are generally run by members of the community who made the goods, and more of the money you spend will trickle down to the actual artisans.

BUYING OUTDOOR GEAR

If you're considering **hiking** or **camping** in Panama, you'd be wise to bring all the necessary **equipment** and clothing with you – there's limited availability here and prices are high. However, if you find yourself short of a few essentials, the following sellers are worth checking out:

Do It Center ⓦ doitcenter.com.pa. General hardware store that also stocks camping and outdoor gear, such as camping stoves and fishing tackle. Outlets in Albrook Mall and Multiplaza (see above), and across the country.

Matawi Gear Sky Business Centre, Av Balboa ⓦ matawigear.com; map p.84. Specialist stockists of expensive, good-quality Patagonia and North Face hiking and rock-climbing gear and equipment. Mon–Fri 11am–7pm, Sat 11am–3pm.

Novey ⓦ novey.com.pa. Amid the hardware, agricultural and household goods of this nationwide chain, Novey also offers outdoor equipment from cheap tents and sleeping bags to snorkel masks. The most convenient outlets are in Albrook Mall (see above), on Av Central in Calidonia, close to Basílica Don Bosco and opposite Multicentro on Av Balboa in Paitilla.

Outdoor Adventure ⓦ facebook.com/outdoor adventurepa. Located in several malls in the capital – Albrook, Multicentro and Multiplaza (see above) – this place supplies general camping and hiking equipment and clothing, including tents, sleeping mats and bags, solar-powered battery chargers and headlamps.

Casa Latina Panamá Av "A" at C 5, Casco Viejo ☎ 228 9828; map p.56. Very pricey offerings, of exquisite quality: the absolute very best of Panamanian handicrafts as well as beautiful Peruvian alpaca knitwear. Daily 10am–7pm.

Centro de Artesenías Amador Causeway, south of the Centro de Convenciones Figali ☎ 314 1439 or ☎ 6674 3071; map p.54. The pick of the craft markets, selling hammocks, *molas* made into place mats, basketry, earrings, glasses cases and the like, as well as offerings from other Latin American countries. Mon–Sat 9am–6pm, Sun 10am–5pm.

Galería de Arte Indígena C 1, Casco Viejo ☎ 228 9557; map p.56. The best selection of Wounaan and Emberá basketry in the capital at suitably elevated prices, alongside high-quality *tagua* and *cocobolo* carvings. Daily 9am–8pm.

Mercado de Buhonería y Artesanías C 24 Este, just off Plaza Cinco de Mayo; map pp.62–63. A series of bright-pink shipping containers, housing craft stalls selling Panama hats, Guna *molas*, *tagua* carvings and the like. Mon–Sat 9am–5pm.

Reprosa Av "A" at C 4, Casco Viejo ☎ 228 4913, ⊛ treasuresofpanama.com; map p.56. Beautifully crafted gold and silver reproduction pre-Columbian and Spanish colonial jewellery. There's another branch at Av Samuel Lewis on the corner with C 54, Obarrio (☎ 269 0457). Daily 9am–6pm.

La Ronda C 1, Casco Viejo ☎ 211 1001; map p.56. Excellent selection of arts and crafts at Casco Viejo prices. Daily 9am–7pm.

BOOKS

Gran Morrison Vía España, next to El Rey supermarket, El Cangrejo ☎ 202 0029; map pp.62–63. This small department store has a reasonable selection of English-language books on Panama. Mon–Sat 9am–6pm, Sun 9.30am–6pm.

STRI Earl S. Tupper Research Centre Av Roosevelt ☎ 2212 8029, ⊛ stri.si.edu; map p.69. The Smithsonian bookshop stocks an excellent selection on wildlife, ecology and environmental issues in Spanish and English. Mon–Fri 10am–4.30pm.

DIRECTORY

Embassies and consulates Australia – refer to the embassy in Mexico (⊛ mexico.embassy.gov.au); Canada, Torres de las Américas, Tower A, 11th floor, C 53 Este, Punta Pacífica (☎ 294 2500, ⊛ canadainternational.gc.ca /panama); Colombia, Edif. Oceania, Torre 2000, 17th floor, Punta Pacífica (☎ 264 9513, ⊛ panama.embajada.gov.co); Costa Rica, Torre BICSA, 30th floor, Av Balboa (☎ 264 2980, ⊛ embajadacostaricaenpanama.com); Ireland, Honorary Consul, Torre Delta, 14th floor, Vía España (☎ 264 6633, ✉ irishconsulatepma@gmail.com); South Africa, Edif. Plaza Guadalupe, fourth floor, Oficina 404, C 50 at C 69, San Francisco (☎ 226 2559, ✉ jmantovani@westmar.com.pa); UK, Humboldt Tower, fourth floor, C 53, Marbella (☎ 297 6550, ⊛ gov.uk/world/panama); US, Av Demetrio Basilio Lakas, Clayton (☎ 317 5000, ⊛ pa.usembassy.gov).

Health Excellent care is available in the public and private sectors, with many US-trained and English-speaking staff. Recommended public hospitals include Hospital Santo Tomás, C 34 Este at Av Balboa (☎ 227 4122, emergencies ☎ 507 5600) and Hospital Santa Fé, Vía Simón Bolívar at Av Frangipani (☎ 227 4733, ⊛ hsantafe.com). Good private options include Clínica Hospital San Fernando, Vía España, Las Sabanas, next to *McDonald's* (☎ 305 6300, ⊛ hospital sanfernando.com) and Centro Médico Paitilla, Av Balboa at C 53 (☎ 265 8800, ⊛ centromedicopaitilla.com). The Centro de Medicina Natural on C 42 Este at Av Mejico, Edif. Guadalupe (☎ 225 0867) offers natural and traditional treatments. For a dentist, try Clínica Dental Fábregas (☎ 399 4251) in Hospital Punta Pacífica or the Eisenmann Dental Clinic (☎ 269 2750), C 53 at Av Samuel Lewis. Staff at both speak English.

Immigration The immigration office (*migración*) is at Av Ricardo J. Alfaro, Tumba Muerto (Mon–Fri 8.30am–3.30pm; ☎ 507 1800, ⊛ migracion.gob.pa).

Internet Many public places are free wi-fi hot spots, provided you register your laptop. Most hotels and hostels also offer free wi-fi, at least in the foyer; they also often have a PC or laptop for guest use. The city also has a sprinkling of internet cafés, notably along Vía Veneto in El Cangrejo and Parque Santa Ana, near Casco Viejo (usually $1/hr).

Money If you need to change currency, head for Panacambios (Mon–Fri 8am–5pm; ☎ 223 1800, ⊛ panacambiossa.com) on the ground floor of Edif. Plaza Regency on Vía España; alternatively RedPlus (⊛ gruporedplus) has branches in the Albrook, Multicentro and Multiplaza shopping malls.

Pharmacies Farmacias Arrocha (⊛ arrocha.com) is the largest chain, often open 24hr, with huge branches in Albrook Mall and in front of the *Hotel El Panamá* on Vía España. The large 24hr supermarkets also have pharmacy counters.

Phones The main Cable & Wireless office (Mon–Fri 8am–6pm, Sat 8am–4pm) is on Vía España, next to the National Bank and Plaza Concordia. It has comfortable facilities to make international phone calls, as do some internet cafés (see p.47).

Police Policía de Turismo, Vía España opposite the *Riande Hotel Continental* (☎ 269 8011) and Av Central at C 3, Casco Viejo (☎ 511 9261).

Post office The main post office is opposite the Basílica Don Bosco, on Av Central, between C Ecuador and C 34 Este. Other convenient branches are in Plaza Concordia (below the *Hotel El Panamá*), in El Cangrejo, and in Balboa at the end of the Prado on Av Arnulfo Arias Madrid.

Isla Taboga

1

Just 20km off the coast and a short boat-ride away, the lush hills of **Isla Taboga** have provided a popular weekend escape for Panama City residents since the capital's sixteenth-century foundation. After the frenetic energy of the capital, the island's relaxed atmosphere makes for a welcome break and the views from its vantage points are well worth seeking out. Packed on summer weekends and holidays, at other times the place can feel gloriously deserted. Most visitors are day-trippers who spend their time lounging on the indifferent **Restinga beach**, bathing in the shallow waters and strolling the traffic-free streets of **San Pedro** fishing village, where most of the island's thousand-odd inhabitants live. However, it's definitely worth summoning up the energy to do one of the island's two **walks**; other popular diversions include **boat trips**, which, in the nesting months of January to June, allow close-ups of pelicans thrusting fish down the gullets of their squawking chicks. There is also reasonable **snorkelling** on the far side of Taboga and Isla El Morro and around a wreck off Isla Urabá, though currents can be strong.

Much of the island, together with neighbouring Isla Urabá, comprises a wildlife refuge for a large colony of brown **pelicans** – check with MiAmbiente (see box, p.42) if you want to visit. Elsewhere, hibiscus, bougainvillea and sweet-smelling jasmine are in evidence, but the succulent pineapples for which the island is traditionally famous are now a rarity.

Brief history

Taboga's present-day tranquillity belies a turbulent past. The Spanish arrived in 1515, and wasted no time in enslaving and removing the native Cueva Indians before populating the island with freed slaves from elsewhere and constructing a fort on the adjoining **Isla El Morro** – its cannons are sprinkled round the island. Taboga's excellent natural harbour has crucially shaped the island's history, forming the base for Francisco Pizarro's expeditions against the Incas, as well as for pirates including Morgan and Drake. After an English steamship company established its headquarters on Isla El Morro, Taboga became a

ISLA TABOGA

▲ Panama City

■ ACCOMMODATION	
Cabañas Verde Mar	1
Cerrito Tropical B&B	3
Hotel Vereda Tropical	2

● EATING	
Calaloo	2
Restaurante Mundi	1

Playa Restinga
Isla El Morro

Jetty
Playa Honda

✝ **Iglesia San Pedro**

Sendero de las Tres Cruces

Golfo de Panamá

▲ **Las Tres Cruces**

▲ *Cerro Vigía (307m)*

REFUGIO DE VIDA SILVESTRE DE TABOGA

✝

MIA office ▲ *Cerro de la Cruz*

N

Isla Urabá

0   1
kilometre

1

buzzing port for supplies and repairs and, though the island's maritime importance has dwindled, many contemporary Taboganos still live off the sea, either through small-scale fishing or unloading tuna from fishing boats to larger trans-shippers.

The beaches

Approaching Isla Taboga's floating pier, you are greeted by the sight of the whitewashed buildings and red rooftops of San Pedro, strung out to the left behind **Playa Honda**, a shingly strip dotted with small fishing boats, which extends to a swathe of tan sand at low tide. Turning right after leaving the pier takes you to Taboga's main beach, **Playa Restinga**, a golden crescent, half of which forms a sand bar reaching to Isla El Morro; at high tide the sandbar becomes submerged. The beach's appeal is somewhat diminished by the piles of overgrown rubble from the demolished *Hotel Taboga* at the back, and by the rubbish that can wash up on the shore after heavy rains. Even so, crowds of Panamanians happily swim from here, and from Playa Honda. Beach umbrellas ($5) and deckchairs ($3) are available for rent.

San Pedro

Heading back towards **San Pedro**, along the jasmine-scented Calle Abajo, a steep path to the right leads up to the **plaza**, the social hub of the island – where villagers of all ages gather to watch or play football or volleyball, dance or simply hang out. At one end, steps lead up to the gleaming white stucco walls of the **Iglesia San Pedro**, built in 1550 and reputedly the second oldest church in the western hemisphere. Leaving the square via Calle Arriba at the opposite end, and turning left, you come across a shrine to the Virgen del Carmen and the house where Pizarro apparently lived, while a brightly tiled plaque nearby commemorates the French painter Paul Gauguin, who had a short stint working on the Canal before heading off for the South Seas.

Cerro de la Cruz

The shorter of the island's two hikes, to **Cerro de la Cruz**, takes an easy thirty minutes. Leaving town along Calle Abajo, you pass the delightful **casa de la concha** on the right, decorated by its former owner, a one-time pearl fisher, with scallop and pearl shells. Further on is the site of an old French canal-era **sanitorium**, which the Americans converted into a rest and recuperation centre for "gold roll" Canal employees (see p.297) before upgrading it to a hotel. Beyond the weed-strewn **cemetery**, take the dirt road down to the left, then a path up an embankment to the right 100m later, after which it's an easy walk to the gigantic sixteenth-century cross, where you can soak up the sweeping sea view.

Cerro Vigía

The panorama is truly spectacular from the mirador at the top of **Cerro Vigía** (370m), Taboga's highest point, making the hour-long hike a rewarding experience. Heading along the main path out of the village, you pass the turn to Cerro de la Cruz, before arriving at a junction. Straight ahead lie the MiAmbiente offices (signposted but not open to the public), the island's desalination plant and the refuse dump; to the right, the widening dirt road meanders slowly up the hill. The more direct route to the summit, up the **Sendero de las Tres Cruces**, presents a more challenging but shorter climb through lush forest, not least because of poor signposting. After heavy rain, the path becomes a mudslide, but the rewards are almost-guaranteed sightings of green and black poison dart frogs and tarantulas. The route is indicated from the plaza, by the phone box; after the housing ends, turn sharp right and keep to the right of the stream until, ten minutes into the forest, the route bears left across a stream, which the path crisscrosses several times

1

before arriving, forty-five minutes later, at three well-tended crosses – the burial sites of a trio of buccaneers who foolishly tangled with some Taboganos. Bearing left again, the trail soon emerges from the undergrowth onto the dirt road to the summit.

ARRIVAL AND INFORMATION
ISLA TABOGA

By boat Two companies run boats to Taboga. The traditional way to travel is on the *Calypso Queen* (☎ 314 1730), which offers great views from the open top deck and affords close-ups of the ships waiting to transit the Canal. There are usually two daily departures from La Playita on the Amador Causeway, near the entrance to the Punta Culebra Nature Centre (50min; $14 return), with extra crossings at weekends and on public holidays when you'll need to get there 1hr beforehand to be sure of a seat, or even buy a ticket a day in advance. There are fewer departures in the rainy season; call to confirm. *Taboga Ferry Express* (☎ 6234 8989, ⊚ tabogaexpress.com) runs a more frequent, faster and more expensive daily service from Balboa Yacht Club, on the causeway (30min; $20 return).

Tourist information The English-language website ⊚ taboga.panamanow.com is a useful resource.

Money Take sufficient cash with you; there is no ATM on Taboga.

ACTIVITIES AND TOURS

Kayaking One- or two-person kayaks are available at Playa Restinga ($5/30min).

Taboga taxi and tours 30m to the right of the jetty, as you leave the ferry ☎ 6061 7986. This little outfit can fix you a couple of hours in a *panga*, including a spot of snorkelling, for around $60 for the boat. They also run an ATV excursion up to the island's three main summits ($20/person) and historical walking tours round San Pedro.

Whale Watching Panama ☎ 6758 7600, ⊚ whalewatchingpanama.com. Half-day trips from Panama City to spot humpback whales in the migration season (July–Oct; from $175; minimum six people), accompanied by a naturalist guide.

ACCOMMODATION

Accommodation on the island is limited and generally overpriced. Some locals rent out **rooms** informally for $20–40; they'll often meet the morning ferry to drum up custom, otherwise ask at *Restaurante Mundi* by the jetty.

★**Cabañas Verde Mar** Opposite the jetty ☎ 6410 9641, ⊚ verdemartaboga@gmail.com. Six simple, cosily decorated self-catering cabins spread around shady tropical gardens, each with two bedrooms (with a/c, and sleeping four; $30/person) and a spacious veranda with a hammock. $60

Cerrito Tropical B&B Up the hill from the village centre ☎ 6489 0074, ⊚ cerritotropicalpanama.com. This friendly B&B offers plain double rooms with a/c, fan, private bathroom and shared balcony, and one- to three-bedroom apartments with kitchenettes and private balconies. $100

Hotel Vereda Tropical Above the main path ☎ 250 2154, ⊚ hotelveredatropical.com. The most comfortable of the island's accommodation exudes a Spanish hacienda-style feel in its tasteful rooms with rustic tiling and fans (a/c costs $15 more); some overlook the ocean. The terrace provides lovely views to accompany excellent food – try the house corvina in coconut and passion fruit sauce ($15) – but prices are high and service is hit-and-miss. $72

EATING

The island's **eating** options are restricted and service is slow, so if you join the summer weekend crowds it's probably worth bringing a picnic.

★**Calaloo** Main path, 50m to the left when leaving the jetty ☎ 6000 5172, ⊚ facebook.com/CalalooPanama. Cheery, breezy café-restaurant looking across the main path to Playa Honda – great for people-watching. The tasty, varied menu ranges from hummus and roast vegetables to fresh fish with *patacones* and salad, plus fresh fruit juices and ice-cold cocktails. Mon–Fri 8.30am–4pm, Sat & Sun 8.30am–9pm.

Restaurante Mundi 50m to the right when leaving the jetty ☎ 250 2292 or ☎ 6429 4803, ⊚ hospedaje munditaboga.com. Small restaurant with an agreeable prow-shaped deck over the water and rustic wooden furniture, serving fried breakfasts and tasty seafood with rice or *patacones* at tourist prices ($14–18). They can deliver to the beach. Daily 8.30am–4pm.

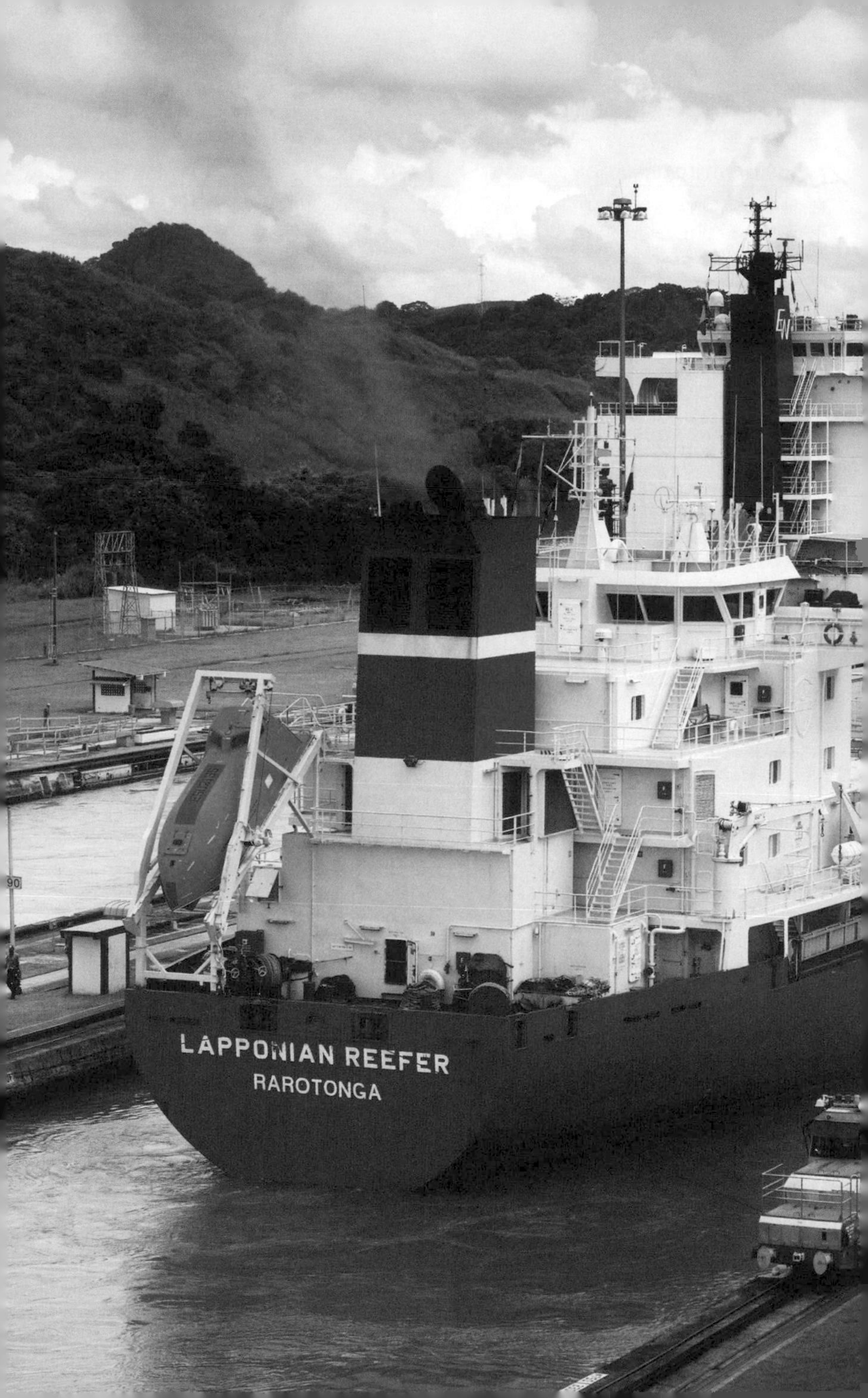
LAPPONIAN REEFER
RAROTONGA

The Panama Canal and central isthmus

The Panama Canal and central isthmus

2

Running 80km across the isthmus between the Pacific and Atlantic oceans, straddling the provinces of Panama and Colón, the Panama Canal remains a colossus among engineering achievements, a truly awe-inspiring sight and justifiably the country's prime tourist attraction. What's more, it can easily be explored on an excursion from Panama City, with the Centro de Visitantes de Miraflores offering the best location from which to view the action. Though the corridor that flanks this vital thoroughfare is home to almost two-thirds of Panama's population, for much of its length the waterway cleaves through pristine rainforest, large tracts of which are protected within national parks.

Parque Nacional Soberanía is one of the most accessible tropical rainforest preserves in Latin America, while **Isla Barro Colorado** is home to the world-renowned Smithsonian Institute. Both support an exceptional degree of biodiversity and are easy day-trips from the capital. The quiet town of **Gamboa** is the embarkation point for excursions to Barro Colorado and for most tours offering partial transits of the Canal; it is also the starting point for rainforest hikes and birdwatching outings along the famous **Camino del Oleoducto** (Pipeline Road). Three of the area's national parks – Soberanía, the smaller adjacent **Parque Nacional Camino de Cruces** and the larger, less accessible **Parque Nacional Chagres** – also offer the opportunity to walk along the remnants of the historic, partially cobbled **Camino de Cruces** and the **Camino Real**. These paths were carved by mule trains across the forested spine of the isthmus in colonial times to transport Spain's plundered treasures from Panama City to the Caribbean coast.

The Canal reaches the Atlantic at **Colón**, Panama's second city, synonymous with poverty and crime in the minds of many Panamanians, yet compelling and rich in history, with a strong Afro-Antillean and Afro-Colonial heritage. Either side of Colón stretch kilometres of Caribbean coastline, peppered with small communities more or less untainted by tourist development. To the west, along the **Costa Abajo**, the formidable remains of the **Fuerte San Lorenzo** are the country's most impressive colonial ruins, still guarding the mouth of the Río Chagres amid untouched tropical rainforest. To the northeast lies the **Costa Arriba**, an isolated region of rich coral reefs and laidback fishing villages, much of which is nominally protected by **Parque Nacional Portobelo**, set around the ruins and beautiful natural harbour of the old Spanish port of **Portobelo**.

At the Pacific end of the Canal, some two hours by boat from Panama City, lies the **Archipiélago de las Perlas**. A former hideout of privateers and pirates and a long-standing weekend refuge for the capital's social elite, the archipelago's translucent waters and powdered beaches offer a pricey slice of tranquillity.

FUERTE SANTIAGO, PORTOBELO

Highlights

❶ Canal transit Experience the great, iconic waterway on a boat and marvel at the tropical scenery. **See p.95**

❷ Canal locks Get a close look at the precision manoeuvring of gargantuan container vessels as they squeeze through the lock chambers at Miraflores or Agua Clara. **See p.97 & p.109**

❸ Rainforest hiking Follow in the footsteps of the conquistadors along the old booty trails of the Camino de Cruces through tangled, lush rainforest. **See p.98 & p.99**

❹ Birdwatching in Soberanía More than five hundred bird species have been recorded here:

grab your binoculars and scan the canopy at dawn. **See p.99**

❺ Stay in an Emberá village Overnight in a traditional thatched home, experiencing Emberá culture and learning about the surrounding rainforest. **See p.104**

❻ Spanish colonial forts Step back in time at the desolate, evocative ruins of Fuerte San Lorenzo or the well-preserved forts of Portobelo. **See p.110 & p.112**

❼ Archipiélago de las Perlas Picturesque islands offering near-deserted beaches and fine snorkelling and diving. **See p.120**

HIGHLIGHTS ARE MARKED ON THE MAP ON P.94

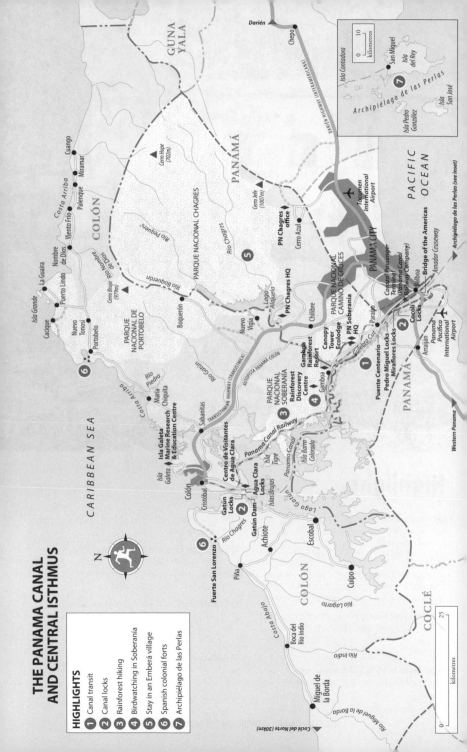

The Panama Canal

The **PANAMA CANAL**, which runs between Panama City on the Pacific coast and Colón on the Caribbean, or Atlantic side, is the country's most recognizable landmark, crucial to its economy and inextricably entwined with its historical and cultural development. One of the world's most important waterways, it has seen around fourteen thousand vessels and more than three hundred million tonnes of cargo passing through its locks every year, a figure which has the potential to double following the Canal's recent ambitious expansion, which was inaugurated in 2016 (see box, p.303). A gargantuan feat of engineering, the original Panama Canal, completed in 1914, set the standards for twentieth-century engineering. At $352 million it was the most expensive project ever undertaken, with the world's largest earthen dam creating the world's largest artificial lake. The most enormous locks ever built contained the greatest amount of concrete ever used – just over three million cubic metres, the equivalent of sixty Empire State Buildings – and possessed the largest-ever swing doors. Statistics notwithstanding,

2

TRANSITING THE CANAL

To fully appreciate the Canal, you need to see it up close. Things may not be quite as you'd expect – the gargantuan Panamax vessels (the biggest ships the original locks could hold), and the even larger Neopanamax, are manoeuvred with surprising delicacy, while the banks of this vast commercial enterprise are lined with jungle and spotted with unspoilt islands. In a **partial transit**, from the tip of the Amador Causeway in Panama City to Gamboa (or vice versa), you get to experience the excitement of passing under the impressive Bridge of the Americas, through the narrow Culebra Cut and being raised and lowered in the lock chambers of both Miraflores and Pedro Miguel locks. The **full transit** from Panama City to Colón takes in the most breathtaking scenery, crossing Lago Gatún and weaving among tiny forested islands. You'll glide past a silent stream of giant ships before passing through the enormous Gatún Locks and terminating in Colón, from where it can be up to a two-hour bus journey back to the capital.

Although completing a full transit might hold a certain cachet, the advertised eight to nine hours can often be a lot longer if you get caught up in one of the frequent log jams in Gatún Locks. A partial transit provides enough excitement and interest for most people, and if you take a northbound trip, docking at around 1pm in Gamboa, you can skip the bus transfer back to the Amador Causeway and enjoy a drink at the *Gamboa Rainforest Resort* (see p.101) before catching the public bus back to Panama City.

The cheapest way to see the Canal is to get a job as a **line-handler** – a person who helps keep the boat positioned in the locks; it's a requirement for all transiting cruising vessels to have four line-handlers. If you're interested, check out ⓦpanlinehandler.com.

INFORMATION AND TOURS

The two companies listed below offer similar trips, charging $195 for the full crossing and $150 for the partial transit, which includes a transfer between the relevant marina on the Amador Causeway and the boat, bilingual guided commentary, soft drinks, meals and snacks. In the tourist season (Dec–April) there are frequent transits and boats can be very crowded; out of season there are fewer, with a full crossing often only once a month. Various other tour operators offer Canal transits, though they all use the boats from the companies listed below. The scheduled times given below are subject to change and will need to be confirmed the day before.

Canal and Bay Tours ☏209 2009, ⓦcanaland baytours.com. Two larger craft are used for full transits, while the partial transit sometimes employs the smaller *Isla Morada*, a 1912 wooden vessel said to have been owned by Al Capone. A partial night transit tour is also available. All tours leave from La Playita, Isla Naos, at 8am, and most are northbound; contact the office for dates of the occasional southbound partial transit.

Panama Marine Adventures ☏226 8917, ⓦpmatours.net. Panama Marine Adventures caters predominantly to foreign tourists. Southbound partial transits usually leave from the Flamenco Marina at 9.30am (starting with a bus journey to Gamboa); northbound partial transits and full transits usually leave at 7.30am.

it is the combination of the scale and ingenuity of the achievement with its ruggedly beautiful tropical setting that makes the Canal so special.

There are several ways to appreciate what the Canal has to offer, all of them within easy striking distance of the capital. Most people take a trip to **Miraflores Locks** – a convenient bus ride out of Panama City – which has a well-situated visitor centre with a museum and viewing platform, offering a fine view of ships as they pass through. The Canal's other main observation point, across the isthmus at the new **Agua Clara Visitor Centre** takes longer to reach, and looks down from a hilltop, offering a more panoramic and holistic view of the Canal expansion programme in particular (see box, p.303). Different perspectives again are offered by fishing or boating trips on **Lago Gatún**, and by speeding across the isthmus and alongside the Canal by **train**. But by far the best way to get your head around the technical brilliance, natural beauty and sheer magnitude of the feat is to travel along the Canal ("transit") by **boat**.

The Canal by train: Panama Canal Railway

Corozal Passenger Terminal, Building T376, Corozal West, Panama City • Mon–Fri departs 7.15am (1hr), returning from Colón at 5.15pm; reservations are advisable and it's worth getting there early (6.30am) to secure your vantage point • $25 one way • ☎ 317 6070, ⓦ panarail.com • A taxi costs around $6 from the centre of Panama City to the Corozal terminal

The Corozal Passenger Terminal of the **Panama Canal Railway** is the departure point for the scenic transisthmian train journey. The original Panama Railroad, built in the 1850s during the California Gold Rush (see box, p.294), transported more than $700

THE BIG DITCH

Erroneously nicknamed the **Big Ditch**, the 77km Canal eschews straight lines as it weaves its way from the Pacific to the Caribbean or Atlantic entrance, which is actually 42km to the west, on account of Panama's eel-like shape. British politician and historian James Bryce dubbed the waterway "the greatest liberty Man has ever taken with nature", though ironically it has resulted in a symbiotic relationship between the two: the Canal's constant thirst for water to feed the locks is highly dependent on the preservation of the adjacent national parks to protect the water catchment area. This is even more true since the Canal's recent expansion; despite the new locks' ingenious basins, which can recover sixty percent of the water used, the overall water loss from the Canal has increased.

The original **lock chambers** measure 304.8m by 33.53m, affording colossal Panamax vessels a mere 0.6m of leeway either side, yet they function in much the same way as they did when they were first used. Once the gates are closed, these vast vessels are kept aligned by cables attached to pairs of electric locomotives known as mules (*mulas*). The huge tunnel-like culverts then kick in with phenomenal efficiency, taking only eight minutes to fill the giant chamber with the equivalent of 43 Olympic swimming pools. The new locks, which are more than half as big again, demand an arguably even trickier operation, since the mules have been abandoned in favour of tugboats, which are attached to the bow and stern of the ships, and squeezed into the same lock chamber as the towering metal behemoths they're guiding.

Tolls for ships are calculated depending on type of vessel, and size and type of cargo. The average toll for the largest Panamax vessels is $126,000 for the 8–10hr journey plus $13,000 each for up to three tugboats required for the more difficult stages of the transit, as well as fees for the obligatory Canal pilot. For Neopanamax vessels, which can carry up to fourteen thousand containers, costs are set to rocket: at the time of writing the record stood at $800,000, with the first million-dollar crossing likely over the next few years.

It is no wonder then that the Canal's annual revenue is well in excess of $1 billion, and expected to rise to $2 billion by 2021, though the repayment of a $2.3 billion loan to finance the expansion – not to mention the litigation fees to decide who pays the vast cost overruns – will swallow up some of the profits for the first few years. For the ships, despite the eye-watering costs, the Canal still represents a major saving in time and money, as it avoids them having to make the difficult 15,000km-journey around the treacherous seas of Cape Horn.

The **history** of the Canal is covered in more detail in our Contexts chapter (see pp.295–298).

million in gold before the completion of the Union Pacific Railroad across the US in 1869 made it obsolete, forcing it into bankruptcy. Following a short revival during the Canal's construction, the railway fell into disrepair until 1998 when the government agreed to privatize it. Though the railway company predominantly ferries freight to and from the Atlantic and Pacific container ports, it offers a commuter passenger service to Colón that is very popular with tourists. A supremely comfortable way to enjoy the Canal, it serves up old-world elegance in wood-panelled, carpeted carriages with large windows. In fine weather, make sure you also get out onto the open viewing deck.

2

Miraflores Locks and around

A mere fifteen minutes from downtown Panama City, along Avenida Omar Torrijos, the **MIRAFLORES LOCKS (Esclusas de Miraflores)** are home to the four-storey **Centro de Visitantes de Miraflores**, which provides a prime location for observing the Canal in action. Marking the Pacific entrance to the waterway, the locks raise or lower vessels 16.5m between sea level and the artificial Lago Miraflores in two stages, a process best appreciated from the visitor centre's observation deck.

Southwest of Miraflores, action in the new three-chambered **Cocolí Locks** can be enjoyed from a small concrete **mirador** along the road that skirts the western flank of the new channel, leading to the Puente Centenario (see p.98), while just over 3km beyond Miraflores lie the smaller **Pedro Miguel Locks**. These are closed to the public, but if you park in the small layby, you can peer through the chainlink fence and watch the ships manoeuvring, saving yourself the $15 Miraflores entry fee in the process.

Centro de Visitantes Miraflores

Daily 9am–5pm (4.15pm last entry), including holidays • Museum and viewing decks $15 • ☎ 276 8617, ⓦ pancanal.com • Take any Gamboa or Paraíso bus from Panama City's Albrook terminal (see box, p.74) to the Miraflores stop; a taxi costs $8–10

The **Centro de Visitantes Miraflores** houses an informative introductory museum on the Canal's history and workings as well as a three-tier **observation deck** just metres from the locks. Optimum viewing times for vessels transiting are before 11am, when ships are usually entering the Canal from the Pacific, and after 3pm, when they are exiting. It's advisable to get there early in high season as the viewing platforms can get very crowded.

The **museum** serves to promote the Autoridad del Canal de Panamá (ACP) – particularly though the 3D film (shown in Spanish and English at different times) – as much as to inform you about the Canal. Both the French and US construction efforts are squeezed into the ground-floor exhibition – for more in-depth coverage, head to the Canal museum in Casco Viejo (see p.57). Against a vast montage of historical photos and a soundtrack of blasting dynamite, the bare bones of the enterprise are covered through impressive scale models and bilingual texts. Sound effects continue on the first floor as the focus shifts to the biodiversity of the Canal's catchment area, while on the floor above, the spotlight turns to engineering. Highlights include a virtual high-speed transit of the Canal, complete with illuminated 3D topographic map, and the chance to experience life inside a lock culvert (thankfully without the water). The centre also houses a couple of thinly stocked cafés, a **restaurant** (see below) and a **gift shop**.

ACCOMMODATION AND EATING	MIRAFLORES

Atlantic & Pacific Co Restaurant Centro de Visitantes Miraflores ☎ 232 3120, ⓦ atlanticpacificrestaurant.com. High-quality organic food in special surroundings. The superior buffet spread ($45; until 4pm) upgrades to a champagne brunch on Sun ($51); in the evening (Mon–Sat) it's à la carte (mains from $25). Panamanian flavours are given a twist – grilled *corvina* in pineapple skin with green plantain, perhaps. Mon–Sat 11.30am–11pm, Sun 11.30am–5pm.

Holiday Inn Ciudad de Saber (City of Knowledge), Clayton ☎ 317 4000, ⓦ ihg.com/holidayinn. Bang opposite the Miraflores Locks; from upper-floor rooms you can watch the action night and day. The well-appointed, spacious rooms have giant plasma-screen TVs, crisp white sheets, sparkling bathrooms and the usual business amenities. But you are a long way from the city, so you'll need to budget for taxi fares (around $6). **$80**

The road to Gamboa

Once beyond the Miraflores and Pedro Miguel locks, the road to the somnolent Canal-era town of **Gamboa** (Carretera Gaillard) skirts the emerald rainforest of the contiguous **Parque Nacional Camino de Cruces** and **Parque Nacional Soberanía**, both of which have trails to suit hikers, bird-lovers and anyone interested in the Spanish conquest. It then ascends to the continental divide at the **Parque Municipal Summit**, before swooping down to the bridge across the Río Chagres, which marks the entrance to Gamboa. Unfortunately buses to Gamboa, though regular, are infrequent, so visiting several sites in one day is tricky unless you have your own transport. A saloon car will do for most sights, though for the road to Camino de Cruces you will need high clearance or 4WD in the rainy season.

The Culebra Cut

Beyond the Miraflores Locks the Canal narrows into the infamous **Culebra Cut** (formerly the Gaillard Cut), where more than two-thirds of all the original Canal excavation occurred. Its 13km stretch posed the most persistent technical headache for engineers, and severe landslides continued long after the eventual opening of the Canal. On the left, a little beyond Paraíso, the Canal's former dredging headquarters, rows of small white crosses mark the **French Cemetery**, which sits on the continental divide, a poignant reminder of the doomed French attempt to build a canal in the 1880s (see p.295).

The road then climbs, passing a turn-off to the elegant, cable-stayed **Puente Centenario**, opened in 2004 to celebrate Panama's hundred years of independence. After 3km of dense rainforest the road forks: to the right it cuts through Parque Nacional Soberanía to the Transístmica and the new motorway, both of which link Panama City with Colón, while to the left it continues to Gamboa.

Parque Nacional Camino de Cruces

The park entrance is 2km up the Carretera Chivo Chivo, a right turn a couple of bends beyond the Miraflores Locks • Daily 8am–4pm • $5; camping $6/person • ☎ 500 0839 • Any Paraíso or Gamboa bus from Albrook's bus terminal (see box, p.74) will drop you off at the bottom of the Carretera Chivo Chivo, which requires a high-clearance vehicle, or 4WD in the rainy season

Despite bearing the name of the conquistadors' famous trade route across the isthmus (named after the now-submerged settlement of Cruces), **Parque Nacional Camino de Cruces** is often overlooked as a tourist destination. Yet, while it is hard to escape the sound of nearby traffic in places, the reserve is a prime location for spotting **sloths** and provides important traces of colonial history.

There are four **trails**: the **Sendero Capricornio** provides an easy 1km circular stroll from the park office through mainly dry semi-deciduous forest. But it's worth expending slightly more energy on the **Sendero Mirador** (3.2km total), which offers a moderate hike up to a breezy wooden watchtower, affording an impressive panoramic view of the Canal and distant city skyscrapers. The remaining two trails, the **Ruinas de Cardenas** and a section of the **Camino de Cruces**, are both still in need of clearance work, though you don't need to venture far along the latter before you'll come across some of the original cobblestones.

Camping is permitted near the park office, though there are no facilities beyond a toilet and running water.

Parque Nacional Soberanía

Providing the most accessible substantial body of tropical rainforest from Panama City, a mere thirty-minute drive away, **PARQUE NACIONAL SOBERANÍA** is one of the country's most visited national parks and well worth exploring. Stretching north and west from the **park office**, it hugs the Canal and encircles Gamboa, covering more than 190

WILDLIFE IN PARQUE NACIONAL SOBERANÍA

With 525 recorded bird species, 105 mammals, 79 reptiles and 55 amphibians, Parque Nacional Soberanía offers good opportunities for wildlife-spotting. White-tailed deer, agoutis, coatis, pacas, howler monkeys and Geoffroy's tamarins are fairly commonplace, but you'll need a good guide to locate the rarer, more elusive nocturnal kinkajous or **silky anteaters**. Following an extensive breeding programme, a number of **harpy eagles** have been released into the park in recent years, so there is even a (slim) chance of catching sight of these endangered birds (see box, p.285). Other **birds** to look out for include crested eagles, red-lored amazons, great jacamars and trogons – the park's symbol.

2

---

square kilometres. It encompasses a stretch of the majestic **Río Chagres**, the Canal's lifeblood, which you can explore by boat; there are also several well-maintained **trails** either side of Gamboa, including a stretch of the historic **Camino de Cruces** and a world-renowned birding hot spot, the **Camino del Oleoducto**. The trails are not particularly close to each other or the park office, however, arguably making the area best enjoyed with a car, parking at the various trailheads or – especially if you want to walk the Camino de Cruces, which you are advised to do with a guide – on a **tour**. Several Panama City operators offer trips to the caminos de Cruces and Oleoducto, or you can **hire a ranger** from the park office as a guide – a much cheaper option, though they are unlikely to speak English.

The trails

Although most of Soberanía's trails are easy and safe enough to walk on your own, you're strongly advised to hike the **Camino de Cruces** on a tour or with a **guide**. The trail is overgrown and difficult to follow in places – and the occasional robbery has been known at the eastern end (though with police now patrolling the area there has not been an incident since 2015). Independent travellers can pick up a **map** and pay the park fees at the office or at the entry barrier to the **Camino del Oleoducto**, if there is someone there when you arrive.

Camino del Oleoducto

By far the most tramped trail in Soberanía is the unpromising-sounding **Camino del Oleoducto** (Pipeline Road), so named because it was originally built to service an oil pipeline constructed across the isthmus by the US in World War II. The pipeline was never used but the 17.5km dirt-road service track, which lies 1km beyond Gamboa, draws birding enthusiasts from around the world. Though it's visually unremarkable – this is no wilderness trail – the likely wildlife sightings more than compensate. Even if you can't tell a white-whiskered puffbird from a band-tailed barbthroat, you cannot fail to be impressed by the array of brightly coloured birds; you'll see a great deal more if you go with a good guide (see p.38 & p.76).

Camino de Cruces and Sendero de la Plantación

A 10km section of the isthmus-crossing **Camino de Cruces** traverses the park's dense vegetation from the borders of Parque Nacional Camino de Cruces (see opposite). The trail begins 6km up the road that forks right at the park office, ending up at the shores of the Río Chagres, site of the barely distinguishable remains of the Ruinas de Venta de Cruces, which served as a resting post for weary, booty-laden mules and conquistadors. You don't have to venture that far to get a flavour of the history – after a ten-minute hike your guide should be able to point out a restored section of the original sixteenth-century paving stones.

If you decide to walk the whole trail – preferably with a guide (see above) – you can avoid returning along the same route (in an exhausting eight-hour trek) by hopping across the Chagres to the *Gamboa Rainforest Resort* (see p.101) and reviving yourself with a drink before catching one of the regular buses back. You would need to organize a boat to meet you in advance ($5/person); the park wardens can arrange this for a couple of dollars. Alternatively, hike half of the Camino de Cruces in a westerly direction, breaking off down the 5km **Sendero de la Plantación (Plantation Trail)**. This is the gravelly remnants of a paved thoroughfare that once led to the largest private agricultural venture in the old Canal Zone, harvesting rubber, coffee and cocoa, which you can still occasionally spot growing wild amid the rainforest. It eventually disgorges you onto the road to Gamboa, where you can flag down one of the regular Gamboa–Panama City buses.

Canopy Tower Ecolodge

Semaphore Hill, on the main road to Gamboa, 6km south of Gamboa and around 20km from Panama City • Half-day visits $120, including meal, park fee and guided walk • ☎ 264 5720, ⓦ canopytower.com • It's a steep 1km to the lodge from the drive entrance

For serious nature lovers who can't afford the overnight rates (see below), it's still worth considering a half-day trip to the **Canopy Tower Ecolodge**, which has to be organized in advance, and includes a guided walk on which you're likely to spot manakins, antbirds, tinamous, sloths, coatis and agoutis, as well as an abundance of butterflies and insects. You also get time on the truly special canopy-level **observation deck**, which is equipped with a telescope and sun loungers, allowing you to indulge in some spectacular armchair birdwatching.

Rainforest Discovery Centre

2km along the Camino de Oleoducto from central Gamboa • Daily 6am–4pm • Peak hours (6–10am; maximum 25 people) $30, other hours $20; advance booking is advisable • ☎ 306 3133 in Panama City, visitor centre ☎ 6450 6630, ⓦ pipelineroad.org

The **Rainforest Discovery Centre**, on the park boundary, boasts an impressive canopy observation tower with multilevel viewing platforms, a series of short trails and an interpretive centre, whose main draw is the **observation deck**, where bird feeders attract scores of hummingbirds. The drawback is the hefty entrance fee, especially if you arrive during prime birding time (6–10am), though it's definitely worth the outlay if you're keen on birds or you make a day of it with a picnic. Profits go towards environmental education, research and conservation projects.

ARRIVAL AND INFORMATION — PARQUE NACIONAL SOBERANÍA

Park entrance and fees Fees ($5) are payable at the park headquarters (Mon–Fri 8am–4.30pm, though there is always a warden on site out of office hours; ☎ 232 4192), 15km northwest of Panama City on the road to Gamboa where the road forks.

By bus Gamboa-bound buses from Panama City's Albrook terminal can drop you off at the park HQ, several kilometres away from the main trails, and 2.5km further along the road, at the entrance to the Sendero de la Plantación – also the turn-off for the *Canopy Tower Ecolodge* (see below). For

the Camino del Oleoducto, alight at the park in Gamboa, walk 1km along the road parallel to the railway and Canal, then follow the signs up a dirt road to the right to the entrance barrier.

By car There are car parks at the trailheads.

By taxi A taxi from central Panama City will cost around $20–30 depending on where in the park you want to go.

Tours Panama City tour operators (see p.76) run a variety of day-trips to the park, which can involve birdwatching, hiking, kayaking or even mountain biking.

ACCOMMODATION

Canopy Tower Ecolodge Semaphore Hill, Parque Nacional Soberanía ☎ 264 5720, ⓦ canopytower.com. US radar tower converted into a four-storey, twelve-room ecolodge with a genuine commitment to conservation. Simple, functional single rooms with shared bathroom are offered alongside more comfortable en-suite doubles and suites; all have screens, fans and hot water. Guests get a free guided walk each day, with excursions available that also cater to non-birders. Rates (multiday packages offer better deals) include full board, with tasty meals served from the panoramic dining lounge. Minimum two-night stay. $534

MIA camping It is possible to camp at the park headquarters (where they have an ablutions block) or, if you prefer, you can arrange to camp wild along the Sendero de la Plantación or the Camino del Oleoducto; though there are no facilities, several of the available spots are near running water. Per tent $6

Gamboa

Surrounded by the luxuriant vegetation of Parque Nacional Soberanía and bordered by the impressive Río Chagres and Lago Gatún, into which the river spills, the sleepy former Canal Zone town of **GAMBOA** is the portal to many attractions on and off the water, most of which are organized as day-trips from Panama City. For nature lovers and birding enthusiasts in particular, Gamboa provides access to the legendary **Camino del Oleoducto** and the adjacent Rainforest Discovery Centre (see opposite). It is also the departure point for excursions to the scientific research station on **Isla Barro Colorado** (see p.102), for boats offering Pacific-bound partial Canal transits (see box, p.95), fishing trips or wildlife viewing on **Lago Gatún** (see p.102), and for cultural excursions to indigenous **Emberá communities** upriver (see box, p.104). The town is easily accessed by bus and though some activities need organizing in advance, others can be arranged on the spot.

Beyond the activities hosed by the *Gamboa Rainforest Resort* (see p.101), there's little to do in town but soak up the tranquil yesteryear feel, taking in the attractive (and often empty) Canal-era architecture, indulging in a little birdwatching around the wooded fringes or strolling along the Chagres, looking out for iguanas and turtles sunning themselves along the riverbanks and marvelling at the constant procession of container ships.

Brief history

Isolated Gamboa – its only road access via an old single-track bridge shared with the Panama Railroad – was built in 1911 as a settlement for around seven hundred "silver roll" employees and families (see p.297), its population did not increase significantly until the Canal's dredging division relocated here much from Paraíso in 1936. By 1942, Gamboa's residents exceeded 3800, much more than the current population, and the community boasted a cinema and golf course. But once the Panama Canal Authority started to transfer operations to Panama City following the 1977 treaties, services began to close and the town dwindled, although the **golf course** has recently been upgraded (ⓦsummitgolfpanama.com).

ARRIVAL AND INFORMATION
GAMBOA

By bus Gamboa is a 50min bus ride from Panama City. Buses (16 daily: Mon–Fri 5am–11.15pm, Sat & Sun 6am–11.15pm; last bus back to Panama City 9pm) depart from the very far end of the Albrook terminal (by *Niko's Café*). After crossing the bridge into Gamboa, the bus circles the tree-filled park, where you alight for the Sendero del Oleoducto or Rainforest Discovery Centre, before it heads up towards the *Gamboa Rainforest Resort*, where it turns, taking the same route back. Catch it back to Panama City outside the entrance to the dredging division, at the park corner.
By taxi A taxi from Panama City costs around $35 (30min).
ATMs There are two ATMs in Gamboa, one by the entrance to the Canal dredging division by the park, the other at the *Gamboa Rainforest Resort*.

ACCOMMODATION AND EATING

During the week, inexpensive lunches are available from the **fondas** opposite the Canal's dredging division. Otherwise there is a hard-to-locate – ask around – small **shop** at the back of a set of houses on the way to the Sendero del Oleoducto. You could also bring a **picnic**.

Canopy B&B 114a Jadwin Ave ⓣ883 5929, ⓦcanopy tower.com. This beautifully restored two-storey Canal-era house provides five tasteful, airy rooms with a/c, fan and private bathrooms. Common areas are comfortable, and they offer reductions on day-passes to the Canopy Tower (see opposite). A set dinner can be pre-ordered for $24/person. **$154**
Gamboa Rainforest Resort ⓣ314 5000, ⓦgamboa resort.com. This luxury hotel is the best bet for a bite to eat, though you'll be paying tourist prices (around $30 for a full lunch) and the quality of food and service is variable. A lunch buffet is available at the main *Corotú* restaurant, while snacks and cocktails are served at the *Monkey Bar* terrace, a breezy spot with fabulous views across the Chagres. The riverside *Los Lagartos*, whose specialities include fish and ribs, offers splendid opportunities for wildlife viewing. Corotú: daily 6.30am–10.30pm; Monkey Bar: Aug–Oct Mon–Fri 11am–7pm, Nov–July

2

daily 11am–11pm; Los Lagartos: April–July Sat & Sun noon–4pm; Dec–March daily noon–4pm.

Ivan's Bed & Breakfast 111 Jadwin Ave ☎ 314 9436 or ☎ 6981 4583, ✆ gamboaecotours.com. In a delightful old wooden Canal house, this friendly establishment is aimed primarily at birdwatchers, with four simple, comfortable en-suite rooms with fans and hot water. Continental breakfast is included, with other meals on request. Ivan leads birding tours and can help organize other excursions. $100

Mateo's Bed & Breakfast C Humberto Zárate 131a ☎ 6690 9664, ✆ gamboabedandbreakfast.com. You'll get a warm welcome in these simple fan-ventilated cabins with large windows and two single beds (cold water only). Surrounded by tropical vegetation and a well-tended garden, there is plenty of space to indulge in armchair or hammock birdwatching. Excellent value. Use of kitchen or other meals on request. $35

Lago Gatún

Following the damming of the Río Chagres in 1910, the waters took three years to rise, culminating in the formation of **LAGO GATÚN**, at the time the largest artificial lake in the world, covering 425 square kilometres. The lake now provides 33km of the waterway's total 77km length – with the ships following the original course of the Río Chagres, where the lake is at its deepest – and collects and releases the 43 million gallons of water necessary for each vessel to transit the Canal.

The undulating topography ensured that this impressive body of water developed into a place of great beauty, with dozens of peninsulas and tree-topped islands, and a myriad of inlets easing their tentacles into the lush rainforest, all of which are best explored by boat. Favourite destinations are **Isla Barro Colorado** and the archipelago of **Isla Tigre** and **Islas Brujas**. You can't land on the seventeen or so islands, but with a good pair of binoculars you can usually observe from your boat the islands' monkeys cavorting in the trees. Several tour operators include the islands on their wildlife-viewing trips (see p.76) though some, unfortunately, can't resist the urge to feed the monkeys.

Other **wildlife** to look out for, which can easily be spotted while on a fishing trip, includes crocodiles and caimans slithering in the muddy shallows, as well as sloths and snakes entwined round branches. The lake is famous for its prolific peacock bass, and fishermen hanging out at the public dock, before the bridge, will happily take you out for a few hours **angling** for around $70 for the boat.

Isla Barro Colorado

Tours depart from the Smithsonian Tropical Research Institute (STRI) jetty, 1km beyond Gamboa • Tours Tues, Wed & Fri 7.15am–4.10pm, Sat & Sun 8am–4.10pm • $80 including boat transfer from Gamboa and lunch • Book through the STRI (☎ 212 8951, ✆ stri.org) or in person at the STRI's Earl S. Tupper Building (see p.64), or via a tour operator

Isla Barro Colorado (BCI), whose name derives from the dominant reddish clay (*barro colorado*), is home to the most studied patch of tropical forest in the New World. Administered by the Smithsonian Tropical Research Institute (STRI), it draws scientists from all over the world to pore over the sixteen square kilometres of flora and fauna, but can also be visited on a day-long **tour**, which makes for a diverting outing.

After a short **talk**, you set out on a **guided walk**, during which you'll learn about some of the island's 1300-plus plant species and 110-odd species of mammal, more than half of which are bats. A favourite route leads to the "Big Tree", an enormous 500-year-old kapok with a 25m diameter, laden with epiphytes. Although the small island is home to both ocelots and pumas, you're unlikely to see more than their prints in the mud. Much more visible are the vast colonies of leafcutter ants, estimated to chew fifteen percent of all leaves produced in the forest to feed the fungus they eat in their subterranean nests. After **lunch** in the cafeteria, you can watch for wildlife in the immediate vicinity of the research station, where you're likely to see howler monkeys, but you are not allowed back in the forest unaccompanied.

Parque Nacional Chagres

North of Panama City, encompassing large tracts of Colón and Panama provinces, the vast, sprawling rainforested wilderness of **PARQUE NACIONAL CHAGRES** stretches from the northern rain-soaked mountains overlooking the Caribbean to the park's highest peak, **Cerro Jefe**, in the south. The tropical vegetation harbours large but elusive populations of tapirs, endemic salamanders and an abundance of birdlife, including harpy eagles and the rare Tacarcuna bush tanager, and is laced with waterfalls and rivers rich in fish as well as otters, caimans and crocodiles. Hikers are also drawn to the area, particularly by the prospect of following in the steps of the conquistadors along the **Camino Real**, which slices across the western edge of the reserve.

At the heart of the park, the powerful **Río Chagres** and its tributaries – home to several **Emberá and Wounaan villages** that welcome visitors (see box, p.104) – carve their way through rugged terrain. They spill into the elongated **Lago Alajuela** reservoir at the park's southwest corner, built to help regulate the water level in Lago Gatún further downriver.

Supplying 45 percent of the water necessary for the Canal to function and providing all the water for domestic and industrial consumption – as well as electricity through **hydroelectric power** – in Panama City and Colón, the Río Chagres is of vital importance to the country. In order to protect the river and its catchment area, the national park was formed in 1985, its 1296 square kilometres making it one of the country's largest reserves.

Río Chagres and around

Most tourist activities rely on the area's main artery, the **Río Chagres**, be it **whitewater rafting** the cascading torrents of the upper river or more leisurely **kayaking** along the slower, lower stretches, both of which are generally organized as day-trips from Panama City (see p.76). One of the best ways to explore the park is by visiting one of the numerous **Emberá** communities sprinkled along the banks of the Chagres and its tributaries (see box, p.104). The Emberá, together with the closely related Wounaan, have been relocating from the Darién since the late 1960s. Since their traditional means of livelihood – seminomadic subsistence agriculture and hunting – are now largely denied to them thanks to the restrictions of living within a national park, they are being encouraged to make a living from tourism.

As with the neighbouring parks of Camino de Cruces and Soberanía, Parque Nacional Chagres also includes important traces of the country's colonial past, containing a lengthy portion of the **Camino Real**, one of the conquistador mule routes across the isthmus, which skirts the eastern shores of Lago Alajuela. There is currently no clearly marked route but several tour companies offer day- or multiday guided hikes along this historic trail (see p.76).

Cerro Azul

On the southern edge of Parque Nacional Chagres, 40km northeast of Panama City, the area known as **Cerro Azul** is one of two entry points to the park – the other being at Lago Alajuela (see p.105). It's very popular with affluent Panamanians – and increasingly with foreign retirees – attracted by the fresh mountain air and great views (when the mists clear); many have second homes peppered along the fringes of the park boundary. It's not particularly wild, but its highest point, the antenna-covered **Cerro Jefe** (1007m) has an impressive **mirador** and a couple of overgrown **birdwatching trails** near the summit, which is a 4.5km hike from the park office – the warden can give you directions.

2

VISITING AN EMBERÁ COMMUNITY

Just a couple of hours' travel away from Panama City and Colón, the **Emberá village tour** is an established favourite with cruise ships and tour operators (see p.76). Publicity brochures glibly talk about the Emberá "living much as their ancestors did centuries ago" although you don't need to look further than the use of outboard motors, mobile phones and Spanish – not to mention the jeans and T-shirts often donned once the tourists have evaporated – to see that the Emberá are undergoing radical change. Staying **overnight**, or preferably for several nights, affords a better opportunity to interact with villagers and venture deeper into the forest. That said, the day-tours can still offer a fascinating partial snapshot of traditional Emberá life and culture, and there are obvious benefits to communities: income that will afford them greater self-determination, renewed cultural pride and a revival of ancestral skills and traditions.

For a less touristy scene, visit an Emberá community in the **Darién** (see box, p.283), where with far fewer, and smaller tour groups, it's easier to learn about village life without disrupting it.

THE TOUR ITINERARY

Although villages vary in setting and character, excursions are similar. **Prices** ($110–185, not necessarily including the $5 park entry fee) and tour-group sizes vary; even travelling in a small party is no guarantee you won't be cheek by jowl with other tourists once you're in the village, especially during the cruise ship season (Oct–April). Morning pickup (8am–8.30am) is followed by an hour's bus journey to Lago Alajuela, where life-jacketed tourists fan out towards different villages in motorized dugouts. The **boat trip** (30–60min depending on the village location and river water levels) is itself a highlight, gliding through vine-laden forest with raptors wheeling overhead and metallic kingfishers flashing past. At the **villages**, traditional wood-and-thatch buildings sit on stilts, and you'll be greeted by enthusiastic kids and women who form a dazzling collage of fluorescent sarong-like skirts (*uhua*) and multicoloured bead-and-silver-coin necklaces, their hair often adorned with hibiscus flowers.

Activities generally include a village tour, a talk about the traditional Emberá way of life (see box, p.275) and a demonstration of basketry or woodcarving as well as a short walk into the rainforest with a village elder to learn about medicinal plants. A simple lunch precedes traditional dances accompanied by drums, bamboo flutes and maracas, after which tourists can get their bodies painted with jagua dye, frolic with the kids in the river and peruse the finely made crafts on display. Unlike the Guna, the Emberá are fairly comfortable being photographed and general shots of the village (though not inside homes) and dances are allowed, though permission should always be sought from individuals. Most tours pile back into the dugouts at 2.30–3pm for the return trip.

VISITING INDEPENDENTLY

It is possible and cheaper to visit **independently from Panama City** – several of the communities have their own website with mobile phone contact numbers (listed below). They generally charge around $70 per person (for up to two people, less for larger groups) for the day, which is approximately what they receive per tourist from the tour operators. But you'll still need to call in advance to ensure a boat ride. Getting **from Panama City to Puerto de Corotú**, the departure point for most villages on Lago Alajuela, is time-consuming on public transport (2hr 30min) and will probably also require some travel by taxi. Take any bus signed "Transístmica" from the front of Albrook bus terminal, and change at San Miguelito onto a bus bound for La Chibima. After the bus stop, turn into the first road on your right, where you should be able to find a taxi to take you to the port (around $10).

CONTACTS FOR INDEPENDENT TRAVELLERS

Comunidad Drua ☎ 6709 1233 (Ivan, in Spanish) or ☎ 333 2850 (community phone, Panama City – ask for Johnson for English) ⊕ trail2.com/embera. Day-tours cost $90/person, for two people. Scenic location and great river trip.

Comunidad Emberá Quera ☎ 6703 9475, ⊕ emberaquera.net. This almost too perfectly maintained village sits on Río Gatún, so departure is from Puente Río Gatun – a $6 taxi ride from Sabanitas. $70/person for two people, or from $140/person overnight, including all transport, meals and activities.

Comunidad Tusipono Emberá ☎ 6539 7918 (Antonio Tócamo), ⊕ emberatusipono09.blogspot .com. Day-tours only, which can include the community's new butterfly breeding conservation project, and a visit to a waterfall. $45 for two people; $80 including transport from Panama City.

ARRIVAL AND GETTING AROUND	PARQUE NACIONAL CHAGRES

Despite its proximity to Panama City, the reserve's vastness and the lack of tourist development make **access** difficult if you're reliant on public transport. Most tourists visit with a tour operator (see p.76), generally bound for the western end, round **Lago Alajuela**, around 35km north of the capital by road. There, several jetties serve as departure points for kayaking, fishing or rafting excursions, or for visiting an Emberá village or hiking along the Camino Real. Other than die-hard birdwatchers, few tourists head for the **Cerro Azul** entrance.

LAGO ALAJUELA

By bus Take a Colón bus from Albrook bus terminal, getting off at Mini Super Mario along the Transístmica, and walk the remaining 3km.

By boat The jetties at Madden Dam, Nuevo Vigia and Victoriano Lorenzo, further round the lake from the park headquarters (see below), are the embarcation points for visits upriver to Emberá communities (see box opposite).

By car The headquarters at Campo Chagres are about a 40min drive from Panama City, possible in an ordinary car.

CERRO AZUL

By bus Take any transport bound for 24 de Diciembre or Chepo from Albrook terminal, getting off at La Doña Super 99 (just before Xtra); cross the road to the bus terminal at the back of the shopping centre, where minibuses wind their way up to Cerro Azul (6am–6pm; every 30–45min; 30min).

By car Head east along the Corredor Sur from Panama City; 6km past the airport turn-off, you enter the nondescript district of 24 de Diciembre, where Cerro Azul is signposted off to the left, just before Supermercado Xtra. The park office – not the headquarters (see below) – is at the end of the main road.

INFORMATION

The **park headquarters** is at Campo Chagres (Mon–Fri 8am–4pm; no phone), a small headland jutting into Lago Alajuela; there's also a new **visitors' centre** at nearby Nuevo Caimitillo and a **park office** (Mon–Fri 8am–4pm; no phone) at the end of the main road that winds up from the Interamericana, in Cerro Azul. In theory you can pay the $5 park fee at either the HQ or the park office – though the latter may well be unstaffed.

ACCOMMODATION

MIA camping Lago Alajuela and Cerro Azul. Both places offer camping space by the park wardens' office-cum-bunkhouse. You can share their rudimentary bathroom and kitchen facilities, but you'll need to bring your own food. Cerro Azul has running water; Campo Chagres does not.

Both prefer advance notice, since the park wardens may be away. Go to the Áreas Protegidas department at the Ministry of the Environment head office in Panama City (see box, p.42) to make arrangements. 56

Colón

Situated at the Atlantic entrance to the Panama Canal, with a population of around 42,000, **COLÓN** makes it into few holiday brochures; for most Panamanians its name is a byword for poverty, violence and urban decay. Sadly, most visitors come here solely to shop at the **Zona Libre**, or **Free Zone**, a walled enclave on the eastern edge of the city where goods from all over the world can be bought at very low prices – it's the world's second largest duty-free zone after Hong Kong. Vestiges of the city's former grandeur do remain, however, and it's worth exploring (by taxi, for **safety** reasons) for an hour or so before heading out to several tourist destinations within striking distance. The people of Colón, mostly descendants of West Indians who came here to build the Canal, are as warm and friendly as anywhere in the country and just as fond of partying.

Brief history

As work began on the construction of the **Panama Railroad** in 1850, the settlement now known as Colón began to mushroom on a low-lying lump of coral known as **Isla Manzanillo**. Surrounded by mosquito- and sandfly-infested mangrove swamps and lacking a source of fresh water, the location was so unfavourable that the workers initially lived on a brig anchored in the bay rather than on the island itself. American historian H.H. Bancroft, on his arrival in 1851, summed up the general view: "The very ground on which one trod was pregnant with disease, and death was distilled in every breath of air". Nonetheless the

COLÓN

ACCOMMODATION

Hotel Internacional	2
Marina Hotel	3
Radisson	1

EATING

Arrecifes	2
The Dock	3
Nuevo Dos Mares	1

0 — 500 metres

Americans in charge of the railway bewilderingly insisted on establishing the **Atlantic terminal** here, and in 1852 unilaterally named the place **Aspinwall** after one of the railway's owners. This upset the New Grenadan (present-day Colombia and Panama) authorities, who insisted that it be called Colón, after Cristóbal Colón (Christopher Columbus), leading to a long-running dispute that the Colombians finally won by ingeniously instructing the postal services not to deliver letters from the US if addressed to Aspinwall.

The railway brought many immigrants and a degree of prosperity to the town despite the constant threat of yellow fever, malaria and cholera. Since then, wealth – via Canal construction, a spell as a fashionable cruise-ship destination in the 1950s and the success of the Free Zone, founded in 1949 – has come and gone, and Panama's main port predominantly remains a slum city. In the face of extreme **poverty** and soaring unemployment levels, it is little surprise that many have turned to crime, particularly drug and arms trafficking, as a way to survive. It remains to be seen whether the government's ambitious plan to renovate the city centre that was kick-started in 2015 will turn out to be a case of too little too late.

SAFETY IN COLÓN

Although sometimes exaggerated, Colón's reputation throughout the rest of the country for **violent crime** is not undeserved, and if you come here you should exercise extreme caution – mugging, even on the main streets in broad daylight, does happen, with the preferred method a knife discreetly pointed at some point of your anatomy until you hand over the goods, which you should do without fuss. Don't carry anything you can't afford to lose, try and stay in sight of the police on the main streets, and consider hiring a taxi driver (your hotel will recommend one) to take you around, both as a guide and for protection.

2

The city centre

At the entrance to Colón, opposite the train station, is the rather dull **Aspinwall monument**, honouring the American founders of the city and owners of the Panama Railroad. A left turn takes you past the bus terminal, behind which lies the port enclave of **Cristóbal**, then north up dilapidated **Avenida del Frente** until you reach the **New Washington Hotel** (ⓦnewwashingtonhotel.com), which overlooks the Caribbean. Initially constructed in wood around 1870 to house railway engineers, the current concrete and cement-block edifice dates from 1913. It's worth stopping to have a peek at the entrance hall, with its chandeliers and ornate double marble staircase – poignant reminders of Colón's former splendour. To the right of the hotel as you face the sea is the dark-stone Episcopalian **Christ Church by the Sea**, the first Protestant church in Central America, built in the mid-1860s for the railroad workers; it has some delightful stained-glass windows.

Four blocks east along the seafront, a statue of Christ the Redeemer, arms outstretched, faces down Avenida Central, the city's main street, which is lined with monuments. The **Catedral de la Inmaculada Concepción de María**, built between 1929 and 1934 with high, neo-Gothic arches and some attractive stained-glass windows, can be found three blocks west of Avenida Central on Calle 5.

Along the waterfront of the Bahía de Manzanillo, on the eastern side of the city, **Colón 2000**, the cruise-ship terminal, holds a collection of shops and restaurants primarily catering to cruise-ship passengers. The Super 99 has an inexpensive café and an ATM.

ARRIVAL AND INFORMATION   COLÓN

By train The most comfortable way to reach Colón is on the fabulous Panama Canal Railway train, which costs $25 one way (see p.96) to the Atlantic terminus, from where it's a short taxi ride ($1–2) or 10min walk to the bus terminal. If you walk, keep to the left-hand side of the road, hugging the fence, otherwise you are likely to get mugged.

By bus There are regular buses from Panama City (4am–midnight; every 20min; 1hr 45min), though it's worth paying a little extra for the express coaches (every 30min; 1hr 15min). The bus terminal (on the corner of Av del

Frente and C 13) is fairly safe during the day, but avoid arriving after dark.

Destinations Achiote (6.30am–7pm; every 45min; 45min–1hr); Escobal (6.30am & 8am, then every 40min until noon & hourly until 7pm; 45min–1hr); La Guaira, for Isla Grande (9.30am–5.30pm; approx every 2hr; 1hr 40min); Portobelo (Mon–Sat 6am–9pm, Sun 6am–6.30pm; every 30min–1hr; 1hr).

Tourist information The tourist office is on Paseo Washington at Av Central (Mon–Fri 8am–4pm; ☎ 500 0877).

GETTING AROUND

By taxi Though the city centre is compact, you are strongly advised not to wander around but to use licensed yellow taxis or the fancier, pricier tourist taxis (white with a yellow band) wherever possible. Consult your hotel about hiring a reliable driver to do your sightseeing; hourly rates

(approximately $15–20) depend on where you go and the number of passengers.

By car Budget (☎ 441 7161) and Hertz (☎ 321 8312) have car rental offices in Colón 2000; both are closed on Sun.

ACCOMMODATION

Colón's budget options are in areas best avoided but there are sufficient **business hotels**, some of which are quite affordable. It's worth splashing out on a place that has armed security and a restaurant, so you won't have to go out at night.

2

BUILDING THE PANAMA RAILROAD

So often overshadowed by the building of the Panama Canal, the **Panama Railroad** was the world's first transcontinental railway and a phenomenal engineering feat in its own right. Anticipating the Gold Rush, wealthy American businessman William Aspinwall constructed a 76km track linking the Atlantic and Pacific oceans to facilitate trade between New York and the East Coast and rapidly developing California. At a total cost of almost $8 million (six times the original estimate), it became the most expensive track per mile in the world, though the hefty first-class transit fee, $25 in gold, also made it one of the most profitable.

The **human costs** were brutal. During the five years of construction an estimated six thousand to ten thousand workers died, though appallingly records were only kept of the white employees, who constituted a fraction of the workforce. The high death toll enabled the railroad to sustain a grisly sideline in pickling bodies in barrels to sell to hospitals worldwide. Although most of the labourers came from the Caribbean, others migrated from as far as India, Malaysia and Ireland. Despite the constant influx, work occasionally stalled since at any one time only a third of the men, who spent long days up to their waists in swamp, attacked by mosquitoes and disease, were fit enough to wield a shovel.

Little sign of the dreadful human cost remained when the inaugural transit was made in 1855 amid much pomp. As one passenger wrote, "It affords the observant traveller an opportunity of an easy enjoyment and acquaintance with intertropical nature unsurpassed in any part of the world". The same is still true today (see p.96).

Hotel Internacional Av Bolívar at C 12 ☎ 445 2930, ✉ hotelinternacionaldecolon@gmail.com. A good deal on one of the safest streets in the city (all things being relative), within a stone's throw of the bus terminal. Rooms are basic but comfortable, with cable TV and clean bathrooms; there's a (sporadically open) rooftop bar and a reasonable restaurant (closed Sun). **$45**

Marina Hotel Shelter Bay, 28km south ☎ 433 0471, ⊕ marinahotelatshelterbay.com. Though aimed at yachties wanting on-shore pampering these new, simple and nicely appointed rooms above a restaurant (see below) provide a comfortable base from which to explore Fuerte San Lorenzo and the Atlantic side of the Canal. **$154**

★ **Radisson** Paseo Gorgas, C 13, Colón 2000 ☎ 446 2000, ⊕ radisson.com. Probably the best in town, this hotel offers unremarkable business-standard rooms with the usual amenities, plus a spa and casino on site. It's in the cruise-ship terminal, Colón 2000, so be prepared for cruise passengers to be peering over you when you're lounging by the pool. There's a varied buffet spread for breakfast ($16). **$100**

EATING

For **safety** reasons you should eat in or near your hotel, especially in the evening. If you have to go out, take a taxi for all but the shortest journeys.

Arrecifes C 11 and Paseo Gorgas, behind Colón 2000 ☎ 441 9308. Nice terrace overlooking the sea slightly away from the cruise-ship crowds, and with a/c dining too. There's a superior *menú del día* for $7 on weekdays and plenty of seafood dishes. Mon–Sat 11.30am–10pm, Sun 11.30am–8pm.

The Dock Shelter Bay Marina, 28km south ☎ 433 0471, ⊕ shelterbaymarina.com. Lovely bayside setting for sipping a cocktail or enjoying a leisurely lunch on your way back from San Lorenzo (see p.110). The food's nicely presented and freshly prepared – soups and salads, gourmet sandwiches and burgers ($8–10) and succulent flame-grilled seafood options (from $15). Cash only. Daily 7.30am–9.30pm.

Nuevo Dos Mares C 5, between Av Central and Arosemena ☎ 445 4558. Specializing in Caribbean cuisine, this restaurant offers a wide range of tasty fish and seafood (from $11) with coconut rice, fried yuca or *patacones*. Take a taxi and organize a pickup time, or get a takeaway. Mon–Sat 11am–7pm.

Around Colón

Southwest of Colón, a road runs through to the enormous **Gatún Locks**, where you can get up close to gigantic container ships being raised and lowered between sea level and Lago Gatún. Once across the Canal, the road divides: to the right it meanders 22km through dense forest to the evocative ruins of the colonial **Fuerte San Lorenzo**, standing guard at the mouth of the Río Chagres; to the left, it rises above the shoreline of Lago Gatún, offering splendid views across the water and its sprinkling of tree-topped islands before undulating through agricultural land to the rarely visited coastal communities of the **Costa Abajo**. Meanwhile, anyone interested in marine ecology should consider heading to the coast northeast of Colón to visit **Isla Galeta**, where the Smithsonian has a research centre.

Isla Galeta marine research and education centre

Isla Galeta • Tues–Sun 9am–3pm • $5; groups of less than ten people need to pay the guide's fee ($20) • ☎ 212 8191, ⓦ stri.si.edu • No public transport, but a taxi from Colón including wait time will cost around $20, or it's easily accessible by car (see the website)

About 12km northeast of Colón lies **Isla Galeta**, which is actually a headland and home to the Smithsonian's **marine research and education centre**. A far lesser known attraction than Isla Barro Colorado, the centre is more on the scale of Punta Culebra (see p.68), its main attraction a modest boardwalk through the **mangroves**, where crabs and tree snakes can be spotted. There's also an **interpretive centre** and a handful of exhibits, including touch pools and the 15m skeleton of a Bride's whale. Given the cost of a taxi here, it's only worthwhile if you have your own transport.

The Atlantic locks and around

Eight kilometres southwest of Colón, accessible by bus (and a walk) or taxi, are the Canal's **Atlantic locks**. First up are the new mammoth three-chambered **Agua Clara Locks** for the Neopanamax ships, overlooked by a visitors' centre. Beyond lie the famous **Gatún Locks**, the largest and most impressive of the original locks; comprising three sets of double lock chambers, they stretch for 3km – if you include the approach walls – which made them the greatest concrete structure in the world until the Hoover Dam's completion in 1930. Unfortunately, the viewing platform has now been closed, but as you drive across the swing bridge below the locks you are afforded a rare close-up of the tremendous studded steel plate breastplates of the lock's mitre gates – an experience which will be lost once the new **Atlantic Bridge** across the Canal has been completed (due 2018). To your left, a couple of kilometres west along the road after crossing the bridge below the locks is **Gatún Dam**.

Centro de Visitantes de Agua Clara

Lago Gatún, on the eastern side of the new locks • Daily 8am–4pm • $15 • ☎ 443 5727

The **Centro de Visitantes de Agua Clara** overlooks the three new larger lock chambers and the adjacent water-saving basins, with the original Gatún Locks in the background – bring your binoculars. Although you're further from the action than at Miraflores, the elevated position on the side of a hill affords a **panoramic view** of both the locks and Lago Gatún, which you don't get at the other sites. For the steep entry fee, you also get two short videos (in English or Spanish) and access to a very short **interpretive trail** through a patch of rainforest. There's also a snack bar, a tourist-priced restaurant, and lots of shade and seating for picnics.

Gatún Dam

Despite being the longest in the world when it was built, at 2.3km, and a brilliant technical achievement, the earthen **Gatún Dam** is not as visually impressive as it should be, though the curved concrete **spillway** at its centre can be an awe-inspiring sight when the floodgates are opened following heavy rains.

ARRIVAL AND DEPARTURE	**THE ATLANTIC LOCKS AND AROUND**
By bus Catch any Costa Abajo bus from Colón (see p.107). For the Centro de Visitantes de Agua Clara, ask the driver to let you off before you cross the Canal and walk 2.5km up the access road to your left. For the dam, take the first left after the Gatún Locks and walk 2km.	**By taxi** A taxi from Colón will take you to the Agua Clara visitors' centre (around $20, including wait time; around $30 to include the dam). Taxis waiting around the cruise terminal are always more expensive.

Fuerte San Lorenzo

Mouth of the Río Chagres, 13km northwest of Gatún Locks • Daily 8am–4pm • $5

Perched high on a rocky promontory, standing guard over the mouth of the Río Chagres, the well-preserved ruins of **FUERTE SAN LORENZO** bear witness to its importance during Spanish colonial times. Its spectacular location, commanding views of both the brooding river and the glistening Caribbean, coupled with its isolation and forest surroundings, make it a far more evocative place than the more accessible and more visited Portobelo (see p.112). Along with the forts at Portobelo, the place was declared a World Heritage Site in 1980 and is now a popular destination on the cruise-ship circuit, but if you get there early (or visit during the rainy season) you can often have the place to yourself.

The fort is set within the 120-square-kilometre **Área Protegida San Lorenzo**, amid a swathe of secondary forest and swampland, which provide excellent **birdwatching**. Though the only developed trail lies close to the village of Achiote (see opposite), a wander down any of the tracks off the road to the fort with your binoculars is likely to be productive. Some areas are still out of bounds on account of unexploded mines that the US military left behind after deciding it was too expensive to clear – there are warning signs about the dangers but they are not everywhere, so stick to the paths.

Brief history

Construction of the original sea-level earth-and-wood fort began in 1595 to protect loot-laden Spanish boats sailing down the Chagres to Portobelo from attack by foreign vessels. Though Francis Drake failed to take the place in 1596, it fell to one of **Henry Morgan**'s privateers in 1670, enabling Morgan and his band to pass unhindered up the river and destroy Panama City. The fort was rebuilt in coral stone in the 1680s in its present cliff-top location, where it was eventually ruined in 1740 by the British. Although San Lorenzo was rebuilt and further strengthened, the fortifications were never really tested again, though they were used as part of the US military defences in World War II – note the still visible antiaircraft platform next to the tower.

Exploring the fort

As you cross over the **drawbridge** (not the original one) and through the smart, squat stone-and-brick **guardhouse**, the main entrance to the fort, you come out onto the **esplanade**, which offers the best view of the fort and served to collect rainwater that was channelled off into a **water tank** over the parapet in front of you. The vast grassy area below is the **parade ground**, containing the ruined troops' and officers' quarters. Taking the ramp down, follow the wall along to the ruins of the **powder magazine** and the **tower** built into the side of the hill, now scarcely more than a deep hole filled with litter. Though the adjacent wall parapets and cannons have now gone, the view is as it always was, and it's easy to picture watchmen anxiously gazing out towards the horizon for enemy ships. Before climbing back up towards the guardhouse, peer inside some of the many remarkably preserved **vaults** underneath the esplanade, used to store equipment and food and, much later, prisoners. Crossing the drawbridge once more you'll find yourself on the **exterior platform**, with the one surviving sentry box to the left. Here the parapet is still intact, as are the nine **cannons** pointing out towards the putative enemy.

ARRIVAL AND DEPARTURE   FUERTE SAN LORENZO

On a tour With no public transport to San Lorenzo, your best bet is to go on a tour – Ecocircuitos (see p.76) runs day-trips from Panama City (approximately $210), via the Atlantic-side locks.

By taxi A taxi (including waiting time at the fort) from Colón will cost about $70.

By car Renting a car allows you to stop off at the Agua Clara Locks and Gatún Dam on the way, enjoy a bite to eat

at the *Shelter Bay Marina* (see p.108), or explore more of the protected area. Note that to cross the Gatún Locks you can use the swing bridge or get a roll-on roll-off car ferry, just north of the bridge. Once over the Canal, take the well-signposted road straight ahead towards Shelter Bay (formerly the US base Fort Sherman). After crossing the remains of excavations made for the French canal, the road continues for 12km, reaching a checkpoint at the entry to the former fort, where you may need to show ID. The road to San Lorenzo bends off to the left, continuing for another 10km along a tarred road to the fort. You'll come across the park office after a couple of kilometres, where there may be someone to relieve you of your park fee.

Costa Abajo

The area to the west of the Canal is known as the **COSTA ABAJO**, which includes a number of inland communities sandwiched between Lago Gatún and the Caribbean coast as well as a handful of coastal villages. A hinterland in tourist terms, the area will really only appeal to avid birdwatchers and those who want to get off the beaten track.

Two villages here earn a trickle of visitors. **Escobal**, attractively situated on Lago Gatún, is a pleasant spot to engage in a little kayaking, fishing or horseriding while **Achiote**, further inland, is a prime location for birdwatching. The other settlements strung out along the wild, windswept coastline rarely see tourists.

Escobal

The road to the sprawling lakeside fishing village of **ESCOBAL** (and Cuipo beyond) periodically offers glimpses of sparkling Lago Gatún and its many wooded islands through the trees and prolific elephant grass. After about 10km the road divides: to the right it heads back up towards the coast via Achiote; ahead it continues to ethnically diverse Escobal, primarily populated by descendants of Canal labourers and communities displaced by the damming of the Río Chagres. It's an attractive spot to relax; you can engage a boatman to explore the tiny islands and secret inlets on the vast reservoir, or go horseriding or hiking in the forest.

ARRIVAL AND DEPARTURE   ESCOBAL

By bus Buses from Colón marked "Costa Abajo Cuipo" pass through Escobal (6.30am & 8am, then every 40min until noon & hourly until 7pm; 45min–1hr).

ACCOMMODATION AND EATING

Restaurante Doña Nelly Main road by main bus stop ☏ 434 6029. Simple local restaurant with outside seating dishing up decent fried chicken or fish with rice or *patacones* and beans. Daily 7am–8pm.

Sra Raquel de Tuñon's Down the last road on the left when leaving the village ☏ 6638 4912. If you have a tent, head for this lovely camping spot down by the lakeside, where you can enquire about a boatman to take you out on the lake. Facilities are limited – a *rancho* under which to pitch your tent and use of the owner's cold shower. Per tent $13

Achiote

Located in a flat-bottomed valley just outside the Área Protegida San Lorenzo – its five hundred inhabitants primarily survive on livestock rearing and subsistence agriculture, with coffee the main crop – the hamlet of **ACHIOTE** provides a good base for exploring the area. Strung along the main road, backing onto a flower-filled and forested hillside and surrounded by bucolic countryside, it is also home to a community-based ecotourism project in the **Centro El Tucán**, which focuses on **birdwatching** and **hiking** as well as offering a tour of a local **coffee** farm and a **boat trip** on Río Lagarto.

Some 435 recorded bird species are spread across the **Área Protegida San Lorenzo**, which encompasses tracts of mangrove, cativo and palm swamps and vast swathes of other secondary forest types, including some deciduous growth.

Sendero El Trogón

$5 combined entry to trails and the Área Protegida San Lorenzo

The main **birdwatching trail** is the **Sendero El Trogón**, which lies 4km before Achiote, within the park boundary, and was so named on account of the three types of trogon that frequent the area. Although it's a pleasant walk, the birding is often easier (and

2

free) along the more open areas of the main road. If you're willing to dodge the occasional speeding bus or truck, you'll get a chance to see brilliant chestnut-mandibled and keel-billed toucans, blue-headed parrots and beautiful blue cotingas.

ARRIVAL AND DEPARTURE ACHIOTE

By bus From Colón, take the bus bound for Miguel de la Borda (6.30am–7pm, approximately every 45min; 45min–1hr to Achiote; 2hr 30min to Miguel de la Borda) or, more commonly, Río Indio, also confusingly marked "Costa Abajo". The last bus back to Colón passes through Achiote from Miguel de la Borda at around 4pm.

Tours To visit the reserve, you can arrange a guide for hiking or birdwatching (around $30); contact Centro El Tucán (see below), which can also organize homestays and a visit to the local coffee farm ($2) in the harvesting season (Dec–Jan).

ACCOMMODATION AND EATING

La Cascá Main road, towards the far end of the village. This inexpensive community restaurant serves up tasty, filling food – it's often a case of being offered whatever's in the pot that day. Daily 7am–7pm.

Centro El Tucán Main road at the village entrance ☎ 6626 9790 or ☎ 6091 3055, ⍟ centroeltucan.org. The centre has camping space plus two basic dorms (fans

and mosquito screens) with shared cold-water showers and kitchen. They also have a *cabaña* that sleeps up to six people, sharing the communal kitchen. Mobile coverage is intermittent; if you fail to make contact in advance you can usually find someone to let you in if you arrive before nightfall. Camping $5, dorms $12, *cabaña* $50

Piña to Miguel de la Borda

There are regular buses from Colón to Miguel de la Borda, passing through Piña (6.30am–6pm; every 45min; 2hr 30min); boats to Coclé del Norte cost around $15/person, and a road is planned

Beyond Achiote the road rises, twists and turns through pleasantly undulating pastures before reaching the coast at the village of **PIÑA**. Here bracing winds and waves batter the rugged coastline while treacherous currents throw up driftwood and fishing debris on the black-streaked beaches. The coastal road meanders a further 40km through a string of settlements to the village and river of **MIGUEL DE LA BORDA**. Here, the truly adventurous can negotiate passage by boat to the small community of **Coclé del Norte**, which maintains links with the rest of the country via motorized dugout up the river of the same name to Coclecito, followed by a *colectivo* to Penonomé (see pp.140–143). The boats leave infrequently, particularly when the sea is rough (Nov–Feb).

There are currently no **places to stay** along this stretch of coast though, with a little Spanish and perseverance, you can probably find a very basic bunk or hammock for the night, or pay to pitch a tent.

Portobelo

In colonial times the scenically situated town of **PORTOBELO** was the most important settlement on the isthmus after Panama City, since all the plunder from South America passed through here en route for Spain. The main tourist sites are the **ruined fortresses**, remnants of the conquistadors' attempts to safeguard the treasure from the envious grasp of pirates and privateers. A soldier's-eye view across the turquoise bay from the forts' rusting Spanish cannons is one of the most popular postcard images in Panama, conveying the impression of a remote military outpost surrounded by dense vegetation – it therefore comes as a shock to find the forts smack in the middle of an economically deprived modern town, with dilapidated houses propped up against the historical ruins and kids playing football in what was once a parade ground. The town itself is mostly squeezed along a thin strip of land between the main road and the bay, which spills into the Caribbean, and is easily walkable. A half-day provides ample time to explore the colonial relics, leaving you

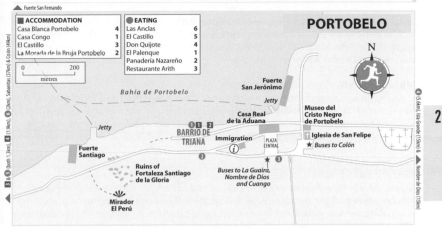

the afternoon to enjoy a nearby beach, a spot of **snorkelling** or **diving**, a **kayaking** session or a **boat trip** around the bay (see box, p.116).

Portobelo gets busy during two famous **festivals** (see box, p.115): the Festival del Nazareño in October and the hugely enjoyable Afro-Colonial Festival de los Diablos y Congos, held biannually in March. Smaller annual celebrations take place along the coast in the weeks leading up to Carnaval.

Note there is no **bank** or ATM in Portobelo or in any of the villages further along the coast, nor any reliable place to get **petrol**. The last ATM and petrol station are by the supermarket in Sabanitas (see p.115).

Brief history

It is said that **Christopher Columbus**, believing himself to be on the verge of death after days on a storm-tossed sea, spotted a beautiful sheltered bay surrounded by forested hills and gratefully exclaimed, "Che porto bello". While the name stuck, the strategic importance of the natural harbour was not truly appreciated until 1585, when it became clear that Nombre de Dios – then the principal Spanish port on the Panama's Caribbean coast – was too exposed and should be relocated to Portobelo. As if to reinforce the point, Sir Francis Drake destroyed Nombre de Dios in 1595 before dying of dysentery – his coffin supposedly lies at the bottom of the ocean at the entrance to the bay, near an islet which bears his name.

In 1597 **San Felipe de Portobelo** was officially founded, prompting further fortification and providing a new target for spoil-hungry **pirates** and privateers, including notorious buccaneer Henry Morgan, who pounced at night in 1668, and squeezed one hundred thousand pesos from the Spanish authorities in exchange for not levelling the place. British naval commander **Sir Edward Vernon**, attacking seventy years later, made no such concession and destroyed the two fortresses. Though new forts were built in the mid-eighteenth century – those still visible today – they were smaller, since Portobelo's commercial importance was already waning as the Spanish had rerouted their ships round Cape Horn. When the Spanish garrison finally abandoned the town in 1821, its 150 years of strategic significance came to an end.

Fuerte Santiago and around

Main road • Open access • Free

Fuerte Santiago is the first fort you encounter from the west before entering the town proper, built in the mid-eighteenth century following the destruction of the original fortifications by the British. The main entrance takes you through a vestibule protected by gun ports to the grassy **parade grounds**, where the ruined walls of the officers' quarters, barracks, kitchen and artillery emplacement are visible. More impressive are the lower and upper **batteries**, their cannons pointing out across the bay.

Mirador El Perú

If you've time, it's worth crossing over the road from Fuerte Santiago for the steep five-minute climb to the **Mirador El Perú**. The mirador is on the site of a watchtower of the former **Fortaleza Santiago de la Gloria**, whose scarcely visible overgrown ruins are now bisected by the main road below.

Fuerte San Fernando

Across the bay from Fuerte Santiago • Open access • Free • Take a water-taxi ($5) from the jetty by Fuerte Santiago

Across the bay from Fuerte Santiago you can make out what little remains of **Fuerte San Fernando** peeking through dense foliage. As with the other forts, many of the original stones were plundered for construction of the Canal. Though smaller than its sibling fort, the scenic spot gives a different perspective on the town.

Casa Real de la Aduana

Plaza Central • Daily 8am–4pm • $5

The small **Plaza Central** in the town centre is dominated by the two-storey coral stone and brick **Casa Real de la Aduana**, built in 1638 to replace an earlier wooden structure. A third of the world's gold, alongside copious other treasures, passed through this customs house for more than a century; there was only one entrance and one exit to reduce fraud and theft and to ensure the Crown got its full royal cut of the spoils. Destroyed in an earthquake in 1882, it underwent a $1 million restoration in 1997 and now houses a small, diverting two-room **museum** containing models of the original forts, costumes and other exhibits including the obligatory pile of cannon balls. It's debatable whether it merits the entrance fee.

Fuerte San Jerónimo

Behind the Casa Real de la Aduana • Open access • Free

Down by the waterside and hemmed in by housing lies **Fuerte San Jerónimo**, the town's largest and most impressive ruin. The former **parade ground** stretches along the eighteen gun emplacements of the lower battery, with nearly all the original rusting cannons intact. It's worth walking along to the high battery, where you can still see the rainwater reservoir, storage rooms for gunpowder and the latrines, and get a great view of the entrance of the bay.

Iglesia de San Felipe

Main road • Daily 6am–6pm • Free

One of the town's major landmarks, and focus of the annual Festival del Nazareño (see box opposite), is the **Iglesia de San Felipe**, which overlooks a bare square. Although construction started in 1606, the church was only completed in 1814, making it the conquistadors' last religious building in Panama, with the bell tower added in 1945. Inside you'll find white walls and a large, carved gilt mahogany altarpiece, though the focus inevitably is on the object of so much devotion, the so-called **Cristo Negro**, a dark-skinned, lifelike statue of Jesus bearing the Cross that peers out from behind a glass casement. Check to see whether the **museum** at the back of the church has reopened; showcasing a splendid collection of luxurious velvet robes donated by wealthy devotees for the Nazareño to wear, it has been awaiting sufficient funding to reopen.

PORTOBELO FESTIVALS

Two very different **festivals** bring this otherwise lethargic town to life, causing traffic to grind to a halt well before the first fort, and streets to heave with people, as you find yourself knee-deep in discarded polystyrene containers, beer cans and chicken bones.

EL FESTIVAL DEL NAZAREÑO

In mid-October, Portobelo bursts into a frenzy of religious fervour and wild partying at the Festival del Nazareño – more commonly dubbed the **Festival del Cristo Negro** (Black Christ Festival) after Panama's most revered religious icon, a striking, dark-skinned Christ with a penetrating gaze and bearing the Cross, which resides in the Iglesia de San Felipe. The effigy's iconic status was cemented in 1821 when it apparently spared the townsfolk from an epidemic that was sweeping the isthmus.

Though the main **procession** occurs on October 21, the build-up begins days before as up to forty thousand pilgrims, including general party-goers and a small number of criminals wanting to atone for their crimes, march into town. Thousands walk the 35km from Sabanitas and a handful hoof it from further afield, many in ankle-length purple robes. Some crawl the last stretch on their hands and knees, urged on by faithful companions wafting incense, rocking miniature shrines in front of their eyes or even pouring hot wax on their backs. To compound the suffering, the pilgrims are frequently overdosing on carbon monoxide from the festival traffic, which weaves in and out of the bodies struggling along the scorching asphalt. Shelters, food stalls and medical posts are set up along the route while the town itself is jam-packed with makeshift casinos, stalls selling religious paraphernalia and food outlets dishing out chicken and rice.

At 8pm an ever-changing cohort of robed men begin to parade the icon, bedecked in a claret robe, round the packed town in a rhythmical swaying, to the accompaniment of brass and drum, followed by the penitents. Once the candlelit litter has been returned to the church around midnight, the pilgrims discard their robes at the entrance as an explosion of fireworks marks the start of a hedonistic feast of drinking, gambling and dancing that continues through the night. **"El Naza"**, as the statue is affectionately known, gets another celebratory town outing on the Wednesday of Holy Week, this time clothed in purple, though the festivities are not quite as grand.

CONGOS AND DEVILS

In the weekends leading up to **Carnaval**, **Congo** societies along the Costa Arriba erupt in colourful explosions of traditional song, dance and satirical play-acting that originated in the sixteenth century among outlawed communities of escaped slaves, known as *cimarrones*. Congregating in mock palaces, each with its king (*Juan de Dios*) and queen (*Mecé*) togged out in extravagant costumes and ludicrously large crowns, they communicate in their own dialect. The general view is that the characters represent a **parody** of the Spanish court, though a more recent interpretation maintains that they refer back to the Kingdom of Konga in Central Africa. The men sport painted faces, conical hats and outlandish tattered clothes, worn inside-out and decorated with everything from empty beer cans to teddy bears; the women wear multicoloured *polleras*, their hair garlanded with flowers, and dance to beating drums and choral chants. In the many comic rituals, "prisoners", including the odd unsuspecting tourist, are taken and released for ransom – a few coins or an offer of a beer will usually do. The celebrations reach their climax on Ash Wednesday with the **Festival de los Diablos**. The ferocious scarlet-and-black devils (representing the evil spirits of the Spanish colonials), who have been previously running amok in frightening masks, brandishing whips, are captured by a posse of angels, who drag them off to be baptized.

Aware of its potential to generate tourist income, the Portobelo authorities support a more formalized biennial **Festival de los Diablos y Congos** in March, which is well worth seeing.

ARRIVAL AND INFORMATION   PORTOBELO

Most people visit Portobelo as a **day-trip** from Panama City, though there is an increasing number of places to stay.

By bus Take any Colón-bound express bus, getting off at the El Rey supermarket at the Sabanitas junction (the last chance to get money from an ATM). Here you can hop on a Portobelo bus (Mon–Sat 6am–9pm, Sun 6am–6.30pm; every 30min–1hr; 1hr). At busy festival or holiday times, it's worth going into Colón itself to make sure of a seat. Return

2

buses to Colón leave from the square in front of the Iglesia de San Felipe (every 30min–1hr); the last bus is at 6.30pm. **Tourist information** The tourist office is in a beautifully restored old merchant's house at the corner where the road forks coming into town (daily 8am–4pm; ☎448 2200); information is limited.

ACCOMMODATION

If you're hitting town for a festival, you will need to make a **reservation** well in advance, or book a homestay through the tourist office (see above). There's nowhere safe to **camp** around the town itself but you could pitch a tent on one of the beaches if you get a boat out there.

Casa Blanca Portobelo La Escucha, north of the main road, 2.5km west of Portobelo, by the police sub-station ☎6989 9218. Lovely waterside spot out of town, with a grassy outdoor area dotted with picnic tables and hammocks – a great place to chill – and an alfresco kitchen barbecue area. The three four-bed dorms and two simple doubles (with a/c) all have shared bathrooms. Bike rental available, with boat trips to come. Breakfast included. Dorms $\overline{\underline{\$18}}$, doubles $\overline{\underline{\$40}}$

Casa Congo Waterfront, west of the Casa Real de la Aduana ☎202 0800, ✉info.casacongo@gmail.com. Four light, modern en-suite rooms filled with local Congo art, plus a/c and fan and a mini-fridge. It's worth splashing out the extra $10 for a room with a private balcony overlooking the bay. $\overline{\underline{\$100}}$

El Castillo 2km west of Portobelo on the main road ☎448 2244, ⊕elcastillopanama.com. This long-standing restaurant (see opposite) now offers hostel accommodation: a dorm and one private room, which share a rudimentary cold-water shower. With no mosquito

---

ACTIVITIES AROUND PORTOBELO

Portobelo may be famed for its forts and festivals, but there are plenty of outdoor activities to keep you occupied.

DIVING AND SNORKELLING

With numerous reefs and scuttled ships in the waters round Portobelo, this is one of the country's top **diving** and **snorkelling** destinations – though you won't get the diversity and quantity of fish that you can find in the Pacific. **Popular dive spots** include a B-45 plane wreck by Drake's Island, where some still hold out hope of uncovering the privateer's sunken lead coffin amid the encrusted coral; the varied marine flora and fauna of the Three Sister Islands; and the labyrinth of canyons off Isla Grande. The two main **scuba companies** are on the main road on the left shortly before you reach Portobelo from the west; both are PADI-certified with good reputations. **Panama Dive Adventure** (☎6747 3297, ⊕dive.com.pa) operates out of *Coco-Plum Eco-Lodge Resort*, offering a two-tank dive for $107 (equipment rental extra), whereas the pricier **Scuba Panama** (☎261 3841, ⊕scubapanama.com; $155), a little further out, includes equipment rental and has its own lodgings.

KAYAKING, HIKING AND BIRDWATCHING

For **kayaking** in the mangroves or **hiking**, **camping** or **birdwatching** in the rainforest, contact Jason (English- and Spanish-speaking) of **Portobelo Adventures** (☎6954 7847, ⊕portobeloadventures.com; or ask at *Coco-Plum*), who charges around $10 per person per hour for most activities (minimum two people).

BOAT TRIPS

You can contract boatmen hanging round the main **jetty** by Fuerte Santiago: a two-hour trip around the bay and up the mouth of the Río Congo will be around $40–50 (one to three people) whereas a drop-off and pickup at **Playa Blanca**, Portobelo's prettiest beach, reachable only by boat, usually costs around $50 per boat.

ACTIVITIES IN RÍO PEDRA

Twenty kilometres west of Portobelo, and 4km up a dirt track along the picturesque Río Piedra valley – 4WD or high-clearance truck necessary – **Panama Outdoor Adventures** (☎6605 8175, ⊕panamaoutdooradventures.com) offers a **nine-line Canopy Tour** ($60), along with **river tubing** ($25) and a day's **horseriding** ($85; lunch extra). You can hike in from the road or arrange a pickup or transport from Panama City, but should contact them at least a day in advance, especially if you want to avoid the tour groups for which they predominantly cater.

nets, and only a fan, you could be in for a hot, itchy night when the wind drops, but the view from the deck, and the mellow vibe, make up for any discomfort. Breakfast included. Dorm $12, double $22

★**La Morada de la Bruja Portobelo** Waterfront west of the Casa Real de la Aduana ☏6528 0679, ⓦlamoradadelabrujaportobelo.com. Striking Congo-themed murals invite you to this welcoming spot, which runs art workshops and has kayaks for rent. They offer three artistically decorated flats (two for six people, one for four), with a shared grassy lawn by the water's edge. $200

EATING

Las Anclas Coco-Plum Eco-Lodge Resort, main road, 2.6km west of town ☏448 2102. Don't let the fun fishy decor distract you from the tasty squid, lobster, crab and the like – try the mixed seafood in coconut milk ($14), washed down with coconut lemonade. Daily 8am–8pm.

El Castillo 2km west of Portobelo on the main road ☏448 2244, ⓦelcastillopanama.com. Get beyond the kitsch pirate-themed exterior, and you've a mellow, rustic over-the-water bar-restaurant, where you can gaze out across the bay while lolling in a hammock and sipping a cocktail. Food is tasty, and portions are generous, and there are some good-value daily specials ($8) among the more expensive dishes (mains from $12); try a Thai or Vietnamese speciality. Mon–Thurs 8am–8pm, Fri & Sat 8am–10pm.

Don Quijote Main road, 6km east of Portobelo at Nuevo Tonosí ☏6697 9793. A large roadside restaurant serving delicious, moderately priced French/Italian cuisine, including home-made pasta and tasty thin-crust pizzas along with an assortment of *parilladas* and Panamanian favourites. Fri–Sun & public hols 9am–8.30pm.

El Palenque Casa Congo, waterfront, west of the Casa Real de la Aduana ☏202 0111. A cheerfully painted Congo-themed interior and an excellent terrace right by the water's edge, offering a small but varied menu, from wraps to substantial seafood dishes (from $8). Part of the Fundación Bahía de Portobelo's local development programme (ⓦfundacionbp.org/es). Daily noon–8pm.

Panadería Nazareño On the main street ☏6957 7088. This bargain bakery is open all day and sells juices for $2, tasty sandwiches from $4, cheap pizzas and a delicious variety of fresh bread. Tues–Sun 7am–9pm.

Restaurante Arith Main road, south side of Plaza Central. Thatched and open-sided with wooden beams draped with fishing nets, this busy place serves breakfasts and lunches of inexpensive staples, including fantastic *patacones*. Daily 8am–7pm.

Parque Nacional de Portobelo

Bordering Parque Nacional Chagres, **PARQUE NACIONAL DE PORTOBELO** covers 360 square kilometres of varied landscape around Portobelo. From Cerro Bruja (979m), the carpet of **rainforest** sweeps down to a 70km wriggle of **coastline**, taking in coral reefs, mangroves – home to crab-eating raccoons – and golden beaches, where four species of **turtle** come to lay their eggs. There are also significant populations of green iguana. Deforestation was already a major concern before the area was declared a park in 1976, but continued surreptitious tree-felling is putting even greater strain on the scarcely protected and highly fragmented natural resources. As yet, no trails or accommodation have been developed, though the lodgings in and around Portobelo and Puerto Lindo usually offer **guided walks** of some description.

Puerto Lindo and around

PUERTO LINDO, a small fishing village en route to Isla Grande, consists of little more than a clutch of simple dwellings strung out along a sheltered, palm-fringed bay, where fishing vessels and yachts bob nonchalantly in the natural harbour. It's become a popular transit point for travellers heading to or from Colombia by sailboat (see box, p.25). The consequent increase in backpacker traffic has meant that – as well as a shop selling basic supplies and a reasonable **restaurant** and bar – there's some inexpensive **accommodation**, offering meals and tours, making Puerto Lindo a fine spot for relaxing. It's also a short hop to the popular island beach of **Isla Mamey** ($6 return by boat) and within easy reach of **Isla Grande** ($10–15 return by boat).

ARRIVAL AND DEPARTURE

By bus The La Guaira bus from Colón (see p.107) passes through Puerto Lindo (10.30am–6.30pm; approximately every 2hr; 1hr 10min; last bus back to Colón passes at

PARQUE NACIONAL DE PORTOBELO

around 1.10pm Mon–Fri, 4.10pm Sat & Sun). If there is sufficient demand, it may detour via Cacique.

ACCOMMODATION AND EATING

Bambu Guest House Overlooking the bay, Puerto Lindo ☎6353 0798, ⓦpanamaguesthouse.com. German-run establishment nestled in a luscious garden overlooking the bay with three stylish en-suite rooms and a communal dining balcony affording great ocean views. Rainforest walks with a local guide can be arranged. A sumptuous breakfast costs $6.50. $60

Casa X Water's edge, by the yacht club, Puerto Lindo. Informal restaurant serving delicious, freshly prepared seafood with a side of salad, *patacones* or rice ($9), to be washed down with a glass of wine. Daily noon–8pm.

Hostal Wunderbar On the left, main road, just after the turn-off to Cacique, Puerto Lindo ☎6700 7790, ⓦhostelwunderbar.com. The traditional Guna cane house has dorm beds, and there are small, individually and cheerily

decorated doubles in a two-storey building. Bag an upstairs room ($15 more, with a/c and satellite TV) opening onto the shared balcony hung with hammocks. There's a communal kitchen, pool table and traditional *cayucos* (dugout canoes) for rent. Breakfast available ($4–6). Dorm $11, doubles $40

Tesoro Verde 3km along the road to Cacique, 600m after the turn-off to the Panamarina ☎6735 0598, ⓦtesoroverdepanama.com. Delightful back-to-nature retreat still being developed by a British couple. It currently has two bamboo "bothies" – open-sided shelters – each with a double bed under a mosquito net, looking out onto the forest teeming with howler monkeys, sloths and other wildlife. Loll in a hammock, go horseriding or birdwatching, or get lost in the amazing hibiscus maze. The introductory rate, quoted here, includes breakfast. $69

Isla Grande

ISLA GRANDE's popularity as a day or weekend getaway for Panamanian urbanites has often led to hyperbolic descriptions of its beaches and overall beauty. In truth, it doesn't measure up to the stunning islands of Guna Yala or Bocas del Toro, but if you're in the area and want a quick shot of Caribbean vibe, a dose of fresh air and a splash in the sea before tucking into Creole cuisine, then Isla Grande will do very nicely. As there is no **ATM** on the island you'll need to bring cash, although most of the accommodation options take credit cards.

The main village

At just 3km long and under 1km wide, with only a couple of paths and no roads, it's easy to orient yourself on the island. Most of its four hundred residents of predominantly Afro-Antillean descent live off fishing and tourism and reside in the **main village**, which is strung out along a coastal footpath running the length of the island. The village jetty, by *Cabañas Jackson*, constitutes the hub of "downtown" Isla Grande, where most accommodation options, bars and restaurants are located and the reggae vibe is at its most pronounced. At weekends in the dry season and peak holiday times, when the island bulges with up to a thousand fun-loving Panamanians, the place is throbbing, often with music blaring from portable stereos (despite the island's attempts to ban them) and the one decent stretch of sand at **La Punta**, on the southwestern tip, is inevitably packed. Apart from a thimble-sized public beach, most of the sand, grass and the shade lies within the confines of the **Hotel Isla Grande**; a $8 pass allows you to use the facilities, including showers, toilets, sun loungers, picnic tables and a volleyball court.

The rest of the island

Behind the village, a steep flight of concrete steps pushes through the dense foliage across the island to a decent **snorkelling beach** (of a now defunct resort). If you don't

EXCURSIONS FROM ISLA GRANDE

A popular **boat trip** from Isla Grande leads you through a mangrove "tunnel of love" to the best local white-sand beach and **snorkelling** destination, **Isla Mamey**. A half-day excursion (about $60 for up to ten people) can be arranged through your hotel or directly with one of the boatmen hanging out at the main jetty – note though, that it's a shorter, cheaper boat ride from Puerto Lindo ($6). **Surfers** should head for Playa Grande ($60 for up to ten) on the mainland, towards Nombre de Dios.

2

fancy the climb, hop in a water-taxi. The island's highest point is crowned by the 85m **lighthouse** built by the French in 1894; though in poor condition, it affords superb panoramic views from the top.

ARRIVAL AND DEPARTURE   ISLA GRANDE

Access to the island is generally from the fishing village of **La Guaira**. Alternatively, boat transport from Puerto Lindo costs $10–15 return.

TO LA GUAIRA

By bus A number of buses make the journey from Colón to La Guaira (9.30am–5.30pm; approximately every 2hr; 1hr 40min) via Sabanitas and Portobelo. The last bus back to Colón usually departs at 1pm (4pm on Sun), but check with the bus driver that these times still hold.

By car Cars can be left by La Guaira dock for free, or in the more secure partially fenced area nearby ($5/day). Either way, don't leave valuables in the vehicle.

FROM LA GUAIRA TO ISLA GRANDE

By water-taxi At La Guaira a water-taxi ($3–5) takes you 200m across the water to the main jetty by *Cabañas Jackson*, which is the unofficial information point – for a little extra you can be taken directly to lodgings further afield.

ACCOMMODATION

There's a reasonable range of basic **accommodation** on the island, none of it particularly cheap, though midweek in low season you can bargain for better rates.

★ **Hotel Sister Moon** Northeastern tip of the island ☏ 6034 6187, ⓦ hotelsistermoon.com. Scattered over the breezy hillside overlooking the island's only surf break, these thatched cabins on stilts (with fans and mosquito screens) offer the island's nicest accommodation – make sure you get a full sea view. Next to the cosy bar-restaurant a small pool and sun deck provide an excellent view of the waves. Rates include a welcome cocktail and there are decent off-peak reductions. Dorms $28, doubles $83

Macondo Hostel 50m from main jetty ⓦ facebook .com/macondo-hostel-isla-grande. The gaudy artwork makes this friendly new hostel unmissable. You've the choice of a mixed dorm, a double room or a family room. There's plenty of chill-out space where you can play board games or pool, or simply mull over tour options. The communal, well-equipped kitchen is spotless. Breakfast included. Dorms $15, doubles $35

EATING

The island's **restaurants** predominantly serve fresh seafood almost straight from the boats, often accompanied by coconut rice or plantain. The opening hours below are for the dry season; you'll be lucky to get anyone to serve you a meal midweek during the rainy season.

El Bucanero Close to La Punta. Relaxed beach bar-restaurant, where you can sit with your toes in the sand at a couple of tables with umbrellas, or under a makeshift awning, or up at the bar. Fairly inexpensive seafood dishes (from $9) are served. Daily 11am–8/9pm.

El Nido del Postre Between the main jetty and La Punta ☏ 448 2061 or ☏ 6550 5587, ⓦ elnidodelpostre .net. The plushest place on the island, with tablecloths, table decorations and a dining area bedecked in artificial lilac flowers. The food – mainly seafood – lives up to the surroundings, being tasty and expensive (mains from around $20). Daily 8am–8pm.

Restaurante Villa Ensueño Villa Ensueno ☏ 448 2964. Built out over the water next to the island's Cristo Negro – a large stone crucifix – this is one of the best places to dine, offering inexpensive delights including *fufú* (fish soup in coconut milk; $8) and lobster. Daily 11am–9pm.

The eastern Costa Arriba to Cuango

For most people the Costa Arriba stops at Portobelo; very few venture much further along the windswept coastline, though bearing right at the fork after Nuevo Tonosí takes you through a string of **surfing beaches** and sparsely populated **villages** – Viento Frío, Palenque and **Miramar** – before terminating at Cuango.

Nombre de Dios

The most compelling of the coastal settlements, **NOMBRE DE DIOS** is famed as the Atlantic terminus for the Camino Real, where in colonial times treasure was transferred from exhausted mules to ships bound for Spain. Apocryphally, the village derived its name from the words of its founder, Diego de Nicuesa, who, desperate to land his starving crew, espied the spot and cried out, "Paremos aquí en el nombre de Dios!" ("Let's stop here in the name of God!"). Sadly no trace remains of the town's historical past, largely thanks to Sir Francis Drake, who razed the place to the ground in 1595, thus persuading the Spanish to move their operation to Portobelo.

Nevertheless, Nombre de Dios is a scenic place to stroll through, situated on the palm-fringed Río Fato, and with a pleasant five-minute meander up to a **mirador** offering a view of the village and the turquoise sea beyond. **Playa Damas**, a short hop away by boat, is the best local beach.

Miramar and around

There's little reason to stop off in **Viento Frío** and **Palenque**, but the forlorn cargo port of **MIRAMAR**, the next village along – and the only place you can (sometimes) get **petrol** – supports a small beachside hotel and a couple of restaurants. At the end of the tarred road lies **Cuango**, with a tangible end-of-the-road feel, though the vast new *Decameron* resort planned on the other side of the river may change all that.

ARRIVAL AND DEPARTURE

THE EASTERN COSTA ARRIBA TO CUANGO

By bus Buses to Cuango from Colón (9am, 11am, 1pm, 3pm & 4.30pm; 2hr 30min) are marked "Costa Arriba–Cuango"; the last return bus departs at 2–3pm. They all stop at Nombre de Dios (1hr 30min) Viento Frío, Palenque and Miramar (2hr 10min) en route. Nine more buses (6am–5.45pm; 1hr 30min) run from Colón to Nombre de Dios.

ACCOMMODATION AND EATING

★**Casita Río Indio** 5min along the Nombre de Dios road from Portobelo after the fork to La Guaira ☎ 6650 6634, ⓦ panamacasitarioindio.wordpress.com. Set well back from the road in verdant surroundings by a stream is a simple wooden *cabaña* with two very rustic rooms at bargain rates, joined more recently by two cosy modern cabins costing an extra $25. The friendly French owners can provide inexpensive breakfast and dinner but you'll need to venture out to the kiosk down the road, or bring supplies, for lunch. Activities such as horseriding, jungle hikes or night outings to look for caimans can be organized. Ask the Nombre de Dios bus to drop you off, or catch a taxi ($10) from Portobelo. $25

Archipiélago de las Perlas

Set in coral-rich crystalline waters in the Golfo de Panamá just a twenty-minute flight southeast of Panama City, the 220 islands and islets that comprise the **ARCHIPIÉLAGO DE LAS PERLAS (Pearl Islands)** were named by Vasco Nuñez de Balboa in 1513 after their once prolific black-lipped pearl oysters. Sprinkled over an area of around 1700 square kilometres, only a handful of islands are inhabited and many remain under-explored.

Currently, the attractive **Isla Contadora** is the only island with a developed tourist infrastructure, though the golden beaches of nearby **Isla Saboga** and the cream-coloured sands of **Isla Viveros** – close to the archipelago's largest island, **Isla del Rey** – are beginning to draw visitors, particularly on good-value day-trips from Panama City (see box, p.122). On the other hand, if you're not on a budget, then consider the wonderful coral and sand of **Isla San José**, only accessible via the exclusive *Hacienda del Mar* (Ⓦhaciendadelmar.net).

In addition to the lure of countless deserted sugar-sand **beaches** and **reefs** teeming with multicoloured fish, a visit to the archipelago between June and October can be rewarded with sightings of humpback **whales** that come to breed. As elsewhere in Panama, high season coincides with the dry season but since the archipelago receives

2

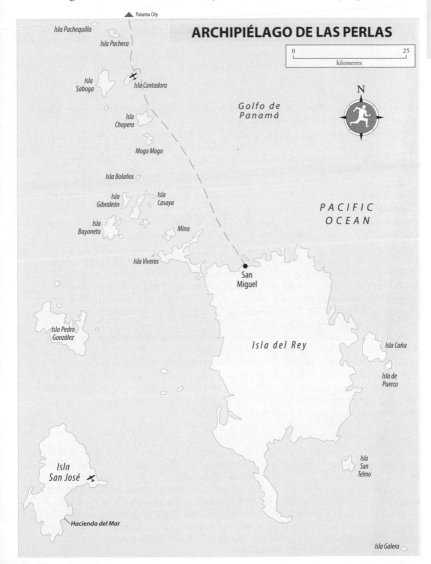

2

DAY-TRIPS TO THE PEARL ISLANDS

The advent of faster and more frequent ferries from Panama City has helped increase the demand for **day-trips** to the Pearl Islands; while you can just book a return ferry passage (from $90 return to Contadora) and pack a picnic, the full-day packages are good value, especially when on special offer ($120–160). These **all-inclusive** rates include the return trip by ferry, a welcome drink, use of hotel or beach club facilities, including towels and umbrellas, and lunch – usually a main dish and a dessert.

The three day-trip **destinations** are: **Contadora**, where the meal deal is usually with *Mar y Oro* on Playa Cacique; the beach club at Playa Encanto on **Isla Saboga**, which additionally includes use of sea-kayaks, stand-up paddleboards and the beach volleyball court; and the most upmarket option, the *BALU Beach Club* on smaller **Isla Viveros**, which is another half-hour boat ride away but has a sparkling infinity pool as well as the sand.

Ferries (see opposite) set off around 7.30am, arriving back in Panama City at around 5.30pm. Day-trips with **Sea Las Perlas** (Ⓦsealasperlas.com), which offers daily tours to Contadora and Saboga but Viveros only as a weekend destination, are the cheaper option, giving a good view of the Canal and causeway. **Ferry Las Perlas** serves all three destinations throughout the year (Wed–Sun; Ⓦferrylasperlas.com).

far less rainfall than the mainland, it's worth considering a visit at other times when prices are lower and beaches less crowded.

Air Panama has **flights** to Isla Contadora and Isla San José. In addition to various day-trips (see box above), Sea Las Perlas (Ⓦsealasperlas.com) provides a **ferry service** from Panama City to Isla del Rey, predominantly for the island's inhabitants (see opposite).

Isla Contadora

Home to the main public airstrip, **ISLA CONTADORA** is by far the most developed and most popular destination in the archipelago. It derives its name from the counting house the conquistadors established on the island to tot up their riches from the pearl trade before shipping them off to Europe. As well as possessing its own fine selection of lovely soft-sand **beaches**, Contadora provides a sound base for **snorkelling** trips to the corals and crystalline waters of neighbouring islands, visits to **seabird colonies** and **whale watching**. Away from the shoreline, the wooded areas provide shelter and food for a surprising array of **wildlife** – deer, agoutis and iguanas can all be spotted here.

Only a handful of families are permanently resident, while workers from nearby Isla Saboga commute daily to service the 180 luxury villas, which remain empty for much of the year. **Inland**, the centre of the island is occupied by a football pitch, which comes alive in late afternoon. South of the pitch there's a small whitewashed church, while the road up the eastern side of the pitch passes one of the island's two **ponds**, on the left. Both ponds are magnets for thirsty wildlife such as magnificent frigatebirds that skim the surface scooping up water at dusk.

The beaches

Playa Larga, on the island's eastern side, provides the longest stretch of sand and the most sheltered swimming in the warmest water; an abandoned ferry is the only eyesore. South round the headland, **Playa de las Suecas** ("Swedish Women's Beach"), Panama's only public nudist beach, is suitably secluded and also offers the island's best snorkelling round the headland towards Playa Larga, where sharks, stingrays and turtles can often be seen. Another few minutes' stroll, skirting the end of the runway, brings you to the island's loveliest swathe of soft, sugary sand, **Playa Cacique**. Backed by lush vegetation, it looks across turquoise waters to Isla Chapera.

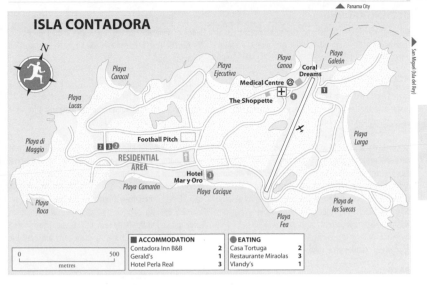

On the northern side of the island the charming sheltered cove of **Playa Ejecutiva** stands out, backed by manicured grass dotted with shady trees. Further east, at the northern end of the airstrip, the *Point Hotel* surveys **Playa Galeón**, where the ferries arrive and depart, and fishermen can take you to Isla Saboga or further afield.

ARRIVAL AND DEPARTURE
ISLA CONTADORA

By ferry Two ferries operate from Panama City. The cheaper, run by Sea Las Perlas (☎ 391 1424, ◍ sealasperlas .com), leaves the Balboa Yacht Club on the Amador Causeway (7.30am, returning 3pm from Playa Galeón; 1hr 30min; $49 one way, $90 return). Tickets are sold online and at their offices in Albrook Mall (8am–7pm). The more expensive and luxurious Ferry Las Perlas (☎ 6200 0080, ◍ ferrylasperlas.com) leaves from the Trump Tower, Punta

Pacífica (7.20am, returning 3.40pm from Playa Galeón; 1hr 30min; $57 one way, $98 return). Tickets are sold online, where you can also choose your seat.
By plane Air Panama flies from Albrook Airport (1 daily Mon–Thurs, Sat & Sun; 2 on Fri; 20min; $52 one way, $94 return), and has an office on Contadora by the airstrip (8am–noon & 2–6pm; ☎ 250 4009).

SLAVES, PIRATES AND PEARLS

Little is known about the **indigenous population** of the archipelago, which was wiped out in the sixteenth century after news of the abundance of **pearls** reached the conquistadors' greedy ears. Needing labour to harvest them, the Spanish brought over African slaves, the ancestors of most of the current population. Over the next few centuries, the maze of islands provided hideouts for pirates plundering Spanish galleons en route from Peru, often with the help of local bands of *cimarrones* (escaped slaves).

The end of Spanish rule did not spell the end of the pearl trade, which thrived until the oyster beds became diseased in the 1930s. Though they have recovered to an extent – pearl fishers still operate from Isla Casaya – there's little chance of a new pearl rivalling the archipelago's most famous find, the pear-shaped Peregrina ("pilgrim"). Plucked in the sixteenth century, it belonged to Spanish and English royalty before ending up with Hollywood legend **Elizabeth Taylor**. Following her death in 2011, it fetched a record $11 million at auction.

Tourism in the islands took off in the 1970s when businessman and diplomat Gabriel Lewis Galindo bought the island for a bargain $30,000. By constructing roads and selling off plots to other wealthy Panamanians, he established Panama's first resort island.

2

GETTING AROUND

By golf cart Most hotels and the dive operator Coral Dreams do a thriving trade in golf cart and ATV rental. Prices vary (starting from $15/2hr or $75/24hr), with lodgings generally offering better rates to their guests. **By taxi** Golf cart taxis can also take you to your destination for around $5.

ACCOMMODATION

There's no such thing as budget **accommodation** on Contadora and most lodgings are overpriced for what they offer. All places listed below have a/c. Off-season midweek rates drop considerably and are often negotiable. **Camping** is frowned upon, though you can easily arrange transport to camp on one of the nearby, uninhabited islands.

★**Contadora Inn B&B** Paseo Urraca ☎6699 4614, ⓦcontadoraislandinn.com. Gorgeous B&B offering excellent service with nine beautifully appointed en-suite rooms spread across two houses. Guests share a spacious kitchen and lounge area that opens out onto a large balcony, backed by luscious forest, with books and games and a cool hammock-strewn *rancho* below. $126

Gerald's Above the airstrip ☎250 4159. Ten well-appointed, comfortable and cool tiled rooms with flatscreen TV, fridge and spacious bathroom. The real treat is the rooftop sun deck with plunge pool and sea views. Breakfast with tasty home-made bread included. $110

Hotel Perla Real Paseo Urraca ☎6982 0962, ⓦperlareal.com. Lovely modern rooms incongruously set round a Spanish colonial-style courtyard with fountain (only running in the rainy season!), strangely juxtaposed with a jacuzzi. Two suites with kitchenette are available ($182). $140

EATING

As with accommodation, **eating** options are limited and supply problems from the capital can mean some dishes are not always available – though the vast stocks of Möet & Chandon in the village shop on the main square look unlikely to run out.

ACTIVITIES ON ISLA CONTADORA

Most organized **activities** on Contadora involve getting on or in water, which your hotel can usually arrange for you. If you're on a day-trip some activities may be included – such as use of kayaks on Saboga – but other activities will need to be booked separately with the operator in advance. Although there's reasonable **snorkelling** off some of Contadora's beaches, there is more to see a little further afield. Snorkelling and **diving** excursions usually take in the islands of **Chapera**, **Mogo Mogo** and the sandy cay of **Boyarena**, which lie in a cluster south of Contadora, but trips sometimes also chug round **Isla Pacheca**, to the north, to see the seabird colonies. Alternatively, you could simply arrange to be dropped at one of the nearby islands, with a tent (or sheet sleeping bag and mosquito net) and supplies, and ask to be picked up a day or two later. On a clear night the stars are truly scintillating.

ACTIVITY OPERATORS

Coral Dreams By the airport ☎6536 1776, ⓦcoral -dreams.com. PADI-certified outfit offering good-value half-day snorkelling ($50 including equipment and soft drinks; minimum four people, maximum sixteen) and diving for both beginners and certified divers ($95 for a two-tank dive). Tourists can be packed rather sardine-like in the boat in the busy summer months, so check on numbers in advance.

Força 3 Playa Ejecutiva ☎6839 8187, ⓦsailing clubpanama.com. Outings with this sailing school are highly recommended; fun and experienced sailing instructors provide sailing or windsurfing lessons, day-trips combining sailing and snorkelling ($250 for the boat for one to three people) or – best of all – a four-day sailing cruise around the islands, cooking over a campfire and camping on deserted beaches (from $550/person for two people).

Pearl Island Paddle Playa Ejecutiva ☎6688 6065, ⓦpearlislandpaddlepanama.com. Stand-up paddle lessons ($120 for 1hr 30min for two people) and guided tours ($40/person for groups), with SUP board rental for more experienced paddlers.

Whale Watching Panama Panama City, no office ☎6758 7600, ⓦwhalewatchingpanama.com. Day-trips from Contadora ($175) in small boats – and even kayaks – around the archipelago to spot migrating humpback whales (July–Oct). Sightings are almost guaranteed. They also offer trips from Panama City ($150/person for a minimum of six people).

Casa Tortuga Paseo Urraca ☎ 6253 6000. Authentic Italian restaurant in a family environment (which may mean sharing a table with other guests). Pricey but tasty set three-course menus cost around $30, with wine on top. Reservations are a must. Wed–Sun 6–10pm.

Restaurante Miraolas Hotel Mar y Oro, Playa Cacique ☎ 250 4067. The grilled seafood, including lobster and crayfish – the house speciality – is usually decent enough (mains from $20), but the delightful breezy cliff-top setting is the real draw. Service is variable. Daily 7am–3pm & 6–10pm.

Vlandy's By Vlandy's supermarket, close to the Air Panama office ☎ 250 4037. Friendly *fonda* on a shady patio overlooking the airstrip, offering a handful of tables. Tuck into a plate of *comida corriente* ($5), usually involving chicken or fish with abundant rice, or have a simple dish from the small à la carte menu, such as pork chops with *patacones* ($6–8). Daily 7am–3pm (lunch noon–3pm).

Isla Saboga

Just across from Contadora lies the slightly larger **Isla Saboga**, whose four hundred inhabitants populate the main village, **Puerto Nuevo**, perched on the hilltop above the main pink-shell beach, spilling off a central paved path. Many villagers commute to Contadora to work; others fish and ferry tourists in their boats or carry out subsistence agriculture. The island's eighteenth-century hilltop **church** – a rare trace of Spanish occupation left in the archipelago – is worth a quick peek before you head across to the delightful **Playa Encanto**, where a new multimillion-dollar resort development has yet to secure its stranglehold.

At low tide, it's an exciting two-hour scramble south over rocks and across coves to the soft salt-and-pepper expanse of the island's premier beach, **Playa Larga**, from where you can hike down a dirt road back to the village in less than thirty minutes.

ARRIVAL AND DEPARTURE   ISLA SABOGA

By boat The daily ferries from Panama City to Isla Contadora (see p.123) will drop off/pick up passengers at Saboga if there is demand; otherwise you will have to get a transfer to/from Contadora. A 10min boat ride from Contadora's Playa Galeón costs $5 if a boat's going your way, but it will cost more for a private charter.

ACCOMMODATION AND EATING

Beyond the expensive, high-quality cuisine available at **Playa Encanto**, there's little culinary enjoyment to be had in any of the village *fondas* on Saboga; value for money, service and quality are all highly variable.

Community house At the top of the steps from the beach, by the police checkpoint; contact Sra Mare (see below). With a superb hilltop location, this community house has four small, basic en-suite rooms, beds with decent mattresses and a shared balcony overlooking the bay. Great value. **$25**

Paula Nani Beach Bar Saboga Playa Encanto ☎ 6693 2002. Catering mainly to middle-class day-trippers from Panama City and chalet residents, this sophisticated raised-deck *rancho* at the back of the beach offers a small selection of delicious mains ($15–17), ranging from burger and chips to succulent seafood, as well as refreshing home-made lemonade, expensive cocktails and superlative sea views. Daily 9am–9pm (kitchen until 5pm).

★ **El Remanso Villa** 30 El Encanto, Playa Encanto ☎ 6575 2447, ⓦ sabogavacations.com. Part of the exclusive *El Encanto* development, above a secluded spot on the beach, peering through trees to the sea. Two lovely studio apartments with fully equipped kitchens ($175) and two spacious rooms, tastefully designed and rich in wood, with all mod cons as well as expansive balconies and easy beach access. The owners also manage other property owners' house lets. Minimum two-night stay. **$150**

Señora Mare's Puerto Nuevo, main street ☎ 6641 0452. The warm Sra Mare offers a handful of clean, simple double and single rooms in the heart of the village, with ceiling fan. **$25**

Central Panama

PANAMA'S HATS

Central Panama

Speeding west along the Interamericana, in a hurry to reach the loftier peaks of Chiriquí or the golden beaches of Bocas, foreign tourists often ignore Central Panama. It might be better known for the arable and cattle farmland that extends over its denuded Pacific lowland slopes, and its peasant farmers who claim varying mixtures of indigenous, African and Hispanic ancestry, but central Panama does possess its own swathes of sand. What's more, strung out along the Pacific coast across the provinces of Panamá and Coclé, the region's beaches are within easy access of Panama City. Central Panama also boasts some impressive mountain scenery harbouring a wealth of wildlife, and a couple of the country's most important archeological sites.

After grinding through the urban sprawl of **La Chorrera**, 40km southwest of Panama City, the **Interamericana** crests at Loma Campana, where you've scarcely time to gasp at the views across the sparkling Golfo de Panamá and the brooding peaks of the Cordillera Central – assuming you dare risk taking your eye off the hair-raising traffic – before it swoops down like a roller coaster onto a narrow alluvial plain hemmed in between the mountains and the Pacific. Fringing these lowlands is a string of **beaches** that lure surf- and sand-loving urbanites in equal measure. While ill-conceived developments have reduced their charm in recent years the accessibility of these beaches – most are less than a ninety-minute bus journey from the capital – is still a draw. Further west lie the towns of **Aguadulce** and **Penonomé**, which have a low-key appeal and provide access to some of the country's main historical attractions, such as the old colonial church at **Natá**, which contains wonderful wooden carvings, and the pre-Columbian remains of **El Caño**, an important ancient ceremonial and burial site.

Yet it is the **mountains** that hold the greatest allure in central Panama, offering a splendid array of hiking and birdwatching opportunities. The volcanic tors of **Parque Nacional Altos de Campana** afford sweeping vistas of the coastline, while the scenic crater town of **El Valle** makes a good base for a range of outdoor activities. Further west, **Parque Nacional Omar Torrijos** offers mist-shrouded peaks and a chance to explore the little-visited rainforested Caribbean slopes north of the continental divide.

Parque Nacional Altos de Campana

Established in 1966 as part of the protection for the canal basin, **PARQUE NACIONAL ALTOS DE CAMPANA** is Panama's oldest national park, and at only 55km from the capital, just off the Interamericana, one of the most accessible. It's often overlooked by tourists, visited only at weekends by enthusiastic birdwatchers or fleeing urbanites in search of cool fresh air and exercise. But the stellar views from the park's summits – the highest, **Cerro Campana**, tops 1000m – make Altos de Campana a worthwhile hiking

PARQUE NACIONAL ALTOS DE CAMPANA

Highlights

❶ Parque Nacional Altos de Campana
Spectacular views greet hikers in this rugged landscape, just an hour from Panama City. **See opposite**

❷ Punta Chame This spit, much loved by kitesurfers and birdwatchers, offers vast stretches of sand on both sides. Perfect for long beach walks, with fabulous views inland and out to sea. **See p.132**

❸ El Valle Lovely crater town filled with flowers and fruit trees, its surroundings home to horseriding, hiking, zip lines and fabled golden frogs. **See p.134**

❹ Parque Nacional Omar Torrijos Hire a local guide to scale the rainforested peaks of this little-explored park or get the binoculars out for a spot of birdwatching. **See p.145**

❺ El Caño While many of the recent finds are still being analyzed, the two open burial chambers still make poignant viewing in this significant pre-Columbian site. **See p.148**

❻ Natá This sleepy town boasts one of the oldest churches in the Americas, with a dazzling white exterior and intricate wooden carvings inside. **See p.148**

HIGHLIGHTS ARE MARKED ON THE MAP ON P.130

day-trip, and its dramatic and singular landscape of craggy tors and lava fields hosts a surprising range of species.

Although the denuded lower western and southern slopes have suffered from deforestation, elsewhere peaks are cloaked in pre-montane and tropical forest. Of the park's 39 **mammal** species, the black-eared opossum is the most numerous, though it'll be tucked up in its den during the day. More likely sightings include two- and three-toed sloths, coatis and Geoffroy's tamarin monkeys. Colourful **birds** also abound, including the striking orange-bellied trogon, rufous motmot and collared aracari. Above all, though, the fifty square kilometres of park is renowned for its 62 **amphibian** and 86 **reptile** species, including the near-extinct golden frog (see box, p.136) in the area's western fringes.

If you've time after exploring the park, head for the village of **CHICÁ**, a few kilometres along the road at the end of the bus route. It makes a pleasant postscript, with bougainvillea-filled gardens and several *fondas* serving traditional **food**.

The trails

The park's network of five interconnecting **trails** is concentrated in the southeastern section. Easily accessible and relatively well demarcated, most are shady strolls, with one a moderately strenuous hike through scenic forest.

Sendero Panamá

The main trail, the flattish **Sendero Panamá** (1.5km), leads to the other trails: first to the moderately strenuous Sendero La Cruz, then *senderos* **Rana Dorada** and **Zamora** – both are only a few hundred metres long. The slightly longer **Sendero Podocarpus** is the next

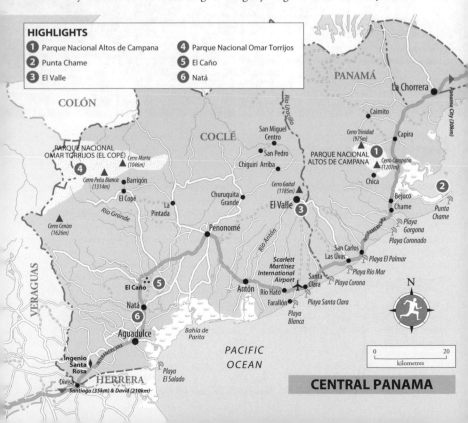

HIGHLIGHTS

1. Parque Nacional Altos de Campana
2. Punta Chame
3. El Valle
4. Parque Nacional Omar Torrijos
5. El Caño
6. Natá

CENTRAL PANAMA

turn-off and worth a detour (see below). The trail eventually peters out; either return the way you came, or turn right to descend a disintegrating asphalt road down to the main road, where you can flag down a bus, or walk back down to the park entrance.

Sendero La Cruz

About 800m along the Sendero Panamá, the **Sendero La Cruz** climbs steeply to the right, through trees dripping with epiphytes. Twenty minutes later the path forks: to the left it climbs to the 1000m domed peak of **Cerro Campana**, the park's highest point, while to the right it descends and then climbs again for another forty minutes, culminating in a giant boulder topped with an enormous cross. Unless you're a proficient rock-climber, follow the trail under the boulder for an easier clamber to the other side. Although at 860m **Cerro La Cruz** is lower than Campana, it affords a slightly better panorama, taking in the meandering Río Chame and the distant Pacific beach resorts, with the rugged ridge of the Cordillera Central disappearing into the distance.

Sendero Podocarpus

The **Sendero Podocarpus** (600m), a loop trail off the Sendero Panamá, takes you through some of Panama's only native conifers of the same name, ending up in the park's campsite at *Refugio Los Pinos*. To return to the Sendero Panamá, turn left at the T-junction below the campsite, then left again once you reach the main path to return the way you came, or right at the second junction to reach the main road.

3

ARRIVAL AND DEPARTURE
PARQUE NACIONAL ALTOS DE CAMPANA

By bus Take any San Carlos, Capira or Chame bus from the Albrook bus terminal to the town of Capira, about 50km west of Panama City. Ask to be dropped off on the Interamericana a few hundred metres after the Shell garage at *Restaurante Lily's*, where minibuses bound for the mountain village of Chicá, via the park, depart (hourly 7am–8pm, returning on the hour; 40min).

By car The park is signposted off the Interamericana to the right 5km beyond Capira. You can leave the car at the park entrance. Follow the path up beside the large house, where a sign marks the trailhead.

INFORMATION AND FEES

MIA office The park office (daily 8am–4pm; ☎254 2848 in Panama City), where you should pay the $5 fee (and may get a map), is on the left-hand side of the road, 4km from the Interamericana turn-off. Unfortunately, it's more than 3km further up the mountainside to the park itself – on the right-hand side, after a sign declaring "No Estoy". You may be able to persuade the bus to wait while you sort out the formalities; if not, you'll have to wait for the next bus, or hike up to the park.

ACCOMMODATION AND EATING

★**Quesos Chela** Interamericana ☎223 7835, ⓦfacebook.com/quesoschela. Stock up with supplies in Capira at one of Panama's gastronomic gems, which makes fresh yoghurt, croissants, *empanadas* and fancy breads, as well as renowned cheeses. Daily 8am–8pm.

Refugio Los Pinos In the park (see above). A pleasant camping spot surrounded by pine trees, about a 30min hike from the trailhead. Facilities are limited to toilets, water and space to make a campfire. Make sure at the MIA office (see above) that the ablutions block is unlocked. $6

The Pacific beaches

Once the Interamericana hits the coastal plain at the western edge of Panama province, roads start to branch off the main artery like blood vessels, feeding the various **beaches** along the Pacific coast. With locations to suit surfers, swimmers and sunbathers, and sand ranging from charcoal grey through tan to pale cream, these beaches have become increasingly **built up** over recent years. The developments – beyond the odd surf spot – primarily cater to weekending capital-dwellers, a few expat communities and Latin Americans on package holidays. Travellers looking for less developed beaches will find offerings in the Azuero, Chiriquí and Bocas with greater appeal.

Punta Chame

The nicest and least built up of the Pacific beaches is **Punta Chame**, which you access by taking the first beach exit as you travel west along the Interamericana. The road travels the length of a 12km sandy spit to a low-key fishing village, where the vast flat beach, strong winds and choppy waters have transformed this otherwise deserted swathe into Panama's **kitesurfing** centre (season Dec–May) – though beware the stingrays at low tide. **Birdwatching** is also good here as the tidal pools and mud flats attract a variety of waders. Looking northwards across the more sheltered **Bay of Chame**, you get lovely views of the mainland.

Playa Gorgona to Playa Río Mar

Playas Gorgona and **Coronado** were once the most fashionable weekend destinations for middle-class residents of Panama City, with beachfront properties overlooking the marbled charcoal sand; Coronado now has a growing expat community. There are two good **surfing spots** here – Playa Malibu in Gorgona and Punta Teta (predictably dubbed "Tits" by surfing gringos), 3km down a dirt road not long after the Coronado exit. The only substantial settlement in the area, 12km on from El Rey, just off the Interamericana, is **SAN CARLOS**, worth noting mainly as a place to buy provisions and catch a bus. The other surfing hot spots in the area lie down two asphalt roads a few kilometres west of San Carlos at **Playa El Palmar** and **Playa Río Mar**. Playa El Palmar hosts one of Panama's longest-established **surf schools**, which specializes in courses for beginners (ⓦpanamasurfschool.com). Non-surfers should continue a further 20km to hit the best beaches on this stretch of coast.

Playa Santa Clara

Although large concrete developments are beginning to encroach, and quad bikes and jet skis roar about the place at weekends, **Playa Santa Clara**, 30km east of Penonomé, is probably the loveliest beach in the area, and you can have it all to yourself midweek. A seemingly endless belt of pale sand lapped by calm waters, it features a number of pleasantly informal bars and restaurants.

Farallón

A few kilometres further along the coast from Playa Santa Clara, at the equally impressive beige swathe of **Farallón (Playa Blanca)**, things are even busier, and the local fishing village is becoming increasingly hemmed in among greedy resorts, condominium complexes and gated retirement communities. Most accommodation can fix up some gentle **horseriding** along the beach or a **boat trip** with one of the local fishermen.

ARRIVAL AND DEPARTURE   THE PACIFIC BEACHES

BY BUS

Buses generally only drop off passengers at the "entrada" (exit) on the Interamericana, from where a 10min stroll or a sweaty 8km hike – depending on the destination – will get you to the beach (taxis are sometimes available).

FROM PANAMA CITY

For Punta Chame Take a Chame-bound bus as far as the Plaza Imperial, Bejuco, just east of the turn-off to Punta Chame (5.30am–9pm; every 20min; 1hr 10min), and transfer to the hourly bus (20min) or take a taxi ($25) for the 12km journey.

For Gorgona Take a San Carlos bus (6am–8.30pm; every 20min; 1hr 20min) alighting at the Gorgona exit, 8km further west of the Punta Chame junction; the beach is within walking distance.

For Coronado Take a San Carlos bus – at the Coronado exit minibuses and taxis ($4–5) will shuttle you to the sand. The highly visible El Rey supermarket, which contains an ATM and is next to a petrol station, marks the turn-off.

For Playa El Palmar and Playa Río Mar Take an Antón or Penonomé bus (5.20am–8pm; every 20min; 1hr 30min); you will probably need to hike the 2km down the road from the Interamericana stop to the beach.

For Santa Clara To get to Santa Clara, 13km west of Playa Corona, take an Antón or Penonomé bus (5.20am–8pm; every 20min; 1hr 40min); taxis are likely to be hanging round the turn-off from the highway, or arrange a pickup in advance.

For Farallón (Playa Blanca) To get to Farallón, 3km west of the Santa Clara exit, take an Antón or Penonomé bus and get off at the turn-off. Walk the 2km or get a taxi ($3–5).

BY PLANE

Scarlett Martínez International Airport – a renovated old military airstrip at Río Hato – has been receiving charter flights of package holidaymakers from Canada and a variety of Latin American countries since it opened in 2014.

ACCOMMODATION

The **accommodation** is as varied as the sand along this stretch of coastline; you can take your pick from a thousand-room all-inclusive resort to a tent on the beach. Our list below runs from the surf-happy eastern stretch, where Playa Coronado offers the best options, westwards towards Santa Clara, which boasts a mega-resort and a hammock and tent spot.

PUNTA CHAME

★**Hostal Casa Amarilla** ☎6032 7743, ⓦhostalcasaamarilla.com. Charming guesthouse set in lush gardens offering a range of accommodation, all beautifully decorated and immaculately maintained, from simple wooden cabins (with shared bathrooms) to larger, more comfortable en-suite lodgings in the main house. Delicious, moderately priced French cuisine tops off the experience (breakfast $8, lunch and dinner around $15). Closed June–Oct. Cabins $35, doubles $77

Nitro City ☎209 2166, ⓦnitrocityresort.com. With a prime beachside location, this family-friendly place is all about action and adrenaline, on land or in the sea, indoors or out. Free activities include volleyball, table tennis, table football and air hockey, while motorcross, wakeboarding, kitesurfing, jet-skiing and SUP – the list is endless – cost extra. Rental and lessons are available for the more energetic options. Slick, modern rooms have large windows and private sea-facing patios. Midweek discounts and day-passes available ($30). $219

PLAYA GORGONA TO PLAYA RÍO MAR

BlueBay Coronado Golf & Beach Resort Av Punta Preita, Playa Coronado ☎240 4444, ⓦbluebayresorts .com. A sprawling, hacienda-style place 1km off the beach in extensive, landscaped grounds. There's plenty to entertain guests: an eighteen-hole golf course, Olympic-sized pool, tennis courts, stables and chocolate massage at the spa, and that's before you've even thought about the

sea. Note that wi-fi in your room costs extra. Very busy at weekends. All-inclusive. $190

El Littoral Av Punta Prieta, Playa Coronado ☎240 1474, ⓦlitoralpanama.com. Classy health-centre-cum-B&B offering yoga, pilates, acupuncture and massage, and with a swimming pool and comfy common areas. $105

PLAYA SANTA CLARA

★**Las Sirenas** ☎6973 7567, ⓦlasirenasdesantaclara .com. Tranquil, fully equipped one- or two-bedroom self-catering cottages (sleeping four or six) located either over the hilltop among the bougainvillea or right on the beach. Add to each a large patio, hammock and BBQ, and you have the nicest lodgings in the area. Midweek reductions. $165

★**Villa Botero By Casa Mojito** C Aviación at C Arroyo ☎6012 7074, ⓦcasamojitopanama.com. A short hop from the beach, this charming B&B offers a couple of beautifully furnished rooms in a colonial-style tiled-roof cottage with all mod cons – wi-fi, flatscreen cable TV, fridge, coffee-maker – overlooking a pool and surrounding garden. Use of a shared stove and BBQ. $143

FARALLÓN

★**Togo B&B** C La Venta. Thoughtfully designed and exquisitely appointed rooms (one with kitchenette) in an airy house within a verdant, tree-filled garden. Living space is shared with the owners though there are plenty of hammocks and shady patio spots for privacy. Additional meals can be ordered. $121

EATING

The large **resorts** take care of the catering and evening entertainment for their guests. Otherwise, there is a sprinkling of local bars and *fondas* amid a handful of restaurants aimed exclusively at tourists and expats, where prices are high. The **opening hours** we quote in our listings are for high season; in the rainy season, hours depend a lot on the weather and some places may shut down completely for a few weeks.

PLAYA GORGONA TO PLAYA RÍO MAR

★**Los Camisones** La Ermita, Km 104 off the Interamericana to the right between San Carlos and Santa Clara ☎993 3622, ⓦloscamisones.com. Its reputation for serving the best seafood in the country

(including paella) has pushed the prices up in recent years, though this Spanish-Panamanian restaurant rarely disappoints. A changing menu using fresh produce is enjoyed in a relaxed large *rancho* in a pleasant garden. Most mains $18–26. Daily 11.30am–10pm.

PLAYA SANTA CLARA

Tortugas Beach Bar and Grill Playa Santa Clara ☎6678 2066. Two-storey, open-sided, breezy bar-restaurant at the back of the beach, with a small beer garden in front, and sun loungers, *ranchos* and umbrellas for rent. They also rent SUP boards, and have showers. Fresh, succulent seafood from $9. Daily 9am–6pm.

Xoko Interamericana, entrance to Santa Clara ☎908 8090. It won't win any architectural awards, and the highway location is hardly conducive to intimate dining, but the cuisine at this highly acclaimed Basque restaurant more than compensates. Specializing in tapas, paella and other seafood dishes, they also do a fine portion of *papas bravas*. Don't be in a hurry to be served, though. Mon–Thurs & Sun noon–9pm, Fri & Sat noon–10pm.

FARÁLLON

La Fogata C Central Arriba ☎908 3975, ⓦlafogatapanama.com. Cosy *rancho* in a garden setting, specializing in Caribbean-Panamanian cooking, with plenty of coconut rice. Try the signature "Sexy lobster special", a veritable seafood orgy of prawn cocktail, lobster, jumbo shrimp, dessert and coffee for $40. Reservations essential at weekends. Daily noon–3pm & 6–10pm.

★**Pipa's Beach Bar** ☎6252 8430, ⓦpipasbeach.com. At the end of the sandy road, past the landmark *Decameron* hotel, this informal bar-restaurant is smack on the sand. The excellent lobster and trimmings will set you back a hefty $30, but you can tuck into other fresh seafood dishes for just over $12. Also rents out *ranchos* ($30/day), sun loungers and umbrellas. Daily 9am–6pm.

3

El Valle

About 100km southwest of Panama City, just beyond San Carlos, a winding road ascends 600m into the cordillera to **EL VALLE**, a small town of around seven thousand inhabitants nestled in the crater of a now-extinct volcano. Undulating hills rise to the south and west, ascending to more dramatic, forested peaks to the north, often shrouded in mist. The picturesque location, cool climate and relative proximity to the capital (90min by car) have made El Valle the holiday-home location of choice for Panama City's elite – a fact which becomes immediately obvious after a quick peek at the immaculately kept gardens and luxury residences down the aptly named **Calle de los Millonarios** (Millionaires' Road). Quiet during the week, the place comes alive at weekends and on public holidays as a stream of 4WDs arrives from the city and the otherwise still roads resound with the sound of clopping hooves or revving quad bikes.

The huge explosion that blew the top off the volcano three million years ago left a vast caldera that over time filled with rainwater. When the crater-lake drained, it left behind a flat layer of rich volcanic soil. Perfect for agricultural production, the fertile earth also nourishes the vast expanses of trimmed lawn, abundant fruit and flower-laden trees, and attendant hummingbirds tucked away down El Valle's side streets, which are central to the place's charm.

The surroundings are instantly impressive. Spectacular stream-filled cloud forests envelop the elevated mountain reserve of **Monumento Natural Cerro Gaital**, which provides first-rate birdwatching, and visitors can also explore the puzzling petroglyphs of **La Piedra Pintada** and the spectacular falls of **Chorro El Macho**. If you enjoy fresh mountain air, meanwhile, there are enough decent hiking, horseriding and cycling opportunities to keep you in El Valle for several days.

The market

Av Central • Daily 7am–6pm

Town life revolves round the daily **market**, which draws the largest crowds at weekends, especially on Sundays, when farmers and artisans pour in to sell fruit, vegetables, flowers and handicrafts. Though small, it's Panama's best-known **craft market** outside the capital; as well as straw hats you'll find a decent range of ceramic figurines, painted wooden trays (*bateas*) and soapstone carvings (mostly by Ngäbe or Buglé artists) alongside Guna *molas* and Emberá or Wounaan basketry.

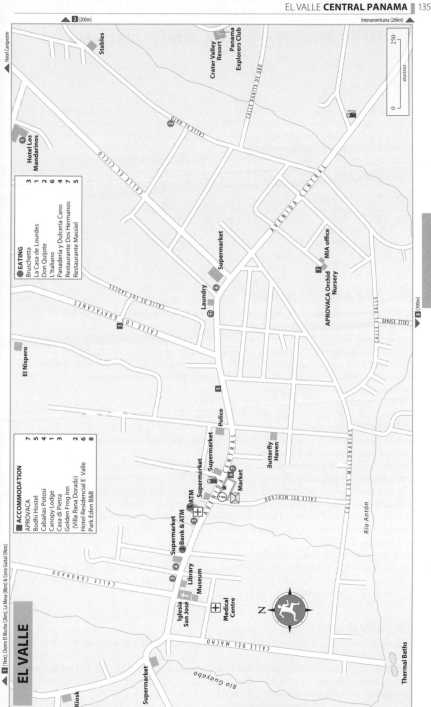

EL VALLE

3

Hotel Campestre

2 (200m)

Interamericana (26km)

Stables

Crater Valley Resort

Panama Explorers Club

CALLE RANITA DE ORO

Hotel Los Mandarinos

CALLE EL HATO

CALLE EL CICLO

AVENIDA CENTRAL

● EATING	
Bruschetta	3
La Casa de Lourdes	1
Don Quijote	2
L'Italiano	6
Panadería y Dulcería Cano	4
Restaurante Dos Hermanos	7
Restaurante Massiel	5

MIA office

APROVACA Orchid Nursery

CALLE EL VALLE

CALLE ESPAVÉ

B (300m)

CALLE DE LOS SAUCES

CALLE LOS GUAYACANES

Laundry

@

Supermarket

El Níspero

Police

Butterfly Haven

CALLE CENTRAL

Supermarket

Market

AVENIDA CENTRAL

CALLE DEL MERCADO

CALLE LOS MILLONARIOS

Río Antón

■ ACCOMMODATION	
APROVACA	7
Bodhi Hostel	5
Cabañas Potosí	4
Canopy Lodge	1
Casa di Pietra	3
Golden Frog Inn (Villa Rana Dorada)	2
Hotel Residencial E Valle	6
Park Edén B&B	8

Supermarket

Bank & ATM

ATM

CALLE CORONADO

Supermarket

Library

Museum

Iglesia San José

Medical Centre

N

CALLE DEL MACHO

Río Guayabo

Supermarket

Kiosk

Thermal Baths

1 (1km), Chorro El Macho (2km), La Mesa (8km) & Cerro Gaital (9km)

La Piedra Pintada (600m)

La Piedra Pintada

4 (500m), Chorro Las Mozas (1km) & La India Dormida (5km)

0   250   metres

3

LA RANA DORADA – PANAMA'S THREATENED GOLDEN FROG

Decorating everything from pre-Columbian talismans to tacky T-shirts and lottery tickets, Panama's **golden frog** (*rana dorada*, *atelopus zeteki*) is one of the country's most enduring cultural icons, associated above all with El Valle since the surrounding cloud forest provides its only known habitat.

In **ancient times** the Guaymí (or Ngäbe) revered the frog, carving ceramic and golden likenesses for jewellery and *huacas* – precious objects buried with chiefs and other prominent citizens – of this symbol of fertility and prosperity. Indeed legend had it that possessing one of these "true toads" in life would ensure good fortune in the afterlife as it would transform into a golden *huaca*. Even today it is believed that a glimpse of this tiny dazzling amphibian in the wild will bring good luck, though a sighting is highly improbable thanks to the deadly **chytrid fungus**, which decimated amphibian populations worldwide and wrought devastation in the area in 2006. The waterborne fungus, which attacks the skin and suffocates the animal, was until recently thought to have wiped out the wild population. You can see captive frogs at El Valle's zoo, **El Nispero** (see below) and, promisingly, there have been recent isolated sightings in the forest. Successful breeding in captivity through the Amphibian Conservation and Rescue Project (Ⓦamphibianrescue .org) in El Nispero, the Smithsonian's amphibian centre in Gamboa and several US zoos, gives hope for their eventual recovery in the wild.

APROVACA Orchid Nursery

Signposted to the left on the way into town from the Interamericana, next to the MIA office • Daily 9am–4pm • $2 • ☎ 983 6472, Ⓦaprovaca.com

The **APROVACA Orchid Nursery** nurtures around five hundred of Panama's twelve hundred orchid species, including the country's rare endemic national flower, the delicate *flor del espíritu santo* – named for the centre of each bloom, which resembles a white dove. The centre aims to reintroduce many of the endemic species – threatened by poaching – back into the wild.

El Nispero

1km north of Av Central • Daily 7am–5pm (EVACC closed on Tues) • $5 • ☎ 983 6142 • Take the turning between the police station and the ATM and follow the rocky unmade road for about 1km

For many, El Valle is synonymous with **golden frogs** (see box above). Your best chance of glimpsing the diminutive amphibians is at the local zoo, **El Nispero**, where they form the proud centrepiece of the impressive Centro de Conservación de Anfibios de El Valle (EVACC for short). Sixteen other threatened native species of frog, toad and salamander have also been collected for study and breeding in captivity, with a view to releasing them back into the wild once the chytrid fungus is no longer a threat.

Unfortunately the rest of the zoo, which started life as a plant nursery and still functions as such, crams 55 species of bird, alongside ocelot, margay, capybara, several types of monkey and even the progeny of Manuel Noriega's tapirs – adopted after the US invasion – into inadequate cages.

Butterfly Haven

Signposted left off Av Central, just before the police station • Jan–Sept & Dec Mon & Wed–Sun 9am–4pm • $5 • ☎ 6062 3131, Ⓦbutterflyhavenpanama.com

The **Butterfly Haven** has a butterfly house with around 250 multicoloured butterflies flitting around as well as a nursery where you can learn all about the life cycle of lepidoptera. There's also a garden café and gift shop.

The museum

Av Central, behind Iglesia San José • Sun 10am–2pm; ask around for access on other days • 50¢

On the south side of the main street, west of the market, protrude the whitewashed twin towers of the small **Iglesia de San José**, behind which is a modest one-room **museum**. Many of the displays – lumps of volcanic rock, household objects and contemporary crafts – are forgettable, but there are some striking polychromatic pre-Columbian ceramics and interesting carved faces.

Thermal baths

End of C del Macho • Daily 8am–5pm • $4; $3 for pot of exfoliating mud • ☎ 6621 3846

In the south of town, the low-key **thermal baths** (*pozos termales*) by Río Antón allegedly have medicinal powers. The weekends are hectic, but the warm cement pool can be a pleasant experience midweek – take your swimming costume. A mud facepack is included in the entry price; an extra $3 gets you a pot of exfoliating, mineral-rich mud (*barro*), which is fun to slather all over your body before rinsing off and taking to the pool.

La Piedra Pintada and Chorro Las Mozas

After crossing the bridge over the Río Guayabo at the west end of Avenida Central, the road forks: a fifteen-minute walk along the central prong leads to a massive petroglyph known as **La Piedra Pintada** ($1.50), where there's no shortage of kids offering to guide you to the giant rock face and attempt to explain the mysterious pre-Columbian carved spirals and anthropomorphic and zoomorphic figures. You can continue up the path that follows the stream, which becomes more of a scramble as it forges through the forest, passing three pretty waterfalls. Ten minutes beyond the third one, to the right, stands the smaller petroglyph of **Piedra El Sapo**, named after the toad-like shape of one of its hieroglyphs, before the path continues up to the mythical ridge of **La India Dormida** (see box, p.138).

The left fork from the bridge leads to the **Chorro Las Mozas** falls; fifteen minutes' stroll from town, it's a popular place for the local youth to splash around, especially at weekends.

Chorro El Macho

Road to Cerro Gaital, 2km northwest of the town centre • Daily 8am–5pm • $5 • Cross the bridge over the Río Guayabo at the west end of Av Central, then take the right-hand fork; alternatively, take the bus to La Mesa from the market (hourly 5am–7pm), which passes the entrance

One of El Valle's most popular excursions is to **Chorro El Macho**, a picturesque 35m **waterfall** set in a private ecological reserve. A short circular path leads to a viewing platform at the base of the falls, where lizards bask on the rocks and hummingbirds dart through the foliage. Though you can't take the plunge here, near the entrance there is a delightful **natural swimming pool** in the river, or you might prefer a guided nature walk with a bilingual guide.

Canopy Adventure

Chorro El Macho • Daily 8am–4pm • Five platforms $65 • ☎ 983 6547

The **Canopy Adventure**, accessed via the park entrance, adds adrenaline to the delightful flora and fauna and its five cables – one taking you across the face of the falls – forms one of El Valle's major attractions. If you're heading for Chiriquí you might want to save your cash to do the more impressive Boquete Tree Trek (see p.187). But here the adventure has the potential to combine thrills with a guided (uphill) hike through the rainforest (around 30min).

3

LA INDIA DORMIDA

The undulating hilltop at the western end of El Valle, known as **La India Dormida**, is believed to be the slumbering silhouette of Flor del Aire, beautiful daughter of Urracá, the indigenous chief famed for his fierce resistance to Spanish colonization. The story goes that while battles were raging, Flor fell in love with one of the conquistadors, unaware that she was admired by Yaraví, the tribe's most courageous warrior. Failing to get Flor's attention, Yaraví took the drastic measure of hurling himself off a mountain in front of the whole village. Understandably distraught, Flor renounced her love for the Spaniard and wandered off into the forested hills, where she eventually died of grief. Her body, it is said, is immortalized in the shape of a mountain. With a great deal of imagination and a little prompting from a local resident, you can usually make out her recumbent form, denuded of trees except for the distinct forested section to the right-hand side, which more clearly resembles the tresses of her hair.

ARRIVAL AND GETTING AROUND   EL VALLE

By bus Buses pull in across from the market on Av Central (also known as Av or C Principal), which acts as the town's unofficial bus terminal. Among them are regular services to and from Panama City (7.30am–7pm; every 20min; 2hr); the last return bus is 4pm. To travel west from El Valle, take a San Carlos minibus (6.30am–6pm; every 30min; 20min) and get off at the "entrada" at Las Uvas, on the Interamericana; here you have to flag down a westbound bus coming from Panama City. The large ones to Santiago or David are almost always full and rarely stop; your best bet is to get a smaller bus to Penonomé (see p.140) and change, though on Fri afternoons or at the start of a public holiday you could be in for a long wait for any bus to have space. There are also infrequent buses (4–5/day) that go to Penonomé via a back route; ask around at the market.

By bike Though most places can be reached on foot, cycling is convenient; bikes can be rented ($3/hr, $15/day) at the central *Hotel Don Pepe*, by the market, or at several other lodgings in the town.

By taxi Taxi rides should not cost more than a couple of dollars to most places, though finding one available is about as easy as locating one of El Valle's fabled golden frogs.

By local minibus During the day, occasional blue minibuses circulate the town and will drop you off wherever you want, while yellow school buses shuttle back and forth from Capirita, at the eastern end of the town to La Pintada to the west (every 30min). Minibuses also head from outside the market up the mountain to La Mesa (5am–7pm; hourly), the access point for Cerro Gaital.

INFORMATION

Tourist information The small, helpful tourist kiosk (daily 8am–4pm; ☎ 983 6474) next to the market may have a map, although the owners of Artesanías Don Pepe (below *Hotel Don Pepe* on Av Central near the market), or the adjacent Davi's Gift Shop, sell better area maps and are excellent sources of local information.

Websites A couple of town websites are kept relatively up to date: ⓦ el-valle-panama.com and ⓦ antonvalley.com.
MIA office Signposted to the left off Av Central on the way into town from the Interamericana (Mon–Fri 8am–4pm; ☎ 983 6411).

ACTIVITIES AND GUIDES

ACTIVITIES

Birdwatching Enthusiasts can join one of the tours offered by the *Canopy Lodge* (see opposite) from $80/person.
Horseriding The long-established stable at El Hato, south of *Hotel Campestre* (☎ 6646 5813), offers horseriding ($15/hr); it's worth paying a few extra dollars for a guide (Spanish-speaking) to accompany you. A popular route, lasting around 4hr, takes you round Cerro Gaital: $60–80/person (for one to two people; cheaper rates for larger groups) including guide.
Panama Explorers Club Crater Valley Resort, C Ranita de Oro and C Caiprita, at the eastern end of town ☎ 983 6942, ⓦ pexclub.com. Organizes a range of outdoor activities in the area, including abseiling (rappelling), kayaking, mountain biking and hiking.

GUIDES

Note that many of the hotels also have their own local guides whom they regularly call on.
Mario Bernal ☎ 231 3811 or ☎ 6693 8213, ✉ mario bernal@gmail.com. An internationally renowned naturalist from El Valle; he is in great demand, so often away on tour. English and Spanish spoken.
Mario Urriola ☎ 6569 2676, ✉ info@panamabirdguide .com. A professional biologist and enthusiastic ornithologist, who also runs the serpentarium. English and Spanish spoken.
Rodolfo Méndez ☎ 6607 5174, ⓦ hotelresidencialelvalle .com/tour. For Spanish-speakers seeking less specialized naturalist expertise, Rodolfo, better known as "El Chacal", has a good general knowledge of the area, and charges modest rates.

ACCOMMODATION

Most of El Valle's accommodation can be found within walking distance of Av Central. **Prices** can be higher than elsewhere in the interior and are often higher at weekends than during the week. Holiday weekends are busy, when a minimum two- or three-night booking may be required.

APROVACA Signposted to the left on the way into town from the Interamericana next to the MIA office ✆ 983 6472, ⓦ aprovaca.com. Small, quiet hostel attached to the orchid nursery (entry included in the room rates). The comfortable en-suite dorm, which has a small kitchen, patio area and laundry facilities, is good value; the spotless en-suite rooms less so. Dorm $\overline{\$13}$, doubles $\overline{\$54}$

★**Bodhi Hostel** Av Central, by Melo ✆ 908 7120, ⓦ bodhihostels.com. This friendly hostel makes the most of its small space: plant-filled patio, with comfy chairs and hammocks; coffee bar; tidy kitchen; bikes for rent ($12/day); and an upstairs cine-lounge for a rainy afternoon. Sleep in a three-tiered bunk on a quality mattress – each with curtain, reading light, fan and charger – or in one of the small private rooms. Pancake breakfast included. Dorm $\overline{\$15}$, doubles $\overline{\$35}$

Cabañas Potosí On the road to Chorro Las Mozas, 1km west of town centre ✆ 983 6181, ⓦ elvallepotosi.com. A welcoming place with four simple, clean concrete rooms (with double and single bed – two with kitchen attached) sharing a long patio facing La India Dormida. The cockerels in the flower-filled grounds should ensure an early start. Camping nearby. Camping per tent $\overline{\$10}$, camping per rented tent $\overline{\$20}$, doubles $\overline{\$59}$

★**Canopy Lodge** On the road to Chorro El Macho ✆ 264 5720, ⓦ canopytower.com. Though not in the canopy, unlike its Gamboa cousin (see p.100), this lodge overlooking the Río Guayabo is superbly situated in a private nature reserve. It's aimed at birders, but the fine surroundings, tasteful furnishings and comfortable common areas make it a fine spot for anyone to unwind. Minimum two-night stay – three nights gets you a free birding tour. All meals included. $\overline{\$544}$

Casa di Pietra 46 C Los Guayacanes ✆ 6675 6901, ⓦ casadipietra.net. Surrounded by greenery and birdlife, this large house boasts a pebbled exterior with more stones than a cobbled street, and contains six suites, each with private balcony. A delightful place to unwind, offering splendid breakfasts (included) and a restaurant supported by an extensive wine cellar. $\overline{\$110}$

★**Golden Frog Inn (Villa Rana Dorada)** C Las Veraneras ✆ 983 6117, ⓦ goldenfroginn.com. You get satisfying views across the crater valley floor from this superior hillside inn, a 20min walk from the town centre. A handful of rooms and suites, some with private verandas and fully equipped kitchens, are set in a nicely landscaped garden with a decent-sized pool, shared kitchen and hammock deck for enjoying the daily happy hour. Breakfast included. Doubles $\overline{\$110}$, suites $\overline{\$149}$

Hotel Residencial El Valle Av Central, by the market ✆ 983 6536, ⓦ hotelresidencialelvalle.com. The unpromising motel-like exterior belies light, clean en-suite

---

HIKING AROUND EL VALLE

Though not as lofty as the peaks of Chiriquí, the mountains encircling El Valle still offer a wealth of **hiking** opportunities. For most hikes you'll need a **guide**, since trails are not well marked and if the mist descends it's easy to lose your way, though on a clear day you can manage **La India Dormida** (see box opposite) without being accompanied. There are several routes up the legendary hill, the most direct being to follow the path up past the Piedra Pintada, hugging the stream until you reach the top. A better circular route heads out past the baseball stadium, bearing left at the next fork. When the road ends, a path off to the right brings you out on the lower part of what is presumed to be Flor's body (see box opposite). Walking north along the deforested ridge, you can enjoy the splendid views across the crater before taking the path down from the "head" that eventually passes the refreshing waterfalls and natural swimming pools near La Piedra Pintada, where you can cool off.

A more challenging hike scales the area's highest peak, the forbidding forest-clad **Cerro Gaital** (1185m), for which you'll need a permit from MiAmbiente ($5) either from the office in town (see opposite), or the one at the northern entrance to the **Monumento Natural Cerro Gaital** reserve near La Mesa, which is often unstaffed. The most direct route involves a steep climb from a path behind *Hotel Los Mandarinos*, for which you'd need a guide. Alternatively, you can labour 7–8km up the road to La Mesa (or take the bus), bearing right at the fork after the village and arriving, a few hundred metres later, at the entrance to the reserve. The orchid-rich area is a haven for **birdwatchers** as well as hikers, harbouring a rainbow of hummingbirds, honeycreepers, toucanets, tanagers and trogons, as well as the elusive black guan. A 2.5km loop trail, Sendero El Convento, winds through cloud forest, circling the summit, with a turn-off to a mirador, which on a clear day affords stellar views down to the coast.

rooms with sizeable windows and cable TV. A great open-sided hammock deck provides views across to the hills. Other benefits include bike rental and use of communal kitchen and laundry service. **$55**

Park Eden B&B C Espavé ☎ 983 6167, ⓦ parkeden.com.

The old-fashioned decor may not be to everyone's taste, but the comforts (microwave, cable TV, coffee-maker, fridge) and fabulous tree-filled grounds together with friendly service make this a sound choice. Birding packages available. **$99**

EATING

There are a variety of places to eat in El Valle, mainly on the main road, but quality is uneven. At **summer weekends**, it pays to eat early before the crowds gather and the kitchens struggle to cope with the influx of people and quality and service can suffer.

Bruschetta Anton Valley Hotel, west end of Av Central ☎ 983 5118. The lively but cosy atmosphere here, together with the moderate prices (salads $9–11; seafood dishes from $13), makes this a popular place. The menu features Panamanian dishes, some international favourites and pseudo-Italian bruschettas. Since there's only a sprinkling of the sought-after patio tables, it's worth booking ahead at weekends. Service can be slow. Daily 7–9.30am & 11.30am–10pm.

La Casa de Lourdes C El Ciclo, tucked behind Hotel Los Mandarinos, 1km north of town ☎ 983 6450, ⓦ lacasadelourdes.info. Lovers of fine dining should make the pilgrimage to the spectacular Tuscan-style villa-restaurant of celebrity chef Lourdes Fábrega de Ward, where inventive gourmet Panamanian cuisine (such as *corvina* in cashew fruit) is served on the elegant poolside terrace. Leave room for an extravagant dessert. Mains from around $26. Reservations a must at weekends. Mon–Sat noon–3pm & 7–9.30pm, Sun noon–9pm.

Don Quijote C El Hato 1 ☎ 983 6210, ⓦ facebook.com /LosGabirros. No-frills Spanish home-cooking – paellas, Spanish omelettes, stews, roasts and tapas – at affordable prices ($8–10). Inexpensive breakfasts too. They're planning to offer budget accommodation, but in the meantime they rent out floor space for visitors with their own sleeping bag ($8). Tues–Sun 8am–10pm.

L'Italiano Av Central ☎ 6682 9398. Eat outside or step inside and feel like you're in an Italian home with all the photos, knick-knacks and checked tablecloths. The two amiable Italian owners make their own pasta ($11–15) and buffalo mozzarella, and there's a fine wine cellar, but prices are quite high. Try the pumpkin ravioli with pesto. Pizzas from around $10. Wed–Sun 11am–10pm.

Panadería y Dulcería Cano Av Central ☎ 983 6420. Just the place to stock up on sticky buns, cakes and bread to keep you going on a hike. Daily 7.30am–8pm.

Restaurante Dos Hermanos Av Central ☎ 983 6201. This great, cheerful café-restaurant is a favourite lunchtime stop for Panamanian families. Tasty traditional mains ($7–13) include top-quality *patacones* with a few Peruvian additions – try the fried *ceviche* – washed down with delicious home-made juices and *batidos*. Daily 7am–10pm.

Restaurante Massiel Av Central, beyond the market ☎ 6214 4480. Friendly, efficient place serving *comida típica* and fast food – chicken with salad, rice and beans is around $6 and hamburger combos go for much the same. It's also a good choice for a breakfast fry-up. Daily 7am–8pm.

Penonomé and eastern Coclé

The capital of the province of Coclé, **PENONOMÉ** was founded by Spanish colonizers in 1581 and briefly served as capital of the isthmus after the destruction of Panamá Viejo. Standing at the geographical centre of Panama (a plaque marks the fact), this bustling market town remains important both as a transit point and for the surrounding land, which is used for fruit, vegetables, rice and maize as well as for pig, poultry and cattle farming. The seventeen thousand inhabitants are predominantly *mestizo*, while some have Arab and Chinese origins. Fittingly for a town that served as a *reducción de Indios* – a place where conquered indigenous groups were forcibly resettled – Penonomé was named after Nomé, a local chieftain cruelly betrayed and executed.

Though a provincial capital and major agricultural centre, Penonomé is surprisingly small, with a very rural feel, with just a couple of modest sights and a pretty river within walking distance. Its aquatic celebrations for **Carnaval** are a real crowd-puller (see opposite), and it makes a decent base for visiting places of interest nearby. Chief among them are the tranquil village of **La Pintada**, famed for its finely woven **sombreros**, and the scenic mountains to the north, including **Chiguirí Arriba**, with its hiking trails and spectacular views and the vibrant Cucuá community of San Miguel

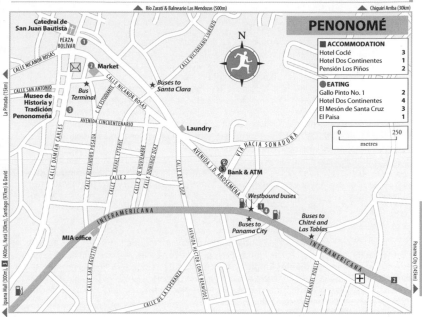

Centro. Topping the mist-swathed peaks to the northwest, **Parque Nacional Omar Torrijos** is a treat for birdwatchers and hikers.

Plaza Bolívar and around

The town's main drag, Avenida J.D. Arosemena (also known as Vía Central), runs a few hundred metres from the Interamericana to the pleasant **Plaza Bolívar** (also known as Plaza 8 de Diciembre). Featuring a statue of Simón Bolívar, the square is flanked by government buildings and the **Catedral de San Juan Bautista**, where the early morning or evening light projects dancing rainbows of colours through the new stained-glass windows. East of the cathedral, a small *plazuela* features monuments to Penonomé's glitterati, including a bust of **Victoriano Lorenzo**, a local nationalist hero who was eventually tricked into capture and executed by firing squad (see p.296).

Museo de Historia y Tradición Penonomeña

C San Antonio • Tues–Sun 9am–4pm • $1 • ☏ 997 8490

Located in quiet San Antonio, the oldest part of town, the **Museo de Historia y Tradición Penonomeña** occupies a tiled blue-and-white *quincha* (wattle and daub) building and contains a modest collection of pre-Columbian ceramics, colonial religious art and period furniture.

Balneario Las Mendozas

If the heat gets too much, take a five-minute walk northeast out of town to the **Balneario Las Mendozas**, a popular swimming area in the Río Zaratí – this is the location of the aquatic parade at Carnaval, when the floats literally float down the river. Though it's a party place at weekends and during holidays, you can enjoy a quieter dip here at other times, or upstream at **Las Tres Peñas**, a more attractive pool.

3

FESTIVAL DEL TORO GUAPO

The small agricultural town of **Antón**, just off the Interamericana almost midway between Farallón and Penonomé, really only registers on the tourist radar once a year, during the festival of **Toro Guapo** ("Fierce Bull") in mid-October, when the pleasant colonial square and whitewashed church are transformed by hordes of visitors.

The fun-filled five-day extravaganza takes its name and much of its action from the cattle farming that has defined the area for centuries and is well worth sampling. Alongside the usual array of folkloric dancing, colourful street parades, beauty pageants and progressively more drunken revelry are **toros** – men who cavort around the streets, charging at all and sundry. They dress in fantastic costumes draped over wooden or bamboo frames, topped with a bull's head adorned with ribbons and mirrors.

Many of the surrounding villages produce such a beast, with the creativity of the costume and acrobatic skills of the wearer a source of local pride, to be displayed during the parade on the final morning. After being blessed in the church, the bulls are led round the town as they playfully harass the *pollera*-swishing dancers, accompanied by bands of drummers. Listen out among the beats for the distinctive chime of the *almirez* – a bell-shaped bronze mortar of Afro-Colonial origin that pharmacists once used to grind their medicinal herbs, and is now a musical instrument unique to Antón.

Other festival highlights include **water fights** (*mojaderas*), competitions testing traditional **rural skills** such as carrying firewood, peeling coconuts and milking a cow, and dancing by extravagantly dressed **diablos limpios**, or "clean devils" (see box, p.163). Strangest of all is the **cutarras**, when a poor cow is wrestled to the ground by several farmers, often the worse for wear, who then struggle to fix sandals (*cutarras*) over the hooves, recalling an old trick of cattle rustlers attempting to hide the telltale hoof prints.

ARRIVAL AND ACCOMMODATION

By bus Antón is well served by bus from Panama City (5.20am–8pm; every 20min; 2hr), especially as additional buses are laid on during the festival.

Hotel Rivera Interamericana ☏ 987 2245, ⓦ hotelrivera-panama.com. Well-maintained a/c rooms with cable TV, and a pond-sized pool. $39

ARRIVAL AND INFORMATION

PENONOMÉ

BY BUS

From/to Panama City Buses from Panama City (4.50am–10.45pm; every 20min; 2hr) pull in at the "bus terminal", which comprises a couple of streets by the market, just southeast of the main square. Through buses also drop passengers off at the Interamericana turn-off (*entrada*) into town, where you can catch other long-distance buses. From the junction it's a 10min walk to the area where the local buses leave. Transport leaves for Panama City from the south side of the Interamericana opposite the *Hotel Dos Continentes* (4.45am–10.45pm; every 20–30min; 2hr).

Westbound buses The large buses to Santiago, Chitré and Las Tablas pull in for a pit stop at the *Restaurante Universal*, just east of the *Hotel y Suites Guacamaya*; David buses rarely stop since they're usually full. Other westbound transport picks up passengers at the petrol station at the Interamericana junction with Av J.D. Arosemena.

BY MINIBUS

Regular minibuses for the beachside resort of Santa Clara leave from J.D. Arosemena at the junction with C Victoriano Lorenzo; all other minibuses can be located around the marketplace.

Destinations Aguadulce (5am–7/8pm; hourly; 1hr); Chiguirí Arriba (6am, 9am then every 60–90min until 6.30pm; 1hr 15min); El Copé (6am–7pm; every 20min; 1hr); La Pintada (6am–8pm; every 10min; 20min); San Miguel Centro (infrequently; 1hr 30min).

INFORMATION

MIA office The regional MIA office (Mon–Fri 8am–4pm; ☏ 997 7538) is on the Interamericana at the junction with C San Agustín. Call in if you want to book accommodation for Parque Nacional Omar Torrijos.

ACCOMMODATION

All the accommodation options reviewed here are suitably motel-like, with midweek **reductions**.

Hotel Coclé Interamericana, Iguana Mall, west of Av J.D. Arosemena ☏ 908 5039, ⓦ hotelcocle.com. Bland

business hotel offering the highest level of comfort in town: modern rooms with large beds, room service, safe, large flatscreen TV and laundry service. Plus there's a business centre, gym, pool and bar-restaurant. Buffet breakfast included. **$77**

Hotel Dos Continentes Interamericana, at the junction with Av J.D. Arosemena ☎997 9326, ⒲hoteldoscontinentes.net. Long-standing labyrinth of

rather faded en-suite rooms with decent beds and noisy a/c units, offering reasonable value nevertheless. **$40**

Pensión Los Piños Interamericana, 200m east of Av J.D. Arosemena ☎997 9518. Easily missable, squat building offering eleven cheap basic rooms with bathroom, a/c & cable TV. **$25**

EATING

Inexpensive places serving **traditional food** are dotted along the main street and around the market, with more varied cuisine served in the **hotel restaurants**.

Gallo Pinto No. 1 C Nicanor Rosas. One of several in town in this local chain, which offers *comida típica* for $3–4 in all its outlets; you can't beat this branch for people-watching, on the corner overlooking the market. Daily 6am–8pm.

Hotel Dos Continentes Interamericana, at the junction with Av J.D. Arosemena ☎997 9325. The glass-fronted hotel restaurant is justifiably popular, serving a good range of international dishes and Panamanian staples. Breakfasts are excellent. Daily 6.30am–10pm.

El Mesón de Santa Cruz Paseo Andaluz, off C Damian

Cortés ☎908 5311. Delightful restaurant in a converted church, with a spacious courtyard decorated with artwork laden with religious motifs. Specializing in Panamanian, Chifa (Chinese-Peruvian) and Spanish dishes, it offers plenty of choice and the quality is good. Don't miss the sangria. Mains from around $16. Daily 11am–10pm.

El Paisa Av J.D. Arosemena, near Plaza Bolívar. Bakery with a couple of stand-up tables and some outdoor seating. Good for a cup of coffee or a fruit juice and a sticky bun. Daily 6am–9.30pm.

La Pintada

Aficionados of **Panama's hats** – as opposed to Panama hats, which are made in Ecuador – should consider making a detour out to the village of **LA PINTADA**, 15km northwest of Penonomé in the foothills of the cordillera, which is famed for its high-quality palm-woven *sombrero pintado* or "*pintao*" (see box below). It is a major and expanding business in the village and surrounding area, involving several thousand individuals. The **Mercado de Artesanías La Pintada** (daily 9am–4pm), which displays the crafts of around a hundred local families, sells a wide range of hats in addition to decorated gourds, soapstone carvings, pots and various knick-knacks, though finding the place open can be tricky, especially in the rainy season. Not so with master hat-maker Señor Quirós, next door, who lives at the back of his shop, **Artesanías Reinaldo Quirós** (daily 8.30am–4pm; ☎6963 0945), and also has a good collection. Both are on the left-hand side of the football pitch and are easy to spot.

PANAMA'S HAT – THE SOMBRERO PINTADO

Though not as famous nor as sought after as its Ecuadorian cousins, Panama's own straw hats are growing in reputation. Ubiquitous in rural Panama, worn by men and women, both as everyday work attire and a luxury accessory, they vary in style according to province and function. But while the hats have their origins in indigenous societies, Coclé's **sombrero pintado** or *pintao* ("painted hat"), which takes its name from the black and white design, has become the most popular and emblematic.

Quality (and therefore price) is principally determined by the number of **rings** (*vueltas*), but takes into consideration the consistency and fineness of the weave. A coarse seven-ring weave takes a week to make and costs around $20–30 whereas a 22-ring *fino* usually requires four to six weeks and can sell for more than $700. The cost may seem high, but immense and skilled labour is involved. Once cut, the fibres are stripped from the leaves and cooked to be made pliable before being dried and bleached in the sun. For a high-quality *sombrero pintado*, the finest fibres are culled from bellota alongside coarser junco fibres, naturally dyed by being boiled with chisná leaves and buried in earth for several days, to form the distinctive black rings, while fine threads of sisal (*pita*) are used to stitch everything together.

Another place of potential interest is the local **cigar factory**, Cigarros Joyas de Panamá (Mon–Sat 7am–5pm; ☎6660 8935, ⓦfacebook.com/joyasde.panama), garnering an international reputation for its hand-rolled organic Cuban-seed-tobacco cigars. Drop by and witness the dexterity with which workers roll up to six hundred cigars a day. Single or boxed cigars can be bought on the spot.

ARRIVAL AND DEPARTURE   LA PINTADA

By minibus Minibuses leave Penonomé for La Pintada (6am–8pm; every 10–15min; 20min) from behind the market. Return buses run to a similar timetable.

ACCOMMODATION AND EATING

★**La Pintada River Inn** 4km north of La Pintada ☎6519 7848, ⓦlapintadainn.com. If you'd like a base up in the hills, head for this new eight-room B&B in a lovely location beyond La Pintada and accessible by bus. It has a sparkling pool and pleasant woodland walk down to a river, where you can bathe; you could also cross the river and hike further into the forest. With advance notice you can order the *cena del día* ($12.50) to enjoy in the lovely *bohío*. $75

Chiguirí Arriba and Churuquita Grande

From the market area in Penonomé, *chivas* head off through the surrounding cultivated fields to villages scattered in the folds of the cool, forested mountains that rise to the north. **CHIGUIRÍ ARRIBA**, 30km to the northeast, makes an easy day-trip, with plenty of good hiking trails, spectacular views across forested limestone hummocks and a 30m waterfall, **Cascada Tavida** ($5 entry) within *Villa Tavida*'s private reserve (see opposite). More adventurous trips can be organized across the mountains to El Valle, or over to the Caribbean rainforests; contact *Villa Tavida* for the name of a reliable local guide.

If you're in the area in late January, it's worth dropping by the village of **CHURUQUITA GRANDE**, halfway between Penonomé and Chiguirí Arriba, for the citrus-filled **Festival de la Naranja**, to marvel at the elaborate and inventive wood-and-thatch displays overflowing with local produce, all vying for the prize of best stall.

LOS CUCUÁS DE SAN MIGUEL CENTRO

San Miguel Centro, 35km northeast of Penonomé, is home to the **Cucuá** community, who are famed for their devil dance conducted in elaborate, cream-coloured, pyjama-like costumes made from cucuá bark, painted with geometric shapes using natural dyes and topped with a fanciful deer mask complete with real antlers and a peccary's jawbone. As with other devil dances, it was originally associated with Corpus Christi celebrations; at one time in danger of dying out, it is now regularly performed at folk festivals across Panama. The dance is the central attraction of the annual **Festival de los Cucuás**, which takes place in March in San Miguel Centro. The bark "material" used for the costumes is beaten against a tree until smooth, then washed in soap and hot water before being laid out to dry. Such has been the demand for the costumes in recent years (they can sell for around $500) that the cucuá tree has become endangered, prompting a recent reforestation programme.

Descended from the Guaymí, like the Ngäbe and Buglé, and originally from Veraguas, the Cucuás fled the Spanish colonizers centuries ago to settle in the mountains of Coclé. These days they make a living primarily from coffee cultivation and the sale of *artesanías*; the latter, along with the devil dance, forms a major part of a community-based **ecotourism** project aimed at preserving and promoting Cucuá culture.

ARRIVAL AND ACCOMMODATION

By bus *Chivas* for San Miguel Centro (1hr 30min) leave infrequently from Penonomé bus terminal (see p.142). **San Miguel Centro homestays** Simple homestay lodging is offered by the eco-community project for a modest fee; extra is charged for a performance by the dance troupe. To organize a visit, ask around the market in Penonomé (see p.142), where members of the Cucuá community often sell their crafts.

ARRIVAL AND DEPARTURE

By bus Buses leave Penonomé by the market (6am, 9am then every 60–90min until 6.30pm; 1hr 15min) for Chiguirí Arriba, via Churuquita Grande.

By car An ordinary saloon car is fine as far as Chiguirí

CHIGUIRÍ ARRIBA AND CHURUQUITA GRANDE

Arriba, and will reach *Villa Tavida* (a 15min drive from the main road) unless it's very wet. Otherwise, it's a 1hr walk from the turn-off.

ACCOMMODATION

★**Villa Távida Lodge & Spa** Chiguirí Arriba, 28km northeast of Penonomé ✆ 6485 0505, ✆ villatavida .com. Set in the Reserva Privada Tavida, this delightful lodge offers six spacious, light double and family rooms (sleeping two to six). All have cable TV and a/c; four have private balconies with a hammock to admire the wonderful forest views. Day-visitors are welcome to enjoy the birdwatching trails and dine at the moderately priced restaurant (whole grilled fish and sides for around $16). The new camping area gets you even closer to nature:

electricity and cold-water showers are available, and mattresses are provided in the tents, but you'll need to bring your own bedding. There's a spa with sauna, offering massages and other treatments ($25–80). You can also organize a local guide here (with advance notice) if you want to hike further afield. Breakfast included in room price (not for campers). Restaurant daily 8am–6pm for visitors, daily 8am–8pm for residents. Camping/tent **$15**, camping/rented tent **$25**, doubles **$150**

3

Parque Nacional Omar Torrijos

PARQUE NACIONAL OMAR TORRIJOS may be tricky to get to, but this little-visited, 250-square-kilometre protected carpet of lush forest astride the continental divide is well worth the trip. Its full name, **Parque Nacional General de División Omar Torrijos Herrera**, was given on its formation in 1986 in remembrance of Panama's flamboyant populist leader, whose plane mysteriously crashed into one of the area's highest peaks, Cerro Martha, in 1981. These days it is more usually referred to as "Parque Omar Torrijos" or "El Copé" after the nearby village. Averaging 20°C in the cloud-forested peaks of the Cordillera Central, the canopy cascades down to the more moist vegetation of the Caribbean side, where temperatures average 25°C and the area receives 4m of rainfall annually.

There's some fine **wildlife**: tapirs, peccaries and all five of Panama's species of large cat roam the undergrowth, while red-fronted parrotlets, orange-bellied trogons and the extraordinary bare-necked umbrellabird draw bird-lovers. You're more likely to hear than see the three-wattled bellbird, which has one of the loudest birdcalls in the world – a bizarre metallic "dong" that carries for almost 1km.

Around the visitor centre

A few hundred metres beyond the park entrance, an informative **visitor centre**, with a rear balcony offering splendid views, marks the start of a couple of fairly short, well-kept circular routes (2km and 4km) and an interpretive loop, aimed at enhancing visitors' appreciation of the abundant and diverse flora. For **longer hikes**, to Cerro Peña Blanca or La Rica for example, you will need to arrange a **guide**, either via the MIA office in Penonomé (see p.142) or by contacting the Navas family (see p.146).

Cerro Peña Blanca

With a guide, **hikers** should consider aiming for **Cerro Peña Blanca** (1314m), which occasionally peeks out from the mist to the west of the park entrance. The moderately strenuous four-hour trail ascends west from the village of **BARRIGÓN** and on a rare clear day you are rewarded at the summit with spectacular views of both oceans.

La Rica

The other popular route heads over the continental divide from the park entrance down to the community of **LA RICA**, a good four-hour hike away. Set in verdant surroundings laced with waterfalls and natural swimming pools and within reach of giant guayacán, cuipo and cedar trees, La Rica is the perfect spot to appreciate the

LA CASCADA LAS YAYAS

A worthwhile diversion on the way to Parque Nacional Omar Torrijos from Barrigón is **La Cascada Las Yayas** (daily 8am–6pm; $2; ☎6809 6372). A shady 300m trail offers several viewpoints from which to appreciate the series of three falls, the highest of which is 25m. The falls, inevitably, are at their most impressive in the rainy season, though in the dry season there's the pleasure of taking a dip in the pool at the base of the main cascade. The surrounding rainforest is excellent for spotting hummingbirds and amphibians, especially in the late afternoon. A couple of very rudimentary wooden **rooms** with shared kitchen are available at the entrance ($10/person).

park's natural beauty, though getting there can be a very muddy affair for much of the year – a guide is essential.

ARRIVAL AND DEPARTURE | PARQUE NACIONAL OMAR TORRIJOS

By bus First, take a bus to the mountain village of El Copé. There are direct buses from Panama City (6am–6.30pm; hourly; 3hr); minibuses from Penonomé are even more frequent (6am–7pm; every 20min; 1hr). There are also services from Aguadulce (6am–6pm; every 45min–1hr; 1hr). Occasional minibuses from El Copé (7am–5pm) make the journey to the even smaller village of Barrigón, after which only a 4WD can crawl the remaining steep 4km to the park entrance – on foot that hike will take well over an hour. For the return, the last bus back from Barrigón to El Copé is around 5.30pm, and from El Copé to Penonomé it is at 7pm, slightly earlier for Aguadulce. Buses heading west along the Interamericana will pick up/drop off passengers at the junction.

By 4WD taxi To arrange 4WD transport in advance, contact Faustino Ortega (☎983 9265). Costs are approximately $20 from El Copé to the park entrance, $8 from Barrigón. Alternatively the Navas family (see below) can give you a number.

INFORMATION

Park entrance The park entrance is 4km beyond Barrigón, which is 3km northwest of El Copé.

MIA office According to the new park regulations, you should pay your park entry and accommodation fees into the MiAmbiente bank account in advance (see box, p.42). Check with the regional MIA office in Penonomé (☎997 7538) however, as you may be allowed to pay the $5 entry fee there, or at the MIA office (no phone) at the park entrance. The warden will then show you the way to the shorter trails. If you want to hire a park warden to accompany you as a guide on a longer hike, it's advisable to make arrangements in advance via the Áreas Protegidas department of the regional MIA office in Penonomé, or to contact *Albergue Navas* (see below); if you just turn up on the day nobody may be available.

Centro de Visitantes The visitors' centre, a few hundred metres from the park entrance, provides information on the park's flora and fauna.

ACCOMMODATION

★**Albergue Navas** Barrigón ☎983 9130. Warm, long-standing hosts Anna and Santos Navas provide three simple cinder-block rooms with shared outside toilet and shower; meals, made with fresh produce from their *finca*, are served in the family kitchen. Santos and his son are wonderfully knowledgeable guides, whose services can also be hired by non-guests ($20/group), though you'll need some Spanish. The family also owns a rustic cabin at La Rica, within the park. Full board. **$90**

MIA cabin Park entrance; contact Hellington Ríos at ☎997 7538 in the MIA regional office, Penonomé. A spacious solar-powered self-catering cabin near the entrance affords sweeping vistas, though conditions are often misty, and comprises a large lounge, a dorm with four bunks and a kitchen with a stove, fridge and basic utensils. Bring a sleeping bag, as it's chilly at night. Camping is possible, but there is no electricity and it is likely to be very wet. Camping **$6**, dorms **$15**

Western Coclé

West along the Interamericana from Penonomé, past the new windfarm – Panama's first and Central America's largest – across the flatlands of Coclé, the terrain becomes duller and drier. Skirting endless fields of sugar cane and cattle, you enter the crescent known as the **Arco Seco** (Dry Arc), which sweeps round the Bahía de Parita west of the

Pacific beaches to the eastern section of the Azuero Peninsula. Plum in the middle of what transforms into an unpleasant dust bowl in the dry season stands the important agroindustrial town of **Aguadulce**, synonymous with sugar, salt and – more recently – shrimp. Though the town itself is unremarkable, at the right time of year you can observe its agricultural processes first-hand, while avid birdwatchers head for the saltpans of **Playa El Salado** to the southeast. East of Aguadulce lie two of Panama's major historical attractions, the intriguing pre-Columbian site **Parque Arqueológico El Caño** and the fine colonial church at **Natá**.

Aguadulce and around

As ever, town life in **AGUADULCE** centres on the main square, **Plaza 19 de Octubre**, where the **Iglesia de San Juan Bautista** exhibits a mishmash of styles, the original altar frescoes having disappeared beneath an expensive pile of red brick – the current altarpiece.

El Museo de la Sal y el Azúcar

Plaza 19 de Octubre • Tues–Sat 8.30am–3.30pm • Free • ☎ 997 4280

The charming two-storey nineteenth-century building that was once the post office now houses the **Museo Regional Stella Sierra** (named after a local poet, whose work is on display), much better known by its previous title, **El Museo de la Sal y el Azúcar**. You'll see a modest assortment of pre-Columbian relics, photos and instruments from the early days of the salt and sugar industries, plus weaponry and uniforms from the civil war, during which two major battles were fought in the town. Space is also devoted to Aguadulce's two most famous citizens – the aforementioned poet, Stella Sierra, and Rodolfo Chiari, one of Panama's former presidents.

Ingenio Santa Rosa

14km west of Aguadulce, north of the Interamericana • Jan–March Tues–Fri 8am–noon; 24hr notice needed to book a tour (in Spanish); to see the cane-processing, you need to wear long sleeves, trousers and closed shoes; otherwise you can only visit the museum • Free • ☎ 987 8101, ⓦ azunal.com • Take a taxi from Aguadulce ($16–20), or any bus heading along the Interamericana; they can drop you off at the entrance, from where it's a 2.5km hike north

Of greater interest than Aguadulce's sugar museum is a tour around Panama's oldest and most important sugar mill, the **Ingenio Santa Rosa.** Here, during the harvesting season, you learn about the fascinating process of production, following the action from the cane fields to the bags of sugar. A small on-site museum, inside the reproduction wooden house of the pioneering DelValle family, is stuffed with period furniture and memorabilia. Outside, the grounds are sprinkled with early mill machinery, including old sugar cane presses.

ARRIVAL AND DEPARTURE   AGUADULCE AND AROUND

By bus Buses from Panama City to Aguadulce (4.15am–9pm; every 25min; 3hr) halt at two bus stops on the Interamericana. The main halt is the western one, by the *Hotel Interamericana*; return buses to Panama City (similar timetable) leave from the nearby junction with Av Rafael Estévez, which leads into the town centre. Regular minibuses ferry people to and from downtown Aguadulce for a few centavos, while taxis only charge $1. Buses to other destinations leave from the new bus terminal on the Interamericana just west of Aguadulce.
Destinations Chitré (4am–6pm; every 20min; 1hr); El Copé (6am–6pm; every 45min; 1hr); Penonomé (5am–7pm; hourly; 1hr); Santiago (5.30am–6.30pm; every 20min; 1hr).

ACCOMMODATION AND EATING

Fonda la Fula Av Rodolfo Chiari, towards the Interamericana. This place has the best reputation for traditional food; a basic affair with long aluminium tables under a corrugated iron roof, it is famous for its *sancocho*. Thurs–Sun 6am–late.

Hotel Interamericano Interamericana ☎ 997 4363, ⓦ hotelinteramericano.com.pa. Bland but functional en-suite rooms (hot water, cable TV, a/c and fan); the main attraction is the excellent large swimming pool, which transforms into a local party place at weekends, so select your room carefully. The on-site restaurant has a vast menu to suit most tastes (mains $9–12) and lunchtime family meal deals. **$44**

Hotel Sarita Behind Super Carnes on Av Alejandro T.

Escobar ☎ 997 4437. This long-standing central hotel offers cheap beds for shoestring travellers. Choose between a basic double with fan, cold water and local TV, or, for $17 extra, one with a/c, hot water and cable TV. **$18**

Parque Arqueológico El Caño

18km north of Aguadulce, just off the Interamericana • Tues–Sat 8am–3.30pm • $1 • ☎ 228 6231 (not working while the museum's closed for restoration) • Buses between Aguadulce and Penonomé can drop you on the Interamericana at the entrance to the village of El Caño, from where it's a further 3km walk to the site – a taxi from Natá ($7) might be easier

Parque Arqueológico El Caño is one of Panama's most significant pre-Columbian archeological sites, which narrowly escaped bulldozing in the 1970s. Sadly, a combination of plunder, vandalism and neglect means there is relatively little for the lay visitor to appreciate, while the park's floodplain location makes it a mosquito-infested quagmire in the rainy season. Even so, the well-preserved skeletons are quite impressive and definitely worth a look if you're in the area.

An important ceremonial site from 500 to about 1200 AD, El Caño later became a cemetery, and was still in use as such after the Conquest. One of the most fascinating finds was a set of more than a hundred basalt statues that formed what was described as the "Temple of the Thousand Idols". These were illegally decapitated by an American Indiana Jones-style adventurer in the early twentieth century, and the best of their zoomorphic and anthropomorphic heads are now scattered in museums in the US, with a few in Panama City's anthropological museum. Only the **stone pedestals** remain. There are also **funeral mounds**, two of which have been excavated, displaying fairly complete skeletons. One, presumed to be a chief's burial mound, has thrown up a number of gold and emerald items, which are currently being examined by archeologists, so are not yet on display. Many more burial sites are thought to lie under the nearby sugar cane fields, likely to contain more gold items.

A small **museum** displays ceramics and lesser stone statues found on the site, though its reopening following restoration has been delayed due to funding shortages.

Natá

It's hard to picture **NATÁ**, a quiet backwater 11km north of Aguadulce, as the major Spanish settlement it once was, until you arrive at the plaza to be confronted with the dazzling white Baroque facade of the expansive **Basílica Menor Santiago Apóstol**. Possibly the oldest church in the Americas still in use, and recently fully restored to its former glory, the church bears testament to the town's historical importance.

Founded in 1522 by Gaspar de Espinosa (whose bust surveys the church from the square) and named after the local indigenous chief, the town supposedly gained its subsequent full name, **Santiago de Natá de los Caballeros**, from a hundred knights (*caballeros*) – hand-picked by King Charles V of Spain – who were sent to subjugate the local population and spread the Catholic Word. The surrounding fertile plains made Natá a perfect base for confronting the main indigenous resistance forces under Cacique Urracá, who relentlessly attacked the site (see box, p.292), and for providing supplies to the now long-abandoned gold mines on the Caribbean coast.

Basílica Menor Santiago Apóstol

Plaza 19 de Octubre • Daily 8am–6pm • Free

Apart from the splendid belltower, the main attractions of the **Basílica Menor Santiago Apóstol** are the ornately **carved wooden altars** framed by exquisite columns laden with vines, flowers and angels, which adorn an otherwise simple wooden interior. Though the least elaborate, the main altar importantly contains images of the patron saint, Santiago el Menor (James the Lesser), and the co-patron, San Juan de Díos, who are removed from their niches and paraded round the town on their saint days of July 25 and March 8, respectively.

ARRIVAL AND DEPARTURE

NATÁ

By bus Regional buses westbound to Aguadulce or eastbound to Penonomé drop and pick up passengers at the entrance to Natá on the Interamericana (every 15–20min), a 10min walk from the village. Local shuttles between Aguadulce and Penonomé may even enter for a quick sweep of the plaza.

Playa El Salado

Heading southeast out of Aguadulce, a tarred road navigates 8km between mud and salt flats and shrimp farms to the mangrove-lined coast at **Playa El Salado**. In the dry season, salt is heaped like snow by the evaporation pools while September and October are the best months to catch flocks of migrating **waders**; among the numerous sandpipers and plovers, look out for striking black-necked stilts probing the mud for crustaceans and lovely roseate spoonbills filtering the tidal pools.

At weekends, many Aguadulceños head this way to escape the heat of the town and to lounge on the pleasant **beach** or to loll about in **Las Piscinas**. These shallow stone baths are built on the flats, offering views of the bay. As the tide moves out they become warm pools of salt water, but you need to get out quickly once the tide turns, as they soon become submerged. The biggest attraction for many, though, are the **jumbo shrimp** for which the fishing village is famous, and which you can sample at one of the restaurants dotted along the road.

3

ARRIVAL AND DEPARTURE

PLAYA EL SALADO

By minibus The only scheduled bus leaves Aguadulce's main square at 7am (15min) with the return bus leaving Playa El Salado at 8am. Other departures depend on demand and at weekends the bus sometimes doesn't run at all.

By taxi Taxis from Aguadulce charge $6–7.

EATING AND DRINKING

Restaurante Johnny y Los Mauditos (formerly Johnny Tapia) Just beyond the village mirador, on the main road ☏ 6774 5386. This unpromising concrete block with a tin roof, overlooking mangroves, is justifiably famed for its jumbo shrimp – a plateful will set you back a mere $10, or you can go the whole hog and share a vast seafood platter for $45. Mon & Thurs–Sun 11am–10pm.

Restaurante Reina del Mar Main road, almost at the end of the village ☏ 997 2960. Boasting a pleasant view across the scrub, this friendly restaurant dishes up moderately priced, freshly prepared seafood, including Ngäbe clams, shrimps, *ceviche* and fish. Mon–Thurs noon–10pm, Fri–Sun 11am–10pm.

The Azuero Peninsula

CORPUS CHRISTI, LA VILLA DE LOS SANTOS

The Azuero Peninsula

Mention the Azuero Peninsula, the box-shaped land mass that protrudes into the Pacific, and clichéd images abound of smiling women dancing in *polleras*, cowboys lassoing cattle and quaint village squares with whitewashed colonial churches. And the peninsula often delivers on such images: peasant farmers stride off to the fields at the crack of dawn, *sombrero* on head and machete slung across shoulder; some hamlets still contain tile-topped adobe houses, adorned with bougainvillea; and small villages celebrate their saint's day with bands of accordionists and fiddlers playing foot-tapping folk melodies. That said, the pace of development is increasing: trucks rattle along tarred rather than dirt roads; unprepossessing cement-block mini-supers with zinc roofs dot the townscapes; and vast tracts of land are being gobbled up by mushrooming real-estate agents and mining companies, looking to force rapid and irrevocable social change. For the moment, though, cattle farming and agriculture still prevail in the interior while coastal communities continue to derive their livelihood from fishing.

The peninsula, which covers a substantial 7616 square kilometres, is sometimes referred to as Eastern and Western Azuero; there is no connecting road across the dividing mountainous spine that runs down the western flank. The former comprises the vast bulk of the terrain and the small provinces of Herrera and Los Santos, clustered around their respective provincial capitals of **Chitré** and **Las Tablas**, which make good bases for exploring the region. The Western Azuero, on the other hand, is an oft-forgotten sliver of Veraguas province that trickles down the western seaboard. Dotted with small ranching and fishing communities – with a few developments sprouting up – it ends in one of Panama's least explored wilderness areas, Parque Nacional **Cerro Hoya**, with its sparkling waterfalls and several endemic species of animals and plants. That and the little-visited **Reserva Forestal El Montuoso** contrast acutely with the rest of the peninsula, which more than anywhere else in the country has been stripped of forest due to excessive logging and slash-and-burn agriculture. The desert-like **Parque Nacional Sarigua**, at the heart of the **Arco Seco** (Dry Arc) – Panama's driest, hottest region, which curves around the eastern shore of the Azuero – is a compelling reminder of the consequences of such practices. For a visitor, this means choosing your time to visit carefully; when fed by the rains (roughly May to mid-Dec), the verdant rolling pastures punctuated by villages ablaze with flowers and fruit trees create a picturesque landscape, but when the clouds dry up, they lose much of their natural beauty, becoming parched and dusty as temperatures soar.

Panama's Spanish **colonial heritage** is also at its most visible and vibrant in the Azuero, from the cattle ranching, bullfighting and Baroque churches to the elaborate costumes – the best examples of which are crafted on the peninsula – and distinctive music that

Festivals in the Azuero p.155
Mask-makers p.159
Ocú's festivals p.161
La Villa's Festival de Corpus Christi p.163
Festival de la Mejorana p.165

Carnaval and other Las Tablas festivals p.167
Turtle watching at Isla de Cañas p.173
Turtle conservation in the Western Azuero p.176

MAGNIFICENT FRIGATEBIRD, ISLA IGUANA

Highlights

❶ Azueran artesanía Catch artisans at work in village workshops, crafting exquisite ceramics, devil masks and straw hats, as well as embroidered *polleras* and *montunos*. **See p.159**

❷ Festivals The peninsula excels in fiestas: devil dances for Corpus Christi in La Villa; the nation's biggest folkloric jamboree, the Festival de la Mejorana, in Guararé; and the glitz of Carnaval at Las Tablas. **See p.163, p.165 & p.167**

❸ Isla Iguana A wildlife retreat of black and green iguanas, chest-puffing frigatebirds and shoals of rainbow-coloured fish. **See p.170**

❹ Playa Venao A lovely swathe of beach best appreciated by surfing the waves or horseriding along the sands. **See p.171**

❺ Isla de Cañas Camp out among the turtles that arrive in their thousands to nest along glorious sand each year. **See p.172**

❻ The Western Azuero Explore the undulating hillsides and rugged coastline of the peninsula's western flank, whose near-deserted beaches offer spectacular sunsets. **See p.175**

HIGHLIGHTS ARE MARKED ON THE MAP ON P.154

enliven the numerous religious festivals. This has led to the region being fondly dubbed the *cuña* (cradle) of national culture and traditions by many Panamanians – a statement that takes little account of the cultural affinities or contributions of the country's non-*mestizo* populations and conveniently ignores the existence of much earlier cultures. Vestiges of **pre-Columbian** communities, the most ancient of which was an 11,000-year-old fishing village at Sariguá – currently the oldest known settlement on the isthmus – provide evidence both of an earlier history and of the conquistadors' brutal efficiency in wiping it out. Still today you'll notice the region's lack of indigenous communities.

The Azuero's greatest appeal may lie in its many **festivals** (see box opposite), but there's more to the peninsula than partying. For nature lovers, **Isla Iguana** and **Isla de Cañas** offer very different but fascinating wildlife experiences; the former is a major nesting site for the chest-puffing frigatebirds, boasting coral beaches and rich snorkelling, while the latter affords a rare opportunity to witness the mass breeding of olive ridley **turtles**. On the eastern seaboard **Cenegón del Mangle** and **La Ciénega de las Macanas** are important **wetlands**, teeming with birdlife; while deserted **beaches** – broad tan, chocolate and black stretches of sand – welcome top-notch **surfing** waves and world-class **sport fishing** takes place off the legendary "Tuna Coast", with many enthusiasts using understated **Pedasí** as a base. In contrast, the more undulating, and slightly greener western flank of the peninsula offers a chance to get off the beaten track and explore a more rugged coastline, boasting more **surfing** hot spots and glorious **sunsets**.

THE AZUERO PENINSULA

HIGHLIGHTS

1. Azueran artesanía
2. Festivals
3. Isla Iguana
4. Playa Venao
5. Isla de Cañas
6. The Western Azuero

FESTIVALS IN THE AZUERO

The Azuero's **festivals** reel in thousands of Panamanians from all over the country, particularly for the major parties of **Carnaval** in Las Tablas and Chitré, **Corpus Christi** in La Villa de Los Santos and the **Festival de la Mejorana** in Guararé. Despite being championed as fine examples of the country's Spanish heritage, the festivities actually illustrate its hybridity: solemn religious ceremonies combine with pagan rituals and hedonistic excess; traditional folk groups are followed by DJs blasting out reggaeton, bachata and salsa; and stylized Andalusian-inspired dances such as the tamborito (Panama's national dance) and punto are imbued with African and pre-Columbian rhythms using drums, gourds and seed pods. More than five hundred festivals are held annually in the region, so you could spend a whole year here in a permanent alcoholic haze drifting from one celebration to the next, soaking up (literally and metaphorically) the legendary Azueran hospitality.

MAIN EVENTS

Jan 6 Fiesta de los Reyes Magos and Encuentro del Canajagua, Macaracas.
Jan (second Sat) Desfile de las Mil Polleras, Las Tablas (see box, p.167).
Late Jan (date varies) Feria de San Sebastián, Ocú (see box, p.161).
Feb (date varies) The country's biggest Carnaval celebration, Las Tablas (see box, p.167).
March/April (date varies) Semana Santa, celebrated most colourfully in La Villa de Los Santos, Pesé and Guararé.
Late April Feria Internacional de Azuero, La Villa de Los Santos.
May/June (date varies) Festival de Corpus Christi, La Villa de Los Santos (see box, p.163).
June 24 Patronales de San Juan, Chitré.
July (third week) Festival de La Santa Librada and Festival de la Pollera, Las Tablas (see box, p.167).
Aug (second week) Festival del Manito, Ocú (see box, p.161).
Late Sept Festival de la Mejorana, Guararé (see box, p.165).
Nov 10 The "First Cry for Independence", La Villa de Los Santos.

Chitré and around

CHITRÉ, the provincial capital of Herrera province and the main urban centre in the Azuero Peninsula, makes an ideal base for exploring the surrounding area and for attending the region's numerous festivals. A laidback commercial town with an attractive colonial centre, Chitré was founded in 1848, though indications are that conquistadors had been there since the mid-1500s. Life centres on the bustling streets around **Calle Manuel María Correa** (where you'll find the interesting regional **museum**) and the well-manicured **Parque Unión** with its splendid **cathedral**, notable for its wooden interior. The compact colonial quarter of Chitré can easily be explored in a couple of hours, leaving time to peruse the crafts in the northern suburb of **La Arena**, noted for its garish ceramics. Nature lovers will also be drawn to the nearby mud flats of **Playa El Agallito** and the wetlands of **Cenegón del Mangle** and **La Ciénega de las Macanas**, which attract prolific birdlife, particularly migratory waders. Of more general interest is the picturesque village of **Parita**, possessing a delightful church and, further afield, the surreal desert-like **Parque Nacional Sarigua**. Some of these destinations are not easily accessible without your own transport, especially in the rainy season.

Catedral de San Juan Bautista

Parque Unión • Daily 6am–8pm • Free

The imposing **Catedral de San Juan Bautista**, built between 1896 and 1910, underwent a major restoration in the late 1980s, which took the unusual step of exposing some of the exterior stone walls to provide a striking contrast with the snow-white facade and bell towers. The restrained, polished wooden interior also makes a refreshing change from the ornate decor in many Catholic churches, especially the gilded mahogany altar, which is complemented by bright stained-glass windows.

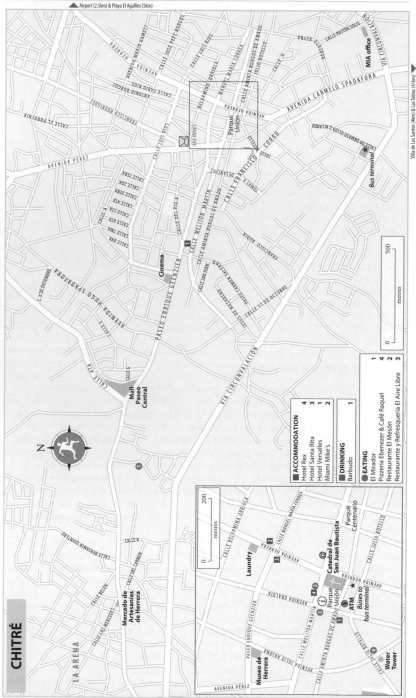

CHITRÉ

Airport (2.5km) & Playa El Agallito (5km)

Villa de Los Santos (4km) & Las Tablas (41km)

cerámica Calderón (50m) & Panama City

ACCOMMODATION
Hotel Rex	4
Hotel Santa Rita	3
Hotel Versalles	1
Miami Mike's	2

DRINKING
Barbudo	1

EATING
El Mirador	1
Pizzería Ebenezer & Café Raquel	4
Restaurante El Mesón	2
Restaurante y Refresquería El Aire Libre	3

Parque Unión and around

The cathedral is flanked by the formal gardens of **Parque Unión**. Neatly clipped flowerbeds and swaying palm trees around a stately bandstand provide the backdrop for a melding of modernity and tradition: young suited executives hold forth on their mobile phones while elderly *campesinos* in *montunos* and *sombreros de junco* – the traditional embroidered shirts and workday straw hats – discuss the local news. A two-block stroll east brings you to **Parque Centenario**, a more low-key affair, surrounded by squat red-tiled houses with wrought-iron grillwork.

Museo de Herrera

Parque Bandera, C Manuel María Correa • Mon–Sat 8am–4pm, Sun 9am–noon • $1

Though quite modest (with captions only in Spanish), the **Museo de Herrera**, in an elegant converted colonial mansion and former post office, is probably the best museum outside Panama City. Downstairs focuses on the pre-Columbian era: a couple of fine ceremonial **metates** stand out, as well as the impressive collection of **ceramics**. A reproduction **burial chamber** shows a life-size model *cacique* decked out in his gold arm- and leg bands, while copies of gold **huacas** from the anthropological museum in Panama City line the walls. Upstairs, fast-forward several hundred years to the colonial and post-colonial periods, with displays of **traditional musical instruments** and **costumes**, including elaborate *polleras* and devil outfits, and various **tools** from rural life. Don't miss the pouch made from a bull's scrotum used to carry staples for mending fences. The museum also offers Spanish-language **cultural tours** of the area.

4

ARRIVAL AND DEPARTURE CHITRÉ

By bus Chitré's bus terminal (☎ 996 6426) is 1km south of the town centre on the bypass, Vía Circunvalación. Frequent minibuses shuttle to Parque Unión, where you can catch the return bus to the terminal. Taxis from the bus terminal cost around $2 to most places in town. Getting to Chitré from Panama City involves taking a bus from Albrook bus terminal (6am–7pm; hourly; 3hr 30min). The last bus bound back to the capital leaves at 6pm.

Destinations Aguadulce (4am–6pm; every 20min; 1hr); La Arena (6am–9pm; every 10–15min; 10min); La Villa de Los Santos (6am–9.30pm, with a last bus at 10.30pm; every 10–15min; 15min); Las Minas (6am–6pm; every 30min; 45min); Las Tablas – change for Pedasí and Tonosí (6am–9.30pm; every 20min; 40min); Macaracas (6am–6pm; every 30–45min; 1hr); Ocú (6.30am–7pm;

every 30min; 1hr); Panama City (1.30am, 2.45am, then hourly 4am–6pm; 3hr 30min); Pesé (6.30am–6.30pm; every 15–20min; 30min); Playa El Agallito (6am–6pm; every 30min; 20min); Santiago – change for David (5am–6.30pm; every 30min; 1hr 10min).

By plane Air Panama (☎ 316 9000, ☎ airpanama.com) offers two daily flights to Chitré from Panama City's Albrook Airport (30min; $81 one way, $150 return).

By car It might be worth renting a car for a couple of days, especially to get to the less accessible protected areas or to explore further inland. There are several international rental companies in town – ask the tourist office for contact details. Alternatively, hire a taxi driver for the day; rates are usually $12–15/hr, but around $80 for the whole day. The tourist office or your lodgings can recommend a driver.

INFORMATION AND TOURS

Tourist information There is an ATP kiosk in the northwestern corner of Parque Unión (Mon–Fri 8am–4pm; ☎ 974 4532, ☎ atp.gob.pa).

MIA office The regional MIA office is on C Pastor Solís, just north of Vía Circunvalación on the southeastern side of town (Mon–Fri 8am–4pm; ☎ 996 7675); get in touch for permission to visit La Reserva Forestal El Montuoso (see p.162) or Parque Nacional Sarigua (see p.159).

Tours Cubitá Tours (☎ 978 0200, ☎ cubitatours.com) offers pricey bilingual day-trips round the Azuero. These include the usual jaunt to Isla Iguana or to the rum distillery (see p.160), visits to artisan workshops, hiking in the hills or even taking part in traditional communal activities such as harvesting rice or building an adobe house. Tours $40–130; minimum four people.

ACCOMMODATION

Hotel Rex Parque Unión, C Melitón Martín ☎ 996 4310, ☎ facebook.com/hotelrexchitrepanama. You're paying

for the prime location on the plaza so it's worth splashing out for the French windows and a view over the park.

Slightly faded furnishings, and a sullen front desk, but pleasant wooden panelling and comfy beds make it a reasonable option if you're not too fussy. **$55**

Hotel Santa Rita C Manuel María Correa, at Av Herrera ☎ 996 4610. Offering good value in a prime location, this ageing but well-maintained hotel has dark, simple en-suite rooms (fan or a/c, cable TV, good bed and hot water) off long corridors. Mattresses are variable so check out several rooms. Weekdays are cheaper. Wi-fi only at reception. **$33**

Hotel Versalles Paseo Enrique Geenzier ☎ 996 4422, ⊛ hotelversalles.com. Don't delude yourself with visions of regal French splendour; that said, rooms in this functional business hotel on the main approach road are comfortable and well equipped (a/c, phone, cable TV, room service and hot water), if lacking in character. Small pool and bar-restaurant. **$76**

Miami Mike's Av Herrera, at C Manuel María Correa ☎ 6603 9711, ⊛ miamimikeshostel.com. Small, cheerily decorated, fan-ventilated hostel offering little more than a bunk, a kitchen-cum-living area and a fantastic rooftop view. It's run by an affable American, with rock-bottom rates. Dorms **$11**, doubles **$22**

EATING

El Mirador Up the hill off the Carretera Nacional between Chitré and La Arena ☎ 974 4647. Atmospheric open-air hilltop spot (well signposted) to enjoy a cheap beer while admiring the sunset or the twinkling night lights of Chitré. Specializes in whole fish and seafood (mains from $9). Mon 4–10pm, Tues–Sat 10am–10pm, Sun noon–5pm.

Pizzería Ebenezer & Café Raquel C Julio Botello, opposite the water tower ☎ 996 8831. *Ebenezer* serves the town's best pizzas (mid-sized from $10), with a wide selection of toppings, but also Greek specialities, tacos, burritos and other comfort food. Adjacent *Café Raquel* is a top spot for a healthy fruit juice or a strong coffee to start the day. Pizzería Ebenezer: Mon–Fri 10am–10pm, Sat 8am–10pm, Sun 4–10pm; Café Raquel: Mon–Sat 7am–10pm, Sun 4–10pm.

Restaurante El Mesón Downstairs at Hotel Rex, Parque Unión ☎ 996 2408. Eschew the a/c dining room for the much nicer open-air café overlooking the park. Breakfasts are just over $5; well-prepared snacks (toasted sandwiches, burritos) cost slightly more. Lunch and dinner items ($9–12) include the usual Panamanian and international staples and Spanish specialities such as paella, chorizo and tongue. Free wi-fi. Daily 6am–11pm.

Restaurante y Refresquería El Aire Libre Parque Unión, Av Obaldía ☎ 996 3639. Pleasant open-sided restaurant overlooking the park. It's packed at breakfast and lunchtime, when they serve a cheap *menú del día* ($4) – the customary plateful of rice, beans and chicken or fish. Mains $6–8. Daily 6am–10pm.

DRINKING

Barbudo C Aminta Burgos de Amado, at Av Obaldía ☎ 6399 5027, ⊛ facebook.com/chitrebarbudo. A welcome interruption to the otherwise staid ambiance of central Chitré, this new rock-bar offers indoor and outdoor seating, beers galore and a bar menu (chicken wings, burgers and the like) accompanied by a rock soundtrack. Local bands occasionally let rip at weekends. Daily 10am–11pm.

Parita

11km northwest of Chitré, a few hundred metres off the Carretera Nacional; take any bus bound for Santiago or Aguadulce from Chitré (6am–8pm; approx every 30min; 15min)

Founded in 1556, **PARITA** is one of the oldest, best-preserved and most picturesque villages on the peninsula. Particularly attractive is the sparkling white eighteenth-century **Iglesia Santo Domingo de Guzmán**, with its attractive clay-tiled roof; peek inside and you'll see some ornately carved wooden altarpieces and an elaborate pulpit. Surrounding the plaza, terraces of pastel-coloured traditional adobe (*quincha*) cottages with tiled roofs take you back in time, though a line of telegraph poles remind you that the village was not totally bypassed by the twentieth century. The days leading up to August 8, the anniversary of the village's foundation, mark a big **fiesta** in Parita.

Playa El Agallito

5km northeast of Chitré • Buses run from Chitré, via Av Herrera (6am–6pm; every 30min; 15–20min); a taxi should cost $4–5

Despite the continued clearing of mangroves to make way for shrimp farms, the silty mud and salt flats of **Playa El Agallito** still provide sustenance for thousands of **shore birds** and **waders**, many migratory, who return to the same spot to feed each year. It's one of the country's top spots for sighting the splendid roseate spoonbill as well as American

---

MASK-MAKERS

Ghoulish **devil masks**, which form the centrepiece of Corpus Christi celebrations (see box, p.163) across the country and feature in other festivals throughout the year, make great souvenirs. They are made predominantly from papier-mâché coated onto a greased clay or earthen mould; their horns, wooden teeth and eyes – usually ping-pong balls or marbles – are added later. They're available in various craft centres and agricultural fairs, and you can also visit some of the mask-makers in their workshops. Expect to pay less than $10 for a small mask and up to $150 for a larger and more elaborate one. The most renowned artist, with almost fifty years' experience, who makes both *diablicos sucios* and *limpios* (see box, p.163), is **Darío López** (☎974 2933 or ☎6534 1958); his hard-to-miss home-based workshop is on the Carretera Nacional, just north of **Parita**, beyond the petrol station, on the other side of the road. Another well-known artisan is **José González** (☎996 2314); taxi drivers should be able to find his workshop in **Llano Bonito**, on the outskirts of Chitré, or ask at the Museo de Hererra for directions (see p.157).

---

oystercatchers and wood storks, amid a potpourri of terns, egrets, herons and sandpipers. The best time to visit – bring the binoculars – is at high tide, when birds feed close to shore.

Parque Nacional Sarigua

A little further up the coast from Playa El Agallito, and 25km north of Chitré, the eighty-square-kilometre **Parque Nacional Sarigua** is squeezed between ríos Santa María and Parita on land, and stretches out into the Bahía de Parita. **Birdlife** is restricted to a coastal sliver of threatened mangrove; further inland lie vast salt flats and tracts of dry forest, and bleak saline-streaked gullies dotted with cactus, acacia and snowy blobs of wild cotton. Less a tourist attraction, as it is often heralded, than a cautionary tale, this desert-like wasteland is testament to the devastating consequences of a century of slash-and-burn agriculture and overgrazing. Covered with a layer of surreal bronze-coloured dust and home to a vast solar farm, it is the country's hottest and driest area.

The silver lining in this sad tale of environmental degradation is that the resulting erosion helped uncover important **archeological remains**, including evidence of an 11,000-year-old fishing village, the oldest known settlement on the isthmus, and more recent traces (between fifteen hundred and five thousand years ago) of an ancient farming community. When walking around the park it's easy to stumble on shards of ancient ceramics or discarded shells, just as the sparse vegetation makes it easier to spot boas curled around parched branches, armadillos digging in the undergrowth or lizards and iguanas sunning themselves. The landscape is best appreciated from the top of the rickety **mirador** by the **ranger station**, from where you can also make out distant shrimp farms. Rangers offer **guided walks** for a tip, but note that the park is rather undeveloped, with only a couple of short **trails**.

ARRIVAL AND INFORMATION   PARQUE NACIONAL SARIGUA

Park entrance and fees The park entrance is signposted off the Carretera Nacional just north of Parita (daily 8am–4pm). You can pay the park fees ($5) here.
By bus and taxi Either catch a bus to Parita and pick up a

taxi ($6) there, or take a taxi from Chitré ($15).
By car The turn-off is well signposted off the Carretera Nacional; note that 4WD is necessary in the rainy season.

Refugio de Vida Silvestre Cenegón del Mangle

At the mouth of the Río Santa María, the **Refugio de Vida Silvestre Cenegón del Mangle** boasts around eight square kilometres of wildlife-rich mangrove. Though numbers have been decreasing in recent years, it's still known for its heronries, packed with grey and tricoloured herons and great white and cattle egrets. There is a 500m boardwalk through the mangroves to better view the birds, especially during the nesting season (June–Sept). In the dry season, the water dries up and there's little reason to visit.

Refuge entrance and fees The entrance (daily 8am–4pm) is at the mouth of the Río Santa María off the Carretera Nacional, east of París (a far cry from its namesake in Europe, this Paris is named after a local indigenous chief). Pay your admission fee ($3) here.

By car You'll need 4WD in the rainy season. It's a 45min ride from Chitré: 7km northwest of Parita on the highway, turn right

at a bus shelter and petrol station to París. At the fork by the village church, bear right and then right again at an unmarked crossroads a few hundred metres later. The tarred road soon peters into dirt, which continues another 4km before signs to the reserve re-emerge, which you follow to the park office.

By taxi To get here by taxi (4WD in the rainy season) will cost around $25 from Chitré or $15 from Parita.

La Ciénaga de las Macanas

4km east of El Rincón, which is 32km northwest of Chitré • Daily 8.30am–3.30pm • $3 • Take a bus to El Rincón from Chitré; you can then walk the 4km to the marsh (right at the church, then right at the fork); the local environmental organization GEMA (☎ 976 1040; or Hector Escudero ☎ 6021 4919) offers guiding services (in Spanish) and boat trips, and can arrange transport for you

Set on Río Santa María's floodplains, **La Ciénaga de las Macanas** is the region's largest freshwater wetland area. It attracts an abundance of resident and migratory **birdlife**, visible from the **observation tower** near the water's edge. In addition to waders and ducks you might see Brahman cattle chomping through the greenery; they help regulate the invasive water hyacinth, though conservationists are keen to reduce the number of grazing livestock.

Amenities are better here than at nearby Cenegón del Mangle: beside the tower are toilets, picnic tables, a short interpretive path and a jetty protruding over the water, with a couple of boats tethered. If you fancy **boating** on the water to get closer to wildlife or throw a fishing line, contact one of the ecotourism groups in the nearby village of **El Rincón** (de Santa María).

The central peninsula

The best way to get a feel for rural life in the Azuero is to head west of the Carretera Nacional into the **agricultural heartland** of the peninsula. Here you pass rolling hills of pastureland sprinkled with giant hardwoods, fields of sugar cane and flower-filled towns and villages where the unhurried pace of life is infectious. There is precious little accommodation in these places, but the main population centres, such as **Ocú** and **Pesé**, are well connected by public transport on decent roads and two or three can easily be combined into a day-trip.

Pesé

One of the prettiest towns within reach of Chitré, lying 24km southeast and surrounded by a carpet of sugar cane, **PESÉ** is known for its liquor and its Good Friday re-enactment of the Passion of Christ. The ironic juxtaposition of faith and booze is evident the moment you set eyes on the church, which looks disapprovingly across the road at the Varela Hermanos **distillery**.

Varela Hermanos distillery

Hacienda San Isidro • Tours in English or Spanish $102, including rum tasting and lunch • ☎ 974 9401, ✉ reservaciones@varelahermanos.com

Founded in 1908 by Spanish émigré José Varela – ancestor of Panama's current president – as a sugar mill and refinery, **Varela Hermanos** became a **distillery** in 1936 and has never looked back. Today it supplies ninety percent of Panama's spirits, including the country's top **rum**, Ron Abuelo, and the national knockout tipple, seco (35 percent). A million cases of spirit a year are produced here, much of which ends up down the throats of revellers at the Azuero's many celebrations, including the **Festival de la Caña de Azúcar** held in Pesé at the end of March to mark the end of the harvest.

ARRIVAL AND DEPARTURE

PESÉ

Regular **buses** leave Chitré bus terminal for Pesé (6.30am–6.30pm; every 15–20min; 30min).

EATING

Restaurante Marithel C José Varela Blanco, 50m from the church ☎ 6648 9901. This friendly restaurant, with a shady patio draped with foliage and hibiscus flowers, serves a decent beef stew and the like for around $4. Daily 7am–3pm.

Ocú

Twenty kilometres west of Pesé, the larger village of **OCÚ** makes up for its lack of quaint charm with its **festivals** (see box below) and its **hat-making** – above all the distinctive white sombrero Ocueño, with a thin black trim, which is still produced in home-based **workshops**. Try **Artesanías Ocueña** (daily 9am–4pm; ☎ 6458 4529), a women's cooperative in the centre of town, on Plaza Sebastian Ocú, which also produces fine *polleras*, *montunos* and other embroidered items.

ARRIVAL AND DEPARTURE

OCÚ

By bus Buses leave Chitré bus terminal for Ocú via Pesé (6.30am–6.30pm; every 20min; 1hr) with the last bus back to Chitré at 7pm. Buses from Santiago terminal also run to Ocú (6am–6pm; every 20min; 1hr); the last return bus is at 6pm.

ACCOMMODATION AND EATING

El Punto Ocueño Main plaza opposite the church. Busy cafeteria dishing up an inexpensive *menú del día* or *cena* for $4 or plates of roast chicken or chow mein for around $4–5. Mon–Fri 6am–6pm, Sat & Sun 6am–noon.
Residencial Ocú 50m downhill from the main square, by the church ☎ 974 1374, ⊕ residencialocu.com. A dozen simple en-suite rooms with cold-water showers are set round a nice shady patio with rocking chairs and hammocks. Rooms are spotless and offer a/c, local TV and beds with decent mattresses. **$28**

Las Minas, Los Pozos and Macaracas

Though Pesé and Ocú are the more common day-trip destinations in the central peninsula, it is a pleasant drive, by car, to cover the further 30km through **LAS MINAS** and **LOS POZOS** before returning to Chitré or continuing southeast to **MACARACAS** – by bus you'd probably need to return to Chitré and take another bus back out into the countryside. There's nothing particular to see or do in any of these places, except chill out and watch rural life unfold. The party most likely to attract outsiders occurs in Macaracas; celebrated in the church plaza every January 6 for almost two hundred years, the **Fiesta de los Reyes Magos** (Three Wise Men) features a two-hour dramatization of the Adoration of the Magi.

ARRIVAL AND DEPARTURE

LAS MINAS, LOS POZOS AND MACARACAS

By bus Buses leave Chitré for Las Minas (6am–6pm; every 30min; 1hr); Los Pozos, via Pesé (6am–7.25pm; every 25min; 45min) and Macaracas (6am–7pm; hourly; 40min) en route to Tonosí (1hr 30min).

OCÚ'S FESTIVALS

The **Festival del Manito** (second week of Aug) is Ocú's premier event. Apart from the usual parades, there are two stand-out elements: the **tamarind duel** (*duelo del tamarindo*) and the **peasant wedding** (*matrimonio campesino*). The latter is a wonderful sight: following a mock church wedding, the bride, decked out in an all-white *pollera*, is paraded on horseback through the streets while the groom holds an umbrella above her head to protect her from the sun (or rain). In contrast, the tamarind duel harks back to the bygone days of testosterone-fuelled fights to the death over women, family honour or simply from overdoing the liquor; such fights are re-enacted with swords and sabres in the centre of the plaza. The town's other five-day extravaganza, **La Feria de San Sebastián** (late Jan), is an agricultural fair honouring the patron saint.

Reserva Forestal El Montuoso

Up the valley from Las Minas, the seriously denuded peaks of the optimistically named **RESERVA FORESTAL EL MONTUOSO** pale in comparison with the richly forested mountain ranges in Chiriquí, Bocas or the Darién, so if you're heading for one of those locations, El Montuoso can easily be skipped. But if you're lingering in the Azuero and aching to get into the hills, this is the best place to come, until the rugged wilderness of Parque Nacional Cerro Hoya (see p.174) becomes more accessible.

The 120-square-kilometre reserve, dubbed the "*pulmón*" ("lung") of Herrera, was created in 1977 to safeguard the five rivers that rise in the mountainous region and to protect the rapidly vanishing tracts of forest being eaten away by illegal farming and timber extraction. In response, several reforestation projects have been initiated. Though only twenty percent of the reserve is now forested, what remains is concentrated around the reserve's highest point, Cerro Alto Higo (953m). Steep-sided mountains cleaved by river-eroded ravines harbour plenty of wildlife to interest the visitor, such as red brocket and white-tailed deer, howler monkeys, white-faced capuchins and collared peccaries. This is also one of the easiest places to spot the endemic brown-backed dove while other specialities include violet sabrewings and blue-throated goldentails – both hummingbirds – and the ever-acrobatic orange-collared manakin.

Exploring the reserve

The park office is set in a lovely orchard, where a short, pretty **trail** crisscrosses the nascent Río La Villa up to a cascading pool. The main trail, **Sendero Alto Higo**, leads up the mountain of the same name, heading off to the left after Chepo, at a place known as the Caras Pintadas (Painted Faces), an imaginative reference to the petroglyph near the start of the path, where rare sundews are in evidence in winter. A moderately strenuous hike of just over an hour brings you out at a peak by a radio mast, which offers a tantalizing restricted view – thanks to some unfortunately located trees – towards the Golfo de Montijo.

ARRIVAL AND ACCOMMODATION   RESERVA FORESTAL EL MONTUOSO

Park entrance and fees The entrance (daily 8am–4pm) is at Tres Puntas, 4km before the village of Chepo. It's advisable to contact the MIA regional office in Las Tablas beforehand (see p.167); at the time of writing, however, all payments (including the $5 admission fee) were still being taken in the reserve.

By bus Buses run from Chitré bus terminal to Las Minas (6am–6pm; every 30min; 1hr), where you take one of the infrequent *chivas* bound for Chepo, alighting at Tres Puntas (30min).

MIA bunkhouse 5min walk from the road at Tres Puntas. The reserve bunkhouse has two comfortable dorms, a shared kitchen and a camping area. You'll need to stock up with food before you reach the limited shopping options of Las Minas; note that alcohol is prohibited in the reserve. Camping $6, dorms $15

The road to Las Tablas

Just south of Chitré, the Carretera Nacional crosses the Río La Villa, the peninsula's longest river, which marks the provincial boundary between Herrera and Los Santos, and continues southeast, running parallel to the coast. After skirting the diminutive yet historically important town of **La Villa de Los Santos**, whose small museum and impressive church interior merit a detour, the road bypasses tiny **Guararé**, host to the country's largest folkloric festival, before arriving in the provincial capital, **Las Tablas**, about halfway down the peninsula.

La Villa de Los Santos

LA VILLA DE LOS SANTOS is famous for the vibrant costume-clad celebrations of **Corpus Christi**, a historic rebellion against Spanish colonial rule, and the Feria Internacional de

Azuero, the peninsula's annual ten-day agricultural jamboree in April. If you arrive outside party time, though, it's easy to be disappointed. "Los Santos", or "La Villa" as the town is usually called, is much smaller and quieter than neighbouring Chitré, and not as spruced up or as vibrant as Las Tablas.

You'll need little more than an hour to check out La Villa's two main attractions, the **church** and **museum**, both on the **central plaza**. The plaza is named after the great Latin American liberator **Simón Bolívar**, to whom the town's influential citizens addressed a letter on November 10, 1821, asking to join his revolutionary movement against Spain. This unilateral declaration, called the *Primer Grito de la Independencia* (**First Cry for Independence**), started the domino effect that led to national independence from Spain eighteen days later; it is celebrated annually with the customary flag-waving parades of marching bands, traditional folk costumes, speeches and fireworks.

Museo de la Nacionalidad
North side of Parque Simón Bolívar • Tues–Sat 9am–4pm, closed for lunch • $1 • ☎ 966 8192

The room in which the townspeople's famous letter to Simón Bolívar was penned, complete with original furniture, forms part of the beautifully restored – and moderately interesting – **Museo de la Nacionalidad**. Much of the museum, which was formerly a school and a prison (though not at the same time), overflows with details (in Spanish) of leading figures in the independence movement.

LA VILLA'S FESTIVAL DE CORPUS CHRISTI

By far the most fascinating and famous of La Villa's celebrations is the **Festival de Corpus Christi**, a heady mix of **Christian** and **pagan** imagery in an exciting narrative of dance, drama and dialogue. It features a cast of larger-than-life characters and dancers decked out in extravagant costumes, interwoven with a series of religious ceremonies. Corpus Christi became an important tool in Spanish colonization across Latin America, as the invaders attempted to woo the indigenous population to the Christian faith by incorporating elements of their traditions and rituals into the ecclesiastical ceremonies. Though there is plenty of local variation, the basic good-versus-evil plot is the same.

The action starts on the Saturday before Corpus Christi when church bells at noon bring hordes of *diablicos sucios* (dirty devils) rampaging onto the streets. Clad in crimson-and-black-striped jumpsuits, wearing ferocious devil masks with flame-coloured headdresses and letting off firecrackers at will, they terrify all and sundry to the beat of drums and whistles. Fast forward to Wednesday, several Masses later, when at 11.30am on the Eve of Corpus Christi, the Diabla or Diablesa (though as with all roles, performed by a male) also races around the town announcing the arrival of her husband, the Diablo Mayor, who convenes with three other devils in the central plaza. Joking and knocking back the booze, they carve up the globe in a bid for world domination. Before dawn on Corpus Christi, Santeños roam around town, on foot and on horseback, in search of the Torito Santeño – a man in a bull's costume – who is causing havoc, but is eventually rounded up in the **Danza del Torito** as the party proceeds through the streets to a large communal breakfast. The centrepiece of the drama unfolds mid-morning before the church, on a magnificent carpet of petals, as the Archangel Michael and the *diablicos limpios* (clean devils), distinguishable from the bad guys by their white sleeves and a rainbow of handkerchiefs attached to the waist, vanquish the villains in the Danza del Gran Diablo or Diablicos Limpios before allowing them in to the service. All the dance troupes – including an assortment of dwarves, roosters, vultures, Mexican conquistadors and escaped African slaves – attend the Mass, which then relocates outside as Holy Communion is offered to the townsfolk before the serious partying begins.

Further merrymaking takes place a week later, culminating in Saturday's **Día del Turismo**, which provides a highlights show on stage in the plaza, and Sunday's **Día de la Mujer**, offering Santeñas, whom tradition has prohibited from participating thus far, the chance to dust off their *polleras* and join in the fun.

4

Iglesia San Atanasio
Northeastern side of Parque Simón Bolívar • Free

The central attraction in the main plaza is the gleaming white **Iglesia San Atanasio**, which contains a series of magnificent carved altars – a profusion of spiralling columns adorned with vine leaves, winged cherubs and flowers, all dripping with gold. Most splendid of all is the main altar, framed by an even more opulent archway that predates the completion of the church. Though the first stones were laid some time between 1556 and 1559, the edifice was not completed until 1782. Note also the painted wooden tracery above the nave and the life-size entombed Christ figure in the glass sepulchre, which is paraded around the streets on Good Friday in a candlelit procession. The church is also the focal point for the town's famous **Festival de Corpus Christi** (see box, p.163). Although it is celebrated throughout Panama, the festivities in La Villa stand head and shoulders above the rest.

Parque Rufina Alfaro
Av 10 de Noviembre, three blocks southeast of Parque Simón Bolívar

At the southeastern end of town, **Parque Rufina Alfaro** celebrates the possibly apocryphal local heroine of the independence movement, **Rufina Alfaro**. A monument to the plucky Santeña has her seemingly emerging from a swamp. The story has it that she exploited the local Spanish commander's affections and secured crucial intelligence about when to attack the army barracks, and that she then headed the march there that cemented the bloodless coup.

ARRIVAL AND DEPARTURE

LA VILLA DE LOS SANTOS

By bus Local buses shuttle between Chitré and La Villa (6am–9.30pm; every 10–15min; 15min) and can drop you off at Parque Simón Bolívar. Direct buses leave Panama City for La Villa (6am–7pm; hourly; 3hr 30min); for the return to Panama City, or other major destinations, board a Chitré-bound minibus and change there.

ACCOMMODATION AND EATING

Hotel La Villa A few hundred metres off the Carretera Nacional ☎ 966 8201, ⬤ hotellavillapanama.com. The better of the town's two hotels – though service can be indifferent and you'll either love or hate the folkloric-themed decor – is a low-key place with good-value rooms (a/c, hot water, cable TV and firm beds), ranging from singles to suites, in a garden setting with a pool and moderately priced restaurant. $55

Hotel Restaurante Kevin Just south of the bus terminal ☎ 966 8276. Set back from the main road, offering compact, clean, functional rooms set round a grassy area. Filling *comida criolla* is served at the adjacent restaurant. $45

Restaurante Los Cuates Main road, close to the fairgrounds ☎ 6755 2112. This gringo-run joint under a breezy *rancho* sells tacos, burritos and the like from less than $6, plus a *menú ejecutivo* on weekday lunchtimes. It's a good place for a drink, too. Tues–Sun 3pm–midnight.

Guararé

The somnolent town of **GUARARÉ**, 6km north of La Tablas, springs to life once a year when enthusiastic crowds arrive in droves to enjoy the famous **Festival de la Mejorana** (see box opposite). That aside, Guararé's other claim to fame is as the birthplace of Panama's greatest sporting legend and one of the all-time greats of world boxing, **Roberto Durán**, better known as Manos de Piedra ("Hands of Stone").

Casa Museo Manuel Fernando Zárate
Five blocks north of the main square • Mon–Sat 8am–4pm, Sun 9am–noon • Free

The Festival de la Mejorana, first held in 1949, was the brainchild of a local teacher, Manuel Zárate, whose nostalgia for Panama while studying abroad made him realize the need to promote and preserve the country's cultural traditions. The **Casa Museo Manuel Fernando Zárate** chronicles Zárate's life and the festival's history. Walls are plastered with photos, including portraits of previous *reinas*, some antique *polleras* and menacing devil costumes.

FESTIVAL DE LA MEJORANA

Panama's largest and best folk festival is Guararé's **Festival de la Mejorana** (ⓦfestivalnacional delamejorana.com), named after Panama's five-stringed guitar, the *mejoranera*. The five-day jamboree, which coincides with the *patronales* for the Virgen de la Mercedes in late September, is for lovers of Hispanic traditions; there's not a techno-beat in earshot and although, just as at most Panamanian festivals, the booze flows, it's a less hedonistic affair than many. The plaza resounds with folk music day and night, with dancers and musicians from around the country converging to entertain and compete. Adults and children vie for medals in playing violin, accordion or *mejoranera*, and drumming, singing or dancing. There are even competitions for traditional work clothes – a kind of beauty pageant for both men and women. Bullfights are also on the agenda, usually dominated by seco-sodden guys staggering around a muddy field waving a filthy rag at a tired bull, cheered on by supporters – a far cry from the celebrity matadors of Spain. The festival highlight on Sunday morning is the **Gran Desfile de Carretas**, when superbly decorated ox-carts parade through the town, accompanied by *tunas* (African-inspired bands of call-and-response singers and drummers).

Inevitably all eyes are on the float carrying the **Reina del Festival de la Mejorana**, decked out in her *pollera de gala* finery and wearing a gold crown. It's an incredibly prestigious position, a national honour that lasts beyond the queen's year-long reign. Families are prepared to shell out $15,000 for the privilege, and that's just for starters. Should there be more than one candidate at the pre-fiesta deadline, a run-off is held over three rounds (*escrutinios*) lasting several months, during which the candidates' families have to outdo each other in fundraising – a prospect that has the organizing committee rubbing its hands in glee, since it means more cash for the festival coffers. The belle with the most financial backing at the end gets to wear the crown; her rivals have to settle for being princesses. The highest sum paid so far to secure festival glory is $70,000, some of which the queen gets to spend on her regalia – the elaborately embroidered *polleras de gala* cost several thousand dollars – and on other necessities such as dancing lessons and float decoration.

ARRIVAL AND ACCOMMODATION GUARARÉ

Dy bus Any Chitré–Las Tablas bus (see p.157) can drop you off on the Carretera Nacional at Guararé.

Hotel La Mejorana Main road ☎ 994 5794. Virtually the only place to stay in town, and it's near impossible to get a bed during the festival. Rooms are small but fairly comfortable with lots of highly varnished wooden furniture. $33

Las Tablas

Famed for hosting Panama's wildest **Carnaval** (see box, p.167), the provincial capital of **LAS TABLAS** moves at a much more sedate pace for the rest of the year. In comparison with neighbouring Chitré, Las Tablas is a modest town, but it possesses a sprinkling of tourist amenities, as well as an attractive **church** and a small **museum** dedicated to Belisario Porras, three-time president and Las Tablas's most famous citizen. Besides these, the only other building of note is the **Escuela Presidente Porras**, with a smart maroon-and-cream exterior, and a distinctive clock tower and majestic portal. Built in 1924, this immaculately kept state school possesses high ceilings, large windows and beautiful louvred shutters.

Most business in Las Tablas is conducted along the two main streets, Avenida 8 de Noviembre (also Av Carlos López) and Avenida Belisario Porras, which converge in the leafy main plaza, Parque Belisario Porras. The vortex of the maelstrom that is Carnaval, at any other time **Parque Porras** is a tranquil shady spot to enjoy a snow-cone or ice cream. Midweek evenings are quiet unless there's a baseball match on at the **Estadio Olmedo Solé** (Jan–May; ⓦfedebeis.com) – a highly entertaining party atmosphere to be savoured even if you don't know a home plate from a dinner plate.

At weekends, many Tableños head for the nearest beach at **Playa El Uverito**, a broad belt of chocolate-covered sand 10km east of town, and reachable by bus; here families tuck into platefuls of **fresh fish** at the beachside restaurants, or picnic on the sand.

La Villa de Los Santos (37km) & Chitré (41km)

LAS TABLAS

0   500
metres

■ ACCOMMODATION	
Hospedaje Martha	2
Hotel Don Jesús	1
Hotel Presidente	3
Hotel Sol del Pacífico	4

● EATING	
La Maestra	1
Restaurante Hotel Piamonte	3
Restaurante y Pizzería El Caserón	2

MIA office (700m), Pedasí (40km) & Playa Venao (70km)

Brief history

Spanish nobles apparently founded the town in 1671; having fled Panamá Viejo after its sacking by pirate Henry Morgan, they were swept by fierce winds onto the shores of the Azuero. Here – so the story goes – an image of the **Virgen de Santa Librada** appeared before them as a statue, which they interpreted as a sign that their new settlement should be established on that very spot. Santa Librada, unsurprisingly, was adopted as the patron saint. The name Las Tablas is thought to have derived from the planks (*tablas*) salvaged from the ships and used to construct the initial houses.

Iglesia Santa Librada

Parque Porras

Iglesia Santa Librada features a figurine of the patron saint set at the façade's apex. The magnificent golden altar, which suffers from an overdose of pale-faced cherubs, illuminates the otherwise pedestrian interior – look out for the reliquary said to contain a segment of the saint's leg. Although originally built in 1789, a lot of the church structure visible today dates from the late 1950s.

Museo Belisario Porras

Parque Porras • Tues–Sat 8am–4pm • $1 • ☎ 994 6326

Diagonally across the square from the church the neat, red-tiled **Museo Belisario Porras** celebrates the life of Panama's most illustrious president in the house of his birth.

Ironically its most striking exhibit is the Napoleonic-size tomb intended to house Porras's remains, which lies empty as family members wrangle over whether the bones should be moved from the prestigious Cementerio Amador in Panama City, where they are currently interred. Walls in the single display room are plastered with faded photos, certificates and memorabilia, which only partly succeed in conveying (in Spanish) the extent of his many achievements (see p.295 & p.298). On one famous occasion the statesman's bust, which stands outside the museum, was stolen and discarded in a latrine. On hearing the news, Porras wryly remarked: "*Mis enemigos, no pudiendo llegar hasta mí, mi han hecho descender hasta ellos*" ("Since my enemies cannot reach me, they have dragged me down to their level").

ARRIVAL AND INFORMATION   LAS TABLAS

By bus Buses from Panama City arrive at the main terminal, four blocks north of Parque Porras down Av 8 de Noviembre. All the other main bus stops are within a few blocks of the main square.

Destinations Cañas via Pedasí (1 daily, 1.30–2pm; 2hr); Chitré (6am–9pm; every 20min; 45min); Panama City (6am–7pm; hourly; 4hr); Pedasí (6.30am–7.30pm; every 45min; 40min); Playa El Uverito (7am–5pm; 6–7 daily;

20min); Tonosí (8am, 10am, then hourly until 5pm; 1hr 20min).

MIA office The regional MIA office for Los Santos province lies along the main road to Pedasí, around 1.7km east of Parque Porras (Mon–Fri 8am–4pm; ☎ 500 0921). Stop here if you intend to visit Isla Iguana, Isla de Cañas or Cerro Hoya from the Los Santos side.

CARNAVAL AND OTHER LAS TABLAS FESTIVALS

For many people Las Tablas is synonymous with **Carnaval**, the nation's wildest party, which sees an estimated eighty thousand people squeeze into the narrow streets and central plaza for the five-day bacchanal. Though scaffolding is erected and bodies cram every window and balcony ledge, it is still a crush, so it's not for the claustrophobic or faint-hearted. The festivities revolve around a Montagues-versus-Capulets-style feud that divides the town down the middle in their loyal support for either **Calle Arriba** (ⓦ carnavalescallearriba.com) or **Calle Abajo** (ⓦ calleabajolastablas.com), during which water pistols are substituted for swords and the calles shell out at least $500,000 each year to compete for the best music, supporters, fireworks, costumes, floats and queen.

The proceedings start on the Friday night in a blaze of fireworks with the coronation of the new queens, followed by dancing until dawn in a swirl of seco and sweat. Mornings kick-start around 10am with *culecos* or *mojaderos*, which essentially entail being doused by hosepipes from large water tankers as you dance in the street. The queens parade around the square enthroned on gigantic themed floats followed by percussion and brass *murga* bands, who work themselves up into a frenzy to inspire the *tunas* – the all-singing all-dancing support groups – to pump up the volume and outdo the opponents with insulting lyrics. The glam factor is ratcheted up a few notches at night, both on the streets and on the even more extravagant and glitzy floats, and general hedonism takes off until people flake out, often in cars or in the park, before starting all over again the next day. The good times are formally ended when a sardine is symbolically buried in the sand at dawn on Ash Wednesday to mark the start of Lent.

OTHER FESTIVALS

The **Festival de Santa Librada** is commemorated annually in the third week of July. This event is less frenetic and a shade less hedonistic than Carnaval, though there is no shortage of boozing and carousing, plus all the usual attractions of traditional costumes, dancing and music, street food, bullfighting, fireworks and, of course, religious devotions. These start as the pilgrims file into town, bearing an effigy of the saint, who is dripping in gold jewellery given by devotees. For tourists the most interesting aspect is the **Festival de la Pollera**, which offers a chance to see streams of women in Panama's glorious national dress sashaying through the streets. A more recently established dusting off of the *polleras* occurs at the end of the second week of January in the **Festival de las Mil Polleras**. Thousands of women from all over the country converge on Las Tablas to show off regional variations of the national dress, accompanied by *tuna* bands.

4

ACCOMMODATION

Hospedaje Martha C Moisés Espino ☎ 994 1012. Ideal for budget travellers, offering small, clean a/c en-suite doubles plus cheaper options ($18) with fan and shared bathroom off a long corridor. **$25**

Hotel Don Jesús C Ramón Mora, north of Parque Porras ☎ 994 6593, ⓦ hoteldonjesus.com. Pleasant lodgings in a converted family home with neat rooms and good service. Guests share a comfortably furnished lounge-balcony area for breakfast ($4–5) and relaxing. There's also a pond-size pool. **$44**

★ **Hotel Presidente** C Pablo Arosemena, half a block east of Parque Porras ☎ 848 3071, ⓦ hotelpresidente .com.pa. An attractive three-storey building boasting 34 rooms, with pale stone-tiled floors, set around an interior courtyard. Standard business-style decor is offset by the stylish bathroom with decorative floor tiles. Other pluses are the rooftop pool and bar, a decent restaurant and welcoming staff. Pay the extra $17 for a balcony. Cheaper midweek rates **$93**

Hotel Sol del Pacífico C Agustín Cano Castillero ☎ 994 1280. This fairly central three-storey modern block offers the best value in town, with clean, comfortable rooms with a/c and TV – though it's worth checking out several – and hot-water showers of varying temperatures. For an extra $16 you can get a larger, more modern and comfortable room. **$50**

EATING

★ **La Maestra** C Pablo Arosemena, half a block west of Parque Porras ☎ 6758 9866. Great, chilled spot featuring psychedelic art inside and out, and with an alternative vibe. Prop up the bar and try out the craft beers, or sprawl across cushions and sip a glass of sangria while browsing one of their books. They offer great soups and salads, burgers and chips, deli sandwiches ($6–8) plus a weekday *menú ejecutivo* ($6), and also host occasional jam sessions on Fri nights. Free wi-fi. Mon–Sat 8.30am–10pm, Sun 3–10pm.

Restaurante Hotel Piamonte Av Belisario Porras ☎ 994 6372. Nicely prepared Panamanian dishes at reasonable rates (mains from around $11), ensuring that the restaurant attracts more than just the hotel guests. Daily 7am–10pm.

Restaurante y Pizzería El Caserón C Moisés Espino at C Agustín Batista ☎ 994 6066. This congenial open-sided joint with outdoor terrace is a reliable choice, serving moderately priced seafood and *parrilladas* (mains $8–12) and cheap pizzas (from $6); you can bring a beer to have with the meal. Daily 7am–10pm.

The southern coast

At the flat southeastern tip of the peninsula, the tiny, quaint colonial town of **Pedasí**, 40km south of Las Tablas, is the centre of an unlikely development boom, attracting tourists and luxury real-estate agents in equal measure; as yet, though, its character remains relatively intact. The nearby wildlife refuges of **Isla Iguana** and **Isla de Cañas** draw wildlife enthusiasts, while the waves that batter the headland and southern coastline act as magnets for **surfers**. As the main road turns southwest, beyond Pedasí, skirting the golden arc of Playa Venao and the mangrove-lined bay encircling Isla de Cañas, the farmland becomes hillier and more rugged, eventually arriving in **Tonosí**, the peninsula's last main town, nestled in a valley. Heading south from there, a tarred road heads south to the remote coastal community of **Cambutal** – another surfing destination – halfway along the coast. To the west, the Azuero's western massif looms, containing its highest peaks, which top 1500m and crown the little-explored **Parque Nacional Cerro Hoya**.

Pedasí

The town of **PEDASÍ** lies near the southeastern corner of the peninsula. A former small fishing village, it was catapulted into the national consciousness in 1999 as the birthplace of Panama's first female president, **Mireya Moscoso** (see p.302), whose picture greets you on arrival. There's nothing much to do here once you've glanced around the main square, but it is a tranquil place to hang out, and provides a base for trips to Isla Iguana and Isla de Cañas, as well as being within easy reach of a string of great **surfing beaches**. Other **activities** that can be organized, depending on the season, include snorkelling, kayaking, horseriding and turtle watching. The growing expat community means there is some comfortable **accommodation** and decent **restaurants**, though places tend to come and go.

ARRIVAL AND DEPARTURE

By bus Minibuses run from Las Tablas to Pedasí (6am–6.45pm; every 45min; 45min). Heading back to Las Tablas, buses leave from outside the supermarket at similar intervals, with the last service at 5pm. The elusive buses bound for Cañas via Playa Venao (see p.167 & p.172) stop outside The Bakery on Av Central, theoretically at 7am and noon, though timings are vague.

By plane There are three Air Panama flights a week to and from Panama City (Wed, Fri & Sun; 45min; $99 one way). The airport is 2km west of town.

INFORMATION

Tourist information The tourist office (Mon–Fri 8am–4pm; ☎ 995 2339) lies 50m off Av Central on the road to Playa Arenal.

MIA office On a backstreet southeast of the main square (Mon–Fri 8am–4pm; no phone); note that, despite the offical opening hours, it is often closed.

Money Pedasí's two banks lie on Av Central; both have ATMs, though they sometimes run out of money. Note that Pedasí is the last place to get cash (and petrol) until Tonosí.

TOURS AND ACTIVITIES

TOUR OPERATORS AND GUIDES

Naturalist guides Recommended (Spanish-speaking) local independent guides Edison Cedeño (☎ 6660 9709) and Mario Espino (☎ 6789 7272) offer tours to Isla Iguana or can take you birdwatching elsewhere.

Pedasí Sports Club Av Central on the way into town ☎ 995 2894, ⓦ pedasisportsclub.com. Pedasí's longest established tour operator is PADI-certified, offering snorkelling ($60) and two-tank dives to Isla Iguana ($100), and dives at Islas Frailes ($125). It also organizes horseriding in the hills ($84), and, in season, whale watching ($73) and nocturnal turtle tours to Isla de Cañas ($73). Day-trips include a packed lunch; two people minimum for all tours.

Pedasí Tours Av Central ☎ 995 2466, ⓦ pedasitours .com. Similar tours to, though cheaper than, Pedasí Sports Club; the bare-bones boat trip to Isla Iguana costs just $37, while the whole package with picnic lunch and snorkel rental is $75. Other excursions include SUP, zip lining, turtle watching and horseriding.

ACTIVITIES

Bike rental Baba House (one block east of Av Central, behind the supermarket) rents out bicycles ($10/day).

Horseriding Contact Javier for horseriding on the beach (☎ 6502 3902; $20/hr).

ACCOMMODATION

★**Casa de Campo** Av Central ☎ 995 2733, ⓦ casacampopedasi.com. Exquisitely designed, locally owned B&B offering spacious, elegant rooms with tiled floors, plenty of wood and chic bathrooms, as well as comfortable outdoor areas (including one with TV) to retreat to, spread out among the landscaped, tree-filled compound. The large swimming pool is another plus. Dinner ($25) can be preordered. $99

Casita Margarita Av Central ☎ 995 2898, ⓦ pedasihotel.com. This American-owned boutique B&B offers five spotless, well-appointed rooms furnished

PEDASÍ

Las Tablas (40km) & Chitré (81km)

■ ACCOMMODATION	
Casa de Campo	2
Casita Margarita	6
Dim's Hostal	3
Pelicanos Hostel	5
La Rosa de los Vientos	4
Tortuga's Lodge	1

● EATING	
Bohemia Pizzería & Restaurante	4
Dulcería Yely	3
Restaurante Ejecutivo	2
Tortuga's	1

Pedasí Sports Club

Police

Bank & ATM

AVENIDA CENTRAL

Laundry

CALLE ESTUDIANTE

Supermarket

Buses to Playa Venao & Cañas

Pedasí Tours

Buses to Las Tablas & Taxis

Bank & ATM

CALLE AGUSTIN MOSCOSO

Library

Parque Pedasí

CALLE LAS TABLAS

CALLE OFELIA RELUZ

CALLE LA POLICIA

AVENIDA CENTRAL

Airport (2km)

(300m) & Playa Arenal (2.6km)

(1km), Playa El Toro (3km) & Playa La Garita (3km)

MIA office (50m)

Playa Venao (30km) & Cambutal (85km)

N

0   100
metres

in wood, with elegant shared living area and hammock-strung balcony. A vast buffet breakfast is included and trips can be organized. Reductions for long stays. $99

★**Dim's Hostal** Av Central ☎ 995 2303 or ☎ 6274 4156, ✉ reservacionesdimshostal@gmail.com. The attraction here is the wonderful hammock-filled *rancho* beneath two vast mango trees at the back of the glorified eight-room treehouse. Cosy and quirky, the rustic en-suite rooms offer a/c, cable TV and hot water. Breakfast is included and the welcoming owners can arrange excursions for modest sums. $55

Pelícanos Hostel C Las Tablas ☎ 995 2844. Basic, spotless locally owned hostel with two family rooms and two mixed dorms, a shared bathroom and kitchen plus small lounge area. Bikes available for guests. Dorms $12, doubles $28

★**La Rosa de los Vientos** On the road to Playa El Toro ☎ 6778 0627, ⊛ bedandbreakfastpedasi.com. Delightful, colonial-style architecture set in tropical grounds 1km outside Pedasí and within walking distance of the beach. Three crisp, bright rooms open out onto a shared porch. $65

Tortuga's Lodge On the road to Playa Arenal ☎ 6419 4465, ⊛ hostalrestaurantpedasi.com. Five no-frills, modern self-catering units of varying sizes and prices, aimed at long-term rental ($110–360/week, $300–650/month). Most possess fully screened windows, a/c and some have private terrace and hammock space. $30

EATING

Bohemia Pizzería & Restaurante Av Central ☎ 995 2950 or ☎ 6905 2330, ⊛ facebook.com/bohemiapedasi. The cosy, rustic interior creates a mellow ambiance to enjoy varied pasta dishes – try the ricotta and artichoke ravioli – but the deli-pizzas top the bill: super-fresh ingredients piled onto a crispy base ($9–18). Cash only. Mon, Tues & Thurs–Sun 5–10pm.

Dulcería Yely C Ofelia Reluz, just off Av Central ☎ 995 2205. Dalila Vera's bakery is a national institution that has served delicious home-made cakes to locals, Hollywood stars and presidents. Specialities include *queques* (coconut cakes made with local sugar-cane honey and a touch of aniseed) and *flan casero*, all washed down with a cup of *chicha* or *chicheme*. Daily 7am–9pm.

Restaurante Ejecutivo C Las Tablas, on the main square ☎ 995 2753. Solid Panamanian dining option with nonstop TV, inexpensive, heaped platefuls of rice and noodles in various guises, plus seafood and meat options (from $8). A good variety of traditional fried breakfasts for around $4. Daily 8am–11pm.

★**Tortuga's** On the road to Playa Arenal ☎ 6419 4465, ⊛ hostalrestaurantpedasi.com. Pleasant breezy *rancho* with wooden dining furniture, saddle-seats at the bar and a comfy lounge area. The small Mexican-themed menu – sizzling fajitas or juicy tacos – helps soak up the beer and cocktails. A good Fri-night party venue, with occasional DJ plus food and drink specials. Mon & Wed–Fri 5–10pm, Sat & Sun noon–10pm.

Refugio de Vida Silvestre Isla Iguana

Undoubtedly the best day-trip from Pedasí is to **Isla Iguana**, 4km offshore. This tiny lump of basalt, covered in dry scrub and grass, forms the centrepiece of the **REFUGIO DE VIDA SILVESTRE ISLA IGUANA**, created in 1981 to protect one of the largest and oldest coral reefs in the Golfo de Panamá. Home to more than two hundred species of colourful fish, the coral itself is not in great condition since a large chunk of the reef was blown off in the 1990s when two large bombs – relics of US training during World War II – had to be detonated.

Avoid travelling to the island during **major holiday periods**, when tourist numbers can top six hundred in a day, which puts huge pressure on the island's natural resources. Isla Iguana is a far better destination between May and December, when the calmer conditions mean crossings are smoother and snorkelling more rewarding; the sea can be so rough between January and March that it's sometimes too dangerous to set out. In the migratory season (June–Dec, especially Sept & Oct) **humpback whales** are visible, sometimes in the company of **dolphins**. The area's rich marine life also makes it popular with **scuba divers** (see p.169).

Playa El Cirial

The rugged coastline of guano- and cactus-covered basalt is interrupted by two coral-sand beaches: the larger **Playa El Cirial**, where all boats pull up, accommodates the park office and a modest visitor's centre. Playa El Cirial's small crescent of silky sand backs a sheltered cove of translucent water barely covering coral formations inhabited by a rainbow of reef fish, making it a superb spot for **swimming** and **snorkelling**.

Playita del Faro

From Playa El Cirial, a 200m **path** across the island through iguana-favoured scrub takes you to **Playita del Faro**. Strong offshore currents mean swimming and snorkelling are sometimes prohibited here, but at low tide rock pools offer plenty to explore. The basalt outcrop to the left as you reach the beach provides a vantage point for one of the island's main attractions: Panama's largest colony of **magnificent frigatebirds**, estimated to be around five thousand. January to April offers the best chance of seeing males puffing out their extraordinary inflatable scarlet pouches, yet nesting goes on all year.

ARRIVAL AND INFORMATION   ISLA IGUANA

Refuge entrance and fees Admission is $10, payable on the island; you will need to present your passport on arrival.

On a tour Pedasí Sports Club and Pedasí Tours both arrange snorkelling and diving trips to the island, as do some of the hotels and private guides (see p.169).

By taxi and boat Most Pedasí lodgings, or the tourist office, should be able to give you contact details of a fisherman with a boat at Playa Arenal – the nearest beach

to the island, 3km from Pedasí – and a taxi driver to get there ($2.50 one way). There are no buses. Arrange a pickup time with the taxi. An average price is $70 for a small boat for a half-day trip; the crossing can take upwards of 40min depending on conditions.

MIA office The Pedasí MIA office (see p.169) can, in theory, provide information about the island, though this branch is often closed.

ACCOMMODATION

Camping Rudimentary camping facilities – a latrine and a *rancho* to pitch a tent under, no electricity, and collected rainwater providing the only water for showering. You'll

need to bring drinking water as well as food and a camping stove. $\underline{\$10}$

Surfing beaches near Pedasí

The southeastern tip of the Azuero Peninsula offers desolate beauty: kilometres of smooth dark sands punctuated by rocky outcrops and pounded by surf, with a few (foreign-owned) intimate lodgings spaced along the coast, ranging from informal surf camps to boutique hotels. Though the best **surfing** conditions are encountered between March and November, the coastline is surfable all year round.

Playa El Toro and Playa La Garita are a walkable 3km or short taxi ride ($4–5) from Pedasí; follow the road out of the main square until the fork, heading left to El Toro and right to La Garita. Three kilometres south of Pedasí at the village of El Limón, a road leads off 7km to the band of chocolate sand and rocks at **Playa Los Destiladeros** (bear right at the fork), which offers point and beach breaks as well as fabulous views across the ocean ($10 taxi ride).

Playa Venao and Islas Frailes

The imposing 3km swathe of charcoal-coloured sand that is **Playa Venao** (or Venado), 30km southwest of Pedasí, is the region's best-known surfing spot, providing waves suitable for beginners and more experienced surfers alike – for lessons, contact Surf Dojo (☎838 3070, ☯surfdojo.com) at the west end of the beach. A glorious arc, Playa Venao's beauty has been somewhat diminished in recent years by ill-considered hotel developments on the sand itself, though it still manages to hold some appeal. A few kilometres out from the bay, the guano-flecked rocky stacks of **Islas Frailes** are at times covered in thousands of nesting sooty terns and other passing seabirds; you'll need a good pair of binoculars to get a decent view from the boat, since landing is impossible.

ARRIVAL AND DEPARTURE   PLAYA VENAO AND ISLAS FRAILES

By bus Buses from Las Tablas (see p.167) and Pedasí (see p.169) bound for Cañas pass through Playa Venao (1hr). Return buses from Cañas, 15min from Playa Venao, leave at

7am for Las Tablas, and at 9am and 3pm for Pedasí. Note that these timetables are only loosely adhered to.

By taxi A taxi from Pedasí to Playa Venao costs around $30.

ACCOMMODATION

Prices are often much higher for **weekends**. If you're **self-catering**, note that a truck from Las Tablas trawls the main beach resorts on Mon, Thurs and Sat mornings to sell fresh vegetables.

La Choza 200m from the beach break; contact Hotel El Sitio ☏832 1010, ⊛facebook.com/la-choza-de-playa-venao. Compact, comfortable fan-ventilated rooms, a breezy balcony and intimate garden-*rancho* kitchen facilities – all at the back of the beach, in a shady spot. Dorms $15, doubles $35

★ **Eco Venao** 1km west of the beach entrance ☏832 0530, ⊛ecovenao.com. On a hilltop overlooking the bay, this lovingly restored wooden farmhouse offers eight bunks and a couple of simple private rooms with shared kitchen and bathrooms, plus some moderately priced cane-and-thatch *cabañas* and two stone bungalows spread across the grounds. Campers share the lodge facilities, including the numerous hammocks and a volleyball court. Boat trips can be arranged, or you can explore the bay on horseback or in a kayak. There's a great on-site restaurant, *Los Sombreros*, too

(see below). Camping $7, dorms $12, doubles $33

★ **Venao Cove** West end of beach ☏6427 2129, ⊛playa-venao-panama.com. Brightly painted hostel in a great setting, overlooking the beach, with two comfortable eight-bed dorms, shared kitchen and bathroom facilities and bags of hammock room for lazing around. There are also ten spacious, light private rooms with shared kitchen and balcony; it's worth paying extra for the rooms overlooking the beach. Camping $7, dorms $12, doubles $50

Villa Marina East end of beach ☏263 6555, ⊛villamarinalodge.com. Tucked away at the back of the sand, this spacious hacienda-style boutique hotel is set in lush grounds surrounded by tropical forest with a stone infinity pool overlooking the beach. Tastefully designed with all mod cons (a/c, cable TV and safe). Continental breakfast included. $99

EATING

La Bicicleta 50m east of the beach entrance ☏6201 9338. Cosy, quirkily decorated café, with a handful of seats inside and out, offering a few cheap eats – *menú del día* ($5) or whole grilled fish – plus inexpensive beer and juice. Daily 7am–5pm.

Pizzería Gavilán Beach Break Surf Camp, east end of the beach ☏832 1124. Excellent pizzas and a fabulous location bang on the beach – no wonder it's a popular hangout. Thin-crust pizzas range from $9 to $16 and beer

goes for $3. Daily 8–10am & noon–11pm; kitchen closes at 9.30pm.

Los Sombreros Eco Venao, 1km west of the beach entrance. Hilltop restaurant under a *rancho* with a good atmosphere and good food, though the menu is limited. Veggie or meat burgers or a whole fish ($9) are served with various accompaniments, charged separately ($4–6). Healthy or traditional breakfast fry-ups are available, too. Daily 7am–9pm.

Refugio de Vida Silvestre Isla de Cañas

In the bay to the west of Playa Venao, nestled among the mangroves and a stone's throw from the swampy shoreline, lies the long sliver of land that is **REFUGIO DE VIDA SILVESTRE ISLA DE CAÑAS**. The island is synonymous with **turtles**, which arrive annually in their thousands, availing themselves of a glorious 14km band of sand to lay their eggs.

Turtles are not the only attraction, however. The reserve extends into a muddy tangle of mangroves both on the island's shore-side and along the mainland, providing roosting and nesting sites for **waterbirds**, which can be seen close up on a round-the-island **boat tour**, which also takes in a pre-Columbian archeological site (with little to see) and a strangely formed cave dubbed the "*casa de piedra*". You can also enjoy a couple of hours' gentle **fishing** or a ride in a **horse and cart** around the island's beaches and cultivations – rice, maize, banana and cocoa are all grown alongside vast quantities of juicy watermelons, which should definitely be sampled.

ARRIVAL AND DEPARTURE   ISLA DE CAÑAS

TO THE JETTY

By bus Take the bus from Las Tablas (1–1.30pm; 2hr) or Pedasí (7am & noon; 1hr) to Cañas village; you may be able to persuade the driver to drive the extra distance to the island dock (El Encerrao) for a few extra dollars. A very occasional minibus runs between Tonosí and Cañas and will

pass via the island dock if requested. The early-morning bus leaves Cañas at 7am.

By car The turn-off to the jetty is 6km west of Cañas village, opposite *Fonda El Refugio*; from there it's another 2.5km down a tarred road to the dock.

By taxi A taxi from Pedasí costs around $35.

TURTLE WATCHING AT ISLA DE CAÑAS

Five species of turtle nest on Isla de Cañas, the most numerous being the world's tiniest sea turtle, the olive ridley. Their extraordinary mass **nesting**, or *arribada* (arrival), when thousands storm the beach over several nights, is a sight to behold. Pacific green turtles also nest in large quantities alongside significantly smaller numbers of loggerhead, leatherback and hawksbill. Nesting primarily takes place between May and November, with September to November considered the peak months, though timing your visit to coincide with an **arribada** – generally several days either side of a full moon – is tricky. The island was designated a protected area in 1994 and a number of the eight-hundred-strong population are involved in protecting the turtles – for which they are permitted to harvest a percentage of the eggs for consumption and sale. Villagers also act as turtle-watching guides (see p.173), an offer worth taking up if only to increase the likelihood of more eggs hatching rather than being sold on the black market. Since female turtles are easily spooked by bright lights, it's better not to bring cameras, or torches, unless infrared; rely on the guide and let your eyes adjust to the light (see below).

TO THE ISLAND

By boat The island is only about 50m across the water, so shout across if you haven't arranged transport in advance, or ring ☎6716 4095 to call for a boat to be sent over ($3) – though ideally not at low tide as it means wading through swamp to meet it.

DAY-TRIPS AND PACKAGES

Isla Cañas Tours (☎6718 0032, ✉islac2010@hotmail .com), a local operation run by Daniel Pérez, offers all-inclusive day or overnight packages to the island.

INFORMATION

Park entrance and fees There is a small MIA office on the island, but there is rarely anyone there to collect the $5 admission charge.
Guides Trained community guides are assigned to visitors ($20) to lead the turtle watch. Fernando Domínguez

(☎6716 4095) is a reliable local guide with a couple of boats who can take you to explore the mangroves and nearby river estuary, on the lookout for crocodiles, or on fishing trips.

ACCOMMODATION

Community accommodation The village has very rudimentary cabins with fans or a/c for an extra $10; alternatively you can pitch a tent, or stay with a family.

There are also a couple of small inexpensive *fondas*. Camping $\overline{\underline{\$5}}$, cabins $\overline{\underline{\$20}}$

Cambutal and around

For most people Playa Venao is remote enough, but die-hard surfers may want to try the even more out-of-the-way spots around **CAMBUTAL**, a small fishing village 60km west. The journey takes you through undulating cattle country – spectacularly lush in the rainy season, desperately barren once the moisture has been sucked out of it. Picturesque, charcoal **Playa Cambutal** and some of the surfing beaches further west get serious 3m waves; non-surfers, meanwhile, can explore the caves, blowholes and crevices of this impressively rugged coastline.

Fifteen kilometres east, around Punto Morro, the less publicized **Guánico Abajo** enjoys a fabulously scenic location. There is a new surf camp here, plus good waves at **Playa Guánico Abajo** and mangroves to explore; at the nearby **Playa Marinera,** where cream-coloured sands are hemmed in by cliffs, more than thirty thousand olive ridley turtles lay their eggs each year. To reach both Cambutal and Guánico Abajo, you first have to head inland and pass through **Tonosí**, which is little more than a glorified regional crossroads surrounded by hilly cattle ranches; it does, however, offer all the basic amenities around the main square, including an ATM and the local **MiAmbiente office**.

ARRIVAL AND DEPARTURE

CAMBUTAL AND AROUND

By bus To reach Playa Cambutal or Playa Guánico Abajo you first need to take a bus to Tonosí from Las Tablas (8am, 10am, then hourly until 5pm; 1hr 20min). From Playa Venao, take the first bus to Cañas, and catch the 8am minivan to Tonosí. From Tonosí local buses depart from outside the two supermarkets in the town centre, near the main square. Cambutal departures are at approximately 8am, 10am and 2pm, returning to Tonosí at 7am and 11am; Guánico Abajo departures are at 7am and 1.30pm, returning to Tonosí at 10am and 3pm.

By car The roads to Cambutal and Guánico Abajo are tarred, but at the time of writing sections of the road between Playa Venao and Tonosí were in a poor state; seek advice before driving a saloon car there in the rainy season.

By taxi A taxi from Tonosí to Playa Cambutal or Playa Guánico Abajo costs $15.

INFORMATION AND TOURS

MIA office Just off the main square in Tonosí (Mon–Fri 8am–4pm; ⓣ995 8180). They may be able to help with information on Isla de Cañas, and on accessing Parque Nacional Cerro Hoya (see below).

Bank The only bank (with ATM) in the area is on the main square in Tonosí.

Turtle patrols Tortuagro (ⓣ6264 9124, ⓦfacebook.com/agrotortugasc), Cambutal's local turtle conservation group welcomes visitors on nightly beach patrols and for hatchling releases (July–Dec), for a small donation.

ACCOMMODATION AND EATING

PLAYA CAMBUTAL

★Hostal Kambutaleko ⓣ6677 0229, ⓦhostalkambutaleko.com. Breezy hilltop *hostal* with charming hosts, boasting five simple fan-ventilated doubles and one family room with a/c, all sharing a wraparound, ocean-view terrace. All have a private bathroom and some have a fridge. No kitchen, but there's an affordable patio restaurant. $45

Hotel Playa Cambutal ⓣ832 0948, ⓦhotelplayacambutal.net. The new colonial-style hotel on the beach offers ten spacious ocean-view rooms. Fishing charters, kayaking, horseriding and hiking excursions can all be arranged and service is friendly and professional. Buffet breakfast included. $135

PLAYA GUÁNICO ABAJO

Jorón On the beach. Large attractive *rancho* with carved wooden pillars, where you can tuck into large plates of *concha*, *camarones* or fish with rice or *patacones* from $8. Beer is cheap ($1) and flows at weekends. Daily 9am–9pm.

Surf Camp Guánico ⓣ6677 2899, ⓦsurfcampguanico.com. In a great beachside location, this stylish surf camp has one six-bed dorm with rustic bunks, lockers and shared cold-water facilities, as well as pricier doubles and family rooms upstairs at various rates (shared or private bathroom; fan or a/c), some of which boast a fabulous ocean-facing balcony. The bar-food menu is limited, but you can use the kitchen (for $3 extra) or eat nearby. Surf lessons are available, as is board, SUP and kayak rental and excursions to Cerro Hoya. There's also a delightful private "love nest" beach shack aimed at longer-term lets. Dorm $16, doubles $50, beach shack $80

TONOSÍ

Hotel Mi Valle Main square ⓣ995 8089, ⓔhotelmivalle@gmail.com. Modern, functional hotel facing the park in the centre of town, offering 24 bland but clean en-suite rooms with the usual amenities (a/c, satellite TV, wi-fi); some have fridges. The on-site restaurant serves inexpensive Panamanian food. $30

Parque Nacional Cerro Hoya

Tucked away in the southwest corner of the Azuero Peninsula, **PARQUE NACIONAL CERRO HOYA** covers 325 square kilometres of the isthmus's most ancient volcanic rocks, and contains more than thirty species of endemic plant. This is one of the country's most inaccessible parks; transport is tricky, and formal trails and accommodation are lacking – which is why MiAmbiente currently does not collect an entry fee. But the rewards are plenty: giant mahogany, cedar, cuipo and ceiba trees soar above the forest canopy, and carpets of moist **forest** rise up from the sea to lofty Cerros Hoya (1559m), Moya (1478m) and Soya (1326m). A few scarlet and great green **macaws** maintain a fragile foothold in the forest, as does the endemic Azuero **parakeet**; other critically endangered species include the **Azuero spider** and **howler monkeys**, while substantial populations of **white-tailed deer** pick their way through the forest floor, shared with agoutis, collared peccaries and coatis. As the park's name suggests (*hoya* means river bed), the massif nourishes more than ten major rivers, home to caimans and otters, and hundreds of streams that tumble down to the coast, leaving natural **swimming pools** and **waterfalls** in their wake. The protected area extends out into the sea, including precious mangroves and secluded coves enclosed by sheer cliffs, providing sheltered sands for hawksbill, olive ridley and even some leatherback turtles to lay their eggs.

Created in 1985, in a desperate attempt to stop the Azuero's haemorrhaging of forest through destructive agricultural practices, the national park and its protecting agencies are helping the population of about two thousand – scattered around 25 communities – to make a livelihood from sustainable agroforestry, ecotourism, animal husbandry and fishing projects. The best time to visit is early in the **dry season** when the views are more spectacular, the mud less overwhelming and the hiking more pleasurable, yet the waterfalls and rivers – two of the major attractions – still hold sufficient water to impress.

ARRIVAL AND DEPARTURE PARQUE NACIONAL CERRO HOYA

FROM THE WEST

The park is most accessible from the Western Azuero, via the community of Flores, close to the northern park boundary, or, less easily, via the coastal hamlet of Restingue, which marks the southwestern park boundary.

To Flores A tarred road leaves the Interamericana just east of Santiago, skirting the coast for more than 90km down to the village of Arenas, where it heads east the last 6km to Flores. There are infrequent buses from Santiago to Arenas and Flores (see p.176).

To Restingue Getting to Restingue means travelling south from Arenas along an 18km dirt road (high-clearance 4WD necessary) and crossing two major rivers. This is only possible in the dry season, when the occasional *chiva* also makes the journey; once the rains start, horses may be able to pass, or you have to travel by boat.

Guides In Flores seek out Miguel Moreno (☎6597 0280), who runs a small shop opposite the primary school, and can guide in the park – though note he can only receive text messages (in Spanish) on weekday mornings. Juan Velásquez is also recommended. The village public phone is ☎333 0596. You will also be able to find someone to guide you in Restingue.

FROM THE EAST

To El Cobachón To get to Cerro Hoya from the east, take the dirt road west from Cambutal for 22km to the hamlet of El Cobachón, close to the park boundary. Whether on horseback, in a 4WD or on foot (which entails some shortcuts along the beach at low tide, so a tide timetable is essential), the road from Cambutal is only accessible in dry season, since several rivers need to be forded. Alternatively, take a boat from Cambutal or neighbouring Los Buzos to El Cobachón, which will be costly ($80), unless you get a lift with MIA staff or catch a *colectivo* heading that way. Marcelino Rodríguez usually accepts campers in El Cobachón.

Guides Daniel Sáenz, based in El Cobachón, comes highly recommended, and can arrange horses. Contact his sister, Regina Caballero, in Cambutal (☎6221 5060), or the MIA representative (see below).

ORGANIZED TOURS

Organized tours You can explore the park with Tanager Tourism, run by the owners of *Hotel Heliconia* south of Mariato (see p.176); other accommodation options also offer excursions.

INFORMATION

MIA offices However you choose to get to Cerro Hoya, you will need to consult MIA: in Cambutal (contact Armodio Ortega ☎6215 7408), Las Tablas (☎500 0921), Tonosí (☎995 8180) or Santiago (☎998 4387).

The Western Azuero

The little-explored coastline of the **Western Azuero** has a very different feel to the dry, flat stretches of sand that line the eastern seaboard. Receiving much more rain, the countryside is greener and lusher, despite the cattle ranching and occasional rice cultivation. As the sole access road threads its way more than 90km south from the Interamericana through an increasingly undulating landscape, it offers tantalizing glimpses of rocky coastline, hidden coves and foaming surf. Best of all, since the beaches face west, they witness glorious **sunsets**. Sprinkled along the coast some delightful new lodgings offer perfect places to unwind for a few days.

Settlements are few and far between in the Western Azuero, and transport is sporadic: the first place of note, some 50km south of the turn-off from the Interamericana, is

Mariato, with a broad central boulevard dotted with *fondas*. Its main feature is its temple-like bank and ATM, and with a couple of small supermarkets and a petrol station, it's a good place to stock up with essentials if you're travelling in your own vehicle or self-catering. Three kilometres southwest of Mariato, the pebble-and-sand **Playa Reina** stretches south to the mouth of the Río Negro, where you can find transport to Isla Cébaco (see box, p.210).

Fifteen kilometres south of Mariato on the main road, the tiny hilltop hamlet of **Torio**, and its surrounding area, is the unlikely centre of the area's nascent tourism scene, offering several places to stay and eat. The increasingly roller-coaster road then bypasses **Punta Duarte** and the new surfing hot spot of **Playa Morillo** – home to one of the country's most isolated surf camps (ⓦvillaventosurfhostels.com) – before arriving in **Arenas** and **Flores**, where the tarred road comes to a halt before the massif of Parque Nacional Cerro Hoya.

ARRIVAL AND INFORMATION   THE WESTERN AZUERO

MARIATO AND TORIO
By bus Buses run from Santiago to Mariato (Mon–Fri 5.30–7am every 30min, then hourly until 7pm; 1hr 15min), with some buses continuing to Torio (1hr 40min). The last return bus from Torio to Santiago leaves at 4.45pm. At weekends, and Sunday in particular, transport is far less frequent, and less reliable.

ARENAS AND FLORES
By bus At least one bus a day from Santiago is scheduled to go as far as Arenas and Flores (Mon–Fri 5am; 2hr 30min–3hr), and other Mariato and Torio buses from Santiago may go that far depending on demand; if there are no local passengers, you'll have to pay extra for the driver to take you the full way. On weekdays a bus leaves Flores for Santiago at 6am; other, infrequent buses tend to leave Arenas, though you should be prepared to hitch a ride.

By car The road is tarred all the way to Flores but note that the last petrol station is in Mariato – and it is often closed, so fill up in Santiago or Atalaya (see p.205).

ACCOMMODATION AND EATING

MARIATO
Hotel Heliconia Main road, Palmilla, 8km south of Mariato ☏6676 0220, ⓦhotelheliconia.com. Modern, nicely furnished, four-room B&B with a porch offering comfortable seating and surrounded by a lush tropical garden. The Dutch biologist owners are engaged in reforestation projects and ecotourism under the name of Tanager Tourism: the most popular trip is a three-day tour to Isla Coiba ($1300 for two), but outings to Isla Cébaco and Cerro Hoya are also possible. $97

★**Hotel Playa Reina** Playa Reina, 3km south of Mariato ☏6461 2725, ⓦhotelplayareina.com. A relaxing place set in shady surroundings on the beach, this newly renovated hotel has a/c rooms to suit all wallets

---

TURTLE CONSERVATION IN THE WESTERN AZUERO

The tranquil soft sands of the Western Azuero coastline provide prime nesting sites for **turtles**: the vast majority are olive ridley, with the occasional leatherback, green or hawksbill turtles also laying their eggs here. Two established **turtle conservation groups** run nightly beach patrols during the nesting season (July–Nov), monitoring and protecting turtle nest sites: on **Playa Malena** in the hamlet of the same name, 11km south of Mariato, and in the small settlement of **Quebro**, midway between Torio and Arenas. In the latter, the community Asociacion de Agro-Pesca Ecoturística Quebro (AAPEQ), which also works on mangrove reforestation, collaborates with the Fundación de Agua y Tierra (ⓦFacebook.com/www.fundat .org) on turtle conservation on nearby Playa Mata Oscura. You can accompany either organization on a beach patrol for a small donation, or could even offer your services as a volunteer, provided that you speak some Spanish. Both offer cheap **accommodation**, and some volunteers camp on Playa Mata Oscura.

ACCOMMODATION
Centro AAPEQ Quebro ☏6389 5249. Bunks in roadside accommodation – ask for Digna Peralta for the key. $10
Hostal Iguana Malena ☏6865 3908. Ana González, chair of the local turtle association, rents out a few simple rooms with fan or a/c, as dorm beds or privates. Dorms $15, doubles $35

– from superior dorm bunks with lockers to standard doubles and ocean-facing suites (with fridge, kitchenette and various trimmings). Curl up in a hammock with a book, splash in the infinity pool, surf the waves or explore with the free kayaks, SUPs or bicycles; snorkelling excursions to Isla Cébaco are available at extra cost. You can eat nicely prepared fresh food at the restaurant – or find cheaper eats nearby. Midweek reductions. Dorms $\overline{\$16}$, doubles $\overline{\$35}$, suites $\overline{\$95}$

TORIO

Brisas del Mar Main road at the turn-off to the beach. The wooden tables of this no-frills bar-restaurant are packed with locals, expats and tourists during the summer, especially on Fri and Sat nights, reeled in by inexpensive fresh fish, langoustines and lobster ($9–12) plus good-value *comida corriente* ($4) and cheap beer. Mon–Thurs & Sun 8/9am–7pm, Fri & Sat 8/9am–late.

★**Hotel El Sol** 8km south of Torio ☎ 6616 1632, ⓦ ecoelsol.com.pa. This exclusive, design-conscious retreat makes the most of its hillside location, offering stunning ocean views. The dazzling yellow exteriors, reflecting the hotel's name, give way to more sophisticated colour schemes and works of art in the seven guestrooms. It's a place to indulge, relaxing in a hammock or in the pool, or being pampered with massage and spa treatments. The gourmet meals, prepared by the owner-chef, draw on fresh local ingredients. Breakfast included. $\overline{\$100}$

Punta Duarte Garden Inn Punta Duarte, 6.5km south of Torio ☎ 6152 7817, ⓦ puntaduarte.com. Cosy, moderately priced B&B, a stone's throw from a pale grey soft-sand beach, offering five spacious a/c rooms with private balcony and sea views; two have self-catering facilities. There is also an ocean-facing pool and jacuzzi, and they can organize horseriding, plus trips to Isla Cébaco. $\overline{\$85}$

4

Chiriquí and Veraguas

SURFING AT SANTA CATALINA

5

Chiriquí and Veraguas

From the raging torrents of the Río Chiriquí Viejo and the verdant peaks of the Cordillera Central to the marine-rich coral, swampy mangroves and empty sands of the Golfo de Chiriquí, the diverse scenery of Chiriquí and Veraguas offers some of Panama's top natural attractions. Magnificent in their own right, they also provide the setting for a range of exhilarating outdoor adventure activities, including whitewater rafting, kayaking, diving, surfing, hiking and zip lining. Though Veraguas is the only province in the country to border both the Atlantic and Pacific oceans, Chiriquí gets most of the headlines since – as Chiricanos will proudly remind you – the province is the *granero* (granary) or *canasta de pan* (breadbasket) of Panama. As well as growing most of the country's agricultural produce – everything from rice to strawberries – it also boasts the country's second city, David, and its best-known mountain resort town, Boquete.

The **Tierras Altas** (Highlands) at the western end of Panama, north of David, attract the most attention and the most tourists, with the cool, sunny climate and spectacular scenery of **Boquete** drawing North American and European retirees. The town makes a great base for exploring the cloud forests or ascending Panama's highest peak, **Volcán Barú**, which can also be approached from the less touristy settlements of **Volcán** and **Cerro Punta** on its western flanks. The latter provides a convenient springboard for the rugged, little-explored peaks of the **Parque Internacional La Amistad**.

A large area of the forested slopes of eastern Chiriquí forms part of the **Comarca Ngäbe-Buglé**, which includes some of western Veraguas on both sides of the continental divide and extends into much of Bocas del Toro province (see p.218). South of the central cordillera lie the **Tierras Bajas** (Lowlands), home to the tranquil provincial capitals of **David** and **Santiago**, the former coming alive during its annual international agricultural fair in March (see box, p.198); the region's other main festival, celebrating flowers and coffee, takes place in Boquete every January.

South of David lies the **Golfo de Chiriquí**, a vast body of water with beautiful coastal fringes and deserted islands, which stretches from the Costa Rican border to the Veraguas side of the Azuero Peninsula in the east. Surrounded by nutrient-rich waters that attract dazzling aquatic life, including humpback whales, the gulf contains the mangroves and coral of **Parque Nacional Marino Golfo de Chiriquí** and the former penitentiary of **Isla Coiba**, which is renowned for its scuba diving and pristine rainforest. It is most easily accessed from **Santa Catalina**, a mellow fishing village and the country's top surfing venue, tucked away in the southwestern corner of Veraguas.

COFFEE PICKING, BOQUETE

Highlights

❶ **Coffee** Learn to tell a "buttery" from a "chocolatey" aroma on some of the world's finest gourmet coffee estates. **See p.187**

❷ **Birdwatching** Seek out the resplendent quetzal and rare hummingbirds in the eerie cloud forests of the Chiriquí Highlands. **See p.187**

❸ **Whitewater rafting** Dramatic rapids set in breathtaking mountains make the Río Chiriquí Viejo an exhilarating whitewater run. **See p.188**

❹ **Hiking in the Chiriquí Highlands** From the glorious cloud forests of the Sendero de los Quetzales to the breathtaking panorama at the summit of Volcán Barú, the region provides some of Panama's most spectacular trails. See p.190

❺ **Parque Nacional Marino Golfo de Chiriquí** Head out in a boat to explore swathes of mangrove and idyllic tropical islands, with abundant marine life. **See p.202**

❻ **Santa Fé** This tranquil mountain town makes a good base for exploring the surrounding waterfalls and hills, with strenuous hiking on offer in the nearby national park. **See p.207**

❼ **Santa Catalina** The country's capital of surf boasts first-class waves and a laidback ambience. **See p.210**

❽ **Parque Nacional Coiba** You can enjoy outstanding diving, whale watching and pristine rainforests in this penitentiary turned wildlife reserve. **See p.212**

HIGHLIGHTS ARE MARKED ON THE MAP ON PP.182–183

5

To reach here you pass through the provincial capital, **Santiago**, a bustling commercial and agricultural centre that is also the gateway to the **central highlands** to the north. The standout destination in this region is the delightful unspoilt mountain village of **Santa Fé**, which is renowned for its orchids and waterfalls, and provides access to a little-explored national park.

Brief history

The **Ngäbe** and closely related **Buglé** – both recognizable by the women's brightly coloured cotton dresses – were collectively referred to as Guaymí in colonial accounts,

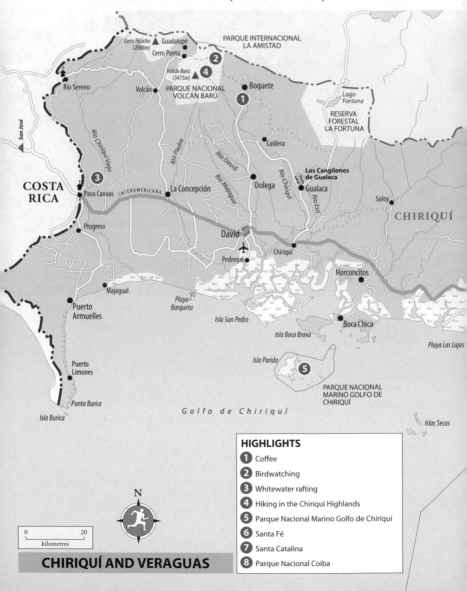

HIGHLIGHTS

1. Coffee
2. Birdwatching
3. Whitewater rafting
4. Hiking in the Chiriquí Highlands
5. Parque Nacional Marino Golfo de Chiriquí
6. Santa Fé
7. Santa Catalina
8. Parque Nacional Coiba

CHIRIQUÍ AND VERAGUAS

featuring prominently as fierce warriors. Their tribes, alongside many others that never survived the colonial struggle, were pushed up into the mountains by the **Spanish**, who moved into the region in the late sixteenth century. Founding major centres in Remedios (1589) and Alanje (1591), the colonizers also established numerous mission towns such as San Félix, San Lorenzo and Tolé. Though some Guaymí succumbed to their evangelizing efforts, others formed alliances among themselves and with passing pirates, and the towns were regularly raided and sometimes destroyed.

Following the separation from Colombia, the province of Chiriquí, which had been established in 1849, gained its own railway – which folded around 1980 – in

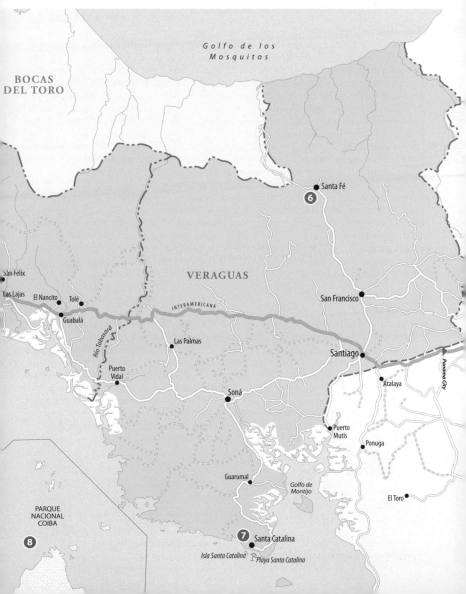

5

recognition of its agricultural importance; soon the United Fruit Company began banana production round Puerto Armuelles in 1927 and coffee plantations started to thrive. It is on such plantations that the Ngäbe and Buglé now work, travelling great distances throughout the provinces of Chiriquí and Bocas del Toro – migrant wage labourers on rich lands that once belonged to their ancestors.

The Chiriquí Highlands

North of David rise the slopes of the eastern limits of the Cordillera de Talamanca, home to Volcán Barú (3475m), the country's highest point. These are the **Chiriquí Highlands**, or Tierras Altas, a region of forested peaks, fertile valleys and mountain villages. The cool, temperate climate and stark scenery give the highlands a distinctly Alpine feel, an impression reinforced by the influence of the many European migrants who have settled here since the nineteenth century. Sadly, their agricultural success poses a threat to the survival of the region's spectacular **cloud forests**, which have been cleared at a devastating rate over the past forty years, while Chiriquí's picturesque rivers have attracted major hydroelectric projects, which are beginning to cause serious environmental damage, as well as posing a major threat to the livelihoods and cultural heritage of the indigenous communities.

More positively, large tracts of forest are now protected by **Parque Nacional Volcán Barú** and **Parque Internacional La Amistad**, whose flanks are home to wildlife including jaguars, pumas, tapirs and resplendent quetzals, and whose trails offer some of the best hiking in Panama.

Two roads wind up into the highlands on either side of Volcán Barú. The first climbs due north to **Boquete**, an idyllic coffee-growing town cradled in a picturesque valley, which has become popular among foreign retirees and tourists and is the easiest place from which to climb **Volcán Barú**. The second runs north from the town of La Concepción, 25km west of David, snaking 32km through countless dairy farms to the smaller settlement of **Volcán**, before threading its way through a steep-sided valley to **Cerro Punta**, the highest village in Panama and the best base for visiting the cloud forests and Amistad.

Boquete

Set in a scenic valley on the banks of the Río Caldera, 37km north of David and 1000m above sea level, **BOQUETE** is the largest town in the Chiriquí Highlands, with a population of more than 22,000. It is to gourmet **coffee** what Bordeaux is to fine wine, with an array of informative *finca* tours to choose from (see p.187). It's also a popular weekend resort, offering some of the country's best **hiking**, **birdwatching** and **adventure sports** in a delightfully refreshing climate. Life in the laidback town revolves around the small Parque Central and the main street, Avenida Central, dotted with souvenir shops, with a couple of low-key attractions on its fringes. There's plenty to occupy you for several days – longer if you take a **Spanish course** at one of the town's acclaimed language schools (ⓦhablayapanama.com; ⓦspanishatlocations.com).

BOQUETE'S FESTIVALS

Boquete's main festival, **Feria de Flores y Café** (ⓦferiadeboquete.com), takes place midway through the coffee harvest in January. Its ten-day riot of craft stalls, flowers, stage shows and throbbing late-night music centres on the fairgrounds bordering the eastern banks of the Río Caldera. Around $20,000 is spent annually on a vibrant floral carpet – which you can still admire once the fair has ended. The fairgrounds burst into colour again for the annual **Feria de las Orquídeas** in April, while the **Boquete Jazz and Blues Festival** (ⓦboquetejazzandbluesfestival.com) reels in visitors in February/March.

Technically, Boquete, spread out along the west bank of the Río Caldera and set against a mountainous backdrop, is separated into **Alto Boquete**, on the lip of the escarpment leading into the valley, and **Bajo Boquete**, considered to be Boquete proper. The surrounding slopes are dotted with shady coffee plantations, lush gardens and orange groves, and rise to rugged peaks. The thick cloud that envelops them often descends on the town as a veil-like fine mist known as *bajareque*, producing spectacular rainbows when the sun emerges. Only when the sky clears, most often in the early morning, can you see the imperious peak of **Volcán Barú**, which dominates the town to the northwest.

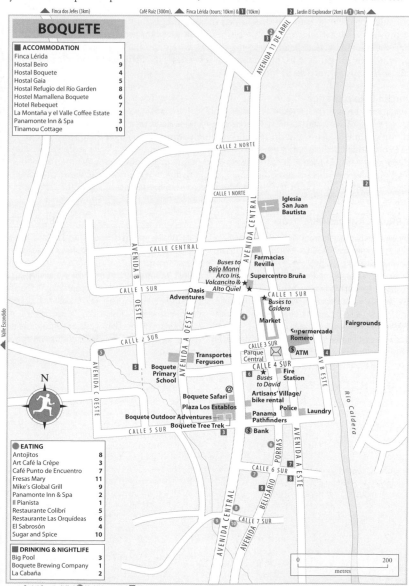

BOQUETE

ACCOMMODATION

Finca Lérida	1
Hostal Beiro	9
Hostal Boquete	4
Hostal Gaia	5
Hostal Refugio del Rio Garden	8
Hostel Mamallena Boquete	6
Hotel Rebequet	7
La Montaña y el Valle Coffee Estate	2
Panamonte Inn & Spa	3
Tinamou Cottage	10

EATING

Antojitos	8
Art Café la Crêpe	3
Café Punto de Encuentro	7
Fresas Mary	11
Mike's Global Grill	9
Panamonte Inn & Spa	2
Il Pianista	1
Restaurante Colibrí	5
Restaurante Las Orquídeas	6
El Sabrosón	4
Sugar and Spice	10

DRINKING & NIGHTLIFE

Big Pool	3
Boquete Brewing Company	1
La Cabaña	2

5

Brief history

Though the **Guaymí** were the first inhabitants of this remote valley, seeking refuge from the conquistadors, formal settlement only started in 1911, when **European and North Americans migrants** joined the existing population. Drawn to Panama during the canal construction eras, these pioneering settlers started up the various coffee estates and hotels as Boquete continued to develop, especially when, in 1916, the (now defunct) national railway improved connections with David and other lowland centres.

In recent years, the increase in **foreign retirees** and associated **real estate boom**, driven by the government's attempts to increase foreign investment, has resulted in considerable deforestation and has forced major changes on the tranquil mountain community. Many Guaymí are only resident nowadays for the duration of the coffee harvest (Oct–March, depending on the estate), when families migrate from across the province for the tiring work of picking the "cherries", the earnings from which have to support many for the rest of the year.

Jardín El Explorador

Jaramillo Arriba, 2km north of Boquete • Mon–Fri 9.30am–5pm, Sat & Sun 10am–7pm (in low season closed Mon and reduced hours) • $7 • ☎ 720 1989 • Cross the bridge in Boquete and follow the road north; turn right at the fork and walk uphill to Jaramillo Arriba

If you've time to spare, and don't mind the high admission charge, the quirky **Jardín El Explorador** northeast of Boquete is worth the forty-minute walk. Its steep gardens are decorated with tin men and scarecrows, with plants protruding from Wellington boots and old TV sets, plus scattered homilies in Spanish. On a clear day the views of the Caldera Valley and Volcán Barú from the rose garden are fabulous, as are the strawberry juices at their café.

ARRIVAL AND INFORMATION   BOQUETE

By bus The only way to reach Boquete by bus is from David's bus terminal (4.50am–9.45pm; every 20min; returning at similar intervals 5.45am–9.45pm; 45min); buses drop passengers on the west side of the Parque Central, and depart just off its southeast corner.

By shuttle *Hostel Mamallena Boquete* (see p.189) runs daily shuttle services to and from Bocas del Toro and Santa Catalina. Shuttles from Bocas del Toro to Boquete leave at 11am (4hr; $30, including water-taxi), whereas shuttles to Bocas leave Boquete at 8am. The service to Boquete from

Santa Catalina departs at noon (5hr; $35) and leaves Boquete for Santa Catalina at 7.30am. There are reductions for hostel guests.

Tourist information The best advice and information is to be gained from the hotels or tour operators. The tourist office (daily 9.30am–5.30pm; ☎ 720 4060) and adjacent café is inconveniently, if splendidly, located on the bluff overlooking the town at Alto Boquete, on the road to David. Few of the staff speak English and their knowledge is limited.

GEISHA COFFEE

In most of the world, the word "**geisha**" evokes elaborately made-up Japanese entertainers. Mention the word in Boquete and you'll be naming a deluxe beverage that took the speciality coffee world by storm in 2004, prompting ecstatic experts to exhaust their thesauruses. As with fine wine, the world of gourmet coffee tasting or **cupping** is full of hype, jargon and poetry. Geisha – a variety of bean named after its village of origin in Ethiopia – has variously been characterized as spicy, honeyish, chocolatey and citrusy, with one critic likening the experience to "diving head first into a swimming pool of mixed fruits". The fuss started when the small Hacienda Esmeralda began sampling individual cups of beans from different parts of the farm – usually combined in blends – and discovered an extraordinary Ethiopian variety that had been growing neglected for some years. Having been declared the world's best coffee on three occasions by the prestigious Specialty Coffee Association of America, the estate's "Esmeralda Especial" is very much in demand, setting an auction record of $350 per lb in 2013. Since almost all the farm's slender annual hundred-bag crop is exported you have a better chance of locating it at Fortnum & Mason than anywhere in Panama. Although you won't get to sample any Esmeralda Especial on a Boquete coffee tour (see p.187), you will at least learn what goes into making a great coffee.

GETTING AROUND

On foot or by taxi Getting around the centre of Boquete is easy on foot, while a $2–3 taxi ride will get you to most places on the fringes of town.

By minibus Local minibuses from outside Supercentro Bruña, close to the Parque Central, head up to the surrounding hillside hamlets such as Volcancito and Alto Quiel. Most drive a loop; no journey will cost more than $2.50 (Mon–Sat 6.30/7am–5/6pm; every 15–40min, depending on demand; less frequent on Sun).

ACTIVITIES AND TOURS

You will need a **guide** for some of the hikes; inevitably, however, in a tourist-boom area everyone wants a piece of the cake, and some "guides" and operators lack the skills and equipment (first-aid kits for mountain guides, for example) for the job. If in doubt, seek **advice** from your accommodation.

GENERAL TOUR OPERATORS

Oasis Adventures C 1 Sur, between Av "A" Oeste and Av Central ☎720 3361, ☎6920 6554, ⓦfacebook.com /OasisAdventuresBoquete. For a less touristy, more local experience (in Spanish) visit this family-run farm in the folds of Volcán Barú. Experience a 2–3hr farm tour and a guided walk in the surrounding hills for $35 or camp overnight – in your own tent ($20/person) or in one of theirs (mattress but no bedding; $50/person, including the tour). Transfer from Boquete included in all rates.

Panama Pathfinders Av Central at C 5 "A" Sur ☎6442 6321, ⓦpanamapathfinders.com. Owned and operated by Chiricano Patricio Ortíz, who combines environmental training with local knowledge and social commentary to enhance the usual tours: Caldera hot springs ($35); Volcán Barú or quetzal trail hikes; day-trips to the Golfo de Chiriquí islands ($75).

COFFEE TOURS

Coffee tours, offered in English or Spanish, range from 45min introductions to 3hr interactive marathons, involving a lesson on how to hone your cupping (tasting) skills and a tour of the estate and roasting facilities. Remember not to wear scent, repellent or any strong-smelling lotion. Apart from the short tour in Café Ruiz, for which you can simply roll up, tours need to be prebooked.

Café Ruiz Av Central, 500m north of town ☎730 9575 or ☎6672 3786, ⓦcaferuiz–boquete.com. Panama's largest producer of gourmet coffee offers a nuts-and-bolts tour of its roasting facility (Mon–Fri 7.15am; 45min; $9) led by multilingual Ngäbe or Buglé cuppers. You'll learn about the production process from plucking to packaging, how to distinguish the different varieties and how to judge quality. All tours end at their coffee shop (Mon–Sat 7am–6pm, Sun 10am–6pm). Longer outings focus on the tasting process (Mon–Fri 7.15am; 90min; $15–20, depending on numbers), while the full works (Mon–Sat 9am & 1.30pm; 3hr; $30) includes a visit to the plantation. The two longer tours include hotel transfer from Boquete.

Finca Dos Jefes El Salto ☎6677 7748, ⓦfincadosjefes .com. Enjoyable hands-on tour (9am & 2pm; 3hr; $30) – including a roasting session – of a small organic farm where coffee is cultivated in accordance with the lunar calendar. The US owners practise Direct Trade. Hotel transfer included.

Finca Lérida Alto Quiel ☎720 2285, ⓦfincalerida .com. Spectacular setting for a comprehensive estate tour (most days 9.30am & 1.30pm; 2hr; $45), which includes watching the action in the original 1922 processing plant. Take the Alto Quiel bus from Boquete or a taxi ($7–8) – transfers are not included.

HIKING, RIDING AND BIRDWATCHING

Feliciano González ☎6624 9940, ⓔfeliciano gonzalez255@hotmail.com. Feliciano has taken people up and down Volcán Barú so often over the last twenty years he almost lives up there. Enthusiastic, popular and with constantly improving English and a little French, he charges modest rates ($25–60 for two). He also offers a four-day trip over the cordillera and down to the coast in Bocas, camping and staying in indigenous villages.

Jason Lara ☎6718 6279, ⓦjasonlaratours.com. Trained English teacher turned renowned birding guide, Jason Lara is the person to take you birdwatching (with his telescope) for a morning ($60/person for two to four people).

Franklin Rovetto ☎6588 5054. Two-hour horseback excursions across the open countryside in the foothills of the cordillera round Caldera ($35, including Boquete transfer; English spoken). It's cheaper to deal directly with Franklin than through the tour operators.

CANOPY TOURS

Boquete Tree Trek Office in Plaza Los Establos, zip line in Palo Alto ☎720 1635, ⓦboquetetreetrek.com. Soar across the valleys along an impressive 3km zip-line tour high above Boquete (1600m) in a series of adrenaline surges that scarcely give you time to admire the breathtaking scenery ($65). Alternatively, take a guided walk through the canopy along eight swing bridges ($30), or combine both activities for $80. After a 90min thrill you can chill at their pleasant terrace café-cum-bar-restaurant – you can even stay overnight in spacious cabins. Transport included (departures daily 8am, 10.30am & 1pm).

5

WHITEWATER RAFTING FROM BOQUETE

Until the completion of a controversial dam a few years ago, the tumbling waters of the 128km-long **Chiriquí Viejo**, hugging the border of Costa Rica, constituted one of the world's great **whitewater rafting** rivers. It's still a top-class route to raft, providing an exhilarating descent with mostly category III rapids carving their way through stunning scenery. There are, however, other equally picturesque and enjoyable rivers within closer striking distance of Boquete, such as the **Fonseca**, **Gariché** and **Majagua**, with category II and III rapids. The rafting **season** predictably dovetails with the rains (May to Dec).

Although the rafting outfits are located in Boquete, by the time all the passengers have been picked up and you've crawled up the spectacularly sinuous road to the drop-off point, Chiriquí Viejo is almost two hours' drive away, whatever the operators may claim. If you are staying in **David**, you can arrange a pickup there (which operators regularly do) or, if you're in **Volcán**, a rendezvous on the Interamericana at the turn-off in Concepción. The descent ends at the Interamericana bridge near Paso Canoas.

The rafting companies in Boquete are professional outfits, but the sport is not without risk. Bring sun block, trainers and a change of clothes (you will get wet and possibly thrown out of the raft); don't be afraid to ask for clarification on safety issues, and know your limits.

RAFTING AND KAYAKING OPERATORS

Boquete Outdoor Adventures Plaza Los Establos ☎720 2284, ⓦboqueteoutdooradventures.com. Known for rafting ($65), but also offers the usual hiking, birdwatching, coffee and adventure day-tours as well as multiday, multi-activity adventures (around $150 for two days) with optional accommodation add-ons.

Boquete Safari Near Plaza Los Establos ☎6627 8829. Whitewater rafting day-trips ($65) and a host of other tours, including on the ever-popular ATVs ($65 and up) and a number of popular hikes – including up Volcán Barú and along the Sendero de los Quetzales.

MOUNTAIN BIKING

Mountain bike rental You can rent new bikes with helmets ($15/day) from a stall in the Boquete Artisans' Village on Av Central.

ROCK CLIMBING

Panama Rock Climbing ☎6764 7918, ⓦpanamarockclimbing.blogspot.com. Rock climbing and abseiling (rappelling) are relatively new to Panama – try this local outfit run by Panama's first internationally certified (bilingual) guide César Meléndez ($45/3hr). The favoured destination is the Gunko de Boquete, a fascinating lump of basalt that was spewed out of Volcán Barú when it last erupted, a 10min drive north of Boquete.

ACCOMMODATION

There's a decent range of predominantly foreign-owned **accommodation**, all with hot water, in a burgeoning mid-range market. Since most places only have a handful of rooms, everywhere fills up during holiday and festival periods – when prices are hiked – so book ahead.

Finca Lérida Alto Quiel, 10km up the valley ☎720 2285, ⓦfincalerida.com. This is less about ambience and all about location: plum in the middle of a historic coffee estate, with cloud-forested slopes and birding trails above. The deluxe rooms have vast windows and private patios affording stellar views down the valley on clear days. In the evenings, snuggle up by the fire in the cosy common room. Pricier rooms with old-world charm are available in the original family home. Breakfast included. $\overline{\underline{$209}}$

Hostal Beiro Av Porras ☎6478 4015. Friendly local landlady offering four compact, clean en-suite rooms in an annexe; they share a small patio with a hammock and rocking chair. A solid budget choice if you want to avoid the hostel scene. $\overline{\underline{$30}}$

Hostal Boquete Av "B" Este ☎720 2573, ⓦhostal-boquete.com. With a great central riverside location (noisy during the festival), these nine compact rooms (mainly doubles) have a shared balcony overlooking the river at the back, and a communal deck. $\overline{\underline{$40}}$

Hostal Gaia Av "B" Oeste ☎720 1952, ⓦhostalgaia.com. Away from the party scene, this tidy, friendly, newly renovated hostel offers excellent value, hosting a mixed clientele of locals and travellers in its two small dorms (each with its own bathroom) and three private doubles. There's a clean kitchen, lounge area with TV and a nice small outdoor terrace overlooking a garden with a stream at the far end. Dorms $\overline{\underline{$11}}$, doubles $\overline{\underline{$33}}$

Hostal Refugio del Río Garden Av "A" Este, at C 6 Sur ☎6878 6433, ⓦrefugiodelrio.com. Recently converted house with small dorms and private rooms (shared or private bathroom) plus a lounge, well-equipped kitchen and delightful garden, filled with fruit trees and hung with hammocks. Dorms $12, doubles $36

Hostel Mamallena Boquete South side of Parque Central ☎720 1260, ⓦmamallenaboquete.com. Set right on the main square, in a lovely renovated wooden property, this friendly, efficient place offers small four-bunk dorms and private rooms with shared or private ($5 more) bathrooms, plus use of a large kitchen, TV lounge and garden, and an abundance of hostel benefits, including free pancake breakfast and reductions on shuttle services (see p.186). Dorms $14, doubles $33

Hotel Rebequet Corner of Av "A" Este and C 6 Sur ☎720 1365, ⓦhotelerebequet.com. This long-established, good-value hotel has nine splendid rooms – spacious and generous with solid wooden furniture, including handsome beds, polished parquet floors and a fridge. Continental breakfast included. $73

★**La Montaña y el Valle Coffee Estate** Jaramillo Arriba ☎720 221, ⓦcoffeeestateinn.com. A deluxe retreat in lush gardens – three bungalows, each with kitchenette, lounge, dining room and a terrace affording spectacular vistas across to Volcán Barú – this intimate B&B enjoys an unparalleled reputation. Light suppers and gourmet candlelit dinners are on offer and a coffee tour is included. Rack rates (quoted here) are stratospheric; pay almost half the price by booking online. Reservations essential. Two-night minimum stay. $410

Panamonte Inn & Spa Av 11 de Abril, off the top end of Av Central ☎720 1324, ⓦpanamonte.com. This historic 1914 hotel has hosted the likes of Roosevelt and Ingrid Bergman, and offers refined elegance in flower-filled surroundings. When the chill nights close in, huddle next to the cosy log fires while you sip your wine. Breakfast included. $275

Tinamou Cottage Finca Habbus de Kwie, Jaramillo de Abajo ☎720 3852, ⓦcoffeeadventures.net. Three snug self-catering cottages tucked away in a small Dutch-owned hillside coffee estate a 10min drive from Boquete; a choice retreat for birdwatchers who don't want to have to stay in town. You'll need 4WD access, or arrange to be picked up in town. Meals can be ordered. Reduced rates for online booking and stays of two nights or more. $153

EATING

Antojitos Av Central ☎730 9332. Pleasant and cheerfully decorated open-sided patio serving inexpensive (from $9) Tex-Mex favourites: enchiladas, quesadillas, chilli con carne and plenty of veggie options. Daily noon–8.30pm.

★**Art Café la Crêpe** Av Central, at C 2 Norte ☎720 1821 or ☎6769 6090, ⓦfacebook.com/BoqueteArtCafe. More Paris than Panama, this cosy US-run French café is as colourful as the art decorating the walls. Enjoy deliciously light but filling sweet and savoury crêpes (from $8) or French classics such as *boeuf bourguignon* ($20), and leave room for the *crème brûlée*. Mon–Sat noon–8.30pm.

Café Punto de Encuentro C 5 Sur off Av Central ☎720 2123. This pleasant terrace overlooking a garden is the top spot for brunch, attracting Panamanians and foreigners alike, who feast on a varied menu of eggs – with great crispy bacon, French toast, tortillas, pancakes or waffles (most $4–8). Service will be slow when it's busy. Daily 7am–noon.

Fresas Mary On the Volcancito road ☎720 3394. Great little kiosk serving delicious *licuados* and *batidos* and fabulous bowls of strawberries with *natilla*, a particularly mouthwatering local cream concoction. Usually daily 10am–7pm; sometimes closed Mon.

Mike's Global Grill C 7 Sur, at Av Central ☎730 9360 ⓦmikesglobalgrill.com. Nice location by a stream, with outdoor seating – inside has the feel of a US sports bar with a friendly vibe. The menu is international and eclectic, listing burgers and pad Thai, falafel and tofu. The Fri fried chicken and open-mic night is popular with the US expats. Free wi-fi. Daily 8am–10pm.

★**Panamonte Inn & Spa** Av 11 de Abril ☎720 1327, ⓦpanamonte.com. Hands-down the most sumptuous dining in Boquete, laid on by celebrity chef Charlie Collins. Inventive gourmet dishes, such as salmon smoked in cedar with parmesan ($23) can be savoured at candlelit damask-covered tables in the formal dining room or more casually in the fireside lounge or on the terrace. Daily noon–2.30pm & 6–10pm.

Il Pianista Palo Alto road ☎720 2728. Intimate split-level stone restaurant, a $3–4 taxi ride northeast of town by a bubbling stream, illuminated at night. The Italian chef produces Boquete's best pizzas – wood-fired – plus *bruschetti*, *antipasti* and excellent home-made pasta (mains from $12). Tues–Sun noon–10pm.

Restaurante Colibri Av "B" Oeste ☎6379 1300, ⓦrestaurantecolibri.com. Imaginative, healthy menu, drawing where possible on locally sourced, organic ingredients. There are several gluten-free and vegetarian options, including passionfruit *ceviche* or quinoa and black bean falafel. Mains from around $16. Tues–Sun noon–9.30pm.

★**Restaurante Las Orquídeas** Av Belisario Porras, at C 5 Sur ☎6628 9108. Small, friendly family-run restaurant in a quiet location with a few outside patio tables. Good-sized portions of nicely presented and tasty Panamanian home cooking, plus fresh juices and *batidos*. Mon–Sat 11.30am–8.30pm.

El Sabrosón Av Central, between C 1 Sur and C Central ☎720 2147. Probably the most reliable of the local *cafeterías* – hence the long but swift-moving lunchtime queues – serving hot, freshly made rice, plantain, beans, salads and a range of meat dishes, plus usually some fish, all for under $5. Daily 7am–3.30pm.

Sugar and Spice Av Central at C 7 Sur ☎730 9376, ⓦsugarandspiceboquete.com. This international bakery

5

and café is a major expat meeting place, serving great cooked breakfasts (around $5), salads, soups and deli-sandwiches using their posh breads, such as sourdough, nine-grain and rye. Sweet snacks include a mouthwatering array of muffins. Mon, Tues & Thurs–Sat 8am–6pm, Sun 8am–4pm.

DRINKING AND NIGHTLIFE

Big Pool C 5 Sur. The nicest of several pool halls, emitting a friendly vibe, and selling cheap beer. A pleasant enough place to while away a rainy evening. Daily 4pm until late.

Boquete Brewing Company Av Central, 200m north of the church ☎ 6403 7576, ⓦ boquetebrewingcompany .com. The place to quench your thirst after a hike, and a favourite expat hangout, offering a changing menu of craft beers ($4.50 a pint or $6.50 for a three-beer tasting tray) and ciders– some packing a punch – along with a bar food menu. Occasional live music at the weekend. Daily 2–10pm.

La Cabaña Left after the bridge, 200m north of the fairgrounda. For a loud blast of a variety of sounds and blinking plasma screens, try dancing or drinking in this joint's dark recesses. Fri & Sat 8pm–late.

Parque Nacional Volcán Barú

Jade-coloured cloud forests sit in the mist high above Boquete, many of them within the boundaries of **PARQUE NACIONAL VOLCÁN BARÚ**, which stretches west towards the town of Volcán. This is prime **birdwatching** territory, and the favoured habitat of the metallic green **resplendent quetzal**, the Holy Grail of Boquete birding. The male in particular, with its ruby breastplate and lengthy trailing iridescent tail, which it only dons for the breeding season, is a dazzling sight. These otherwise elusive birds are at their most visible from the end of December to April, just after first light, when breeding pairs can sometimes be seen on the path.

Hiking **trails** range from a gentle undulating stroll round *Finca Lérida* to an eight-hour slog up and down **Volcán Barú**, with several scenic options in between.

Trails around Finca Lérida

Daily 7am–4.30pm • Guided birdwatching hikes cost $80/person and last about 4hr, including lunch; day-visitors pay $12/person to walk the trails with a map • Take an Alto Quiel bus from Boquete and get off at the entrance (20–25min)

The **Finca Lérida** ecolodge (see p.188) offers good-value hikes through the 10km of trails on its estate; **birdwatching**, you may see quetzals, highland hummingbirds such as the white-throated mountain gem, sulphur-winged parakeets, silver-throated tanagers and the impressive black guan. Much of the trail network actually lies within the **Parque Internacional Amistad** (see p.197), which abuts the Barú national park. You can join a guided hike, or pay for a sketch map and head off up through the coffee fields and cloud forest on your own.

Sendero de las Tres Cascadas

North of Boquete on the Bajo Mono loop • Daily 7am–3pm • $7 • ☎ 6691 9144, ⓦ thelostwaterfalls.com • Driving, turn right at the T-junction 8.5–9km north of Boquete, in the direction of the Sendero de los Quetzales, and park at the sign 1.2km along the road (from where it's a 10min hike to the entrance); otherwise, catch a Bajo Mono bus, get off at the T-junction and walk the rest of the way, or take a taxi (around $7–8)

SAFETY IN THE MOUNTAINS

Although you can enjoy the shorter trails round Boquete on your own, you should really undertake the **longer routes** – including the popular, scenic **Sendero de los Quetzales** – with an experienced **guide** (see p.187), who should have a first-aid kit and emergency equipment with them. Although in fine weather travellers usually successfully negotiate these longer trails without a guide, every year someone gets seriously lost once the bad weather has closed in – most notably in 2014 when two young Dutch backpackers set off on the Il Pianista trail – now off limits – and never returned. Whichever trail you take, don't hike alone and make sure you tell your lodgings where you are going. In recent years, the authorities have tended to close the national park trails altogether when the weather is bad.

Also known as the Lost Waterfalls, the **Sendero de las Tres Cascadas** is a delightfully scenic cloud-forest trail that takes in three waterfalls, each of which tumbles into a (cold) natural swimming pool. The first two are the most accessible, though still involve some moderately strenuous patches, especially when muddy. The last cascade involves more boulder clambering. Inevitably the trail is at its wettest when the falls are at their most impressive, but even in the dry season, be prepared for some mud. Give yourself two or three hours to vist all three waterfalls at a leisurely pace.

Sendero Pipa de Agua

8km northwest of Boquete • Daily 8am–3pm • $3 • Take a Bajo Mono bus from Boquete and ask to be dropped off at the trailhead at the T-junction with the road that leads to the start of the Sendero de los Quetzales

An easy 4km trail, **Sendero Pipa de Agua** – also known as the Cascada Escondida (Hidden Waterfall) – is a birdwatchers' favourite, following a water pipeline up a relatively gentle incline in a dead-end valley to an impressive waterfall. Beware of a scam by the occasional unscrupulous taxi driver who, in order to save petrol, leaves hikers here claiming it's the start of the Sendero de los Quetzales (see below). That said, quetzals can occasionally be spotted on this trail too, which will take a couple of hours to the end and back.

Sendero de los Quetzales

A far more beautiful, rugged hike than the slog up the brooding volcano it skirts, the 8km **Sendero de los Quetzales** offers the additional thrill of a possible glimpse of a male quetzal in full regalia (Dec–April). Though formerly easily doable on your own, severe floods and landslides have made the route difficult to navigate in places, and hiring a guide (see p.187) will substantially enhance your chances of spotting a quetzal as well as allowing you to learn more about other fauna and flora. If you go on an **organized tour**, which is strongly advised, transport to/from Boquete will be provided; if you decide to walk the trail on your own towards Cerro Punta, you can get your luggage transferred for you.

The trail can be hiked in both directions, though conventional wisdom has it that it's easier to start from the Cerro Punta side (over 2400m) because of the drop in altitude between there and the eastern trailhead at Alto Chiquero (over 1800m). A moderately fit person soaking up the scenery and making occasional stops to spot the odd shy bird in the undergrowth should count on five to six hours to complete the trail, including the extra few kilometres to get to/from the official trailhead on the Cerro Punta side.

Climbing Volcán Barú

The unremarkable haul up **Volcán Barú** (3474m), Panama's highest point, is rewarded at the summit, which on a good day boasts a truly breathtaking panorama of the Pacific and Caribbean, both dotted with a myriad of islands. The **dry season** (roughly mid-Dec to April) is the best time to attempt the ascent but even then clouds and rain can close in quickly. To maximize your chance of a clear view, you should attempt some, or all, of the climb at night – for which you'll need a **guide** (see p.187), and a torch – in order to arrive at dawn. If you set off from the small park office, which marks the trailhead, at 11pm or midnight, the 13.5km ascent takes four to six hours, getting you to the peak in time to enjoy a sunrise picnic – you'll need to turn a blind eye to the radio masts and graffiti-covered rocks on one side – before descending. No rock-climbing skills are necessary, just the grit to plod up a boulder-strewn track and endure a little rock-scrambling. You'll need warm, waterproof clothing, as it's cold on the summit, plenty of water and the usual hiking essentials.

Climbing Volcán Barú from the **western side** (see box, p.193) is more physically demanding, and takes longer, but is more rewarding as you are taken up a path, albeit very indistinct in places, rather than a road, and across more varied terrain. This trail should definitely not be undertaken without a guide.

ARRIVAL AND DEPARTURE

MIA STATIONS AND FEES

If you are on a tour or with a guide (see p.187) – which is advisable – the park fee ($5) is often included in the tour price. Independent hikers can pay the fee at the MIA stations at either end of the Sendero de los Quetzales, about 8km apart: the Alto Chiquero ranger station and refuge is at the Boquete side of the trek, while the El Respingo ranger station is at the Cerro Punta end. There are also two small, unnamed MIA offices at the start of the trail that climbs Volcán Barú, on both the Boquete and Cerro Punta sides. These places are often unstaffed.

ALTO CHIQUERO RANGER STATION

By taxi The Alto Chiquero park office, accessible by 2WD is a steep, almost completely tarred 11km up from Boquete, reachable by taxi ($10–12).

PARQUE NACIONAL VOLCÁN BARÚ

By bus You can take a bus as far as the T-junction, followed by a 3km hike.

EL RESPINGO RANGER STATION

By taxi Hiring a 4WD taxi from Cerro Punta to the park office a 40min hike below the trailhead will cost around $8 ($30 to go right up to the refuge); contact taxi driver Ricardo ☎ 6516 8638.

By bus You can get dropped off any Cerro Punta-bound bus from Volcán and walk the rough 5km road to the office.

THE VOLCÁN BARÚ TRAILHEAD

You'll need a 4WD taxi to take you to the trailhead ($8–10) from Boquete; you can arrange a pickup time, or simply walk down to the main road and flag down a taxi or bus there.

INFORMATION

Park information Contact the MIA regional office in David (☎ 774 6671); ask for *Áreas Protegidas*.

Luggage transport service Backpackers wanting to hike the Sendero de los Quetzales one way and who don't want to be encumbered with their rucksack should go to Transportes Ferguson (Boquete ☎ 720 1454, Volcán ☎ 771 4566; both Mon–Fri 8.30am–4pm, Sat 8.30am–noon). They have an office at Av 1 Oeste at C 4 Sur in Boquete, and another behind the petrol station in Volcán, and will charge $5 to courier your rucksack to the other location within 24hr.

ACCOMMODATION

In addition to the **camping** detailed below there is also a small camping spot about two-thirds of the way up Volcán Barú, though it's on an inconvenient slope, with no facilities. The police at the security post by the summit may also allow you to sleep in their hut for a small fee.

MIA bunkhouses/camping Contact MIA's David office (☎ 774 6671) and ask for Áreas Protegidas. You can arrange to sleep in the bunkhouse at the ranger stations at either end of the Sendero de los Quetzales, though you'll need to take warm bedding and food, and be prepared for cold-water showers. At the time of writing payments were still being accepted at the ranger stations. Camping also available. Camping $\overline{\$6}$, dorms $\overline{\$15}$

Mirador la Roca Halfway along the Sendero de los Quetzales. The nicest camping location, at a picnic spot with tables, but with no other facilities. $\overline{\$6}$

Volcán

Spreadeagled on the lower western slopes of Volcán Barú, at an altitude of 1700m, the twelve-thousand-strong town of **VOLCÁN** (formally known as El Hato de Volcán) is little more than a glorified road junction en route to the more appealing fertile valleys of Cerro Punta and the cloud forests of the Parque International La Amistad, or the little-used Costa Rica border crossing at Río Sereno. That said, it does offer the most impressive views of the volcano, and as the retirement and real estate boom gradually seeps west of Boquete, tourism is beginning to take root. There are a few diverting excursions, not least to scale **Volcán Barú** (see p.191), and you could easily spend a couple of enjoyable days exploring the area, but if you're short of time it's probably best to push on to Cerro Punta and Guadalupe. Even if you don't overnight here, a couple of good restaurants and relaxed ambience make Volcán a convenient pit stop and anyone set on self-catering up in the mountains should stock up on supplies (leaving the fruit and vegetables to Cerro Punta) and visit a bank.

ACTIVITIES AROUND VOLCÁN

Hiking and **birdwatching** are very much the order of the day, in particular on the forested slopes of the volcano within the protected boundaries of **Parque Nacional Volcán Barú**, which lies between Volcán and Boquete. The **Sendero de los Quetzales** (see p.191) is by far the most popular destination for hikers and birding enthusiasts, offering a wonderful twisting trail through verdant forest round the northern flanks of the volcano. Accessing the **summit** of Volcán Barú itself (see p.191) from this western side is a much more daunting though potentially satisfying prospect, clambering across overgrown lava flows and navigating round precipitous tors, where you should look out for the spectacular black and white hawk eagle soaring above. Less energetic targets include the **Pozos Termales de Tisingal**, a collection of thermal pools, or the breathtaking 80m cascade of the **Salto de Tigre**, both in a lovely setting off the Río Sereno road.

TOUR OPERATORS AND GUIDES

Highland Adventures Cerro Punto road ✆771 4413 or ✆6685 1682, ✉ ecoaizpurua@hotmail .com. Well-established company run by Gonzalo Aizpurúa (who speaks some English) from an unmissable garden shed-office. Excursions – rates include guiding service and transport – include overnight treks to the summit of Volcán Barú ($180 for two), for which you'll need to bring and carry your own food and equipment, or a day-long slog up the mountain ($160), which only the super-fit should attempt. Guides can also be provided for the Sendero de los Quetzales or to explore other trails in the national park or in Amistad, as well as to the Pozos Termales de Tisignal and the Salto de Tigre.

ARRIVAL AND GETTING AROUND

VOLCÁN

By bus Buses between David and Cerro Punto and Guadalupe pass through Volcán (5am–8pm; every 15min; 1hr 20min; last return bus from Guadalupe 8pm). Buses from David also pass through Volcán en route to and from the Costa Rica border at Río Sereno (6.20am–6.20pm; every 45min–1hr; 1hr 10min).
By taxi Taxis hover near the main junction, charging $1/ person for a short hop round town.

ACCOMMODATION

Hoctal Llano Lindo Av 2A, 1km up the Cerro Punto road off to the left ✆6514 0094, ⊛ hostalllanolindo .com. Basic seven-room hostel with a friendly family atmosphere and a shared kitchen-dining-TV room. Multiday package deals are available and local tours at $75/person. Breakfast included. Dorms $12
Hotel Don Tavo Av Central, on the right ✆771 5144, ⊛ hoteldontavo.com. Reliable, slightly overpriced central hotel with sixteen clean en-suite rooms (sleeping two to five) – with variable mattresses – set around a courtyard garden. Service standards can vary. $43
Las Plumas Paso Ancho, 2km north of Volcán ✆771 5541, ⊛ las-plumas.com. Excellent value for groups or families with their own vehicle, comprising four fully equipped (laundry, cable TV, wi-fi and phone) two- or three-bedroom modern self-catering bungalows set in manicured wooded grounds, bordered by the Chiriquí Viejo. Three-night minimum stay; good long-term rates ($274/ week). $66
★**Volcán Lodge** 100m up the road opposite the bakery ✆771 4709 or ✆6998 6565, ⊛ volcanlodge .webs.com. Lovingly restored 1940s lodge where wooden beams, panelling and flooring create homely rooms and a warm atmosphere. The friendly Panamanian owners are bilingual after living for many years in the US. Cooked breakfast $5. $60

EATING

Burrico's Av Central, next to Hotel Don Tavo ✆6203 7363, ⊛ burricos.wixsite.com/burricos. Bright tables and cheery Mexican decorations make this an inviting spot, even before you see the food: a mix of Panamanian – a superior *menú del día* with a choice of beef, chicken and pork for under $6 – and Tex-Mex favourites for less than $9. Tues–Fri 11am–9pm, Sat & Sun 11am–5pm.
Cerro Brujo Gourmet Restaurant Brisas del Norte, 500m up a dirt road signed off east of Av Central ✆6669 9196, ⊛ facebook.com/cerrobrujo. Overlooking a garden, the delightful, Mediterranean-style stone-and-tile interior is laden with artwork. An eclectic changing menu lists locally sourced, organic gourmet dishes (mains from $17), such as dorado fillet in sesame seeds and mushrooms, and doesn't disappoint; leave room for dessert. Regular musical, artistic and gourmet evenings. Reservations preferred. Tues–Sun noon–4pm & 6–10pm.
La Maná Volcán Lodge, 100m up the road opposite the bakery ✆771 4709, ⊛ volcanlodge.webs.com. A warm

5

wood-panelled dining room where the hospitable hosts serve Panamanian cuisine and US comfort food, spanning the price spectrum: choose from *gallo pinto* ($7), BLTs or burgers, or splurge on filet mignon in red wine ($17). Daily 11am–10pm.

Restaurante Mary Av Central on the left ☎ 6704 1237. Popular local restaurant on a breezy upstairs terrace (with inside a/c seating) serving moderately priced chicken, pork and seafood ($6–8), plus tasty soups and fresh juices. Try the local trout ($9). Daily 6am–6pm.

Around Volcán

A few kilometres west of Volcán lie several modest attractions – a couple of **lakes**, a **coffee estate** and an **archeological site** – which will appeal to enthusiasts or may be worth swinging by if you've a free couple of hours and your own transport. South of the town, the **waterfall** of Cañon Macho de Monte is a spectacular sight in season.

Lagunas de Volcán and Janson Coffee Farm

The **Lagunas de Volcán** (1300m), Panama's highest wetlands and an important sojourn for migrating **birds**, will appeal to birders keen to spot northern jacanas, masked ducks and, in the forested fringes, the rare rose-throated becard. Consider some early morning birdwatching ($35 for two hours) with Laguna Adventures (ⓦ lagunaadventures.com), the tour company branch of the **Janson Coffee Farm** (ⓦ jansoncoffeefarm.com) on whose estate the lakes are located. They also offer guided hikes, horseriding and, of course, coffee tours.

Sitio Barriles

5km west of Volcán, on the road to Caisán · Daily 7am–5pm · Guided tours in English or Spanish $5 · ☎ 771 4281 or ☎ 6575 1828 · A taxi from Volcán will cost $6

The private *finca* of the Landau family harbours one of Panama's most important archeological sites, **Sitio Barriles**, named after the barrel-shaped stones unearthed in 1947 that provided the first modern-day evidence of what is presumed to be the country's oldest pre-Columbian culture, which was prominent around 500 AD. The most interesting artefacts have been carted away to Panama City's anthropology museum (see p.64), but the farm possesses a couple of **petroglyphs** – the *pièce de résistance* is a silky smooth slab of basalt, which when doused with water reveals yet more squiggles. There's also an unconvincing re-creation of an archeological dig chamber and a small, rather chaotic display of ceramics.

Cañon Macho de Monte

Roughly 13km south of Volcán, east of the Concepción–Volcán road · No fixed hours · Free · Any David–Cerro Punta bus can let you off at the hamlet of Cuesta de Piedra; take the turn east at the mini-super and hike 2.5km along the tarred road, crossing two bridges, to the canyon – if travelling by car, park at the hydroelectric project, where a path leads to the precipice above the fall

A worthwhile detour is **Cañon Macho de Monte**, a dramatic (less so in the dry season) waterfall that tumbles into a gorge. It's also a good **birdwatching** site, where orange-collared manakins and fiery-billed aracaris are the stars of the show.

EATING   CAÑON MACHO DE MONTE

Mirador Alan-Her Road to Volcán, 2.5km south of Cuesta de Piedra. A good pit stop for tea or coffee, this place is also a top spot to pick up regional delicacies, from local mozzarella and ricotta to *bienmesabe* – a

slow-cooked dessert of rice, milk and *panela* – and *sopa borracha* ("drunken soup"), sponge cake soaked in cinnamon-flavoured rum. Daily 6.30am–7.30pm.

The road to Río Sereno

From Volcán, a well-paved road snakes its way 42km to the small border town of **Río Sereno** (see box opposite), swooping round tight bends, across cascading rivers and through coffee and banana plantations. Unless you're bound for Costa Rica, the only

CROSSING THE BORDER AT RÍO SERENO

A 35km drive west from Volcán along a spectacular winding mountain road brings you to the somnolent frontier town of **RÍO SERENO** and the least-used **border crossing** with Costa Rica. It is easily reached by bus from David, via Volcán (5am–5pm; every 45min–1hr; 2hr 30min). The last return bus to David leaves Río Sereno at 5pm, passing through Volcán after 1hr 10min. Buses leave Río Sereno from close to the T-junction at the entrance to the town. **Panamanian immigration** (daily 8am–5pm; ☎ 722 8054) is 400m from the bus stop, by the police station (look for the flag); the **Costa Rican immigration** office (same hours) is next door. Don't forget that whether entering Panama or Costa Rica you'll need to get an exit stamp from immigration in the country you are leaving and an entry stamp from immigration in the country you are entering; you will also need to show proof of onward travel and financial solvency. Should you get stranded here for the night, the town's lone **accommodation**, the *Posada Los Andes* (☎ 722 8112) on the main square can provide you with a rudimentary room in a fairly rickety building for $20.

reason to make this spectacular drive is to visit a couple of places favoured by nature lovers. **Mount Totumas**, which abuts Parque Internacional Amistad, is a private reserve tucked away in cloud forest, 7km north of the Río Sereno road, some 10km west of Volcán; it boasts a range of lodgings and trails that make the most of the spectacular natural surroundings. A further 17km west lies **Finca Hartmann**, a birding hot spot and charming coffee estate, which also offers delightful back-to-nature lodgings.

Finca Hartmann

Santa Clara • Coffee tours, in Spanish or English (1hr 15min) $15; trail access for day-visitors $15 • ☎ 6450 1853, ⓦ fincahartmann.com • Any David–Río Sereno bus (via Volcán) can drop you at the entrance, which is signposted – if you are driving, the 1km drive up a dirt track from the entrance is best undertaken in a high-clearance vehicle, or 4WD

A family-run, ecofriendly coffee estate, **Finca Hartmann** has recorded more than 280 species of **bird** – it's the best place in Panama to see the dazzling turquoise cotinga and fiery-billed aracari – as well as 62 different mammals. Birds are most easily spotted round the main farm at Palo Verde, where the coffee roasting and other operations take place. Taking a **coffee tour** (best during harvesting season, Oct–March) also allows you to stroll the five **trails** on the estate, one of which leads up to Amistad park (see p.197).

ACCOMMODATION
THE ROAD TO RÍO SERENO

★**Mount Totumas** 18km northwest of Volcán ☎ 6963 5069, ⓦ mounttotumas.com. A special place in a fabulous setting, surrounded by cloud forest, with three glorious lodgings, made predominantly of wood, to suit a range of budgets. The three economy rooms in the *Homestead* share a bathroom, kitchen and cosy living area; the self-catering two-storey *Cabin* sleeps up to seven; and the *Bellbird Lodge* boasts three rooms, two suites – all with vast windows and skylights – and a fine-dining restaurant open to all guests. All have plenty of deck and hammock space from which to admire the breathtaking views and the iridescent hummingbirds; a vast network of trails to waterfalls, thermal springs and mountains await the more active. Access via high-clearance 4WD, or from Volcán a $60 transfer (one way), or local bus to Los Pozos

(followed by a a 2hr 30min hike). Two-night minimum stay. *Homestead* **$74**, *Bellbird Lodge* **$150**

★**Ojo de Agua Cabañas** Finca Hartmann, Santa Clara ☎ 6450 1853, ⓦ fincahartmann.com. The *finca's* two rustic cabins are tucked away in the forest. The smaller one-bedroom *cabaña* is cosier, with a kitchenette, whereas the larger six-bedroom two-storey cabin with full kitchen and fireplace is more of a bunkhouse, accommodating up to ten people ($140 for up to four, plus $10/person). Both have hot-water showers (though neither has electricity – gas lamps and candles are used) and are regularly visited by howler and white-faced capuchin monkeys. A sturdy 4WD is necessary for access, or you can arrange transfers. *Cabaña* **$90**, bunkhouse for four **$180**

Cerro Punta and around

Shortly after leaving Volcán, the road to **Cerro Punta** starts to twist and turn, threading its way up a mist-filled ravine. The **Río Chiriquí Viejo** gushes through, flanked by almost vertical pine-clad slopes dotted with alpine chalets, some established by early European

5

settlers. Roadside stalls overflow with locally produced vegetables; stop off and gorge on a heaped bowl of strawberries or blackberries and *natilla* (a local creamy custard) or pick up a pot of home-made jam.

Cerro Punta

Set almost 2000m above sea level in a fertile basin-shaped valley – the scarcely recognizable crater of an extinct volcano – and surrounded by densely forested, rugged mountains, **CERRO PUNTA** is the highest village in Panama. In the ninety or so years since it was formally settled, partly by Europeans, agriculture has expanded so rapidly that the area now supplies over sixty percent of all the vegetables consumed in Panama, with fields forming a tapestry of produce from lettuce, onions and carrots to commercial flowers and strawberries. This agricultural boom has come at the expense of the surrounding forests, but the village, frequently swathed in cloud, and the surrounding fields are still undeniably beautiful, filled with abundant flowers and buzzing with hummingbirds.

The spectacular scenery, together with the cool, crisp mountain air (temperatures drop to well below 10°C at night), makes Cerro Punta a superlative base for **hiking**, and the pristine cloud forests of La Amistad (see opposite) and Volcán Barú (see p.190) national parks are both within easy reach.

Guadalupe

Three kilometres beyond Cerro Punta, you arrive at **GUADALUPE**, an enchanting flower-filled hamlet of around four hundred inhabitants, dominated by the rustic *Los Quetzales Lodge and Spa*. From there, the road (and bus) sweeps round to the left in a wide loop, passing the turn-off to Las Nubes and Amistad to the right, then the church, before a steep climb back to the junction with the main road at the police station, where taxi drivers often hang out. Orchid fanatics may fancy dropping in at nearby **Finca Dracula** (wfincadracula.com) while horse lovers can visit a **stud farm** (wharascerropunta.com).

ARRIVAL AND DEPARTURE   CERRO PUNTA AND AROUND

By bus Buses from David via Volcán pull up on Cerro Punta's one main street before heading up to Guadalupe (5am–8pm; every 15min; 1hr 50min). The last return bus to David leaves Guadalupe at 8pm, passing through Cerro Punta 10min later.

ACCOMMODATION AND EATING

CERRO PUNTA

★**Hostal Cielito Sur** Nueva Suiza, main road 5km south of Cerro Punta, 10km north of Volcán ☎771 2038, wcielitosur.com. This outstanding B&B is run by genial hosts, who provide a perfect blend of knowledgeable warm hospitality and privacy. Set amid beautiful grounds, five vast, immaculate rooms, some with kitchens, are decorated with traditional Panamanian artwork and share a homely living room. Rates include a substantial breakfast with plenty of home-made goodies. $116

Hotel Cerro Punta Main road ☎771 2020. Though the rooms at this place are rather run-down, you should bear the restaurant in mind, as there aren't many places to eat in the vicinity. Local dishes are well prepared, with weekday set menus (around $5) and limited à la carte selections at weekends (from $9). Daily 8.30am–7pm.

GUADALUPE

★**Los Quetzales Lodge and Spa** ☎771 2182, wlosquetzales.com. Incredibly versatile place accommodating campers, backpackers, honeymooners, Panamanian families and expats with consummate ease. If you're not camping, choose from superior dorms – chunky wood, quality bedding, bedside lights and really hot showers – standard doubles, suites and glorious cloud-forest cabins that sleep two to eight people. All guests have access to the comfy lounge and games room, full of books and sofas, warmed by a log fire, and with table tennis. Activities include spa treatments, cycling, horseriding and cloud-forest walks. The restaurant caters to a good range of budgets, offering delicious soups with home-made bread ($6), pizza and pasta ($10) and pricier, fancier mains accompanied by more vegetables than you are likely to see in a month elsewhere in Panama ($12–17). Daily 6.30am–8pm. Camping/tent $15, dorms $18, doubles $85, cabins $155

Parque Internacional La Amistad

5

Just 6km from Cerro Punta or Guadalupe, the hamlet of **Las Nubes** provides access to **Parque Internacional La Amistad** (International Friendship Park), often abbreviated to PILA or Amistad. Covering 4000 square kilometres of precipitous forested mountains straddling Panama and Costa Rica, the park forms a crucial link in the "biological corridor" of protected areas running the length of Central America. Given its varied topography, Amistad is the most ecologically diverse park in the region, including more than four hundred different **bird** species (see p.305), making it the most important protected area in Panama after the Darién. Although almost all of the Panamanian section lies in Bocas del Toro, it is far more accessible from the Pacific side of the country. There are three short **trails** with *miradores* offering excellent views of some of the highest mountains in Panama (at least before the cloud descends) and a 50m **waterfall**. A longer, steeper and less distinct trail (8km round trip) leads through virgin cloud forest to the summit of **Cerro Picacho** (2986m), but you'll need to get one of the park wardens to guide you.

ARRIVAL AND INFORMATION   PARQUE INTERNACIONAL LA AMISTAD

On foot or by taxi From Cerro Punta or Guadalupe, walk the 6km – or take a taxi ($6–7) – to the entrance.
By car The road is tarred up until the park entrance; thereafter, you need 4WD. If driving a saloon car, you'll

need to park at the gate and walk from there to the office.
MIA office and fees You can pay the park fee ($5) at the permanently staffed MIA office, a 10min walk uphill from the entrance.

ACCOMMODATION AND EATING

Asociación Agroecoturística La Amistad (ASAELA) Las Nubes, 200m before the park entrance ☎6703 1941 (Fermina Gómez). Run by a local women's cooperative, this place offers a restaurant serving *comida corriente* ($3 for breakfast, $5 for lunch) such as *arroz de guandú* (rice and beans) with chicken, pork or beef, and a couple of clean, tidy en-suite rooms with electric hot-water

showers and cable TV. Daily 8am–4pm. $\underline{\$30}$
MIA refuge One of the larger, better-equipped bunkhouses, with kitchen facilities but cold water only. Bring your own food – though you could walk down to the community restaurant (see above) – and a warm sleeping bag, as it gets cold at night. Camping $\underline{\$6}$, dorm $\underline{\$15}$

Along the La Fortuna road

The serpentine road that traverses the continental divide to the Caribbean coast is Panama's most spectacular drive. On a clear day you get **breathtaking views**; conversely, if you find yourself peering through thick fog to see the edge of the asphalt, it can be one of the scariest journeys you ever make. During the October and November rains, landslides are frequent, sometimes blocking the route for days. Midway across the cordillera, before descending into Bocas del Toro province, you cross the dam wall of **Lago Fortuna**, Panama's main source of hydroelectric power.

Los Cangilones de Gualaca

1km north of Gualaca, which lies 17km north along the La Fortuna road from the Interamericana • Dec–April daily • Mon–Fri $3, Sat & Sun $4 • Buses run from David to Gualaca (every 40min; 35min); get off at the junction by the baseball stadium, from where it is a 1km walk

Just north of the village of **Gualaca** the sparkling waters of Río Este squeeze through a narrow, shallow canyon, known as **Los Cangilones de Gualaca**, creating a refreshing **natural swimming pool** – an ideal place to cool off in the summer, though it's packed at weekends. The flat slabs of volcanic rock either side of the canyon are thought to have come from lava slides from Volcán Barú, through which the river has eroded its path over time. There are no facilities beyond toilets and changing rooms, but it makes a delightfully tranquil **picnic** spot provided you avoid the weekend crowds.

ACCOMMODATION   ALONG THE LA FORTUNA ROAD

Lost and Found Ecolodge Km 42 on the La Fortuna road ☎6581 9223, ⊛lostandfoundlodge.com. This

lodge-cum-hostel with shared kitchen or food provided is worth visiting for the views alone. Perched at well over

5

1300m, on the edge of the Reserva Forestal La Fortuna – established to protect the Fortuna reservoir's catchment basin – it boasts numerous cloud-forest trails, offers a range of modestly priced tours and puts on free fun activities, including treasure hunts. Dorms have single and double bunks, and there are three private doubles. To get here by bus, alight at the Km 42 marker, at the hamlet of Valle de la Mina, where a sign directs you up a lengthy flight of steps to the right. Very popular, so book in advance. Cash preferred. Two-night minimum stay. Camping $\underline{$10}$, dorms $\underline{$14}$, doubles $\underline{$40}$

David and the Chiriquí Lowlands

In contrast to the Highlands – the destination for the vast majority of visitors to the province – the oppressive heat of the **Chiriquí Lowlands** does little to attract the punters. Nor do endless fields of maize, rice, bananas, sugar cane and cattle. Still it's hard to avoid **David**, or at least the city's vast bus terminal, since virtually all the province's public transport passes through here. What's more, Chiriquí's capital is growing in appeal as a place to chill out for a couple of days and enjoy a few city comforts as well as a couple of local attractions.

West of David, the Interamericana speeds along 47km of flattish terrain to the frontier with Costa Rica. Just before the border post, the road veers off left down the narrow **Península Burica**, weaving through plantations and passing the former banana boom town of **Puerto Armuelles**, before an undulating road eventually peters out close to the southern tip, where the handful of travellers who make it this far can stroll along deserted beaches and watch the waves.

David and around

The only one of three Spanish settlements founded in the area in 1602 to survive repeated attacks from indigenous groups, **DAVID** developed slowly as a remote outpost of the Spanish Empire, only beginning to thrive when Chiriquí's population swelled in the nineteenth century. Today, despite being a busy commercial city of more than 140,000 people – the second largest in Panama – and the focus of Chiriquí's strong regional identity, it retains a sedate provincial atmosphere.

Oppressively hot and either humid or dusty, its unexceptional modern architecture spread out on a grid that derives from colonial days, David has few attractions *per se*, but its very ordinariness holds a certain appeal for a few days. It's also a good place to stock up before a trip to the highlands or break a journey between Panama City and Costa Rica or Bocas del Toro. Several **day-trips** – chiefly the mangroves at **Pedregal**, the natural pool at **Balneário Barranca** and the **wildlife reserve** at **Playa Barqueta** – are all possible on public transport, and popular with Davideños at weekends as they attempt to escape the city heat.

Parque Cervantes

David's heart is vibrant **Parque Cervantes**, where snow-cone sellers, shoe-shiners and hawkers peddling sugar cane and fresh fruit juice all vie for business, overlooked by the nondescript **Iglesia de la Sagrada Familia**. The park's curved stone seating maximizes the leafy shade, making it a prime spot for watching urban life unfold.

THE INTERNATIONAL AGRICULTURAL FAIR

David's annual highlight is its international agricultural fair, **Feria Internacional de San José de David** (⦿ feriadedavid.com), whose ten days of festivities coincide with the patron saint day for San José on March 19. Although principally a trade show, there's plenty to entertain, with rodeo and lasso competitions, music and dancing, not to mention the annual *cabalgata*, a colourful horseback parade through the city streets.

Barrio Bolívar

A stroll three blocks southeast of Parque Cervantes down Calle "A" Norte takes you back to the city's colonial past in **Barrio Bolívar**, where the district's ever decreasing sprinkling of russet tiles, balconies and intricate wrought iron holds out against encroaching modern architecture. The historic colonial mansion on the corner with Avenida 8 Este was occupied by successive generations of the distinguished Obaldía family – José Vicente was the president of New Granada (combined Colombia and Panama) and his son José Domingo became the second president of Panama. Just east of here, a crumbling bell tower stands over the messily restored nineteenth-century **Catedral San José de David**. See what you make of the renovated colonial Romanesque facade and the interior's gaudy murals.

Pedregal

10km south of David • Buses leave from Av 2 Este between C Central and C "A" Norte (6am–11pm; every 10–15min; 15min)

Beyond the airport, the road fizzles out at **Pedregal**, David's small port and marina, which provides entry by **boat** into the morass of mangroves and islands in the **Golfo de Chiriquí**. At weekends, **La Cocaleca** (☎730 5583, ⊛lacocalecapty.com; $5–20), a popular cruising boat, leaves the jetty at set times to tour the mangroves or venture further out into the gulf.

5

Balneario Barranca

20km west of David • Daily 11am–6pm • Take any bus heading west to the border, Volcán or Concepción, getting off on the Interamericana just before the Boquerón turn-off (about 20min) and walking 100m up a track to the right

A more appealing place to cool off from the sweltering heat than David's local beach is **Balneario Barranca**, a natural swimming pool with a *rancho* bar-restaurant and hammocks on a meander of Río Chirigagua. While a festive family atmosphere prevails at weekends you can have the Tarzan swing all to yourself midweek.

Refugio de Vida Silvestre de Playa Barqueta Agricola

25km southwest of David • Daily 6am–3pm • $5 • Park warden ⓣ 6602 5770 • Buses leave David at 6am, 8am & 11.20am (40min), returning at 2.30pm & 5pm, or take a bus to Guarumal, then a taxi to the beach ($6)

Unremarkable, grainy **Playa Barqueta** is the nearest spot to dip in the sea, and has a couple of informal places to eat and enjoy a beer. A large portion of the beach lies within the boundaries of the low-key **Refugio de Vida Silvestre de Playa Barqueta Agricola** whose 14km stretch of sand, scrub and mangrove protects nesting sites for hawksbill, olive ridley, leatherback, loggerhead and green sea **turtles**. Visits to check out the night-time nesting (late May–Nov is best) can be arranged with the park warden or at the MiAmbiente office outside David (see opposite). The reserve entrance lies east of *Las Olas Resort*, where the bus stops; alternatively the warden will come and pick you up. Visitors in their own vehicle will need a 4WD.

ARRIVAL AND DEPARTURE — DAVID

BY PLANE

Airport Flights from Panama City arrive at Aeropuerto Enrique Malek, about 4km south of town, a $4 taxi ride away.

Flights Air Panama (ⓣ 316 9000, ⓦ airpanama.com) offers three daily flights to and from Panama City's Albrook Airport (40min; $128 one way). Copa Airlines (ⓣ 217 2672, ⓦ copaair.com) also has code-share connecting flights to/from North American and European destinations via Tocumen International Airport in Panama City.

Airline offices Air Panama has an office at the airport and in town, on Av 2 in the Plaza Oteima shopping mall (Mon–Fri 8am–5pm; ⓣ 775 0812). Copa Airlines also has an office at the airport and in town on Av Central at C "B" Norte (Mon–Fri 8am–5pm, Sat 8am–noon; ⓣ 775 7073).

BY BUS

Bus terminal The main bus terminal, for local services and long-distance routes, including to Costa Rica (see box below), is on Paseo Estudiante, a 15min walk north of the town centre. It has good facilities, including a self-service restaurant, toilets, ATMs, a left-luggage office (daily 6am–8pm) and internet café.

Buses to Panama City Terminales David-Panama (ⓣ 775 7074), with its own a/c waiting room at the far end of the terminal, has 17 departures daily (6am–1pm hourly, then every 1hr 30min–2hr until 8.30pm; 4 overnight express buses). Panachif (ⓣ 777 4217) has twelve daily departures (7.30am–10pm) from its own terminal on Av 1 Este between calles "E" and "F" Norte, a 5min walk from the main bus station.

Other destinations Boquete (6.30am–9.45pm; every 30min; 50min); Caldera (10 daily 6am–7pm; 1hr); Cerro Punta (5am–8pm; every 15min; 1hr 50min); Las Lajas (5 daily 11.45am–5pm; 1hr 30min); Puerto Armuelles (via the Costa Rican border at Paso Canoas; 5.30am–10pm; every 15min; 1hr 30min); Río Sereno (5am–4.15pm; every 45min–1hr; 2hr 30min); Santiago – from a terminal across the road from the main bus terminal (5am–7.30pm; approx every 45min; 3hr) or take one of the faster buses to Panama City; Soloy (7am–7pm; approx every 30min when full; 1hr 30min); Volcán (5am–8pm; every 15min; 1hr 20min).

BUSES TO COSTA RICA

Tracopa (ⓣ 775 0585, ⓦ tracopacr.com) operates two daily services to San José, Costa Rica, at 8.30am and noon (8–9hr; $21 one way). Buses leave from the main bus terminal on Paseo Estudiante, where the company has an office (daily 7am–5pm). Tickets should be prebooked for peak holiday periods.

It is often quicker, though, to take one of the frequent **minibuses** from the bus terminal to the border at **Paso Canoas** (see box, p.202) and walk across, getting exit and entry stamps at Panama and Costa Rica immigration respectively, before hopping on one of the regular shuttles to Ciudad Neily, the first sizeable population centre over the border 18km away, where there are connections with San José.

GETTING AROUND

By taxi Taxis are plentiful and should not cost more than $2–3 for a ride in town.
By car Most of the major rental chains have offices at the airport; a good local operator is Arrendadora Económica (☎ 229 5257).

INFORMATION

Tourist information The tourist office (Mon–Fri 8.30am–3.30pm; ☎ 775 2839), on C Central between avs 5 Este and 6 Este, is friendly and courteous but thin on information.
MIA office For the latest information on Chiriquí's several national parks, contact the MIA office, on the road to the airport (Mon–Fri 8am–4pm; ☎ 775 3163).
Immigration and consular services The Costa Rican consulate (Mon–Fri 9am–1pm; ☎ 774 1923) is in Torre del Banco Universal, C "B" Norte and Av 1 Este; Panamanian immigration (Mon–Fri 8am–4pm; ☎ 775 4515) is on C "C" Sur near Av Central.

ACCOMMODATION

A broad range of good-value **accommodation** exists in David, most of it near the city centre. Even so, it's difficult to get a room during the Feria Internacional de San José de David (see box, p.198) and the festival periods in Boquete (see box, p.184). The places reviewed below all have hot water and a/c.

★**Bambú Hostel** C Virgincita, San Mateo ☎ 730 2961, ⓦ bambuhostel.com. Further out than most places, though within reach of amenities on C "F" Sur. Appealing both to mellow-minded folk and party enthusiasts, this place offers en-suite dorm bunks, and private rooms, both with excellent mattresses, as well as cheaper beds protected by mosquito nets in a wood-and-bamboo jungle house. The standout feature is the lush tropical garden containing a small pool with *rancho* bar and open kitchen; plus there's a table-tennis table out front. Dorms $11, doubles $35

Chambres en Ville Av 5 Este between C "A" Sur and C "B" Sur ☎ 775 7428, ⓦ chambresenville.info. A good choice for couples and mature travellers, with cosy, if dark en-suite private rooms enlivened by colourful murals. The large open-air kitchen leads to a fruit-filled garden, with hammocks and a decent-sized swimming pool – though the caged toucan might upset some visitors. French, English and Spanish spoken. Dorms $11, doubles $33

Hotel Gran Nacional C Central and Av 1 Este ☎ 775 2221. Before the arrival of the *Hotel Ciudad de David*, this was the top hotel in town with marble lobby to match. Recently refurbished rooms are stately, furnished with flatscreen cable TV and other mod cons. There's also a bar, pool, 24hr casino, cinema and three restaurants. Promotions offer huge discounts. Buffet breakfast included. $193

Hotel Toledo Av 1 Este, between C "D" Norte and C "E" Norte ☎ 774 6732. Handy for the bus terminal, this clean, comfortable hotel offers good value, with firm beds, cable TV and friendly service. There's an on-site bar-restaurant (closed Sun). $35

EATING

★**Entrepan** C "D" Norte between Av Central and Av 1 Oeste ☎ 787 0560. Delicious fresh juices, gourmet salads, wraps and deli-sandwiches, including mozzarella, smoked ham or pulled pork. The *almuerzo del día* ($6.50) consists of a flavoursome soup plus sandwich and drink. The quality and professional service is no surprise given that a top chef is at the helm. Mon–Sat 11am–9pm.

Multi-Café No. 2 C "A" Norte between Av 2 Este and Av 3 Este ☎ 774 5236. Modern self-service restaurant with a/c and parking that attracts a busy weekend crowd. There's a vast array of local and international staples on offer, each rarely more than $5, with omelettes for breakfast. Mon–Sat 7am–8pm, Sun 7am–3pm.

Restaurante Bar El Fogón Av 2 Oeste, between C "C" Norte and C "D" Norte ☎ 775 7091. Recently expanded, spacious and airy restaurant, painted in warm colours.
There's a friendly atmosphere, and it's a real favourite with Davideños. You can choose from grilled meat, poultry and seafood mains (from $9) – try the *pescado parmesano* – or a selection of burgers and sandwiches. The quality can suffer when it gets busy. Mon–Sat 11.30am–11pm, Sun 11.30am–9pm.

★**Restaurante Bocachica** C "A" Sur between avenidas 4 and 5 Este ☎ 730 4057. Favoured by university students drawn by the cheap beer, the pleasant elevated patio here is a prime spot to tuck into tasty, good-value dishes, with seafood a speciality (mains $10–12). Daily 11.30am–10pm.

Restaurante La Típica Av 3 Este and C "F" Sur ☎ 777 10780 Busy, no-nonsense Chinese-Panamanian *cafetería* serving palatable food around the clock at reasonable prices. A reliable budget choice. Daily 24hr.

5

THE BORDER WITH COSTA RICA

The **border at Paso Canoas** is by far the busiest of the three border crossings Panama shares with **Costa Rica**; in recognition of this, **immigration** is open longer hours (7am–11pm Panamanian time). Don't forget that whether entering Panama or Costa Rica you need to get an exit stamp from immigration in the country you are leaving and an entry stamp from immigration in the country you are entering; proof of onward travel and financial solvency is also required.

Paso Canoas is reached by frequent **minibuses** from David, with regular **onward transport** to San José and other destinations in Costa Rica (see box, p.200). If you are arriving from Costa Rica, you can find transport to both Panama City and David 100m down the Interamericana from the border. The Panachif (☎ 727 7054) office here sells tickets for buses to Panama City via David (12 daily; 7am–9pm; 8–9hr; $17) plus two overnight express services (10pm & 11pm; 7hr; $21). Small minibuses also scoot off down the highway to David (4am–10pm; every 10–15min; 40min), from where onward transport is easy (see p.200); after the last shuttle, you'll need a taxi ($25–30). Less frequent minibuses also head north to the mountain border town of Río Sereno (6am–6pm; every 1hr 30min; 2hr).

Península Burica

Aside from a handful of die-hard surfers and fishing enthusiasts, few tourists venture down to the distant tip of the **Península Burica**, resembling an upside-down skittle straddling the Costa Rican border. Here, 50km southwest of David, the remoteness is tangible and the sunsets spectacular. The gateway to the peninsula is **Puerto Armuelles**, for more than seventy years Panama's thriving Pacific hub of the infamous United Fruit Company (now Chiquita Brands) until it pulled the plug in 2003 (see p.221). The rotting pier and abandoned wooden houses serve as poignant reminders of the town's former importance.

ARRIVAL AND DEPARTURE   PENÍNSULA BURICA

By bus Frequent minibuses run from David's main bus terminal to Puerto Armuelles (4am–10pm; 1hr 30min). A daily *chiva* (1hr 30min–2hr) makes the 30km trip down the peninsula from the town's waterside transport depot to the community of Bella Vista; timing depends on the tides, since much of the "road" is on the beach, only accessible at low tide – make sure you arrive before noon and bring your passport.

Paso Canoas and the Costa Rican border

It's a short hop from David along the Interamericana to Panama's main border crossing with Costa Rica at **Paso Canoas** (7am–11pm). Others are at Río Sereno, west of Volcán (see box, p.195) and Guabito (see p.243), over the cordillera in Bocas province. The busy frontier town exudes an edgy tackiness, with stalls, money changers and taxi drivers all competing for business.

Parque Nacional Marino Golfo de Chiriquí

There's not much to the laidback fishing village of **BOCA CHICA** – 30km southeast of David as the vulture flies – beyond a small supermarket, an upmarket fishing lodge and a couple of inexpensive *fondas*. It does, however, provide the gateway to one of the province's most prized natural treasures: **Parque Nacional Marino Golfo de Chiriquí**, a nirvana for **scuba-diving**, **snorkelling** and **sport-fishing** enthusiasts. Created in 1994 to protect almost 150 square kilometres of terrestrial and marine wildlife, the park comprises 25 islands – some with places to stay – and nineteen coral reefs, teeming with hundreds of fish in a rainbow of colours. The coastline to the west of Boca Chica, meanwhile, is thick with **mangroves** – which means you'll have to venture to the more distant islands to find white sand or crystalline waters. Note that when the wind drops in the rainy season, sandflies can be a nuisance, so bring repellent.

Islas Parita and Paridita

Isla Parita, by far the largest land mass, together with the much smaller **Isla Paridita**, are the only two inhabited islands on account of their fresh water sources; the rest are generally small, low-lying sedimentary outcrops that enjoy a tropical savannah climate, with beaches backed by coconut palms and manchineel trees, where the only visitors to disturb the hermit crabs and iguanas are nesting hawksbill and leatherback turtles.

Boca Brava and beyond

Across the narrow water channel in front of Boca Chica's jetty is **Boca Brava**, an island hosting two contrasting lodgings, while on the mainland a couple of upmarket fishing lodges and a small guesthouse do little to disturb the tranquillity of the place. Snorkelling trips head out into the national park, to the gorgeous white-sand coves of **islas Bolaños and Gámez**, but there is even better snorkelling and diving to be had around the more remote (and pricier) **Islas Secas**, **Islas Ladrones** and **Isla Montuoso**. The marine life is breathtaking, from sea horses and starfish to giant manta and eagle rays, pods of dolphins, turtles, sharks and vast schools of fish swirling round volcanic pinnacles, with humpback whales arriving to calve from June.

ARRIVAL AND DEPARTURE   PARQUE NACIONAL MARINO GOLFO DE CHIRIQUÍ

BOCA CHICA

By bus and taxi There are no direct buses from David to Boca Chica. Infrequent buses leave David for Horconcitos, 36km to the east (5am–5pm; approximately every 1hr 15min–1hr 30min; 45min), 5km south of the Interamericana on the road to Boca Chica. From there, you could catch the occasional (and unreliable) Boca Chica bus (12.30pm, 2.30pm & 4.30pm), take a taxi ($15 from the Interamericana) or hitch a ride, paying the *colectivo* rate ($3). Returning, the daily bus leaves Boca Chica at 9.15am and 1.30pm-ish, and will drop you at the Interamericana. In the not entirely unexpected event of a no-show, you'll need to negotiate a ride.

By car Boca Chica is down a paved road, accessible in a saloon car; turn off from the Interamericana to Horconcitos, 36km east of David, and then take the middle road at the three-way fork in the village, coming to a halt at the Boca Chica jetty 16km later. There are a couple of places where you can leave your car safely overnight ($2/night).

TO THE ISLANDS

By boat Transfer to *Hotel Boca Brava* from Boca Chica is $3. *Cala Mia* and *Isla Paridita* can organize a transfer, or you can usually find someone at the dock to take you; the going rate is $60 return.

ACCOMMODATION

Bocas del Mar Boca Chica, signposted to the left 2km before entering the village ☎6395 8757, ⓦbocasdelmar.com. Gaze out at the wooded landscape and glistening sea through the vast French windows in

---

PARQUE NACIONAL MARINO GOLFO DE CHIRIQUÍ ACTIVITIES

Snorkelling outings in the park can easily be arranged through the hotels, or you can hire the services of one of the local boatmen. Trips usually visit islas Bolaños and Gámez and cost $100 for up to six people – bring a picnic. Contact reliable boatmen Marcelo Rios (☎6209 6420) or "Jaye" (☎6214 6883) in Boca Chica.

    For **scuba diving**, the highly recommended Carlos Spragge at Boca Brava Divers (☎775 3185 or ☎6600 6191, ⓦbocabravadivers.com) offers a one-day all-inclusive dive excursion ($250, minimum four people; visibility best Dec–April) and multiday dive trips sleeping on his dive boat.

    Alternatively, you can explore the area's islands, inlets, caves and mangroves in a **kayak**; most of the accommodation options that we review have kayaks available for guests (usually to rent).

5

your spacious bungalow, or from your private porch or your luxurious bathroom. Stylish rooms have a contemporary feel, and include all the comforts (a/c, satellite TV, minibar); some even have a private outdoor hot tub. The pleasant open-air restaurant is set round an infinity pool and there are a variety of inland or water-based activities to choose from. Breakfast included. Promotions and low-season discounts are substantial. $208

Cala Mia Isla Boca Brava ☎851 0059, Ⓦboutiquehotelcalamia.com. A sophisticated yet rustic retreat comprising eleven a/c bungalows, each with a gorgeous private *rancho* looking out to sea. The lovely bar-restaurant deck serves gourmet Mediterranean cuisine – the three-course dinners ($32) use organic garden produce. Boat rides, horseriding and a visit to a Ngäbe community can be arranged, and there's a small spa. Breakfast and use of kayaks included. $209

★**Hotel Boca Brava** Isla Boca Brava ☎851 0017, Ⓦhotelbocabrava.com. Possessing simple tiled rooms with fan or a/c, and private or shared (for $10 less) bathroom, this long-standing retreat offers an affordable rub with nature. Awake to the cries of howler monkeys, and stroll along to the modest beach. The cliff-top bar-restaurant (daily 7.30am–10pm) serves excellent food at reasonable rates (from $7) and inexpensive drinks. Minimum two-night stay. $60

Howler's Bay Hotel Isla Boca Brava ☎6740 8812, Ⓦfacebook.com/islabocabrava.com. This is by no stretch of the imagination a hotel, but instead an informal camping spot in a delightful forested location – which

you'll share with the eponymous howler monkeys – affording serene sea views. There's a handful of small dome tents with mattress, sheets and fan, plus a couple of rustic wooden cabins (one semi-open), and a larger stone bungalow – facing the sea. All share a well-equipped kitchen and sea-facing dining patio, plus ablution block and BBQ hearth. Apart from beer and water, you need to bring all supplies with you. Kayaks for rent. Camping $11, cabins $38, bungalow $66

Isla Paridita Isla Paridita ☎6464 2510, Ⓦexpeditionpanama.com. Tranquil eco-getaway on a gorgeous private island with beaches, rainforest trails and freshwater lagoons, offering simple open-sided bamboo-and-thatch *cabañas* (fans, solar energy) alongside communal gourmet dining. Rates include all meals, use of kayaks and snorkel gear plus one boat tour and guided hike; scuba diving and sport fishing can be arranged. Return transfer from Boca Chica $60. $290

Pacific Bay Resort Punta Bejuco ☎6678 1000, Ⓦpacificbayresort.net. There's an unequalled panorama of the bay from the hilltop bar-dining area, though you'll earn your food hiking up there from the four well-spaced, solar-powered, wood-furnished duplex cabins. Set on an extensive forested headland with three beaches, and coves to explore by kayak, this is a wonderfully relaxing resort, and is only open two weeks per month to minimize the environmental impact. Meals are included in the room rates; horseriding and moderately priced boat excursions are also on offer. Return transfer from Boca Chica $60–70. $146

Playa Las Lajas and around

The impressive broad belt of flat tan-coloured sand of **Playa Las Lajas** is by far the most popular weekend beach destination for urbanites from David (81km) and even Santiago (124km) in need of sand, sea and surf. However, since the beach, backed by wafting palms, stretches for kilometres both ways, there's plenty of space to escape the crowds – except over the weekends leading up to Carnaval, when you can expect all-night partying on the sands. The benign waves are more suited to body surfing and playing around in than serious surfing.

If you are interested in **Ngäbe** or **Buglé** culture, you should take time to visit the major communities of San Félix and Tolé north of the Interamericana; the latter, which lies east close to the border with Veraguas, is noted for its **handicrafts** – the versatile *kri* (string bag, or *chácara* in Spanish) made of plant fibres, or beaded *nguñunkua* (necklace, or *chaquira* in Spanish) – many sold at stalls along the Interamericana close to the turn-off. For a homestay experience, head for **Soloy** (see box opposite).

ARRIVAL AND DEPARTURE

PLAYA LAS LAJAS AND AROUND

By bus and taxi Although there are direct buses to La Lajas village from David (5 daily; 1hr 30min), most visitors heading to the beach take one of the more frequent buses from David bound for Tolé or San Félix (every 20–30min) and get off at the busy intersection, El Cruce de San Félix, 68km east of David (1hr). You are likely to find a taxi at the petrol station at the junction that can take you the 12km to the beach ($8 one way; $5–6 from the village); make sure to get a contact number for your return trip.

STAYING WITH THE NGÄBE IN SOLOY

Though the **Ngäbe** are Panama's most numerous indigenous citizens by far, they see considerably fewer tourists than the Guna or Emberá, and are understandably wary of outsiders given the recent history of conflict – sometimes violent – with both the Panamanian authorities and international mining and hydroelectric power corporations. Arranging a **homestay** in the mountain community of Soloy (ⓦcomarcangobebugle.com), in the southwest corner of the Comarca Ngäbe-Buglé provides a unique opportunity to begin to learn about the Ngäbe, their traditions and their present-day challenges, though you'll need some Spanish to make the most of it, and be prepared for very rudimentary lodgings and simple food. The village itself has no nucleus, but rather is strung out several kilometres along the main road and the Río Soloy. The river, and the even more powerful Río Fonseca into which it flows, are crucial to community life and are also the basis for **tourist activities** (most around $15–20/person), such as waterfall visits and rafting; visitors can also go hiking (40min–6hr) or horseriding and learn the processes of extracting plant fibres and mixing natural dyes to make a traditional *kri* (string bag).

ARRIVAL AND INFORMATION

By bus Buses leave David's main bus terminal for Soloy approximately every hour when full (7am–7pm; 1hr 30min); alternatively take a bus bound for Horconcitos and get off at the turn-off south to Horconcitos from the Intermericana, where you can hop on a pickup truck heading north for Soloy (approximately every 30min). The last bus returning to David leaves Soloy at around 4pm. Where you get off in the village depends on where you have agreed to meet your guide.

ACCOMMODATION

Homestays Homestays are currently only arranged by a handful of families as many in the community remain suspicious of tourists and tourism. Contact tourist coordinator and experienced whitewater rafting guide, Juan Carlos Bejerano (☎6638 0944, ⓔcarlito559 @hotmail.com); alternatively get in touch with Adan Bejerano (☎6468 5249), or just turn up. Accommodation is usually $10/person/night plus $4–5/meal.

ACCOMMODATION AND EATING

Casa Laguna Las Lajas lagoon; turn left just before the beach T-junction ☎6896 0882, ⓦcasalagunapanama .com. Situated on the wildlife-rich lagoon, this restful B&B has three brightly painted and cheerful en-suite rooms with fan – one of them sleeps four, with a private patio overlooking the garden ($88). Curl up with a book in a hammock or head for the beach. Simple but tasty Italian home-cooking at reasonable rates. Two-night minimum stay. $60

Johnny Fiestas Just off the beach; turn left at the T-junction ☎6240 4728, ⓦfacebook.com/johnny fiestaslaslajas. Small hostel with a garden. Stay in a dorm bunk or a dome tent kitted out with electricity, fan and camp beds. The vibe is relaxed, with hammocks galore and sport on TV, plus board games to play and surfboards to rent. Fast wi-fi. Camping $8, dorm $12

Las Lajas Beach Resort On the beach; turn right at the T-junction ☎6790 1972, ⓦlaslajasbeachresort.com. Set back from the beach, a dozen expansive, tiled, minimally furnished rooms (one with wheelchair access) look onto the lawn through floor-to-ceiling windows. The two upstairs suites have spectacular sea views from the balcony and there's a large pool and bar-restaurant serving moderately priced American-style food. $176

La Pepita de Marañon C Principal, north end of Las Lajas village ☎6225 2027, ⓦlapepitapanama.com. Small B&B, a 20min drive from the beach ($5 for transfers), run by a young, dog-loving Italian couple. There's a quirky "glass house" double room featuring creative use of recycled bottles in the stonework and a two-storey room with two double beds that can sleep up to four ($79). They offer inexpensive tours to Ngäbe communities and the interior. $49

Santiago and the central highlands

The administrative, economic and cultural capital of Veraguas province, **SANTIAGO** is a bustling centre of around forty thousand inhabitants. Founded in its present location in 1637, and previously of great agricultural importance, it is now a thriving commercial hub – evidenced by the proliferation of banks and a state-of-the-art baseball stadium. Situated almost halfway between Panama City and David, Santiago

is a **major transit point** as well as a marketing centre for the livestock, rice, maize and sugar from the surrounding farmlands. If you're travelling round Panama by public transport, it's highly likely that at some stage you will, at the very least, spend time in the bus terminal or stranded on the Interamericana here, though there's little incentive to venture further into town unless you happen to coincide with the **patronales** around July 25, which draw in the crowds for some serious partying.

Of greater tourist interest is the city's status as the entry point to the undulating **Península de Soná**, at the tip of which lies Santa Catalina, Panama's surfing capital (see pp.210–212), and as gateway to the cooler mountain slopes of the **central highlands**, which are sprinkled with tranquil farming villages and the charming hilltop village of **Santa Fé**. Closer to town, a few kilometres outside Santiago, are a couple of delightful **village churches** worth a detour, both accessible by bus.

The town centre

Most of the businesses are strung along the Interamericana and Avenida Central, which branches west off the highway heading into the town centre, coming to an abrupt halt in front of the impressive exterior of the **Catedral Santiago Apóstol**, stunningly illuminated at night. Adjacent is **Parque Juan Demóstenes Arosemena**, the city's main plaza; it takes its name from the former president, revered here for choosing the town as the site for Panama's first teacher-training institution. The college, **Escuela Normal Juan Demóstenes Arosemena**, lies several blocks northeast of the plaza on Calle 8A Norte and is the architectural jewel of Santiago, with a majestic Baroque frontispiece.

Across the main plaza from the cathedral stands the rather uninspiring – save for a few pre-Columbian ceramics – **Museo Regional de Veraguas** (Mon–Fri 9am–4pm, Sat 9am–3pm; free), housed in the former prison where three-time president Belisario Porras was incarcerated during the civil war.

Iglesia Atalaya

Atalaya, 8km southeast of Santiago • Buses from Santiago every 15min (30min)

From the outside, the **Iglesia Atalaya** resembles an inauspicious two-tier wedding cake; inside, its lofty vaulted ceilings covered in splendid frescoes and lovely stained-glass windows more than compensate. Tucked away in a side altar, the Cristo de Atalaya, said to date back to before 1730, is one of Panama's most venerated icons, a magnet for thousands of pilgrims every first Sunday in Lent.

5

Iglesia San Francisco de la Montaña

San Francisco de la Montaña, 16km north of Santiago on the Santa Fé road • Irregular hours • Take a Santa Fé-bound bus from Santiago (see below); hop off at the fork by the police post and bear right a few hundred metres

The **Iglesia San Francisco de la Montaña** lies on the road to Santa Fé, north of Santiago, in a village of the same name. The simplicity of the small stone church, believed to have been built around 1727, belies the wonderfully elaborate wooden interior, with nine intricately carved Baroque altarpieces betraying both Spanish and indigenous influences. You are likely to have to ask around to get someone to open up.

ARRIVAL AND DEPARTURE | SANTIAGO

Panama City–David buses The more luxurious buses running between Panama City and David (see p.200) make their pit stops at one of two service areas: Centro Los Tucanes or the more popular Centro Piramidal, at Santiago's northeastern and eastern exits to the Interamericana respectively. If they have space, they will pick up extra passengers but at peak times – Fri afternoons and holidays – you are better off taking the services from the main terminal.
Bus terminal All other transport leaves from the bus terminal on C 10A Norte, a short walk (or $1–2 taxi ride) from Los Tucanes or the Centro Piramidal. The terminal has a left-luggage office and public toilets.
Destinations Aguadulce (Mon–Fri 5.30am–9pm, Sat & Sun 5.30am–7.30pm; every 15–20min); Chitré (5.30am–9pm; every 30min; 1hr 30min); David (6am–7.30pm; every 50min; 3hr); Santa Fé (5am–7pm; every 30min; 1hr); Soná – change for Santa Catalina (6am–9.40pm; every 20min; 50min).

GETTING AROUND AND INFORMATION

By taxi Taxis are abundant and will ferry you to most places within town for a couple of dollars.
Tourist information The tourist office (Mon–Fri 8am–4pm; ☎ 998 3929) is in the Plaza Palermo shopping centre.
MIA office On the Interamericana, north of the Av Central exit (Mon–Fri 8.30am–3.30pm; ☎ 998 4387).

ACCOMMODATION

Hotel Gran David Interamericana, near Centro Los Tucanes ☎ 998 1866, ⓦ hotelgrandavid.com. Popular with business folk and families on the move (and therefore often full), offering comfortable, if slightly tired, rooms around flower-filled gardens. Breakfast included. **$73**
Residencial del Sol C 10A Norte, across from the bus terminal ☎ 993 0371. A cheap (though uninspiring) place to bed down, especially convenient if you've missed the bus to Santa Fé or Santa Catalina, with functional, clean, dark en-suite rooms. **$39**

EATING

El Maná Av 10B Norte, opposite the bus terminal. Cosy *cafetería* offering filling, inexpensive dishes with the usual mounds of noodles interspersed with more appealing items. A place to hang out while waiting for a bus. Daily 6am–8pm.
Gran Machu Picchu Interamericana, at Av Central ☎ 933 1024. Highly recommended restaurant serving genuine Peruvian *ceviche* ($8) and excellent seafood dishes, including *cazuela de mariscos* (seafood stew; $17), albeit in an uninspiring a/c room. It even sells Inca Kola – Peru's favourite soft drink. Daily noon–10pm.
Restaurante y Asados Alex La Placita, near the main plaza. A busy daytime watering hole, serving up Panamanian breakfast fry-ups and the *almuerzo del día* for less than $4, plus local specialities such as *gaucho de mariscos* (seafood stew and rice). Daily 6am–3pm.
Restaurante Tropicalísimo Av Central, opposite Plaza Palermo shopping centre ☎ 998 3661. Mid-priced Cuban and Panamanian dishes (most mains under $11), such as *lechón habanero,* the house speciality, served on a pleasant terrace or indoors. Mon–Sat 9am–9pm.

Santa Fé

A hilltop village about 60km north of Santiago, **SANTA FÉ** is a jewel of a mountain retreat that has been a well-kept secret for years. Surrounded by a stunning necklace of verdant mountains sprinkled with sparkling cascades and serene stretches of river, with easy access to a forested swathe of national park, it is a hikers' and birdwatchers' dream.

5

HÉCTOR GALLEGO AND THE SANTA FÉ COOPERATIVE

In the middle of the night of June 9, 1971, **Padre Héctor Gallego**, the 33-year-old priest of Santa Fé, was **abducted** by two uniformed men of Omar Torrijos's National Guard (see p.299) and was never seen again. In 2002, the Truth Commission set up by President Moscoso to examine crimes committed during Panama's two dictatorships found what they believed to be the tortured remains of the revered priest. It is generally presumed that Manuel Noriega, then head of the secret service, gave the orders, though it seems likely that Torrijos, even if unaware of events at the time, was complicit in the cover-up.

Gallego had arrived in Santa Fé from Colombia in 1967 as the town's first parish priest. Appalled at the exploitation of the local farmers by the wealthy merchant elite, the energetic priest set about educating and organizing the peasant population into becoming self-reliant, helping them to establish a **cooperative** so their products could be sold directly to the market, bypassing the merchants. For some reason Gallego was perceived as a threat to the authorities, which resulted in a campaign of intimidation, starting with insults and threats, and escalating into arson, culminating in the priest's final "disappearance". "If I disappear," Gallego announced before his death, "don't look for me. Continue the struggle." His prophetic words now figure on the monument dedicated to him in the village.

Thanks to its 500m altitude, Santa Fé de Veraguas – to give it its full name – enjoys a pleasant, fresh climate, and while the arrival of a real-estate office may herald further development, for the moment its absence of traffic and low population density, with houses strung across the tree-dotted hillside, gives it a peaceful village feel. Santa Fé is famous for its flowers, boasting more than three hundred species of **orchid**; the annual three-day orchid festival in August, when most are in bloom, attracts aficionados from around the country – contact the tourist office in Santiago (see p.207) for dates. The annual **agricultural fair** (late Jan–early Feb) also pulls in the crowds.

The village

Daily activity centres on the small covered **market** area, where fresh local produce is on display alongside a smattering of predominantly Ngäbe craft stalls. Across the road stands a monument to Santa Fé's most famous resident, **Padre Héctor Gallego** (see box above), whose kidnap and murder has left the village emotionally scarred. A nonprofit foundation that bears his name continues his community development work, offering support and skills training to local farmers and artisans. More visibly, the priest's legacy resides in the continued success of the cooperative he helped found; it includes a couple of supermarkets, several grocery stores, a restaurant, bus and taxi services, and the jewel in the crown, the local organic coffee mill, **Café El Tute**. Tours (in Spanish) of the processing plant, where you can buy some of the delicious product, and to a nearby organic coffee farm, can be organized via the Fundación Héctor Gallego (see opposite) in the village.

Around Santa Fé

The area's natural beauty makes it perfect for **hiking**, **birdwatching** and **bathing** in clear streams and rivers – provided the weather holds – though the mountainous topography means there'll be steep inclines wherever you wander. A good start is to head down to the river, near the entrance to the village, below the *Hotel de Santa Fé*, or follow the road up towards Alto de Piedra and the Santa Fé national park.

If you intend to tackle the area's loftiest peaks, Cerro Tute (930m) and Cerro Mariposa (1200m), cloaked in montane forest, or want to penetrate the wilderness areas of the park, then hiring a **guide** is a must (see opposite). More accessible hiking destinations include the impressive Salto Alto de Piedra and Salto El Bermejo, as well as the 30m cascade of El Salto, slightly further afield. Your accommodation should be able to provide directions and/or a sketch map. For the hardcore, it's possible to organize a multiday hike over the cordillera to the Caribbean coast.

Two of the most pleasurable activities in the area, given the magnificent scenery, are **horseriding** and **tubing**, floating down the nearby river for more than an hour, gliding past kingfishers, herons and egrets.

ARRIVAL AND INFORMATION   SANTA FÉ

By bus Santa Fé is served by buses from the main terminal in Santiago (5am–7pm; every 30min; 1hr). For the return trip they leave from outside the village bus terminal.
On foot Though hilly, Santa Fé is easily explored on foot.

Fundación Héctor Gallego Up the hill from *Hostal La Qhia* (Mon–Sat 8am–4pm; ☎ 954 0737). This community development organization can fix up a tour of the coffee cooperative (in Spanish) and offers internet access (75¢/hr).

ACTIVITIES AND GUIDES

Farm tour The organic Finca de María y Chong (☎ 6525 4832) can, given notice, happily show you round their small-scale operation – growing citrus fruits, orchids, green vegetables and coffee – before serving a farmhouse lunch ($8 including lunch).
Hiking The experienced and extremely knowledgeable Edgar Toribio (contactable at the *Hotel Santa Fé* or on ☎ 6121 4286, ✉ edgar_toribio@yahoo.es) comes highly recommended for hiking and wildlife trips; he generally charges around $40/person for a full-day tour, such as to Cerro Tute. Fit, adventurous travellers should enquire about

the four-day trek to the Caribbean – though you'll need to take a tent or hammock to sleep in. Other guides charge around $20–25/person/day depending on numbers; ask your lodging or contact the tourism cooperative coordinator, Hernán Aguilar, at *Fonda Hermanos Pineda* (see below).
Horseriding Contact César Miranda (☎ 6792 0571, ⓦ aventurascesamo.blogspot.co.uk; $60 for two).
Tubing Ask your accommodation to organize, or ask for directions to the house of William Abrega (☎ 6583 5944; $8, life jacket provided), whom it's well worth employing to show you the best line into the occasional rapids.

ACCOMMODATION

All accommodation reviewed here can provide home-made **maps** of the area for local self-guided walks to waterfalls, and can organize **guides** for horseriding and more strenuous hikes further afield.

★ **Coffee Mountain Inn** 500m downhill on the right-hand turn before the bus terminal ☎ 6988 0921, ⓦ coffeemountaininn.com. Set in lovely grounds this beautifully appointed lodge offers six options, ranging from a simple compact double with fan, via more luxurious doubles with a/c and cable TV, to an apartment with kitchenette and wraparound balcony. Breakfast, included in the rates, is served on your private terrace. Discounts for online bookings and long-term stays. $89
★ **Hostal La Qhia** 50m from the bus terminal ☎ 954 0903, ⓦ panamamountainhouse.com. Set in a lush garden, this efficient chalet-style hostel has a relaxed, bohemian feel. It has just one six-bed dorm, with adjoining

semi-open kitchen, and four private rooms (three with shared hot-water bathrooms), so book ahead. A lovely hammock-strewn balcony and *rancho* complete the tranquil scene – the cockerels less so. Free morning coffee, plus sketch maps of local hikes. Dorm $12, doubles $40
Hotel Santa Fé Main road ☎ 954 0941, ⓦ hotelsantafepanama.com. Perched on the hillside 500m from the village, this place has for years attracted weekenders fleeing the city in search of fresh mountain air and relaxation. No-frills rooms sleep two to five people, with cold-water showers (hot water, a/c and cable TV cost extra); they're clean and cheap, though a bit dull, and they could do with a coat of paint. On-site bar-restaurant. $28

EATING

★ **Anachoreo** Left after the bus station and first right down a dirt road ☎ 6911 4848. The rather unatmospheric, cavernous dining room is more than compensated for by the delicious Cambodian cuisine – stir-fried vegetables, chicken ginger and fish *amok* ($8–14), for example – using fresh green veg and herbs from the garden. All dishes come with steamed rice. Wed–Sun 5–9pm.
Café Dorado On the main road when entering the village ☎ 6686 4237. You can't beat the mountain views here – a lovely south-facing deck provides an ideal spot to enjoy breakfast, lunch or dinner – soups, seafood and chicken dishes or burgers – or to just chill with a drink. Daily 7.30am–9pm.

Fonda Hermanos Pineda Just off the main road near the bus station ☎ 954 0777. Really friendly local restaurant serving mains from around $6. Try the *picadas* – a sampler platter of deep-fried local favourites chicken, pork, *hojaldres*, *empanadas*, yuca chips and *patacones* ($6). Daily 6.30am–9pm.
Restaurante El Terminal Main road. Small a/c dining room by the bus terminal, dishing up traditional fried Panamanian breakfasts (around $3) and filling lunches: generally chicken, beef or pork in tasty sauces accompanied by a mound of rice, lentils and salad – all for under $5. Daily 5am–6pm.

5

Península de Soná and Isla Coiba

Though dwarfed by the Azuero Peninsula to the west, the hilly **Península de Soná** does attract its own share of tourists. Small cattle farms cover the interior and fishing communities dot the rocky coastline, which protrudes into the Golfo de Chiriquí; meanwhile, Panama's surfing capital, **Santa Catalina**, is expanding. More and more visitors are using the mellow fishing village as a launch pad for excursions to the rainforests and coral reefs of **Isla Coiba**, which offers some of the world's finest scuba diving, snorkelling and sport fishing.

Santa Catalina

At the southern end of the peninsula, the sleepy fishing village of **SANTA CATALINA** reels in visitors for its internationally renowned **surf** spots and as a jumping-off point for **Isla Coiba**. As a result, the village has developed into a pleasantly bohemian tourist centre, with mostly foreign-owned small-scale operations scattered along the main road in, or spilling off the paved road that leads to the main beach, **Playa El Estero**.

ARRIVAL AND DEPARTURE   SANTA CATALINA

By bus There are direct buses from Panama City to Soná (6 daily; 5hr), an unendearing town 47km southwest of Santiago, and 63km north of Santa Catalina; most visitors, however, use the more frequent buses to Santiago (see p.207), where they change onto Soná-bound services (daily 6am–9.40pm; every 20min; 50min). Buses from Soná to Santa Catalina are sporadic (Mon–Sat 7 daily; 4.30am–6pm, returning 7am–6pm; Sun 3 daily). Check ⓦ labuenavida.com for the latest timetable. Note that the last bus from Santa Catalina sometimes does not run, or may only go as far as Guarumal, where there are other bus connections with Soná.

By taxi Taxis, found hanging round Soná bus terminal, charge $30–35 for the trip to Santa Catalina.
By shuttle Hola! Panama (ⓦ hellopanama.com) runs a daily shuttle service between Boquete and Santa Catalina (leaves Boquete 7am, leaves Santa Catalina noon; 5hr; $35).
By car Whether you come from the east via Santiago, or from the west, turning south off the Interamericana at Guabalá, the road is tarred all the way to Santa Catalina. Note that there is no petrol station in Santa Catalina – fill up in Soná. Detailed driving instructions are given on various accommodation websites.

GETTING AROUND AND INFORMATION

On foot Once in Santa Catalina, you'll be on foot unless you've your own transport, but nowhere is further than a 20min hike from the bus stop.

Tourist information ⓦ visitsantacatalina.com and ⓦ santacatalinabeach.com both have plenty of useful information, are reasonably up to date, and have maps and

---

SANTA CATALINA ACTIVITIES AND TOURS

The most popular day-tours from Santa Catalina are to **Parque Nacional Coiba** (see pp.212–215), and **Isla Cébaco**, noted for its sparkling clear waters and good coral; at both you'll be sharing the sea with colourful schools of snappers, jacks, tunas, butterfly, angel and puffer fish alongside moray eels and white-tip reef sharks. At certain times of year, you're likely to have the company of even more impressive marine life such as whales, sharks and rays, especially near Isla Coiba. Most day-trips (specialist dive trips aside) involve a look around the MiAmbiente ranger station and the interpretive centre, a short rainforest walk and a couple of snorkelling stops.

Experienced surfers should head for Santa Catalina's most famous surf break, **La Punta**, which boasts an international reputation, with waves often topping 5–6m in the season (April–Aug); novice surfers will be happier at **Playa El Estero**. *Oasis*, *Sol y Mar*, *Rolo's* and Fluid Adventures, among others, all offer beach-based lessons for beginners at varying rates ($20–35 for a 1–1hr 30min class, including board rental). In addition to the above, various other places rent out surfboards ($15/day).

While the Santa Catalina website mantra of "surf, dive, fish and chill" just about sums up what the village is about, it doesn't do justice to an array of other **activities** that includes yoga and massage (at *La Buena Vida* hotel), horseriding (at *Hibiscus Garden* or *Oasis Surf Camp* hotels), kayaking and birdwatching (see p.211), and SUP ($40/half-day tour; ⓦ supsantacatalina.com).

directions for driving. They only include a selection of accommodation or tour options, though.

Money There is no bank or ATM in the village, and very few places take credit cards, so bring sufficient cash. The nearest ATM is in Soná, but it often runs out of money on busy weekends, so pick up cash in Santiago.

Communications There are still no land lines in the village and erratic internet and mobile phone connections, plus frequent power cuts, so you may have to wait several days for a response when booking anything.

TOUR OPERATORS

For specialized trips you're best off going with one of the **tour operators** listed below, whose offices are spread along the 200m of main road from the junction to Playa Santa Catalina. For general snorkelling, surfing, fishing or jaunts to Isla Cébaco or Coiba you may pay less by organizing things through your accommodation or by negotiating directly with the **fishermen** hanging out on the beach by their *pangas* (small flat-bottomed metal boats) or advertising outside their houses. Make sure you agree on exactly what the fee will cover. Expect to pay $40 (in a boat carrying up to six) for a full day of snorkelling, surfing or fishing, excluding food and drinks; budget more for Parque Nacional Coiba ($60) since it involves extra fuel. Note that park fees ($20) are not usually included in tour prices (see p.215).

BIRDWATCHING AND HIKING

Bird Coiba On the right, just after the junction on the road down to Playa Santa Catalina ☏6544 1806, ⓦbirdcoiba.com. Bilingual (English/Spanish) Javier Elizondo specializes in safety-conscious birding tours to Coiba and surrounding islets ($110/person for one day to $275 for three; assuming six people), including park fees, meals, snacks and lodgings. Also local guided walks.

DIVING AND SNORKELLING

There are several dive shops in Santa Catalina; while the operators are generally of high quality and the diving can be superb, there have been occasional complaints of failing to satisfy all clients when mixing day-trippers with those on overnight excursions, combining novices with experienced divers, and mixing divers with snorkellers (with divers prioritized). Make sure your needs are likely to be fully met when making enquiries.

Coiba Dive Center Main road between Brisas del Mar and the police station ☏6565 7200, ⓦscubadivecenter.com. Established dive shop operating day- or multiday tours to Coiba at similar rates to Scuba Coiba (see below).

Panama Dive Centre Main street, by the junction ☏6665 7879, ⓦpanamadivecenter.com. A newish outfit and a five-star PADI resort, offering courses from three-day regular Open Water ($410 plus park fees and accommodation) to Divemaster, as well as the regular Coiba trips.

Scuba Coiba Playa Santa Catalina ☏6980 7122, ⓦscubacoiba.com. Run by pioneering Austrian Herbie Sunk. Rates are $65 for two-tank trips close to Santa Catalina, $125 for Coiba national park. Multiday trips with three-tank dives to Coiba are also available ($675 for a three-day all-inclusive tour). Gear rental ($15/day) and park fees extra. Also offers PADI certification.

SURFING AND KAYAKING

Fluid Adventures Playa Santa Catalina ☏832 2368, ⓦfluidadventurespanama.com. Acclaimed Canadian outfit specializing in surfing and kayaking – lessons, tours and equipment rental. Kayak tours range from an easy paddle and snorkel round Isla Santa Catalina ($75), or the coastal mangroves, to three- or six-day kayaking and camping adventures in Coiba that offer wonderful access to wildlife ($555/$1208).

ACCOMMODATION

Boarder's Haven Main road, managed by La Buena Vida (see below). This cosy self-catering hostel is an excellent budget choice. Three cheerily painted rooms (with a/c and fans) share two hot-water bathrooms, and open onto a communal lounge. Shared kitchen and outdoor space front and back. Three-night minimum stay. $̄30

★**La Buena Vida** Main road ☏6635 1895, ⓦlabuenavidahotel.com. Laden with original mosaic and wrought-iron work, these variously sized, charming mid-range villas (with a/c, hot-water private bathrooms and patios) were designed by the artistic owners, who continue the theme on the terrace café. Yoga and massage also available. $̄66

★**Cabañas Rolo** Main road, by the beach ☏6494 3916, ⓦrolocabins.net. A Santa Catalina institution,

Rolo's is one of the few locally owned operations, and is the top choice for backpacking surfers. Its brightly painted, clean dorm rooms sleep two to four, with comfy beds, fan and shared bathrooms. There's a kitchen for guest use, and a pleasant dining and social area. Neat pine-furnished doubles with a/c, cable TV and fridge also available. Cheap kayak and board rental. Dorms $̄12, doubles $̄55

Coiba House Off the main street, near the beach ☏6962 6388, ⓦcoibahouse.com. Three spotless, comfortably furnished rooms (with a/c but shared bathroom) open out onto a spacious communal balcony with armchairs and hammocks, overlooking the beach, with steps down to the sand. You'll receive warm hospitality, and breakfast is included. Minimum two-night stay. $̄59

5

Hibiscus Garden 10min drive from Santa Catalina on the Soná road, at Lagartero ☎6615 6095, ⊚hibiscusgarden.com. Spacious, brightly painted rooms with tasteful dark-wood furnishing (shared – for $17 less – or private bathroom), plus a couple of two-bed dorms and space for camping. There's a patio and a serene beach and riverside setting. The terrace restaurant offers a tasty, varied menu (most mains $8–15), or you can self-cater in a shared kitchen. There's no shortage of activities here – table tennis, horseriding and SUP – and a shuttle service is provided to Santa Catalina. Under-14s free. Camping $8, dorms $15, doubles $50

★**Oasis Surf Camp** Playa El Estero, contact David Bortolletti (in David) ☎6588 7077, ⊚oasissurfcamp .com. With a great beach location among the palms, this place offers no-nonsense, fan-ventilated double cabins (a/c $10 extra), good-value *casonas* (large, two-storey wood-and-thatch *cabañas*) for six ($90) and camping – tents with mattresses and bedding provided if needed (only in summer). Italian dinners in the restaurant *rancho* are a highlight. Watch out for the river – you'll need to wade across at high tide. The same people run a cheap wooden hostel in the village. Camping (own tent) $7, camping (tent provided) $12, doubles $45

EATING

If you are headed for Coiba and need to take **food** supplies, you should know that the local mini-super has very limited offerings – you may prefer to bring at least some supplies from Santiago.

La Buena Vida Main road ☎6635 1895, ⊚labuenavidahotel.com. Delightful mosaic-filled terrace that's great for a leisurely breakfast – vast fruit platters or a "Greek scramble" ($5–8) – or a light lunch of salads, tacos and sandwiches (around $8). They also prepare superior packed lunches. Daily 6am–2pm.

Los Pibes Off the beach road ☎6585 1046. Pleasant Argentinian-run open-air bar-restaurant (with TV and pool table) dishing up *empanadas*, home-made burgers, fish and other meats chargrilled to perfection, complemented by fresh salads, and lathered in home-made *chimichurri* sauce. Mains from $8. Mon, Tues & Fri–Sun 6.30–9.30pm.

Mama Inés Beach road just before Playa del Estero ☎6923 6695, ⊚santacatalinasurfpoint.com. Perched on a bluff with a great sea view – an ideal location for lunch or a relaxing drink, while fairy lights and music create a good evening vibe. Tuck into tasty tacos or burgers (around $7–8) or something more substantial; try chicken curry

with coconut rice (around $12). Daily 8am–10pm.

★**Pizzería Jamming** Off the beach road ☎6447 1373. This genuine pizzeria is the hub of the tourist-based nightlife, serving crispy, clay-oven-fired pizzas ($7–12) under thatch or in the garden, accompanied by a steady dose of reggae. Jan–Sept, Nov & Dec Wed–Sun 6.30–11pm.

Restaurante Iguanito 50m up the beach road ☎6549 7464. This pleasant raised patio is a prime spot to sip a cocktail or linger over an intimate dinner. Mouthwatering mains ($12–17) include passion fruit couscous with jumbo prawns; or you could sample some tapas – the $15 *surtido de tapas* (ten items) is a treat. Mon–Sat 6–9.30pm.

Restaurante El Pacífico Just before the village beach on the main road. Local restaurant at local prices, serving filling Panamanian favourites – fish and chicken with beans, rice and salad (around $5 for lunch), and a fry-up breakfast for much the same. Can fix up boat trips too. Daily 7am–7pm.

Parque Nacional Coiba

Some say "Panama" means "abundance of fish", and nowhere is this more apparent than in the crystalline waters of **Parque Nacional de Coiba**. The 2700 square kilometres of reserve encompass Panama's largest island, **Isla Coiba**, plus eight smaller islands and forty islets, but the vast majority consists of ocean brimming with spectacular sea life, including the second largest coral reef along the eastern Pacific. As part of the nutrient-rich Central Pacific Marine Corridor, the park is on the migration route of humpbacks (June–Sept), orcas, pilot and sperm **whales**. Diving conditions are good year-round, but for land-based activities, it's better to visit the island in the **dry season** since the trails are less boggy and there's a better chance of spotting mammals.

The island possesses large tracts of **virgin forest**, most of it still unexplored, home to numerous mammal and bird species. Of the estimated two thousand different types of plant, under half have so far been formally classified. The surrounding **oceans** contain countless varieties of fish, ranging from delicate sea horses to vast manta rays, with 33 species of shark – including tiger, hammerhead and whale sharks, though most are harmless reef varieties.

PARQUE NACIONAL COIBA

For years, the island's gruesome history as a penal colony (see box, p.214) helped protect its forests and waters, but the colony's animals (cattle, buffalo and dogs) are now roaming free, threatening the **ecological balance**. Incursions by large fishing vessels (limited artesanal fishing is permitted), illegal timber extraction and resort development could also damage the reserve, and ongoing negotiations between the government, environmental pressure groups and interested businesses will have a critical impact on Coiba's future.

Isla Coiba

All visitors to **Isla Coiba** report first to the MIA station at Playa Gambute, on the northern tip of the island, to pay the entrance fee and sort out accommodation (for those staying on the island). You can spend a pleasant day just hanging out around the camp. There's an interpretive centre, moderate snorkelling in the sandy cove and a couple of easy short **walks** affording pleasant views and tranquil birdwatching. Iguanas and agoutis are frequent dawn visitors to the lawn-cum-part-time-football-pitch fronting the main beach, and spider monkeys are often sighted swinging through the surrounding vegetation.

Sendero de los Monos and Granito de Oro

The first stop on a tour, just a short boat ride from the MIA station, is usually the 1km **Sendero de los Monos**, though you'll need to be here early to encounter the elusive white-faced capuchins or the island's unique variety of howler monkey. Just across the water from the trail lies one of the most popular snorkelling spots, **Granito de Oro** ("the little grain of gold"), a speck of soft sand surrounded by translucent water, plentiful coral and prolific fish, including the occasional nurse shark and turtle. However, smaller cruise ships (Dec–April) periodically stop off here and smother the sand with deckchairs and assorted aquatic paraphernalia, causing the fish to scarper. The park rangers can advise you on timing.

Sendero de Santa Cruz

The most rewarding hike is the **Sendero de Santa Cruz**, which leads from the ranger station through primeval rainforest, crossing crocodile-infested rivers to the island's

5

THE PENAL COLONY ON COIBA

For almost eighty years Coiba was synonymous with fear and brutality, as horror stories of forced labour and torture, political assassinations and gang warfare leaked from the island. Designated as a **penal colony** in 1919, it was intended to be an open prison, staffed by civilians and aimed at reforming serious offenders – hence the inclusion at the main camp of a school, rehabilitation centre and church. But with up to three thousand prisoners on the island at one stage, scattered around sixteen different camps, most offenders were unable to access these resources, and the planned civilian custodians never materialized. Instead, prisoners worked twelve-hour shifts on farmland and forest on only one meal a day, suffering violence from gangs and guards, malnutrition, poor sanitation and scant medical care. A peek inside the decaying **high-security block** is sobering. Here ten to twenty people used to share a humid, windowless cell no more than 3m across, with nine bare concrete "beds" and a hole for a toilet, incarcerated for 24 hours a day, with no exercise, no visitors and little chance of release. Unsurprisingly, **escape attempts** were frequent but usually failed as those who managed to get through the island's dense undergrowth, avoiding the crocodiles and snakes, generally came to grief in the shark-infested waters and strong sea currents.

Far from the public gaze, the island also gained notoriety during the **military dictatorships** of Omar Torrijos and Manuel Noriega as a prime location for "losing" political opponents, some of whose tortured bodies were unearthed in around 180 graves discovered during President Moscoso's Truth Commission investigations. The penitentiary finally closed in 2004; the only former convict still remaining on the island is "Mali-Mali", now the park's most famous ranger and much-sought-after tourist guide.

west coast at Santa Cruz. You'll need to engage one of the park wardens as a guide (see opposite); if you have your own boat, you can hike the trail one way (2–3hr) and arrange a pickup time to be ferried back to the MIA station – but factor in the extra fuel needed for this.

South to Bahía Damas and beyond

Just south of Punta Damas is the main camp of the former **penal colony** (see box above), whose crumbling, eerie buildings are slowly being reclaimed by nature – though some parts have recently been "cleaned up" for the tourists. Further south, across **Bahía Damas**, the aquamarine reef-filled shallows of the eastern coast provide many of the prime diving and snorkelling sites. Panama's last remaining nesting site of the spectacular scarlet macaw is at the south of the island, near **Barco Quebrado**, though these magnificent birds are more easily heard than seen in the forest canopy. Some tours take a plunge in the invigorating thermal springs at **Punta Felipe** or venture into tangled mangroves at **Boca Brava**, or at **Punta Hermosa**, on the less-explored west coast.

ARRIVAL AND DEPARTURE   PARQUE NACIONAL COIBA

Day-trips from Santa Catalina Day-trips from Santa Catalina can be both costly and a little disappointing since the lengthy journey plus the unavoidable *tramites* (bureaucracy) at the ranger station mean that by the time you actually venture into the rainforest any animal or bird with sense will be hiding from the heat and humidity. However, should you want to go for it, it's straightforward enough – fishermen on the beaches will probably do the return trip for around $60/person (assuming a group of six), or more if you want them to take you round the island to some of the sights, which are inconveniently spaced out along the eastern coastline (see p.213). Each journey to

Coiba from Santa Catalina can take anything from 90min to several hours, depending on the weather conditions and the boat; make sure you establish your itinerary and pickup times beforehand, and check that any boat has a decent-sized engine, and preferably a roof to stop you frying.

Multiday tours Because of the limitations of day-trips, it pays to spend at least one night on Coiba with a boat and guide willing to take you out at first light. It's therefore worth splashing out the extra for a hassle-free multiday deal with a tour operator; particularly rewarding are those that include some beach camping away from the ranger station (see p.211).

INFORMATION

Park permits In theory, independent travellers should buy a park permit ($20/day), in advance at the Santiago regional MIA office (☎ 998 4387; national park desk ☎ 998 4271); in practice, if you turn up in Coiba, the permit can be paid for there. However, if you want to spend the night on Coiba, you need to check availability in advance (the bunks get fully booked in high season) and currently MIA is demanding that half the park entry and accommodation fees are paid into their bank account in advance (see box, p.42) while the other half is settled at the ranger station.

Ranger guides You can usually engage a park ranger to accompany you on trips around the island for around $20; you'll need to negotiate the price with them.

When to visit As there are no limits on visitor numbers to the national park, holiday periods and summer weekends should be avoided at all costs.

ACCOMMODATION AND EATING

Coiba's **accommodation** is, in some ways, a great leveller – whether you're on an exclusive all-in deal or you've hitched a ride with the park wardens, everyone has to stay in the same basic huts, with shared facilities.

MIA cabins Coiba ranger station; independent travellers need to book ahead through the Coiba reservations desk at the MIA office in Santiago (see p.207). Forty-odd beds spread dorm-style around five double cabins with screening and shared bathrooms. Independent travellers will need to bring food supplies from Santa Catalina, in a cool box supplied by your boatman; use of the kitchen, including fridge, is $15/ group/night for the small kitchen, $20 for the large one, plus you need to supply the gas cylinder. Cabins have electricity and a/c after 6/7pm though power cuts are frequent. Other useful items to bring include a mosquito net (some screens have holes), a torch, candles – preferably with citronella to help ward off the bugs – and plenty of insect repellent, plus cream to apply to your bites. Limited camping spaces available. Camping $10, dorms $20

Bocas del Toro

ISLA CARENERO

Bocas del Toro

Isolated on the Costa Rican border between the Caribbean and the forested slopes of the Cordillera de Talamanca, Bocas del Toro ("Mouths of the Bull") is one of the most beautiful areas in Panama. It's also one of the most remote – the mainland portion of the province is connected to the rest of Panama by a single spectacular road that carves its way over the continental divide, often blocked by landslides during the heaviest rains, while the island chain offshore requires a boat ride to reach.

For most people, Bocas – confusingly, the abbreviation for the province, archipelago, provincial capital and even sometimes Isla Colón – means the **tropical islands**, which attract more visitors than anywhere else outside Panama City, offering opportunities for relaxing on pristine **beaches** and snorkelling and diving among **coral reefs** in a maze of tangled **mangroves** and undisturbed **rainforest**. The archipelago's unique history has made it the most ethnically diverse region in Panama outside the capital, its Afro-Caribbean, Panamanian-Chinese, *mestizo* and indigenous Ngäbe residents recently joined by North American retirees and US and European hotel owners. English is the dominant language, though Spanish is still widespread. That said, however cosmopolitan Bocas has become, it is the languid pace of the dominant **Afro-Caribbean culture** and its distinctive vernacular wooden architecture that most clearly defines the place.

The archipelago only constitutes a small percentage of the province, much of which is taken up by the **Comarca Ngäbe-Buglé** in the east and the inaccessible but spectacular Talamanca mountain range to the southwest, whose lofty peaks form the backbone of the vast **Parque Internacional La Amistad**, which boasts an awe-inspiring array of wildlife. The lowlands of the mainland, often dismissed as an endless stream of banana plantations, also offer a couple of notable attractions. Panama's banana capital and the province's main commercial centre, **Changuinola**, provides access to the magical **Humedales de San San Pond Sak**, the country's main refuge for the manatee and an important beach for nesting marine turtles. Inland, on the banks of the picturesque Río Teribe, a stay with the **Naso**, one of the less-well-known indigenous peoples, provides a unique opportunity for intercultural exchange in a stunning natural setting.

Brief history

Archeological evidence suggests that **indigenous peoples** inhabited the islands and mainland of present-day Bocas del Toro two thousand years ago, long before an ailing Christopher Columbus limped into the bay on his final voyage in 1502 in search of a route to Asia. Later, during the colonial era, the calm waters of the archipelago provided shelter for European pirates and by the early nineteenth century the islands were becoming the ethnic melting pot that they are today. British and US trading **merchants** came with their West African slave workforce, founding the town of

COCKTAIL TIME IN BOCAS TOWN

Highlights

❶ Tour an organic cocoa farm Learn how the Ngäbe make chocolate and sample the product while experiencing village life on the Bocas mainland. **See p.228**

❷ Relax in a secluded eco-retreat Disconnect from the modern world in an island retreat, set in fabulous tropical surroundings. **See p.230, p.235 & p.237**

❸ Cocktails in Bocas The finishing touch to a hard day at the beach is an iced cocktail at one of Bocas Town's many waterside bars. **See p.231**

❹ Isla Bastimentos Explore the Caribbean community of Old Bank, Ngäbe villages and windswept surfing beaches while looking out for the famous red frogs. **See p.232**

❺ Cayo Crawl Snorkel among gorgeous soft corals before tucking into a seafood platter at a restaurant over the water. **See p.234**

❻ Humedales de San San Pond Sak This wetland manatee refuge also provides nesting sites for marine turtles and hosts an array of birdlife. **See p.240**

❼ Stay in a Naso village A unique opportunity to learn about Panama's only monarchy and explore the surrounding rainforest. **See p.242**

HIGHLIGHTS ARE MARKED ON THE MAP ON P.220

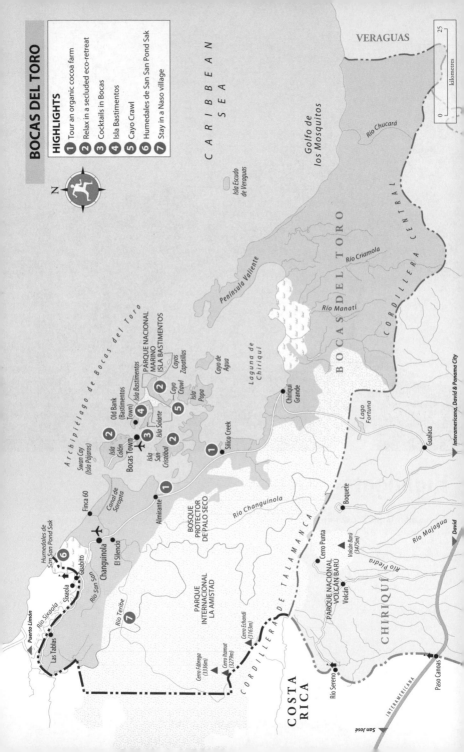

BOCAS DEL TORO

HIGHLIGHTS

1 Tour an organic cocoa farm
2 Relax in a secluded eco-retreat
3 Cocktails in Bocas
4 Isla Bastimentos
5 Cayo Crawl
6 Humedales de San San Pond Sak
7 Stay in a Naso village

N

VERAGUAS

C A R I B B E A N   S E A

Golfo de los Mosquitos

Río Chucará

Isla Escudo de Veraguas

B O C A S   D E L   T O R O

Río Criamola

Río Manatí

Península Valiente

C O R D I L L E R A   C E N T R A L

Archipiélago de Bocas del Toro

Swan Cay (Isla Pájaros)

PARQUE NACIONAL MARINO ISLA BASTIMENTOS

Isla Bastimentos
Cayos Zapatillas

Old Bank (Bastimentos Town)

4

2
Isla Colón

3

Bocas Town

2
Isla Solarte

Cayo Crawl **2**
5

Isla Popa

Cayo de Agua

Laguna de Chiriquí

Chiriquí Grande

2
Isla San Cristóbal

1

Silico Creek

Finca 60

1

Canal de Soropta

Almirante

BOSQUE PROTECTOR DE PALO SECO

Río Changuinola

Lago Fortuna

Gualaca

Interamericana, David & Panama City

Humedales de San San Pond Sak

6

Guabito

Changuinola

El Silencio

PARQUE INTERNACIONAL LA AMISTAD

Cerro Punta

Boquete

Río Majagua

David

Sixaola

Puerto Limón

Río Sixaola

Río San San

Río Teribe

7

Río Echandi (3165m)

Cerro Echandi (3165m)

Cerro Fábrega (3336m)

Cerro Itamut (3279m)

C O R D I L L E R A   D E   T A L A M A N C A

PARQUE NACIONAL VOLCÁN BARÚ

Volcán Barú (3475m)

Volcán

Río Piedra

C H I R I Q U Í

Las Tablas

COSTA RICA

Río Sereno

INTERAMERICANA

Paso Canoas

San José

0   25
kilometres

Bocas del Toro in 1826. Following construction of the **Panama Railroad** and the French canal effort, West Indian migrants continued to drift into the area.

The banana trade

For the last two centuries, the ebb and flow of the **banana trade** has most clearly defined the province. By 1895 bananas from Bocas accounted for more than half of Panama's export earnings, and Bocas Town boasted five foreign consulates and three English-language newspapers. Around 6500 were employed by the United Fruit Company in its heyday, and the company was responsible for building the now-defunct mainland railroad system and constructing canals, hospitals, telegraph networks and entire towns. But following repeated devastation by disease early in the twentieth century, the banana harvests failed, causing the archipelago's economy to languish. When the banana trade started up again in the 1950s and 1960s, Guna and Guaymí workers were also integrated into the workforce, many suffering serious ill-health from noxious pesticides. Now, with the trade in "*oro verde*" (green gold) flagging, the business is confined to the plantations round Changuinola, the headquarters of Bocas Fruit Company, the current incarnation of "the company" and part of Chiquita Brands International. With almost four thousand employees it is still the most important employer in the province, though workers now earn pitifully low wages.

Tourism and real estate

In recent years, **tourism** and **real-estate speculation** have soared, generating employment and income for some residents while leaving others behind to struggle with the inevitable rise in the cost of living, increased pressure on services and the threat of being thrown off their land. Foreign investors have been allowed to purchase huge portions of the archipelago for luxury resorts and holiday homes, despite local opposition. Given the complex ecosystems involved and the lack of infrastructure on the islands due to years of government neglect, much concern exists over the sustainability of such developments.

THE NGÄBE AND BUGLÉ

The province's highest-profile indigenous peoples are the **Ngäbe** (pronounced "No-bay") and the **Buglé**. These two related groups speak mutually unintelligible languages, and are probably the oldest surviving ethnic groups on the isthmus, descended from the great Guaymí warrior tribes, whose best-known chief, Urracá (see box, p.292), graces the 1¢ coin. Forced into remote and mountainous lands by the Spanish, where many have remained, the majority live within the Comarca Ngäbe-Buglé, a semi-autonomous area established in 1997, covering almost 7000 square kilometres in the eastern half of the province and pockets of Veraguas and Chiriquí. With poor access to potable water, health care and education, the *comarca* suffers Panama's highest levels of poverty.

Most Ngäbe and Buglé practise **subsistence agriculture**, supplemented by hunting, fishing and limited cash crop cultivation. Struggling to survive in an increasingly cash-based economy, some make seasonal migrations to the banana, coffee or sugar plantations, where they do the harshest jobs for the worst wages. A few produce traditional handicrafts – the distinctive colourful cotton dresses (*nagua*), necklaces (*nguñunkua*) and woven bags (*kri*) – to sell to tourists; others have abandoned the rural areas altogether.

Traditionally, both groups have lived in small kinship groupings – half a dozen thatched huts with dirt or wooden floors, though coastal communities prefer rectangular lodgings built on stilts – which control access to land and work in cooperation. These, and other cultural practices, such as the Ngäbe custom of polygamy (the Buglé have always espoused monogamy), have been eroded by missionary and other outside influences. One of the traditions that clings on in some places, despite attempts to outlaw it, is the **krün** (*balsería* in Spanish), a violent "sport" in which members of two teams take turns to try and knock their opponent off-balance by hurling a wooden pole at their calves. The contest is a core part of the four-day **chichería**, which involves plenty of its namesake, the potent maize-based *chicha fuerte* brew, alongside dancing and music.

Archipiélago de Bocas del Toro

Most tourists make a beeline for the **Archipiélago de Bocas del Toro**, scarcely setting foot on the mainland except to catch a bus or a boat. Despite the existence of several hundred atolls, islets and cays scattered across the bite-shaped gulf that shelters much of the archipelago, most tourist activity is centred on the handful of larger islands, covered in rainforest and fringed with mangroves, populated by small **Ngäbe** communities or, in the cases of islas Colón and Bastimentos, largely **Afro-Antillean** settlements.

The majority of visitors stay in the laidback provincial capital **Bocas del Toro**, which spills off a peninsula at the southeast tip of **Isla Colón**, the archipelago's largest and most developed island. During the day, launches brimming with tourists scatter outwards, heading for the reefs, beaches, mangroves and forests of the neighbouring islands of **Bastimentos**, **Solarte** and **Carenero** or the distant cays of **Zapatillas**. Other popular destinations include the **Laguna de Bocatorito**, often dubbed Dolphin Bay for the frequent sightings of dolphins, and the seabird colonies of **Swan Cay** off the north coast of Isla Colón. In late afternoon, the sandy streets of Bocas fill as the **waterfront bars** come to life. Dining options are plentiful and varied, reflecting the cosmopolitan population, and at weekends energetic visitors can usually find somewhere to dance till dawn.

Isla Colón

The first port of call in the archipelago for almost all visitors – whether arriving by plane or boat – is **ISLA COLÓN**, or, to be more precise, **Bocas Town**, the provincial capital of Bocas del Toro. Connected to the rest of the island by a slender isthmus, Bocas explodes with tourists in high season (mid-Dec to April), and is the easiest base

ARCHIPIÉLAGO DE BOCAS DEL TORO

ACCOMMODATION

Al Natural	15	Hostal Camping Ygriega	4
Bambuda Lodge	12	Hostal Gran Kahuna	10
Beverley's Hill	5	The Hummingbird	2
Casa Acuario	9	La Loma Jungle Lodge	13
Casa Cayuco	14	Palmar Beach Lodge	11
Casa El Jaguar	6	Playa Bluff Hotel	1
Dolphin Bay Hideaway	16	Rafael's House	8
Hostal Bastimentos	7	Tesoro Escondido	3

EATING

Alvin and Ketch's	4
Bibi's on the Beach	6
Chavela's	5
Leaf Eaters Café	7
Paki Point	2
Up in the Hill	3
Yarisnori	1

DRINKING AND NIGHTLIFE

Aqua Lounge	1

6

SAFETY IN BOCAS

The collapse of the banana trade and the social inequalities exacerbated by the mushrooming tourism and real-estate industries have led to an increase in **petty crime**. Valuables can go missing from even the most apparently empty beach, especially on islas Colón and Bastimentos, despite police patrols. Even in daylight there are periodic robberies on Isla Bastimentos, on the path across to Wizard Beach from Old Bank, with the occasional report of guys threatening with knives. If you hike this path, seek local advice and ensure that you are in a group. However tempting, **camping** on any of the beaches on the main islands outside an official campsite is very unwise.

Another safety issue concerns **boats**. Serious, even fatal collisions have occurred in the bay, usually at night, generally involving an unlicensed or inebriated boatman and/or a lack of lights on the vessel. Don't get into a boat until you've assessed the level of risk. And finally, take note of **riptides**, which are prevalent in the archipelago. Ask locals about currents, riptides and rogue waves before swimming, especially on Bastimentos. Every year, someone drowns.

---

from which to explore the islands, beaches and reefs of the archipelago. It also offers an ever expanding choice of tours and activities, from the traditional pursuits of **surfing**, **diving** and **snorkelling** to options such as forest walks, kayaking and wildlife viewing, as well as yoga and massage. Despite the lush primary and secondary rainforest on the island, most tourist activity happens on the wild and relatively deserted **beaches** of the east coast or the more sheltered shallows of **Boca del Drago**, on the western point close to the mainland.

Bocas Town

Arriving in **BOCAS TOWN**, you are welcomed to the island's casual melee by a spread of rickety, wooden, pastel-painted buildings and a laidback, often English-speaking, population. After falling into decline with the collapse of the banana trade (see p.221), the town was catapulted into another era by a steady trickle of backpackers and American retirees in the 1990s, followed by a country-wide real estate boom. Around twenty years ago there were only three hotels here; now there are more than seventy. There's no sightseeing as such – experiencing Bocas is more about hanging out in the waterfront bars and restaurants, soaking up the relaxed vibe, getting out on the water during the day and partying at night.

The town centre

Bocas is laid out on a simple grid system with most activity centred on **Calle 3**, the broad main street that runs north–south, spilling into Calle 1, which bulges out into the bay, where the decks of attractive wooden hotels, bars and restaurants stretch over the water on stilts. Halfway up the main drag, lined with supermarkets, souvenir shops and stalls, hotels and hostels, sits **Parque Bolívar**, the social heart of the town, shaded by coconut palms and fig trees, with a bust of the Liberator, the town's sole monument.

Playa El Istmito

The nearest stretch of sand and general town beach is tatty **Playa El Istmito**, on the eastern side of the causeway that links Bocas with the rest of Isla Colón. It is a decent place for a beer, especially during September's Feria del Mar festivities (see box, p.226).

WATER IN BOCAS

Tap water is not safe to drink throughout the province; meanwhile, used plastic bottles are a major environmental headache, especially on the islands. Where possible, try to buy the large gallon containers and refill a smaller bottle from them, rather then purchase a succession of small bottles. Better still, try to fill up from the eco-aware establishments that provide filtered water.

6

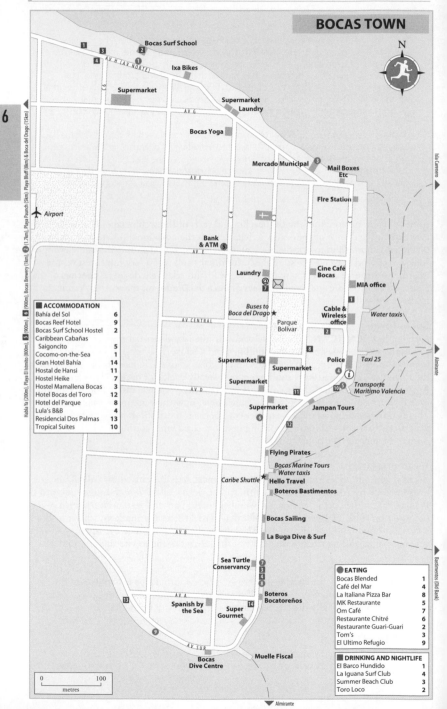

BOCAS TOWN

N

Bocas Surf School
Ixa Bikes
Supermarket
Supermarket
Laundry
AV G
Bocas Yoga
AV H (AV NORTE)
Airport
Mercado Municipal
Mail Boxes Etc
Fire Station
Bank & ATM
AV E
Laundry
Cine Café Bocas
MIA office
Water taxis
Buses to Boca del Drago
Cable & Wireless office
Parque Bolívar
AV CENTRAL
Supermarket
Police
Taxi 25
Supermarket
Supermarket
Transporte Marítimo Valencia
Supermarket
AV D
Jampan Tours
Supermarket
Flying Pirates
AV C
Bocas Marine Tours
Water taxis
Caribe Shuttle
Hello Travel
Boteros Bastimentos
Bocas Sailing
AV B
La Buga Dive & Surf
Sea Turtle Conservancy
Spanish by the Sea
AV A
Boteros Bocatoreños
Super Gourmet
AV SUR
Bocas Dive Centre
Muelle Fiscal

Habla Ya (200m), Playa El Istmito (800m), Playa El Istmito (1.7km), Playa Paunch (5km), Playa Bluff (8km) & Boca del Drago (15km)
Bocas Brewery (1km)
Isla Carenero
Almirante
Bastimentos (Old Bank)
Almirante

■ ACCOMMODATION

Bahía del Sol	6
Bocas Reef Hotel	9
Bocas Surf School Hostel	2
Caribbean Cabañas Saigoncito	5
Cocomo-on-the-Sea	1
Gran Hotel Bahía	14
Hostal de Hansi	11
Hostel Heike	7
Hostel Mamallena Bocas	3
Hotel Bocas del Toro	12
Hotel del Parque	8
Lula's B&B	4
Residencial Dos Palmas	13
Tropical Suites	10

● EATING

Bocas Blended	1
Café del Mar	4
La Italiana Pizza Bar	8
MK Restaurante	5
Om Café	7
Restaurante Chitré	6
Restaurante Guari-Guari	2
Tom's	3
El Ultimo Refugio	9

■ DRINKING AND NIGHTLIFE

El Barco Hundido	1
La Iguana Surf Club	4
Summer Beach Club	3
Toro Loco	2

0   100
metres

Playa Bluff and around

Three kilometres north of Bocas Town, the road divides at "La Ye"; a left turn takes you over the hilly terrain to Boca del Drago, 12km away, while the road to the right, which eventually becomes sand and gravel (4WD needed in the rainy season), hugs the coastline for another 5km past **surfing** hot spots **Playa Paunch** (or Punch) and **Dumpers**, until the start of the glorious 4km swathe of sand that is **Playa Bluff**. An important nesting site for leatherback and green **turtles**, Bluff can be visited at night during the nesting season (May–Sept) by arrangement (see box, p.236). None of these beaches is suitable for swimming, with powerful waves and strong currents, but the thundering breakers on Bluff beach are a sight to behold and the golden sands provide a lengthy, scenic promenade.

La Gruta

Colonia Santeña, 7km along the road to Boca del Drago • No fixed hours • $2 • Take the Boca del Drago bus from Bocas Town; La Gruta is signposted to the right off the main road, from where it is a short walk

Halfway across the island on the bumpy, tarred Boca del Drago road lies the small settlement of **Colonia Santeña**. The main reason to stop here is to visit a sacred cave, often referred to simply as **La Gruta**, a place of pilgrimage on July 16 for the Festival de la Virgen del Carmen. Push the fronds of greenery aside and, depending on the time of year and the amount of rain, you'll be wading in a delightful freshwater creek or a stream of guano. The shrine to the Virgin is near the entrance; flash a torch around and you'll see hundreds of bats clinging to the rock.

Boca del Drago

Northwest tip of Isla Colón, 16km from Bocas Town • Visit on a boat tour (see box, p.228), take the Boca del Drago bus (see p.227), or rent a bicycle: take the left fork at "La Ye" at the north end of Playa El Istmito, and turn left at the T-junction at the north end of the island

One of the most popular day-trips from Bocas Town is to take the bus to the Ngäbe community of **Boca del Drago**, at the northern end of the island. Supposedly the first place in Panama that Christopher Columbus set foot on, Boca del Drago can be a pleasant place to spend a relaxing day, outside holiday weekends. The beach, though slight, consists of lovely white palm-fringed sand, but the real appeal is the sheltered translucent water, perfect for safe bathing and snorkelling while you wait for your seafood order at the beachfront restaurant (see p.231).

Playa Estrella

A fifteen-minute walk along the shoreline from Boca del Drago takes you to **Playa Estrella**, whose shallows were once dotted with an amazing number of orange cushioned starfish. Sadly, thanks to a combination of increasing numbers of water-taxis and thoughtless actions by some tourists, touching or picking up the starfish for photos, numbers have dwindled. Here the beach is backed by a string of informal seafood restaurants and bars, which are packed at weekends and during the holiday season, with music blasting out across the sand. However, if you visit midweek, you'll encounter a more tranquil scene (though fewer options for eating) and by snorkelling a little further out from the beach, you might spot a few more starfish.

Swan Cay

2km off the north coast of Isla Colón • Visit on a boat tour (see box, p.228), or negotiate a rate with a fisherman in Boca del Drago

Swan Cay, a fifteen-minute boat ride off the north coast (accessible only in good weather conditions), is one of the area's main attractions. Known locally as **Isla Pájaros** (Bird Island), this impressive 50m stack, topped with cascading vegetation, is a **bird sanctuary**. Seabirds wheel above, with star billing going to the elegant white **red-billed tropicbird**, which shares this nesting spot with a colony of brown boobies.

6

BOCAS FESTIVALS

Bocas Town's main festival is the **Feria del Mar**, held on Playa El Istmito in late September; endless rows of exhibition stands, craft stalls, mountainous fry-ups and late-night partying on the sands draw visitors in their thousands. Other dates for the diary include November 16, when Bocas' main street becomes the focus of multiday celebrations for the **foundation of Bocas del Toro** province, marked by daytime parades with marching bands and *pollera*-garbed women, and nighttime drinking and dancing to DJs and live music. **Carnavales**, though less wild than in the Azuero, involve a fair amount of partying nonetheless – the strong Afro-Panamanian influence ensures regular street outings of Congo bands and *diablitos* brandishing whips (see box, p.163).

ARRIVAL AND DEPARTURE   ISLA COLÓN

BY PLANE

Airport All flights arrive at, and depart from, Bocas Airport, three blocks west of the main street, C 3.

Airlines and flights Air Panama (☎ 757 9841 in Bocas; ☎ 316 9000 for general reservations; ⓦ airpanama.com) offers several daily flights from and to Panama City (from $105 one way), which get booked up early over long weekends and holiday periods. The carbon-neutral Costa Rican domestic airline Nature Air (☎ 757 9390 in Bocas, ⓦ natureair.com) has daily direct flights between San José and Bocas (50min; from $211 one way, including carbon offsetting). Both airlines have offices at the airport in Bocas.

Luggage allowance Air Panama flights allow 14kg of checked baggage plus hand luggage, and charge supplements for surfboards. For Nature Air the luggage allowance depends upon the fare class purchased.

BY BUS

Almirante, a port on the Caribbean mainland, is the only departure point for boats to Isla Colón, the gateway to the Bocas del Toro archipelago. Whether you're coming from or heading to Costa Rica, Panama City or David by bus, you will be dropped off/picked up at "La Ye" de Almirante (see p.238), the junction between the main coastal road and the entrance to Almirante. Shared taxis shuttle back and forth between here and the water-taxi terminals ($1/person), where boats depart for/arrive from Bocas Town on Isla Colón.

From Costa Rica After crossing the Costa Rican border at Sixaola/Guabito (see p.241), take the bus to Changuinola, the first main town, 17km from the border (5.30am–7pm; every 25min; 30min), and transfer to a bus bound for Almirante (see p.239); alternatively, take a taxi to Almirante (50min; *colectivo* $6/person, private $15–20). A shuttle service also runs between Puerto Viejo, in Costa Rica, and Bocas del Toro (see below).

From/to Panama City Tranceibosa operates buses between Panama City and Changuinola, dropping off/picking up passengers at Almirante. Overnight buses from Panama City leave at 6pm, 6.30pm and sometimes 7pm,

depending on demand (10hr; $28); departures from Almirante to Panama City leave at 8am and 6pm daily. Tickets can be bought at Albrook bus terminal in Panama City, and at the Tranceibosa office by Taxi 25 in Bocas Town (daily 8am–noon & 1–5pm; ☎ 757 9493) up to two days in advance – buying ahead is advisable in high season. You'll need warm clothes to combat the invariably glacial a/c on the overnight buses.

From/to David Buses run frequently between Changuinola and David, stopping at Almirante (5am–7pm; every 25min; 4hr).

Shuttles The Caribe Shuttle (Bocas ☎ 757 7048; Puerto Viejo, Costa Rica ☎ 2750 0626, ⓦ caribeshuttle.com) offers a hassle-free, daily door-to-door a/c service to Bocas from Puerto Viejo (6am, 8am & noon; 4hr; $33) or San José (6am; 10hr; $76) in Costa Rica. Departures from Bocas to Puerto Viejo also leave at 6am, 8am and noon, while for San José the shuttle leaves at 8am. Hello Travel (☎ 757 7004, ⓦ hellotravelpanama.com), which has an office on C 3, Bocas Town, operates a daily shuttle between Boquete and Bocas Town, leaving Boquete at 8am (4hr; $30) and Bocas at 11am. All shuttle prices include water-taxi fares.

BY BOAT

Water-taxis The number of water-taxi companies providing transfer across the bay between Almirante and Bocas ebbs and flows. At the time of writing four companies were active: each has a separate jetty along the same 100m of road in Almirante with departures every 30min (6am–6pm, occasionally 6.30pm; 30min; $6). The most established companies are Taxi 25, which has a dock next to the police station in Bocas Town, and Bocas Marine Tours, which operates from the main jetty, further down C 3. Newer companies Transporte Maritimo Valencia and Torres Tours have jetties on C 1 and offer cheaper rates when business is slack.

Ferries The Palanga car ferry (ⓦ ferrybocas.com) leaves Almirante at 7am and noon Tues–Sun, 7am on Sun (1hr 30min; $2) and will transport a bicycle ($4) or a motorbike ($10). The ferry docks at the southern end of Bocas Town's main street, returning to Almirante at 10am and 3pm.

GETTING AROUND

There are currently two minibus services (see below); otherwise, beyond the town centre – which is easily navigable on foot – you're reliant on taxis.

By taxi Though generally unnecessary in town, taxis are readily available (0.60¢/person *colectivo* rate within town). Travelling further afield, a 4WD taxi to Playa Bluff will set you back $15–20 depending on how far up the beach you are going, and the condition of the road.

By bus There are two bus routes across the island. Transporte Boca del Drago (**☎** 774 9065) operates the more regular and reliable service, to and from Boca del Drago. It leaves from Parque Bolívar approximately hourly (7am–6pm) and departs from outside *Yarisnori* in Boca del Drago (see p.225) at similar intervals for the return trip. In high season, private minibuses leave from just south of Parque Bolívar when full and charge the same rates. There is also a bus service to Playa Bluff, when the road is dry, which also leaves from Parque Bolívar (7am to mid-afternoon; roughly every 1hr–1hr 30min; 20–30min); the last bus returns around 4.30–5pm.

By water-taxi Water-taxis regularly ferry people back and forth from Bocas to Isla Carenero ($1 to the near shore; $2 anywhere else) and to Old Bank on Bastimentos ($3) at fixed rates, from around dawn to dusk. Taxis leave once they've gathered a few passengers, every 10–15min or so, and the rates go up at night. The main water-taxi dock for Carenero is by *El Barco Hundido* on C 1, while for Old Bank, Bastimentos, you should head for the Boteros Bastimentos water-taxi dock, on the main street, opposite Av "C". On C 1, opposite Av "D", Jampan Tours (**☎** 757 9619) runs a regular water-taxi service to Red Frog Beach on a fixed timetable (usually 5–6 daily; $8 one way, $15 return).

By bike The main cycling destinations are Playa Bluff and Boca del Drago. Several places in Bocas Town rent out bicycles (around $10–15/day; $50/week) in varying states of repair. Ixa Bikes, on Av "H" and C 5, is a good choice as they also do bike repairs. Flying Pirates (**☎** 6689 5050, **🖥** flyingpiratesbocas .com) also offers quad-bike rental ($140/day).

DIVING, SNORKELLING AND SURFING IN BOCAS

Diving and **snorkelling** are the most established diversions around Bocas Town. The area offers the healthiest **coral** on the Caribbean coast, covered in sponges and anemones, fed on by colourful reef fish and frequented by turtles and nurse sharks, while moray eels, lobsters and crabs hide in the crevices. The main problem with snorkelling and diving in Bocas is drastically reduced **visibility** caused by run-off from the mainland following heavy rains, which are frequent, even in the dry season. Strong winds and rough seas limit accessibility to more remote dive sites too.

Bocas also has a growing reputation for **surfing**, and while it can't match Santa Catalina (see pp.210–212) for consistency of waves, it offers some excellent rides when conditions are right, generally between December and March.

DIVING AND SNORKELLING

Snorkelling highlights include the distant **Cayos Zapatillas** in the national marine park, though currents are strong, and, off the southern tip of Bastimentos, the magical soft coral gardens of **Cayo Crawl**. Closer to base, the shallows by Hospital Point off **Isla Solarte** are favoured by both snorkellers and divers, who can explore the impressive wall and rocky outcrop sheltering schools of fish. The best diving is undeniably **Tiger Rock**, a group of beautiful pinnacles visited by schools of large fish, which lies 40km offshore and requires a full day-trip and calm seas. The little-visited **Escudo de Veraguas**, an island at the far east of the archipelago, offers a variety of dive sites and can be visited on multiday dive trips with La Buga Dive & Surf (see p.229).

SURFING

Most surf spots are for **experienced** or **intermediate** surfers, though everyone will need reef booties for the sharp reef breaks and to protect against sea urchins. On the east coast of Isla Colón, top billing goes to **Playa Bluff**, which can produce huge tubes when the swell is in and is only for experienced practitioners. **Dumpers** – nearer Bocas Town – provides a tricky reef-bottom left break, whereas the reef break at nearby **Paunch** is usually the place to take **beginners**. Over on Isla Bastimentos the left and right beach breaks of **Playa Wizard** and **Red Frog Beach** are also usually accessible to novice and intermediate surfers. Other hot spots for experts include the reef break that lies off **Isla Carenero** and along the northern coast of Bastimentos; and, between the two islands, the giant waves of **Silverbacks**.

Numerous places rent out **boards** in various states of repair ($15–20/day), and several places offer lessons ($50–60/half-day; $90/day), transfers to surf spots and even guided surf tours (see p.229).

INFORMATION

Tourist information The tourist office (daily 8am–4pm; ☎ 757 9642) on C 1 has toilets, and may be able to provide a map, but is otherwise of limited help. The free monthly *Bocas Breeze* (ⓦ bocasbreeze.com) advertises local events. The sustainable tourism group, Alianza de Turismo Sostenible de Bocas del Toro runs a useful website (ⓦ redtucombo.bocasdeltoro.org) about community-based tourism, and can provide further information.

MIA office C 1 between Av Central & Av "E" (Mon–Fri 8am–4pm; ☎ 757 9244). MIA hands out permits for camping within Parque Nacional Marino Isla Bastimentos ($6/person, plus $10 park fee).

ACTIVITIES AND TOURS

Cocoa farms The mainland communities of Silico Creek (ⓦ urari.bocasdeltoro.org; $10 for a 2hr tour) and Río Oeste Arriba (ⓦ oreba.bocasdeltoro.org; $35 including lunch and transport from Almirante; minimum two people) offer fascinating tours in Spanish and English of their organic cocoa farms, with plenty of tasting along the way.

Horseriding At Playa Bluff, you can arrange horseriding at *Bluff Beach Retreat* (☎ 6677 8867; $45 for 3hr plus tip for the guide). On Isla San Cristóbal, a highly acclaimed but more expensive operator, Panama Horseback Adventures (☎ 6915 3147, ⓦ panamahorseback.com), offers half-day ($50; 2hr on horseback) and full-day tours ($75) to a Ngäbe village, plus a more challenging day for experienced riders ($100) or an overnight trip ($250). Prices include transfer from Bocas Town.

Kayak rental Several lodgings, such as *Bambuda Lodge*, *Cocomo on the Sea* and *Gran Kahuna*, rent out/lend kayaks.

Turtle watching See box, p.236.

Yoga Bocas Yoga (top end of C 4; ☎ 6658 1355, ⓦ bocasyoga .com; $6/session, twenty-class pass $80) gets rave reviews.

TOURS FROM BOCAS TOWN

Generally, you get what you pay for in a **tour**, in that the pricier operators tend to use better and safer boats, take fewer people and show greater customer service and respect for the environment and the indigenous communities. Make sure you establish the itinerary and what's included in the price. If you get a group of about six together, you can usually negotiate a deal for your own itinerary with one of the boatmen hanging out around the dock.

The standard day-trip excursions combine snorkelling with other activities, and cater predominantly to budget travellers ($25–30/person for a minimum of four to six people), depending on the destination and boat quality. Most leave at around 9.30am, returning about 4–4.30pm and stopping off for a seafood meal (not included in price) at a local restaurant along the way, though some trips include a picnic lunch. Bad **weather** can result in a change of itinerary or cancellation and the seas further out can get very rough. We offer a selection of the town's best **tour operators** in Bocas' listings section (see opposite).

THE ITINERARIES

There are three popular itineraries offered by most operators. The first takes you to **Laguna Bocatorito** (Dolphin Bay), where you have a chance of seeing the rather shy **bottle-nosed dolphins** that live there year-round. This should be boycotted in high season when the place is overrun with boats, many engaging in potentially harmful practices. The next stop is the gorgeous, rainbow-coloured soft coral of **Cayo Crawl**, where lunch is at one of the three over-the-water restaurants (around $9–12), before returning to lounge on **Red Frog Beach** ($5 fee), sometimes with an additional spot of snorkelling nearer home.

Another similar but pricier option takes you on from Cayo Crawl to the national marine park and **Cayos Zapatillas** ($10 park entry fee on top) for further snorkelling and beach lounging, stopping off at another snorkelling spot, such as **Hospital Point**, on the way back. Alternatively, boats head round Isla Colón to the easy shallows of **Boca del Drago**, with lunch at a restaurant on the beach, a visit to **Playa Estrella** and a trip out to see the seabirds at **Swan Cay** before snorkel masks are donned once more at **Punta Manglar** on the way back. In an attempt to avoid the crowds or offer some variation, some operators are now offering a visit to a Ngäbe village, such as Bocatorito or Bahía Honda.

Endless possibilities exist for boat excursions further afield: up one of the rivers into the rainforests of the mainland to visit isolated **indigenous communities** or east around the Península Valiente to the remote **Isla de Escudo de Veraguas**, which aficionados consider to be one of the best diving spots in the whole Caribbean – La Buga Dive & Surf (see opposite) offers overnight camping dive trips, though the seas are too rough to reach it most of the year.

TOUR OPERATORS

There are many tour operators in Bocas Town; below is just a small selection of the best.

Bocas Dive Centre C 4 and Av Sur ☎757 9737, ⓦ bocasdivecenter.com. Highly regarded Panamanian-owned dive shop emphasizing safety while having fun. Two-tank dives from $110 at various locations and dive instructor training on offer.

Bocas Sailing C 3 at Av "B" ☎757 9710, ⓦ bocassailing .com. Excellent-value catamaran trips to see dolphins en route to Cayo Crawl ($48 including picnic lunch) or to Boca del Drago, with private charter possible (minimum eight people).

Bocas Surf School Av Norte, between C 5 & C 6 ☎6852 5291, ⓦ bocassurfschool.com. Professional private lessons with qualified instructors ($59 half-day, $89 full day, including board) at all levels; the same people run a small, quiet, on-site hostel.

Boteros Bocatoreños C 3, at Av "A" ☎757 9760. An association of local boatmen formed to try and compete against some of the slicker foreign tour operators, offering the usual tour favourites, often at slightly lower prices, and with bags of local tales to tell.

La Buga Dive & Surf C 3, at Av "B" ☎6781 0755, ⓦ labugapanama.com. Highly recommended, this dive centre (Open-Water $250) also offers surfing, snorkelling and fishing trips as well as SUP and surfboard rental, and has a cool bar to boot.

Jampan Tours C 1, at Av "D" ☎757 9619. You can't miss the bright Jamaican colours of their office or boats, which run water-taxi services to Red Frog Beach and the standard day-tours ($25–30), with one trip that includes a visit to a Ngäbe community on Isla San Cristóbal.

6

ACCOMMODATION

There's a good range of **accommodation** in Bocas, and more hostels here than anywhere else in the country outside Panama City. Even so, rooms are scarce during high season and on holiday weekends. **Advance booking** is a good idea, though backpacker lodgings don't accept reservations, so try to arrive before 11am. A sprinkling of foreign-owned lodges and guesthouses are now opening up in more remote corners of Isla Colón; staying in these you are close to nature but generally reliant on their amenities, since public transport is scarce. And it pays to remember that water shortages, power cuts and floods often affect Isla Colón – and other areas in the archipelago – however much you're paying.

BOCAS TOWN

HOTELS AND B&BS

Bahía del Sol Saigon Bay ☎6695 6286, ⓦ bocasbahiadelsol.com; map p.224. Situated in a local community, a 15min walk from town, this cosy over-the-water guesthouse offers a range of rooms and prices from affordable rustic comfort (in the adjoining three-roomed *Casa Rosada*) to rustic luxury. The most sought-after suite boasts an ocean veranda with open-air jacuzzi and shower (no a/c). Wonderful sunsets, scrumptious breakfasts (included in the rate) and gracious hosts make this place a treat. $80

Bocas Reef Hotel C 3 between Av Central & Av "D" ☎757 9804; map p.224. Functional, characterless hotel in a labyrinthine building offering clean en-suite rooms, hot-water showers, cable TV, modern a/c and solid beds. Service is friendly and efficient and they have a terrace and kitchen for guests' use. You can't ask for more for the price. $40

Caribbean Cabañas Saigoncito Saigon ☎6446 0787, ⓦ panamasparadise.com; map p.224. A collection of nicely renovated traditional wooden houses on stilts with balconies in lush gardens; it's in a residential area 5min from Bocas Town centre, so bike rental is included to help you get about. Some rooms can be rented separately or together as a whole cabin; others are *cabañas* with kitchens. All have fans, hot water and cable TV. Good weekly rates. $55

Cocomo-on-the-Sea Av "H" at C 6 ☎757 9259, ⓦ cocomoonthesea.com; map p.224. Popular, comfortable four-room B&B (with a/c) in a lovely painted wooden Bocatorian house, where you'll be well looked after. Two rooms face the ocean but all have access to a waterside veranda plus free use of kayaks. Substantial breakfast included. $94

Gran Hotel Bahía C 3 at Av "A" ☎757 9626, ⓦ ghbahia .com; map p.224. You're definitely paying more for the history than facilities or service (though refurbished rooms have a/c and cable TV) – the impressive former headquarters of the United Fruit Company (1905) is steeped in it. Hang out on the fabulous first-floor wooden veranda and splash out the extra $17 for the larger, brighter rooms upstairs. Breakfast included. Two-night minimum. $77

Hotel Bocas del Toro C 1 between Av "C" & Av "D" ☎757 9018, ⓦ hotelbocasdeltoro.com; map p.224. Attractive polished wood abounds here and the eleven rooms (with a/c, cable TV and coffee-maker) are elegantly furnished, some with stunning ocean-view balconies. The restaurant deck overlooks the water. They also organize tours, rent kayaks and offer massage. Breakfast included. $143

Hotel del Parque C 2 ☎757 9008, ⓦ hdelparque .webs.com; map p.224. This warm, family-run, no-frills place has two balconies: one overlooking the main square and another, quieter and hung with hammocks, at the back. Rooms (sleeping one to four) include cable TV, good hot-water showers and a/c (or fan); and there's a small kitchen. The next-door hostel can be noisy. $50

★ Lula's B&B Av "H" at C 6 ☎757 9057, ⓦ lulabb.com; map p.224. Professional B&B offering half a dozen spotless rooms (four doubles, four triples) with private hot-water bathroom, a/c or fan, plus a spacious communal balcony, homely, nicely furnished living room and shared kitchenette.

The triples in particular are excellent value ($88). $77

Residencial Dos Palmas Av Sur at C 5 ☎ 757 9906, ✉ residencialdospalmas@yahoo.com; map p.224. On the quieter southern tip of town in a residential area, this local lodging offers the best budget over-the-water deal, with a handful of faded but tidy rooms (a/c, cable TV and hot water) plus a terrace with hammocks and chairs from which to watch the sun set. $35

Tropical Suites C 1 at Av "D" ☎ 757 9880, ⓦ bocastropical .com; map p.224. Aparthotel with helpful English-speaking staff and sixteen well-equipped suites; particularly good value for families, these comprise a kitchenette, large double beds and pull-out double sofa beds, with patio or balcony; you'll pay more for a sea view. Cheaper weekly rates ($651). $103

HOSTELS

Bocas Surf School Hostel Av Norte, between C 5 & C 6 ☎ 6852 5291, ⓦ bocassurfschool.com; map p.224. Quiet hostel in a converted wooden Bocatoreño house. Small dorms, sleeping eleven people (sharing two bathrooms), have ample bunks with decent mattresses, and there's a kitchen and waterside deck at the back. The friendly owners run the on-site surf school (see p.229). $20

Hostal Camping Ygriega The Y, north end of Playa El Istmito ☎ 6921 2125, ⓦ hostalcampinglaygriega.com; map p.222. Basic campsite-cum-hostel a $1 taxi ride or 10min cycle from town. Pitch your own tent or use one of theirs, erected on a wooden deck under a roof, with bedding and a thin mattress provided. Also doubles with shared bathrooms and kitchen. Bikes for rent. Camping $6.50, camping with tent provided $8, dorms $10, doubles $26

★**Hostal de Hansi** C 2 at Av "D" ☎ 757 9932, ⓦ hostalhansi.bocas.com; map p.224. Immaculately clean and tidy, catering to couples and single travellers on a budget who want to avoid the dorm party scene. Fan-ventilated singles ($15; $13 with shared bathroom) and en-suite doubles have use of a communal kitchen. $25

Hostel Heike C 3, between Av Central & Av "E" ☎ 757 9708, ⓦ hostelheike.com; map p.224. Large well-run hostel with packed dorms (fans or a/c and lockers) sharing

spotless, hot-water bathrooms. The communal kitchen, balcony overlooking the main street, roof terrace, free Spanish lessons and purified water on tap make it a popular hangout. Pancake breakfast included. Dorms $11, doubles $28

★**Hostel Mamallena Bocas** Av "H" at C 6 ☎ 760 9934, ⓦ mamallenabocas.com; map p.224. The stunning open-sided lounge-bar-chillout area that melts into an over-the-water sundeck makes this place special. Relax in a deckchair, play pool or sprawl on a sofa amid the pot plants, and soak up the sea views. Fourteen rooms – ten dorms, two doubles and two quads – all have a/c and private (cold-water) bathrooms. Plus, you've the usual hostel essentials: lockers, kitchen, DIY pancake breakfast and weekly BBQ. Dorms $18, doubles $45

PLAYA BLUFF

★**The Hummingbird** ☎ 6949 3694, ⓦ thehumming birdpanama.com; map p.222. Six-room boutique eco-B&B – solar power and rainwater harvesting – in tropical gardens replete with butterflies and hummingbirds. Book a room in one of the raised wooden bungalows with screened louvred windows and folding doors that open onto a fabulous balcony to maximize the breeze and keep out the bugs. There's also a pool and gourmet bar-restaurant (open to non-residents; booking preferred). Breakfast included. $150

Playa Bluff Hotel ☎ 6871 6064, ⓦ playabluffhotel .com; map p.222. Set back in forest midway along the beach road, this place has nine spacious, cool fan-ventilated rooms with private or shared bathroom, all with terraces, in verdant surroundings brimming with wildlife just a stone's throw from the beach. Breakfast included. $138

★**Tesoro Escondido** ☎ 6749 7435, ⓦ tesoroescondido .info; map p.222. Delightful, genuine ecofriendly resort offering rustic rooms, a couple of cottages and a small apartment (sleeping two to four) – all set amid lush tropical forest up on the cliff or down near the beach with plenty of terrace and porch space. Rooms and cabins are simply yet quirkily furnished with recycled artwork; mosquito nets are provided. Self-cater in the communal kitchens or enjoy home cooking at reasonable rates. Good weekly or monthly discounts in low season. $57

EATING

Bocas has an excellent range of **restaurants**, with vegetarians enjoying a decent selection. Lobster, conch and other local seasonal specialities taste particularly delicious in local coconut milk and Caribbean spice preparations. **Opening hours** can be erratic, especially in low season, and service seriously soporific. Note that **tap water** is not safe to drink (see box, p.223).

BOCAS TOWN

★**Bocas Blended** Av "H", by Bocas Surf School ☎ 757 9135, ⓦ facebook.com/BocasBlended; map p.224. Unmistakeable converted sky-blue bus by Bocas Surf School, dishing up smoothies, tasty breakfasts and delectable salads and wraps filled with fresh ingredients at modest prices ($6–9). Take away or eat at the bus and take advantage of the two-for-one "wrappy hour" and excellent-value lunch

combos. There's free wi-fi, too. Mon–Sat 8am–6pm.

★**Café del Mar** C 1a, opposite the tourist office ☎ 6776 8858, ⓦ facebook.com/Café-del-Mar; map p.224. Cosy five-table café with arty decor. Breakfasts and light lunches are not cheap, but everything's freshly prepared and a change from the norm: spinach and feta omelette with coconut bread, say, *gallo pinto* burrito, or tuna steak burger ($7–9). Tues–Thurs 8am–4pm, Fri–Sun 8am–10pm.

La Italiana Pizza Bar C 1, between Av "A" & Av "B" ☎ 757 9812; map p.224. Fronting *La Iguana Surf Club* (see below), this is a favourite spot to eat before hitting the dancefloor – try a $10 bowl of pasta or a great wood-fired, thin-crust pizza. Friendly, efficient service and bags of ambience. Mon, Tues & Thurs–Sun 5.30–11.30pm.

★**MK Restaurante** C 1 at Av "D" ☎ 760 8144, ⓦ facebook.com/MKrestaurante; map p.224. The welcoming French owner-chef ensures a sensory feast, serving exquisitely presented dishes on slates: most seafood comes with the rice and vegetables of the day, including the signature grilled whole lobster ($23). The desserts are melt-in-the-mouth works of art. Mains from $13. Daily 7.30am–10pm.

★**Om Café** C 3, between Av "A" & Av "B" ☎ 6624 0898; map p.224. The Canadian-Indian owner draws from traditional family recipes, dishing up excellent curries (mains $11–14), as well as juices and *lassis*. For breakfast the eggs vindaloo *roti* wrap will set your day off with a blast, or choose from bagels and bowls of fruit, granola and yoghurt. Mon, Tues & Fri–Sun 8am–noon & 6–10pm.

Restaurante Chitré C 3, between Av "C" & Av "D"; map p.224. Probably the best hot sauce and fried chicken in town: tuck into traditional staples for under $4 and watch the world go by from one of the patio tables. Mon–Sat 6am–9pm, Sun 10am–9pm.

★**Restaurante Guari-Guari** 2km from town centre along the isthmus, near the petrol station ☎ 6627 1825, ⓦ bocasdeltoro.travel/guari-guari; map p.224. The gourmet prix fixe, six-course meal ($23) features some of the most innovative dishes in Panama, exquisitely prepared

by a Spanish chef, in intimate open-air surroundings. Reservations essential. Cash only. Daily 6–10pm.

Tom's Av "H" at C 4, upstairs, behind the municipal market; map p.224. Local Caribbean food for $5–7 (over $10–12 for seafood mains). Expect sides of coconut rice, plantain and *escobeche* with hot pepper sauce and watch the boats bobbing in the careenage. Mon–Fri 11am–5pm.

★**El Último Refugio** Av Sur, between C 4 & C 5 ☎ 6726 9851, ⓦ ultimorefugio.com; map p.224. West-facing waterfront venue affording the best sunset views in Bocas, and cheerily decorated with fairy lights. The interesting, daily changing fine-dining menu includes the likes of guava pork tenderloin, or shrimps in spicy cilantro pesto (mains $19–22), and excellent cocktails. Mon–Fri 6–10pm.

THE REST OF THE ISLAND

★**Paki Point** Playa Paunch ☎ 6948 6562, ⓦ facebook .com/PakiPointBocasdelToro; map p.222. Capturing weary cyclists and tired surfers, this touristy open-air bar-restaurant satisfies all, with decent comfort food – burgers (the jalapeño variety is a favourite), *ceviche* and fresh fish – plus great music, vibrant artwork and a vast wooden deck strewn with sunloungers that spill onto the sand. Watch the surfers, soak up the rays or slide into oblivion with a cocktail. Live DJs on "Siesta Saturdays". Daily 11am–6.30pm.

Yarisnori On the beach, Boca del Drago ☎ 6615 5580; map p.222. This mellow open-air restaurant on the beach is the longest established of the casual seafood places along this stretch of coastline. Enjoy succulent snapper, mahi-mahi or grouper in garlic or Creole sauce from around $12 up to $30 plus for lobster. Daily 9am–6pm.

DRINKING AND NIGHTLIFE

El Barco Hundido C 1, beside Cable & Wireless; map p.224. Known as the "Wreck Deck" both for the illuminated shipwreck by the dancefloor and the late-night state of its clientele, this legendary hangout has DJs most nights, playing everything from Latin to reggae. It gets lively after 10pm. Beer $2. Mon, Tues & Thurs–Sun 7pm–late.

★**La Iguana Surf Club** C 1, between Av "A" & Av "B" ☎ 757 9812; map p.224. This popular nightspot, blasting out heavy doses of reggaeton (salsa and rock, too), is a serious party venue, with great cocktails and a waterside deck. Live bands and DJs at weekends. Mon, Tues, Thurs, Fri & Sun 9pm–4am.

Summer Beach Club C 1, between Av "A" & Av "B"

ⓦ facebook.com/summerbocasdeltoro; map p.224. Laser lights, glitzy DJ deck, themed party nights (often offering free body painting and make-up), free drinks for women, fire-dancing acts – all on a vast plant-filled deck over the water. The dancefloor is heaving on party nights, with a central sea swimming pool carved out of the deck to cool off in. Occasional cover charge. Usually Wed & Sat 9pm until late.

Toro Loco Av Central, between C 1 & 2 ☎ 757 7011; map p.224. Beyond NFL and baseball fixtures on the TV screens, this sports bar offers friendly, efficient service, moderately priced drinks (including an extended happy hour) and US comfort food – wings, mozzarella sticks, burgers and pasta – plus live music on Wed nights. Daily 11am–midnight.

DIRECTORY

Cinema For those rainy afternoons: recline in a beanbag at *Cine Café Bocas*, C 2 (Mon, Tues & Thurs–Sun 10am–11pm, Wed 10am–3pm; ☎ 6549 4158, ⓦ facebook.com/cinecafe bocas) with a fistful of popcorn (included) in hand.

Learning Spanish Habla Ya (ⓦ hablayapanama.com) and Spanish by the Sea (ⓦ spanishatlocations.com) are the

best-known language schools, both with good reputations (weekly rates for small group classes around $225–250).

Massage In keeping with the boho vibe of Bocas, there's no shortage of people willing to knead your aching post-surf limbs; check the hostel notice boards and posters throughout town.

6

Isla Carenero

A short water-taxi ride from Bocas Town, **Isla Carenero** presents a 2km sliver of low-lying land surrounded by shallow waters and a thin necklace of beach that periodically dissolves into mud, tangled roots and, around the northeastern end, jagged rocks, where one of the archipelago's best **surf breaks** pounds the reef. Most of the four hundred occupants are squeezed onto the southwestern tip, in makeshift wooden housing on littered and boggy ground. Though the settlement is quieter than Bocas Town, which could be a plus, the island has a reputation for vicious sandflies; moreover, there's not much to do or see. Most visitors hop across for a drink, a bite to eat or just a change of scene.

6

ARRIVAL AND DEPARTURE   ISLA CARENERO

By water-taxi Isla Carenero is a short hop by water-taxi from the dock beside *El Barco Hundido* in Bocas Town ($1 to the nearest, unnamed, bit of land; $2 to La Playita by *Hostel Gran Kahuna*).

ACCOMMODATION

★**Casa Acuario** Southwest side of the island ☎757 9565, ⓦcasaacuario.com; map p.222. This delightful wooden structure, built over the water, has five spacious rooms (fan, a/c and cable TV) with vast windows, some with hammock and deckchairs. Plus, there's a wraparound deck and communal kitchen-dining area. **$97**

★**Hostel Gran Kahuna** South side of the island ☎757 9038, ⓦgrankahunabocas.com; map p.222. Solid budget option on the beach, attempting green practices and offering dorms with lockers and surfboard storage space, and two (overpriced) private en-suite rooms – all with a/c and good beds. Nice garden and social area, with comfy sofas, sea-facing hammocks and a moderately priced bar-restaurant. Surf lessons available, plus board, kayak and SUP rental. Dorms **$15**, doubles **$60**

EATING

Bibi's on the Beach Buccaneer Resort, southeast side of the island ☎757 9137; map p.222. Popular tourist and expat over-the-water watering hole with great Caribbean views. It serves fresh seafood – try the *ceviche* with passion fruit ($7), or larger platefuls from around $13 – and refreshing cocktails. Mon & Wed–Sun 8am–9pm.

★**Leaf Eaters Café** Southwest side of the island ☎757 9543, ⓦleafeaterscafe.com; map p.222. A gem of a vegetarian and vegan café ($8–11), in a breezy over-the-water setting, whose warm decor has Indian and Caribbean touches. Try the specials: a nutty veggie burger or a tripartite salad bowl of the day, or go for the smoothies, cakes and coffee. Healthy eating *par excellence*. Tues–Sat 10am–6pm.

DRINKING AND NIGHTLIFE

Aqua Lounge Southwest side of the island ⓦbocasaqualounge.info. A legendary over-the-water party venue boasting a swimming pool carved out of the deck, swings, a water trampoline – and plenty of cheap booze. All-night parties (Wed & Sat) are wild, but there's something happening every night, from "beer pong" to a games evening. Mon, Tues, Thurs, Fri & Sun 9am–11pm, Wed & Sat 9am–dawn.

Isla Bastimentos

The sprawling and beautiful 52 square kilometres of **ISLA BASTIMENTOS** boasts the mellow, Afro-Antillean fishing community of **Old Bank**, marble-sand **surfing beaches** and lush inland **forest** inhabited by strawberry poison dart frogs. Most visitors are day-trippers: some come independently to tuck into tasty Creole seafood in Old Bank or to hike across the island to the surfing beaches; others visit with organized tours, which generally cut across the western arm of the island to the much vaunted Red Frog Beach. If you want to escape the tourist scene in Bocas, Bastimentos is a good place to hang out and the place where you're most likely to hear Guari-Guari, English patois embellished with Spanish and Ngäbere.

The island's two Ngäbe communities of **Bahía Honda**, in the crook of the bay of the same name on the island's south side, and **Quebrada Sal** (Salt Creek), over towards the eastern end by Punta Vieja, both welcome visitors.

Old Bank (Bastimentos Town)

OLD BANK – affectionately referred to as **Basti** – the island's main settlement, with a population of around nine hundred, sits on the westernmost point, a short jaunt by water-taxi from Bocas. An undulating, cracked concrete path acts as its main thoroughfare, snaking its way between tightly packed houses built out over the water on stilts, passing reggaeton beats, discarded bikes and old men slamming down dominoes, and winding up to a steep, green hillside dotted with precariously built wooden homes. A jungle **path**, occasionally impassable after heavy rains, leads to several glorious **beaches** twenty minutes away on the other side of the island.

6

The beaches

Renowned for riptides that claim lives every year, the sea that pounds the northern surfing **beaches** of Bastimentos is often too dangerous to swim in, but there is lots of good walking to be had along these curved broad belts of creamy sand backed by palms and thick vegetation. Heading along the overland path from Old Bank (see box, p.223), you pass **Playa Wizard** (Playa Primera) after fifteen to twenty minutes, and, further east, Playa Segunda, and then **Red Frog Beach**, though you won't find its namesake waving to you from a beach towel (see box below). A short hike further east brings you to **Playa Polo**, a smaller, sheltered cove protected by a reef; it's good for snorkelling, though it can get busy, and the eponymous Polo, who lives there, happily cooks up the catch of the day with coconut rice for visitors. Even further east lies another surfing stretch of sand, **Playa Larga** (see p.236).

If you're planning a whole day at the beach, take enough water with you; there are a couple of restaurants on Red Frog Beach.

Bahía Honda

6km southeast of Old Bank • $40/person (for two people) including transport, guiding and lunch; one day's notice needed • Community tourism project ✆ 6726 0968 (ask for Rutilio Milton), ⊕ timorogo.org • Pick up from the dock by the *mercado municipal*, Bocas Town

The 25 or so thatched homes of the dispersed Ngäbe community of **BAHÍA HONDA** are hidden among a dense tangle of mangroves at the eastern end of the bay of the same

---

STRAWBERRY POISON DART FROGS

Probably Bastimentos' most famous residents, the dazzling **strawberry poison dart frogs** (*oophaga pumilio*), no larger than a thumbnail, are actually widespread along the Caribbean lowlands from Nicaragua to western Panama. But nowhere is their colouration and size – "morphs" as they are termed – as varied as here. That said, the place you're least likely to spot these amphibians, ironically, is on **Red Frog Beach**, where local kids have captured many of them to impress tourists and charge for photos – or they've simply scarpered.

The most commonly sighted poison dart frog is the smart **"blue-jeans"** morph, whose brilliant scarlet torso fades into cobalt blue or purple legs; on Bastimentos these seductive amphibians span red, orange, gold, green or even white, and are often speckled with black. The "poison dart" title given to the family derived from the likes of the Colombian golden poison frog (*phyllobates terribilis*) that secretes a particularly lethal toxin – sufficient to kill up to twenty people – and which has traditionally been used by the Chocó (ancestors of the present-day Emberá) to coat darts and arrows for hunting.

While the dazzling colouration aimed at alerting would-be predators to the poison beneath their skin is what most attracts tourists to these fluorescent creatures, their **behaviour** is equally striking. Extremely territorial, male dart frogs can be seen locked in combat among the leaf-litter like miniature wrestlers, comically teetering on their hind legs trying to pin their opponent down in submission with the front legs. Mating occurs at any time of year and after the small clutch of eggs has been laid and fertilized, the male periodically pees on them to keep them moist. Once hatched, the female gives each tadpole a piggy-back ride, one by one, up to the canopy, depositing them in separate water-filled bromeliads. Over the next few weeks, she returns frequently to deposit unfertilized eggs in the water for the tadpoles to eat as they mature.

name, with a few across the water on Isla Solarte. In addition to a chapel and primary school, they have a restaurant, the heart of the **community tourism project** – whose star attraction is a guided excursion up the **Sendero del Peresoso** (Trail of the Sloth) to the Cueva Nivida. You'll be paddled up a nearby creek, where you can often see the trail's namesake furled round a branch and crabs and caimans in the shallows, before heading off on foot through forest that was once a cocoa plantation, to wade through a series of caves thick with stalagmites and coated with several species of Bastimentos bats. If you ring a day in advance, you can stop off at the community restaurant on the way back and sample traditional dishes such as *morongodo*, a green plantain pancake.

Cayo Crawl

At the southern tip of Bastimentos amid a myriad of mangrove islets lies tiny **Cayo Crawl**, where three thatched restaurants do a roaring trade in seafood lunches. After rounding the point, you come to the gorgeous soft coral fields of the same name, which feature on many day-trips. In order to protect the coral, fins are not allowed when snorkelling.

Quebrada Sal

Near Punta Vieja • $22/person plus $5 community fee; guide $2 • ☎ 6142 1476, ⓦ aliatur.bocasdeltoro.org

On Bastimentos' southeast coast, close to Punta Vieja, the Ngäbe community of **QUEBRADA SAL** (Salt Creek) is seeing an increasing number of day-trippers, generally from the lodges around that end of the island; they also offer basic accommodation in the village itself. The surrounding wetlands and nearby Playa Larga – part of the marine park that occupies a swathe of the island (see p.236) – can be explored via several trails, which also provides a chance to learn about medicinal plants and other aspects of Ngäbe culture.

ARRIVAL AND GETTING AROUND   ISLA BASTIMENTOS

BY WATER-TAXI
To Old Bank Boteros Bastimentos, from their jetty on C 3 at Av "C", Bocas Town, offers trips to Old Bank (10min; $3); other boats charge $5.

To Red Frog Beach Jampan Tours (see p.229) runs a regular service to a marina on the south side of Bastimentos ($15 return; $8 one way), from where it's a 10min walk (or 3min shuttle) across the island to the beach. A $5 landing fee ($3 if you travel with Jampan) imposed by developers

ostensibly goes towards maintaining the path across the island. To avoid the fee, hike the beach path from Old Bank, though be mindful of security issues (see box, p.223).

REACHING THE NGÄBE COMMUNITIES
If you want to visit a Ngäbe community and are struggling to make your own arrangements, contact the Bocas del Toro Community Tourism Network (ⓦ redtucombobocasdeltoro.org).

CULTURAL ECOTOURISM IN BOCAS DEL TORO

Several **Ngäbe communities** in the province have initiated cultural **ecotourism** projects to supplement their subsistence livelihood: Bahía Honda and Quebrada Sal (Salt Creek) on Bastimentos, Sandubidi on Isla Popa and Silico Creek and Río Oeste Arriba on the mainland are all trying to attract visitors. The less well-known and less numerous **Naso**, too, are also active in community-based tourism (see box, p.242). While several day-tours from Bocas Town include communities in some of their itineraries, you learn and experience much more by staying overnight (see p.233, p.234 & p.238). In addition to the obvious interest of being able to interact with the Ngäbe (or Naso) and learn about their culture, the communities often offer traditional dishes, crafts for sale and guided walks into the rainforest, with good wildlife-spotting opportunities and the chance to learn about medicinal plants. With some of the mainland communities, you can undertake more strenuous hiking.

Details of how to contact the communities directly, and therefore ensure that all your money goes directly to them, are to be found in English and Spanish on the Red de Turismo Comunitario Bocas del Toro **website** ⓦ redtucombo.bocasdeltoro.org.

ACTIVITIES AND TOURS

Bastimentos Alive Sea Monkey, east end of the cement path ☎6514 7961, ⓦbastimentosalive.com. Tom and Titi offer personalized experiences, with a recommended day's hike across the island (10km) taking in the natural environment and finishing up on Polo's beach, where Polo cooks fish while you snorkel ($45).

Red Frog Zipline Red Frog Beach ☎836 5950 or ☎6987 8661, ⓦredfrogbeach.com/bocas-del-toro-zipline. Tours (daily 10am, 1pm & 3.30pm; 2hr; $55) along seven rainforest zip lines and a swing bridge. Transfer from Bocas Town included.

Scuba 6 Diving Old Bank ☎6722 5245, ⓦscuba6diving.com. New dive operator offering two-tank dives ($80–110) and PADI certification (Open-Water $270) and beginners' taster courses ($75).

ACCOMMODATION

The handful of lodgings in Old Bank are mainly **budget-oriented** and attract people wanting to experience the "real" Bocas; be prepared to be lulled to sleep by ear-splitting music on occasions. They are found along, or just off, the cement path that winds through the village. The all-inclusive **ecolodges** elsewhere on the island offer a more back-to-nature, yet luxurious experience.

OLD BANK

Beverly's Hill Turn left from the main dock ☎6323 8013, ⓔbeverlyshill@gmail.com, ⓦfacebook.com/beverlyshillguesthouse; map p.222. A gem on the hillside, this friendly family-owned place offers rustic *cabañas* (shared or private bathroom) in a lush tropical garden that's home to the elusive red frog (see box, p.233), and brimming with birdlife. The pricier room at the top has stunning Caribbean views ($50). **$22**

Casa El Jaguar 50m to the right of the main dock ☎6374 4917, ⓦhostaleljaguar.wixsite.com; map p.222. Owned by local Arnulfo Archibald, who is happy to share his knowledge of the islands, this *hostal* is good value; the spacious over-the-water hammock deck and shared kitchen provide the main appeal. Basic, painted wooden rooms have fans, with private or shared bathroom. **$32**

★ Hostal Bastimentos Turn right from the main dock ☎757 9053; map p.222. A friendly maze of a hostel spread over the hillside behind town, offering dorms, basic doubles with shared facilities ($20) and fancier en-suite rooms with a/c, hot water, fridge and private balcony, plus great views. Two communal kitchens, plenty of hammock space and a mellow vibe. Excellent value. Dorms **$10**, doubles **$25**

Rafael's House 120m to the right of the main dock ☎6446 0787, ⓦpanamasparadise.com; map p.222. Beautifully renovated, two-bedroom Caribbean house with fully fitted kitchen, living room and balconies front and back, one overlooking the main street, the other the sea. Rooms can be rented separately, though the bathroom is shared. Doubles **$50**, whole house **$132**

THE REST OF THE ISLAND

★ Al Natural Punta Vieja ☎757 9004, ⓦalnaturalresort.com; map p.222. Beautiful, isolated spot with single- or double-decker Ngäbe-style palm-thatched huts that open onto the sea. Rustically decorated with hewn driftwood, with solar-powered fans and showers and comfy beds with netting. Delicious meals are served communally in the bar-restaurant *rancho*, with a games and reading room plus an observation deck upstairs. Rates include transfer from Bocas, meals, use of kayaks and snorkel gear. The two-storey superior bungalow is worth the extra $87. Two-night minimum stay. No wi-fi. **$271**

Casa Cayuco Punta Vieja ☎1 313 355 6692 (US), ⓦcasacayuco.com; map p.222. A three-storey lodge and five lovely raised wooden cabins (for two to six people) with private balconies, most tucked away in the rainforest just off the beach. Rates include transport, communal fine dining and use of kayaks, SUPs, boogie boards and a village tour. Three-night minimum stay. **$358**

★ La Loma Jungle Lodge Bahía Honda ☎6619 5364, ⓦthejunglelodge.com; map p.222. On a hilltop surrounded by rainforest, this working cocoa farm offers four private airy Ngäbe-style *ranchos* at modest prices. Rates include transfer, meals and some activities, with other excursions for a fee. Gourmet cuisine, with ingredients from the lodge's organic garden, makes this very popular, so book ahead. Some costs go to the Bahía Honda community development fund. Two-night minimum stay. **$180**

★ Palmar Beach Lodge Red Frog Beach ☎838 8552, ⓦpalmarbocas.com; map p.222. Set in rainforest at the back of the beach, this expanding resort offers wood-cabin dorms, simple, delightful, private safari tents and incongruous wooden bungalows with kitchenette and LED TV (two with a/c). Facilities include solar-powered fans, lamps and showers plus a bar-restaurant, beach volleyball, kayaking, daily yoga, massage and snorkel rental. Dorms **$14**, double tents **$55**, bungalows **$120**

EATING

Most **eating** options in Bastimentos are low-key, with local flavours at locally affordable prices. You're likely to find traditional **Caribbean dishes** such as *rondón*, a fish and vegetable stew in coconut milk, or *pescado escabeche*, a spicy marinated fish dish.

OLD BANK AND AROUND

Alvin and Ketch's 100m left of the main dock, over the water; map p.222. Tasty, simple home-cooking; choose from that ubiquitous Panamanian staple fried chicken, rice and beans or Caribbean seafood dishes with coconut rice and plantain. Daily 8am–7pm.

★**Chavela's** 300m right of the main dock; map p.222. Named after its engaging host, this cosy wooden-deck bar-restaurant, surrounded by lush foliage, is a step back from the main drag. Breadfruit chips make a pleasant change from rice and plantain, with burgers, jerk pork and the like at modest prices ($6–9). Mon–Sat 6pm until late.

Up in the Hill Signposted up the hill from Old Bank police station ☎ 6607 8962, ⊚upinthehill.com; map p.222. Worth the 20min hike, this organic snack and craft shop offers fresh lemonade, delectable brownies and numerous other goodies ($4–5) on a patio surrounded by flowers. Mon–Sat 8.30am–6pm.

Parque Nacional Marino Isla Bastimentos

PARQUE NACIONAL MARINO BASTIMENTOS is one of the archipelago's major attractions. The 130 square kilometres of boomerang-shaped reserve sweep across a central swathe of Isla Bastimentos and include a chunk of the northern coastline, dominated by the 6km **Playa Larga**, an important nesting site for hawksbill, leatherback and green **turtles** (March–Sept).

MARINE TURTLE CONSERVATION

One of the most poignant scenes in the natural world is the laborious nesting process of the female **turtle** as she drags herself up the beach beyond the high tide mark, excavating a hole with her flippers, before depositing fifty to two hundred eggs, their sex later determined by the temperature of the sand. After around sixty days, usually under cover of darkness, the hatchlings break out from their shells en masse and scuttle down to the sea, unless they become disoriented by lights or emerge in daylight and are picked off by seabirds. Each egg has less than a one in a thousand chance of reaching maturity.

Of the five species of turtle found in the country, four are known to nest along the beaches of Bocas del Toro. Historically the **hawksbill** (*eretmochelys imbricata*) and **green turtle** (*chelonia mydas*) reproduced prolifically on the province's sands but over the last sixty years, as eggs were overharvested and adults killed for their meat and shells, the populations were decimated – though significant numbers of hawksbill still nest on Islas Zapatillas (May–Sept). The 29km expanse of Playa Chiriquí, which lines the Golfo de los Mosquitos, east of the Península Valiente, is the most important rookery in all Central America for gigantic **leatherbacks** (*dermochelys coriacea*). Measuring around 1.5m on average and weighing half a tonne, these leviathans dig seven thousand nests annually (March–June). In contrast, there are scarcely any records of **loggerheads** (*caretta caretta*) nesting in Bocas, though they can occasionally be spotted swimming in the archipelago's shallows.

VOLUNTEERING

If you're interested in volunteering (minimum one week; March–July), **monitoring and tagging** turtles and patrolling beaches – most likely on Playa Soropta in the Humedales de San San Pond Sak (see p.240) – contact the Sea Turtle Conservancy in Bocas Town on C 3 between Av "B" and Av "C" (Mon–Fri 9am–6pm; ☎757 9186 or ☎6661 2533, ⊚facebook.com /SeaTurtleConservancyBocas).

TURTLE-WATCHING TOURS

A community tourism organization on Playa Bluff leads two **turtle watches** per evening (8.30pm & 10.30pm; 2hr; $20/person) in the breeding season (April–Aug). Transport from Bocas is not included; taxis charge $35 return (including wait time) at night. The Sea Turtle Conservancy Office (see above) will help to get groups together to reduce transport costs.

While turtle watching can be a captivating experience, bear in mind that female turtles can easily be spooked into not depositing their eggs. Avoid bright clothes and try to go when there is a good moon, so as not to be tempted to use a torch (unless it's infrared). Leave your camera behind and maintain a respectful distance from the turtle.

Cayos Zapatillas

Southeast of Isla Bastimentos, but still within the park boundary, are the **Cayos Zapatillas** (Little Shoes), so named because they resemble a pair of footprints in the sea. The two dreamy, coral-fringed islands, encircled by powdery white sand, offer **snorkelling** off the beach, where you'll find more and larger fish than in Cayo Crawl. The main reef is exposed to the ocean, often with strong currents and choppy water. With permission from MIA in Bocas Town (see p.228), **camping** is possible on the prettier northern island, where there is a short trail, and you can watch the stars and share the sand with nesting turtles.

ARRIVAL AND ACCOMMODATION

By tour or boat The easiest way to visit is with a tour operator on a day-trip (prices don't include the park fee) or by contracting a boat (arrange for an early start to miss the tour groups at Laguna Bocatorito and Cayo Crawl).
Park entry fees The $10 entry charge is generally collected by a MIA warden on Cayos Zapatillas.

PARQUE NACIONAL ISLA BASTIMENTOS

MIA camping Cayos Zapatillas. You can camp by the park warden's hut on Cayos Zapatillas, where you can use the kitchen (bring some food to share). There are toilet facilities but water may be scarce, depending on the rain. You will need permission from MIA in Bocas Town (see p.228). $6

Isla Solarte

Sheltered in the leeward crook of Isla Bastimentos, thin, hilly **Isla Solarte** – also known as Cayo Nancy, a corruption of "nance", the cherry-sized yellow fruit much in evidence on the island – is surrounded by tranquil waters. Its most famous feature, **Hospital Point**, at its northwestern tip, was the location of a hospital built by the United Fruit Company in 1900 during the banana boom to quarantine malaria and yellow-fever sufferers. The point is now one of the most popular **dive** and **snorkel** spots, at the end of many day-trip itineraries, with a healthy reef of cauliflower and brain coral and an impressive wall full of tropical fish, shelving off a pencil-thin strip of beach.

Solarte is home to a **Ngäbe village** of around 250, which has a school and even a football field. Most of the villagers live from fishing and subsistence agriculture.

ARRIVAL AND ACCOMMODATION

By water-taxi A 10min ride from Bocas ($5) will get you to anywhere on Isla Solarte.
Bambuda Lodge 1.3km southwest of Hospital Point, ☎ 6962 4644, ⊛ bambuda.net; map p.222. Wooden lodge – part hostel, part hotel – with a fabulous location and great sea views, a large pool (with daytime music and

ISLA SOLARTE

waterslide) and kayak rental. Wraparound balconies, sofas and hammocks make it a great place to chill – with board games and ping-pong for rainy days. There's no kitchen, but the family-style restaurant serves delicious food (mains $9–15). Fan-ventilated rooms have shared or private bathroom; no mosquito nets. Dorms $16, doubles $74

Isla San Cristóbal

A large mangrove-fringed island, nestled in the Bahía de Almirante facing the mainland peninsula of Cerro Brujo, **Isla San Cristóbal** is home to three **Ngäbe** communities: **Bocatorito**, in the south, which overlooks a bite-shaped lagoon populated by dolphins, much visited on day-trips from Bocas Town; and **Valle Escondido** and **San Cristóbal** to the north. While cacao, yuca and rice cultivation provides much of their diet, fishing is still the mainstay of these villages. Look out for the navigation lights on the north side of the island, used to guide the banana cargo boats into Almirante.

ARRIVAL AND ACCOMMODATION

By water-taxi Bocatorito is a 20–30min journey by water-taxi from Bocas Town.
Dolphin Bay Hideaway Bocatorito ☎ 6886 4502, ⊛ dolphinbayhideaway; map p.222. Intimate eco-retreat among the mangroves, with five individually

ISLA SAN CRISTÓBAL

designed wooden rooms, decorated in tropical colours, affording views of the bay and their gardens. Organic food and healthy activities – SUP, kayaks and *cayucos* – are on hand, as well as tours (extra cost). Half-board (desserts extra) and transfer from Bocas included. $215

Isla Popa

Just off the southern tip of Isla Bastimentos lies the archipelago's second largest land mass, **Isla Popa**, home to five Ngäbe fishing communities and the only island where you can spot toucans. The northern village of **Sandubidi** (Popa 2) has a community-based tourism project that offers walks along a trail with a local guide, and a **community homestay** (ⓦmeringobe.bocasdeltoro.org). Nearby, on the island's northeastern tip, you'll find several thin, sandy **beaches** leading off into coral-filled shallows and acres of **rainforest**.

6

Mainland Bocas

Mainland Bocas covers the vast majority of the province, yet its imperious jagged peaks clad in virgin forest, its boggy wetlands and its powerful rivers are ignored by most visitors. That said, while the three mainland towns of **Chiriquí Grande**, **Almirante** and **Changuinola** have little for tourists, the **Humedales de San San Pond Sak**, home to countless aquatic birds and the endangered manatee, and the spectacular wilderness **Parque Internacional La Amistad** are definitely worth the effort to reach. The two main obstacles to exploring the region – poor accessibility and lack of infrastructure – have helped preserve the province's natural heritage; today, however, the indigenous Bri-Bri, Naso and Bokota populations' livelihoods are under threat from hydroelectric projects (see box, p.241).

Chiriquí Grande to Almirante

From the village of Chiriquí, 14km east of David on the Interamericana, a spectacular road heads over the Fortuna hydroelectric dam, cresting the continental divide that marks the entry into Bocas del Toro, before descending to the small town of **Chiriquí Grande**, the Atlantic terminus of the Trans-Panama Oil Pipeline. The road then hugs the crinkled coastline for 60km to the port of **Almirante**, before continuing to Changuinola (see opposite). Few visitors venture east of Chiriquí Grande into the increasingly deforested **Comarca Ngäbe-Buglé**, where rivers cut through the Caribbean slopes of the Cordillera Central, flowing into the Golfo de los Mosquitos. The 29km Playa Chiriquí here is home to a major turtle conservation programme (see box, p.236).

Silico Creek

Km 25, Punta Peña • Community tourism ☎ 6558 6913, ⓦ uraribocasdeltoro.org • David–Changuinola buses pass through Silico Creek (2hr 30min–3hr from David; 30–40min from Almirante)

Between Chiriquí Grande and Almirante, on the border of the Comarca Ngäbe-Buglé, lies the Ngäbe community of **SILICO CREEK**, a dynamic village that has successfully retained traditional values while adapting to the modern economy. Though day-visits are common, you can also **stay** in the community's thatched *cabañas* ($15/person) or even arrange a homestay ($10/person), giving you more time to learn about the organic permaculture projects in coffee, plantains, banana, yuca and, most successfully, cocoa. In addition to cocoa tours ($10/person), you can hike through the rainforest to a waterfall (4–6hr; $15/person), or undertake a whole-day trek to visit an indigenous organic farm ($30/person). Some English is spoken on tours.

Almirante

The ramshackle town of **ALMIRANTE**, its rusting tin-roofed wooden houses propped up on stilts over the Caribbean, is the departure point for **water-taxis** to the Bocas del Toro archipelago. Like Bocas, the port is a product of the banana boom, and suffered a similar decline. Unlike Bocas, there is no tourism-fuelled renaissance on the horizon. Basic services are lacking, unemployment and its associated ills are a major concern, and most visitors pass through as quickly as possible. If you miss the last water-taxi, try the *Hotel Alhambra* (☎758 3001), on the road to the port – it's basic but clean and safe.

ARRIVAL AND DEPARTURE   **ALMIRANTE**

By bus Through buses from/to Panama City, David or Changuinola will drop you/pick up at the intersection ("La Ye"), on the main road (see p.226).

By minibus Minibuses career between Almirante – the main bus station close to the water-taxi terminal – and Changuinola (6am–10pm; every 20–25min; 30min), where you can get connections for the border.

By water-taxi There are water-taxis to Bocas Town from Almirante (see p.226).

By car, bike or motorbike If you're coming by car to Almirante, it's advisable to leave it in a secure compound at Leiza's ($3/day) near the water-taxi terminal. Anyone wanting to take a bike or motorcycle across should take the car ferry (see p.226).

Changuinola

The hot, dusty town of **CHANGUINOLA**, Panama's most important banana centre, lies 29km west of Almirante and just 17km from the Costa Rica border. Surrounded by flat, drained wetlands, a patchwork of plantations and pastureland, this bustling, unattractive town of around fifty thousand possesses little of interest for visitors but does provide a launch pad for trips to the **Humedales de San San Pond Sak** or **Parque Internacional La Amistad**. It is also the best place to stay if you are too late to make it to the Costa Rican border.

Most of the action occurs along the congested **Avenida 17 de Abril**, whose crowded central pavements overflow with cheap goods. Cut through east to the parallel street, Avenida Omar Torrijos, and you can glimpse rusting carriages in railway sidings and disused tracks, the last vestiges of what was once an impressive rail network built by the United Fruit Company extending along the coast back to Almirante and well into Costa Rica.

Humedales de San San Pond Sak (6km), Costa Rica (Guabito) (17km) ▲ & Las Tablas (35km)

CHANGUINOLA

■ ACCOMMODATION
Hotel Alhambra   2
Hotel Golden Sahara   1

● EATING
Restaurante Ebony   2
Restaurante La Fortuna   1

0   100
metres

Airport

Urracá
Bus Terminal ★

AVENIDA 17 DE ABRIL

AVENIDA OMAR TORRIJOS

Police

SINCOTAVECOP
Bus Terminal

CALLE CENTRAL

MIA office (250m)

CALLE DE EL PURÉ

Immigration

▼ El Silencio (8km) & Almirante (29km)

ARRIVAL   CHANGUINOLA

BY PLANE

The airport lies just northeast of the town centre. Air Panama (☎ 316 9000, ⓦ airpanama.com) operates daily flights to and from Panama City (1hr; from $106).

BY BUS

Urracá terminal On the northern end of Av 17 de Abril, this terminal serves long-distance buses between Panama City and David. Tranceibosa (☎ 758 8455) has daily departures for Panama City, leaving at 7am and 6pm, and at 1pm if there are sufficient passengers (11hr; $29). They fill up fast, so buy tickets as early as possible. Buses to and from David are much more frequent (5.30am–7pm; every 25min; 5hr).

SINCOTAVECOP terminal Set back from the main street, this is the main bus terminal, serving all local destinations. Destinations Almirante (6am–10pm; every 20–25min; 30min); El Silencio, Río Teribe (6.30am–8pm; every 20min; 25min); Guabito and the Costa Rican border (take the Las Tablas bus; 5.30am–7.30pm; every 20min; 30min).

BY COLECTIVO OR TAXI

Colectivos and private taxis run to and from the Costa Rican border at Guabito (see p.243).

6

THE WEST INDIAN MANATEE

Occasionally called a "sea cow", the **West Indian manatee** (*trichechus manatus*) resembles a cross between a sea lion, a hippo and an elephant, its barrel-like greyish-brown body propelled by two flippers and a spatula tail, its large snout equipped with a prehensile upper lip that helps it feed. Adults average 3m in length though can reach 4.5m, including tail, and weigh in at 200–600kg; to sustain such a size, they have to spend six to eight hours a day munching floating or submerged greenery. When not feeding, they often rest, floating like large logs on or below the surface, frequently surfacing to breathe. Moving easily between freshwater and marine environments, the shy yet playful mammals are surprisingly agile, and can exceed 25km/hr for short bursts. In Panama, the vast majority of these aquatic behemoths inhabit the wetlands of Bocas del Toro, though in 1964 a small number were relocated to Lago Gatún by the Americans in a failed attempt to tackle the rampant spread of water hyacinth in the Canal. Though lacking natural predators, manatees are threatened by **human activity**, experiencing collisions with motorboats and getting tangled up in fishing nets or canal locks, while suffering from loss or pollution of habitat. What's more, since they only give birth to a single calf every three to five years, it takes a long time to boost numbers.

INFORMATION

Immigration The immigration office (☎758 6533; Mon–Fri 8am–4pm) is on Av 17 de Abril at Calle de El Puré.

MIA office Several blocks west of Av 17 de Abril (Mon–Fri 8am–4pm; ☎758 6603).

ACCOMMODATION

Hotel Alhambra Av 17 de Abril ☎758 9819; map p.239. Probably the best value in town. Quality varies, but all rooms are clean with a/c, hot water and cable TV. Those at the back overlook a graveyard and are much quieter. $25

Hotel Golden Sahara Av 17 de Abril ☎758 7908; map p.239. This place has 28 reasonably modern rooms (a/c, cable TV, hot water), though some lack windows. Service is friendly. $39

EATING

Restaurante Ebony Av 17 de Abril ☎6547 6600, ⓦfacebook.com/restauranteebony4151; map p.239. Chock-full of Bob Marley memorabilia, inflatable sharks and balsa-wood birds, this popular Afro-Antillean restaurant delivers authentic Caribbean cuisine: salt fish, ackee, rice and peas, spicy shrimp in coconut milk. Prices are high for Changuinola (mains from $10). Daily 11am–11pm.

★**Restaurante La Fortuna** Av 17 de Abril ☎758 9395; map p.239. Very popular Chinese restaurant next to the *Golden Sahara* hotel, offering friendly, efficient service and good value in a/c comfort. The wide-ranging menu has several veggie options and set menus. Choose a sizzling hotplate dish with first-rate chips. Daily 11.30am–10.30pm.

Humedales de San San Pond Sak

One of the premier natural attractions of mainland Bocas is the **HUMEDALES DE SAN SAN POND SAK** (with numerous variant spellings), which encompasses more than 160 square kilometres of coastal wetlands stretching from the Costa Rican border, past Changuinola, to the Bahía de Almirante. Only a small section of the reserve is accessible to visitors but its mix of seasonally flooded swampy forests, dense mangroves and peat bogs makes for a magical boat trip, especially at first light when the prolific **birdlife** – 160 species at the current tally – is at its most active.

As you glide along the river, keep an eye out for caimans and river otters lurking in the waters. A dawn visit will also heighten your chances of spotting the wetlands' most celebrated inhabitant, the shy, endangered **manatee** (see box, p.240). Though there are now an estimated 150–200 in the area, they remain fairly elusive except when banana leaves are provided at the viewing platforms when tour boats enter the reserve. The river eventually fills out into a coastal lagoon before emptying into the sea, its progress blocked by a sandbank on which there is a poorly maintained **refuge**. Behind the hut lies **Playa Soropta**, a long stretch of beach where hawksbill, leatherback and green **turtles** nest (see box, p.236).

ARRIVAL AND INFORMATION

By bus or taxi To reach the reserve from Changuinola, take the Guabito–Las Tablas bus (see p.239) to the Río San San bridge, or take a taxi ($6).

Reserve fees The $5 admission charge, payable to MIA, can be paid at the AAMVECONA office on arrival.

HUMEDALES DE SAN SAN POND SAK

AAMVECONA Activities in the reserve are managed by AAMVECONA (☎ 6679 7238, ⓦ aamvecona.com); the office is by the road bridge on the Río San San, 6km northwest of Changuinola, on the road to the Costa Rica border.

TOURS

The following tours are offered by **AAMVECONA**, from their office (by prior arrangement in Spanish). Note that turtle and manatee tours can be combined. Tours are also offered (for guests only) by one or two of the pricier lodgings in Bocas, but these will be more expensive.

Manatee tours The most popular excursion is the manatee tour ($45/person; less for more than two people), which gives you several hours gliding through the wetlands by boat, with great birdwatching opportunities, and with luck, manatee sightings. Go early in the morning, cover up well and/or douse yourself with repellent as the sandflies on the viewing platform are vicious.

Turtle tours In the season (March–July) evening excursions (8pm) are organized to watch leatherback turtles nesting ($10/person) on Playa Soropta. This means staying overnight in the rudimentary and rather unappealing bunkhouse at the far end of the lagoon ($10), where turtle conservation volunteers lodge. Take your own food, or ask for meals to be prepared ($5 breakfast; $12 dinner).

Parque Internacional La Amistad

Divided equally between Panama and Costa Rica, the remote **PARQUE INTERNACIONAL LA AMISTAD** (International Friendship Park), often abbreviated to PILA or Amistad, covers a vast 4000 square kilometres of the rugged Talamanca massif, with a topography and biodiversity unmatched in Central America. Precipitous volcanic tors clad in prolific cloud forest, containing the greatest density of **quetzals** in the world, plunge into deep ravines in Panama's most dramatic mountain scenery.

From the treeless *páramo* of **Cerro Fábrega** (3336m), the park's highest peak, to the Caribbean rainforests only 40m above sea level, the park encompasses an incredible range of **flora** and **fauna**, including many endemics and endangered species. All five of Panama's resident cat species prowl the forests while the soaring canopy is pierced by impressive specimens of ceiba, almendro and cedar, home to endangered harpy and

THE NASO KINGDOM

When the Spanish arrived in what is now Bocas del Toro (and southeast Costa Rica), the **Naso** (or Teribe) were both numerous and widespread, but centuries of conflict with the conquistadors and other tribes decimated their numbers, which declined further in the early twentieth century due to tuberculosis. Of the remaining 3500 Naso in Panama, around a third have been assimilated into the dominant Latin culture, living and working in Changuinola, while the rest mostly inhabit settlements along the Río San San and Río Teribe. Teribe is believed to be a corruption of "Tjër Di", meaning water of Tjër, the grandmotherly guardian spirit of the Naso, one of the more tangible traces of a sorely eroded culture. Since the Naso language is not taught at school, only an estimated twenty percent still know how to speak it, with Spanish often the preferred language even in the villages, though Naso legends are still widely recited.

The more immediate threat to the Naso lies in the form of the recently completed hydroelectric dam upstream on the Río Bonyik, a tributary of the Teribe, which has ripped the kingdom apart. In 2004, the reigning monarch, **Tito Santana**, approved the project without proper consultation, for which he was deposed and chased into exile. His uncle, **Valentín Santana**, who took over, garnered the support of national and international environmentalists and human rights groups in a battle to stop the dam and safeguard their ancestral lands and livelihood. However, as the Panamanian government refused to recognize his authority, the Naso were forced to elect a new king – Alexis – from the Santana dynasty in 2011, though he too has failed to make progress with the Naso's long-standing petition to establish their own *comarca*.

6

crested eagles and great green macaws. A crucial link in the "biological corridor" of protected areas running the length of Central America, it is now under threat from agricultural incursions, illicit timber extraction and poaching, but most of all from the ill-considered hydroelectric projects under way. As well as imperilling the area's unique biodiversity, the projects are threatening numerous indigenous communities.

Given the park's remoteness and the ruggedness of the terrain, any **visit to Amistad** proper is a major undertaking, to be made with a good guide, suitable hiking and camping gear, a readiness for rain (more than 5m tips down annually in places) and mud, plus a spirit of adventure. Most visitors content themselves with a trip organized through one of the Naso communities dotted along the banks of the Río Teribe (see box, p.241), in the buffer zone of the **Reserva Forestal de Palo Seco**, a haven for colourful butterflies, dazzling birdlife, and a host of other wildlife.

The Naso villages

The **Naso**, boasting Central America's last remaining monarch, are one of the country's least numerous indigenous groups, whose recent history has been particularly troubled (see box, p.241). As well as inhabiting the park, they also live on the San San and Yorkin rivers and around Changuinola, where, seeking further schooling and employment, many have abandoned their traditional lifestyles. Those that have remained generally inhabit wooden houses built on stilts covered in thatch or occasionally zinc, practising animal husbandry and subsistence agriculture supplemented by fishing and hunting. Though the spiritual heart of the Naso lies in their ancestral lands high up the headlands of the Teribe, the present-day capital is **SEIYIK**, the largest Naso community. Around ninety minutes upriver from Changuinola, the five hundred inhabitants are dispersed over a pleasant hillside overlooking the river. In the grassy clearing at the centre of the village stand a medical centre, primary school and the unremarkable **royal palace**.

STAYING IN A NASO VILLAGE

Lodgings are **basic**: rudimentary wooden beds with mosquito nets and sporadic water. You'll need a torch, as there's no electricity. **Meals** consist of simple traditional dishes made from local organic produce. The main **expense** for the trip is the fuel needed to power a dugout against a strong current. Note that a **national park fee** ($5) is generally collected for MIA even though most excursions stay within the buffer zone. Note also that price details quoted online are not necessarily up to date, so enquire before you go.

OCEN Bonyik ☎ 6986 7588 (Raúl Quintero), ⌖ ocen .bocasdeltoro.org. Splinter group from ODESEN, across the river from WEKSO, and nearer the new road. Guests are lodged in several traditional balconied wooden houses. Guided hikes are on offer (4–12hr); bring snacks and make sure you have a water bottle (preferably with purification tablets). Costs are à la carte (accommodation/person $20; three meals $15; return boat from El Silencio to Bonyik, or Bonyik to Seiyik $70; hikes $25–30).

ODESEN WEKSO ☎ 6569 2844 (Adolfo Villagra), ⌖ odesen.bocasdeltoro.org. The original Naso community organization, at WEKSO, the former site of General Manuel Noriega's Pana-Jungla training camp. Accommodation is in a simple balconied wooden lodge set back from the main camp, surrounded by forest, with a communal hilltop dining area overlooking the

river. Rates include meals, transport from El Silencio, a trip to Seiyik and the WEKSO trail ($300 for a three-day all-inclusive tour for two). If you're very fit and adventurous, a multiday guided hike into the mountains to Palenque, the former royal seat of the Naso, is a possibility. Gliding back downriver on a traditional balsa-wood raft is a highlight.

Soposo Rainforest Adventures Soposo ☎ 6631 2222, ⌖ soposo.com. The best advertised and most patronized project was set up by a US-Naso couple. They offer pleasant wooden cabins with porches, lit by solar lanterns, and have pricier rates: $90/person for a day-trip; $140 for a two-day tour, $275/person for a three-day tour, including lodging, meals, transport from Changuinola and a range of excursions. If travelling from Bocas, you can be met at Almirante provided you meet the additional transport costs.

Three communities are involved in **ecotourism** projects, which give visitors the chance to learn about medicinal plants, Naso history and culture, hike in the rainforest, make and travel on a traditional bamboo raft (*balsa*), and visit the capital. The Naso are warm and welcoming and the spectacular **river trips** set against the brooding backdrop of the Talamanca range alone make a visit worthwhile, though to do the place and the people justice you should plan at least a two-night stay. Among the many pernicious effects of the recent controversial hydroelectric dam (see box, p.241) communities now suffer from periodic daytime noise of buses transporting workers to and from the dam. Once you're on the WEKSO trail or up in Seiyik, traffic disturbance is thankfully absent, as it is at night in the communities.

6

ARRIVAL AND INFORMATION

THE NASO VILLAGES

By bus and boat The communities are 45min–1hr 15min (depending on conditions) upriver by boat from El Silencio, the location of the Naso jetty (*embarcadero*) on the Río Teribe. To reach El Silencio take the regular bus from the main bus

station in Changuinola (6.30am–8pm; every 20min; 25min). **Contact details** Contact details for all three communities are on the Bocas del Toro community tourism website (⊕ redtucombo.bocasdeltoro.org).

Guabito and the Costa Rica border

From Changuinola, the road runs 17km to the border with Costa Rica at **Guabito– Sixaola**, where, on the Panamanian side, there is little more than a handful of shops. It's a short walk from **immigration** across the old railway bridge to Costa Rica (an hour behind Panama time), where you can change currency in the town of Sixaola.

ARRIVAL AND INFORMATION

GUABITO AND THE COSTA RICA BORDER

Getting to the border To reach the border from Changuinola, take one of the *colectivos* or private taxis ($8) hanging around the bus terminal, or, if you're in no hurry, the bus marked for the village of Las Tablas (5.30am–7pm; every 20min; 30min).

Onward travel in Costa Rica After getting an exit stamp at Panamanian immigration (8am–5.45pm; ☎ 759 7019), cross the border bridge to Costa Rican immigration (same hours, though Costa Rica is an hour behind Panama time) in Sixaola. There you can catch a through-bus to San José (6am, 8am, 10am & 3pm) or to Puerto Viejo in southeastern Costa Rica (Mon–Sat hourly, Sun every 2hr; 90min).

Arriving from Costa Rica After getting your exit stamp from Costa Rican immigration and paying your $8 exit charge, cross the bridge to Panamanian immigration – where you may have to show proof of onward travel (a return bus ticket will suffice) and the ability to support yourself financially. Beware of the scam that occasionally

operates of being directed to a hut to pay a bogus "municipal tax". Once through immigration, head down the steps for the bus to Changuinola (5.30am–7.30pm; 30min), from where there are frequent connections to other destinations in Panama (see p.239). Alternatively, cross back under the bridge for either a *colectivo* or private taxi to Changuinola (*colectivo* $1.50/person, private $10; 20min) or Almirante (*colectivo* $8–10/person, private $25–30; 50min) for the water-taxi to Bocas Town (see p.226); note that some taxi drivers are not beyond spinning yarns about buses not running or taking longer than they actually do in order to secure clients. Since there is no bank or ATM in Guabito, make sure you are carrying sufficient US dollars for you to reach your next destination.

Immigration office The immigration office is on the railway bridge (daily 8am–5.45pm, though they will close for lunch; ☎ 759 7019).

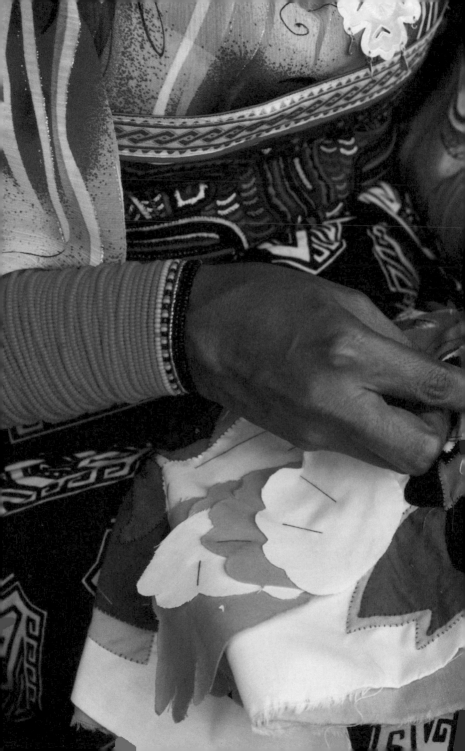

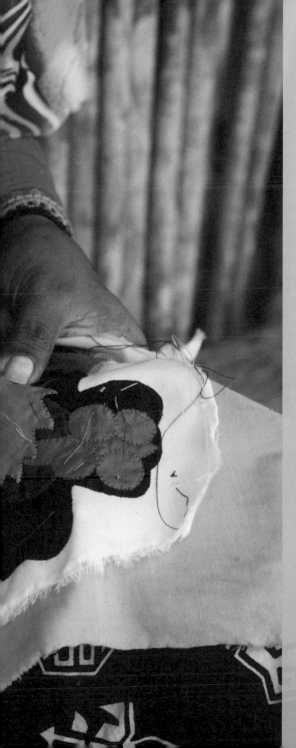

Guna Yala

MOLA MAKING, GARDI YANDUB

Guna Yala

A Guna woman in traditional attire – hair bound in a scarlet headscarf (*muswe*), embroidered blouse (*mola*) tucked into a sarong-like patterned skirt, her forearms and calves bound with intricate beadwork (*wini*) and her nose pierced with a golden ring – is a sight that has launched a thousand travel brochures. Yet the Guna's relationship with tourism remains ambivalent, and their suspicion of outsiders (*uagmala*) and determination to ensure that tourism is conducted on their terms has been born of bitter experience. This can make a trip to Guna Yala fairly challenging, though the benefits far outweigh any frustrations or inconveniences. A visit is an opportunity to engage with an evolving, unique, indigenous culture, to experience village life first-hand, to loll on heavenly white-sand islands and to explore the little-visited, rainforested mainland.

The Guna (pronounced "Guna" or "Kuna" depending upon the dialect) – or the Dule (pronounced "Dule" or "Tule"), as they call themselves – are Panama's highest-profile indigenous people. They inhabit a vast semiautonomous region (or **comarca**) along the eastern Caribbean coast, which stretches some 375km from the Golfo de San Blas to Puerto Obaldía and comprises almost four hundred islands and a swathe of land whose limits extend to the peaks of the serranías de San Blas and the Darién. Around 33,000 Guna live within the Comarca de Guna Yala, with a further 47,000 predominantly spread among two smaller inland *comarcas* in eastern Panama (see p.277) and Panama City, though populations are fluid given the constant toing and froing between the capital and the *comarcas*.

In Guna Yala, for the most part, people are packed onto a chain of 36 low-lying coral outcrops close to the shore, with eleven communities established on the coast and two further inland. Recently, frequent flooding caused by rising sea levels has encouraged some island-based families to relocate to the mainland. Plans are afoot for entire communities to join them over the coming years, as it becomes increasingly likely that their homes will become permanently submerged.

The waters of the western archipelago, in particular, are sprinkled with near-deserted **cays** covered in coconut palms, surrounded by dazzling **beaches** that shelve into turquoise waters, whose coral reefs provide great opportunities for **snorkelling** (diving is prohibited across the *comarca*). Trips to the luxuriantly rainforested mainland are equally magical, whether gliding upriver in a dugout, visiting a Guna burial ground or seeking out the spectacular birdlife. These attributes make Guna Yala a wonderfully idyllic location for a holiday, but to appreciate its unique nature, engaging with **Guna culture** in all its variations, complexities and contradictions is essential.

There are basically two types of islands of interest to tourists. The palm-topped **deserted islands**, surrounded by white-sand beaches, are predominantly distinguished by their accommodation, ranging from simple cane *cabañas* to more comfortable

ISLAND LIFE, ACHUERDUB

Highlights

❶ Village-islands Experience a compelling mix of tradition and modernity in crowded communities such as Gardi Sugdub or Aligandi, taking in the meeting and *chicha* houses and museums. **See p.257 & p.266**

❷ Blissful near-deserted islands Camp out in a thatched *cabaña*, laze in a hammock or float in the turquoise shallows of the palm-topped white-sand islands of western Guna Yala – choose from Isla Perro Chico, Wailidub or Naranjo Chico. **See p.258 & p.260**

❸ Cayos Holandeses and Coco-Bandero The archipelago's best snorkelling; marvel at a marine wonderland of corals and tropical fish. **See p.261**

❹ Isla Tigre The fascinating home of the Guna dance and one of the few remaining places that practises community-based traditions. **See p.263**

❺ Armila A very different Guna village on the forested mainland at the far southeastern end of the *comarca*, where you can explore the jungle by dugout and watch leatherback turtles nesting. **See p.268**

HIGHLIGHTS ARE MARKED ON THE MAP ON PP.248–249

lodges, all owned by families or communities from the more densely populated **village-islands**. These latter – overcrowded coral outcrops chock-full of cane-and-thatch buildings interspersed with cement structures, schools, medical centres and the occasional shop – generally lack beaches. To the casual visitor, the village-islands are very much alike: jetties hold tethered dugouts and traditional over-the-water toilets, with litter often floating among the pilings, while sandy streets gravitate towards the centre, where meeting and *chicha* houses (see box, pp.264–265) and the basketball court stand out. Only by spending a couple of nights in different places will you begin to appreciate the subtle variations between communities.

GUNA YALA

COLÓN

Naranjos Grandes

Ukuptupu
Wichub-Wala
Corbiski
Nalunega
El Porvenir (Gaigirgordub)

Chicheme Grande (Wichubdubdummad)
Archipiélago
Isla Pelicano (Gorgidub)
Banedub
Masargandub
Isla Diablos (Niadub)
Isla Perro Chico (Assudubbibi)
Wailidub

Cayos Limones

Ogobsibudub & Nidirbidub (Coco Blanco)

Golfo de San Blas

Icodub (Isla Aguja)
Achuerdub (Isla Ansuelo)
Aridub (Isla Iguana)
Guanidub
Isla Pelicano (Gorgidub)

Gardi Yandub
Gardi Dubbir
Gardi Sugdub
Nurdub
Naranjo Grande (Narasgandubdummad)
Naranjo Chico (Narasgandubbibi)

Río Sidra (Mamartupu Urgandi)

Carti
Barsukum
Soledad Miria (Mirya Ubgigandub)
Nusadub (Isla Ratón)

Río Barsukum

HIGHLIGHTS
1. Village-islands
2. Blissful near-deserted islands
3. Cayos Holandeses and Coco-Bandero
4. Isla Tigre
5. Armila

Nusagandi (10km), El Llano (30km) & Panama City (78km)

GUNA YALA (CONTINUED)

0 — 5
kilometres

Niadub
Punta Niamulo
Playón Grande (Uggubba)
Irgandí
Playón Chico (Uggubseni)
Yandub

San Ignacio de Tupile (Dadnaggwe Dubbir)

Río Masargandi

Agligandi
Achutupu (Assudub)
Mamitupu (Mammidub)
Ogobsucum
Usdub

There are more than 365 islands to choose from, most with two names (one in Dulegaya, one in Spanish) and a handful with the same name. However, the fact that only 36 of them support villages, and that many are conveniently arranged in identifiable **clusters**, simplifies planning. During one visit most visitors are satisfied to explore just one cluster.

The islands in the **western area** of the archipelago, such as those in the **cayos Limones or Holandeses**, or north of **Río Sidra**, are the most visited, possessing the greatest sprinkling of tiny Robinson Crusoe-style beaches and the best snorkelling, and plenty of accommodation options. Moreover, they – together with a handful of islands in the **central region** – are generally the most geared up for tourism. For these reasons, along

with improvements in the only road link with the *comarca*, which makes it just a three-hour drive from Panama City at most, have led to a great increase in visitor numbers. This in turn has inevitably put great strain on the natural resources, and sometimes on Guna–tourist relations, and has undoubtedly diminished the appeal of this particular group in high season. Visiting the more isolated **eastern islands**, such as **Agligandi** or **Mamitupu**, you'll experience greater cultural engagement with the Guna –

7

GUNA YALA ESSENTIALS

WHEN TO GO

Peak tourist season in Guna Yala, as elsewhere in Panama, is the **dry season** (roughly mid-Dec to April) though for some of the period, you'll suffer from the trade winds (Dec–Feb/March), which whip up the waters into large waves, making travel uncomfortable – and scary at times – impairing snorkelling and leaving the outer islands inaccessible. Late March and April are more appealing times to visit, although water levels can be low on the mainland, restricting river trips.

If possible, avoid the popular palm-topped islets of **western Guna Yala** – Isla Perro Chico above all – at weekends or **public holidays** during the dry season. At this time hundreds of weekenders and day-trippers flock here from Panama City, saturating the beaches with deckchairs, vast cooler boxes and sound systems, making it almost impossible to see the sand, never mind sit on it.

The **wet season** lasts from May to mid-December; in the early months, from May to July, the unbearable humidity and lack of breeze is balanced by a sea that can be millpond-still – perfect for snorkelling, except during the afternoon downpours, when run-off muddies the waters. June to October spells the season for *chocosanos*, terrifying electric tempests that generate monstrous waves capable of flooding an island and dashing a ship onto a reef in an instant.

WHAT TO TAKE

A **mosquito net** may be a good idea, together with lashings of **repellent**, **sun cream**, a basic **first-aid kit** and a **torch** and/or candles (there is limited or no electricity on some islands), plus a **sheet sleeping bag** in high season – if water is short, or the weather bad, sheets may not get a full wash. Some kind of **waterproof protection**, such as a plastic bin liner, is desirable to protect your gear from getting soaked in the boat, and you may want a breathable waterproof for yourself. In **budget accommodation** it's recommended to take snacks with you, as meal portions are often small, plus a toilet roll. It's not advisable to drink **tap water** in Guna Yala. Some hotels provide purified water for guests at meals; most charge. Bottled water is on sale in most islands, but is expensive and its disposal an environmental headache; it's far better to use a water filter or purifying tablets (see box, p.85). Use of **snorkelling equipment** is sometimes included in package deals, or the *cabañas* may rent out masks ($5–6). In either case, masks are often not in good condition, so if you intend to spend some time in the area, consider buying a cheap one in Panama City (see box, p.85).

TAXES AND MONEY

At the road entrance to the *comarca* at **Nusugandi** – around 20km before you get to the coast – all non-Guna have to pay a **tourist tax** ($20 for foreigners), which is not included in transport costs. In addition, there is $2 fee to use the docks at Cartí or Barsukum (see opposite). Visitors generally also have to pay a **community tax** ($3–10 for the village-islands, $3–5 on near-deserted beach islands); these costs are usually not included in tour packages (see box, pp.252–253). You have to take all the cash you might need with you, in small denominations – the *comarca's* only bank, in Narganá, does not accept credit-card withdrawals. Some of the more expensive lodges accept online credit-card payments for a basic package, but extras – drinks, community taxes, extra tours, snorkel rental and so on – will usually need to be paid for in cash.

COMMUNICATION

Mobile coverage has now reached most parts of the *comarca* through the Digicel and Más Móvil networks, though the signal may be weak and the system is often down when the weather is bad. There is virtually no **wi-fi** access across the region (though you may manage to use a signal from a government building by lurking outside). In 2017 the government stated its intention to set up five wi-fi hot spots in Guna Yala, but don't get your hopes up.

provided you can speak Spanish – since you may well be the only outsider there. Even on islands unused to seeing tourists, you are likely to be able to negotiate a hammock for the night in someone's home for a few dollars.

Brief history

Guna **oral history** traces their origins to the Sierra Nevada de Santa Marta of present-day Colombia. Fleeing from tribes such as the Emberá, in the fifteenth or sixteenth century, they took refuge in the mountainous areas of the **Darién**, including Mount Tacarcuna – the highest peak in eastern Panama (1874m), lying just outside the *comarca* – which became a sacred place in folklore. Violent conflict ensued against the Spanish, with the Guna often forming unlikely alliances with English and French pirates, and gradually being forced towards the Caribbean. Though Guna had visited the coast for many years, colonization of the **islands** they inhabit today did not start until the mid-nineteenth century as they sought greater access to passing traders and escape from disease-carrying insects on the mainland.

Panamanian independence

Geographical isolation ensured the Guna were pretty much left alone until **Panamanian independence** in 1903, when the new state refused to recognize the **Comarca Dulenega**, which had been established by Colombia in 1870. It covered Guna territories straddling the two countries and had guaranteed a certain measure of independence.

The Revolución Dule

Tension between the **Guna Congress** and Panamanian authorities escalated as the latter granted concessions to outsiders to plunder resources in Guna territory and persistently attempted to suppress Guna culture – banning women's traditional attire or forcing missionaries and colonial schooling onto the communities. Matters came to a head in 1925, when a gathering of Guna leaders on Ailigandi – today's Agligandi – resolved to declare independence and rose up in what is proudly commemorated as the **Revolución Dule** (Guna Revolution). Around forty people lost their lives, and only the intervention of the US – concerned for the safety of the Canal – prevented further government reprisals. A settlement was finally reached in 1938, when the Guna agreed to recognize Panamanian sovereignty in exchange for a clearly defined *comarca* and a high degree of political autonomy.

ARRIVAL AND DEPARTURE   GUNA YALA

Most visitors, and the Guna themselves, bound for the western or even some of the central islands, travel from Panama City by road, which connects with one of two dock areas at the western end of the *comarca*. The main departure area is by the disused **Cartí** airstrip, which in turn has three jetties: Sugdub, Dubbin and Cartí Tupile. A 15min walk away, close to the mouth of the Río Barsukum, is the much smaller riverside **Barsukum** dock. Cartí is often used as shorthand to refer to both places. From the docks speedboats and motorized dugouts fan out to the various islands; there are few scheduled services, however, so access is limited and unpredictable. You can also reach some destinations by **light aircraft** from Albrook Airport.

BY ROAD

By car It takes 2hr 30min–3hr by road (4WD only) from Panama City to the dock at Cartí or Barsukum. Head east out of Panama City on the Interamericana; the turn-off for Guna Yala is just east of Chepo, where the 40km El Llano–Cartí road crosses the peaks of the Serranía de San Blas to the Caribbean coast. Though now paved, the road is still treacherous as it's incredibly steep, winding, narrow and increasingly potholed; only 4WD vehicles are granted entry. The vehicle fee is $10, payable at Nusugandi (see box

opposite), in addition to the entry fee, and there's a charge of around $3–5 for parking.

Hostel/hotel transfers Hostels and hotels in Panama City can arrange a pickup in a 4WD vehicle – $30 one way to the Cartí/Barsukum dock, plus taxes (see box opposite). Vehicles should only take four or six passengers, though they may try to squeeze in more – check in advance – and will collect you from your accommodation at around 5am. Drivers generally stop at a hypermarket in the suburbs to allow passengers to stock up on supplies.

Independent booking You can also make your own arrangements with Transporte y Carga Kuna Yala in Panama City (C 33, Calidonia; ☎ 225 4900, ⓦ facebook.com/transport ekunayala); or contact Transkuna (see box, p.253). As well as the usual pre-dawn departures for Cartí, they sometimes leave later in the morning. The rates are the same as those offered by the hostels and hotels ($30 one way), though note that unlike the hotels and hostels, the transport company will not arrange onward boat travel from the dock.

Onward travel – packages On arrival at the Cartí/ Barsukum docks, visitors who have arranged their trip via their hotel or hostel pile into a collection of motorized dugouts waiting to transport them to their island lodgings; this cost is sometimes included in the overall deal.

Onward travel – independent travellers It's worth asking the waiting boatmen about vacancies on their vehicle, though bear in mind that transport to popular backpacker islands, such as Isla Perro Chico or Senidub, is often booked up. You could ask to get dropped off in Gardi Sugdub ($3), a transport hub for neighbouring islands, where you can check out departures for that day. Transfer fees vary, starting from around $20 return to one of the islands near Cartí and Río Sidra. Many communities in the western and central isles have daily early-morning departures (5–6am) for Cartí, which can then transport you back to their island, leaving Cartí between 8–9am. For the eastern isles, departures are less frequent, and when sea conditions are rough, boats will be cancelled. For likely departure times, contact the island transport company or one of the lodgings on the island you are heading for.

BY PLANE

Destinations Air Panama (☎ 316 9000, ⓦ airpanama .com) has daily flights from Albrook Airport to Achutupu (Assudub) and Playón Chico (Uggubseni), six departures a week (not Sat) to Puerto Obaldía and three a week (Tues, Thurs and Sun) to little-visited Mulatupo (Muladub) and Ogobsucum (Ogobsuggan).

Fares Prices, including taxes, range from $80 (Playón Chico) to $106 (Puerto Obaldía) one way. Most of the

---

PACKAGE STAYS IN GUNA YALA

Given the complexities of travelling independently around the archipelago, the easiest way to visit the region is on a **package tour**. In fact most hotels only offer package deals – the Guna prefer this as it affords them greater control over tourist activities. The majority of hotels are aimed at budget travellers; there's little mid-range **accommodation** and no luxury lodgings – the nearest lies 25km west of El Porvenir (ⓦ corallodge.com). Panama City hostels and hotels can help organize a multiday trip, or you can make arrangements yourself for the same price – a **minimum stay** of three days and two nights is recommended.

Itineraries may change depending on sea conditions. Most packages in the western region include: return **transport** by boat from the Cartí docks (though some charge $20–40 for the transfer); three basic **meals**; rustic accommodation; and a daily **excursion**. These might entail a trip to a near-deserted palm-fringed island (there's usually someone living there to look after the place), or a cultural visit to an inhabited island or to the mainland to visit a cemetery (see box, p.262) or a waterfall. The *comarca* taxes and the 4WD transport fees are usually additional; check in advance exactly what's included. There is usually a fuel supplement to visit the Cayos Holandeses, which offer the best snorkelling in the *comarca* but are sometimes inaccessible due to rough seas for much of the peak season (Dec–Feb/early March).

On the **sandy atolls**, all of which are privately owned, accommodation is usually in simple white-cane *cabañas*, with either a thin mattress or a hammock and perhaps somewhere to keep your belongings out of the sand. Increasingly, some islands are offering camping, though you usually have to bring your own tent. Whichever option you choose, the often-basic **toilets** (which may have to be flushed with sea water from a bucket) are shared, and **electricity** is not a given; you may have to wash under overhead cold **showers**, or use a barrel of water and a jug or *calabash* (gourd). At weekends in peak season, fresh water for washing may run out on islands that have to transport it from the mainland.

For more **comfort**, several lodges in the central islands, such as *Akwadup* or *Uaguinega* (see p.267), fit the bill, offering cabins with private bathrooms (flush toilets, hand basins and cold-water showers), often with private balconies, fancier cuisine and English-speaking guides.

At the budget end, **package rates** are generally $30–80 per person per night, but you'll pay more than $100 each for more comfortable options. Prices depend heavily on fuel prices, and may be negotiable in low season. Accommodation and package rates in Guna Yala – be they for private or shared/dorm *cabañas*, tents or hammocks – are almost always quoted per person. Throughout this chapter we have quoted the rates two people would pay for a package, staying in a **double room**, with single rates for camping and dorms where those options are available.

airstrips are on the mainland a few hundred metres from the islands themselves. When organizing return flights from the *comarca*, you can ring Air Panama and book a seat with a credit card, paying on arrival at Albrook.

Booking Seats go quickly, especially for Puerto Obaldía, so book well in advance at the Air Panama office in Albrook Airport or on Avenida Balboa (see p.73). Even if the flight is fully booked, it's worth turning up at the airport at 5am on the day, when a couple of standby places are usually available. Note that flights into the *comarca* have an 11kg checked luggage allowance.

Flight times Almost all flights depart from Albrook at 6am – except the plane for Puerto Obaldía, which leaves mid-morning – though schedules are prone to change and delays are common, so always check beforehand. All the early flights return to Panama City almost immediately, generally around 7–7.30am; enquire at Puerto Obaldía airport the day before for departure times on that service.

Transfer to your hotel If you have arranged a package, there will be a boatman from your accommodation at the airstrip to take you to your destination. This transfer may or may not be included in the tour cost. Independent travellers may be able to catch a ride (for a fee); otherwise, other boatmen are usually hanging around with whom you can negotiate a deal.

BY BOAT

The main entry point by sea is Puerto Obaldía in the southeastern corner, where you'll almost inevitably be arriving from Colombia (see p.268). Backpackers travelling to and from Cartagena, Colombia, by sailboat from Puerto Lindo or Portobelo usually spend a couple of days in Guna Yala en route (see box, p.25).

From Puerto Obaldía Smallish fibreglass motorboats (*lanchas*) head up the coast from Puerto Obaldía to Cartí ($100/person) several times a week, depending on demand (see p.268), and will drop you off at other islands en route. Note that the sea is very rough and dangerous between Puerto Obaldía and Achutupu (especially Dec–March), and the experience is likely to be extremely wet and

7

Day-trips (from around $90–110) and **overnight camping trips** (from around $130–150) from Panama City are offered as extras in high season, though the former are rarely worth the time and expense, given the six hours needed to get to and from the dock, plus the boat travel time.

TOUR COMPANIES

In theory only **Guna-owned companies** are entitled to operate within the *comarca*, though several others do, including backpacker boats to and from Colombia (see box, p.25). The overnight stays organized by the tour companies tend to be more expensive than tours arranged directly with the accommodation concerned, though in some cases you're paying the extra for an English-speaking guide.

Expediciones Tropicales (Xtrop) ☎ 387 4582, ⊛ xtrop.com. Excellent sea-kayak tours working with trained Guna guides and communities, and with plenty of beach-lounging and snorkelling opportunities. Their four-day excursion ($550/person) is based on Nurdub and includes return transfer from Panama City by road and boat, including taxes. The longer excursion usually starts from Isla Tigre. Two people minimum.

San Blas Amazing Tour ☎ 6846 7537 or ☎ 6816 8569, ⊛ sanblasamazingtour.com. New Guna company run by operatives experienced in hospitality, providing inexpensive day or overnight camping trips to Cayos Limones; $180/person including food, transport from Panama City, tours and camping equipment (camping only available in high season). Some English spoken.

San Blas Sailing ☎ 314 1800, ⊛ sanblassailing .com. Professional and pricey but providing an idyllic way to see the archipelago, offering sailing tours (in French, Spanish and English; three to 21 days), generally in western Guna Yala, including kayak or dinghy forays to the mainland. Prices depend on the boat capacity and cabin occupation, the degree of luxury, and the season – in high season it's easier and cheaper to share ($150–300/day for a monohull, $215–590/day for a catamaran). Private charters are more expensive. Transport to the *comarca* and Guna taxes are not included.

Transkuna C Ecuador and Av Justo Arosemena, Panama City ☎ 390 2577 or ☎ 6520 9601. Reliable Guna-run transport company providing transport to the *comarca* in comfortable brand-new vehicles. Also all-inclusive day-trips from Panama City and overnight stays in *cabañas* or tents in the Cayos Limones – you'll pay $150 to stay in a tent on Yansailadub.

Viajes San Blas ☎ 6793 1797 (English), ☎ 6138 6312 (Spanish), ⊛ viajessanblas.com. Efficient Guna outfit offering (almost) all-inclusive day- and multiday trips from Panama City to a wide range of islands at much the same rates as the island lodgings themselves charge – $132 for a two-night dorm stay on Isla Diablos, for example (4WD transfer from Panama City and *comarca* tax extra).

uncomfortable. Make sure the boat has two engines and life jackets as a minimum, is robust enough to withstand the waves, and preferably has a roof and satellite phone.

Island-hopping transfer A compromise between the sailboat and the *lancha* transfer is the four-day island-hopping, partying venture offered by San Blas Adventures (ⓦ sanblasadventures.com), which runs between Cartí and Sapzurro in Colombia ($455), hugging the coastline and so avoiding the two-day open ocean crossing involved in sailing to/from Cartagena.

GETTING AROUND

ORGANIZED TOURS

If you are on an organized tour (see box, p.252), inter-island transport will be arranged by your hosts. Included in the package will be one or two tours per day to another beach or village-island, or to the mainland. Some lodgings also offer optional excursions for set prices. Generally though, if you want to visit somewhere not on the schedule you will need to pay for another boat and pilot. Cost will depend on the distance, the boat's engine size and quality (see below) and the number of people wanting to do the trip. It will also depend on whether your lodgings have two boats – not all do – although sometimes they manage to stagger timings for pickups and drop-offs. If you stay on a populated village-island such as Playón Chico, you have more options for additional boat rental.

INDEPENDENT TRAVEL

Inter-island transport Since there are no fixed itineraries or schedules for boats, you need to ask around about transport heading the way you want to go. This is relatively easy in the populated western region of the *comarca*, and not too difficult if you are heading westwards in the general direction of Cartí from other parts of the region, since most islands have early-morning boats carrying Guna bound for Panama City. Transport in such cases is inevitably cheaper than renting a boat privately. The best places to enquire are the main dock or fuel depot.

Private boat rental The further east you travel, the less frequent and more expensive inter-island transport becomes – in part because fuel costs are higher. You are more likely to need to rent a private boat, which is fairly easy (with some Spanish) but you will probably need to cover the fuel costs for the boatman's return trip.

Cartí–Puerto Obaldía Fairly regular speedboat services between Cartí and Puerto Obaldía ($100) leave when they have enough passengers to cover the fuel costs. Alternatively, contact Andutu in Panama City (Av Justo Arosemena and C 34; ☎ 6060 9104, ⓦ andutu.com); they run trips between Cartí and Capurganá in Colombia but can drop you off at Puerto Obaldía and include land transfer from Panama City in their rates.

Types of boat Always check out your boat transport before agreeing a price. It may be a customary paddled dugout (*ulu* in Guna, *cayuco* in Spanish) for short distances, a (sometimes leaking) motorized version with 15HP, or even a traditional canoe sailboat with a cotton-sheet sail attached to a rough-hewn mast and boom. More often than not however, these days, travel is in a fibreglass *panga*, or *lancha*, with a bigger engine, possibly with a roof to shade you from the sun.

Western Guna Yala

Most visitors to Guna Yala stay at the **western end** of the *comarca*. It's more accessible by land, sea and air than the rest of the region, with a good number of idyllic islets and white-sand beaches – especially in the **cayos Limones** and **Holandeses** – better snorkelling and more accommodation (most of it at the budget end). For independent travellers, there is also more inter-island transport available (see above) and more shops for supplies – in **Gardi Sugdub** and **Río Sidra** – though choice is limited and prices high. The downside, of course, is that with greater exposure to tourism, especially in communities that have put up with more than their fair share of insensitive visitors, some Guna are understandably jaded with outsiders.

El Porvenir and around

The diminutive, scarcely inhabited island of **EL PORVENIR (GAIGIRGORDUB)** belies its status as administrative **capital** of Guna Yala. A sliver of bare land, it barely manages to squeeze on an airstrip (no longer in use) alongside a handful of buildings, including a police post, hotel, museum and craft shop, plus a clump of palm trees. Though this is not one of the more popular destinations, the water off El Porvenir's thin strip of sand is cleaner than at the more heavily populated neighbouring islands.

ETIQUETTE WHEN VISITING GUNA YALA

In Guna Yala, particularly in the more remote areas, it is important to remember that you are a guest of the Guna, irrespective of how much you have paid for the privilege, and should abide by their laws. On islands less frequented by visitors it is customary to ask **permission** from the local *saila* when you visit a particular community or wish to stay on an island, as indeed the Guna themselves do. **Photography** is another contentious area: on some islands it is forbidden, on others it is governed by strict regulations. Never photograph anyone without asking. Traditional beliefs still held by some of the older generation maintain that a photograph takes away a part of the soul, which is why you should resist the temptation to surreptitiously snap away. Generally, $1–2 is charged to take a single photograph, more for group shots, whereas filming, if permitted, can cost around $15 (use of drones is forbidden). Women selling *molas* – the distinctive brightly coloured, embroidered cloth panels – will usually allow you to photograph them if you purchase an item, but do not presume that the cost includes the photo charge.

Beachwear is fine when you're lazing in a hammock on one of the coconut islands, but you should **dress** more modestly in villages – no bikini tops or bare chests. Villagers may not say anything, but it doesn't mean you haven't caused offence. The Guna are particularly sensitive about the *onmagged nega* (meeting house) and the cemeteries on the mainland – never enter or photograph these without permission. **Alcohol** too is a thorny issue. Traditionally during ceremonies large clay pots of *chicha* (see box, pp.264–265) would be prepared for the whole village; once the jars were exhausted, the drinking spree was over. Though this is often still the case, outside the ceremonies communities now vary in their regulations on alcohol: in some places drinking is unregulated, but people are fined if found drunk; some allow seco and beer to supplement the *chicha* at celebrations but not at other times; some have licensing hours; and others ban alcohol completely, though may allow its sale to tourists. Always enquire first, and drink discreetly if alcohol is available to tourists but not to villagers.

Museo de la Nación Guna

By the airstrip • Mon–Sat 8am–4pm, though you may need to ask around to get someone to open up • $5 • No phone

It's worth pausing in El Porvenir to call in at the **Museo de la Nación Guna** – unless you're travelling on to Gardi Sugdub, where a privately owned museum (see p.257) covers similar ground. The exhibition hall displays photos of festivals and numerous ceremonial artefacts such as a necklace of pelican bones worn by the *absoguedi's* (chanter's) assistant and a headdress decorated with macaw feathers. There's also a model Guna kitchen and a notable collection of basketry and bamboo flutes. Information is given in English, Spanish and Guna.

Wichub-Wala and Ukuptupu

Wichub-Wala is a bustling yet relaxed island that's often visited by cruise ships, hence the proliferation of arts and crafts on sale. In addition to the usual sandy pathways and cane-and-thatch huts there are some decaying cement structures, including a former swimming pool now full of large tropical fish.

To the west, the tiny semi-submerged private coral outcrop of **Ukuptupu** was formerly home to a Smithsonian marine research station until the institute was ejected from the *comarca* in 1998. The islet, on which the accommodation is the only building, provides a mellow hideaway – there's nowhere to stretch your legs, but Wichub-Wala and Nalunega are a stone's throw away.

Nalunega

Just south of Ukuptupu lies **Nalunega**, "the house of the macaw" in Dulegaya; these brightly coloured birds were resident on the island when it was first colonized. A more appealing village than Wichub-Wala, with a population of around five hundred, it has broader streets dotted with shady trees populated with parrots, while traditional cane-and-thatch buildings rub shoulders with occasional aluminium-topped cement structures. At the centre lie a primary school, the meeting hall and the basketball court.

Nalunega museum

Signposted off the basketball court • Daily 7am–6pm • $3 • No phone

Nalunega's **museum** houses an unusual collection that is particularly worthwhile if you have some Spanish. The curator, Teodoro Torres, offers a fascinating narrative of Guna culture illustrated through his woodcarvings and paintings from recycled materials, such as boat sails that have washed up on the beach.

ARRIVAL AND DEPARTURE   EL PORVENIR AND AROUND

As the airstrip at El Porvenir is no longer in use, you can only arrive by **boat**. The cost from Cartí/Barsukum is usually $30.

ACCOMMODATION

Cabañas Nalunega Nalunega Karina ☎ 6687 9683 or Angelica ☎ 6969 7148, ✉ karinaiglesias0303 @gmail.com. Three over-the-water cane cabins, on solid cement bases and with electricity, share a bathroom. Cloth hung on the inside provides a greater measure of privacy than in many such *cabañas* while also letting the breeze through. Meals, tours and transfer from Cartí included. $130

Cabañas Ukuptupu Ukuptupu ☎ 293 8709 or ☎ 6746 5088, ⊕ facebook.com/ukuptupu. The friendly owner, Juan García, speaks good English, and his family are Ukuptupu's only inhabitants. A maze of wooden boardwalks leads between fifteen spacious, careworn, wooden doubles, each overlooking the sea, with hammocks on the front deck. Good food is served under a communal central *rancho*, and traditional showers (bucket of water and soap) and toilets are shared. Meals, daily tours and transfer from Cartí included. $140

Hotel El Porvenir By the airstrip, El Porvenir ☎ 6718 2826, ⊕ hotelporvenir.com. This long-established hotel, offering the only accommodation on the island, is pleasantly situated in grassy grounds with its own veranda bar-restaurant and eleven rather gloomy concrete rooms with tin roof and private cold-water bathrooms. They also offer package deals that include transfer from Panama City. Rates include full board plus two daily excursions to nearby islands. Cartí transfer $20. $160

GUNA NAMES AND LANGUAGE

All island communities have a **Guna name**, which often has several variant spellings, and a **Spanish name**. Matters have been further complicated by the standardization of the Guna alphabet in 2011 in which the letters "p", "t" and "k" were removed and replaced by "b", "d" and "g", which are sometimes doubled to give "bb", "dd" and "gg"; the letters "l", "m" and "n" are also doubled in some contexts. However, this standardization has not yet permeated all of Guna society. In the Guide, when introducing a place, we have tried to use the more commonly used name first (be it in Spanish or in Dulegaya) and given the alternative – and sometimes a variant spelling – in parentheses.

GUNA GLOSSARY

The most essential word to grasp in Dulegaya (Guna language) is the versatile "**nuedi**", meaning "hello", "yes" and "it's good/OK" or "welcome". "Nuegambi", meaning "thank you" is also useful. Other key cultural terms include:

absoguedi chanter
Bab Dummad and **Nan Dummad** Great Father and Mother, the creators
Baba Nega heavenly spirit world
boni evil spirits
dule masi traditional Guna fish and plantain stew
Iberogun Guna prophet and religion
Innamudigi initial puberty ritual held at a girl's first menstruation
inna nega *chicha* house
innasuid second puberty ritual for girls during which they are officially named

nainumar cultivated lands on the mainland
neg uan burial ground
nele traditional healer or shaman
nuchu carved wooden totem to ward off evil spirits
Onmagged Dummad Sunmagaled Guna General Congress
onmagged nega meeting house
saila chief
uaga (uagmala) outsider(s)
ulu dugout canoe

The Gardi islands and around

The road connecting Panama City funnels backpackers and day-trippers into the Cartí docks. Just a coconut's throw away, the **GARDI (CARTÍ) ISLANDS**, together with the tiny uninhabited palm-covered retreats of **Icodub (Isla Aguja)**, **Achuerdub (Isla Ansuelo)** and **Aridub (Isla Iguana)** nearby, experience the greatest number of tourists in the archipelago, and day-trippers in particular. The best recommendation is to stay on one of the smaller islands – **Gardi Yandub** if you want to sample Guna village life, or Icodub for the desert-island experience – and drop by **Gardi Sugdub** during the day to visit the excellent museum, or in the evening if there's a community event.

Gardi Sugdub

Close to the mainland, densely populated **Gardi Sugdub** – a favourite pit stop for cruise-ship passengers – forms the stadium-sized hub of this island group and, with around two thousand inhabitants, is one of the *comarca*'s busiest communities. Motorized dugouts are constantly coming and going, so it's a good place to sort out onward transport, but it's not a desirable place to spend the night.

The centre comprises a few large, functional cement buildings, including a secondary school, medical centre, library and post office, standing amid a maze of cane and thatch. There are a couple of restaurants, and numerous stalls selling soft drinks and snacks. The large number of people passing through and the increasing proliferation of consumer goods has resulted in rubbish piling up in the streets and at the water's edge, and the place should be avoided at all costs when a cruise ship has dropped anchor, as Guna women selling *molas* appear from every doorway and the population almost doubles.

Museo de Cultura y Arte Guna
Centre of the island • Daily 8am–4pm • $3 • ☎ 669 1390

The main reason to visit Gardi Sugdub is to spend time at the **Museo de Cultura y Arte Guna**. Stuffed full of artefacts, with pictures from floor to ceiling, it covers many aspects of Guna culture – *mola* making, funerary rites, traditional medicine, religious beliefs – with some bilingual signage in Spanish and English. The place really comes alive through the informative explanations of the curator, José Davies, who is happiest conducting tours in Spanish but can manage some English.

Nurdub

Very close to the coast, four families occupy the tiny outcrop of **Nurdub**, welcoming visitors to their simple *cabañas* (see below). Provided your Spanish is up to the task, this intimate environment is ideal for deepening your understanding of Guna culture. Although there's no beach, daily trips are arranged to beaches.

ARRIVAL AND DEPARTURE **THE GARDI ISLANDS AND AROUND**

By boat For independent travellers, there is always transport waiting to transfer passengers to Cartí from the dock (10–20min).

ACCOMMODATION

★**Cabañas Nurdub** Nurdub ☎ 6803 7033 (Elixto Tejada). Six immaculate cane *cabañas*. Day-trips are offered to Isla Perro Chico (see p.258) and to the beautiful, deserted Piderdub, where you can also choose to camp as part of your stay. Lodgings, meals and one daily beach excursion plus transfer from Cartí are included. **$120**

Cayos Limones

Offering perfect tranquillity (provided you don't coincide with a cruise-ship stopover), the gorgeous islands that comprise **CAYOS LIMONES** are clustered east and northeast of El Porvenir. Once dedicated to harvesting coconuts, they now function mainly as prime day-trip destinations. At other times, it's worth staying overnight, allowing you to soak up the tranquillity by a campfire and admire the sparkling night sky.

Isla Perro Chico

Community tax/day-pass $3

Isla Perro Chico (Assudubbibi) – also known as Perro Uno and not to be confused with nearby Isla Perro Grande (Assudubdummad), or its more populated namesake with the airstrip much further east – is the most visited of the Cayos Limones, so can be overwhelmed with day-trippers on summer weekends and holiday periods. It offers the best **snorkelling** in the area, around an accessible reef and a sunken cargo boat in the narrow channel separating it from adjacent Isla Diablos. A further draw is the beachside **restaurant** that offers an à la carte menu, though the two-storey cement structure that houses it is less appealing.

Isla Diablos

Community tax/day-pass $3 (waived if lunch is eaten at one of the restaurants)

A short hop (or strong swim – beware of currents) from the midsummer mayhem and the sunken cargo boat near Isla Perro Chico, **Isla Diablos (Niadub)** has a thin stretch of **beach** with a sheltered swimming area and two pleasant backpacker accommodations with good restaurants, neither of which attracts too many day-trippers during the season.

Chicheme Grande

Towards the outer perimeter of the archipelago, the large palm-covered **Chicheme Grande (Wichubdubdummad)**, home to a handful of families, is a popular day-trip destination. In addition, sailing vessels on the Puerto Lindo/Portobelo–Cartagena route (see box, p.25) often stop here for the night. Waves thunder over the protective outlying reef, which prevents rubbish from washing up on the gorgeous beach, and the island's relative size coupled with its isolation engender an away-from-it-all feel – outside peak periods – though it's not really a place for snorkelling.

Wailidub

Wailidub, tucked away behind a mangrove-fringed islet, is arguably the nicest place to stay in the area. Favoured by passing sailboats, which stop off at the well-known bar-restaurant at *Cabañas Wailidup* (see opposite), it comprises a windward stretch of alabaster sand, shelving into crystalline shallows sprinkled with starfish, and an open grassy patch surrounded by willowy palms. It also has the rare luxury of a fresh water supply. But beware the bugs when the wind drops.

Masargandub

Just off the eastern end of the Cayos Limones, and about an hour's boat ride from Cartí en route to the Cayos Holandeses, lies **Masargandub**. A gem of an island and one of the largest in the *comarca*, it takes a full hour to circumnavigate on foot. Starfish, stingrays and dolphins inhabit its translucent waters, iguanas peek out through the undergrowth and hawksbill turtles dig their nests in the soft sand (late April to July). Two family associations from the central isles run camping-only operations here.

ACCOMMODATION AND EATING | CAYOS LIMONES

Cabañas Iguadaili Nega ☎ 6155 3986 (Ronaldo Linares), ⓦ facebook.com/isla.masargandup. Flexible away-from-it-all camping run by an association of families from Uggubseni that are heavily involved in turtle conservation. Bring your own tent or sling a hammock – rented ($5) or your own – between the palm trees or in a shared cane *cabaña*. Meals are charged separately ($9 for lunch or dinner) or you can bring your own food and pay $5 to use their stove. Cartí transfer is $40. Camping $7, hammocks $7

Cabañas Niadub Isla Diablos ☎ 6654 1467 (Robles). The preferred option on the island, with its own sliver of beach and sheltered waters to loll in. They offer dorm *cabañas* for up to ten, tents (equipped with airbeds and

LOBSTER AND THE CLOSED SEASON

If you're hoping to sample the succulent **lobster** for which Guna Yala is famous, avoid the closed season (*veda*; March–May). During this period conch, crab and octopus are also off-limits. Note that in budget accommodation there is usually a supplement if you want lobster for a meal.

sheets) and four private *cabañas* bang on the beach with private porch and chairs – worth paying extra for. All share tiled-floor bathrooms, which are cleaner than many. There's also a volleyball court and a pleasant open-sided restaurant (mains from around $8 for day-visitors). Lodging, meals and tours included. Transfer from Cartí $30. Camping $30, dorms $35, doubles $90

★**Cabañas Wailidup** Wailidub ⓣ6715 2335, ⓔwailidup@hotmail.com. Four relatively smart, if basic, en-suite *cabañas* at the back of the beach, and six superior ones (an extra $20) built on stilts over the water with sea-facing balconies, solar-powered electricity, private bathrooms and aluminium roofs. The bar-restaurant serving succulent seafood is favoured by yachties. Room rates include transfer from Cartí, meals and trips; $40 reduction per cabin after the first night. Transport from Panama City can be included. Snorkel rental available. $260

Cabañas Wissubub Isla Chicheme Grande ⓣ6772 9481 (Umberto Burgos). One of three lodging options on the island. Thatched huts house dorms and private rooms; you'll hear the waves crashing on the reef at night. Camping is also available, with tents to rent for $5. Toilet and shower facilities are often in a state of disrepair. Meals – slightly more bountiful than many in this price bracket – are included; Cartí transfer $30. Camping $8, dorms $35, doubles $80

Camping Masargandub Masargandub ⓣ6878 8885, ⓔanaisgernado@yahoo.com. You can choose to sleep on a foam mattress in a tent (provided), or lie on an airbed in one of two cane dorm *cabañas* (each with own washbasin and shower). Shared toilets are outside. Three meals are included. Transfer from Cartí $50. Tour to Cayos Holandeses $10. Camping $20, dorms $30

Ogob Nega Isla Chicheme Grande ⓣ6098 4326, ⓦogobnega.com. Five superior *cabañas* gaze out to sea across a swathe of alabaster sand at the quiet end of the island. Each has a raised wooden floor, electricity and decent beds and mattresses, accommodating couples or family-size groups. There's a pleasant raised wooden bar-restaurant area, and congenial host Aaron speaks good English. Rates include food, lodging and a daily tour; $30 Cartí transfer is extra. $130

Restaurante Banedub Banedub ⓣ6119 4743. This efficient restaurant, popular with yachties, has a lovely breezy, over-the-water setting. They serve high-quality fresh seafood (from $8) – fish, conch, octopus – alongside rice and a smidgen of salad, and good lobster ($10–20). Daily 8am–7pm.

7

Río Sidra and around

Some 15km east of Cartí, just off the mainland, lies **RÍO SIDRA**; formerly a key portal into the archipelago until its airport was closed a few years ago, it is still an important settlement within the *comarca*. Originally two separate islands, **Urgandi** and **Mamartupu** combined to make Río Sidra – a community of close on two thousand – by reclaiming the land in between. Each retains its own identity, maintaining separate *sailas*, meeting houses and churches – and each charges a community visitors' tax – though they share a school and basketball court, plus the two nearby public pay phones. As you face the town from the main jetty, Urgandi lies to the right, Mamartupu to the left; the main drag, a broad sandy boulevard with a number of grocery stores, bisects both, running the length of the island.

The island is convenient for visiting **Nusadub** and **Isla Maquina**, famous for its *molas*, and is a popular village excursion for the backpacker islands of **Senidub**, **Naranjo Chico** and **Isla Pelicano**. Other scenic diversions in the area include the lovely sandy island of **Bigirdub** and starfish haven of **Isla Salar**, while the mainland attractions include a boat trip up the **Río Masargandi**, calling in at the cemetery at its mouth, and a trek through luxuriant rainforest to the once-sacred waterfall of **Saiba** ($15/group), where you can cool off in the delightful freshwater pool at its base.

Nusadub and Isla Maquina

A small community of around four hundred just across the water from Río Sidra, the unfortunately named **Nusadub (Isla Ratón)** – "Rat Island" – does not harbour any more of these rodents than anywhere else, though sandflies are a major nuisance here in winter (May–Dec). Nearby, diminutive **Isla Maquina (Mormagedub)**, whose four-hundred-plus inhabitants are less accustomed to visitors, is known for its fine *molas*.

Isla Pelicano and Senidub

The postage-stamp-sized islands of **Isla Pelicano (Gorgidub)** and **Senidub (Isla Chiquita)**, crowned with coconut palms and fringed with strips of soft sand, are perennial favourites with backpackers since they offer the cheapest packages in the *comarca* and stays are easily organized through Panama City hostels. As a result there can often be something of a holiday-camp atmosphere on them. Of the two, Senidub is the slightly larger and better tended, though it's rather cluttered with *cabañas*. Possible **excursions** from both take in the village of Soledad Mirya (Mirya Ubgigandub), which is noted for fine *molas*, or the glorious white-sand beaches of Piderdub.

Naranjo Chico

Belying its diminutive tag, **Naranjo Chico (Narasgandubbibi)** is the second largest island in the area after Naranjo Grande (Narasgandubdummad). It is particularly lovely for its distinctive hourglass shape, its gorgeous swathe of white-powder sand – from which you can snorkel – and its vegetation of coconut palms, shrubs and delightful hibiscus flowers. Several families run lodgings here, but with most *cabañas* set back off the sand, nestled in the undergrowth, the nicest stretch of beach remains unspoilt.

Guanidub

As you approach the wafting coconut palms of **Guanidub**, 10km north of Río Sidra, a serried rank of twelve smart cane-and-thatch *cabañas* at the edge of the sparkling white sand seemingly stand to attention. Though idyllically located, within striking distance of the Cayos Holandeses, the teardrop-shaped island offers relatively little shade and the beach is small.

ARRIVAL AND GETTING AROUND

RÍO SIDRA AND AROUND

By boat Río Sidra is a 45min boat ride ($20 return) from Cartí. Senidub, Naranjo Chico and Pelicano are around a 20–30min boat ride northwest of Río Sidra, or 40min from Cartí.

ACCOMMODATION AND EATING

RÍO SIDRA

Restaurante Petita By the main jetty. Serves fresh home-baked bread and coffee for breakfast, as well as a decent main meal with dessert and coffee for around $6 at other times. Daily 7am–8pm.

SENIDUB

Cabañas Senidub ☎ 6945 4301, ✉ cabanas_senidub @hotmail.com. Run by a family cooperative from Soledad Miria, this place offers dorm *cabañas* packed with beds plus five private *cabañas*, and even has an occasionally functioning toilet/shower. Though solar-powered electricity illuminates the pleasant dining area, a generator runs between 6 and 10pm. There's a shady volleyball court, too. Meals included; transfer from Cartí is $20. Dorms $26, doubles $62

Franklin's Place ☎ 6768 4075. Officially *Cabañas Dubesenika*, this is a legendary party spot with twenty tightly packed cane *cabañas* with sand floors, a large cement over-the-water dining room, a dirt volleyball court and dreamy views of a palm-framed Caribbean. Guests share an oversubscribed, basic communal shower/toilet area, and luxuries such as juice, snacks, beer and cigarettes can be bought at English-speaking Franklin's "office". The generator runs from 6 to 10pm, when the partying begins. Rates include basic and sometimes small meals. Because of the larger numbers, island-hopping boat trips and fishing excursions, though extra, are cheap. Transfer from Cartí $20. Dorms $26, doubles $70

NARANJO CHICO

Cabañas Casso ☎ 6562 6620. A new place on a quiet corner of the island, run by a friendly couple who currently manage three well-maintained sandy *cabañas* (one used as a tiny dorm) – and can string up a couple of hammocks for free – right by the water's edge. The small scale ensures the shower/toilet facilities are in a better state than many, though the owners are looking to expand. Food and transfer from Cartí included. Dorm $30, doubles $70

Cabañas Miro (formerly Robinson) ☎ 6769 5801. Probably the cheapest cane huts (three dorms, four private) in western Guna Yala – so don't expect much, though their

GUNA YALA FESTIVALS

The main party to catch in the *comarca* is the celebration of the **Guna Revolution**, which takes place from February 23 to 25 (Feb 19–21 in Agligandi) in various forms around the archipelago. Skirmishes between Panamanian forces and Guna are re-enacted on land and sea, accompanied by storytelling, parades and drinking. October, meanwhile, sees the splendid dance competitions of the **Feria de Isla Tigre** (see p.263).

patch of island is enlivened by flowers and shells. Avoid the back *cabañas* nearest the generator. Showers and bathrooms are shared. A shop sells home-baked bread. Rates include meals and an excursion to Isla Pelicano or Estrella. Cartí transfer $20. Dorms $20, doubles $50

Cabañas Isla Narasgandup Naranjo Chico; Contact Ausberto El Valle ☎ 6501 6033, ⓦ narasgandup.jimdo .com. On the quiet side of the island, this friendly place has three private sandy-floor *cabañas* set back across a patch of grass that also serves as a volleyball court, and three pricier en-suite beachside *cabañas* with wooden floors and a private porch overlooking the sea ($200). All have solar-powered electricity. Rates include Cartí transfer, daily tours and food. $160

GUANIDUB

Cabañas Kuanidup Guanidub ☎ 6635 6737, ⓦ kuanidup.8k.com. Neat and well-kept *cabañas* with shared toilet and shower facilities plus generator-powered electricity; across the central grassy area there's a bar and a couple of open-sided restaurant areas. Very little shade. Daily tour and transfer from Cartí included. $180

Cayos Holandeses and around

Three groups of predominantly **uninhabited cays** forming an equilateral triangle provide the archipelago's most spectacular underwater scenery. At the top of the triangle, marking the outer limit of the *comarca* 30km from shore, **Cayos Holandeses (Maoki)** are the most remote, yet the most visited, of the three. Effectively out of bounds during the fierce winds and high waves of December to the end of February, at other times this chain of around twenty densely forested islands acts as a magnet for yachts drawn to the sheltered anchorage and shallow, translucent waters. The protection is afforded by the outlying **Wreck Reef**, which has ensnared Spanish galleons and the odd drug-smuggling vessel, parts of which still protrude through the pounding surf. The resulting bays form clear natural swimming pools displaying a stunning array of sponges and soft and hard corals – fire, elkhorn, brain, fan – that attract rays, reef sharks, moray eels, starfish and a plethora of polychromatic fish. At the time of writing, overnight **camping** is possible on the islands, but it is not approved by the Guna General Congress since ever-increasing visitor numbers (and no ablution facilities) is contaminating the area, which is considered to be a marine reserve within the *comarca*.

Cayos Los Grullos and Cayos Coco-Bandero

Strung out along the 30km expanse of sea between Río Sidra and Narganá and Corazón de Jesús, **Cayos Los Grullos** and **Cayos Coco-Bandero (Ordupuquip)** – two clusters of around a dozen or so cays – comprise thin powdery beaches peppered with driftwood encircling densely forested isles and coral-filled shallows. Popular with cruising yachts, they attract Guna dugouts selling *molas* and fresh produce to the visitors.

ARRIVAL AND DEPARTURE   **CAYOS HOLANDESES AND AROUND**

By boat For budget travellers staying on the inner isles near Cartí or Río Sidra, an excursion to Cayos Holandeses often requires a $30 fuel supplement.

Central Guna Yala

The main appeal of **central Guna Yala** lies in **Isla Tigre**, which sustains many traditional Guna practices. Forty kilometres further east, sprawling **Playón Chico** presents an

---

GUNA CEMETERIES

One of the most fascinating tours offered by Guna communities is to their traditional Guna **burial ground** (*neg uan*) on the mainland. From afar the cemetery resembles a miniature village, a mass of thatched rooftops, which turn out to be shelters protecting the graves from the rain. Beneath each one is an elongated mound of earth, representing the pregnant belly of Nabguana (Mother Nature) as she gives birth to the deceased in the heavenly spirit world (Baba Nega), as well as everyday utensils, clothing and food, which are left to accompany the deceased on their journey and serve as gifts for relatives who have already passed away.

Before burial the deceased is bathed in aromatic herbs and dressed in their best clothes, their cheeks painted with the natural reddish dye of *achiote*, a colour believed to ward off the evil spirits (*boni*). After villagers have paid their respects, the body is laid to rest in a deep grave in a hammock oriented towards the rising sun in the east, symbolic of the beginning of new life, which is also sometimes alluded to by laying cotton threads – representing the umbilical cord – across the corpse. A dugout tethered nearby is left to carry the deceased to their ancestors.

7

interesting combination of modernity and tradition – it is generally only visited by guests at the nearby *Yandup Island Lodge* (see p.264). The region possesses a handful of delightful sand-fringed coconut isles on which to idle, and though its beaches don't match the breathtaking beauty of many in the western end of the archipelago, the mainland excursions into primeval **rainforest** more than compensate. Consider also a trip up **Río Azúcar (Uwargandub)**, a few kilometres west of Narganá – it is one of the most beautiful rivers in the *comarca*, brimming with birdlife, with the occasional crocodile idling on the bank.

Narganá and Corazón de Jesús

A quick glance round either **Narganá (Yandub)** or **Corazón de Jesús (Aggwanusadub)** and it's easy to forget you're in Guna Yala. The paved squares are dotted with benches, lampposts flank wide sandy streets, evening sound systems blast out reggaeton and bachata, and traditionally clad women are conspicuously absent. Some Guna see the twin islands as a warning of the fate of the *comarca* if the spread of *uaga burba* – the spirit of outsiders – proceeds unchecked. On the plus side, the location of the two islands is enchanting, nestled in a bay and fringed with mangroves fronting forest-clad hills. Moreover, if you've been travelling around the *comarca*, you might find Narganá's *Hostal Parks* – with cable TV – a welcome relief (see opposite).

Corazón de Jesús, in keeping with its name, has a **statue of Christ** in its central plaza, which is illuminated at night. Other than that, the island's main features are its airstrip, a handful of government buildings and a church; there's a small cemetery at the northern tip. Most of the action occurs down at the wharf and at its opposite number across the dividing channel of water in Narganá: boats load up with supplies and drop off passengers, and yachts bob at anchor.

Across the bridge in Narganá, the gleaming golden **statue of Carlos Inaediguine Robinson**, educator and major player in the 1925 Guna Revolution, stands as if in defiance at the centre of the main plaza. Spacious sandy streets lead off the square in grid formation, in stark contrast to most Guna communities' cramped, labyrinthine layouts. Cement houses, occasionally surrounded by a hedge or garden, alternate with traditional cane-and-thatch dwellings, sometimes sprouting satellite dishes. Given that the first missionaries to the *comarca* settled in Narganá, it's no wonder the place has four churches.

ARRIVAL AND DEPARTURE	NARGANÁ AND CORAZÓN DE JESÚS
By boat Both islands have 5.30am departures for Cartí ($20 one way). Enquire at the wharf in Corazón de Jesús or contact	Transporte Doña Hermalinda (☎6058 4210); in Narganá, Paco, who runs the island's fuel depot by his home at the back

of the primary school, is a good source of information.

By plane At the time of writing, the Corazón de Jesús airstrip was closed, but there are rumours of it reopening in the future – though no one knows when.

ACCOMMODATION AND EATING

Hostal Parks By the primary school, Narganá ☏ 6137 8678, ✉ piolalejandroparks@hotmail.com. Four bland, tiled-floor a/c rooms, with cable TV – overpriced for what they are but it's really the only option, and rates are negotiable. Boat tours can also be arranged; a trip up nearby Río Azúcar (Uwargandub) is recommended. **$50**

Restaurante Narganá At the western tip of Narganá. At the time of writing this was the only restaurant on either island, offering a pleasant view of bobbing yachts and large plates of tasty seafood – mains (from $8) include octopus, conch, fish and lobster with rice, salad or *patacones*. Service is indifferent. Daily 6.30am–10pm.

Isla Tigre

Populous yet spacious, elongated **Isla Tigre (Digir Dubu)** has the rare luxury of a couple of slender beaches. This island is managing better than most to sustain Guna mores while opening up to tourism, partly due to partitioning off the village from the grassy community-run tourist areas. In the latter you can loll in a hammock, enjoy a beer at the community restaurant, or sit on the sliver of **beach** in your swimwear – provided you cover up to go into the village. Possible inexpensive **excursions** ($20–30) include a visit to the mainland cemetery, a three-hour hike to waterfalls or a snorkelling trip around one of the nearby islands, where coconuts are harvested.

Some aspects of **traditional living** are still practised: families rotate to harvest coconuts, and workers take it in turn to staff the community restaurant. The island also has its own NGO and is actively involved in lobster protection and recycling practices. The **Guna dance** – involving men playing panpipes and women shaking maracas – originated here, and during the mid-October **Feria de Isla Tigre** dance troupes from across the *comarca* compete for prizes. You can catch them rehearsing on some evenings and at weekends.

ARRIVAL AND DEPARTURE

ISLA TIGRE

By boat Isla Tigre is a 1hr 30min boat ride from Cartí ($20 one way). It is rumoured that the airstrip on nearby Corazón de Jesús may reopen in the future.

ACCOMMODATION AND EATING

Cabañas Digir On the beach ☏ 6105 9581 (tourist coordinator). A dilapidated dorm-style beachside *cabaña*, with cement floor, squidgy mattresses and electricity, shares a toilet and bucket-shower facilities with three newer and nicer private *cabañas* on stilts – the private *cabañas* have their own small balconies looking out to sea. Rates don't include meals or excursions. Dorm **$10**, doubles **$35**

★**Restaurante Digir Dubu** Across from the cabañas ☏ 6099 2738. This open-sided bar-restaurant offers some of the best cuisine in the *comarca*; $6–7 will get you succulent lobster and crab in a delicious sauce with decent sides. Attracting Guna from other islands for the quality of the food and the relaxed atmosphere, it's a good place for cross-cultural conversation. Daily 7am–3pm & 6–10pm (but will open on request).

Playón Chico

Two cemeteries atop hills on the mainland announce your arrival at the sprawling administrative hub of **Playón Chico (Uggubseni)**, home to around three thousand people. A large, flat, coral-filled pancake packed with cane-and-thatch dwellings, interspersed with functional concrete buildings, the island is wrestling to balance traditional customs with modern developments, but is a vibrant and welcoming place for all that.

The wharf opens out onto the main-square-cum-basketball-court, and a painted stage. A concrete pedestrian bridge leads to the **mainland**, where a football pitch, airstrip and several government buildings, including a secondary school, are located. In the early morning, men armed with machetes stride up the path leading to the

7

THE TRADITIONAL GUNA WAY OF LIFE

Historically the Guna have lived collectively and worked cooperatively. Though some hunting was practised, **fishing** and **subsistence agriculture** – yuca, plantain, rice, maize, sugar cane, cocoa, fruit trees and coconuts – were the mainstay of the economy for many years. In the late 1960s, **coconuts** accounted for seventy percent of the *comarca's* revenue, bartered for dry goods, such as fuel, clothing and cooking oil, sold by the brightly painted Colombian trading vessels that you still see tethered to the main jetty at communities across the region. More than three million coconuts are still harvested annually.

Guna society is traditionally both matrilocal (when a man marries he moves into his in-laws' compound and works for them) and matrilineal (property is inherited down the female line). But these practices are slipping, and while women's views are respected, men play a larger role as chiefs, healers and interpreters in community meetings. Men undertake most of the agricultural labour, and the entire Guna Congress is male.

Families traditionally live in compounds of cane-and-thatch dwellings, the living quarters crammed with hammocks and the rafters laden with clothing, buckets and utensils. Villages without aqueducts bring fresh water by canoe from the mainland. Seafood accompanied by plantain, rice and coconut are staples, and *dule masi* – a fish stew containing boiled green plantains, coconut and vegetables – is effectively the Guna national dish.

At the heart of community life stands the **onmagged nega** (meeting house), where villagers, including children, congregate most evenings, though attendance is dropping off among the young. The *saila* – usually recognizable by his hat – is the leader in all village matters, though some communities now have several *sailas* to fulfil particular functions. A mixture of songs, chants, stories and talk filter through the walls, as Guna history, mythology and religion are as much a part of the reunions as information-giving, public debate and conflict resolution. Another key community building is the **inna nega**, where the *chicha brava*

cultivated lands (*nainumar*). Westernizing influence is evident in the numerous churches scattered round the island, and in the presence of electricity, which allows for a weekend film night at the community hall by the basketball court, and results in the sound of competing TVs penetrating paper-thin walls as you try to sleep.

Attractive **excursions** include hikes into pristine rainforest taking in the cascading waterfall of Saibar Maid; birdwatching up the Río Grande; and lazy sun-lounging, moderate snorkelling and fishing off nearby coconut isles.

ARRIVAL AND INFORMATION   PLAYÓN CHICO

By plane Daily flights leave Albrook Airport, Panama City, at 6am ($80 one way).

By boat The cost (one way) to/from Cartí is $30, $10 to/from Isla Tigre and $5 to/from Agligandi. Contact Genara

Linares Guardia (☎ 6085 8493) for information.

Information The community tax is $4. You may be able to catch a wi-fi signal by the school.

ACCOMMODATION AND EATING

Domy's 200m from the basketball court ☎ 6038 5157. The engaging Domy and Nilka offer a three-bed budget dorm in the top floor of a two-tiered wooden house, with shower below and a breezy deck with hammocks from which to watch the world go by. Breakfast ($5) and tours to a beach or the mainland can be arranged at extra cost. $10

Refresquería Sol 50m from the basketball court ☎ 6136 6541. The best place to eat on the island, offering one of the *comarca's* more varied menus and good value, too (*almuerzos* $3–4). You should book, and choose your dish, in advance – select from fish, langoustines, pork chops or chicken with rice and lentils – since demand often exceeds supply. Daily 7am–8pm.

★ **Yandup Island Lodge** Yandub, 5min from Playón Chico ☎ 394 1408, ⊕ yandupisland.com. One of the *comarca's* standout lodgings, comprising a collection of well-maintained octagonal *cabañas* with private balcony and bathroom; most sit over the water, while three (slightly cheaper) are set further back. The tiny island, covered with grass and with a small beach and nearby reef, has a breezy waterside *rancho*-restaurant with full bar, which serves excellent seafood-based cuisine, and service is friendly and attentive. Electricity is solar-generated. All inclusive; rates include two daily excursions with an English-speaking guide. *Cayuco* or kayak rental $15–20. Credit cards accepted. $244 (*inna* in Guna), the potent mind-numbing sugar-cane-based homebrew, is left to ferment in large clay urns for major celebrations such as a young girl's puberty ritual (see box, p.266).

CHANGES TO GUNA SOCIETY

As in any society, Guna life is evolving: numerous communities now have piped fresh water from the mainland; electricity (albeit limited, and often solar) is available on many village-islands; cement block buildings are increasingly common; shops stock canned food, sweets and biscuits, whose wrappers often litter the streets; the use of mobile phones is mushrooming; and the iconic Guna traditional dress is declining among women. That said, *molas* – the colourful, reverse-appliqué, multilayered panels that make up the most distinctive part of their traditional blouses – are still a major source of income for the Guna.

Christian churches have taken root on some islands, on the understanding that they respect traditional **religion**. Despite the Guna authorities' success in insisting on intercultural bilingual **education**, schooling is primarily about preparing young people for a modern industrialized society. In this respect, many Guna hope that tourism, if managed carefully, may help ensure that changes in lifestyle can coexist with more established mores.

Already, tourism has played a pivotal role in the Guna's reluctant but inevitable metamorphosis from a collective barter economy – the word for "money" does not exist in Guna – to a more individualistic cash economy. The resulting **economic inequalities** have put a strain on communities that are already struggling to deal with major social upheavals due to increasing contact with outsiders (*uagmala*) and returning urbanized Guna who are no longer prepared to live as their ancestors did. **Environmental damage** by outsiders and the Guna themselves constitutes a further challenge, often exacerbated by tourism, especially in western Guna Yala. Issues include waste disposal, overfishing, particularly of lobster, reef degradation and deforestation of the mainland.

7

San Ignacio de Tupile

Ten kilometres southeast of Playón Chico, midway along the *comarca*, lies the well-organized community of **San Ignacio de Tupile (Dadnaggwe Dubbir)**. As you step out of a boat at the community pier, you are greeted by a statue of the Virgin Mary – an indication of the island's fairly widespread evangelization. Though tourists rarely visit, the vibe among the 1500 inhabitants is relaxed and welcoming, particularly if your visit coincides with the **patron saint festivities** (July 28–31), when you can join in the celebrations marked by rowing races and various competitions.

Beyond the statue stands the primary school, where a wide main boulevard peels off left. The streets are kept spick-and-span, as community regulations mean families are held responsible for disposing of rubbish on the mainland. Rules are equally strict about getting a permit to leave the island, aimed at curbing what elders see to be the moral decline among some of the younger members of the community. Squeezed between two public phone boxes, the strangely whitened face of General Inatikuña, the community's first *saila* following relocation from the mainland to the island in 1903, stares out across the street.

Excursions are available to the unremarkable nearby beach on Ilestup ("Isle of the Englishman", after a gent who lived there in the 1700s) and to the Río Yuandub Gandi, where alligators laze on sandbanks and a rainbow of birds flit in and out of the foliage.

ARRIVAL AND DEPARTURE   SAN IGNACIO DE TUPILE

San Ignacio is a 30–40min **boat ride** from Playón Chico, the nearest airstrip.

EATING

Community restaurant By the wharf. The community's only restaurant is up the stairs to the right by the wharf. It serves a decent plate of fried fish with rice and plantain. Daily 6am–7pm.

The eastern isles

What might loosely be described as the **eastern isles** stretch over the whole of the eastern half of the *comarca*, which, outside the sprinkling of lodges near **Achutupu (Assudub)** and **Mamitupu** (Mammidub) sees precious few outsiders beyond the odd yacht and Colombian trading vessel. Here, lacking the protection of an offshore reef, the seas are rough and transport between communities sparse. After storms, rubbish jettisoned from boats will wash up on the shore in places. Islands of note include **Agligandi** – home of the Guna Revolution – while the twin settlement of **Ogobsucum** and **Ustupu** boasts the archipelago's largest population. Marking the eastern limit of the *comarca*, on the mainland, lies the border town of **Puerto Obaldía** and the more appealing mainland community of **Armila**.

Agligandi

Westernmost of the eastern islands, overlooking coastal mangroves (*ailan*), **Agligandi** (previously **Ailigandi**) has its spot firmly cemented in Guna history as the first place of organized resistance in the Guna Revolution of 1925; note the Guna swastika flag (representing an octopus) fluttering proudly above the rooftops. It's a good place to witness the annual revolution celebrations (see box, p.261). A pivotal figure in the rebellion was Chief Olokindibipilelel (Simral Colman), whose **statue** – incongruously clad in suit and bowler hat – claims a central position on the densely populated island of around 1200, next to the obligatory basketball court. A warren of pathways weaves through tightly packed thatched dwellings, in the midst of which is squeezed the tiny **Museo Olonigli**.

Museo Olonigli

No fixed hours • Donations welcome

As with other museums in the *comarca*, **Museo Olonigli** comprises a single room stuffed with artefacts whose significance only becomes clear through the explanations (in Spanish) of the owner-curator, Roy Cortéz Olonigli. He elaborates on traditional culture drawing on his own woodcarvings, which depict Guna symbols and rituals.

ARRIVAL AND DEPARTURE   AGLIGANDI

By boat Agligandi is a 10min boat ride from the Achutupu (Assudub) airstrip (see opposite). The community transport association offers three boats a week (usually Mon, Wed & Fri) to Cartí ($40), which can stop off at other islands including Playón Chico ($10) and Isla Tigre ($20) en route.

PUBERTY RITUALS

Although like many Guna customs, **puberty rituals** are becoming less common, If you spend time in one of the more traditional village-islands you may be lucky enough to be invited to attend one. Whereas adolescent boys pass into adulthood unheralded, a **young girl** traditionally undergoes two important ceremonies. The first, **innamudiggi**, at her first menstruation, prompts several days of confinement in a small ceremonial enclosure cloaked in banana leaves (*surba*) within the house, where she is purified in herbal baths and finally painted from top to toe in the indigo *jagua* dye before being allowed to join the festivities outside. The second celebration, **innasuid**, involving the whole village, entails the young woman being officially named and receiving a ceremonial haircut, a protracted affair signifying that she is now available for marriage. Food is shared, pipes are passed and *chicha* abounds – and the presence of cigarettes and seco in some communities reflects the changing times.

Ironically the young woman at the heart of the festivities misses out on most of the fun, remaining in seclusion until the actual hair-cutting. In an increasing fog of rituals, chants, cocoa-bean incense, tobacco and alcohol, the celebrations, aimed partly at affirming the coexistence of the material and spiritual worlds, continue for several days, until the *chicha* has run out, by which time several people have usually passed out.

Achutupu and Mamitupu

Five kilometres east of Agligandi, the unusual crescent-shaped island of **Achutupu** (**Assudub**), dotted with banana trees and coconut palms, has a deceptively spacious feel. The village has a primary school, health centre and restaurant by the pier, alongside a basketball court. It's inadvisable to swim off the strip of sand that might optimistically be called a beach, due to pollution. There's nowhere to stay on the island itself, but a couple of higher-end lodgings are close at hand.

Just a few hundred metres east of Achutupu, **Mamitupu** (**Mammidub**) has ten *sailas* governing a traditional village of about 1200. Photography is forbidden here, though it is permitted on excursions to the mainland.

ARRIVAL AND DEPARTURE   ACHUTUPU AND MAMITUPU

By plane The airstrip, 200m across from Achutupu on the mainland, receives daily Air Panama flights ($81 one way). Motorized dugouts greet the plane and will ferry you to Achutupu for a few dollars.

By boat There are occasional boats to Cartí, though it can be a 4–5hr haul ($45 one way).

ACCOMMODATION

Akwadup Lodge West of Achutupu ☎832 5144 or ☎6126 0737, ⓦakwaduplodge.com. A 5min boat ride west of Achutupu, this exclusive (by Guna standards) lodge offers comfort and seclusion in a row of seven simple over-the-water wooden bungalows. They're set rather close together but nicely decorated, with two double beds in each, solar-powered ceiling fans and mosquito nets. Rates, which are on the high side, include meals, lodgings and airport transfer. Community taxes ($15) are extra. **$224**

Cabañas Mamitupu Mamitupu ☎6017 2618 (Pablo Nuñez, who speaks English); or contact Agostín Silva, receptionist at Hotel Costa Azul in Panama City (☎225 4703). Set apart from the main village in a palm-shaded grassy end of the island stand four simple sandy-floor cane huts, with decent mattresses protected by mosquito nets, a good-size table, private washing area (for bucket and water ablutions) and solar-powered electricity. Flush toilets are shared, as is the pleasant *rancho* dining area. Rates include community taxes. **$180**

Dolphin Lodge (Uaguinega) Uagitupo ☎396 4805 or ☎6090 8990, ⓔinfo@dolphinlodgesanblas.com. A stone's throw across the water from Achutupu, on a tiny islet, this easy-going place has well-built, if tired, wood-and-cane *cabañas* facing the water. Palm trees are sprinkled over a grassy area with a central *bohío* and a pleasant and breezy restaurant where you can tuck into succulent seafood while gazing out to sea. Community taxes ($15) are extra. **$160**

Ogobsucum and Usdub

Beyond Mamitupu, completing the remaining 75km to Puerto Obaldía, you pass the densely matted, thatch rooftops of the *comarca*'s most populous communities: the four-thousand-strong twin settlements of **Ogobsucum** and **Usdub**, renowned for their gold craftwork. The next notable community is the pine-clad **Isla Pino** (**Dubbag**), which unlike any other island in the *comarca* has a large hill; though only a little more than a square kilometre in size, it boasts a couple of forest trails and a picturesque waterside thatched village.

Travellers rarely venture this far east to these more traditional communities, where you will need to check in with the police and ask **permission** of the *saila* to visit or stay on an island – make sure you are appropriately clad (see box, p.255). It is usually possible to negotiate with a family for a hammock or bed, pay for meals and engage the services of someone to explore the rivers and rainforest on the mainland. The seas along this stretch of coastline are particularly rough and should only be navigated in a decent boat, with life jackets – not the shallow leaking dugout favoured by many boatmen.

ARRIVAL AND DEPARTURE   OGOBSUCUM AND USDUB

By plane Air Panama flies three times a week (Tues, Thurs & Sun) to Ogobsucum ($85) from Albrook Airport in Panama City (see p.252).

Puerto Obaldía

PUERTO OBALDÍA is the last major "town" before the Colombian border. Despite a tidy park, a decent playing field, clean streets and a scenic seaside location, it is an unendearing encampment, where the frontier police in combat gear guard against drug runners, Colombian guerrillas and smugglers. Though technically within the *comarca*, the community has a mixed population of Guna, Colombian refugees and non-Guna Panamanians. You could end up with a more intimate knowledge of the town than you would like unless you've booked an air ticket to Panama City in advance, since seats are often oversubscribed.

ARRIVAL AND INFORMATION

PUERTO OBALDÍA

BY PLANE

Air Panama operates mid-morning flights – check with the airline the day before to confirm the time – from Panama City's Albrook Airport to Puerto Obaldía daily except Sat, with almost immediate return flights to the capital (1hr; $106). The airstrip is a 2min walk from the centre. Flights are in great demand, especially those back to Panama City, so you should book several weeks in advance.

BY BOAT

To Guna Yala Regular unscheduled speedboats head west up the *comarca* to Cartí (6–8hr; $100/person) from Puerto Obaldía, usually departing before 9am when they're full; ask around. You should also be able to negotiate a price if you want to be dropped off at another community along the way. Seas can be particularly rough and dangerous over the first three hours (especially Dec–Feb), even when

conditions are considered "safe". It is imperative that you check the condition of the boat beforehand (see p.254).

To Colombia Visitors travelling on to Colombia from Puerto Obaldía (see p.24) take a launch (1hr; $15) to the resort town of Capurganá, from where a further ferry to Turbo, or Necoclí, and onward bus to Medellín or Cartagena are possible.

IMMIGRATION

Before crossing the Colombian border, or after arriving from Colombia, you'll need to visit immigration (daily 8am–4pm; $20 charge to attend at other times), just off the park, for an entry or exit stamp. When arriving in Panama, you may also be asked for proof of onward travel out of the country and evidence of the means to support yourself financially. You then need to swing by the police post, to register and have your belongings searched (see p.25).

ACCOMMODATION AND EATING

Hotel Doña Primitiva Near the park. Simple but clean fan-ventilated rooms, with cold en-suite shower, accommodating two to four people. $40

Las Tres "L" Corner of the park. Friendly restaurant with

a pleasant patio where you can get a decent breakfast and lunch ($4), though options are limited. Arrive early for lunch, since food often runs out when visitor numbers are high. Daily 6.30am–4pm.

Armila

Highly recommended is a detour to the welcoming Guna community of **ARMILA**, which is idyllically located at the base of a forest-cloaked hill where two rivers empty into the sea. Atypically spacious, and run by five *sailas*, the village boasts an intriguing mix of traditional cane *cabañas* and more substantial Afro-Antillean-style wood-and-thatch houses, sometimes painted or on stilts. Beyond, more than 4km of cream-coloured windswept beach extends along the coast. **Turtle watching** is one of several tourist **activities**; others include jungle walks, river trips by dugout and swimming in the local freshwater lagoon. Provided the sea is calm, beach and

---

SECURITY IN THE FRONTIER ZONE

The **security situation** in the frontier zone is liable to change at a moment's notice so be sure to check out the latest information on the ground before you head into this area. In addition to the relatively safe boat-hopping route (see above), some travellers take the unofficial overland route from Puerto Obaldía via La Miel, hike across the border to Sapzurro in Colombia, and then head on to Capurganá. However, this is not advisable; although many people make the journey without a hitch, a few never arrive.

snorkelling trips can be organized to the lovely Playa Blanca at La Miel, by the Colombian border.

Turtle watching

Armila is one of the world's most important nesting sites for **leatherback turtles**, with several thousand nests protected by the community. The visitor community fee ($6) goes towards the conservation and monitoring project. Nesting occurs between February and August, peaking between late April/May and July. There's a major **turtle festival** during the third week in May, involving traditional music and dancing, during which a three-night package deal is usually offered, and camping is permitted.

ARRIVAL AND DEPARTURE   ARMILA

By boat Although Armila is just a 20min boat ride up the coast from Puerto Obaldía, landing on the beach (there is no jetty) is frequently impossible due to rough waves (especially Dec–Feb and sometimes July and Aug), or water spilling out of the river-mouths following torrential rain.

On foot When conditions are too rough to travel by boat, you will need to make a moderately strenuous uphill hike (1hr 30min–2hr) to reach Armila from Puerto Obaldía, accompanied by a guide.

ACCOMMODATION

★**Cabañas Ibedi** ☎6127 6298, ⬤naky-armila .wixsite.com/ibedialnatural. Run by Ignacio Crespo, known as "Nacho", an engaging, trained multilingual biologist and conservationist. Simple, tidy raised cabins of varying sizes with private porches sit among trees and a lovely hibiscus garden. Basic toilet/shower facilities are shared and there's solar-powered electricity at night. Food is tasty and activities varied, including river kayaking, guided hikes, a snorkelling beach excursion and turtle observation (in the season). Food, tours and transfer from Puerto Obaldía are included in the rates. Cheaper deals, in more rudimentary accommodation, can sometimes be negotiated for budget travellers. Minimum two-night stay. $106

Yaug Galu cabaña ☎333 2060 (public phone). Community *cabaña* attached to the turtle conservation foundation, Fundación Yaug Galu (⬤yauggalu.org). Eight beds are available to tourists in a dorm when it's not hosting visiting researchers. $53

7

The Darién and eastern Panama

DAWN IN THE DARIÉN

The Darién and eastern Panama

Mention of the Darién – Panama's largest province, abutting Colombia – conjures up a host of images, some alluring, others less so; some true, others vastly exaggerated. What is not in dispute is the region's status as one of the last true tropical wildernesses – though even this is under threat – encompassing swathes of mountainous forest containing an astounding array of wildlife. This is most apparent in Parque Nacional Darién, which provides unparalleled opportunities for serious hiking and birdwatching.

The Darién covers a sparsely populated, rugged expanse sprawling across almost twelve thousand square kilometres; it reaches its highest point at Cerro Tacarcuna (1875m) by the border, but includes numerous peaks of more than 1000m. The province also boasts Panama's longest river, the **Río Tuira**, which empties into the Golfo de San Miguel, a vast mangrove-lined body of water that opens out into the Pacific Ocean. Yet travellers are increasingly drawn to the Darién as much by its people as by its compelling scenery; several communities populated by the closely related **Emberá** and **Wounaan** – the region's main indigenous peoples – have opened up to tourists. In the **Comarca Emberá-Wounaan** or in communities outside the *comarca*, such as **La Marea** and **Mogué**, you can stay overnight in a village and learn about the intricacies of basketry or woodcarving, for which they are world-renowned, or hike through steaming rainforest to spot harpy eagles – the area boasts the greatest concentration of these raptors in the world. **Guna** communities also exist, mainly in **eastern Panama province**, historically considered part of the Darién. Their two small *comarcas* stretch along the shores of **Lago Bayano**, a vast reservoir 100km east of Panama City, which enjoys a picturesque setting in an increasingly deforested landscape, and has an impressive network of caves.

Brief history

The Darién bore witness to some of the bloodiest confrontations between the invading conquistadors, greedy for gold and power, and the indigenous groups desperate to defend their territories – most notably at **Santa María La Antigua del Darién**, the first successful Spanish settlement on the mainland since the time of Columbus (across the border in present-day Colombia). Balboa took Santa María in 1510, and later intercepted an attempt to reclaim the city, led by Cacique **Cémaco**, a pivotal figure in the indigenous resistance; he captured all the alliance's chiefs, bar Cémaco, and had them hanged as an example. It is perhaps only fitting that Balboa, who first espied the Pacific from the Darién, also met his end here – beheaded by Pedrerías Dávila in the coastal town of Acla (in present-day Guna Yala) – while Santa María was eventually abandoned by the Spanish in favour of Panama City, and was razed to the ground by indigenous forces in 1524.

The region's population

The indigenous peoples most in evidence today are the **Emberá** and **Wounaan**. Both groups may have migrated from the Chocó regions of Colombia (which is why they are often

THE DARIÉN FROM THE AIR

Highlights

❶ Lago Bayano Take a boat ride in search of caiman lurking in the lake's muddy fringes, and venture into the bat-infested Cuevas de Majé. **See p.277**

❷ Parque Nacional Darién On the banks of a picturesque river, the MiAmbiente refuge Rancho Frío provides the best access to the natural wonders of Parque Nacional Darién. **See p.280**

❸ Staying with the Emberá or Wounaan Spend a few nights in the villages of La Marea, Mogué or Playa Muerto, where you can learn about Emberá culture and the surrounding rainforest. **See p.284 & p.288**

❹ Harpy eagle nests Stake out the nest of the world's most powerful raptor and wait for a parent to swoop into view and deliver a monkey to their needy chick. **See p.284**

❺ Río Sambú A gloriously sinuous river, lined with mangroves and rainforest, and populated with ibis, herons and kingfishers. **See p.286**

❻ The Pacific coast A voyage by boat to Playa Muerto, Bahía Piñas or Jaqué from La Palma hugs a rugged, mountainous coastline, where spectacularly forested steep slopes tumble into the ocean. **See p.288**

HIGHLIGHTS ARE MARKED ON THE MAP ON P.274

referred to collectively as Chocós). **Guna** presence is still recalled in some of the place names, notably the snaking Río Tuira, and though most Guna moved to the Caribbean coast, pockets remain in the more recently formed *comarcas* of Madugandi and Wargandi, and in isolated communities in Panamá and Darién provinces. The other substantial population, dominant in the regional capital of La Palma and in settlements lining the Golfo de San Miguel, are the **Afro-Darienites**, descendants on the whole of the *cimarrones* – escaped slaves brought over by the Spanish, who fled and waged warfare from their own strongholds (*palenques*) in the rainforest, forming strategic alliances with pirates and indigenous tribes. Some of their communities are now mixed with Emberá and Wounaan, and, in some parts, with **Afro-Colombian refugees**, who fled the more recent civil conflict across the border. The completion of the Interamericana to Yaviza in 1979 opened the floodgates to **colonos** (the name often given to migrating *mestizo* cattle ranchers and farmers predominantly from the Azuero Peninsula), who have now cleared vast tracts of land along the highway for pasture, and constitute around fifty percent of the total population of Darién province.

Local conflicts

Though the joint Comarca Emberá-Wounaan was established in 1983, covering around 25 percent of Darién province, there have been increasingly **violent clashes** with *mestizo*

THE EMBERÁ AND WOUNAAN

Two separate but related ethnic groups speaking mutually unintelligible languages, the majority of Panama's **Emberá** (warriors famed for their poisonous blow-darts) and **Wounaan** (more noted for their artistry) inhabit wood-and-thatch huts along the Darién's numerous rivers – though the increasing presence of zinc roofs and cement buildings is indicative of encroaching modernization. As former seminomadic hunter-gatherers, it is only relatively recently that their communities started to live in fixed villages, a government-promoted project primarily to facilitate schooling and access to modern health care; before, family homes, though still sprinkled along the rivers as they are today, formed temporary bases from which to hunt and practise limited slash-and-burn agriculture before moving on, allowing forest to recover.

The groups' wooden **houses** are built on stilts, to protect them from wild animals and unwelcome intruders, as well as rising floodwaters. Semi-open sides permit cooling breezes to enter while preserving a degree of privacy. The platform, accessed by a tree trunk, with notches carved out as steps, constitutes a living space with a fire pit for cooking; crucially, the heat prevents the thatched roof from rotting during the rainy season, and keeps destructive insects at bay. Traditionally, the largest building in the community is the *bujía* or *casa comunal*, a splendid circular construction with a soaring conical ceiling, where meetings are held, guests are received and ceremonies take place. Missionaries have been chipping away at traditional **beliefs** since the time of the conquistadors, and while shamanism persists, villagers are more likely today to head for the government medical centre than put their trust in traditional medicine.

To learn more about Emberá or Wounaan village life, consider **staying the night** (see box, p.283).

8

settlers encroaching on their lands, while overlap with the national park, whose regulations restrict traditional hunting and agricultural practices, fuel frictions between indigenous groups and government. There are also concerns that following the 2016 peace accord between the Colombian government and the Fuerzas Armadas Revolucionarias de Colombia (**FARC**) – the opposition guerrilla movement – there is likely to be an influx of former combatants who are against the agreement.

ARRIVAL AND INFORMATION   THE DARIÉN AND EASTERN PANAMA

Most tourists visit the Darién on a **tour** but it is entirely possible, and becoming more common, to visit **independently** – though you need to be flexible and have time, money and Spanish-language skills.

INDEPENDENT TRAVEL

BY PLANE

To Jaqué and Bahía Piñas Air Panama (☎316 9000, ⓦairpanama.com) flies to Jaqué ($91; 1hr 15min) and nearby Bahía Piñas.

BY BUS AND BOAT

Bus and boat transport in the Darién requires patience and flexibility. Timetables are only loosely adhered to and services may be delayed or cancelled if there are insufficient passengers to warrant a trip. Set out as early as possible from Panama City's Albrook bus terminal to have a chance of reaching your destination the same day. For information on Darién bus schedules, call ☎6792 9493 or visit their office in the terminal.

To Yaviza and Metetí Beyond the expensive express bus to Yaviza (midnight; around 5–6hr; $21), most buses bound for the Darién stop at Metetí, where you transfer to a local minibus for Yaviza. Journey times are approximate,

as the condition of the paved road is highly variable, especially in the rainy season. The last daily direct bus from Albrook leaves at 4.30pm.

To La Palma To reach La Palma and other destinations in the Golfo de San Miguel, take the bus to Metetí, then a minibus shuttle to nearby Puerto Quimba (see p.279), from where there is a water-taxi to La Palma (see p.283).

COMMUNICATIONS

Communication is very difficult and intermittent in the Darién. Some places have no mobile phone reception (Más Móvil and Digicel have the greatest coverage); for others you might need several days and several attempts to make contact either by email or phone, since people may only have access to these services when they visit a large town. Outside Metetí, wi-fi is rarely available; we have indicated in our accommodation listings where it exists. Moreover, unlike in some areas of Panama, virtually nobody will speak any English.

SAFETY IN THE DARIÉN

For many years the rule of thumb for **safety** in the Darién has been to draw an imaginary line from the Caribbean Colombian border, through Yaviza, to Bahía Piñas and Jaqué on the Pacific coast, beyond which you should not travel. Rancho Frío excepted, this still holds; however, due to the occasional flare-up in violence and drug-trafficking-related incidents (see p.43), other places may be temporarily off limits too. Always check before travelling with your consulate, and once on your travels, continue to seek local advice, especially from the frontier police (SENAFRONT) and village authorities.

For a few years, independent foreign travellers were required to obtain a **permit** from SENAFRONT, and although this restriction was lifted in 2016, security is tightened up again after any major incident. SENAFRONT maintains a presence in many Darién communities, and you will be required to sign in with them and present your ID on arrival.

GETTING AROUND

By boat Once in the Darién proper, transport is by boat, often a motorized dugout (*piragua*). It entails waiting around as many communities are on tidal rivers, only accessible at high tide, especially in the dry season. It's infinitely cheaper, though far less comfortable, to travel in a community boat, or *colectivo*, already heading to your destination (*como pasajero*) than to hire a boat privately (*viaje especial*). For the latter you will have to cover the cost of the fuel (often for the return trip, even if you're only travelling one way), the captain and probably a poleman; find out fuel costs and the amount required for your journey from another source before negotiating a price, and note that if hiring someone's services for an overnight stay in a village, you may need to pay for *their* lodging and food too.

Guides You cannot visit the national park without a guide; you will also need to hire a guide in the indigenous villages. Most villages have local guides (around $20/day) who will have varying levels of knowledge about the rainforest and its wildlife.

ORGANIZED TOURS TO THE DARIÉN

Though **customized itineraries** can also be arranged, **all-inclusive tours** generally leave Panama City (usually Dec–April), and include transport to and around the Darién, as well as accommodation, meals and non-alcoholic drinks, activities and bilingual guiding services in Spanish and English. Prices given here are per person.

ANCON Expeditions ☏ 269 9415, ⓦ ancon expeditions.com. The Rolls-Royce of tour operators, with top-notch bilingual naturalist guides, offering four-day all-inclusive tours to its comfortable lodge in the Reserva Punta Patiño, with prices to match ($1065 assuming two sharing), though one night is spent in the Emberá village of Mogué. Minimum four people.

Canopy Camp Border of the Reserva Hidrológica Filo del Tallo, east of Metetí, off the Interamericana ☏ 264 5720, ⓦ canopytower.com. Part of the *Canopy* "family", the camp comprises eight luxurious African safari tents (with electricity and fans) laden with local, sustainably sourced teak, on raised platforms that provide private observation decks. Aimed mainly at birders, packages also include excursions of interest to general nature-lovers. Eight-day tour $2799.

Ecocircuitos ☏ 315 1305, ⓦ ecocircuitos.com. Among a vast array of excursions is a four-day "Jungles of the Darién" tour, which combines visits to indigenous communities with a stay at the refuge at Rancho Frío, in the national park, and a night's camping in the rainforest. Minimum four people; $995.

Ecotour Darién ℂ Villa Nueva, Santa Fé ☏ 6736 1807, ⓦ ecotourdarien. Working with local guides and communities, this sound, Panamanian ecotour company offers several multiday tours including to the MIA refuge at Rancho Frío and a moderately priced trek across the mountains from Sambú to Playa Muerto.

Jungle Treks ☏ 6438 3130, ⓦ jungletreks.com. Former ANCON Expeditions guide Rick Morales operates his own trekking outfit with local guides. The "Deep Darién Adventure" involves two days' travel and six days of backpacking and camping – plenty of sleeping in hammocks and eating dehydrated food – from Sambú across the Serranía del Sapo, then following the Río Piña down to the Pacific coast. Minimum four people; around $2700.

Panama Orgánica ☏ 6079 6825, ⓔ panama organica@gmail.com. Small, reliable outfit that can arrange customized budget transport and adventure tours to hard-to-access areas such as the Darién and Guna Yala, working with local communities. Two weeks' notice needed; minimum two or three people.

Panama province

Aside from the Altos de Cerro Azul, **Panama province** east of the canal is known less for any sightseeing charms than for rampant deforestation and the continuing urban spread out towards Chepo – an unappealing agro-commercial town and former gateway to the Darién. That said, **Lago Bayano**, some 90km east of Panama City is worth a day, while the two adjoining Emberá communities just south of the Interamericana at **Ipetí** provide the other main reason to stop en route to the Darién proper. Popular with day-trippers and budget tours from Panama City, their relatively barren location lacks the rainforest charm of other villages in Darién province. However, if you're keen to drop in, any bus bound for Yaviza, Metetí or Agua Fría will let you off by the roadside, from where it's a twenty-minute walk along a gravel road.

Lago Bayano

Though now earmarked for "development", **LAGO BAYANO** remains a picturesque location, perfect for boat rides and picnics, and with a fascinating cave network at its southeastern tip. Its apparent charm and tranquillity, however, belie the anger of indigenous communities – displaced when the reservoir was formed in 1976 and still awaiting full compensation from the government – and the acres of forest that were submerged when the Río Chepo (or Río Bayano) was dammed to supply Panama City with more hydropower; dead tree trunks protruding eerily from the water act as poignant reminders. The economic mainstay of the sixteen lakeside communities – including those of the Guna **Comarca de Madugandi**, as well as Emberá, Wounaan and Ladino settlements – is the commercial fishing of tilapia.

8

Named after Bayano, a charismatic leader of a major settlement of *cimarrones* (see box, p.278), the 350-square-kilometre reservoir is a popular day-trip destination from Panama City; at weekends, families spill out of vehicles at the impressive **Puente Bayano**, which fords the lake's narrowest point, and pile into motor **launches** for island picnics, fishing trips or tours of the lake, on the lookout for caimans, crocodiles and otters slithering around the muddy banks.

Cuevas de Majé
Southeastern tip of Lago Bayano • $3

Lago Bayano's most fascinating destination is the **Cuevas de Majé**, comprising a 1km-long system of limestone caverns, replete with colonies of bats clinging to calcitic formations. Towards the end of the dry season, it's possible to wade your way (up to your chest) through the entire system, emerging in a steep-sided verdant gully, dripping with mosses and ferns. At other times, the raised water level means you'll need to go partway in a boat before stepping into the water, and may not be able to make it through on foot. In either case, you'll need a headlamp, footwear with a good grip and a minimum amount of clothing that you're happy to get soaked. Make sure your tour also takes in the impressive **rock walls** that enclose the entrance to the nearby Río Tigre.

Comarca de Madugandi
North of Lago Bayano • $3 entry to the *comarca*

The indigenous community of **Akua Guna** (or Loma de Piedra) at the western end of the Puente Bayano marks the entry to the Guna **Comarca de Madugandi**, established in 1996, which includes eighty percent of the reservoir's surface area and extends from the forested northern shores of the lake up the mountainous backdrop of the Serranía de San Blas. Well over three thousand Guna inhabit the *comarca*, dispersed among fourteen communities; some, such as **Icanti**, **Pintupu** and **Tabardi**, are beginning to open up to tourists, but you'll need to stay in someone's home as there's no organized accommodation as yet. Enquire at Akua Guna if you wish to visit.

EL "REY NEGRO BAYANO"

While his origins and date of death remain uncertain, there is no doubt that El "**Rey Negro Bayano**" (also Ballano or Vaino) was the most successful leader of the *cimarrones* and the undisputed king, referred to as such even by the Spanish. Commanding the loyalty of between four hundred and 1200 followers, he constructed an impenetrable hilltop fortress from where he repeatedly attacked Spanish forces and plundered mule trains on the Camino Real. Despite conducting three major campaigns against him (1553–56), the governor of Panama failed to quell the resistance, prompting the viceroy of Peru to charge a certain Captain Pedro de Ursúa with the specific task of crushing the *cimarrones* rebellion. Realizing it would be impossible to take Bayano's mountain stronghold by force, Ursúa used deceit. Pretending to offer Bayano a peaceful settlement and half the land, the conquistador arranged a celebratory feast. There – so the story goes – he drugged the wine, which stunned Bayano and his men, resulting in their easy capture, thus ending six years of revolt against the Spanish Crown.

ARRIVAL AND TOURS   **LAGO BAYANO**

Tour companies offer **bus-and-boat excursions** from the capital (around $150–160), but it's fairly easy, and cheaper, to organize a visit yourself.

By bus Buses depart from Albrook bus terminal for Puente Bayano (4am–4.40pm; every 40min; 2hr), which hosts the first of several police checkpoints. Buses from Yaviza and Metetí can also drop you off at the bridge.

Boat tours Reserve your launch in advance (especially at weekends) as organizing a boat and guide on the spot (from $70/boat for up to five) can take time: for lake tours, contact Noy Ortega (☎ 6959 6833, prefers 24hr notice), who has a house by the bridge, or Panama Caves (☎ 6674 1135, ⓦ panamacaves.com), a local tour company.

The Interamericana to Yaviza

Agua Fría No. 1, a place easily missed were it not for the police checkpoint, marks the entry into Darién province. From here, traffic tends to speed along the remaining 110km of virtually straight (predominantly tarred) road past pastureland, the odd settlement and occasional teak plantation to the end of the tarmac at **Yaviza**, spelling the end of the Interamericana.

Puerto Lara

Five kilometres downriver from the important agricultural community of **Santa Fé** lies **PUERTO LARA**. One of the few communities to receive plenty of technical support and funding, this Wounaan village of around six hundred people has a functioning fishing association and a computer centre, and produces high-quality crafts (see ⓦ puertolara .com). Though both Emberá and Wounaan are renowned for their **basketry** and tagua **carving**, it is the Wounaan who historically have been artists and have the greater reputation; many pieces from Puerto Lara are sent straight to Panama City for sale, but some can still be perused in the village, where workshops in *artesanía* are also held. Beyond the village, **boat trips**, **guided hikes** (within a small patch of forest of modest appeal), fishing and traditional dances can all be arranged by contacting the president of the tourism committee (see opposite).

ARRIVAL AND DEPARTURE   **PUERTO LARA**

TO/FROM METETÍ OR PANAMA CITY

By bus and boat Buses between Panama City and Metetí stop at Santa Fé (every 30min; 40min from Metetí, roughly 4hr 30min from Panama City). From Santa Fé, take a bus or *colectivo* taxi a few kilometres to Puerto La Cantera. Arrange with the tourist coordinator in advance for a *piragua* ($10) to meet you. Boats can only land at La Cantera, a 10–15min boat ride from Puerto Lara, at high tide.

By bus and 4WD Alight from any Metetí–Panama City bus at the turn-off to Puerto Lara on the Interamericana. Ask at the house at the junction for a 4WD taxi (around $15) for the 11km dirt road to Puerto Lara. Occasional *colectivos* leave the village for the Interamericana, from where you can catch a bus. In the rainy season, the road is sometimes impassable.

ACCOMMODATION AND EATING

Community accommodation Contact the president of the tourist committee, Dionisio Negria (☎6765 3086). A plain open-sided wooden "lodge" overlooking the main street offers several partitioned rooms with

TO/FROM PUERTO QUIMBA

By boat Occasional *colectivo* boats leave for Puerto Quimba ($12). Boat rental for a special trip is around $60–80/boat.

mattresses and shared toilet and shower around the back (and one pricier, relatively deluxe room with private bath). Visitors pay for food purchases, plus a $10/group daily fee for the tourist coordinator and cook. Doubles $25

Metetí

A police security checkpoint heralds your impending arrival in **METETÍ**, a long, strung-out settlement that is an increasingly important commercial and administrative hub. It's hardly endearing, but if you're travelling around much in the Darién, you're likely to pass through more than once, since it offers good links with Yaviza – from where it's a shortish hop to El Real, the main gateway to the national park – and **Puerto Quimba**, which provides a water-taxi link to La Palma, capital of the Darién and access point for many of the Emberá and Wounaan communities.

The village's de facto centre lies across the bridge at the turn-off to Puerto Quimba, where there's a taxi rank, a handful of warehouse-like shops and a bus stop.

ARRIVAL AND INFORMATION   METETÍ | 8

By bus The bus station is 1.5km up the Puerto Quimba road from the main junction. There are direct services to Panama City (2am–5.40pm; every 40min; 5–6hr), or you can flag down a bus from Yaviza at the junction with the Interamericana. Buses to Yaviza (5.30am–6pm; every 30min; 50min, depending on road conditions; $5) usually (but not always) leave from the bus station and also pick up passengers at the junction with the Interamericana. Buses also run to Puerto Quimba (5am–5pm; every 30min;

30min), to meet the water-taxi to and from La Palma (5am–6pm; every 30min; 30min; $4).

Taxis Taxis will ferry you from the junction to the terminal for $1/person, charging slightly more to take you to the bank.

Banks One of the Darién's two national banks, with an ATM, is in Metetí, 2km west of the main road junction (Mon–Fri 8am–3pm, Sat 9am–noon). You can pay your park fees here (see box, p.42).

ACCOMMODATION AND EATING

Crown Darién 500m before the bus station on the Puerto Quimba road ☎6609 1451, ✉crowndarien14@gmail.com. This small hotel gets top billing, with thirteen en-suite rooms – some with balcony – offering tepid showers but enhanced by a/c and cable TV. The on-site bar-restaurant (daily 1–10pm) dishes up a few basic meals. Free wi-fi. $25

Hospedaje Aruba 400m before the bus station on the Puerto Quimba road ☎6344 2388, ✉hospedaje arubadarien@gmail.com. Aesthetics are not high on the

agenda in this tatty hotel, offering desultory service and bland rooms. But the tiled bathrooms are clean (cold water), the mattresses firm and you get cable TV, a/c and free wi-fi. $25

Restaurante Bellagio Signposted off the Puerto Quimba road ☎6521 8753. The best place to eat in town, and in air-conditioned comfort. Dishes are roasted or grilled, a rare pleasure in the Darién (mains from $6). Plans are afoot to offer accommodation, too. Free wi-fi. Daily 11am–10pm.

Yaviza

The gently rolling final 50km of the Interamericana to **YAVIZA** – now tarred, though with sections often under repair – is mercifully slightly more tree-lined than the stretch between Chepo and Metetí. It comes to an abrupt halt at the banks of the Río Chucunaque, hidden behind a high chainlink fence and reams of barbed wire.

Marking the official start of the infamous **Darién Gap** (*Tapón del Darién* – literally Darién cork or plug), the highway hiatus between Central and South America, Yaviza simultaneously exudes a lethargic end-of-the-road torpor and an edgy frontier-town feel. The mixed population of around three thousand (Afro-Darienite, Emberá, Wounaan and *mestizo*) eyes outsiders warily, while gun-toting frontier police officers routinely patrol the town togged up in full camouflage combat gear.

Yaviza's only interest to visitors is as a stepping stone to El Real, the gateway to **Parque Nacional Darién**, or to the Distrito Cémaco, the northern segment of the Comarca Emberá-Wounaan, which has been out of bounds to visitors for years on account of the security situation.

During the day, most of the action occurs at the **wharf**, where buses pull in: supplies are loaded onto a flotilla of motorized *piraguas* headed for communities upriver, while mounds of plantain and yuca bound for the city are heaved onto trucks, and the surrounding makeshift *fondas* and restaurants do a thriving trade.

ARRIVAL AND INFORMATION
YAVIZA

By bus Buses for Yaviza, via Santa Fé and Metetí, leave Panama City's Albrook terminal (3.15am–1.30pm; every 40min–1hr; 6–7hrs; $15; express bus at midnight; $21). Many stop at Metetí, if there are few passengers, where you transfer onto a local minibus to Yaviza (see p.279). Buses leave Yaviza for Panama City (3.15am–1pm; every 40min–1hr) and for Metetí (6am–5pm; every 30min).

Police registration On arrival, visit the heavily fortified

SENAFRONT headquarters – take the left-hand pavement from the bus stop.

Parque Nacional Darién HQ If you're bound for the national park, the MIA office (Mon–Fri 8am–4pm; ✆ 299 4495), 100m beyond the SENAFRONT barracks, will definitely want to see proof that you have paid your park fees into their Banco Nacional account (see box, p.42) – there is a branch in Metetí (see p.276 & p.279).

ACCOMMODATION AND EATING

Travellers heading to Parque Nacional Darién should note that Yaviza is a better place to stock up with **supplies** than El Real. After 7pm, you'll be unlikely to find anywhere serving food.

Hotel Yadarien 50m along the pavement from the wharf ✆ 6757 6186. The town's best accommodation, but basic; its grubby twenty rooms contain beds in varying states of repair, with fan or a/c and cable TV ($5 extra) and private bathrooms. A small first-floor balcony affords a prime view of the street below. $20

Restaurante Oderay 40m along the pavement from the wharf. This reasonable eating option, with a small dining patio, dishes up a decent plate of fried chicken or fish (from around $6), is often packed at breakfast, and has a good toilet. Daily 7am–7pm.

Parque Nacional Darién

At 5790 square kilometres, **PARQUE NACIONAL DARIÉN** is the most expansive protected area in Central America. Created in 1972, it outranks all of Panama's national parks in both size and reputation, but is nevertheless one of the least visited protected areas in the country – reaching the refuge at Rancho Frío requires considerable organization. That said, the awe-inspiring greenery, laced with rivers and waterfalls and rich in wildlife, is well worth the time and money, providing a truly magical experience.

The park hugs the Colombian border, a forested carpet rising from the mangroves, coastal lagoons and deserted beaches of the **Pacific**, rippling over the volcanic ranges of the **Serranía del Sapo** and **Serranía del Jungurudó** northeast to the park's highest point of **Cerro Tacarcuna** (1875m), on the continental divide of the **Serranía del Darién**, and stopping just short of the Caribbean coast. Numerous important rivers scythe their way through the green mantle, including the Tuira, Sambú and Balsas.

Now that hiking the Darién Gap has been consigned to history (see p.24), **visiting the national park** these days means hiring a guide and staying at the only permanent camp: MiAmbiente's refuge at Rancho Frío, reached via El Real.

WILDLIFE IN PARQUE NACIONAL DARIÉN

The biodiversity in **Parque Nacional Darién** is staggering even as it is shrinking. More than 450 **bird species** have been recorded, including an array of vibrantly coloured macaws and parrots and strange-named rarities such as the beautiful treerunner, scale-crested pygmy tyrant and Chuck-will's-widow. Mammal species top 168, with numerous endemics and endangered animals lurking in the lush vegetation; the park offers the best chance, albeit slender, of glimpsing any of the big-five cats (see p.306), or a Baird's **tapir** – though spotting their footprints in the early morning mud is more likely – and even the occasional **spectacled bear** has been sighted. Yet the arboreal richness of the **rainforest** in the Darién demands just as much attention, with tracts of primary and secondary growth and a towering canopy of barrigón, spiny cedar and graceful platypodium. A visit in March or April is rewarded with the golden crown of the guayacán, heralding the start of the rains, and the russet bloom of the silvery cuipo trees looking down on the already lofty forest canopy, favourite nesting site of the world's largest concentration of **harpy eagles** (see box, p.285). Most of this can only truly be appreciated from the air, or from breaks in the tree line when ascending the region's peaks. On the forest floor, the scene is very different: dark and dank, and dominated by gnarled tree trunks entwined with vines or studded with vicious spines, vast buttress roots, dangling lianas, ferns and rotting leaf litter.

The park was declared a UNESCO World Heritage Site in 1981 and a Biosphere Reserve in 1983, but the **protection** it is offered in practice is worth little more than the paper it's written on, as illegal hunting, logging, extraction of rare plants and animals, and slash-and-burn agriculture continue unchecked. Ironically, the long list of undesirables that have taken refuge in the rainforest – FARC guerrillas, right-wing paramilitaries, drug traffickers, smugglers and bandits – have acted as unwitting conservationists by frightening off most settlers and major developments, though the fighting over the border in Colombia has also resulted in an influx of refugees, who themselves are clearing land to cultivate.

8

ESSENTIALS
PARQUE NACIONAL DARIÉN

Fees The daily park entry ($5) and accommodation fees (bunk in the refuge $15; camping $6), should be paid into the MiAmbiente bank account in advance (see box, p.42) – there's a branch of the national bank, with an ATM, in Metetí (see p.279).

Guides To enter the park and/or stay at the refuge at Rancho Frío – currently the only accommodation in the park – you need to hire a guide. You can arrange for a warden (*guardaparque*) to guide you (US$15–20/day for one to three people) though they may try to encourage you to go with one of the very expensive, independent local guides ($50/day/person plus costs) – if you don't want to do this, insist politely. MIA-recommended local guides might include Isaac Pizarro (☎6242 5220, ✉ipizarro.3003@hotmail.com), who speaks English, and Luis Pacheco (☎6704 1486). Make sure you have the necessary supplies (see box, p.283) – best acquired in Yaviza – including food for the guide.

El Real

The deceptively fast-flowing waters of the Río Chucunaque snake down 6km from Yaviza through variegated walls of water chestnuts, banana plantations, expansive trees and pastureland to the low-key grassy bank "jetty" of **EL REAL** on the Río Tuira, the jumping-off point for the MiAmbiente refuge at Rancho Frío. From the jetty, it's a sweltering fifteen-minute walk into the town proper – a one-time fortified colonial settlement, now a pleasant if somnolent collection of houses constructed from various combinations of wood, zinc and concrete, and a couple of churches, interwoven with a network of cement pathways.

ARRIVAL AND DEPARTURE
EL REAL

By boat *Piraguas* regularly make the 45min journey from Yaviza to El Real, unless delayed by a major downpour; *piragua colectivo* rates are generally $10.

ACCOMMODATION AND EATING

Hotel El Nazareño On the main path. Housed in a very dilapidated wooden two-storey building, with intermittently functioning plumbing and a DIY shower. $15

Restaurante Doña Lola Near the church. This friendly place serves very tasty food – plantain, lentils and fried chicken – for a few dollars. Daily 7am–8pm.

Rancho Frío

The only national park refuge still in operation within the park, **Rancho Frío**, sometimes called Pirre Station, is scenically situated on the shady banks of the Río Perescenico, with several **trails** leading off from the camp. These include the serious day- or overnight trek to the cloud forest of **Cerro Pirre** (1200m) – which requires lugging tent, sleeping bag and provisions up the mountain; it can be chilly at night, so pack something warm. The **Sendero de las Antennas** provides a stiff all-day alternative that culminates in a hilltop police post, affording sweeping views of La Palma and the Golfo de San Miguel, with the Pacific as backdrop. Less strenuous walks can be had closer to camp, but still require a guide – the most popular is the two-hour circular **Sendero Rancho Frío**, which takes in a waterfall and natural *piscina*. During the wet months, the rivers and waterfalls are truly spectacular, though the refuge and mountain trails are often swathed in mist and the quantity of mud to wade through can scarcely be imagined, making even the shortest hike a major physical achievement. In the dry season, paths are easier to hike, views more frequently glimpsed and your chances of spotting mammal life – driven to the river to drink – is greatly enhanced.

8

ARRIVAL AND DEPARTURE   RANCHO FRÍO

By 4WD In the dry season, the easiest access from El Real is to arrange transport by 4WD as far as the village of Pirre Uno, 12km upriver ($25/vehicle), from where it is a gentle 1hr 30min walk to the refuge. Or you can arrange to be taken by horse from Pirre Uno ($20).

By boat In the rainy season, you can sometimes get further upriver from El Real to Pijebaisal (around $30 for the *piragua* from El Real, plus the cost of three gallons of diesel each way), an hour's hike away.

ACCOMMODATION

★ **Rancho Frío** On the banks of the Río Perescenico. The renovated but basic refuge has limited electricity. Bring all provisions with you, including bedding and food – and enough for the park warden and/or guide. Be sure to pack

bottled water or, better still, a water filter or purifying tablets, since tap water is not drinkable. A mosquito net is advisable. Camping $6, dorm $15

Around Golfo de San Miguel

Stacked up on a hilly peninsula, the ramshackle collection of wooden buildings that constitute the lively provincial capital of **La Palma** jut out into the widening expanse of the Río Tuira as it empties into the **Golfo de San Miguel**, a large bite-shaped body of water penetrating into Panama's southeastern Pacific coastline. Just across the water from La Palma, Isla El Encanto (or Boca Chica) hosts the scarcely visible, crumbling remains of the overgrown **Fuerte de San Carlos de Boca Chica**; though little more than a watchtower, it was a crucial link in a chain of defences that safeguarded the gold mines at Cana. Sprinkled along the coastline amid the mangroves are several predominantly Afro-Darienite communities such as **Garachiné** – comprising a collection of fairly dilapidated buildings and negligible services. The rivers that flow into the Golfo de San Miguel are the means of access to the **Comarca Emberá-Wounaan** and to the villages of **La Marea**, **Mogué**, **La Chunga** and, of course, **Sambú** itself.

VISITING AN EMBERÁ OR WOUNAAN VILLAGE

Staying overnight in an **Emberá or Wounaan village** is a great way to interact with villagers and learn about their day-to-day activities, as well as giving you access to the rainforest. Accommodation will either be in a traditional communal house (raised, thatched and open-sided) or in a family home. Communities that are used to greeting tour parties tend to offer slightly better **facilities** (showers, flush toilets and maybe even mattresses and mosquito nets), whereas others may provide little more than a wooden floor or a hammock for you to sleep on, and possibly a fire to cook your own food and a bucket of water for washing.

As many settlements are located on tidal rivers only accessible at high tide you may well have to hang around by jetties waiting for the water level to rise – generally, you need to be flexible and organized, taking **food** with you where possible, since many communities expect you to provide the food to cook and village shops are thinly stocked. **Bottled water** – or the means of purifying it – is both necessary and scarce; beer is more widely available, though check on the village etiquette before indulging and be discreet in your drinking, except when the whole village is having a party.

Most visitors head for villages round the **Golfo de San Miguel** or in the **Distrito Sambú** section of the **Comarca Emberá-Wounaan**, where you first need to report to the *comarca* office in Puerto Indio (see p.287) and pay the $10 entry fee. Mobile phone signals are fickle, and some communities have no coverage at all; given the difficulties in communication in the Darién, most independent travellers just turn up. The tourist coordinator (or president) is the person to ask for on arrival. They can tell you the prices and whether money needs to be paid to them (to be disbursed later to the relevant people) or directly to anyone who provides a service. They may also allocate you a personal tourist coordinator (usually $10/group – or solo traveller – per day), who will organize all aspects of your stay. Families usually take turns in hosting visitors to ensure that wealth is distributed across the community, but it is essential to sort out what's to be paid to whom from the outset to prevent misunderstandings. **Costs** are charged per person and itemized separately: village community fee (usually $5–10, but word is that it may soon be increased to $20); accommodation ($10/night); meals ($4–5); services of a cook ($10/day per group or solo traveller); fishing trips or guided hikes ($10–15; more to a harpy eagle nest); body painting with *jagua* – (dye from the juice of a tropical berry mixed with charcoal; $5); and dance performances ($40/group). Assuming you take one excursion and three meals a day, you should budget around $50–60 per person per day, plus **transport** ($15–30/person, depending on the distance and the number of people, if you manage to catch a *piragua colectivo*; $80–200 for a private hire).

Sales of **handicrafts** are also an important aspect of village visits, displayed in a small shop or by the artisans themselves, and at set prices (usually from $20) that are inevitably lower than in Panama City. If you don't intend to buy anything, alert the tourist coordinator to avoid embarrassment; otherwise, try to spread your purchases round several artisans.

8

La Palma

Resembling no other town in Panama, **LA PALMA**, a predominantly Afro-Darienite settlement of around six thousand, is the regional administrative and commercial hub, where motorized dugouts from the coastal and riverine communities jostle for position at the narrow and non-too-salubrious main jetty. The town's one sultry street is chock-full of hole-in-the-wall restaurants, bars and hotels, and shops selling welcome piles of fresh produce and other goods that are regularly shipped in from Panama City. Most visitors gravitate to La Palma to connect with transport to Emberá communities such as La Marea and Mogué, or those further afield up the Río Sambú, and you'd be well advised to stock up with supplies while here – the (pricier) village stores are unlikely to provide much beyond tinned fish, rice and biscuits. If you don't have the means to purify **water**, make sure you pick up a flagon or two of the bottled variety.

ARRIVAL AND DEPARTURE   LA PALMA

By water-taxi Water-taxis to La Palma run from Puerto Quimba (daily 5am–5.30pm; every 30min; 40min; $4). The last return water-taxi to Puerto Quimba leaves around 5.30pm.

ACCOMMODATION AND EATING

Hotel Biaquirú Bagará C Principal ☎ 299 6224. This basic, family-run hotel is your best bet, with a dozen neat wood-panelled rooms, some with fan and shared (cold-water) bathroom, others en suite with a/c. There's a shared waterside deck with hammocks. $25

Lola's Grill C Principal, near the basketball court. The ebullient Lola serves inexpensive seafood with coconut rice or yuca (from $6) in her upstairs restaurant, but like most places in La Palma it can close early and suffer from a lack of provisions. Mon–Sat 7am–3pm & 6–9pm.

Pension Tuira C Principal ☎ 299 6316. For shoestring travellers who fancy being in the thick of the noisy action – there's a *cantina* next door – this friendly hotel provides rooms with fan or a/c ($5 extra) and communal balconies overlooking the estuary. $20

La Marea

Forty minutes' boat ride southeast from La Palma up the sinuous tree-lined Río La Marea, the small, welcoming community of **LA MAREA** provides a perfect introduction to the Emberá way of life. The "*marea*" (tide) is crucial to village logistics since the place is only reachable at high tide, and even then, at the backend of the dry season, the *piragua* scrapes along the riverbed. Traditional open-sided wood-and-thatch dwellings are dotted across a sloping expanse of neatly trimmed grass ending at the riverbank, where a small *rancho* is used for dance performances and craft displays; opposite this, a tiny shop sells beer and a few tinned essentials.

An infectious tranquillity pervades the settlement – aside from the two hours in the evening when the generator is on – and for most of the night it is illuminated by starlight and kerosene lamps. Unlike in some communities, many of the 160 villagers choose to go about their business clad in traditional attire, except when heading into town. The surrounding forest abounds in **wildlife**, worth exploring with a guide following a trail leading to a waterfall or a lake, or embarking on a substantial hike or a shorter horseride. Otherwise, the days can happily slip by interacting with villagers, getting your body painted in *jagua* dye and cooling off in the river.

ARRIVAL AND ACTIVITIES   LA MAREA

To visit the community, contact the tourism coordinator Turiano (☎ 6742 3615).

By boat Ask around at La Palma on a weekday and you may be able to catch a *piragua colectivo* ($15).

Hiking The village trail goes straight into the rainforest ($10); guiding services cost $20/group.

ACCOMMODATION AND EATING

Community accommodation A traditional house is set aside for visitors, with space to hang a hammock or spread a sleeping bag, and a family allocated either to cook food (which they prefer you to provide; $10–20/group or solo traveller) or lend you their fire pit and utensils to prepare your own meals. $8

Mogué

There's a *Heart of Darkness* feel about entering the **Río Mogué**, enclosed by forbidding walls of mangroves, flecked with perching white ibis, which eventually clear at a scenic mooring, ten minutes' walk from the village of **MOGUÉ**. The name derives from Mogadé, a mythical Emberá creature that lived in the mountains and ate people – though Panama City would seem to have devoured more of the dwindling village population as they leave in search of employment. Besides a little tourism, agriculture – plantain, yuca and a variety of other fruits and vegetables – constitutes the economic mainstay of the community, though a minority still fish or hunt iguanas, agoutis and other small animals with traditional arrows or a gun. Another important source of income is **basketry** – especially masks – for which Mogué is justifiably renowned. Mogué is also the most likely community to have an active **harpy eagle nest** (see box opposite), where a willingness to stake the place out for several hours can often be

SAVING THE HARPY EAGLE

Instantly recognizable for its splendid slate-grey back, brilliant white chest and distinctive crest, the **harpy eagle** (*águila harpía*) is the largest eagle in the Neotropics and one of the most powerful worldwide, with talons the size of a grizzly bear's claws. The larger female can weigh up to 9kg and be more than 1m long, and despite its vast wingspan of more than 2m, it can reach speeds of up to 80km/h while accelerating through trees to stab its prey.

After declining in numbers for many years due to loss of habitat and hunting, the harpy eagle is making a comeback: an increasingly successful breed-and-release programme run by the Peregrine Fund (❿peregrinefund.org) has resulted in Panama now having the greatest concentration of harpy eagles in Mesoamerica, with more than two hundred pairs. It will be a long recovery process, though, as harpy eagles are lethargic breeders, laying two eggs once every three years; worse still, once the first egg has hatched, the second is discarded as the pair focus on nurturing the single chick in the nest for another six months, and taking care of it for a further two years.

Working with local communities and conducting educational campaigns in schools, the conservation project has succeeded in heightening public awareness and interest in the harpy eagle. Fittingly, the raptor is now the **national bird**, topping the national coat of arms, and has its own national day on April 10. All this publicity, it is hoped, will help ensure the harpy eagle's continued survival.

For more on the efforts to save this majestic bird, check the sites of Fondo Peregrino-Panamá (❿peregrinefund.org) and Patronato Amigos del Águila Harpía (❿aguilaharpia.org). To find out which communities have an active harpy eagle nest in any given year, contact the Darién desk of Áreas Protegidas in the MIA offices in Panama City (see box, p.42) or Metetí (see p.279).

rewarded by a truly special sighting: a parent returning with a monkey in its talons, which is ripped apart, before tiny morsels are fed to the chick with incredible delicacy.

The focus of community life is the zinc-roofed **casa comunal**, where on Saturdays or Sundays the leaders preside over the weekly village gathering. The tri-weekly Evangelical services are also a draw for a large number of the community, while late afternoon the football pitch provides an important social focus for both the men's and women's teams, and visitors are welcome to join in.

ARRIVAL AND ACTIVITIES   MOGUÉ

By boat Transport to the village makes the journey expensive unless you catch a village boat ($15 one way from La Palma). Enquire at the main jetty, as boats leave with the rising tide most days (especially Mon, Wed and Fri). Otherwise, ring the *presidente de turismo*, Alberto Rito (❷6653 3379), to arrange a boat pickup in La Palma. Ask for the cool box to be brought along, which you can fill with fish, chicken or shrimp from the market for meals; otherwise your diet will be very limited.

Hiking and birdwatching It takes 15min to reach the more luxuriant rainforest from Mogué, and a further 1hr 30min along a well-trodden trail to an active harpy eagle nest, though there are numerous less-frequented paths to explore with a guide ($10/group for the guide, $10/group trail fee – $25 to visit a harpy eagle nest), populated with toucans, sloths and monkeys.

Horseriding and fishing These activities can be organized for $10.

ACCOMMODATION AND EATING

Community accommodation Visitors can sleep on a mattress in a small tent or in a hammock in the *casa comunal*, whose breezy raised platform, where food is served, affords a prime spot to eavesdrop on village life. $12/day for the cook's services/group or solo traveller, plus $5/meal. **$10**

Reserva Punta Patiño

Established in the early 1990s, **Reserva Punta Patiño** is Panama's first and, at 300 square kilometres, largest private reserve, occupying the entire headland at the tip of the choppy Golfo de San Miguel, just beyond the lively Afro-Darienite fishing village of **Punta Alegre**.

While the landscape is nowhere near as dramatic as the jungle-carpeted peaks of the interior, the regenerating hinterland forest – once devastated by cattle ranching, timber extraction and coconut plantations – is filling up with native hardwoods, though it's an hour's hike to primary forest. The area also covers a stretch of charcoal **beach**, an important expanse of **mangroves**, and mud and **salt flats** that attract an abundance of resident and migratory seabirds.

Managed by the environmental organization **ANCON**, the reserve is not without its critics, not least the Emberá, who feel the land should be theirs. Moreover, the area can only be visited by splashing out on an all-inclusive four-day tour through ANCON Expeditions (see p.276), which includes a day or overnight excursion to Mogué (see p.284). Still, there's no denying that this is a magical spot to soak up glorious sunsets, aerial displays by diving pelicans and occasional sightings of bottle-nosed dolphins and humpback whales. On land, mammals to look out for include the weasel-like tayra, grey foxes and the extraordinary-looking capybara, the world's largest rodent, which resembles a giant guinea pig and weighs in at 55kg. Needless to say, the location necessitates lashings of insect repellent to ward off the prolific uninvited guests.

ARRIVAL AND ACCOMMODATION

RESERVA PUNTA PATIÑO

By bus and boat Included in the ANCON Expeditions package, you travel from Panama City to Puerto Quimba, and back, by minibus (4–5hr), then take a boat (1hr 30min) to the reserve.

Punta Patiño Lodge Comfortable accommodation in ten *cabañas* with twin beds, a/c, private cold-water bathrooms and balconies. Perched on a bluff overlooking the bay, the main lodge offers great views, best appreciated from a hammock on its wraparound balcony. Package includes full board, transport from and to Panama City, and bilingual naturalist guide. Additional $192 to overnight in Mogué. **§3212**

Garachiné

Set against the imposing backdrop of Cerro Sapo (Toad Hill), the small, neglected fishing community of **GARACHINÉ** is only of interest to visitors who intend to hike the overland route to Playa Muerto (see p.288), or are trying to reach Sambú via a bumpy road which then loops back to the coastal Wounaan community of Taimatí. Unless you arrive at high tide, you'll be wading knee-deep across alluvial mud flats to the shore.

ARRIVAL AND INFORMATION

GARACHINÉ

By boat Boats regularly depart from La Palma ($15) and Puerto Quimba ($20).

By road Getting a ride to Sambú by road is tricky, with transport only going early in the morning and returning in the afternoon ($4–5). Wait by the bus shelter (*la caseta*) at the end of the main cement path.

SENAFRONT registration There is a police checkpoint (where you need to register) on the beach, where the boats pull up.

ACCOMMODATION AND EATING

There's little to tempt the palate in Garachiné and the few **fondas** that exist have irregular hours; it's usually a case of looking around to see what's open.

AJ's Hospedaje C Principal ☎ 6501 3234 or ☎ 6506 2097. Behind the hardware store are five surprisingly nice, simple rooms, offering ample space, gleaming tiled floors and bathrooms and comfortable beds, plus a/c and cable TV. **§25**

Río Sambú and the Comarca Emberá-Wounaan

Portal to the twelve communities of the **Distrito Sambú** of the **Comarca Emberá-Wounaan**, 12km up the serpentine **Río Sambú**, the twin settlements of **Sambú** and **Puerto Indio** are generally only reached by river at high tide. The boat trip, sweeping round the river's tortuous bends, causing flocks of white ibis to fly off in unison, is highly atmospheric. As the Río Sambú's waters swell during the rainy season, *piraguas* can penetrate as far upstream as the tiny village of Pavarandó; more easily accessible downriver is the fairly dispersed community of **La Chunga**, which lies a few minutes' paddle up a quiet tributary.

TOURS FROM SAMBÚ AND PUERTO INDIO

In **Puerto Indio**, the tourism committee, based in the Oficina del Congreso, offers a range of day **excursions to the Distrito Sambú** (for which you'll need to provide your own food and water). These include a guided walk round the village, taking in a nearby lake, a half-day excursion to a waterfall involving a 45-minute boat ride and a modest rainforest walk, and lengthier ventures to the communities of La Chunga or Pavarandó. In all cases, **overnight stays** can easily be arranged, either in the *casa comunal* or in someone's house. Arquinio Dogirama (✉ emberaguia@yahoo.es) and Domicilio Cardena (La Chunga public phone ☎ 333 2516) are **guides** authorized by the *comarca*'s tourism committee, though each village has its own guide.

Sambú guides are not allowed to guide within the *comarca*, but can offer excursions to rainforest and Emberá communities that lie outside the *comarca* boundaries.

Sambú and Puerto Indio

While **SAMBÚ** and its counterpart **PUERTO INDIO**, connected by a footbridge, are pleasant enough places, they serve more as a gateway to swathes of primeval **forest** and a serpentine waterway leading to **Emberá** and **Wounaan communities** further upriver.

The contrast in mood and architecture between the two villages is striking. In bustling Sambú – where all accommodation and eating options are located – cement pathways wind between tightly packed houses of various architectural styles, accommodating a mixed population of Emberá, Wounaan, *mestizos* and Afro-Darienites. Across the river, quieter Puerto Indio, at the western limit of the Distrito Sambú, of which it is the capital, comprises an indigenous population living in traditional wooden housing raised on stilts, where afternoon social activity centres round the basketball court or football pitch.

ARRIVAL AND INFORMATION   SAMBÚ AND PUERTO INDIO

By boat Most commercial boat traffic to Sambú and Puerto Indio ($20 from La Palma, $25 from Puerto Quimba) leaves on Mon and Fri.

By boat and 4WD If there isn't a boat going directly to Sambú, in the dry season you could go to Garachiné (see opposite), where you can usually hitch a ride to Sambú along the dirt road ($5–6/person for a *colectivo*, $40–60 in total if a special trip is necessary).

SENAFRONT registration The SENAFRONT checkpoint is halfway down the disused airstrip in Sambú.

Fees The $10 entry fee to the *comarca* should be paid at the Oficina del Congreso in Puerto Indio.

ACCOMMODATION AND EATING

Aquí me Quedo Close to the airstrip. In a sturdy cane building behind the shop, Benedicta prepares good breakfasts and solid lunches for around $4. Evening meals are a case of what's left over. Daily 7am–8pm.

Mi Sueño By the airstrip ☎ 6902 8327. Eleven small, wooden-fan-ventilated rooms with shared bathroom, and a large communal balcony affording a pleasant view of the surrounding hillside. The occasionally functioning restaurant offers cheap meals. Tours to Emberá village of Villa Queresia can also be arranged. $15

Villa Fiesta By the airstrip ☎ 6792 9493. Four bright, good-value rooms (two with a/c, two with fan) with excellent beds, private bathroom and fridge; meals can also be arranged. Former Emberá *cacique* Ricardo Cabrera, the genial owner and proprietor of the downstairs shop, is fluent in English and a mine of local knowledge. $25

La Chunga

Closer to the mouth of the Río Sambú, a small tributary navigable only at high tide leads to the hamlet of **LA CHUNGA**, named after the ubiquitous palm used for basketry. At other times, you land at a pontoon on the main river, from where it's a twenty-minute walk along a boardwalk through mosquito-infested swamp to the village.

An avenue of cedar trees marks the entrance, opening out onto an overgrown basketball court surrounded by a handful of traditional homes. **Basketry** is still widely practised by the women. Make sure you check out the village **stocks** (*sepo*); miscreants who commit an offence and are unable to pay the fine are placed there for a couple of hours, an experience made particularly painful by being made to sit on a pile of cooked rice, which attracts vicious ants that tuck in to the penitent's buttocks. The Wounaan community of **Semaco**, known for its exquisite basketry, music and dance, is just a two-hour hike away. A village guide can take you **birdwatching** upriver, or perhaps to a **harpy eagle nest**.

ARRIVAL AND ACCOMMODATION   LA CHUNGA

By boat Although La Chunga has its own motorized transport that occasionally travels to and from La Palma ($20) on weekdays, you can also catch a ride in the Sambú/Puerto Indio boats, which will drop you at the La Chunga pontoon on the Río Sambú, from where it is a 20min walk.

Community accommodation ☎ 333 2516 (public phone). Overnight guests are made comfortable in someone's home on mattresses with mosquito nets and even sheets and pillows. Bathrooms are shared and rudimentary. You pay $12 for someone to prepare your three meals. $̲1̲0̲

The southeastern Pacific coast

The Darién's **Pacific coast** is as remote and unexplored as the jungle-filled interior: to the northwest of the Golfo de San Miguel, the coastline is dominated by mangroves, but to the southeast it comprises kilometres of deserted beaches interspersed with rocky outcrops, cliffs and expanses of pristine forest, with the brooding serranías del Sapo and Jungurudó a dramatic backdrop. Three places of interest stand out here: the Emberá village of **Playa de Muerto**; the luxury sport-fishing magnet of **Bahía Piñas** (ⓦtropicstar .com), staffed primarily from the adjacent village of **Puerto Piñas**; and **Jaqué**, the last sizeable community before the Colombian border. Note that Bahía Piñas and Jaqué are the only places in the Darién accessible by **plane**.

Playa Muerto

Attractively situated amid serried ranks of coconut palms backing a chocolate swathe of sand, **PLAYA MUERTO** is the only Emberá community on the Pacific coast. Its gruesome name ("Beach of the Dead") derives from the corpses that used to wash ashore following sea-battles between bullion-laden Spanish galleons and pirate ships in colonial times. Isolated, and inaccessible by boat in winter, when the waves are huge, the village is well worth a visit; note that there is no **mobile phone** coverage. Beyond the village stocks – which are still used to punish wrongdoers – Playa Muerto has lost most of its traditions but the setting is attractive, and the pace relaxed. You can have your body painted in *jagua* dye, hike through the rainforest or take a short stroll to a nearby **waterfall** and natural pool.

ARRIVAL AND DEPARTURE   PLAYA MUERTO

By boat Boats from La Palma for Jaqué will call in at Playa Muerto provided sea conditions are favourable ($30) – they have to land passengers on the beach – as will the *Halcón* from Panama City (see opposite).
On foot A couple of Darién tour operators include the

overland two-day trek from Sambú or Garachiné (see p.286). Alternatively, you could arrange for a local community guide (and mule if you don't want to carry a pack) by contacting the authorities in Puerto Indio or Playa Muerto (see p.287 & below).

ACCOMMODATION

★**Community accommodation** At the back of the beach ☎ 386028 (satellite phone). Choose between a traditional, raised wood-and-thatch building with ocean-facing open sides (sleeps ten), or a smaller, two-person wooden *cabaña* with porch, slightly back from the beach.

Sleep on a mattress or in a hammock and watch the pelicans and the sunsets. Shared bathroom with flush toilet and cold-water showers. Simple meals are cooked in a villager's home ($4). $̲1̲2̲

Puerto Piñas

Less edgy and much smaller than the neighbouring frontier community of Jaqué, **PUERTO PIÑAS** has a more impressive setting, encircled by forested mountains, in a protected bay – the safest anchorage along this part of the coast – boasting a substantial beach and riverside location. From here you can organize a day-hike over the mountains to the cream-coloured sands of **Playa Blanca**, which offers sheltered **snorkelling**, or to the Wounaan village of **Biroquera,** from where it's a half-hour boat trip down to Jaqué.

Jaqué

Though actually around 40km from the Colombian border, **JAQUÉ** is Panama's Pacific border town, and as such heavily garrisoned – you'll need to check in with SENAFRONT. The three-thousand-strong mixed population, including many Colombians, live around a vague grid of cement paths. Though enlivened somewhat by the generous sprinkling of plantain, mango trees and coconut palms, Jaqué is still an unappealing place: heavily littered, with loud *cantinas* blaring out reggaeton and surprisingly lacking anywhere that serves coffee. Yet the setting is impressive, with the mountains of the Cordillera de Jungurudo forming a distant backdrop, a 4km stretch of beach pounded by surf, and a sweeping river-mouth rich in birdlife. Stroll along the sands, surf the waves, birdwatch or contract a boat to take you upstream to the Wounaan community of **Biroquera**, where you can sort out a place to sling up a hammock, or contract a guide to accompany you on a splendid three-hour **hike** to the fishing hamlet of Piña.

ARRIVAL AND INFORMATION   PUERTO PIÑAS AND JAQUÉ

By plane Air Panama (☏ 316 9000, ⓦ airpanama.com) operates mid-morning flights from Albrook Airport to Jaqué (Mon & Fri; 1hr 15min; $91 one way). Return flights to the capital leave on the same days, almost as soon as the plane has landed. There are also flights to Bahía Piñas.

By boat in Panama It is possible to catch a ride in a boat from La Palma to Jaqué or Puerto (around $50/person; 3–5hr, depending on the engine and the ocean conditions). The sea can be very rough, especially in the rainy season, so be sure to make the relevant safety checks beforehand (see p.28). Enquire at Terraplén, by the Mercado de Mariscos in Panama City, about departures on the *Halcón* (☏ 6846 4594 or ☏ 6523 0316), a new vessel that offers a bunk bed ($35; $30 bench seat only) for the 14hr voyage between Panama City and Jaqué (via Playa Muerto and Puerto

Piñas) every four or five days, depending on demand and ocean conditions. Snacks are sold on board, but it is best to bring your own food. The boat leaves on the second high tide of the day, so check the departure time the day before. Boat services to Colombia are planned.

By boat from Colombia There is currently no immigration office in Jaqué, so immigration formalities have to be undertaken on arrival in Panama City – at Balboa Yacht Club on the Amador Causeway – but your details will be taken by SENAFRONT at Jaqué's beach (the de facto port) on arrival.

Transfers Jaqué–Puerto Piñas Though only a small headland separates the two communities, the short hop by boat costs $10.

ACCOMMODATION AND EATING

PUERTO PIÑAS

Fonda Laura 200m down the cement path from the airstrip. You'll get a hearty welcome from the ebullient Laura as well as a tasty plateful of *mondongo* or chicken, rice and beans ($6). She also has rooms to rent, though usually for long-term lets. Daily 7am–8pm.

Hospedaje Nemecia By the church near the airstrip ☏ 6802 3808. Four neat, clean tiled-floor rooms, the odd frilly bedspread, plus a/c and satellite TV, and shared cold-water showers. $25

JAQUÉ

Fonda Alex On the main cement path, near the riverside SENAFRONT headquarters. Like everywhere

else in town, you won't get coffee and the menu has few options, but this friendly wood-and-thatch hut is still the pick of the *fondas*, serving reasonable platefuls of fish or chicken with plantain, rice and salad (around $6). Daily 7am–7pm.

Hospedaje Hermanas Hurtado 300m northeast of the SENAFRONT checkpoint ☏ 6000 9730. The only place to stay – until a rumoured new surf camp opens – is this extremely basic, wooden two-storey building with shared cold-water showers (plus a bucket in case of water outages), torn lino-covered floorboards, rusty fans and shutters. Beds are serviceable, however, with clean sheets. Bring your own mosquito net in the rainy season. $16

8

GOLD PLAQUE, COCLÉ PROVINCE

Contexts

History

Though the Republic of Panama is only a little over a century old, humans have lived on the isthmus for thousands of years. Its location as a slender bridge between two vast land masses has been as crucial to its development as its eventual link between two expanses of ocean.

Pre-Columbian society

Panama's scarce archeological remains give little clue to the societies that inhabited the region, in part because many early excavations were poorly executed and finds were damaged or looted. Lacking the huge structures and sophisticated carvings that epitomize the Maya, Aztec and Toltec civilizations of Mesoamerica, the trading societies of Central America have always taken a historical backseat. Yet central Panama boasts the earliest traces of **pottery-making** in the Americas with ceramics from Monagrillo, in the northern Azuero Peninsula, carbon-dated to 2500–1200 BC. A nearby fishing village in Sarigua is considered to be the isthmus's **oldest settlement**, dating from around 11,000 BC.

The most sophisticated societies inhabited central Panama, with the richest archeological finds in the **necropolis** of Sitio Conté, outside Penonomé. Excavations by American academics in the 1930s opened up around a hundred **tombs** to reveal thousands of intricate **gold pieces of jewellery** alongside sophisticated **polychrome ceramics** and other artefacts dating back to the first century, most of which were shipped off to the States.

At El Caño, near Natá, lies a **ceremonial site** believed to have become a cemetery dating from 500 to 1200 AD, though its original function and significance is unknown, not helped by the fact that a US adventurer decapitated more than a hundred basalt **standing stones**. In the Western Highlands, outside Volcán, another important site indicates the existence of what has been termed the **Barriles culture**, at its apogee around 500 to 600 AD, whose curious **stone statues** of a figure wearing a conical hat carrying another on his shoulders are on display at Panama City's anthropological museum (see p.63). A large **ceremonial grinding stone**, or *metate*, adorned with human heads – also in the museum – has led to speculation about human sacrifice. Sprinkled round Sitio Barriles and elsewhere in western and central Panama on moss-covered boulders are numerous **petroglyphs**; the largest is La Piedra Pintada outside El Valle.

Arrival of the Spanish

The first European credited with setting foot on the isthmus was the Spanish aristocratic notary **Rodrigo Galván de Bastidas**, who in 1501 made a low-key arrival, trading his way peacefully up the Caribbean coast as far as present-day Colón. In contrast, **Christopher Columbus** (Cristóbal Colón), who arrived a year later on his fourth and final voyage to the "New World", headed for the western and central Caribbean coast, keen to lay his hands on the legendary gold. He attempted to establish the first European settlement on

11,000 BC	2500–1200 BC	500–600 AD
The first settlement is established on the isthmus, a fishing village, in the Azuero Peninsula.	The earliest traces of pottery-making in the Americas are also found in the Azuero Peninsula.	An eruption by Volcán Barú is thought to have brought an end to the Barriles culture – one of the most important pre-Columbian societies.

CACIQUE URRACÁ

The most famous of three Guaymí (forefathers of the Ngäbe) heads in western Panama – the others being Natá and Parita, after whom the Spanish named settlements – was the mighty indigenous chief **Urracá**, who provided the colonizers' fiercest resistance over a nine-year period. Managing to unite tribe leaders who were traditional enemies, he conducted guerrilla-type raids from his mountain stronghold above Santa Fé de Veraguas. After repeatedly failing to defeat Urracá, the Spanish resorted to deception, luring him down to Natá under the pretence of negotiating a peace settlement. Here he was immediately seized and taken in chains to Nombre de Dios, from where he was to be deported to Spain. Managing to escape, he returned to his people, vowing to fight the invaders to the death. By this stage, however, the Spanish were so afraid of his warriors that they avoided conflict with them whenever possible, while the chief continued his resistance until he died in 1531.

---

the isthmus, prompting violent conflicts with indigenous populations. Though relations between Columbus and the local chief or *cacique*, **Quibián**, known as "El Señor de la Tierra", were initially friendly, the mood changed once it was clear the Spanish intended to stay. When Columbus left his garrison at Santa María de Belén (in present-day Veraguas) to seek reinforcements, Quibián rallied local leaders to destroy the settlement but was captured by Columbus's brother Bartolomé, who had been left in charge. While being transported as a prisoner downriver to Belén, the chief dived out of the dugout and was presumed drowned. He survived, however, and went on to lead an assault against the invaders, forcing them to flee.

The respite was short-lived. In 1505 the king of Spain, Ferdinand II, intent on expanding his empire, dispatched two men to take charge of what had been named "*Tierre Firme*" (extending from present-day Venezuela to Panama): **Alonso de Ojeda** was to govern the land between Cabo de la Vela in present-day Colombia through to the Golfo de Urabá, known as Nueva Andalucía, while **Diego de Nicuesa** was to oversee the west from the gulf to Gracias a Dios on what is now the border between Honduras and Nicaragua (and was known as Castilla de Oro, after its supposed riches). Both campaigns ended in disaster.

Though estimates of the indigenous population at the time of the Spanish conquest vary from two hundred thousand to two million, what is not in dispute is the speed at which the local communities were decimated, as much by **disease** brought by the conquistadors as through **massacre** and **enslavement**. The remainder retreated to inhospitable remote mountain areas, where they either lay low or continued their resistance against the invaders. The Spanish instituted a feudal-style system of **encomiendas**, theoretically entrusting "free" indigenous peoples to the stewardship of colonizers for their well-being and instruction in the Catholic faith in return for labour; in practice, workers were more often treated like slaves. Though the system was abolished in 1720, it did not spell the end of intense hardships for many of the rural population.

Balboa and the Mar del Sur

There's little in **Vasco Núñez de Balboa**'s inauspicious early life to suggest he would rise to prominence. After setting foot on the isthmus as a member of Bastidas's expedition, he settled on Hispaniola, where, failing as a pig-farmer, he fled his creditors by stowing

---

1501–02	1505	1513
Spanish explorers Rodrigo de Bastidas and Christopher Columbus visit modern-day Panama.	The Spanish conquest intensifies; indigenous populations are massacred or enslaved, though some resist.	Vasco Núñez de Balboa crosses Panama, becoming the first European to see the Pacific Ocean.

away on a boat bound for the mainland. Upon discovery, he was saved from being thrown off the ship thanks to his knowledge of the isthmus. As the incipient Spanish settlements struggled to survive, including the new regional centre **San Sebastián de Urabá**, founded by Ojeda, Balboa recommended relocating across the gulf. **Santa María de la Antigua del Darién** (on the other side of the current Panama–Colombia border) was thus established on a site that had been seized from followers of Cacique **Cémaco**, a pivotal figure in the indigenous resistance. It was the first successful Spanish settlement on the isthmus, eventually becoming the capital of **Castilla de Oro** until the seat transferred to Panama City in 1524.

Meanwhile Balboa continued his acquisition of power by subjugating, negotiating and making peace with local tribes. Hearing from the locals about another sea to the south and land dripping in gold and pearls, Balboa found a route through the forests of the Darién to become the first European to look out onto the **Pacific Ocean** on September 25, 1513. Several days later, in true imperialist fashion, Balboa waded into the water in full body armour, sword in one hand, statue of the Virgin Mary in the other, and claimed possession of the "Mar del Sur" in the name of the king of Spain. Yet he received scant reward for his "discovery" – in 1519 his jealous superior **Pedro Arias de Ávila**, known as Pedrarias the Cruel or *Furor Domini* (Wrath of God), the first governor of Castilla de Oro, had him beheaded.

Panama City and the Camino Real

In the face of appalling losses from disease, Pedrarias moved his base from the Caribbean side to the slightly more salubrious Pacific coast, where he **founded Panama City** (Panamá La Vieja) in 1519. The new settlement became the jumping-off point for further Spanish inroads north and south along the coast, and, after the conquest of Peru in 1533, it began to flourish as the transit point for the fabulous riches of the **Incas** on their way to fill the coffers of the Spanish Crown. From Panama City, cargo was transported across the isthmus on mules along the paved **Camino Real** to the ports of Nombre de Dios and later Portobelo, on the Caribbean coast. A second route, the **Camino de Cruces**, was used to transport heavier cargo to the highest navigable point on the Río Chagres, where it was transferred to dugout canoes to be carried downriver to the coast.

The flow of wealth attracted the attention of Spain's enemies, and the Caribbean coast was under constant threat from European **pirates**, the first of whom, the Englishman **Francis Drake**, successfully raided Nombre de Dios. He received support from the **cimarrones**, communities of escaped African slaves who lived in the jungle and often collaborated with pirates in ambushing mule trains and attacking their former masters. In the most daring assault, in 1671, Welshman **Henry Morgan** and his men sailed up the Río Chagres, having destroyed the fortress at San Lorenzo at the river-mouth en route, and crossed the isthmus to ransack Panama City. Though Morgan is generally blamed for the fire that then engulfed the place, it was more likely due to the detonation of the city's gunpowder supplies ordered by the defeated Spanish governor.

The city was rebuilt in 1673 on today's Casco Viejo behind defences so formidable that it was never taken again, but the raiding of the Caribbean coast continued until finally in 1746 Spain rerouted the treasure fleet around Cape Horn. With the route across the isthmus all but abandoned, Panama slipped into decline.

1519	1533	1595–1739
Panama City is founded on August 15 by conquistador Pedro Arias de Ávila (known as Pedrarias).	The Camino Real flourishes as the main transit route for plundered riches from South America bound for Spain.	The Spanish are constantly threatened by European pirates and privateers; Henry Morgan sacks Panamá Viejo in 1671.

Independence from Spain

By the turn of the nineteenth century independence movements in South America, headed by **Simón Bolívar** and **José de San Martín**, were gathering pace. Though the isthmus initially remained fairly detached from the process, it was not devoid of nationalist sentiment. On November 10, 1821, the tiny town of La Villa de Los Santos unilaterally declared that it would no longer be governed by Spain, in what was known as the *Primer Grito de la Independencia* (First Cry for Independence); the rest of the country followed suit, declaring **independence** on November 30. It retained the name of Panama, as a department of what historians have subsequently termed "Gran Colombia"; with the secession of Ecuador and Venezuela it quickly became Nueva Granada. Almost immediately conflicts emerged between the merchants of Panama City, eager to trade freely with the world, and the distant, protectionist governments in Bogotá, leading to numerous, if half-hearted, attempts at separation. As the century wore on, US influence asserted itself, most notably in the 1846 **Mallarino-Bidlack Treaty**, which granted the US government rights to build a railroad across the isthmus and, significantly, accorded them power to intervene militarily to suppress any secessionist uprisings against the New Granadan government – a theoretically mutually beneficial accord that was to seriously backfire on Bogotá.

The **discovery of gold** in California in 1849 sparked an explosion in traffic across the isthmus. Travel from the US east coast to California via Panama – by boat, overland on foot, and then by boat again – was far less arduous than the trek across North America, and thousands of "Forty-niners" passed through on their way to the goldfields. In 1850 a US company began the construction of a **railroad** across Panama. Carving a route through the inhospitable swamps and rainforests proved immensely difficult – thousands of the mostly Chinese and West Indian migrant workers died in the process – but when the railroad was completed in 1855, the Panama Railroad Company proved an instant financial success, earning $7 million in profit in the first six years, despite having cost $8 million to construct. The railroad also marked the beginning of a new

THE WATERMELON WAR

The completion of the **Panama Railroad** left many Panamanian labourers, including the new immigrant workforce, unemployed and resentful of their well-paid US counterparts, some of whom showed scant respect for their hosts or local customs. On April 15, 1856, tensions spilled over. An intoxicated (white) American named Jack Oliver, who had been killing time in the bars waiting for the boat, grabbed a slice of **watermelon** from a local (black) stallholder and refused to pay. When the trader drew a knife, Oliver's mate tossed a dime at him, further enraging the merchant, and as he advanced on Oliver, the latter drew a gun. An attempt to disarm the American resulted in a bystander getting shot, prompting a full-scale anti-US **riot**. Many Americans holed up in the railway depot and gunfire was exchanged with the crowd, which was attempting to batter down the door. Rather than control the situation, the **police** joined in the affray, which continued until a trainload of the vigilante **Isthmus Guard** arrived to disperse the mob. While the number of casualties in the so-called "Watermelon War" – seventeen dead and 29 wounded, predominantly American – was not disputed, blame for the violence was. Amid claims and counterclaims of racism, the US government dispatched two **warships** to Panama and occupied the railway station – albeit only for three days – but their demand for total control of the railroad was refused.

1746	1821	1830
Spain reroutes the treasure fleet around Cape Horn, resulting in economic decline.	Panama declares independence from Spain, and joins the confederacy of Gran Colombia (Bolivia, Peru, Ecuador, Venezuela, Colombia and Panama).	Panama becomes a province of Colombia after the dissolution of Gran Colombia.

era in foreign control: within a year, the first **US military intervention** in Panama had taken place (see box opposite).

The French canal venture

In 1869 the opening of the first transcontinental railway in the US reduced traffic through Panama, but the completion of the **Suez Canal** that same year made the long-standing dream of a canal across the isthmus a realistic possibility. Well aware of the strategic advantages such a waterway would offer, the French secured a concession to **build a canal**, as well as purchasing the Panama Railroad, from the New Granadan government. In 1881, led by ex-diplomat **Ferdinand de Lesseps**, the driving force responsible for the Suez Canal, the Compagnie Universelle du Canal Interocéanique began excavations.

Despite de Lesseps' vision and determination, the "venture of the century" proved to be a disaster, not least because of his technical ignorance and arrogance. In the face of impassable terrain – forests, swamps and the shifting shales of the continental divide – the proposed sea-level canal proved unfeasible, while yellow fever, malaria and a host of other unpleasant diseases ravaged the workforce. In 1889 the Compagnie collapsed; $287 million had evaporated as a result of financial mismanagement and corruption, implicating the highest levels of French society. Hundreds of thousands of ordinary French investors lost everything.

The War of the Thousand Days

At the end of the nineteenth century the simmering feud between the Conservative and Liberal parties erupted into a bloody three-year **civil war** called the **War of the Thousand Days** (*Guerra de los Mil Días*). Though there were ideological differences – ruling elite **Conservatives** supported strong central government, limited voting rights and close bonds between Church and State, whereas the merchant class and educated **Liberals** wanted more decentralized, federal government, universal voting rights and a greater division between Church and State – there were also many factions within each party. The violence was triggered by alleged election fraud by the landed Conservatives in their bid to remain in power, but by the time the bloody conflict had ended in 1902, claiming a hundred thousand lives, it was hard to pinpoint what much of the fighting had actually been about. It's also unclear whether key Liberal protagonists were motivated more by the desire for separation than social justice; regardless, most Liberals were subsequently elevated to the status of nationalist heroes.

The initial Liberal revolt was led by **Belisario Porras**, the popular exiled lawyer, who later won three periods of office as president of Panama. With the support of the presidents of Nicaragua and Ecuador, Porras entered western Panama on March 31, 1900, with an invasion force commanded by Colombian **Emiliano Herrera**, at the insistence of President Zelaya of Nicaragua. Their antagonism was a major factor in the ultimate Liberal failure. Moving towards Panama City, they gathered numerous supporters, but slow progress allowed reinforcements to arrive from Colombia. On arrival outside the capital, Herrera rejected Porras's attack plan and led a botched single-pronged assault on the city in which a thousand died. Though the Conservatives reasserted their authority, small bands of Liberal sympizers ran riot in the interior,

1850–55	1881	1902
The California Gold Rush prompts construction of the Panama Railroad across the isthmus.	French architect Ferdinand de Lesseps begins excavations for the Panama Canal. Some twenty thousand workers die before the venture is abandoned in 1889.	End of three-year civil war between the Conservative and Liberal parties – La *Guerra de los Mil Días* – which claimed one hundred thousand lives.

PEDRO PRESTÁN AND THE FIRE OF COLÓN

One of the uglier episodes in the factional feuding between Liberals and Conservatives occurred in 1885, with the public hanging of **Pedro Prestán**. Prestán, a Liberal revolutionary, had taken advantage of the absence of Colombian troops in Colón – they had headed over to Panama City to quell an attempted coup – by seizing control of the city. After looting businesses to raise money, he and his band of rebels purchased arms from the US, which arrived on a steamship anchored in the bay. When the ship agent refused to unload the arms, Prestán took the agent, US consul and several other Americans **hostage**, threatening to kill them if the US naval vessel stationed nearby landed troops and the arms were not handed over. Though the weapons were promised and the hostages released, the Americans reneged on the deal. Fleeing to Monkey Hill outside the city, Prestán and his poorly armed combatants got caught up with the Colombian troops now back from Panama City. The rebels were routed and the **city caught fire**; built of wood, it was totally destroyed, killing eighteen and leaving thousands homeless. Prestán, who had fled by boat to his native Cartagena, became the scapegoat. Many of his men were rounded up and **executed** while Prestán himself was captured, tried and convicted by a partisan jury, and left to hang above the railway tracks in Colón.

especially in the central rural areas under the leadership of **Victoriano Lorenzo**, a local official of mixed heritage from Coclé and a champion of the indigenous population.

In 1901, a second Nicaraguan-backed Liberal force managed to take Colón and effectively immobilize the railway, forcing the Colombian government to ask the US to broker an armistice. The Liberals, fearing intervention by the US government, agreed to the peace conditions but Lorenzo refused to accept the terms. In a sordid collusion between both Conservative and Liberal social elites, Lorenzo was tricked into capture. In disregard of the amnesty detailed in the accord, he was summarily tried and executed by firing squad on May 15, 1903, in the Plaza de Armas (today's Plaza de Francia) of Panama City. Six months later Panama separated from Colombia.

Separation from Colombia

Despite the French canal debacle, the dream of an interoceanic waterway remained as strong as ever. US President **Theodore Roosevelt**, in particular, felt that the construction of a canal across Central America was an essential step to becoming a major sea power. At first the favoured route was through Nicaragua, but the persuasive lobbying of Philippe **Bunau-Varilla**, former acting director and major shareholder in the French company, swung the Senate vote in Panama's favour. His masterstroke was to buy ninety Nicaraguan stamps that showed an erupting volcano – a major argument against the Nicaragua route – and send one to each senator just three days before the vote. In 1903 a **treaty** allowing the US to build the canal was negotiated with the Colombian government, whose senate refused to ratify it, understandably wary that the US would not respect their sovereignty. Outraged that "the Bogotá lot of jackrabbits should be allowed to bar one of the future highways of civilization", Roosevelt gave unofficial backing to Panamanian secessionists.

In the event, the **separation** was a swift almost bloodless affair with only one casualty. The small Colombian garrison in Panama City was bribed to switch sides and a second force that had landed at Colón agreed to return to Colombia without a fight after its

1903	1914	1925
Backed by the US, Panama declares separation from Colombia but essentially hands the US control of the future Canal Zone "in perpetuity".	The Canal is completed. Around 56,000 people from 97 countries have a hand in its construction.	The successful Dule Revolution results in the Guna people being promised a measure of cultural autonomy.

officers had been tricked into captivity by the rebels. On November 3, 1903, the **Republic of Panama** was declared and immediately recognized by the US, whose gunship standing offshore prevented Colombian reinforcements from landing to crush the rebellion.

The Canal

A new **canal treaty** was quickly negotiated and signed on Panama's behalf by the slippery Bunau-Varilla, who had managed to get himself appointed a special envoy, theoretically only with negotiating powers. The Hay-Bunau-Varilla Treaty gave the US "all the rights, power and authority … which [it] would possess and exercise as if it were the sovereign", in perpetuity over an area of territory – the **Canal Zone** – extending five miles (8km) either side of the canal. In return, the new Panamanian government received a one-off payment of $10 million and a further $250,000 a year. (Of particular interest to Bunau-Varilla was the $40 million the French canal company received for all its equipment and infrastructure.) Even American secretary of state John Hay admitted the treaty conditions were "vastly advantageous to the US and we must confess … not so advantageous to Panama". Panama's newly formed national assembly found the terms outrageous, but when told by Bunau-Varilla that US support would be withdrawn were they to reject it – a claim he invented on the spot – they ratified the treaty, and work on the Panama Canal began.

It took ten years, 56,000 workers from 97 countries and some $352 million to complete the task, an unprecedented triumph of organization, perseverance, engineering and, just as crucially, sanitation, during which time chief medical officer Colonel **William Gorgas** established a programme that **eliminated yellow fever** from the isthmus and brought malaria under control. As a result the **death toll** – though still numbering some 5600 workers, predominantly of West Indian descent – was substantially lower than it would otherwise have been. Meanwhile the two men in charge, **John Stevens**, a brilliant railway engineer, and his successor **George Goethals**, a former army engineer, managed to solve the problems that had stymied the French. The idea of a sea-level canal was quickly abandoned in favour of constructing a **series of locks** to raise ships up to a huge artificial lake formed by damming the mighty Río Chagres. Stevens was responsible for maximizing the potential of the railway, devising an ingenious pulley system that enabled them to excavate over 170 million cubic metres of earth and rock, three times the amount removed at Suez. The 13km **Gaillard Cut**, which ran through the continental divide, required a mind-boggling 27,000 tonnes of dynamite. The end result, overseen by Goethals, was the largest concrete structure, earth dam and artificial lake that the world had ever seen, accomplished with pioneering technology that set new standards for engineering. On August 15, 1914, the SS *Ancón* became the first ship to officially transit the Canal, which was completed six months ahead of schedule.

An enormous **migrant workforce**, at times outnumbering the combined populations of Panama City and Colón, was imported to work on the Canal's construction, and many of these workers – Indians, Europeans, Chinese and above all West Indians – stayed on after its completion, indelibly transforming the racial and cultural make-up of the country. Work was carried out under an apartheid labour system, where white Americans were paid in gold and the rest – the vast majority of whom were black – in silver. Employees were "**gold roll**" or "**silver roll**", a categorization that permeated every

1936	1940	1953
Despite a treaty limiting US rights, tensions continue to build between Panama and the US territory of the Canal Zone.	Fascist president Arnulfo Arias Madrid sets about disenfranchising Afro-Antillean and Chinese-Panamanians while pursuing racist immigration policies.	The first *comarca* is legally established in Panama under the authority of the Guna General Congress.

aspect of life. The gold roll employees and their families enjoyed higher wages, superior accommodation, better nutrition, health care and schooling; even toilets and drinking fountains were set aside for the exclusive use of one group or the other. Unsurprisingly, the mortality rate among black workers was four times higher than among whites.

The New Republic

Though their economy boomed during the Canal's construction, it was soon apparent to Panamanians that they had exchanged control by Bogotá for dominance by the US. The government, largely controlled by a ruling **oligarchy** known as the "twenty families", was independent in name only; the US controlled everything – trade, communications, water and security. Moreover, the de facto sovereignty and legal jurisdiction that the US enjoyed within the Canal Zone made it a strip of US territory in which Panamanians were denied the commercial and employment opportunities enjoyed by the US "**Zonians**", a situation that lasted well beyond the completion of the Canal. The US agreement to guarantee Panamanian independence came at the price of intervention whenever the US considered it necessary to "maintain order", a right they exercised on several occasions.

One such action followed the Dule or **Guna Revolution** in 1925, an eventual result of the Panamanian government refusing to recognize the relative autonomy granted by the Colombian authorities in 1870 through the Comarca Tulenega. Pressure mounted when outside groups were given concessions to plunder Guna resources and persistent attempts made to suppress Guna culture. Following an **armed revolt** led by Sailas (chiefs) Nele Kantule and Olokindibipilele (Simral Colman), which resulted in around twenty fatalities on each side, the Guna declared independence. Forestalling government retaliation, the US stepped in and mediated a **peace agreement** that granted the Guna the semiautonomous status they still retain.

The Republic of Panama's first president, the respected Conservative **Manuel Amador Guerrero**, was actually from Colombia, but the first Panamanian president of real impact was **Belisario Porras**, elected to office in 1912 for the first of three terms (1912–16, 1918–20 and 1920–24). A trained lawyer and prominent Liberal leader from the War of a Thousand Days, he is largely credited for establishing the basic infrastructure necessary for a newly independent state – roads, bridges, hospitals, schools, libraries, a legal system, communication networks and even the cherished national lottery.

The rise of nationalism

Despite a **new treaty** limiting the US right of intervention in 1936, resentment of American control became the dominant theme of Panamanian politics and the basis of an emerging sense of national identity. **Arnulfo Arias Madrid**, a fascist and Nazi-sympathizer – earning him the nickname "Führer Criollo" – exploited this while going on to become one of the country's most popular leaders. Of middle-class farming stock from Coclé, and a Harvard graduate, he founded Acción Communal, the political precursor to the Partido Nacional Revolucionario and present-day **Partido Panameñista (PP)**, which espoused his nationalistic and initially racist doctrine of **Panameñismo**. After assisting his older brother Harmodio Arias Madrid to the presidency in 1932, he won office himself in 1940, for the first of three periods (1940–41, 1949–51 and 1968).

1964	1968	1977
"Martyrs' Day" flag riots leave 21 Panamanians dead and more than five hundred injured.	Omar Torrijos, chief of the National Guard, overthrows President Arnulfo Arias and imposes a military dictatorship.	Torrijos secures a new canal treaty with US president Jimmy Carter, who agrees to transfer the Canal to Panamanian control in 1999.

During his first term he set about disenfranchising Afro-Antillean and Chinese-Panamanians and pursuing **racist** immigration policies. On the positive side he instigated the social security system, improved many workers' rights (a policy strand abandoned in his later term), modernized banking and gave the vote to women. Crucially, he was adamant about pushing for a better deal with a US government intent on expanding its military defences outside the Canal Zone. But the US-backed Panamanian Policía Nacional (National Police) and its successor, the Guardia Nacional (National Guard), made sure that no president who challenged the status quo lasted long in office and Arias was ousted by military coup each time, the last after only two weeks.

Nevertheless, **anti-US riots** erupted periodically over the next thirty years. The ten-thousand-strong protest in 1947 against the US attempt to extend the lease on World War II-era bases outside the Canal Zone helped persuade the deputies not to ratify the proposal. By 1948, the US military had withdrawn from outside the Zone. The most infamous disturbances, however, were the so-called **flag riots** of 1964. The flying of flags was a trivial but symbolic battleground for Panamanian-US antagonism. When the US flag was flown on its own for two days in succession in Balboa High School – not along with the Panamanian flag, as had been agreed – two hundred Panamanian students arrived at the school to rectify the situation. A skirmish broke out and the Panamanian flag was torn, prompting full-scale mob violence. The 21 Panamanians who died were later elevated to the status of **national martyrs**, commemorated annually on January 9, *Día de los Mártires* (Martyrs' Day).

Omar Torrijos and the new canal treaty

After a brief power struggle following the coup to oust Arnulfo Arias in 1968, Lieutenant Colonel **Omar Torrijos** of the National Guard established himself as leader of the new military government. Fracturing the political dominance of the white merchant oligarchy (known disparagingly as the *rabiblancos*, or "white tails") in his pursuit of a pragmatic middle way between socialism and capitalism, he was a charismatic, populist leader. Over twelve years he introduced a wide range of reforms – a new constitution and labour code, nationalization of the electricity and communications sectors, expanded public health and education services – while simultaneously maintaining good relations with the business sector, establishing Colón's **Zona Libra** and initiating the banking secrecy laws necessary for Panama's emergence as an international financial centre. Rather more darkly, he was extremely intolerant of political opposition and his critics were often imprisoned or simply "disappeared". Several **mass graves** from the period were unearthed during a Truth Commission instigated by President Moscoso, though there was no evidence of Torrijos' direct involvement in the atrocities.

Central to Torrijos' popular appeal was his insistence on gaining Panamanian control over the Canal. After lethargic negotiations with the Nixon and Ford administrations, Torrijos signed a new canal treaty with US president Jimmy Carter on September 7, 1977. Under its terms the US agreed to a gradual withdrawal, passing complete control of the Canal to Panama on December 31, 1999; in the meantime it was to be administered by the **Panama Canal Commission**, composed of five US and four Panamanian citizens. Even so, the US retained the right to intervene militarily if the

1983	**1988**
Colonel Manuel Noriega becomes de facto military ruler. He is initially supported by the US, but also cultivates drug-cartel connections.	US charges Noriega with rigging elections, drug smuggling and murder; Noriega declares state of emergency, dodging a coup and repressing opposition.

Canal's neutrality was threatened. Under pressure from Washington to democratize, Torrijos formed a political party, the **Partido Revolucionario Democrático (PRD)**, and began moving Panama towards free democratic elections. In 1981, however, he died in a plane crash, which was rumoured to have been plotted by the **CIA** or Colonel **Manuel Noriega**, Torrijos' former military intelligence chief.

Manuel Noriega and the US invasion

After a period of political uncertainty, Noriega took over as head of the National Guard, which he restructured as a personal power base and renamed the Fuerzas de Defensa de Panamá (**Panama Defence Forces** or **PDF**), becoming the de facto military ruler in 1983. Although the 1984 elections gave Panama its first directly elected leader in nearly two decades, Nicolás Ardito Barletta, the real power lay in the hands of **Noriega**, backed by the US government.

A career soldier, Panama's new military strongman had been on the US Army's payroll as early as the 1950s and the CIA's from the late 1960s, before becoming chief of intelligence for the National Guard in 1970. In the early 1980s, Noriega assisted the US by supporting its interests elsewhere in Central America, especially Nicaragua. Whereas Torrijos had supported the leftist Sandinistas in Nicaragua's civil war, Noriega allegedly provided covert US military support for the Contras, helping to funnel money and weapons to the guerrilla force – a charge he denies. At the same time, Noriega was busy building relations with the Colombian cocaine cartels in Medellín. Although this extracurricular activity was ignored by the US for years, in 1986 the **Iran-Contra Affair** – in which the US government sold weapons illicitly to Iran and used the proceeds to fund the Contras – brought an unwelcome glare of publicity on the cosy arrangement between Noriega and the CIA. Deciding it was politically expedient to drive Noriega from power, the US government began economic sanctions in 1987, followed by Noriega's indictment on drug charges in the US in February 1988.

On December 20, 1989, US president George H.W. Bush launched the ironically named "**Operation Just Cause**", and 27,000 US troops invaded Panama. They quickly overcame the minimal organized resistance offered by the PDF. Bombers, helicopter gunships and even untested stealth aircraft were used against an enemy with no air defences, and hundreds of explosions were recorded in the first twelve hours. The poor Panama City barrio of El Chorrillo was heavily bombed and burned to the ground, leaving some fifteen thousand people homeless; a Human Rights Watch report noted that civilian deaths were more than four times higher than military casualties among the PDF. Noriega himself evaded capture and took refuge in the papal nunciature, before being forced to surrender on January 5 after a round-the-clock diet of ear-splitting heavy metal and rock music blasted from the car park. He was taken to the US, **convicted of drug trafficking** and sentenced to forty years in a Miami jail.

Estimates of the number of Panamanians killed during the invasion vary from several hundred to as many as ten thousand. That the invasion was **illegal**, however, was clear: it was condemned as a violation of international law by the United Nations and the Organization of American States, both of which demanded the immediate withdrawal of US forces. Despite most Panamanians being relieved to see the back of Noriega, they were outraged at the excessive use of force and America's blatant disregard for Panamanian sovereignty.

1989	1992	1999
US troops invade Panama and oust Noriega, but also kill and leave homeless thousands of civilians.	US court finds Noriega guilty of drug charges, sentencing him to forty years in prison.	Mireya Moscoso, widow of Arnulfo Arias, becomes the country's first female president, and presides over the handover of the Canal to Panama in December.

PANAMA'S INDIGENOUS POPULATION

While Panama's national economy enjoys one of the highest growth rates in Latin America, the distribution of wealth remains highly skewed, the poorest twenty percent living below the poverty line, receiving less than 1.5 percent of the earnings. This includes most of Panama's 415,000 **indigenous citizens**, who comprise around thirteen percent of the total population according to the 2010 census. Some have been assimilated to varying degrees into urban life; most, though, inhabit the rural regions, with around half living in the various *comarcas* – semiautonomous areas demarcated by the state over the last sixty-plus years – many without access to clean water, health care, electricity, decent schooling or paid employment.

Panama has eight indigenous groups, the most numerous by far being the **Ngäbe** (180,000), who share a vast *comarca* in western Panama, spanning Bocas del Toro, Chiriquí and Veraguas, with the less numerous **Buglé** (ten thousand). The groups are culturally similar but speak mutually unintelligible languages. The first *comarca* established was Guna Yala in 1953, the result of a revolution by the **Tule** (or **Guna**) people (62,000) in 1925, which stretches out along the coastal strip of eastern Panama to the Colombian border, incorporating more than four hundred tiny islands. Much later, the smaller inland *comarcas* of Wargandi and Madugandi were added. The **Emberá** (23,000) and **Wounaan** (seven thousand) inhabit the forests of the Darién, though some have now migrated to the Chagres river basin nearer Panama City. Around 35 percent remain in the two *comarcas*; many others are scattered among around forty riverside communities across the province. At the other end of the isthmus in Bocas del Toro province, the **Naso**, also known as the Teribe, number just over three thousand and live around Changuinola and along the rivers heading up into the mountains. A few kilometres north, on the banks of the Río Sixaola, live the **Bri-Bri** (2500). The often forgotten **Bokota**, which number less than a thousand, are often mistakenly considered Buglé since they speak Buglere; they live around the Bocas–Veraguas provincial boundary in the Comarca Ngäbe-Buglé.

Suffering the highest levels of poverty, some Ngäbe and Buglé migrate for seasonal jobs on banana, coffee and sugar plantations to earn cash to sustain them the rest of the year. Guna, Emberá and Wounaan women, in particular, earn an income from their fine craftwork – though villages in remote areas more or less compete with each other for the small percentage of visitors who venture past Panama City and the Canal.

Although the *comarcas* cover a fifth of Panama's land, these territories as well as those of indigenous communities residing outside their boundaries are under constant **threat**. Some lands lie within national parks and reserves, which has enabled government, generally through MiAmbiente (and previously ANAM), to apply restrictions on traditional lifestyles in the name of conservation, while simultaneously allowing mining or hydroelectric projects to go ahead often with minimal or no consultation with indigenous authorities and no compensation to those forced to move. Government and big business are not the only threats: poor cattle farmers, *colonos*, desperate for fresh grazing land, have been encroaching on indigenous lands for years, particularly in eastern Panama.

By far the most **organized politically** are the Guna, who have had the greatest success in defending their rights against the state and possess three representatives at government level. The other main indigenous groups have tended to follow the Guna model, electing a **General Congress** consisting of a *cacique* and community representatives. Leaders from indigenous parties have begun working together to tackle attempts to marginalize them or incorporate them into models of development they do not espouse. In 2008, a petition listing indigenous peoples' grievances against the state was presented to the Inter-American Commission on Human Rights (IACHR). The resulting landmark victory for the Ngäbe living along the Río Changuinola, who secured an injunction to halt the dam threatening their village – albeit only temporarily – has been the only bright light in an otherwise bleak narrative.

2004

Martín Torrijos, son of former dictator Omar Torrijos, is elected president; plans for a Panama Canal expansion plan are passed with an overwhelming majority.

2009

Right-wing supermarket magnate Ricardo Martinelli becomes president after a landslide victory. Meanwhile, the government ignores a landmark IACHR ruling in favour of the Ngäbe, and continues working on the Río Changuinola dam.

The dawn of the twenty-first century

In an interesting twist, the presidential elections of 1999 were contested between Martín Torrijos, illegitimate son of the former military ruler, and the widow of Arnulfo Arias (the man Torrijos ousted in 1968), **Mireya Moscoso**, who became Panama's first female leader. On December 31 she presided over the seamless **handover of the Canal**, which is now efficiently managed by the independent Autoridad del Canal de Panamá. The US withdrawal was a mixed blessing for Panama's economy: many jobs disappeared with the closure of the bases, but the valuable real estate and infrastructure Panama inherited created investment opportunities. Still, a number of the former US buildings lie abandoned, and relations with the US remain complex.

Moscoso's term in office got off to a rocky start when, before the first budget vote, she gave Cartier watches and jewellery as "Christmas presents" to the 72 members of the legislative assembly. It set the tenor for the presidency, which was scarred with accusations of **corruption** and incompetence. Her term ended in similarly controversial fashion as she tried to push through construction of a tarred road linking Boquete and Cerro Punta through the national park of Volcán Barú. Opposition to the outrageous plan successfully united numerous national and international environmental groups and became a major election issue allowing **Martín Torrijos**, heading the PRD, to become president.

Though Torrijos junior was elected on a platform of "zero corruption" it did not take long before scandals started to emerge; nor was his administration's record on the environment particularly memorable, approving countless hydroelectric projects in Chiriquí and Bocas del Toro provinces with scant environmental assessment studies and little negotiation with the indigenous populations most affected. He did, however, help to tighten measures against drug trafficking and money laundering. And in his biggest gamble, he green-lighted the **Canal expansion** project (see box opposite).

To the present day

The elections in May 2009 broke the political stranglehold that the PRD and PP had enjoyed for the previous seventy years as conservative multimillionaire supermarket magnate **Ricardo Martinelli** swept to power. Head of the new **Cambio Democrático** (Democratic Change) party, he immediately launched popular initiatives, increasing the minimum wage, establishing pensions and ensuring free books and uniforms for school children. Panama enjoyed sustained economic growth – though the gap between the "haves" and "have-nots" continued to increase – and the government spent a staggering $20 billion on roads, schools and bridges across the country. In the capital countless skyscrapers sprang up, the new Metrobus and metro systems were established and the Cinta Costera – an ambitious land reclamation project – was extended, including a highly controversial ring-road round Casco Viejo.

However, as with Martinelli's predecessors, corruption scandals flourished and his increasingly autocratic ruling style, curtailment of the press and overuse of police force – especially against indigenous communities – provoked much criticism at home and internationally. In the 2014 elections, Martinelli's estranged vice-president, **Juan Carlos Varela**, who had fallen out with his former ally after being dismissed as foreign minister, won a surprising victory for the Partido Panameñista.

2011	2012
Silvia Carrera is elected the first female *cacique* of the Ngäbe. Noriega is extradited back to Panama, after prison terms in the US and France, to serve another twenty years.	Countrywide protests by the Ngäbe and Buglé over mining and hydroelectric concessions on their land end in police violence, leaving thousands wounded and three dead.

THE BILLION-DOLLAR GAMBLE: EXPANDING THE PANAMA CANAL

Two years overdue and several – as yet unspecified – billion dollars over budget, the **Panama Canal expansion** was finally inaugurated on June 26, 2016 amid much fanfare, fireworks and flag waving. The bold investment aimed to accommodate Post-Panamax vessels (ships that don't currently fit in the Canal) through two larger sets of locks and by widening the Culebra Cut, thereby tripling the size of the ships it can accommodate and doubling the Canal's capacity. Initially budgeted at $5.3 billion, with a completion date of 2014, to coincide with the Canal's centenary, the project has not been without its setbacks: for a start, the $1.6 billion in cost overruns are likely to keep the courts busy for years to come, as neither the Panamanian government nor the Spanish and Italian contractors are willing to foot the bill. Another concern is the huge amount of fresh water needed to ensure the smooth passage of the vast container ships through the Canal. Although the new Cocolí and Agua Clara locks include water-recycling devices, overall the Canal now needs twice the amount of water than it did previously, which, given current climatic variability, may prove difficult in the future. Add to that the economic uncertainty in world shipping, and it remains to be seen whether this massive investment will ultimately pay off. Unperturbed, the Canal authorities are already contemplating a **fourth set of locks**.

Meanwhile, the economic ramifications of the delayed and overbudget **Canal expansion** project, which was finally inaugurated in June 2016 (see box above), were compounded by a series of **huge corruption scandals**. Involving many of the country's elite, they ranged from the "**Panama Papers**" – a massive leak of Panama's offshore financial dealings that implicated numerous world leaders, criminals and celebrities in tax evasion – to revelations about successive governments' widespread acceptance of kickbacks in awarding mega-construction contracts. At the time of writing, former president Martinelli, for one, had been holed up in Miami since January 2015, evading charges of bribery, embezzlement, illegal phone-tapping and insider trading. His continued resistance to extradition seemed to generate greater public interest even than the **death of Manuel Noriega**, on May 29, 2017, whose passing President Varela tweeted "closes a chapter in our [Panama's] history."

The long-term, endemic lining of pockets by top government and business officials has diverted funds and attention away from addressing the Panamanian people's more pressing concerns: inadequate health, transport and education services; continued erosion of indigenous populations' rights; widening social inequalities; worsening environmental degradation and rising levels of unemployment and crime. In the wake of the scandals, 2017 witnessed widespread anticorruption and antigovernment street protests, but it remains to be seen whether popular opinion will succeed in kick-starting real social change.

2016

Overbudget and overdue, the new Panama Canal locks are inaugurated while spiralling corruption scandals threaten to undermine the country's financial credibility.

2017

Manuel Noriega dies following unsuccessful brain surgery.

Wildlife

One of Panama's major attractions is its varied and abundant wildlife. For its diminutive size – slightly larger than the Republic of Ireland, smaller than the US state of South Carolina – Panama's biodiversity and level of endemism is astounding. Located at the barely touching fingertips of two continents, the country hosts fauna from both land masses: deer and coyotes more readily associated with temperate North America as well as jaguars and capybaras from the tropical South, and a cornucopia of astounding marine life. The flora is equally diverse: an estimated ten thousand vascular plant species grow on the isthmus, predominantly in the country's luxuriant tropical rainforests, which cover an estimated 45 percent of the land.

Flora

Panama's **tropical wet forests**, or **rainforests**, which by definition receive an annual rainfall of more than 2m and can receive up to three times that amount on some of the Caribbean slopes, are what most excite nature-lovers. **Primary** rainforests – original, undisturbed growth – are highly prized for their greater biodiversity, comprising seventy percent of the country's forested area. In these complex ecosystems most animal and plant activity occurs in the forest "roof" or **canopy** and the **sub-canopy**, where dangling vines and lianas provide vital transport links. Poking out of the canopy, which filters out more than ninety percent of the sunlight, are a sprinkling of robust **emergent trees**, generally around 60–70m tall, able to withstand being buffeted by storms and scorched by sunlight. Most easily recognized, and visible from a great distance, is the ringed silvery grey trunk of the **cuipo** (*cavanillesia platanifolia*), which exhibits a bare umbrella-like crown during the dry season; particularly abundant in the Darién, it is a favourite nesting site of the harpy eagle. Equally distinctive from above is the lofty **guayacán** (*tabebuia guayacan*), whose brilliant golden crown stands out against the dense green canopy carpet, blooming a month in advance of the first rains. Not atypically, both species drop their leaves in the dry season to reduce water loss through evaporation. From the forest floor, the vast buttress roots of the **ceiba** (silk-cotton or kapok tree; *ceiba petandra*), or thinner versions on the **Panama tree** (*sterculia apetela*), are more striking; so, too, the vicious protective spines on the **spiny cedar** (*pachira quinata*), or the swollen midsection of the aptly named **barrigón** (*pseudobombax septenatum*) – *barriga* meaning "pot belly" in Spanish – which can double its waist size to store water and whose pretty pompom flowers open for evening pollination.

Dominated by vines, ferns, saplings and shrubs typically 10–25m tall, the forest **understorey** and **forest floor** below are relatively sparsely populated in the cathedral-like primary forest, in contrast to the dense and tangled vegetation of **secondary** forest. It's in these lower layers that you'll come across the pinkish hues of **heliconias**, such as the vividly named **lobster's claw** (*heliconia rostrata*), edged with yellow, and the more solid **beefsteak** (*heliconia mariae*), a "medium-rare" dark pink, or the pouting scarlet bracts of the Warholian **hotlips** (*psychotria poeppigiana*), which lure butterflies and hummingbirds to the almost invisible central flowers.

Topping the higher mountainous ridges, especially in western Panama, and almost permanently enveloped in mist, are dense patches of eerie fern-filled **cloud forest**, characterized by shorter, stockier trees covered in **lichen** and dripping with **mosses**. Boughs here are more heavily laden with **epiphytes**, including many of Panama's thousand-plus species of delicate **orchid** and **bromeliads**, whose leaves trap moisture, providing water for numerous tree-dwelling organisms. Back down on the coast, some 1700 square kilometres of mostly **red, white** and **black mangroves** constitute a vital buffer zone, serving both terrestrial and marine ecologies.

Fauna

Though most visitors yearn to catch sight of a jaguar or tapir, you'll likely have to settle for smaller **mammals** and the less elusive members of the **avian** and **amphibian** populations, which can be just as fascinating.

Birds

Panama lays claim to more than 990 recorded species of **bird**, more than Canada and the US combined, and greater than any Central American state. The 17km Camino del Oleoducto (Pipeline Road) in the former Canal Zone alone boasts a species list of more than four hundred. Even Panama City harbours egrets to elaenias, parakeets to pelicans: avian-rich locations within the greater city boundaries include the Metropolitan and other parks, Panamá Viejo, the Amador Causeway and round Cerro Ancón and Balboa.

Acting as a continental funnel, Panama sees many **migrants**, with numbers peaking in September and October and returning in more dispersed fashion from March to May. During this period, more than a million shore birds carpet the Pacific coastal mud flats, though it is the **raptor migration** that captures the imagination. Hundreds of thousands of **turkey vultures**, interspersed with **Swainson's** and **broad-winged hawks**, ride the thermals, wheeling their way along the isthmus (late Oct to Nov), a spectacular sight best appreciated from the summit of Cerro Ancón or one of Gamboa's several canopy lookouts.

While twitchers may get excited locating a dull-coloured rare endemic in the undergrowth, average nature-lovers will be more impressed by the visually dazzling birds. The cloud forests of Chiriquí afford an unparalleled opportunity to spot the iridescent emerald-and-crimson **resplendent quetzal** – especially visible and striking during spring courtship displays – while the Darién jungle maintains a similar reputation for the **harpy eagle**, Panama's gigantic national bird and arguably the world's most powerful raptor, with its distinctive tousled crest and ferocious giant talons (see box, p.285). Other glamour birds include the country's multicoloured, raucous **parrots** (*loros*), including five species of endangered **macaw** (*guacamaya*). Sadly depleted through the pet trade, loss of habitat and hunting – their flashy tail feathers make a customary adornment for some traditional costumes and dances – they have been forced into more remote areas, with the **scarlet macaw** making its last stand on the island of Coiba. Panama's seven varieties of **toucan** (*tucán*), including toucanets and aracaris, are another psychedelic feature of the landscape; their oversized rainbow-coloured bills help pluck hard-to-reach berries and regulate body temperature. Abundant in the Canal area and round Cerro Ancón, they are most easily spotted croaking in the canopy early morning or late afternoon. Panama's 55 types of **hummingbird** (*colibrí*) are spellbinding as they hover round flowers and feeders as if suspended in air, or whizz past your ear at some 50km/h. Lustrous **tanagers**, smart **trogans** and the distinctive racquet-tailed **motmots** will also turn heads.

Some birds are more notable for their behaviour: **jacanas**, whose vast, spindly feet enable them to stride across floating vegetation, are nicknamed "lily-trotters"; minute fluffy **manakins** conduct manic acrobatic courtship displays in their communal mating arenas known as *leks*; and the prehistoric-looking **potoo** is a nocturnal insectivore that camouflages itself on the end of a tree stump during the day, invisible to would-be predators. Spend enough time in the Western Highlands, especially in the breeding season (March–Sept), and you're likely to hear the distinctly unbell-like metallic "boing" of the strange-looking **three-wattled bellbird** complete with what look like strands of liquorice hanging from its beak; audible from almost a kilometre away, it is considered one of the loudest bird songs on earth. Mention should also be made of the ubiquitous **oropendola** (gold pendulum); these large, generally russet-toned birds, with outsize pointed beaks and golden tails, are renowned for their colonies of skilfully woven hanging nests, which dangle from tall trees like Christmas decorations.

Terrestrial mammals

Spotting any of Panama's 230-plus mammal species – half of which are small **bats** – requires luck and persistence and is nigh on impossible when it comes to Panama's "big five" wild cats, which in descending size order are the **jaguar**, **puma**, **jaguarundi**, **ocelot** and **margay**. Nocturnal and shy at the best of times, from years of human predation, they are most numerous in the country's two remaining wilderness areas at either end of the isthmus: the Darién and Amistad.

Spotting tracks in the morning mud is the closest you're likely to get to a jaguar in the wild. Referred to as a "*tigre*" (tiger) by indigenous populations and revered as a symbol of power and strength, the jaguar is the world's third largest feline after the lion and tiger, weighing in at around 60–90kg, and with leopard-like markings. It's more probable you'll encounter its dinner, be it **deer** (*venado*), the raccoon-like **coati** (*gato solo*) or large rodents such as the **agouti** (*ñeque*) or the nocturnal **paca** (*conejo pintado*, literally "painted rabbit" on account of its white spots). Panama also harbours the world's largest rodent, the **capybara**, which can tip the scales at 65kg; resembling a giant guinea pig, it wallows in the shallows round Gamboa and grazes at Punta Patiño, in the Darién. A more ambitious feature of the jaguar's diet is the **peccary**, a kind of wild boar. Two barely distinguishable species forage through the rainforest undergrowth in Panama: the more frequently seen **collared** peccary (*saíno*), which lives in small herds, and the elusive, aggressive **white-lipped** peccary (*puerco de monte*), which can travel in battalions of several hundred and be dangerous when threatened.

One of the largest, most extraordinary-looking mammals in the Neotropics is **Baird's tapir** (*macho de monte*). Another endangered nocturnal creature, it resembles an overgrown pig with a sawn-off elephant's trunk stuck on its face, which is actually a stubby prehensile nose and upper lip used to grip branches and eat the leaves and fruit. Though the adults are dull brown, baby tapirs have spotted and striped coats for camouflage. More commonly espied are **sloths** (*perezosos*) and **anteaters** (*hormigueros*), both of which arrived on the planet shortly after the demise of dinosaurs. Panama's **two-toed** and **three-toed** sloths spend much of their time literally hanging around treetops, either curled round a branch camouflaged as an ants' nest, or gripping with their long curved claws, doing everything in slow motion to conserve energy. Inexplicably, they make a near-suicidal descent to ground level once a week to defecate. In contrast, the **northern tamandua**, a type of anteater, moves nimbly along the branches, hoovering up ants and termites. Not an uncommon sight in the Metropolitan Park, even though mainly nocturnal, they are widespread across the country, whereas the wholly terrestrial **giant anteater** is verging on extinction nationally, as is the **spectacled bear**, named after the cream-coloured markings around its eyes.

Monkeys are an almost guaranteed sighting in Panama, which hosts all seven Central American species. A distinctive feature of the tropical landscape, the large, shaggy **mantled howler monkey** (*aullador negro*) is more likely to be heard before being seen; the ape's stentorian cries travel for kilometres, with large troops announcing dawn and dusk and even the onset of heavy rain. The other two more widespread species are the cherub-like **Geoffroy's tamarin** (*mono tití*), found in central and eastern Panama, and the larger, highly intelligent **white-throated capuchin** (*mono cariblanco*). Named for their physical resemblance to brown-robed Capuchin friars, though also somewhat misleadingly dubbed "white-headed" or "white-faced", the monkey's pink anthropomorphic face makes it a popular pet. Catching sight of a troop of **black-headed spider monkeys** (*mono araña negro*) – one of several types of endangered Panamanian spider monkey – elegantly gliding through the canopies of eastern Panama is a magical experience. At the other end of the isthmus, the **owl** or **night monkeys** (*mono de noche*), with their saucer-like eyes, are restricted to the Caribbean lowlands of Bocas, while over on the Pacific side, the delicate **squirrel monkey** (*mono ardilla*) is occasionally sighted in the Burica Peninsula in southwestern Chiriquí.

Reptiles

Mention the fact that you intend to hike in the jungle, and someone is bound to alert you to the dangers of **snakes**, though a relatively small percentage are venomous and snakebites are rare – most serpents are as wary of humans as humans are of them. The most feared, accounting for almost all fatal snakebites in Panama, is the **fer-de-lance** pit viper, which inhabits a variety of lowland habitats. Commonly dubbed "*equis*" ("X") for the markings on its well-camouflaged brown, cream and black skin, it often exceeds 2m in length. The female gives birth to fifty to eighty live young, which incredibly are already 30cm, not to mention venomous, when born. Initially arboreal, feeding on frogs and lizards, they become terrestrial with age. The world's largest pit viper, the dangerous **bushmaster**, can reach 3m, but fortunately is only encountered in remote forests and, like most pit vipers, is nocturnal. In contrast, Panama's various species of **coral snake**, both venomous and benign, all possess striking black, red and yellow-banded markings; since it's difficult to differentiate among them, it's best to assume danger. Positively mellow in comparison – though packing a powerful bite if provoked – the giant **boa constrictor** is Panama's only endangered snake, hunted for its prized skin.

Similarly threatened is the **green iguana**, which ranges from lime-green to dusty brown in colour and is pursued for its eggs and tasty meat, earning it the nickname "*gallina de palo*". Despite its dragon-like appearance, it is a docile forest-living herbivore that likes to be near water; the large flaps of skin under its chin (dewflaps) are used to regulate body temperature and for courtship and territorial displays. The tetchier, charcoal-grey **spiny-tailed** or **black iguana** is most commonly found on the Azuero Peninsula. The world's fastest lizard, it escapes predators by hitting speeds of up to 35km/h; the miniature version, a 30cm **basilisk**, takes flight across water on its hind legs and partially webbed feet, earning it the nickname "**Jesus Christ**" lizard.

In Panama's mangrove-filled estuaries and mud-lined waterways, including around Lago Gatún and Lago Bayano, **crocs** and **caimans** lurk. The endangered, aggressive **American crocodile** has actually increased its numbers here, as has the smaller, more docile **spectacled caiman**.

Amphibians

Of all Panama's amphibians, **frogs** are the most compelling. The country's emblematic and revered **golden frog** (see box, p.136) is, sadly, under grave threat due in part to the **chytrid fungus**, which has been decimating amphibians worldwide; this has prompted an Amphibian Ark rescue mission (🅦amphibianrescue.org) to seek out healthy specimens to breed in captivity (see p.136). The brilliantly coloured miniature **poison dart frogs**, with markings as varied as wallpaper, are relatively easy to see, especially in Bocas del Toro (see box, p.233), as they hop around the leaf litter under trees by day. But the rainforests harbour other equally extraordinary specimens, less visible since they're primarily nocturnal: the tiny lime-green **glass frog**, whose inexplicably transparent belly affords you the dubious pleasure of observing its viscera and digestive processes; the **flying frog** with giant webbed feet that help parachute it through the air; and the **milk frog** – so named after the toxic mucous it secretes when threatened – which possesses two giant vocal sacs either side of the head that also act as buoyancy aids in water.

Insects and arachnids

Although **insects** don't generally set the pulse racing, **butterflies** are the exception. With sixteen thousand species, Panama hosts approximately ten percent of the world's Lepidoptera, from the enormous **owl butterfly**, so-called after the large "eyes" on its mottled brown wings, to the tiny delicate **glasswing**, whose translucent wings are reminiscent of a stained-glass window. Most magnificent of all, is the iridescent **blue morpho**, whose drunken zigzagged flight makes it particularly hard to photograph.

Ants can be found in abundance; tiny Isla Barro Colorado alone has 225 species. Most distinctive are the packed highways of industrious **leafcutter** ants bearing enormous segments of leaf to their vast underground complex, where they are pulped to cultivate a "fungus garden", which in turn feeds the ants. Also easy to spot is the enormous black **bullet ant**; the size of a large grape and prevalent in low-lying forests, it holds the dubious distinction of causing the world's most painful insect sting.

Panama also possesses more than a thousand species of **spider**, a fair proportion of which are poisonous though rarely lethal to humans. One such is the innocuous-sounding **wandering spider** – until you realize its scientific name derives from the Greek for "murderous" (*phoneutes*) – which is a hairy arachnid that stalks the forest floor at night rather than ambushing prey in a web or lair. It is often mistaken for the stockier, hairier and relatively harmless **black tarantula**; also a night-time predator, it can be seen poking out of its lair, in a hollowed-out log or semi-submerged under leaf litter, during the day. Worth avoiding is the female **black widow spider**; recognizable by the glossy black abdomen and red hourglass mark on the underbelly, she has a potent venom with which to inject her prey. The **golden silk orb-weaving spider** makes the largest web; a magical sight on a sunlit morning in the rainforest, it really does glisten like gold thread.

Marine life

With coastlines on two oceans, Panama's **marine biodiversity** is impressive, especially where warm ocean currents and upwellings of cool nutrient-rich waters converge along the Pacific's Golfo de Chiriquí. **Humpback whales** calve in this area (July–Oct) and can also be sighted off the Pearl Islands and the tip of the Azuero Peninsula. These 15m giants are exciting to behold though **whale watching** in Panama is in its infancy. Earlier in the year (Feb–July), you may be lucky enough to catch sight of the gargantuan but placid **whale shark**, the world's largest fish, as it moves submarine-like through the waters round Coiba. **Hammerhead** and **tiger** sharks are occasionally spotted though **white-tipped reef** sharks are more common. The distinctive black-and-white **killer whales**, or **orcas** – actually the world's largest dolphin – prey on younger and weaker marine mammals, but aren't as widespread as **bottle-nosed** dolphins. From October to December schools of diamond-shaped **golden rays** glide like floating autumn leaves, occasionally leaping 2m into the air, as do more solitary **manta** rays; boasting a colossal 6m wingspan, one weighs as much as a small car.

In general the Pacific coast boasts a greater number of large fish – **blue** and **black marlin**, **amberjack**, **wahoo**, **dorado** and **tuna**, to name a few – while the **coral reefs** on the Caribbean side, particularly around the archipelago of Bocas del Toro and parts of Guna Yala, are populated with a greater variety of soft and hard corals. These feed and shelter aquatic life from sinuous **moray eels** and spiky **sea urchins** to delicate **sea horses** and a rainbow of dazzling fish. Iridescent **parrot fish** (30–50cm) are among the most distinctive, named less for their technicolour coats than for their serrated parrot-like "beaks" that gnaw algae and coral polyps off the reef. The ground coral is digested and excreted as sand – up to an estimated 90kg per fish annually – a major factor in the formation of Panama's glorious **white-sand beaches**. The Caribbean's other mammalian draw is the **manatee**, or sea cow, an amiable elephantine herbivore with a paddle-like rudder and flabby fleshy snout, found in the Humedales de San San Pond Sak in Bocas del Toro.

Five species of **marine turtle** lay their eggs on both Atlantic and Pacific shores, roughly between March and October/November – timings depend on species and location (see box, p.236). In the Caribbean, Bocas del Toro is the easiest place to visit **hawksbill**, **leatherback** and, to a lesser extent, **green** turtle nesting sites while **loggerheads** frequent the shallows. On the Pacific side, Isla de Cañas, off the Azuero Peninsula, is renowned for the mass **olive ridley** nesting (May–Nov), though the other species also deposit their eggs there in smaller numbers.

Environmental issues

As elsewhere in the tropics, the rainforests of Panama are disappearing at an alarming rate, threatening wildlife and, ultimately, human survival. While 45 percent of the country is still covered in forest, and deforestation rates have slowed since the millennium, the country is losing around one percent of its species-rich primary growth a year. A third of the land lies in national parks and reserves, but many of these are "paper parks" since the perennially underfunded Ministry of the Environment is short of cash and, in some cases, political clout and/or the will to enforce the regulations.

Deforestation

Although the large-scale extraction of mahogany, cedar or purpleheart destined for European and North American markets has come under greater control in recent years, the timber industry continues to be a major contributor to **deforestation** as illegal logging, and more insidiously, selective thinning continues.

By far the main driver of deforestation is **colonization**, clearing the land for cattle ranching and subsistence agriculture, and more recently, palm oil cultivation. Having already denuded the entire Azuero Peninsula and most of the Pacific slopes of central and western Panama, *colonos*, or "colonists", have been moving into eastern Panama in recent years along the Darién highway and Caribbean coast, sometimes into protected areas, often with the collusion of government officials. Despite the richness of tropical forests, the layer of nutritious topsoil is particularly thin so that once cleared it soon becomes worthless, forcing farmers to move on to fell new areas. Though usually contesting this encroachment onto their lands, some indigenous communities are also contributing to deforestation thanks to population increases and forced changes in lifestyle; in some cash-strapped settlements they are even leasing land to farmers for cattle grazing or colluding with illegal timber extraction. Panama's coastal mangrove forests – considered to be the most extensive, healthiest and most diverse in all Central America – are critically threatened, from agricultural expansion and coastal development on the mainland and water pollution, overfishing and sedimentation on the islands and marine areas.

Small-scale initiatives across the country aim to improve **environmental awareness**, ranging from assistance for micro-enterprises such as plant nurseries and agroforestry projects to tree-planting and recycling, often backed by NGOs and international environmental organizations. One such programme, started in 2003, was supported through Fundación Nacional Parque Chagres, the result of a "debt-for-nature" swap whereby $10 million of debt to the US government was eradicated over a 14-year period in return for the Panamanian government banks spending $700,000 annually on green-oriented projects and education. Of course it's no coincidence that the focus was the Chagres river basin, which is vital to the functioning of the Panama Canal, the lifeblood of Panama's economy and not insignificant to the US.

Reforestation programmes in Panama have become more common in the last few years. Initially they were all teak plantations, which arguably further degrade the soil, do nothing to sustain biodiversity and, being a monoculture, are more susceptible to disease; however, there has been a positive recent move towards more sustainable mixed plantations of native species. The Azuero Earth Project (ⓦazueroearthproject.org), another Panama–US collaboration, is attempting to establish a biological corridor in the Azuero Peninsula, working with local landowners to regenerate tropical dry forest, as well as carry out community outreach and education programmes.

Mining and hydroelectric projects

Another area of environmental concern is the **mining industry**. After the hiatus in mineral exploitation during the 1990s due to its unprofitability, prices have begun to rise again, and the threat looms once more. In 2008, Panamanian environmental watchdog CIAM (Centro de Incidencia Ambiental) revealed that the amount of land involved in mining concessions that had either already been granted or were awaiting consideration totalled three times the country's surface area. Though many projects have not yet been realized or have stalled since then, significant degradation has been caused by those mining operations that have been pushed through. Top of the list of offenders is the vast Petaquilla open-cast copper and gold mine in Colón province, which restarted operations despite still owing $2 million in fines and damages for environmental negligence and trampling on local people's rights. Although the mine is now bankrupt and its CEO, "father of Panamanian mining" Richard Fifer, is behind bars for non-payment of employees' social security, the damage has been done.

Cerro Colorado, potentially one of the world's largest copper mines, lies in the middle of the Comarca Ngäbe-Buglé, where the indigenous population is also defending its territory against the many **micro-hydroelectric projects** underway or planned for western Panama – more than seventy in Chiriquí at the last count – one of which has already resulted in intervention by the Interamerican Human Rights Commission. In 2012, the Ngäbe and Buglé managed to bring the country's economy to a standstill by blocking the Interamericana for six days, though the protest ended in violence as the police were sent in, leaving at least three dead and many wounded.

Thankfully, Panama is now also looking towards alternative, more renewable energy sources, establishing its first wind farm outside Penonomé in Coclé province in 2015 – the largest in Central America – as well as a huge photovoltaic power station on the Azuero Peninsula.

Tourism and environmental impact

It's a difficult balance between promoting tourism and limiting its environmental and social impact. **Indigenous communities** are being encouraged to engage in **cultural ecotourism**, inviting visitors to learn about their traditional ways of life and selling their handicrafts. With little financial support from the government, some groups have benefited from assistance from NGOs or local Peace Corps workers. Emberá communities along the Chagres, in particular, have gained valuable income from cruise-ship tours and day-trip groups from travel agencies in Panama City because of their proximity to the capital. But the long-term effect when large groups swamp small villages in high season, eroding the land and tramping en masse down the same rainforest trail, is more difficult to gauge. Moreover, the impact on the marine environment of the cruise-ship industry – the area of tourism in which the government has invested most heavily – is also unknown.

Visitor numbers are small in most indigenous communities that engage with tourism, except in the western end of **Guna Yala**. This is partly due to the road across the cordillera from the Panamerican Highway, which has allowed faster, cheaper access. Day-tripping Panamanians and beach-loving backpackers make up the bulk of the visitors: for small, overpopulated islands with inadequate sanitation and often ad hoc waste disposal, there's untold pressure on the natural resources. The beautiful islands of **Bocas del Toro**, the most visited region outside the capital and Canal area, suffer from similar problems as water, sanitation and electricity systems struggle to cope with pressure from high visitor numbers and the substantial expat population. On the positive side, turtle watching is taking off here, and in other areas of Panama, which as an income-generating project might eventually help protect their nesting sites.

Books

Bookshops are far from plentiful in Panama. Most are located in Panama City (see p.86), generally stocking a small, pricey selection in English. The colossus of contemporary Panamanian literature is Enrique Jaramillo Levi – internationally acclaimed short-story writer, poet, essayist, editor and critic, who, despite such accolades, has had relatively few works translated into English. New authors, such as Afro-Panamanian Melanie Taylor Herrera, have short stories and poetry translated into English scattered round various journals, some of which are accessible online.

THE CANAL

Rosa Maria Britton and Eduardo Montaina *The New Panama Canal: A Breathtaking Journey Between the Pacific and Atlantic Oceans*. Expensive coffee-table book published to mark the 2016 opening of the expansion of the Canal, offering spectacular colour photos and stunning views.

William Friar *Portrait of the Panama Canal: Celebrating its history and expansion*. Updated edition to include the recent Canal expansion, this readable account by former Zonian and *New York Times* journalist is a paperback coffee-table offering containing a few wonderful historical photos as well as some more mundane contemporary glossies of the Canal and Panama.

★ **Julie Greene** *The Canal Builders: Making America's Empire at the Panama Canal*. Long overdue focus on the men and women who, in dreadful conditions and facing all sorts of discrimination, worked to achieve the realization of America's grandiose dream of empire. You also meet the big players whose ambition ignored the human cost.

Ulrich Keller *The Building of the Canal in Historic Photographs*. A clear case of pictures speaking louder than words, as 164 detailed black-and-white photos evoke the lives of both rich and poor engaged in the monumental struggle to build the Canal.

★ **David McCullough** *The Path Between the Seas: The Creation of the Panama Canal, 1870–1914*. Though this is a detailed scholarly work of seven hundred pages, the plot-twisting narrative and larger-than-life characters sweep the reader along, together with a focus on understanding the underlying causes of events.

★ **Matthew Parker** *Hell's Gorge: The Battle to Build the Panama Canal* (also published as *Panama Fever*). A gripping account of the struggle with jungle, disease, engineering impossibilities and disastrous ignorance, which is a meticulously researched yet wide-ranging narrative that focuses on the oft-neglected labour force that lived and died digging the Big Ditch.

OTHER HISTORY AND POLITICS

Kevin Buckley *Panama*. Written by a former *Newsweek* correspondent, this book provides what many consider to be the most reliable account of events leading up to the US invasion of Panama in 1989. Buckley vividly brings the complex web of corruption and political intrigue to life.

Peter Earle *The Sack of Panama: Captain Morgan and the Battle for the Caribbean*. Swashbuckling account of the real-life pirates of the Caribbean and the Spaniards' efforts to defeat them, focusing on the Welsh privateer Henry Morgan and his exploits, culminating in the sack of Panama in 1671.

John Esquemeling *The Pirates of Panama: True Account of the Famous Adventures and Daring Deeds of Sir Henry Morgan and Other Notorious Freebooters*. Based on a lively firsthand account originally written in Dutch, the first English edition was published in 1684. The author was barber surgeon to Henry Morgan and accompanied him on his notorious expedition against Panama City.

Aims McGuinness *Path of Empire: Panama and the Californian Gold Rush*. A look at the key role played by the isthmus during the Gold Rush in the mid-1800s as the fastest link between New York and San Francisco, the consequences of building the Panama Railroad and the first of many military interventions by the US.

Bastian Obermayer and Frederik Obermaier *The Panama Papers: Breaking the Story of How the Rich and Powerful Hide Their Money*. Both gripping and disheartening in equal measure. Insights into the exposé on how the global political, commercial and celebrity elite use perfectly legal offshore accounts for tax avoidance, while their funds are used to launder drug money.

Andrew Parkin *Flames of Panama: The True Story of a Forgotten Hero, Pedro Prestán*. Dramatized true story of a lawyer of mixed heritage who rose to eminence in Colón and became a member of the Assembly, only to be hanged as a leader of rebel forces, falsely accused of burning Colón to the ground in 1885. A poignant tale that would have worked better as a factual account.

John Lindsay Poland *Emperors in the Jungle: The Hidden History of the US in Panama*. A human-rights campaigner and investigative journalist explores the role of the US military in Panama and the dubious uses to which it put the land it acquired.

John Prebble *The Darien Disaster*. Highly detailed and often turgid exploration of the doomed attempt by the Scots to colonize the Darién. The minutiae, such as the numbers of cases of rum loaded onto the ships, obscure the depth of the tragedy that bankrupted Scotland.

Sonja Watson *The Politics of Race in Panama*. This thoughtful, scholarly work, which examines the way that race and identity are inscribed differently by authors from the Afro-Caribbean and Afro-Hispanic communities, leads you to wish more of these authors' writings were available in English.

John Week and Phil Gunson *Panama: Made in the USA*. Written in 1991, this much-praised analysis of the 1989 American invasion of Panama and its historical background deals with the legal implications and political consequences, while shining a light on the part Noriega played leading up to the attack.

GUNA CULTURE

James Howe *Chiefs, Scribes and Ethnographers: Kuna Culture from Inside and Out*. Written by a professor of anthropology who has spent considerable time among the Guna over a 35-year period, this recent book deals with accounts that the Guna chiefs themselves have given of their life and culture. Like his previous books – *A People Who Would not Kneel: Panama, the United States and the San Blas Kuna* and *The Kuna Gathering: Contemporary Village Politics in Panama* – it's a serious but rewarding read.

★ **Salvador Mary Lyn (ed.)** *The Art of Being Kuna: Layers of Meaning among the Kuna of Panama*. Glossy coffee-table book full of fascinating photos and scholarly insights on the interweaving of Guna art, culture and environment.

Michael Perrin *Magnificent Molas*. Lavishly illustrated, this book explores the *molas* or fabric "paintings" of the

Guna women, tracing the links between the patterns used and traditions and rituals in the lives of the women.

Joel Sherzer *Stories, Myths, Chants and Songs of the Kuna Indians*. The author, a linguistic anthropologist, lived among the Guna people photographing and recording their oral tradition of songs and ritual performances. He reveals their close association with plants and animals and their belief in myths and magic.

Jorge Ventocilla, Heraclio Herrera and Valerio Nuñez *Plants and Animals in the Life of the Kuna*. Written by two Guna biologists and a Panamanian colleague, this book is aimed at the Guna reader as well as outsiders, providing fascinating insights into the Guna perspective on ecology and cosmology as they relate to environmental issues.

FICTION

Iain Banks *Canal Dreams*. More nightmare than dream, in which an unloveable, famous Japanese cellist is trapped on a ship in the Panama Canal that is captured by guerrillas. The violence she and her lover suffer at their hands leads her to an equally violent revenge.

Jane Bowles *Two Serious Ladies*. An avant-garde classic of 1943, this story follows two women seeking freedom from the confines of social convention. On holiday in Panama, one falls in love with a young prostitute and leaves her husband to live in the brothel in Colón. Offering a glimpse of the city's red-light district, it also includes a scene in the historic *Washington Hotel*.

Cristina Enríquez *The World in Half*. Debut novel from US author who draws on her Panamanian heritage to narrate a young woman's search for identity as she leaves her ailing mother to find in Panama the father she never knew. Though the book is heavy-handed with the geological symbolism, the protagonist's physical and existential journey keep the pages turning. The same author's award-winning *Come Together Fall Apart* contains a novella and a handful of short stories, which provide deft close-ups of a range of Panamanian characters in the turbulent 1980s, just before the fall of Noriega.

Douglas Galbraith *The Rising Sun*. A detailed, somewhat rambling historical novel about the Scottish expedition to the Darién, fuelled by human greed but leading to unbelievable hardship and the eventual bankruptcy of Scotland. It is difficult to warm to the main character who tells the story, but the horror comes across.

James Stanley Gilbert *Panama Patchwork Poems*. A fascinating collection, published between 1901 and 1937, by a one-time employee of the Panama Railroad Company. Though "Poet Laureate of the Isthmus" may be a tad exaggerated, his accessible verse provides a powerful evocation of pre-Canal hardships for settlers in Colón.

Robert Hatting *Murder in Panama*. Though it won't win any awards for writing, this first of a trilogy of Kindle thrillers set in Panama will happily pass time on the plane, taking you round the country at a breathless pace.

★ **John Le Carré** *The Tailor of Panama*. With an explicit nod to Graham Greene's *Our Man in Havana*, this satirical spy thriller is a classic. Set just before the US handover of the Canal, a young unscrupulous British agent embarks on an elaborate fiction of intrigue, which spirals out of control. While both American and British intelligence services are lampooned as much as Panamanian high society, the novel, nevertheless, caused some upset in Panama upon publication.

Enrique Jaramillo Levi *The Shadow: Thirteen Stories in Opposition*. Short stories by Panama's pre-eminent (post) modern writer, though some tales are scarcely more than vignettes. You'll either be seduced by the originality of his imagination and fluid prose or left baffled and irritated as meaning slips through your grasp. More accessible is his edited collection of short stories by Costa Rican and Panamanian women, *When New Flowers Bloomed*, tackling

a range of subjects from gender relations to political events.
William Penn *The Panama Conspiracy*. A thriller that manages improbably to link all the US's enemies, from Fidel Castro through Red China to Osama Bin Laden, in a complex plot culminating in a plan to blockade the Panama Canal.

★ **Eric Zencey** *Panama*. All but the first chapter is actually set in Paris, with a deftly drawn cast of real and imagined characters woven into a historically intriguing murder mystery that centres on the financial scandal surrounding the Panama Canal debacle.

BIOGRAPHY AND MEMOIR

Darrin Du Ford *Is There a Hole in My Boat? Tales of Travel in Panama Without a Car*. The author sets out to explore Panama using public transport or hitching a lift, by dugout or on foot, aiming to get closer to the life and culture of the people than the average tourist; he never seems to turn down a new experience.

Christian Giudice *Hands of Stone: The Life and Legend of Roberto Durán*. Meticulously researched biography of Panama's most famous boxer and one of the sport's all-time greats, drawing on plenty of fascinating, original interview material. A warts-and-all rags-to-riches tale that tracks his rise to fame from the slums of Panama City, giving a view of his contradictory character inside and outside the ring.

Graham Greene *Getting to Know the General: The Story of an Involvement*. Greene provides a personal slant on Omar Torrijos, the country's most charismatic leader, whom the author befriended during his time in troubled late 1970s and early 1980s Panama.

Malcolm Henderson *Don't Kill the Cow Too Quick: An Englishman's Adventures Homesteading in Panama*.

Entertaining and informative, especially for expats thinking of following a dream, this book follows a couple's retirement in Bocas in the late 1990s, where they eventually established an organic farm.

Leo Mahon *Fire Under My Feet: A Memoir of God's Power in Panama*. The moving story of a compassionate Roman Catholic priest sent in 1963 to a poverty-stricken town in Panama to found a church.

Martin Mitchinson *The Darien Gap: Travels in the Rainforest of Panama*. An entertaining account of eighteen months spent in the trackless jungle trying to retrace the route to the Pacific made by the first European, Balboa, in 1513. It's a successful blend of personal experience, history and local lore.

Manuel Noriega and Peter Eisner *America's Prisoner: The Memoirs of Manuel Noriega*. The other side of the story of a leader who was vilified, arrested and put on trial by the US. A controversial book, it is worth reading for its revelations about the American attitude to Panama and Latin America.

WILDLIFE

George Angehr, Dodge Engleman and Lorna Engleman *A Bird-finding Guide to Panama*. You need to read the title carefully – this excellent, detailed guide tells you where to find the birds and how to get there by car, but is not a bird identification manual. Details updated on the web at ⓦ audubonpanama.org.

Juan Carlos Q. Navarro *Panama National Parks* (Ediciones Balboa). Bilingual Spanish/English guide to Panama's national parks accompanied by gorgeous glossy photos that will make you want to pack your rucksack and head immediately for the hills.

★ **Rainforest Publications** *Panama Field Guides* (numerous titles). This company has produced an excellent series of illustrated laminated concertina-style pocket field

guide pamphlets on Panama's flora and fauna, giving scientific, Spanish and English names. Available in Panama or online (ⓦ rainforestpublications.com).

Robert Ridgely and John Gwynne *A Guide to the Birds of Panama*. This weighty tome is *the* birding bible for Panama, although it's in desperate need of updating.

★ **Jorge Ventocilla and Dana Gardner** *A Guide to the Common Birds of Panama City* (Smithsonian Tropical Research Institute & Panama Audubon Society). Excellent, beautifully illustrated pocket book aimed at the average nature-lover – perfect for anyone basing their stay in the capital and wanting to identify the city's surprisingly abundant birdlife.

Language

Spanish is the national and official language of Panama and the first language of more than two million of the population. A recorded thirteen other first languages are spoken across the country, including English, which is used by many black Afro-Antilleans (see p.44) – though outside Panama City and the touristy areas of Bocas del Toro and Boquete, it's not widely spoken. Learning at least the basics of Spanish will make your travels considerably easier and reap countless rewards in terms of reception and understanding of people and places.

Pronunciation and word stress

In Spanish, each word is **pronounced** as written according to the following guide:

A somewhere between the "A" sound of "back" and that of "father"

E as in "get"

I as in "police"

O as in "hot"

U as in "rule"

C is soft before E and I, otherwise hard; *cerca* is pronounced "SERka".

G works the same way – a guttural "H" sound (like the "ch" in "loch") before E or I, a hard G elsewhere; *gigante* is pronounced "HiGANte".

H is always silent.

J is the same sound as a guttural "G"; *jamón* is pronounced "ham ON".

LL sounds like an English Y; *tortilla* is pronounced "torTIya".

N is as in English, unless there is a "~" over it, when it becomes like the N in "onion"; *mañana* is pronounced "maNYAna".

QU is pronounced like an English "K" as in "kick".

R is rolled, **RR** doubly so.

V sounds like a cross between B and V, *vino* almost becoming "beano".

X is a soft "SH", so that *Xela* becomes "SHEla"; between vowels it has an "H" sound – *México* is pronounced "ME-hi-ko".

Z is the same as a soft C; *cerveza* is pronounced "serVEsa".

Getting the **word stress** right makes a big difference: *PAgo* means "I pay", *paGÓ* she/he paid. The rule is simple: if a word ends in a vowel, "s" or "n", the stress is on the syllable before last. If it ends in any other consonant, the stress is on the last syllable. Exceptions are marked with an accent on the vowel of the stressed syllable.

Latin American Spanish lacks the lisp common in Spain, where *cerveza* is often pronounced "therVEtha". One feature of the speech of many Panamanians which makes understanding more difficult is the aspiration of the "S" sound at the end of a syllable or word, such that the word *cascada* is pronounced more like "cahcada". Also, words containing a "ch" such as *muchacho* may sound more like "mushasho". Generally the Spanish of indigenous Panamanians is easiest to understand.

Formal and informal address

For English-speakers one of the most difficult things to get to grips with is the distinction between formal and informal address. Generally speaking, the third-person **usted** indicates respect and is used in business, for people you don't know and for those older than you. Second-person **tú** is for children, friends and contemporaries in less formal settings. (Remember also that in Latin America the second-person **plural** – *vosotros* – is never used, so "you" plural will always be *ustedes*.)

Verbal courtesy is an integral part of speech in Spanish and one that – once you're accustomed to the pace and flow of life in Panama, especially out of the city – should become instinctive. Saying *Buenos días/Buenas tardes/Buenas noches*, or the abbreviated *buenos* or *buenas*, and waiting for the appropriate response is usual when asking for something at a shop or ticket office, for example, as is adding *señor* or *señora* (in this instance similar to the US "sir" or "ma'am").

On meeting, or being introduced to someone, people are likely to say *con mucho gusto*, "it's a pleasure", and you should do the same. On departure you will more often than not be told *¡Que le vaya bien!* – literally meaning "May all go well with you", it often translates better as "Take care" or "Travel safely".

BASIC WORDS

a lot	mucho	more	más
afternoon	tarde	morning	mañana
and	y	night	noche
bad	mal(o)/a	no	no
big	gran(de)	now	ahora
boy	chico	open	abierto/a
closed	cerrado/a	or	o
cold	frío/a	please	por favor
day	día	she	ella
entrance	entrada	sir/mister	señor
exit	salida	small	pequeño/a
girl	chica	thank you	gracias
good	bien/buen(o)/a	that	eso/a
he	él	their	suyo/de ellos
her	ella	there	allí
here	aquí	they	ellos
his	suyo	this	este/a
hot	calor/caliente	today	hoy
how much	cuánto	tomorrow	mañana
if	si	what	qué
later	más tarde/después	when	cuando/cuándo
less	menos	where	dónde
ma'am/missus	señora	with	con
man	señor/hombre	without	sin
maybe	talvez	yes	sí
miss	señorita	yesterday	ayer

BASIC PHRASES

Hello	¡Hola!	I (don't) speak Spanish	(No) Hablo español/
Goodbye	Adiós		castellano
See you later	Hasta luego	What (did you say)?	¿Mande?/¿Cómo?
Good morning	Buenos días	Could you... please?	¿Podría...por favor?
Good afternoon	Buenas tardes	...repeat that	...repetirlo
Good evening/night	Buenas noches	What's your name?	¿Cómo se llama usted?
Sorry	Lo siento/Discúlpeme	My name is...	Me llamo...
Excuse me	Con permiso/Perdón	Where are you from?	¿De dónde es usted?
How are you?	¿Cómo está (usted)?/	I'm from...	Soy de...
	¿Qué tal?	How old are you?	¿Cuántos años tiene?
Nice to meet you	Mucho gusto		(usted)
Not at all/You're welcome	De nada/para servirle	I am...years old	Tengo...años
I (don't) understand	(No) Entiendo	I don't know	No sé
Do you speak English?	¿Habla (usted) inglés?	Do you know...?	¿Sabe...?

I want/I'd like	Quiero/Quisiera	There is (is there)?	Hay (?)
What's that?	¿Qué es eso?	Do you have…?	¿Tiene…?
How much is it?	¿Cúanto es/Cuesta?	What time is it?	¿Qué hora es?
What is this called in Spanish?	¿Cómo se llama este en español/castellano?	May I take a photograph?	¿Puedo sacar una foto?
		It's hot/cold	Hace calor/frío

BASIC NEEDS, SERVICES AND PLACES

ATM	cajero automático	market	mercado
bank	banco	money	dinero/plata
bathroom/toilet	baño/sanitario	museum	museo
beach	playa	pharmacy	farmacia
border crossing	frontera	post office	el correo
church	iglesia	restaurant	restaurante
internet café	cibercafé	supermarket	supermercado
laundry	lavandería/lavamático	telephone	teléfono
map	mapa	tourist office	oficina de turismo

NUMBERS (NÚMEROS), MONTHS (MESES) AND DAYS (DÍAS)

1	un/uno/una	second	segundo/a
2	dos	third	tercero/a
3	tres		
4	cuatro	January	enero
5	cinco	February	febrero
6	seis	March	marzo
7	siete	April	abril
8	ocho	May	mayo
9	nueve	June	junio
10	diez	July	julio
20	veinte	August	agosto
21	veintiuno	September	septiembre
22	veintidos	October	octubre
30	treinta	November	noviembre
40	cuarenta	December	diciembre
50	cincuenta		
60	sesenta	Monday	lunes
70	setenta	Tuesday	martes
80	ochenta	Wednesday	miércoles
90	noventa	Thursday	jueves
100	cien	Friday	viernes
1000	mil	Saturday	sábado
		Sunday	domingo
first	primero/a		

GETTING AROUND

bus	autobús	engine	motor
minibus	buseta/colectivo	4WD/4X4	doble tracción/ cuatro por cuatro
bus station	terminal de autobuses		
bus stop	parada de autobús	taxi	taxi
boat	barco/lancha/panga	lorry/truck	camión
dugout canoe	cayuco/piragua	pickup	camioneta
dock/pier	muelle	bicycle	bicicleta
airplane	avión	motorcycle	moto
airport	aeropuerto	petrol/diesel/gas	gasolina
car	carro/auto(móvil)	ticket	billete/pasaje

ticket office	taquilla/ventanilla	Where does...to...	¿De dónde sale...para...?
I'd like a ticket to...	(Necesito) un billete	leave from?	
	(pasaje) para...	What time does the...	¿A qué hora sale...para...?
...one way	...sólo ida	leave for...?	
...return/round trip	...ida y vuelta	What time does the...	¿A qué hora llega...en...?
I would like to rent a...	Me gustaría alquilar un/	arrive in...?	
	una...		

DIRECTIONS

Where is...?	¿Dónde está...?	east	este
How do I get to...?	¿Por dónde se va a...?	west	oeste
I'm lost	Estoy perdido/a	street	calle
Is it far?	¿Está lejos?	avenue	avenida
left/right	izquierda/derecha	block	cuadra
straight ahead	derecho/recto	corner	esquina
north	norte	(main) road	carretera
south	sur		

ACCOMMODATION

Is there (a)...nearby?	¿Hay...aquí cerca?	...two people	...dos personas
...hotel	...un hotel	...for one night	...una noche
...cheap, small hotel	...una pensión/	...one week	...una semana
	un hospedaje	Does it have...	¿Tiene...?
...hostel	...un hostal	...a shared bath	...baño compartido
Do you have...?	¿Tiene...?	...a private bath	...baño privado
...a room	...un cuarto	...hot water	...agua caliente
...with two beds	...con dos camas	...air conditioning	...aire-acondicionado
...a double bed	...con cama matrimonial	... a fan	... abanico
...a dorm room	...cuarto colectivo/	...a mosquito net	...mosquitero
	dormitorio	May I see a room?	¿Puedo ver un cuarto?
...a cabin	...una cabaña	May I see another room?	¿Puedo ver otro cuarto?
It's for	Es para	Yes, it's fine	Sí, está bien
...one person	...una persona		

FOOD AND DRINK

BASIC DINING VOCABULARY

almuerzo	lunch	plato vegetariano	vegetarian dish
cafetería	self-service restaurant	silla	chair
carta	menu	vaso	glass
cena	dinner	Soy vegetariano/a	I'm a vegetarian
comedor	basic restaurant	Tengo hambre/sed	I'm hungry/thirsty
comida corriente	cheap set menu, usually		
	lunch	**BASIC FOOD VOCABULARY**	
comida típica	traditional cuisine	aceite	oil
cuenta	bill	ajo	garlic
desayuno	breakfast	arroz	rice
fonda	inexpensive, informal	azúcar	sugar
	local restaurant	chile	chilli
menú del día	cheap set menu	galletas	biscuits/crackers
menú ejecutivo	a fancier and pricier set	hielo	ice
	menu than the *menú*	huevos	eggs
	del día	mantequilla	butter
mesa	table	mermelada	jam
plato fuerte	main course	miel	honey
		natilla	sour cream

pan (integral)	bread (wholemeal)
pimienta	pepper
queso	cheese
sal	salt
salsa de tomate	tomato sauce

FRUTAS (FRUIT)

aceitunas	olives
chirimoya	custard apple
coco	coconut
fresa	strawberry
guanábana	soursop
guayaba	guava
guineo	banana
limón	lemon
manzana	apple
maracuyá	passionfruit
marañon	cashew
melón	melon
mora (zarzamora)	blackberry
naranja	orange
papaya	papaya
piña	pineapple
plátano	plantain
sandía	watermelon
uva	grapes

LEGUMBRES/VERDURAS (VEGETABLES)

aguacate	avocado
cebolla	onion
champiñón (hongo)	mushroom
ensalada	salad
espinaca	spinach
frijoles	beans
gallo pinto	mixed rice and beans
lechuga	lettuce
lentejas	lentils
maíz	sweetcorn/maize
menestra	bean/lentil stew
papa	potato
papas fritas	chips/French fries
tomate	tomato
zanahoria	carrot

CARNE (MEAT), AVES (POULTRY) AND MENUDO (OFFAL)

bistec/lomo	steak
carne	beef
cerdo	pork
chuleta	pork chop
jamón	ham
mondongo	tripe and chorizo stew
patas	trotters
pollo	chicken

res	beef
ropa vieja	shredded spicy beef and rice
sancocho	thick red meat or chicken soup with root vegetables

MARISCOS (SEAFOOD) AND PESCADO (FISH)

almejas	clams
anchoa	anchovy
atún	tuna
calamares	squid
camarón	shrimp
cangrejo	crab
ceviche	raw seafood marinated in lime juice with onions
concha	conch
corvina	sea bass
langosta	lobster/crayfish
langostina	king prawn
mejillónes	mussels
mero	grouper
pargo rojo	red snapper
pulpo	octopus
trucha	trout

BOCADOS OR BOCADITOS (SNACKS)

carimañola	mashed boiled yuca stuffed with beef
carne en palito	meat on a little stick
churro	ribbed, tubular doughnut-cum-waffle
empanada	cheese-/meat-filled pastry
emparedado	sandwich
hamburguesa	hamburger
hojaldre	deep-fried doughy pancake
patacones	fried green plantains
platanitos	plantain crisps
salchichas	sausages
tortilla	thick fried maize patty
tortilla de huevos	omelette
tostada	toast

BEBIDAS (DRINKS)

agua mineral	mineral water
…con gas	…sparkling
…sin gas	…still
agua potable	drinking water
aromática	herbal tea
batido	fresh fruit milk shake
café	coffee
cerveza	beer
chicha	maize and/or fruit drink